MW01631318

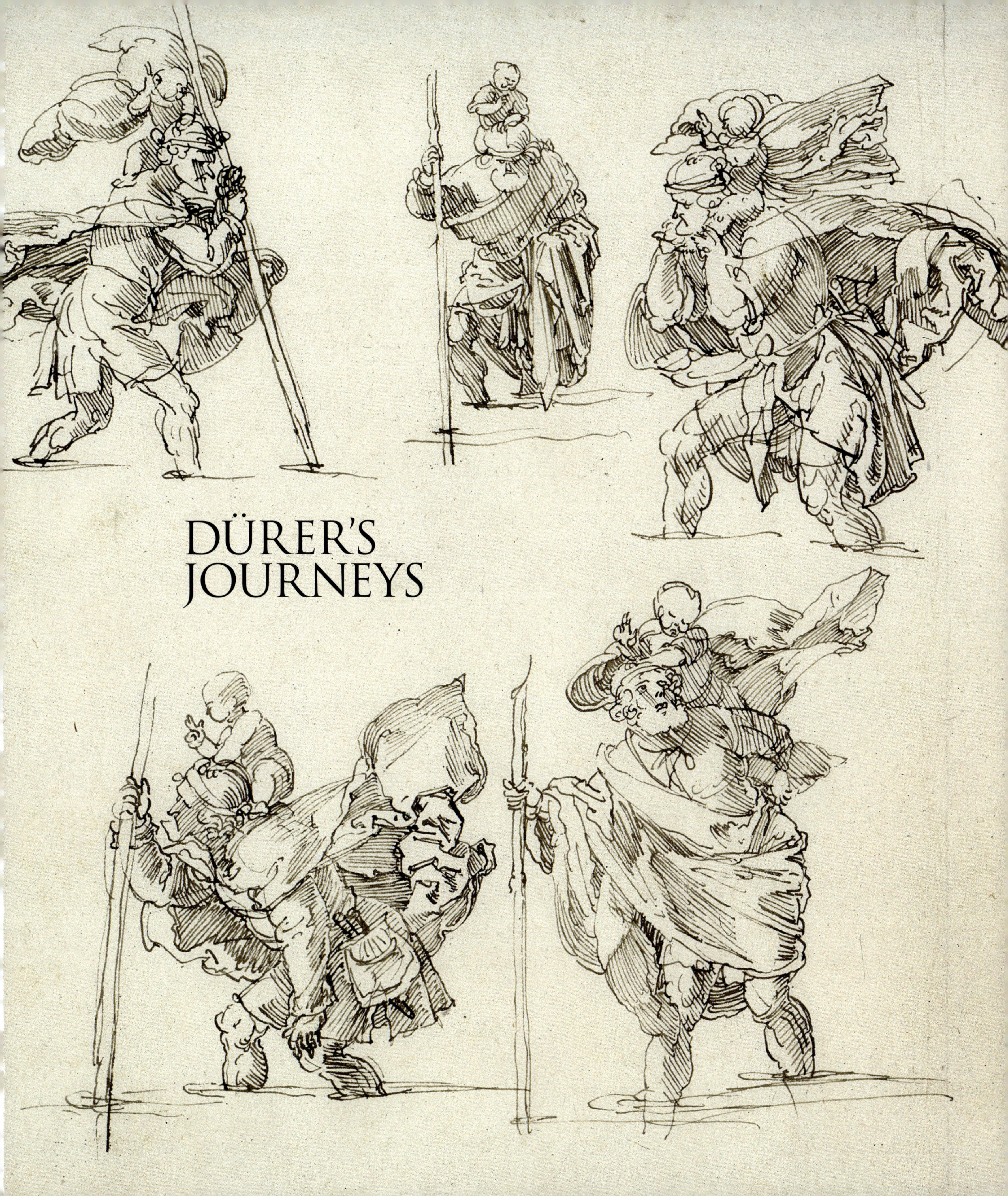

DÜRER'S JOURNEYS

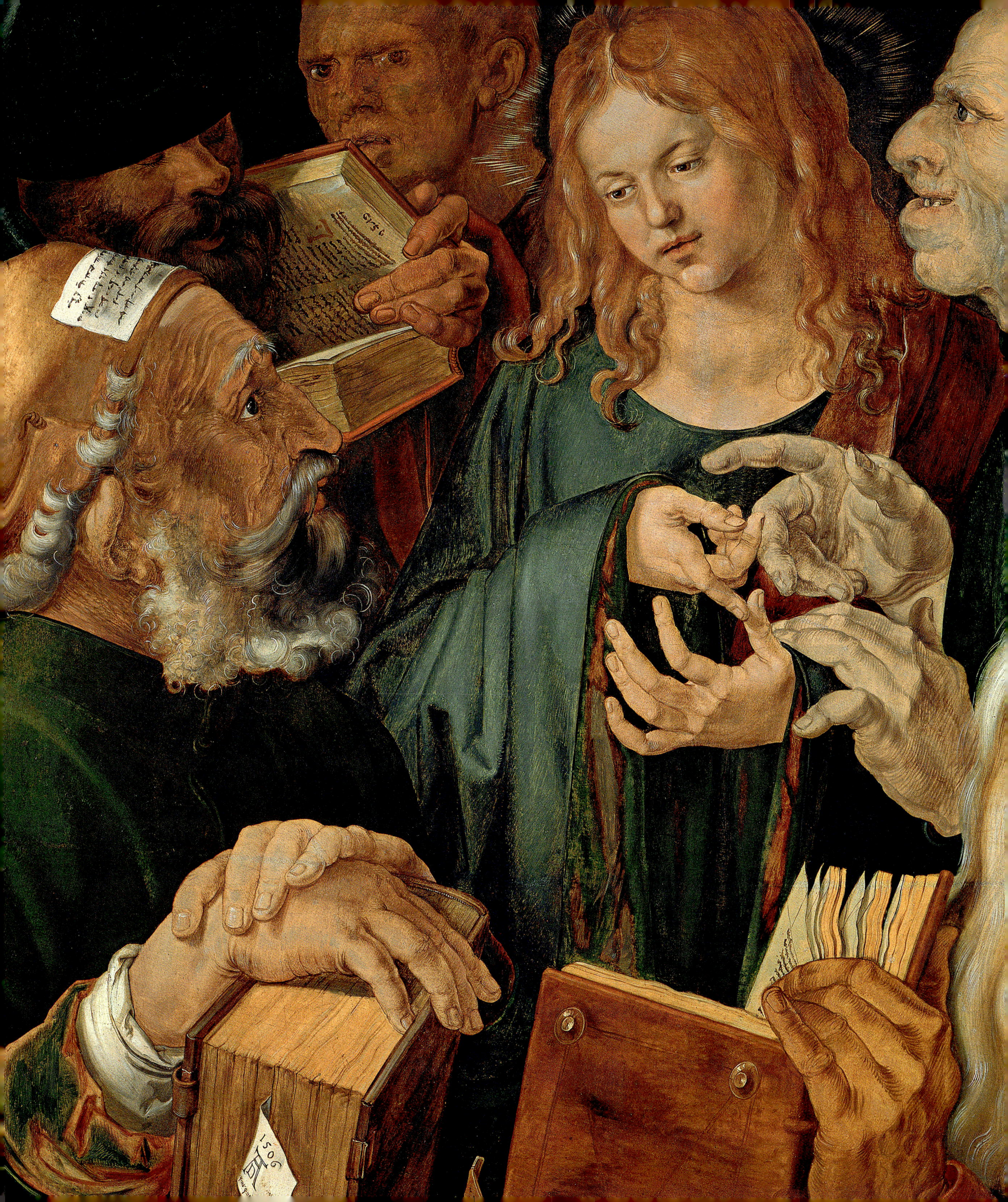

DÜRER'S JOURNEYS

TRAVELS OF A RENAISSANCE ARTIST

SUSAN FOISTER AND
PETER VAN DEN BRINK

NATIONAL GALLERY COMPANY, LONDON. DISTRIBUTED BY YALE UNIVERSITY PRESS

Published to accompany The Credit Suisse Exhibition

DÜRER'S JOURNEYS: TRAVELS OF A RENAISSANCE ARTIST

The National Gallery, London
6 March–13 June 2021

Exhibition sponsored by

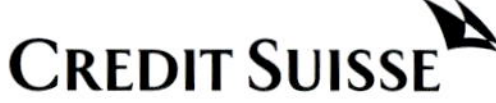

Partner of the National Gallery

Publication supported by

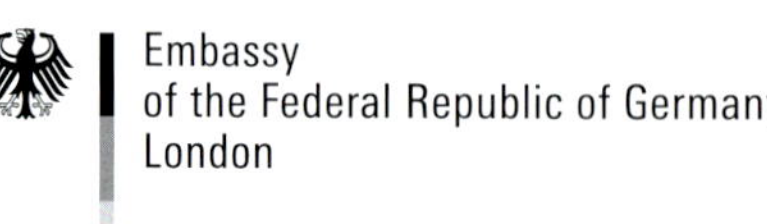

Supported by

KYTHERA
KULTUR-STIFTUNG
Düsseldorf

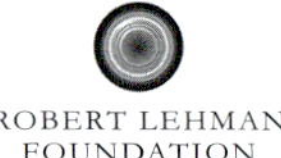

Katrin Henkel

Elizabeth and Daniel Peltz OBE

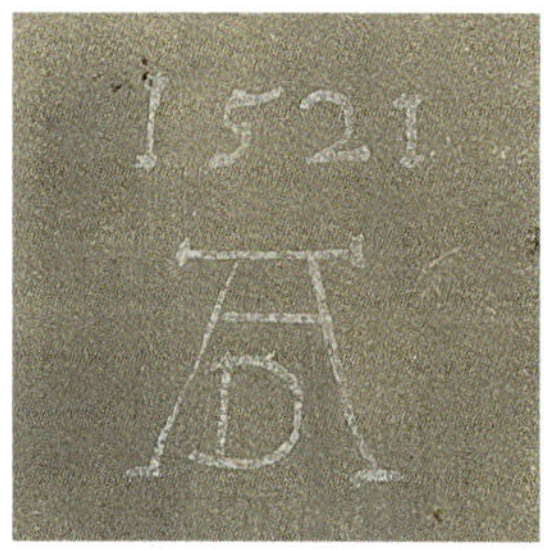

All texts in section openers by Susan Foister.
Chronology, Provenance and Selected Literature
compiled by Imogen Tedbury.
Map designed by Karoliina Hujanen.

This exhibition has been made possible by the provision
of insurance through the Government Indemnity Scheme.
The National Gallery would like to thank HM Government for
providing Government Indemnity and the Department for
Digital, Culture, Media and Sport and Arts Council England
for arranging the indemnity.

First published in Great Britain in 2021 by
National Gallery Company Limited
St Vincent House
30 Orange Street
London WC2H 7HH
www.nationalgallery.co.uk

ISBN: 9781857096675
Product code: 1049755

British Library Cataloguing-in-Publication Data
A catalogue record is available from the British Library
Library of Congress Control Number: 2020932683

Publisher: Laura Lappin
Commissioning Manager: Sarah Derry
Project Editor: Diana Adell
Editor: Johanna Stephenson
Picture Researcher: Suzanne Bosman and Rebecca Thornton
Production: Jane Hyne
Designer: Raymonde Watkins

Translation from German by Kristin Lohse Belkin (A. Beyer,
D. Eichberger), Sophie Duvernoy (A. Nesselrath) and
Noah Harley (A. Nesselrath, S. Ayooghi and H. Lange-Krach,
T.-H. Borchert, C. Metzger).

Designed and typeset in Trajan, Minion and Gotham
Colour origination by DL Imaging
Printed in Italy by Verona Libri

Front cover: detail from *Saint Eustace* (cat. 50)
Back cover: detail from *A Lion* (cat. 82)
p. 1: detail from *Nine Studies of Saint Christopher* (cat. 17)
p. 2: detail from *Christ among the Doctors* (cat. 31)
pp. 7, 304: detail from *Adam and Eve*, 1504. Rijksmuseum,
Amsterdam (RP-P-OB-1156)
p. 10: detail from *Head of the 12-Year-Old Christ* (cat. 29)
p. 13: detail from *Self portrait* (fig. 18)

Quote on p. 12: A. Dürer, Drafts of the Introduction to the
Handbook on Painting, 1512, in Ashcroft 2017, vol. 1, p. 367

All measurements give height before width.

CONTENTS

SPONSOR'S FOREWORD

We are delighted to be supporting the Credit Suisse exhibition: *Dürer's Journeys: Travels of a Renaissance Artist* at the National Gallery, London. This exhibition will bring together works from a wide range of collections from different parts of the world, presenting Albrecht Dürer as a painter, draughtsman and printmaker from the perspective of his journeys. The exhibition will be the first to chart his travels across Europe, bringing to light some of the artists that Dürer encountered, as well as the experiences that fuelled his curiosity and creativity, and increased his fame and influence.

Credit Suisse has been a proud partner of the National Gallery for over ten years supporting a range of exhibitions and educational programmes. We have a long-standing commitment to help widen access to fine arts with leading cultural institutions bringing fresh ideas and experiences to existing and new audiences alike.

DAVID MATHERS
CEO
Credit Suisse International

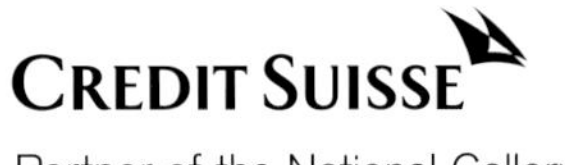

Partner of the National Gallery

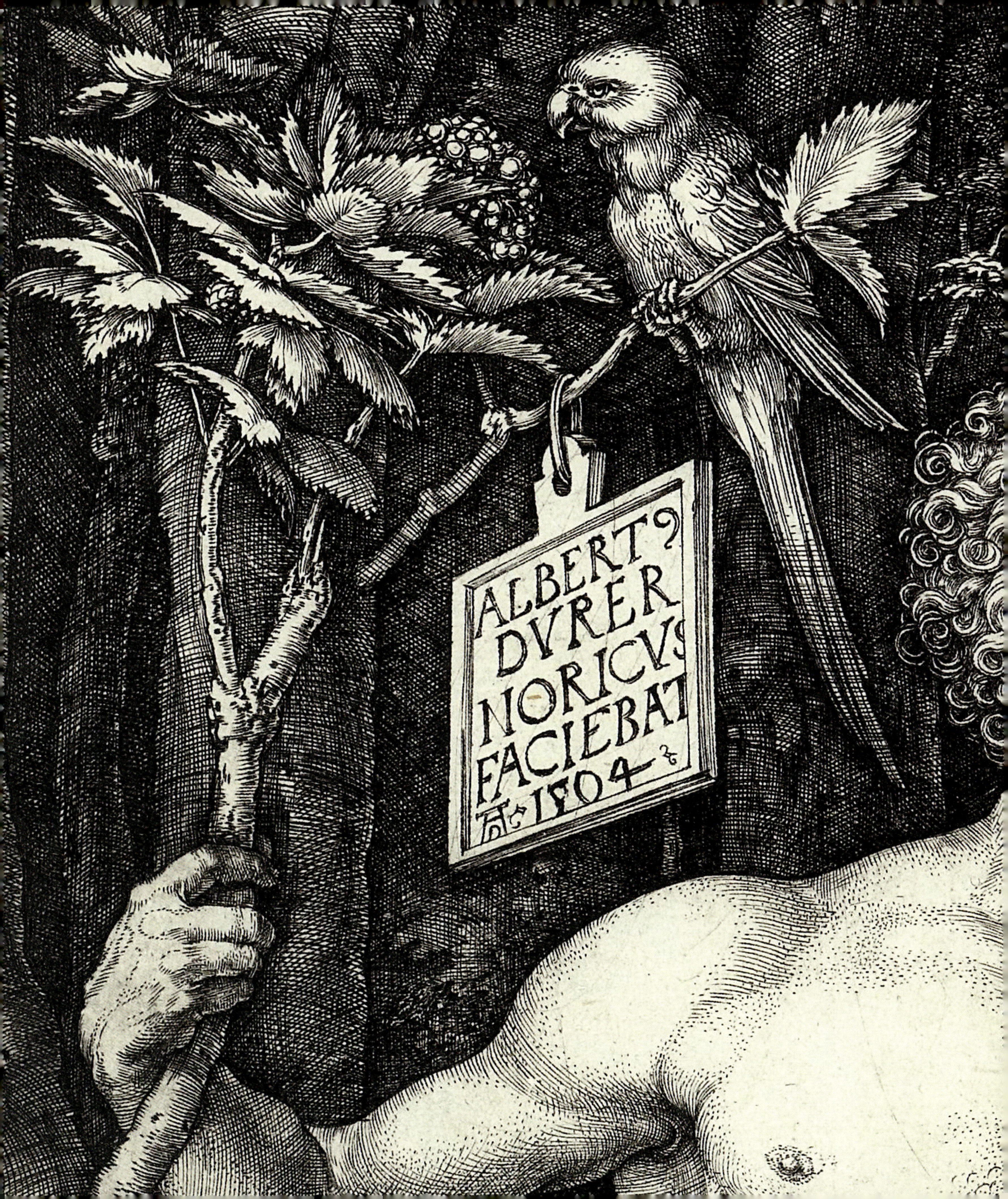
ALBERTꝰ
DVRER
NORICVS
FACIEBAT
1504

AMBASSADOR'S FOREWORD

We are delighted to be supporting the publication that accompanies the exhibition *Dürer's Journeys: Travels of a Renaissance Artist* at the National Gallery in London. The exhibition and catalogue are prime examples of German-British cooperation in the field of culture. They are the fruit of a close collaboration between the Suermondt-Ludwig-Museum in Aachen and the National Gallery.

The exhibition in Aachen focuses on Albrecht Dürer's journey to that city in 1520 – when he attended the coronation of Emperor Charles V and renewed a pension granted him by the previous emperor – as well as a trip to the Netherlands in 1520–1. The exhibition at the National Gallery in addition encompasses his earlier travels to Italy, the Alps and Venice.

Dürer's Journeys sheds light on the breadth of Dürer's interests as an artist and author through his painting, engravings and woodcuts, as well as his writings on art theory, geometry, perspective and proportion; his entrepreneurial spirit in founding his own publishing enterprise to sell his prints; his wide-ranging correspondence, with Erasmus, among others; his searching introspection evident in his numerous self portraits and extensive diaries; and his openness and curiosity, as demonstrated by the travels that took him away from his native Nuremberg for long periods of time. All of these characteristics have established Dürer as a modern European figure who has inspired generations of art lovers and will surely continue to do so in the future.

I would like to congratulate Director Gabriele Finaldi and his team for granting us this fascinating insight into Albrecht Dürer's artistic travels, and I wish them every success with the new show.

ANDREAS MICHAELIS
German Ambassador to the United Kingdom

DIRECTOR'S FOREWORD

Albrecht Dürer's astounding artistic achievement, his intellectual curiosity, his inexhaustible versatility and his engagement with the great events of his time, make him deeply fascinating to us.

A painter, printmaker, draughtsman and designer, he was widely admired throughout Europe in his lifetime and his fame has never waned. His skill as a maker of woodcuts, etchings and engravings was unrivalled and these were quickly disseminated from Germany across the whole continent from Portugal to Sweden, introducing his compositions into the artistic bloodstream of European art and exerting a powerful influence on sixteenth-century artists as varied as Jan Gossaert and El Greco. From his home town of Nuremberg he travelled south across the Alps to Venice, almost certainly twice, and later north to the Low Countries. This latter journey, which began in July 1520 and lasted nearly two years, is supremely well documented and forms the main focus of this exhibition.

Dürer's Journeys: Travels of a Renaissance Artist is a collaboration with the Suermondt-Ludwig-Museum in Aachen. The Director there, Peter Van den Brink, conceived an exhibition to celebrate the 500th anniversary of the coronation of Charles V in the Imperial City and Dürer's visit there as part of his 'Netherlandish journey' in 1520–1. The London exhibition, under the expert guidance of the National Gallery's Deputy Director and Curator of German Painting, Susan Foister, has broadened its scope to explore the artist's journeys to Italy and to northern Europe over the course of his career. I am delighted that the collaboration has been a particularly happy and rewarding one for both our institutions.

I want to thank Credit Suisse, Partner of the National Gallery, for supporting this exhibition but also to express my appreciation for more than ten years of loyal friendship towards the Gallery. The Embassy of the Federal Republic of Germany has supported this publication and I am grateful for the personal commitment to the project demonstrated by HE Ambassador Andreas Michaelis.

In addition, I am grateful to KYTHERA Kultur-Stiftung, Düsseldorf, the Robert Lehman Foundation, Katrin Henkel, Elizabeth and Daniel Peltz OBE and other donors, who have supported *Dürer's Journeys*.

My final thanks are to the numerous lenders from 11 different countries who have allowed works from their collections to undertake the journey to Trafalgar Square. Their contribution has been fundamental and I especially want to express our gratitude to colleagues in the Berlin State Museums, the Prado and Thyssen-Bornemisza Museums in Madrid, the Museu Nacional de Arte Antiga in Lisbon, the Musée du Louvre, the Albertina in Vienna and the Washington National Gallery of Art, to HM The Queen, the British Museum and the British Library. The Bojmans van Beuningen Museum in Rotterdam have made available to us – in rather special circumstances – the painting by Patinir that Dürer himself was pleased to own. This exhibition could not have happened without our lenders' friendship and goodwill.

GABRIELE FINALDI
Director of the National Gallery

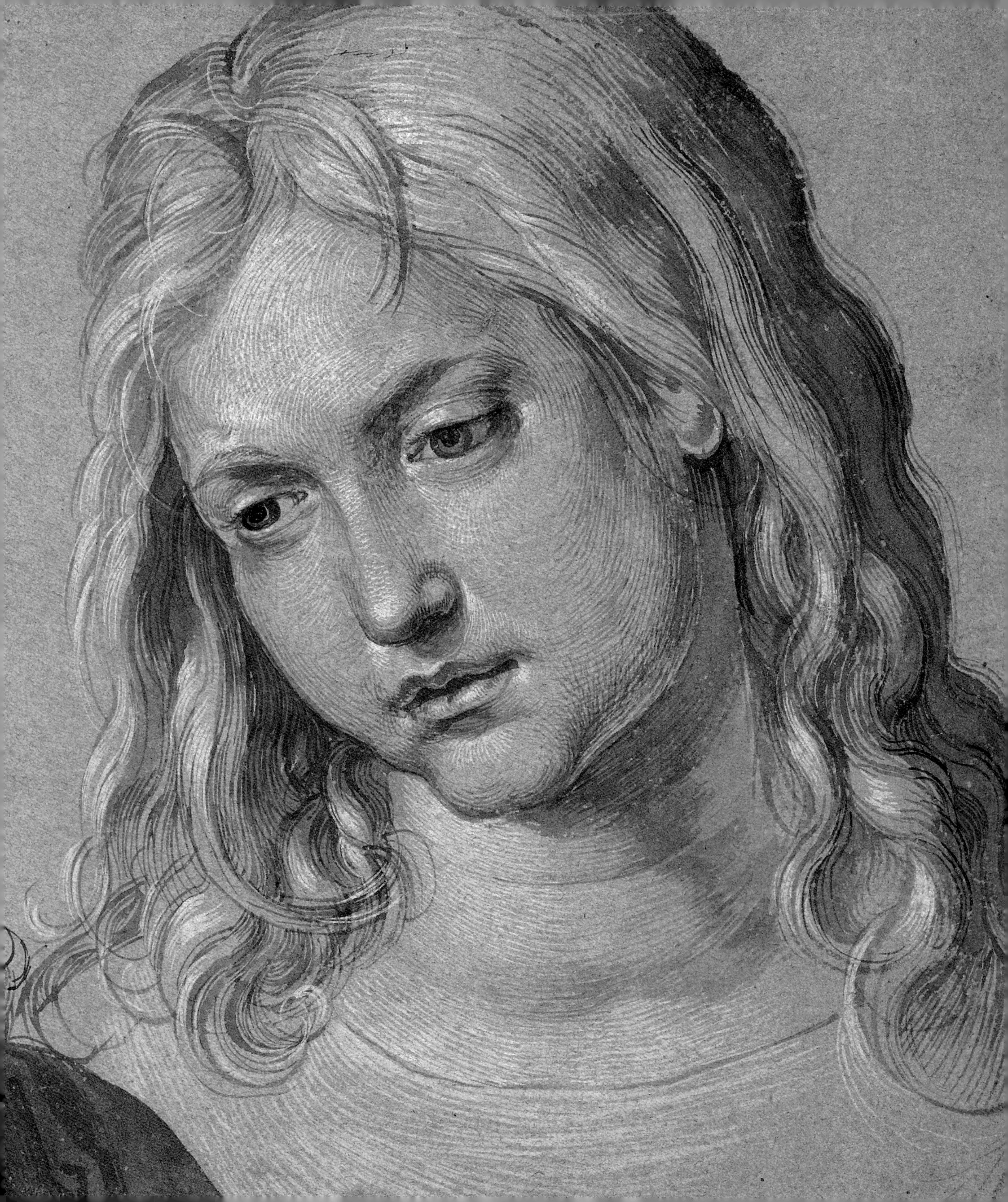

ACKNOWLEDGEMENTS

All exhibitions are highly collaborative projects, and as the curators of an exhibition on the subject of an artist of the stature and significance of Albrecht Dürer we have inevitably relied on the scholarship and support of a wide range of professional colleagues beyond those in our two institutions in London and Aachen. Thanks to their willingness to participate, we have been able to bring together an exceptional range of works and publish new scholarship in this book and online, which we anticipate will greatly enhance our understanding of Dürer's journeys and their significance for his career as a whole. We would like to thank most warmly all the contributors to this catalogue for sharing these new and significant insights. We also gratefully acknowledge the generous support of the Ludwig Foundation for the exceptional facilitation of scholarly interchanges in Aachen in the most propitious manner in advance of the commissioning of the catalogue essays.

We would like to express our special thanks to the following colleagues: Bernard Aikema, Maryan Ainsworth, Giulia Bartrum, Mar Borobia, Claire Breay, Till-Holger Borchert, Magali Briat-Philippe, Véronique Bücken, Hans Buijs, Hugo Chapman, Barrie Cook, Martin Clayton, Philipp Demandt, Taco Dibbits, Yasmin Doosry, Emily Dourish, Iris Ellers, Miguel Falomir, Matthieu Deldicque, Georg Dietz, Michael Eissenhauer, Marzia Faietti, Rupert Featherstone, Anisio Franco, Joris van Grieken, Christoph Grunenberg, John Hand, Babette Hartwieg, Daniel Hess, Erik Hinterding, Max Hollein, Wolfgang Holler, Joachim Homann, Holger Jacob-Friesen, Nicola Kalinsky, Richard Kelleher, Stephan Kemperdick, Miroslav Kindl, Joseph Leo Koerner, Dagmar Korbacher, Friso Lammertse, Huigen Leeflang, Severine Lepape, Elenor Ling, Ger Luijten, Scott McKendrick, Alexander Markschies, Christien Melzer, Christof Metzger, Hermann Mildenberger, Liz Miller, Jürgen Müller, Julia Nauhaus, Uta Neidhardt, Arnold Nesselrath, Jan Nicolaisen, Joaquim Oliveira Caetano, Corinna Otto, Tobias Pfeiffer-Helke, Michael Roth, Amandine Royer, Gill Saunders, Olivia Savatier, Cécile Scaillièrez, Thomas Schauerte, Eike Schmidt, Stacey Sell, Manfred Sellink, Desmond Shawe-Taylor, Guillermo Solana, Martin Sonnabend, Freyda Spira, Andreas Stolzenburg, Nathalie Strasser, Martha Tedeschi, Timo Trümper, Jane Shoaf Turner, Matthias Ubl, An Van Camp, Jan Van der Stock, Joost Vander Auwera, Christiaan Vogelaar, Caroline Vrand, Gregor Weber, Alfred Weidinger, Robert Wenley, Lucy Whitaker and Jill Whitelock, as well as to all our generous private lenders.

At the National Gallery under the leadership of Head of Exhibitions Jane Knowles, Sunnifa Hope, Phoebe Newman and Joanna Weston have managed all aspects of the exhibition with energy and efficiency. Imogen Tedbury, Simon Sainsbury Curatorial Fellow, has been extremely supportive and has contributed the provenances and bibliographical references to the list of works, as well as the essential chronology.

At the Suermondt-Ludwig-Museum a small and dedicated group of a people worked together wonderfully as a team, including two of the museum's curators, Dr Dagmar Preising and Sarvenaz Ayooghi, assistant curator Wibke Birth, researcher and registrar Dr Heinrich Becker and our press agent, Peter Motz. They did a tremendous job, sharing responsibility with the utmost efficiency. They were supported by other staff members Gabriela Borsch, Gabriele Jansen and Michael Rief, as well as engaged colleagues from outside the museum's organisation, of whom Pascaline Blanchaud as well as Irit Tirtey and her staff should be mentioned.

It has been a pleasure to work on the catalogue with our attentive colleagues from the National Gallery Company, Diana Adell, Jan Green, Sarah Derry, Laura Lappin, Suzanne Bosman, Lea Viehweger and Jane Hyne, as well as with editor Johanna Stephenson and designer Raymonde Watkins.

We would like to offer our special thanks to all those in London and in Aachen who have supported the making of the exhibition and its catalogue throughout the exceptionally difficult circumstances of 2020 and, despite these extraordinary challenges, have enabled us to look forward to presenting Dürer's journeys to the public in 2021. We thank them for their forbearance.

SUSAN FOISTER
AND PETER VAN DEN BRINK

'For human curiosity can be so sated by an excess of all worldly things that it becomes weary of them, with the sole exception of knowing a great deal, of which no one tires.'

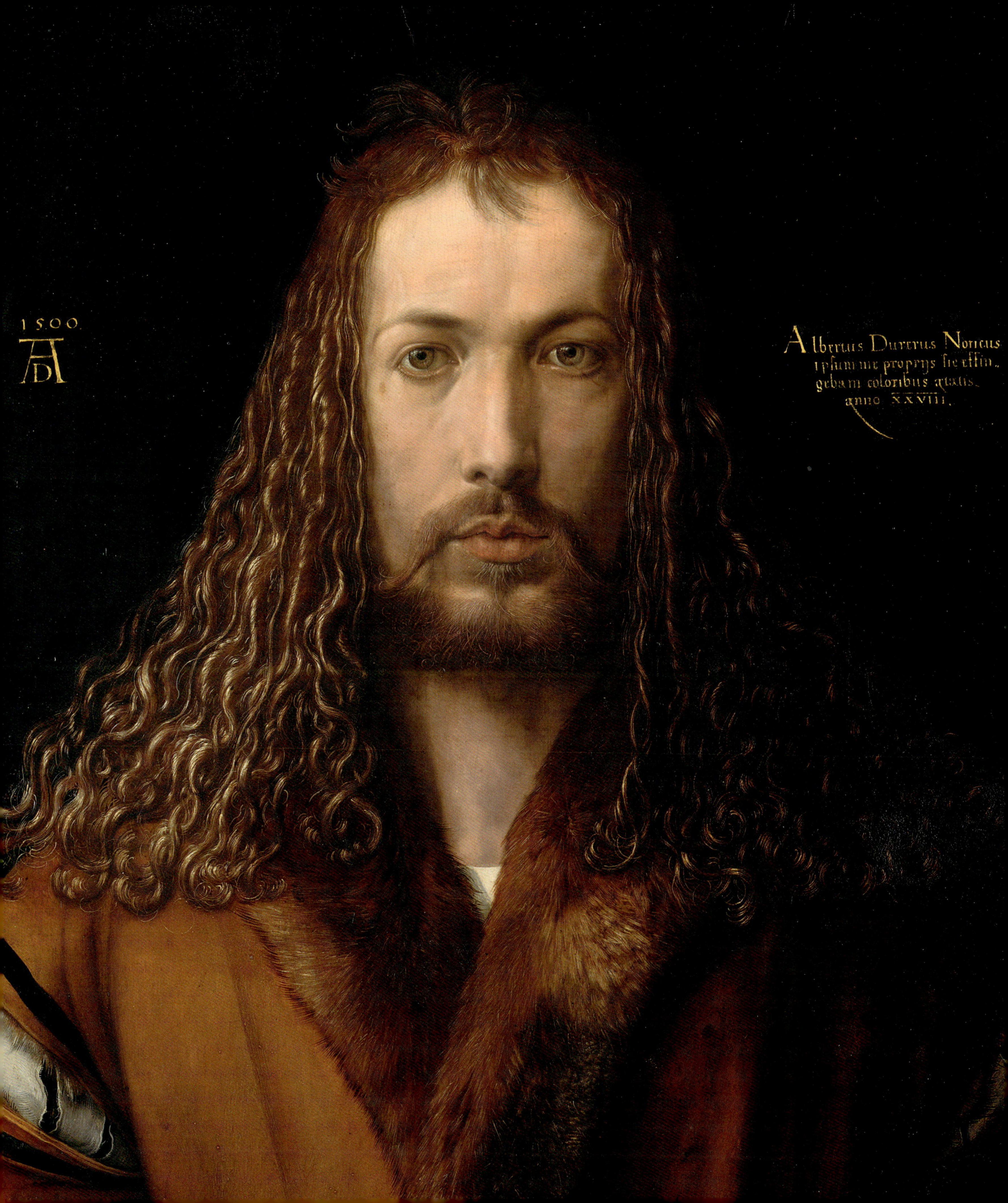
1500.
AD
Albertus Durerus Noricus
ipsum me proprijs sic effin.
gebam coloribus ætatis.
anno XXVIII.

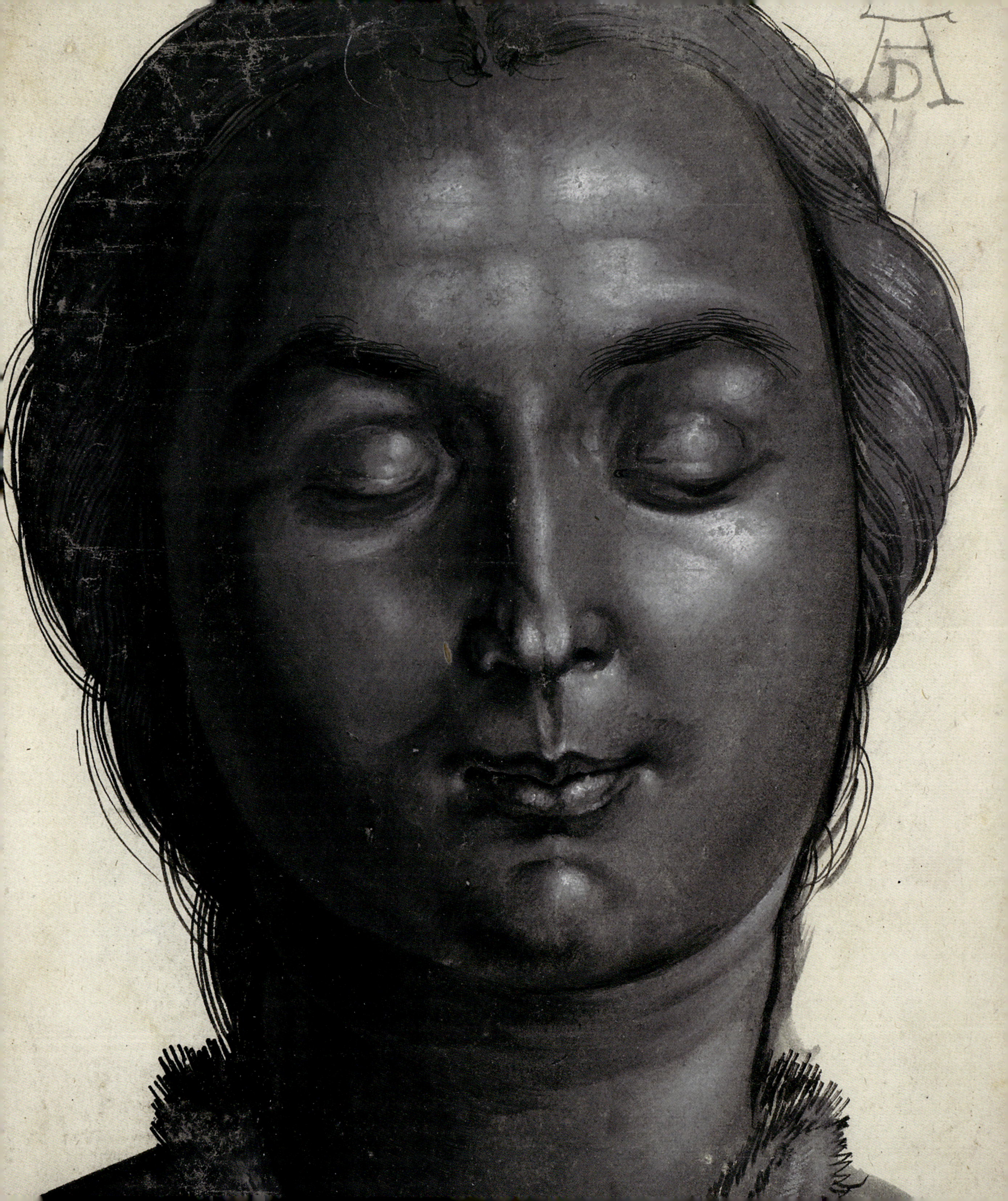

SUSAN FOISTER AND
PETER VAN DEN BRINK

INTRODUCTION

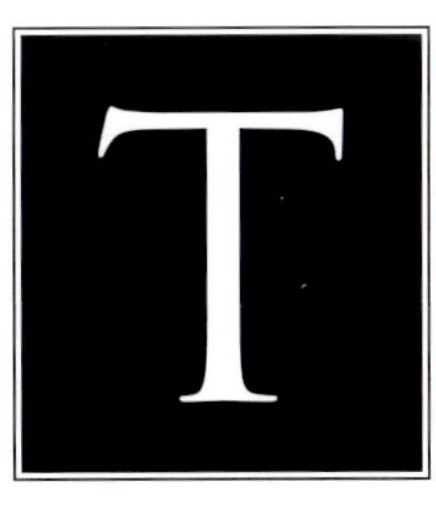

THE ART OF ALBRECHT DÜRER (1471–1528) recognised no boundaries, territorial or intellectual. The excellence of his innovative printmaking allowed his reputation to travel far beyond his home town and base in Nuremberg, and to proceed in advance of the journeys he took in his lifetime south over the Alps and north as far as the North Sea, as Joseph Koerner eloquently explains in his opening essay. Dürer's constantly questing intellectual curiosity opened up exchanges with artists such as Giovanni Bellini (about 1435–1516) and Raphael (1483–1520) on the one hand, and Lucas van Leyden (active 1508; died 1533) on the other. His art reflected his changing engagement with questions that preoccupied many artists of the time – including Dirk Vellert (about 1480; after 1547; cat. 2) and Jacopo de' Barbari (active 1500; died 1516?) – such as theories of proportion and perspective (cats 1, 3, 4), but also larger, more universal issues concerning the meaning and conduct of earthly life following the challenges to conventional beliefs raised by Martin Luther (1483–1546).[1]

The essays in this book illuminate Dürer's career as an international artist, with a special focus on what we can learn from his particularly well-documented journey to the Low Countries in 1520–1. Recent research has focused on situating Dürer in his home town of Nuremberg, and showing how his artistic achievement was strongly grounded in the circumstances of the city and the people connected with it.[2] Scholars have also investigated Dürer's connections to Italy in some detail, showing how the artist made extensive use of Italian source material, and how this material, wholly absorbed within his own production, then created a legacy for Italian artists.[3] At times these studies have appeared to be in tension with each other, as though Dürer must be aligned either with Germany or with Italy. This serves to highlight the ways in which his career also transcends the boundaries of art-historical scholarship, which have tended to be drawn within geographical limits. It also opens up the consideration of the place of the

Detail from *Head of a Woman*, 1520 (cat. 13)

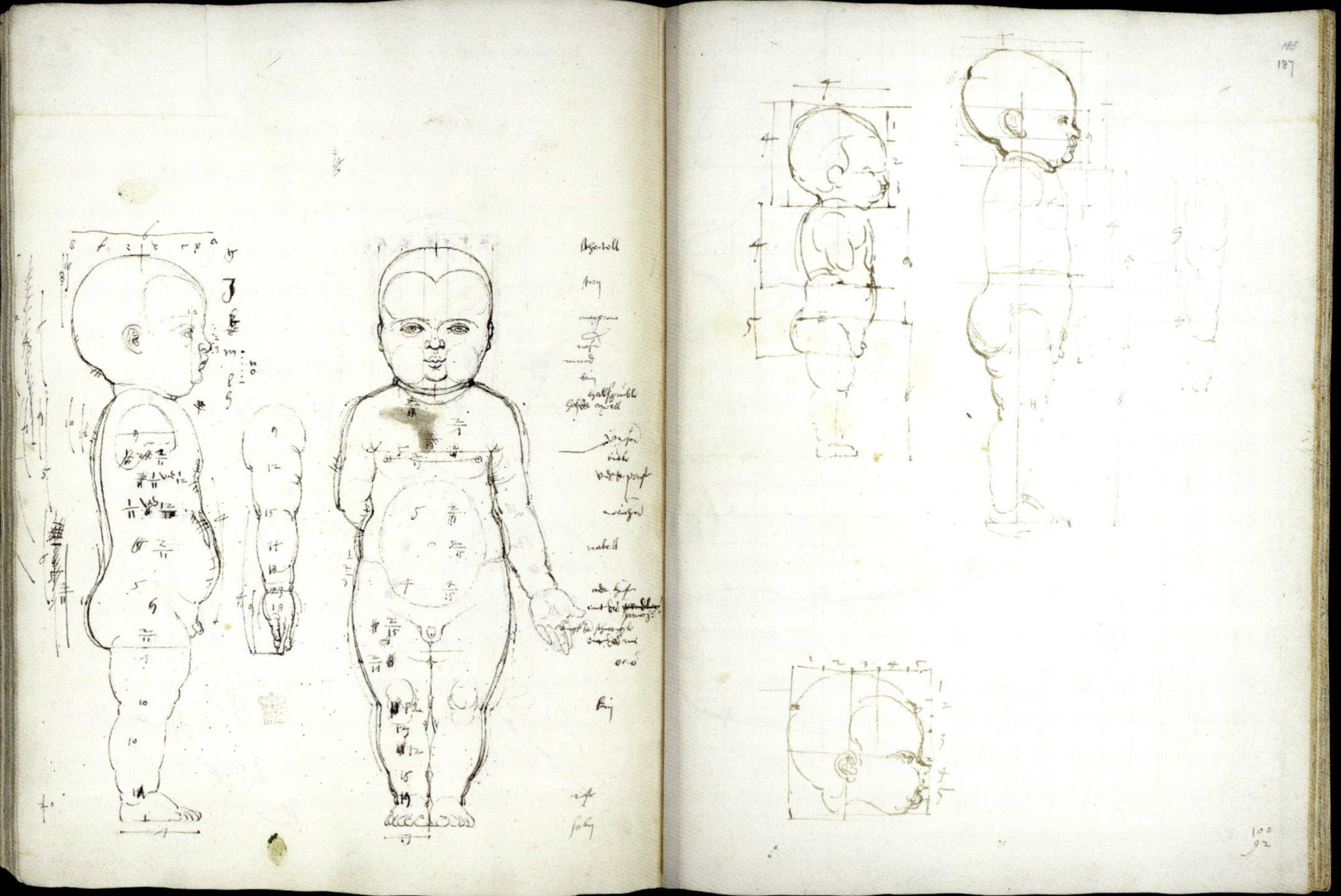

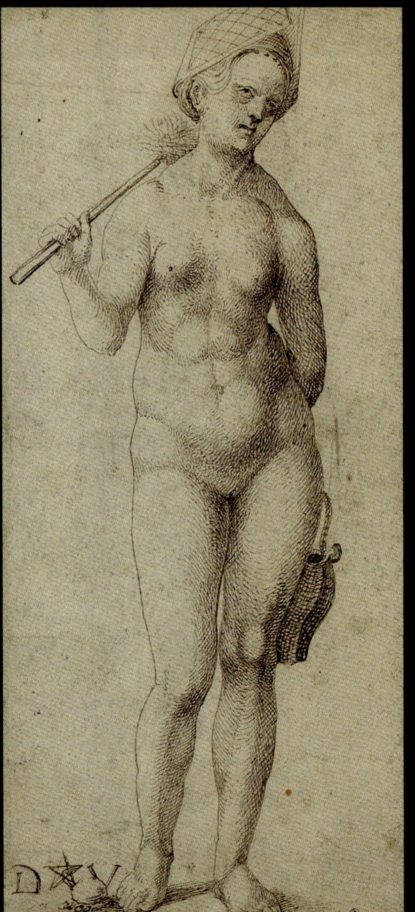

1
ALBRECHT DÜRER
Proportion Drawings of Infants, before 1513
Ink on paper, 28 x 20 cm
The British Library

2
DIRK VELLERT
(1480–1547)
A Woman bathing holding a Brush and a Small Bucket, about 1521
Pen and brown ink, 27.9 × 12.5 cm
Musée du Louvre, Paris

OPPOSITE
3, 4
ALBRECHT DÜRER
Recto: *Study of a Female Nude seen from the Front with Construction Lines and Alteration to her Left Leg;*
verso: *Study of a Female Nude seen from the Front with a Foreshortened Circle*, 1500
Recto: pen and brown ink; verso: pen and brown ink with green wash, 33 × 43.6 cm
British Museum

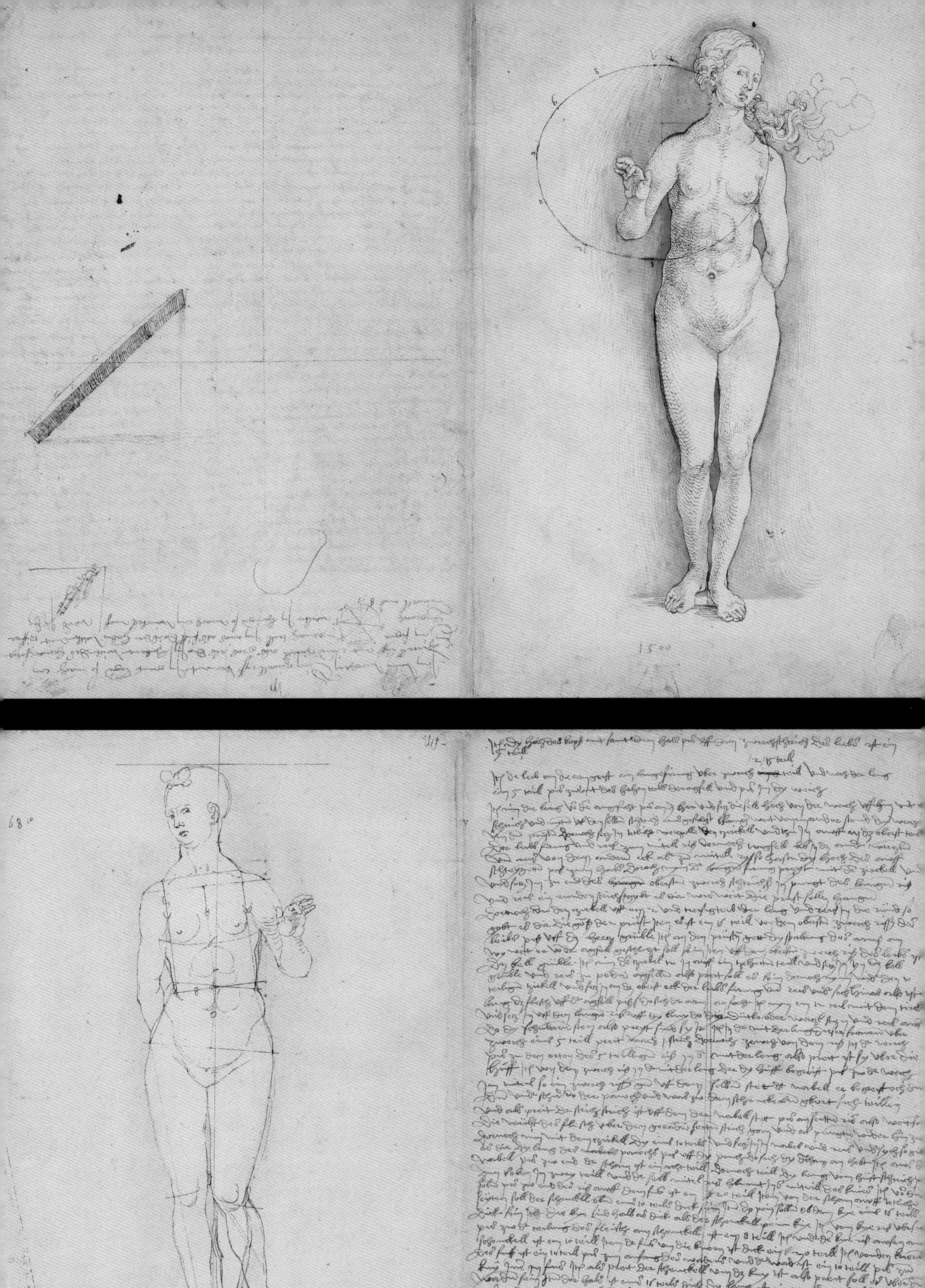
1500

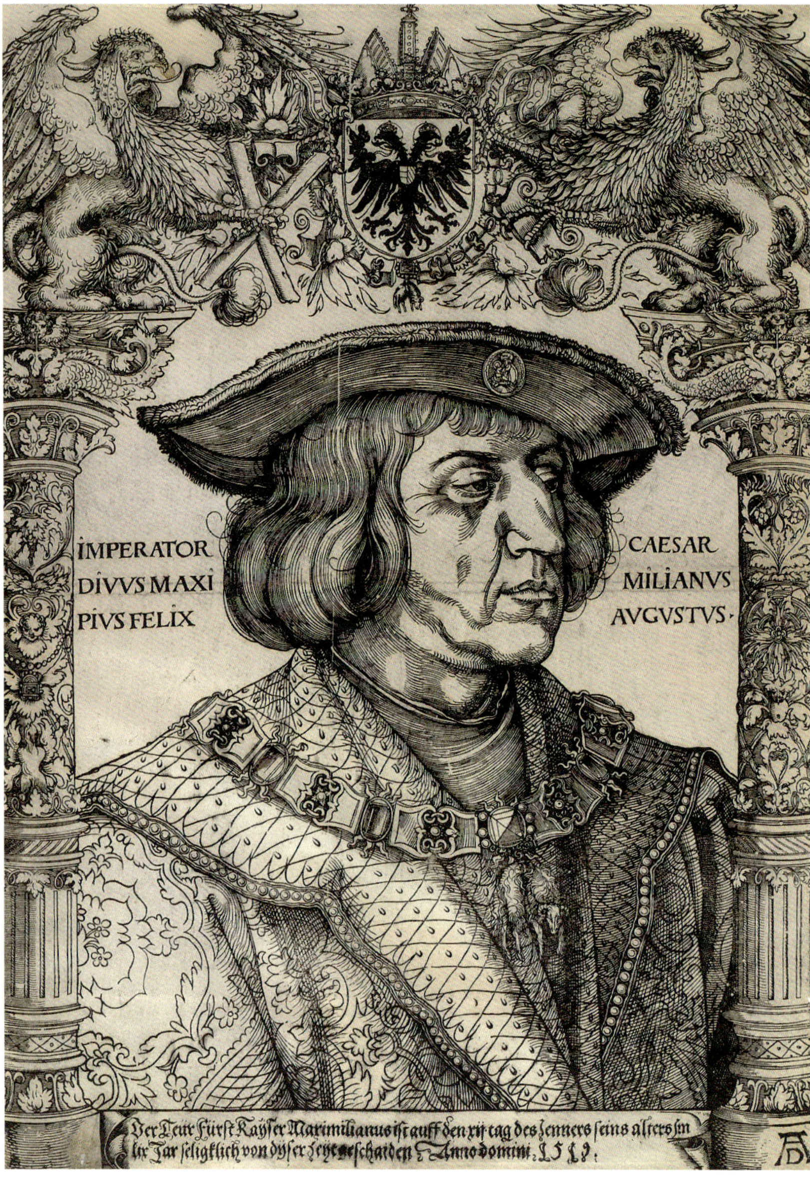

5
HANS WEIDITZ (1495–1537) AFTER ALBRECHT DÜRER
Emperor Maximilian I, 1519
Woodcut on parchment, 54.8 × 37.8 cm
The Albertina Museum, Vienna

Low Countries in Dürer's career: by 1520–1 he was a mature artist with three decades of achievement behind him, coming to a region of Europe in which artists had long flourished. He took the opportunity to admire, for instance, the achievements of Jan van Eyck (active 1422; died 1441) in painting the nude body nearly a hundred years earlier, but also seeking out the work of his own contemporaries. Basing himself in Antwerp, a fast-growing centre for international trade, Dürer mingled not only with artists but also with Portuguese traders, who were already engaging with a world beyond Europe selling ivory, gold, spices and, soon, slaves.

Cities like Antwerp and Nuremberg were vitally important for the exchange of ideas as well as of goods. Such freedom of thought might be seen as a peril needing control by those who ruled the larger areas of Europe in Dürer's time. Indeed, shortly after Dürer left Antwerp in the summer of 1521 attempts were made to proscribe Lutheran beliefs circulating there, as Jeroen Stumpel argues in his enlightening essay. Dürer returned to Nuremberg, where the City Council by 1524 allowed Mass to be celebrated in German, but took strong measures to ensure that traditional beliefs were maintained so that the ceremony did not become merely symbolic, and reference to religious imagery continued to be supported (elsewhere in Europe the questioning of such imagery led to outbreaks of destruction, and damage to the livelihoods of artists).

Antwerp and other nearby cities visited by Dürer, such as Brussels, Bruges and Ghent, formed part of the Holy Roman Empire, ruled over by members of the Habsburg family. In the Low Countries this ruler was Margaret of Austria (1480–1530), widowed daughter of the Emperor Maximilian I, who died in 1519 (cat. 5). Margaret had an important art collection and was a noted patron of artists at her court. Nuremberg was known as an imperial city on account of the particular privileges it had been granted by emperors and the important role it played in their rule: the imperial diets or assemblies were held there, and the special regalia worn by the emperors on ceremonial occasions were kept in the city from 1423 onwards. Dürer was paid in 1513 for painting two panels of the emperors Charlemagne and Sigismund, to be shown in the Treasure Chamber in which the regalia were regularly displayed. But at this period he was also employed directly by the Emperor Maximilian on a number of projects, with other artists illuminating a prayer book, and separately designing monumental woodcuts, one series making up an enormous triumphal arch and another making up a procession. He also took the Emperor's portrait. Maximilian valued Dürer's work and ensured that he was granted a pension in 1515, although this was not paid directly out of the Emperor's own coffers but from those of the city of Nuremberg – and indeed was not paid regularly. Three years later the Emperor promised Dürer a grant of 200 Rhenish guilders, again to be paid out of the Nuremberg city tax. However, in 1519 Maximilian died, to be succeeded by his grandson as Emperor Charles V (1500–1558). Concerned at the potential loss of income, Dürer first tried to persuade the Nuremberg City Council to pay him the promised grant, in a letter dated 27 April 1519. When this approach failed, in October 1520 Dürer decided to attend the coronation of the new emperor in the cathedral of another imperial city, Aachen, a building originally erected as part of Charlemagne's palace.

Dürer was accustomed to travelling. Although Nuremberg remained his base for his entire career, his clients came from a wider region and he himself travelled for extended periods at different times of his life. As a printmaker it was particularly important for him to ensure the distribution of his work, and although for much of his career he employed agents for this, he and his immediate family, his mother and his wife, Agnes, would take prints to sell on journeys to, for example, the Frankfurt fair. When Dürer travelled to the Low Countries in 1520–1 he took with him a substantial number of prints which, he records, he sometimes sold and sometimes gave away. Some of these were individual subjects, but a number were the great series he created, such as the Apocalypse woodcuts of 1497–8, the Life of the Virgin and the series of the Passion of Christ in both engravings and woodcuts, although selling prints was not his only source of income during this journey.

As Susan Foister points out in her essay, Dürer made the traditional journeys as a newly qualified artist at the start of his career, seeking experience in the workshops of masters up and down the Rhine, from Basel to Strasbourg. Still early in his career, now married and possibly escaping plague in Nuremberg, he evidently travelled to the Alps and beyond, to Venice in 1495–6. Settling back in Nuremberg, he created highly innovative engravings and woodcuts and designed work including stained glass and metalwork. He also produced paintings, especially for local clients, such as the Haller family, for whom he painted a *Madonna and Child* now in Washington (cat. 7). However, before long his clients included prestigious rulers such as the Elector of Saxony, Frederick the Wise (1463–1525), based in Wittenberg. Travelling to Venice in 1505–7, perhaps again escaping plague, Dürer painted a large altarpiece for the German merchants there, as well as a number of portraits. On his return to Nuremberg he was commissioned to paint an altarpiece for the Dominican church in Frankfurt for the wealthy cloth merchant Jakob Heller (1460–1522). His life-size paintings of Adam and Eve had been acquired by the Bishop of Breslau, to whom he sold a painting of the Virgin and Child as well. He also painted commissions for the Bishop of Bamberg. The Heller Altarpiece commission tried Dürer's patience; following this he produced fewer paintings, mostly on a smaller scale. His work for the Emperor Maximilian aligned with his renewed focus on printmaking. In 1513 and 1514 he produced three great engravings, *The Knight, Death and the Devil, Melancholia I* (cat. 116) and *Saint Jerome in his Study* (fig. 140).

In the Low Countries in 1520–1 Dürer made many drawings, perhaps more than he usually produced, in different techniques: silverpoint and leadpoint, chalk and charcoal, pen and brush, as well as a few watercolours.

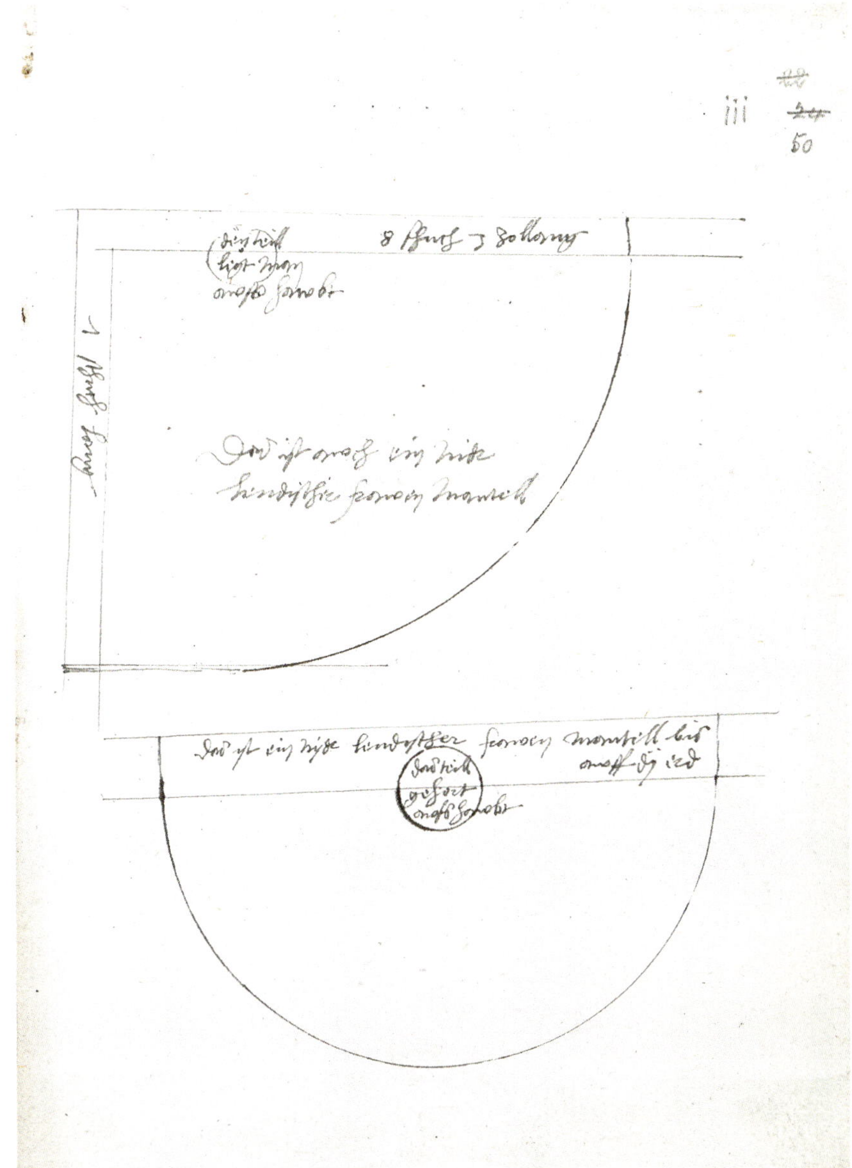

6
ALBRECHT DÜRER
Page from Dürer's original diary of the Netherlandish journey, 1520
Ink on paper, 22.5 × 16 cm
The British Library

He favoured unfamiliar costumes and animals, as Heidrun Lange-Krach and Sarvenaz Ayooghi demonstrate here, but he took numerous portraits as well. However, he also appears to have been considering new approaches to represent the story of Christ's Passion. This hugely important subject is discussed here by Dana Cowen. On his return to Nuremberg he made one further large painted work, the two panels of the Four Apostles, which he presented to the City Council. In 1526 he finally completed the engraved portrait of the humanist Desiderius Erasmus (1466–1536), whom he had sketched in Brussels (cat. 94).

Dürer's life is exceptionally well documented in his own records. Many letters written by him survive, for example those he wrote from Venice to his friend Willibald Pirckheimer (1470–1530) in 1506 and those to Jakob Heller about the altarpiece commission in

OVERLEAF
7, 8
ALBRECHT DÜRER
Recto: *Madonna and Child*; verso: *Lot and his Daughters*, about 1496–9
Oil on panel, 52.4 × 42.2 cm
National Gallery of Art, Washington

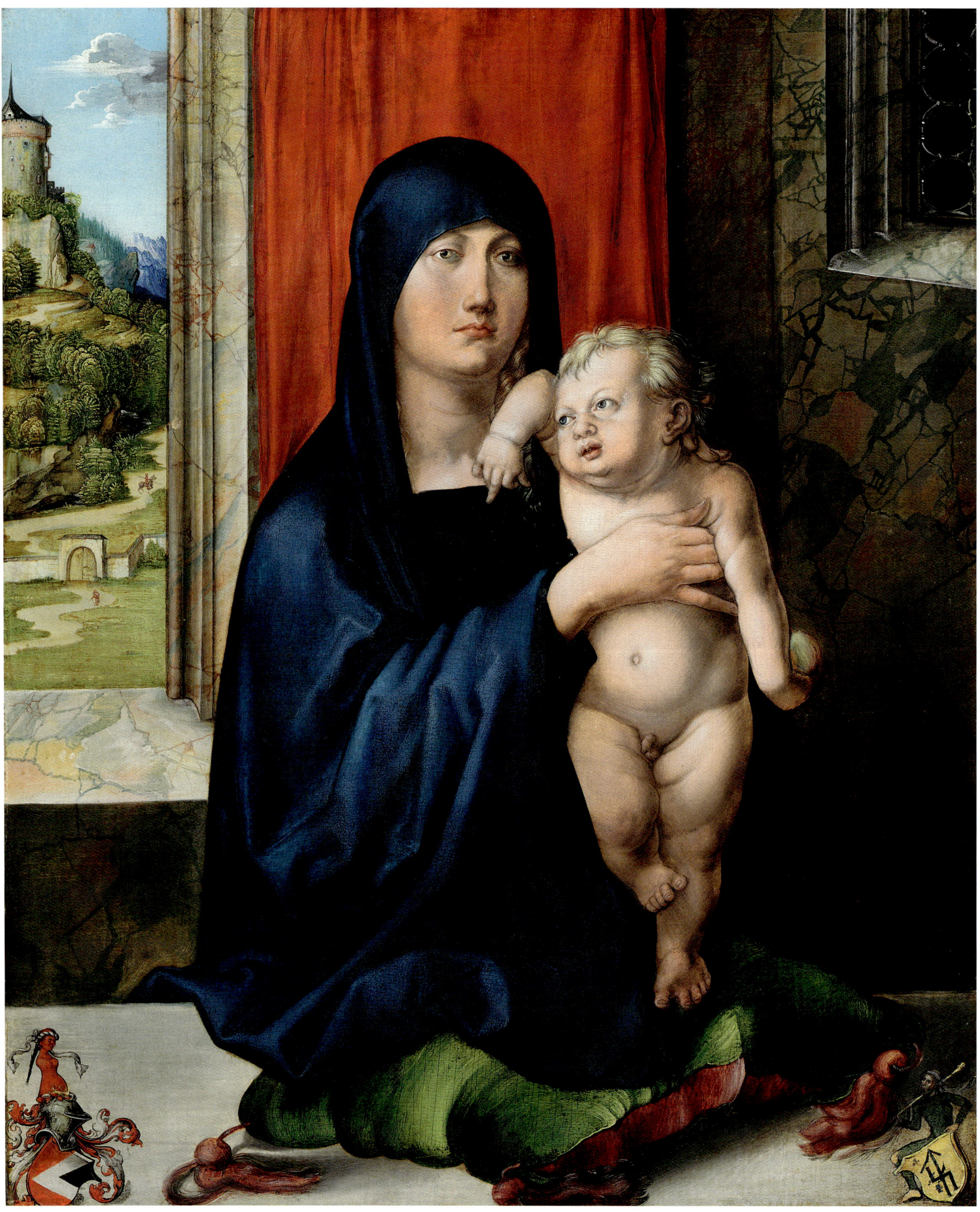

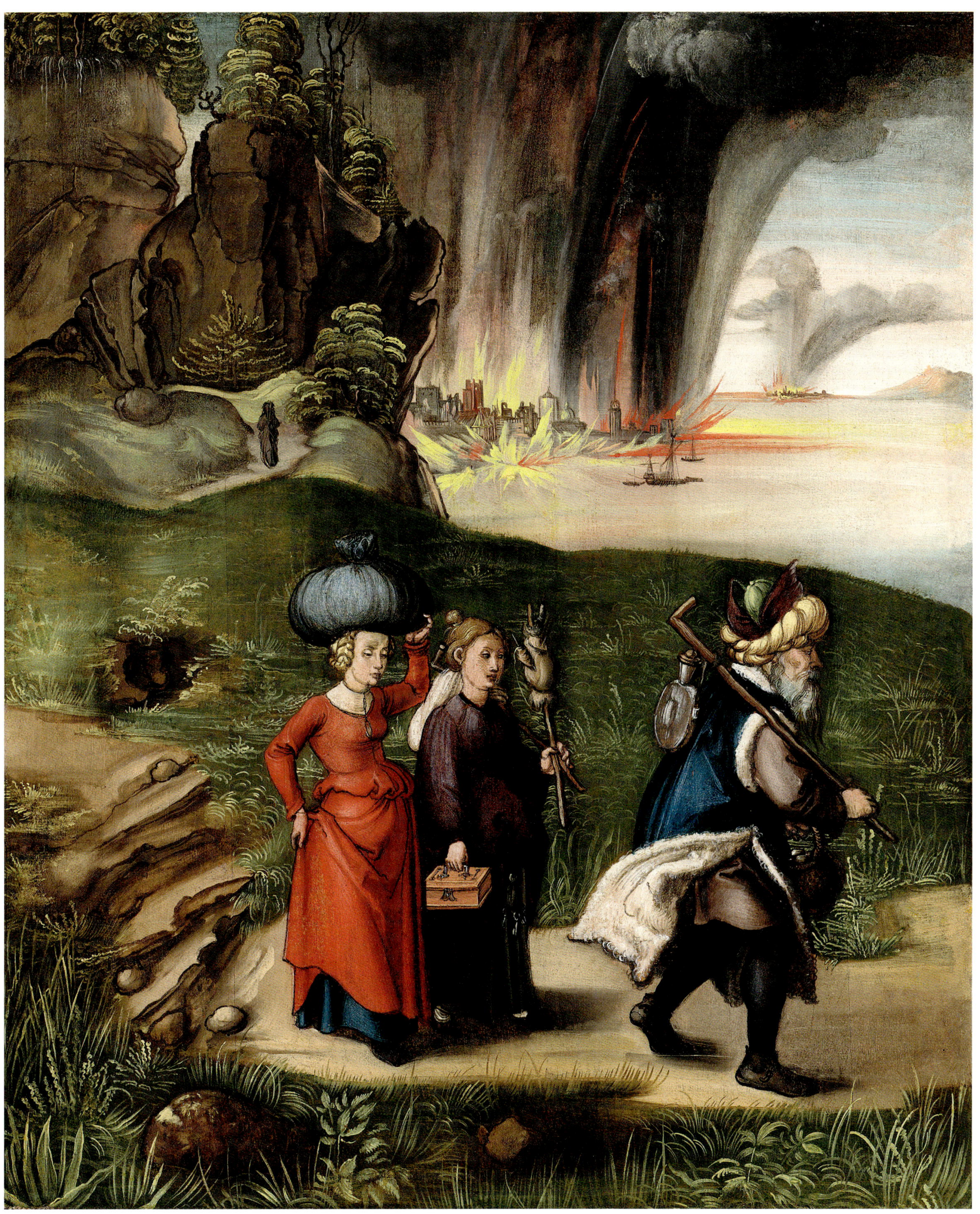

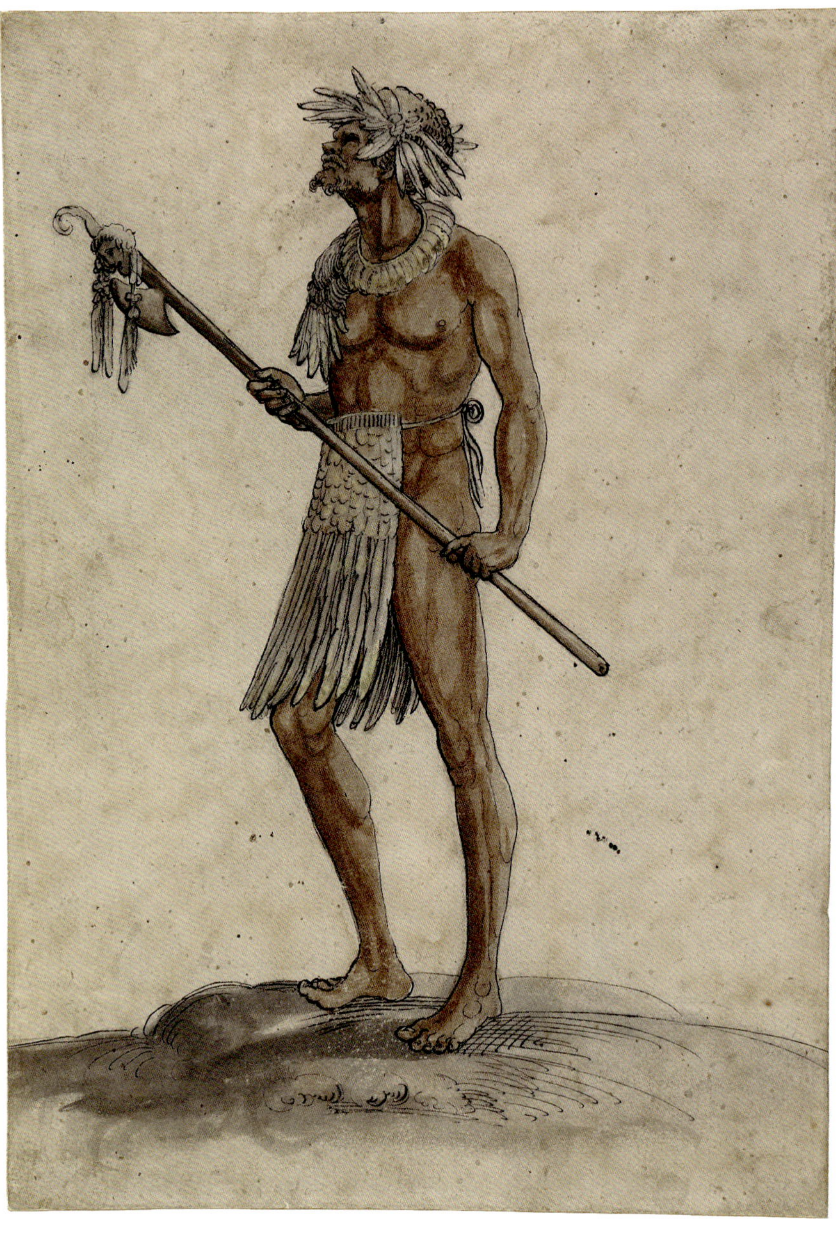

9
HANS BURGKMAIR
THE ELDER (1473–1531)
Standing Black Youth Dressed in a Feather Skirt, Cape and Headdress, 1520–30
Pen and black ink, with grey, brown and green wash, 15 × 16.1 cm
British Museum

1507–9. But the journal from his visit to the Low Countries in 1520–1 is exceptional, as Andreas Beyer discusses in his essay (p. 35). Beyer even considers the journal to be a self portrait in writing. Although the text of the journal itself only survives in two early copies, at least one single sheet of Dürer's original remains, preserved in the British Library (cat. 6). This page shows sketches of a piece of folded cloth with instructions on how to make a type of woman's cloak worn in the Low Countries. A number of Dürer's drawings, notably those of the Passion, show women wearing similar enveloping cloaks. We know that he was interested in the intricacies of clothing: later, in 1526, he drew out a pattern for making a shoe, for example, and a year later a linen Nuremberg headdress. But the sheet in the British Library appears to be untypical of the manuscript as a whole, which details Dürer's movements from leaving Nuremberg on 12 July 1520 to his return the following summer. It also lists the payments he made as he went, including his bills for accommodation at inns, for food and drink and endless tips to smooth the way. He records the people he met and with whom he spent time, some of them other artists, but also merchants and court officials, as discussed by Dagmar Eichberger in her insightful text.

The journal exists today in two complete copies, one in Nuremberg and one in Bamberg, the former made at the end of the sixteenth century, the latter at the beginning of the seventeenth.[4] Although the original has been lost, these copies were made either directly from it or from an earlier copy. The journal mentions a silverpoint drawing book in which Dürer noted his observations of people and places, making it a visual pendant to the

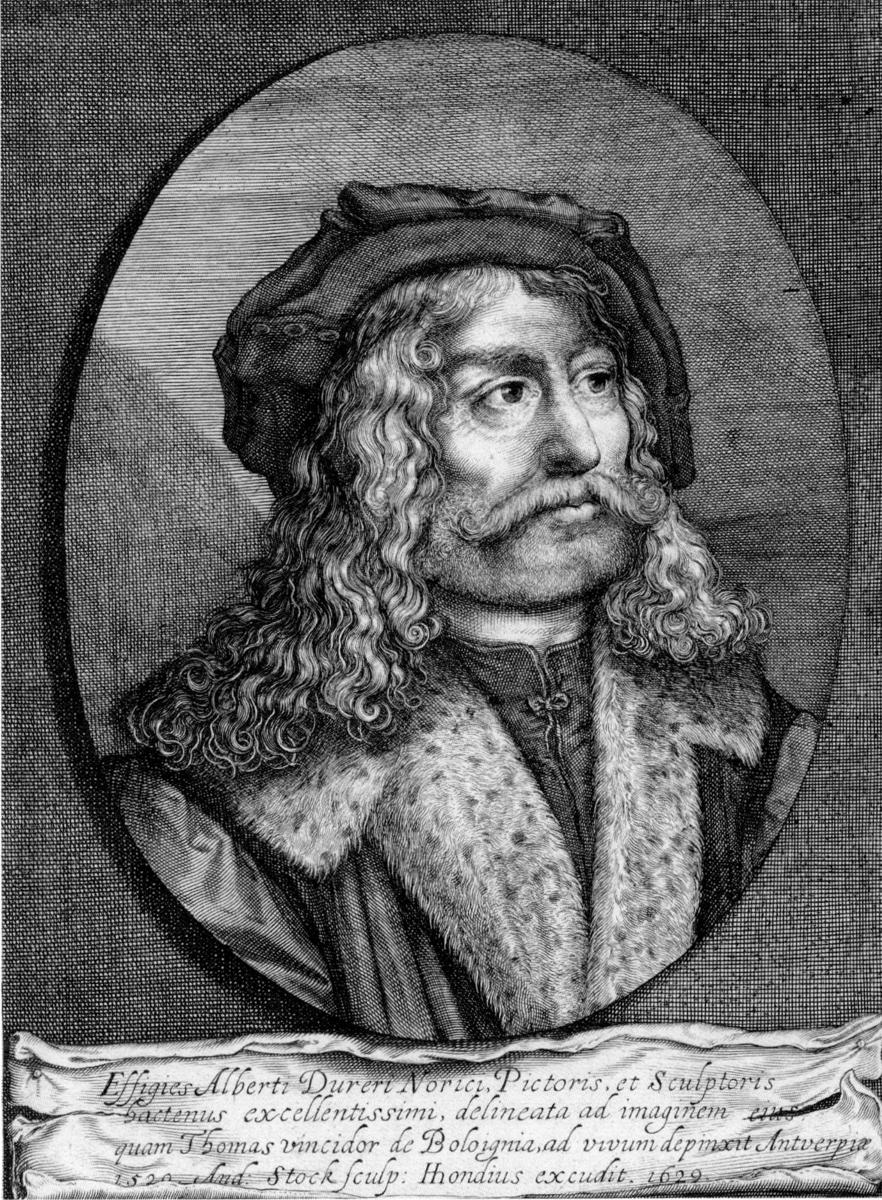

10
ANDRIES JACOBSZ STOCK (ABOUT 1580–AFTER 1648) AFTER TOMMASO VINCIDOR (1493–1536)
Portrait of Albrecht Dürer, 1629
Etching and engraving, 24.2 × 16.4 cm
Rijksmuseum, Amsterdam

journal itself. Fifteen sheets from this silverpoint drawing book survive today. In a stimulating essay Arnold Nesselrath unravels the secrets of this 'Büchlein', as Dürer called it himself with pride. He may have kept a sketchbook for pen drawings as well, from which again some drawings survive, although Christof Metzger is adamant that these small pen drawings were actually part of the journal itself, an intriguing and convincing hypothesis he presents here. Dürer's journal also documents a number of other drawings, especially large portraits, which can be matched against those that survive.

First and foremost the journal enables a complete reconstruction of Dürer's itinerary to, from and around the Low Countries, no doubt using a map such as the one produced by his countryman Erhard Etzlaub (1455–1532). He travelled from Nuremberg to Antwerp, which he made his base, passing through Frankfurt and Cologne and reaching Antwerp on 2 August. At the end of the month Dürer visited Brussels and Mechelen, the seat of Margaret of Austria, seeking support for his petition to Charles V to renew his pension. In Brussels he was astonished by the sight of golden objects, as well as shields and clothing, sent from Mexico, recording that 'I have never in my life seen anything that gave my heart such delight as these things' (cat. 9).[5]

In Antwerp in October, Raphael's pupil Tommaso Vincidor (1493–1536) sought out Dürer in order to give him a gold ring and take his portrait (cat. 10). Here Dürer recorded Charles V's triumphal entry into Antwerp. On 3 October he left for the coronation of the emperor at Aachen, where he gambled and enjoyed the hot springs. He returned to Antwerp after a stay at

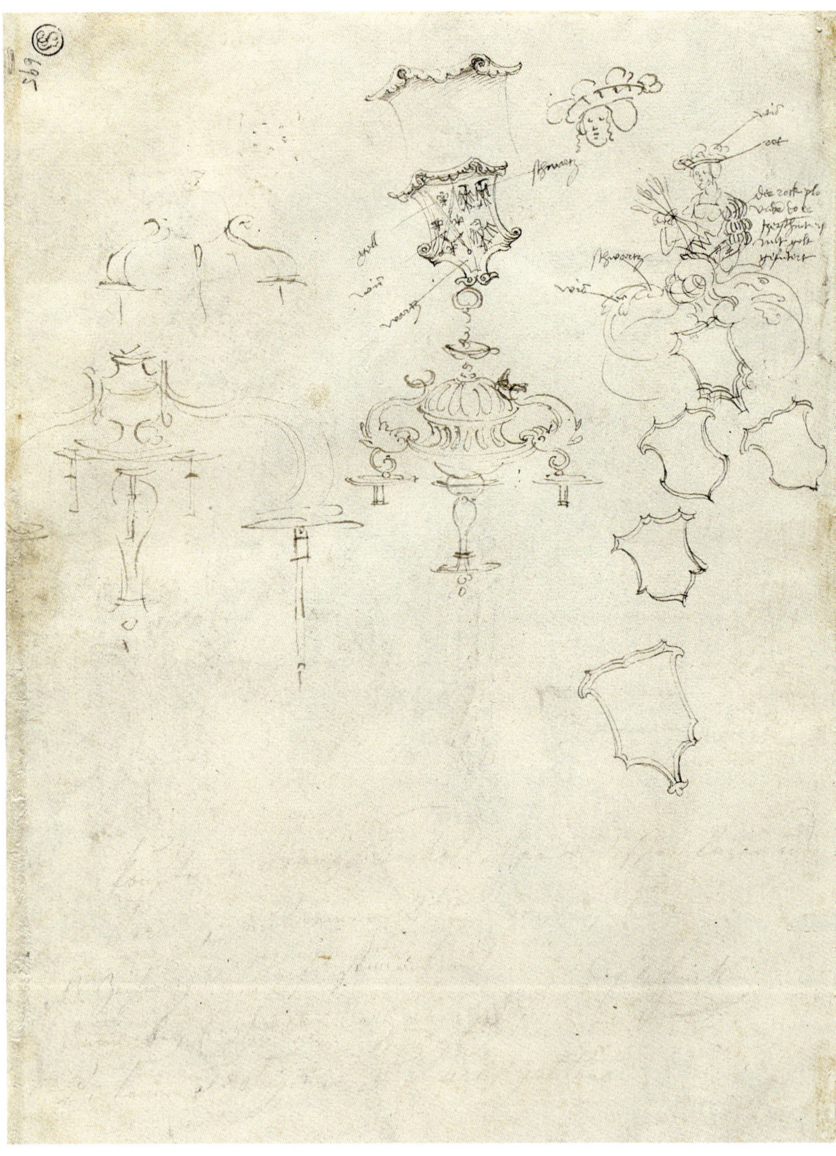

Fig. 1
ALBRECHT DÜRER
Chandelier and Coat of Arms of the Abarrow Family, 26 May 1521
Pen and brown ink, 20.6 × 29.3 cm
Städel Museum, Frankfurt am Main (695 verso)

Cologne, where on 12 November he received the good news that his pension had been granted; ten days later he was back in Antwerp. From 3 to 14 December he travelled to Bergen op Zoom and Zeeland, where he fell ill, possibly suffering from malaria; he also sailed around the islands here, narrowly avoiding shipwreck. Returning to Antwerp on 14 December, he stayed here until the following spring. On 6 April, together with Jan Provoost (1491–1529), he made a boat trip to Bruges and Ghent, where he was able to see works of art including Michelangelo's *Bruges Madonna* and the van Eyck brothers' Ghent Altarpiece. He returned to Antwerp on 11 April and fell ill again. On 6 June he travelled once more to Mechelen and met with Margaret of Austria, who rejected his portrait of her father. He was back in Antwerp on 8 June, where he met with Lucas van Leyden. On 3 July he answered the summons of King Christian II of Denmark and travelled to Brussels for a banquet, leaving on 12 July to return to Nuremberg via Aachen and Cologne.

In his remarkable journal Dürer writes about the drawings and paintings he himself made and sold, including the prints he had brought with him. As he had done in Venice, he painted portraits, among others of his best friend in Antwerp, the Portuguese merchant Rodrigo Fernandes de Almada (about 1465/70–1546/8). As Till-Holger Borchert asserts very convincingly in his essay, Dürer remained close to the portrait style he had developed in Venice, small and relatively modest pictures that appear not to be touched by new developments taking place in the Low Countries at the time. However, as Peter van den Brink states in his contribution, Dürer was especially successful as a portrait draughtsman, a strategy he had tried before at the Diet of Augsburg in 1518 and which would result in more than eighty impressive large portrait drawings that would generate an important income during his year-long absence from home.

Of all the small paintings that Dürer produced in Antwerp, only five survive. Gone are the four paintings of Saint Veronica's cloth he noted in his journal, painted for the imperial councillor Jakob Banisius (1466–1532), the Portuguese traders Francisco Pesão and João Brandão, as well as the goldsmith Jan van de Perre (died 1559), leaving only the model drawing in the Albertina, Vienna (fig. 77).[6] One painting that did survive, and became an icon of sorts, was his *Saint Jerome* (cat. 110), painted for his close friend Rodrigo Fernandes de Almada. Astrid Harth and Maximiliaan Martens unravel the picture's humanistic meaning with care and precision, explaining Dürer's position between Erasmus and Martin Luther. However, Dürer would never finish his large project of the altarpiece of the *Virgin and Child with Saints and Angels*, intended as a Netherlandish 'pendant' of sorts for the *Feast of the Rose Garlands* (fig. 19) he had painted in Venice. As Stijn Alsteens argues in his essay, Margaret of Austria, the patron Dürer had in mind for the unpainted masterpiece, declined the honour he bestowed upon her; or perhaps he did not dare to ask her after she failed to accept his gift of Maximilian's portrait.

But Dürer did not limit himself to finished works of art, drawings or paintings. He made designs as well, whether a house, a seal, a chandelier or a coat of arms for an Englishman, as he describes in his journal between 26 and 30 May. A scribbled sketch survives today on the verso of a drawing of the *Agony in the Garden* he had made at the same time (fig. 1). Examples of his worked-up designs can be seen in a sheet now in Hamburg, on which a drawing for a medallion of Saint George slaying the dragon and another showing Saint Christopher

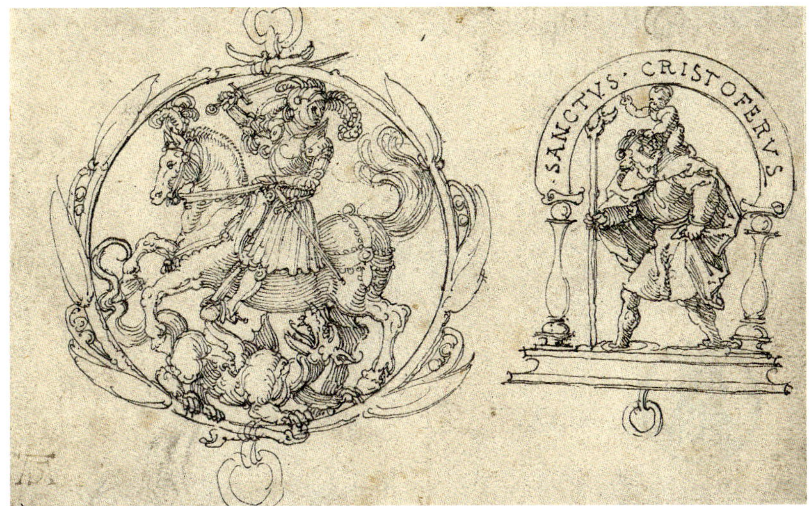

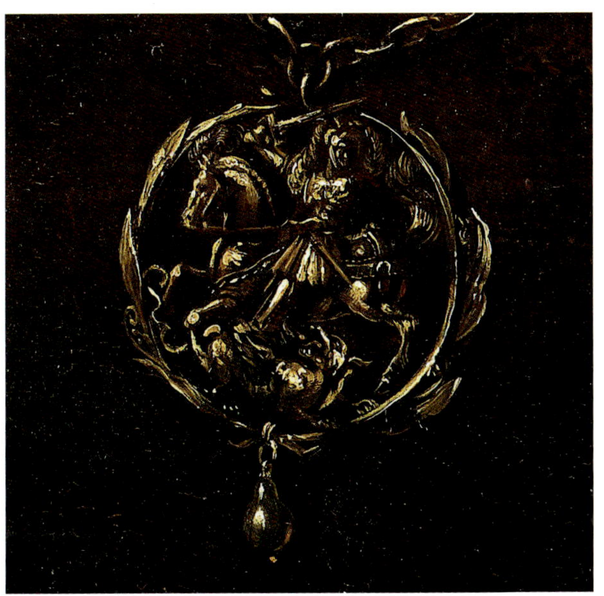

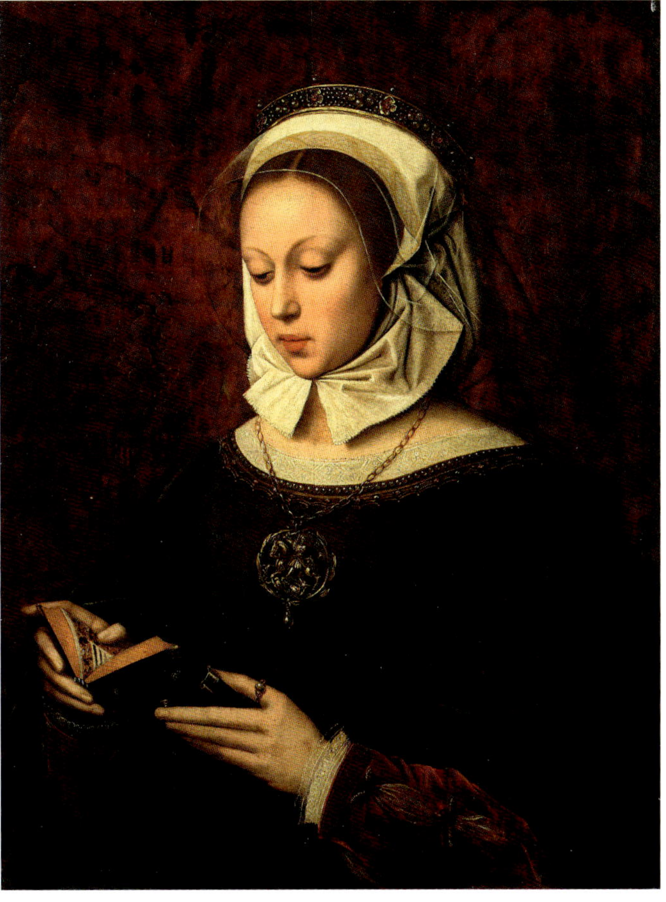

Fig. 2
ALBRECHT DÜRER
Saint George and Saint Christopher, Designs for Medallions, about 1520–1
Pen and black ink, 7.4 × 11.6 cm
Hamburger Kunsthalle, Hamburg (23.003)

Fig. 3
AMBROSIUS BENSON
(active 1519; died 1550)
Portrait of a Woman reading a Book and wearing Dürer's Medallion of Saint George, 1520–3 (and detail, left)
Oil on oak, 75 × 55 cm
Musée du Louvre, Paris

appear side by side (fig. 2). The Saint George design was actually executed: it appears in a painting by Ambrosius Benson (active 1519; died 1550; fig. 3). Interestingly, Dürer was personally involved in the making of his own portrait medal (he designed the reverse) by the famous Augsburg medallist Hans Schwarz (1492–1550), to whom he paid 2 guilders in gold, which was sent from Antwerp on a Fugger Bank shipment in September 1520.

No doubt Dürer saw many works of art on his travels in the Low Countries, by contemporaries and great masters of the past alike, although his journal is rather unforthcoming on this. He comments on Michelangelo's sculpture in Bruges, mistaking the marble for alabaster; he sees an altarpiece by a Master Steffan in Cologne – usually taken to be the altarpiece of the *Adoration of the Kings* now in the city's cathedral, but not necessarily so; and he is impressed by the small panels by Juan de Flandes (active from 1496; died 1519) seen in Margaret of Austria's bedroom, where he is also faced with van Eyck's *Arnolfini Portrait* (fig. 53). He praises the famous Ghent Altarpiece, especially the naked figure of Eve, but the Virgin and God the Father, too. However, he was clearly less enthusiastic about that great contemporary work of art about which everyone was talking, the majestic altarpiece in the Abbey of Middelburg by Jan Gossaert (Jean Gossart; active 1508; died 1532), which was probably the secret reason for Dürer's journey to Zeeland. His small drawing now in Besançon (cat. 11) may actually be the sketch he made of the then already famous *Deposition*, a work of art that would survive fewer than fifty more years before being destroyed by fire.[7]

There is, however, so much more he does not mention. When he pays a visit to the palace of Hendrik van Nassau in Brussels, he does note the now-lost altarpiece by Hugo van der Goes (1440–1482) with the Seven Sacraments in the chapel, and even a meteorite

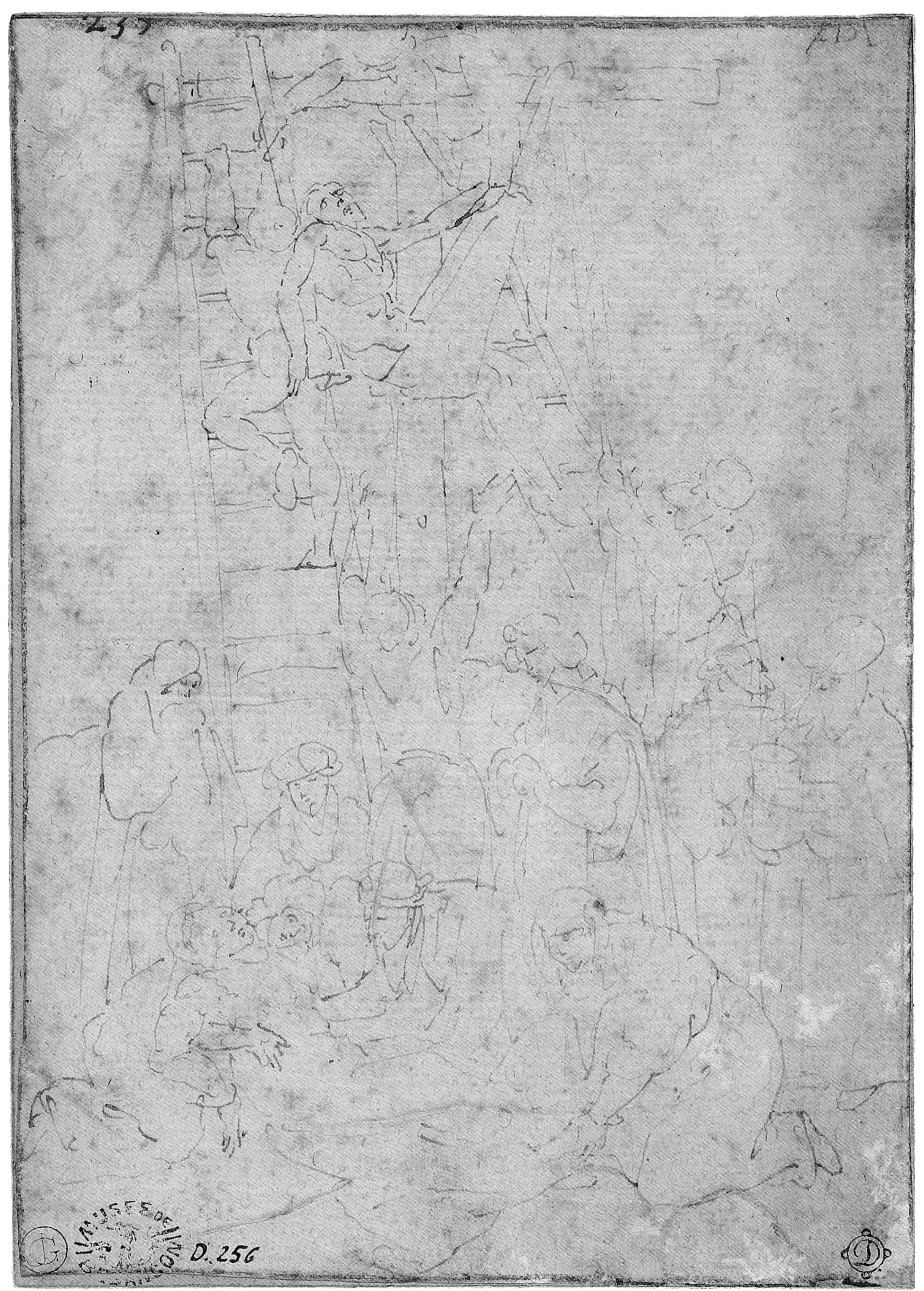

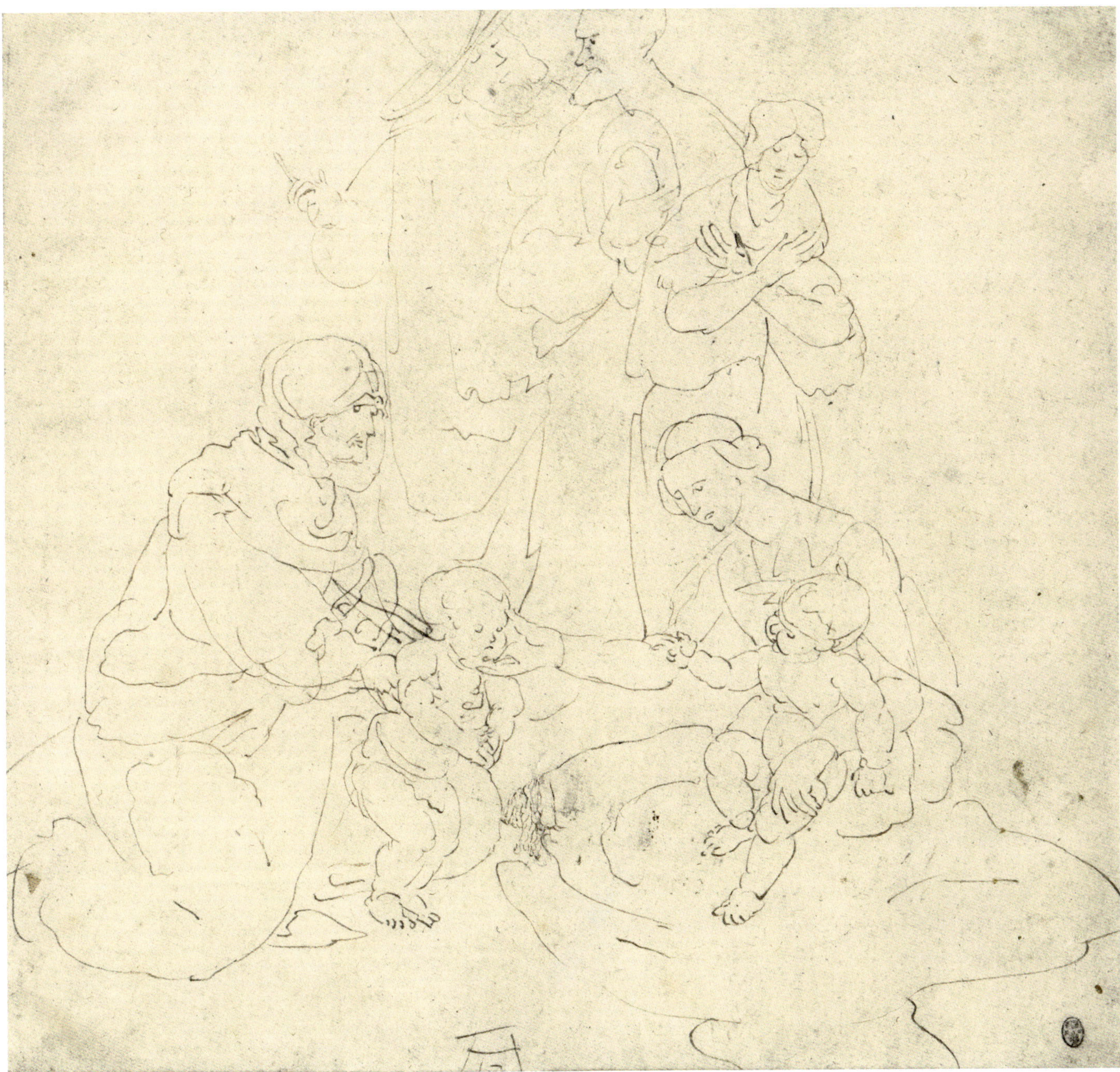

Fig. 4
ALBRECHT DÜRER AFTER RAPHAEL (?)
(1483–1520)
The Holy Kinship, about 1520–1
Pen and brown ink, 19.4 × 20.3 cm
Staatliche Museen zu Berlin. Kupferstichkabinett
(KdZ 4670)

OPPOSITE
11
ALBRECHT DÜRER
Descent from the Cross, about 1520
Pen and iron gall ink on paper, 14.6 × 10.2 cm
Musée des Beaux-Arts et d'Archéologie, Besançon

or the apparent famous large bed with place for fifty people, but he fails to mention the spectacular triptych of the *Garden of Earthly Delights* by Hieronymus Bosch (1450–1516), another indication that he remained rather untouched by contemporary art. And should we consider the absence of Raphael's cartoons from his journal in the same light? These were accessible in the workshop of the weaver Pieter van Aelst (about 1450–1532/3) in Brussels, as no doubt Bernaert van Orley (1487/91–1541) and Tommaso Vincidor would have informed him. However, there is no word on these works of art by this renowned painter and draughtsman who died just before Dürer left Nuremberg for the

12
ALBRECHT DÜRER
Head of a Sleeping Child, 1520
Black chalk, black bodycolour heightened with white, 25.9 × 18.2 cm
Hamburger Kunsthalle, Kupferstichkabinett

13
ALBRECHT DÜRER
Head of a Woman, 1520
Brush drawing in black and grey bodycolour, heightened with white, 32.4 × 22.8 cm
British Museum

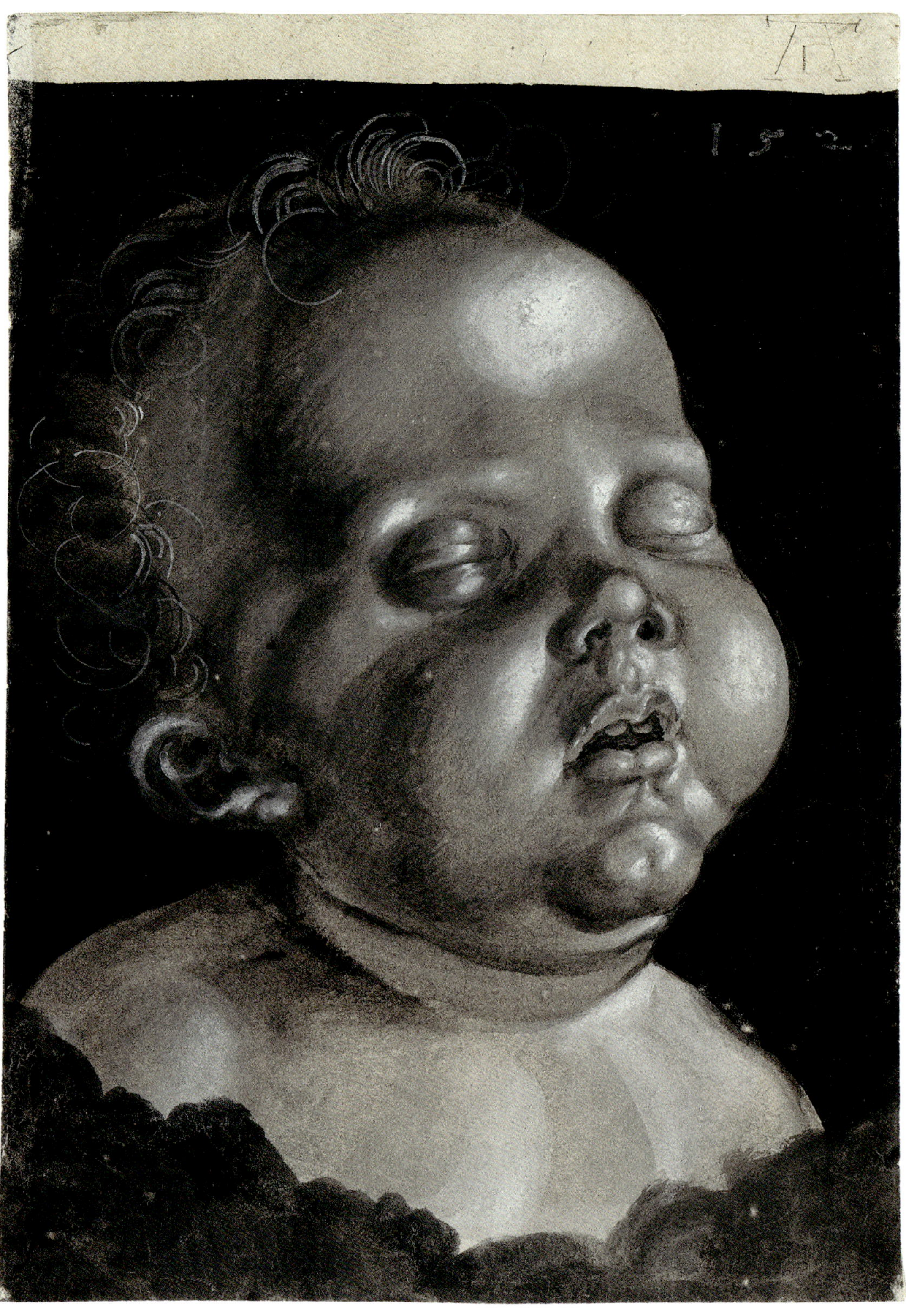

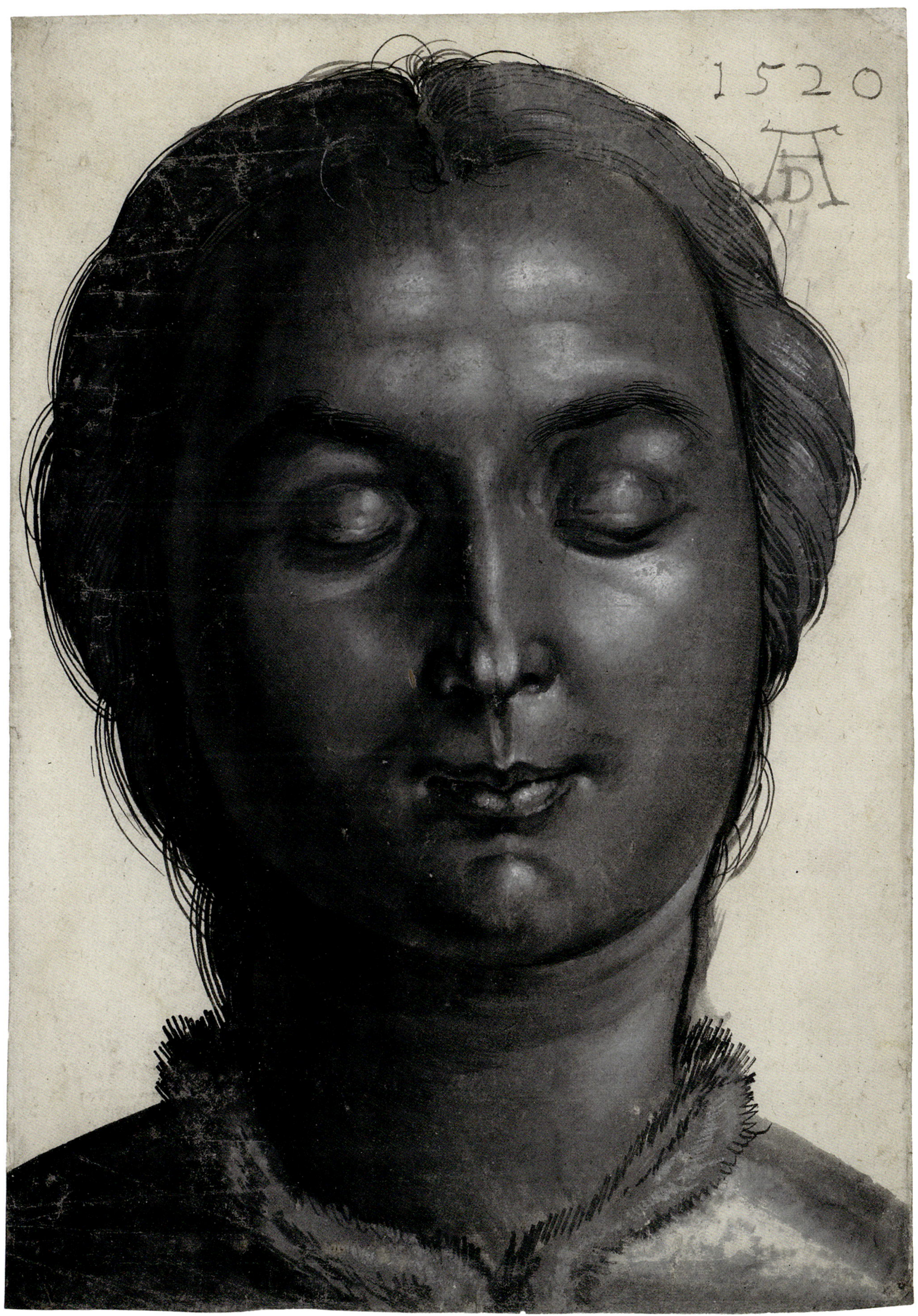
1520

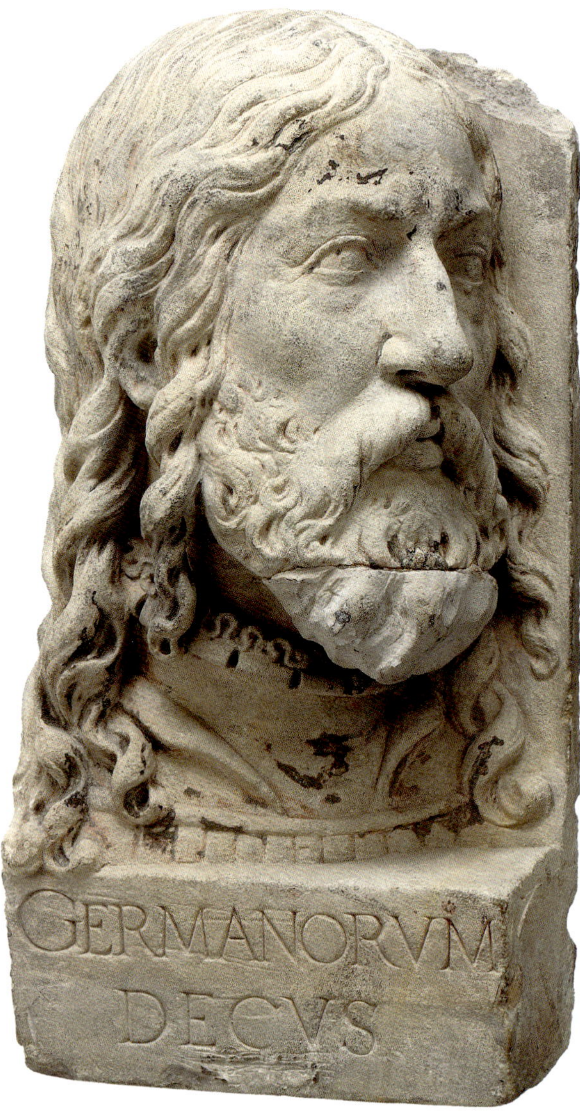

Fig. 5
WILLEM VAN DEN BROECKE, CALLED PALUDANUS (1530–1579)
Portrait Bust of Albrecht Dürer, about 1563
Sandstone, 39.5 × 19.3 × 12 cm
Museum aan de Stroom, Antwerp (AV5920 x)

Low Countries. Although they had never met, the two great Renaissance artists had exchanged gifts and highly respected each other. It is hardly conceivable that Vincidor would not have taken Dürer to see Raphael's large cartoons.[8] Interestingly, Hans Mielke regarded Dürer's pen sketch of the *Holy Kinship* (fig. 4) as a copy after an Italian painting, probably by Raphael.[9] It is possible that Vincidor may have played a role in helping Dürer access works of art by his teacher.

Like Raphael, Albrecht Dürer and his works of art would have an enormous impact in the Low Countries. His engravings and woodcuts paved the way before his arrival in Antwerp. These prints were used by every artist, painter and sculptor alike, and were therefore greatly in demand. In the present volume (pp. 103–15) Larry Silver studies in depth the relationship between Dürer and Netherlandish artist Jan Gossaert, whose relationship with his Nuremberg contemporary was much more personal. Nevertheless, Dürer's prints rather than his paintings or drawings remained their prime source of inspiration, notwithstanding the pivotal role that his *Saint Jerome* (cat. 110) would play for several decades to come or the impact of his large portrait drawings on Lucas van Leyden. Dürer's role as a printmaker would initiate a new generation of engravers and etchers in the Netherlands – not only Gossaert and Dirk Vellert, who began to make prints from 1522 onwards, but others such as Jan Rombouts (around 1475; died 1535/6) and Frans Crabbe (about 1480–1553) as well.

It would be Albrecht Dürer the artist who would become the focus of veneration, even before the end of his stay in the Low Countries. In every city he visited he would be the centre of attention, and banquets would be organised everywhere to celebrate the presence of the first superstar of art history. In Antwerp a banquet was organised almost immediately upon his arrival and all the artists in the city paid tribute to him. This places a remark in a letter by Dürer to the Nuremberg City Council in an interesting light. When on 17 October 1524 he requests an annuity from the Council, he writes that the City of Antwerp wished to pay him a salary of 300 Philip guilders a year, as well as providing tax exemption and a house to live in for free, but that he turned the offer down out of love for his hometown of Nuremberg. Although no other evidence of this is known today, there can be no doubt that Dürer's status in the Low Countries knew no boundaries.

Some forty years later, Dürer still had no equal in Antwerp, perhaps with the exception of Jan van Eyck. It is hardly surprising that the Antwerp painter Cornelis van Dalem (about 1528–1573) added the busts of these two painters to the façade of his house in the Lange Nieuwstraat, with its iconography of Mercury (trade) and Minerva (the arts).[10] Dürer's bust carrying the inscription 'GERMANORVM DECVS' (fig. 5), 'the jewel of the Germans', balances that of Jan van Eyck, 'BELGARVM SPLENDOR'.[11] Cornelis van Dalem, both a merchant and a painter, a true *pictor doctus* with a famous library, was a great admirer of Albrecht Dürer. Many of van Dalem's mesmerising landscapes pay tribute to Dürer's prints; in some cases he actually produced painted versions of Dürer's engravings, such as the 1568 *Nativity*.[12] However, van Dalem's high regard for Dürer's graphic work cannot be separated from that of the successful print-making industry around the publisher Hieronymus Cock (1517/18 –1570) and his Antwerp publishing house, 'Aux Quatre Vents'. In fact, it is entirely possible that van Dalem did not paint his *Nativity* directly after Dürer, but took as his model a copy of 1566 by Jan Wierix (1539–1620).[13]

The importance of Hieronymus Cock for the renewed passion for old masters, such as Bosch and Dürer, cannot be overlooked, as is discussed by Giulia Bartrum in her incisive essay on the *Crucifixion in Outline*. This engraving was long thought to be an original by Albrecht Dürer, but must be regarded as a key work in the Antwerp Dürer Renaissance, thanks to both Cock and his friend, the prominent collector Cardinal Antoine Perrenot de Granvelle (1517–1586). Granvelle's enormous collection of Dürer drawings, largely acquired in Nuremberg from Ursula and Endres Dürer between 1543 and 1560, came into the possession of Emperor Rudolf II (1552–1612) in 1589, who had obtained the remnants of Dürer's estate from the Imhoff family one year earlier.[14] As Christof Metzger describes in his essay, it was Granvelle's collection that accommodated most of Dürer's drawings from his journey to the Low Countries, among them the silverpoint drawing book.

Dürer's fame would receive a new impulse in 1828, with the commemoration in Nuremberg of his death 300 years earlier. Festivities and modern works of art were created for the occasion, and Dürer's journal of his Netherlandish journey was published for the first time in German, edited by Joseph Heller and Friedrich Campe. However, it was Frédéric Verachter's translation into Flemish 12 years later that inspired many artists in Belgium, a country born only a decade earlier. In the search for heroes for an artistic Olympus, Dürer turned out to be an ideal role model and the story of his journey enabled and stimulated many artists to put the Nuremberg master on a pedestal. The same was true in Germany, where even a lock of his hair became a relic in the hands of the Nazarene painter Eduard von Steinle (1810–1886), and France, where the sculptor Albert-Ernest Carrier-Belleuse (1824–1887)transformed Dürer into an artist with godlike features.

Many new discoveries have been made in the preparation of this exhibition and the accompanying publication. Thankfully, however, not all questions have been answered and a new young generation of Dürer specialists will no doubt endeavour to solve more of them. To give just one example: we are still in the dark on the function of two remarkably beautiful drawings that Dürer must have made shortly after his arrival in the Low Countries, the *Head of a Woman* (cat. 13) and the *Head of a Sleeping Child* (cat. 12), now respectively in the British Museum and the Hamburger Kunsthalle. Their high finish and remarkable technique may give the impression of being independent drawings; their subject most certainly does not.

It is a great privilege to have been able to combine our efforts with so many of our esteemed colleagues. All the authors are aware of this great opportunity to make an outstanding exhibition and a book that may be a lasting legacy to all those readers who seek to understand more of Albrecht Dürer and his remarkable journeys.

1 For a comprehensive and accessible biography, see Hutchison 1990. The primary sources are published in Rupprich 1956–69 and Ashcroft 2017.
2 See Nuremberg 2012 and London 2013.
3 See most recently Milan 2018; also Evans 2004 and Crawford Luber 2005.
4 Dürer's original journal has not survived; it was possibly destroyed around 1800 during the so-called Coalition Wars in Europe. The generally accepted view, that it was burned more than a century earlier, when it was in the collection of Thomas Howard, 21st Earl of Arundel (1585–1646), cannot be corroborated. There is not the slightest evidence that Arundel ever owned the original journal; it probably remained in Nuremberg, as Christof Metzger convincingly writes in his contribution to this publication. The most precise German transcription of the texts of the two copies is still Rupprich 1956–69, vol. 1, pp. 146–202. Publications that have added new insights to our knowledge of Dürer's Netherlandish journey are: Veth and Muller 1918; Goris and Marlier 1970; Brussels 1977; Sahm 2002, pp. 133–84; Unverfehrt 2007. The most recent translation in English is Ashcroft 2017, vol. 1, pp. 545–628.
5 Ashcroft 2017, vol. 1, p. 560. See Feest in Frankfurt 2013, esp. pp. 368 and 372.
6 The Albertina drawing seems unconnected to the known prints that Dürer produced much earlier in his career. The drawing fits stylistically much better in 1520–1 and must have been the model for at least one of the four lost paintings.
7 On this drawing and the Middelburg Altarpiece, see van den Brink 2020.
8 Mark Evans has suggested that Dürer may have modelled the figures of Saint Mark and Saint Luke (here Evans was actually referring to Saint Paul) of the *Four Apostles* from 1526 on Raphael's cartoon *Christ's Charge to Saint Peter*. See M. Evans, 'The impact of the Cartoons', in London 2010, pp. 50–2.
9 H. Mielke in Anzelewsky and Mielke 1984, p. 117.
10 L. van Opstal, *Das Haus Cornelis van Dalems an der Lange Nieuwstraat, Antwerpen*, about 1844, Museum Plantijn Moretus, Antwerp (inv. PK.MT.01915).
11 On the iconography of the façade and Dürer's bust, see B. Decker in Frankfurt 1981, pp. 100–1, no. 48; J. van Damme in Antwerp 1993, pp. 165–6, no. 16.
12 Cornelis van Dalem after Dürer, *The Nativity*, 1568, Suermondt Ludwig Museum, Aachen (inv. LS 2493).
13 Jan Wierix after Dürer, *The Nativity*, 1566, Suermondt Ludwig Museum, Aachen (inv. DK 624).
14 Vienna 2019, pp. 59–62.

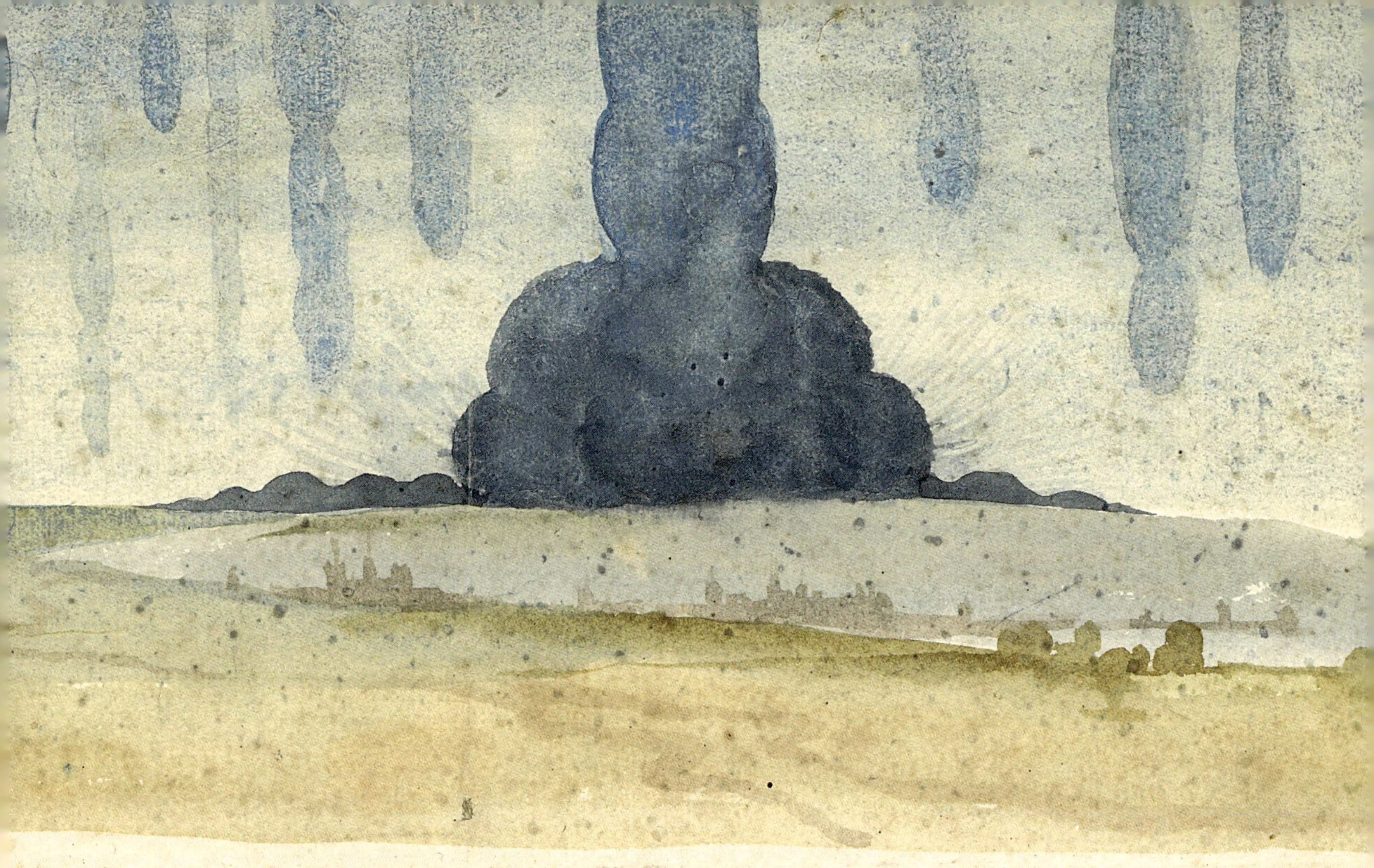

m pfingstag zwischen dem ~~pfin~~ mitwoch und pfintzdag in der nacht im sch

grosser wassern vom himell fillen und das erst traff das ertrich ungefer 4

grausamkeitt mit einem uber grossen rauschen und zersprützen und er

erschrak ich so gar schwerlich das ich doran erwachett. dan dy andern wa

woren fast gros und der fill etliche weit etliche neher und sy kamen so hoch

n filn. aber do das erst wasser das das ertrich traff schir herbey kam do fill es m

t und brausen das ich also erschrack do ich erwacht das mir all mein l

t zu mir selbs kam Aber do ich am morgen auff stund molet ich hy oben

alle ding zu besten

Albrecht Dürer

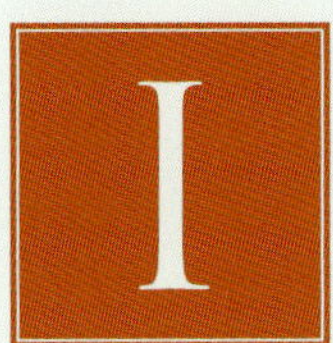

ALBRECHT DÜRER ARTIST, WRITER, TRAVELLER

ALBRECHT DÜRER WAS AN EXCEPTIONAL ARTIST, AND self-consciously so. This is evident not only in the confidence with which he presents himself in his self portraits and in his use of the 'AD' monogram to identify the authorship of his prints. It is also clear in the unusually extensive and varied legacy of writings in the German language that he has left, from autobiographical writings, letters and even comic poems, to theoretical texts intended to aid other artists.

The Dürer family chronicle – begun by his father, Albrecht Dürer the Elder, a goldsmith from Hungary – gives a detailed record of the artist's life and that of his family: Dürer's father died in 1502 and his mother, Barbara, in 1514, after giving birth to 18 children. Both deaths are recorded in the chronicle, in conventional form; but in another document, of which only fragments survive, Dürer gives vivid details of the last painful struggles of both parents, and records his own regret at leaving the room to sleep while his father died. An exceptional insight into Dürer's imaginative life is given in the description he made in 1525 of a terrifying dream of the world engulfed by a deluge, accompanying a rapidly made watercolour.

Dürer frequently annotated his own drawings, such as those he made in silverpoint on his journey to the Low Countries in 1520–1, reminding himself whom he drew and where. He admired the painter and printmaker Martin Schongauer (active 1469; died 1491) and, on a drawing by him that he had managed to acquire, carefully recorded Schongauer's authorship and the date it was made. He similarly annotated the drawing of three male nudes that Raphael sent him in 1515, although the self portrait Dürer apparently sent to him is lost, as is any correspondence they had.

Ten letters that Dürer wrote from Venice in 1506 to his friend the Nuremberg humanist Willibald Pirckheimer survive in his own handwriting but the responses and letters to other correspondents he mentions are lost. As well as demonstrating Dürer's command of Venetian dialect, they show a shared sense of masculine humour. The journal he kept day by day during his visit to the Low Countries similarly shows Dürer's constant curiosity as well as his concern to safeguard his business interests.

From early in his career Dürer had planned a book of instruction for young painters, but over the course of his career his focus shifted towards his own theoretical enquiries, above all into human proportion, which are recorded in a series of notebooks. Towards the end of his life he produced his *Treatise on Measurement* (1525), advice for artists who wanted to use geometrical constructions, including methods for drawing in perspective. His four books on human proportion were published shortly after his death in 1528. SF

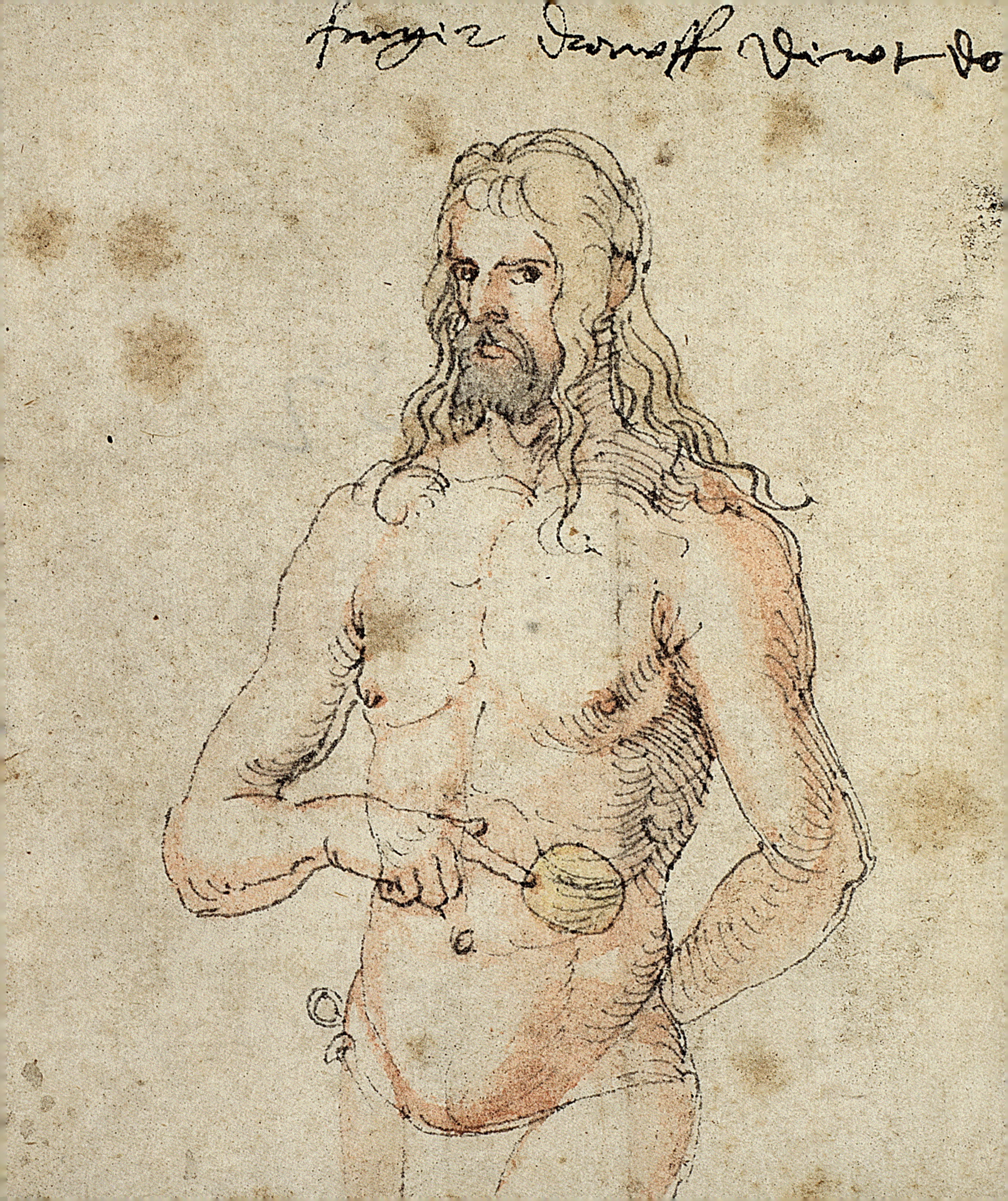

ANDREAS BEYER

DÜRER ON HIS JOURNEY TO SELF-DISCOVERY

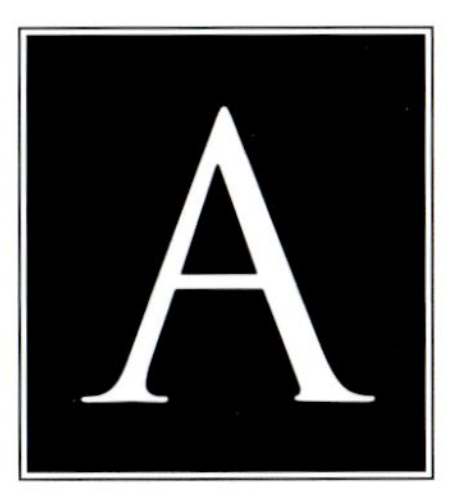

LBRECHT DÜRER, AS ALMOST NO OTHER artist of the early modern era, bore witness to his own persona in self portraits describing his looks, his physical condition and the changes in his appearance in the early and middle phases of his artistic career. Also numerous surviving records in other formats articulate Dürer's unceasing self-awareness and introspection, reflecting his self-assertion, especially in the examination of the world around him. His family's biography, as recorded in the family chronicle or the so-called memorial book (*Gedenkbuch*), enabled him in his search for identity to reflect on his own origins and the path his life had taken. His numerous letters meanwhile, specifically those to Willibald Pirckheimer and Jakob Heller, articulate his self-discovery as artist and entrepreneur. With his *Visions of a Cloudburst* of 1525 (fig. 6), a nightmare recorded in words and watercolour, Dürer becomes the first artist ever to document his own dream and at the same time he distances himself, in the role of observer. When he awakens from the dream, his body trembling all over ('zitternd'), noting that he was not himself for a long time ('lang nit recht zu mir selbs kam'), he describes in spectacular manner both proximity and at the same time distance from himself, being the proper object of self-reflection.[1] Dürer's travels also increased his self-awareness, not only in weighing his life in Nuremberg against his experiences in foreign lands but also in the sense of true self-recognition.

If Dürer's Netherlands travel journal is to be regarded here as an important 'ego document' or autobiography, an essential part of himself as a self-constituted individual, then it is important to understand that it should not be seen as getting closer to his 'being' or character. It was long believed that above all, his written legacy would provide a

PREVIOUS PAGE
Detail from *Visions of a Cloudburst* (fig. 6)

OPPOSITE
Detail from *Self Portrait, III* (fig. 7)

close connection with the communication-friendly artist. Hans Rupprich believed that in the case of Dürer, 'the practical necessities of life, feelings of piety, experiences of a joyfully observing soul … urged him more than other artists of his time to write down his communications … from which we sense even today: he had a faithful and warm heart and was a good person'.[2] Heinrich Wölfflin was of the opinion that the letters and journals contain information 'in which a most congenial man reveals himself almost entirely'.[3] Even Erwin Panofsky inferred from these documents that Dürer was a man 'at once great, good and human'.[4] Jan-Albert Goris and Georges Marlier wrote as late as 1970 that: 'The Diary and his journey also tell us in a very direct way much about Dürer's character'.[5] Finally, Ernst Ullmann gave his Dürer study of 1994 the descriptive title *Albrecht Dürer – Selbstbildnisse und autobiographische Schriften als Zeugnisse der Entwicklung seiner Persönlichkeit* ('Albrecht Dürer – Self Portraits and Autobiographical Writings as Testimonials of the Development of his Personality').[6]

Dürer's personality – whether he was sympathetic or 'good and human' – should not perhaps concern art historical research, quite apart from the question of whether this could even be ascertained in hindsight. This empathetic evocation of a personality, which possibly reveals more about the authors than about the artist anyway, is no longer pursued by recent scholarship, which furthermore strives not to subordinate individual texts into a single category but rather to recognise them within their respective contexts. Therefore Dürer's journal of his travel to the Netherlands has been newly assessed in terms of literary study. Heike Sahm asserts that, because of its disparate content, the journal should be regarded at best as an account book and not as an actual diary – an observation already made by earlier commentators.[7] Indeed, by subdividing her analysis of the content into 'Expenses and earnings', 'Gift practices', 'Tributes', 'Sightseeing and visit to Zeeland', as well as 'Lament over Luther',[8] Sahm confirms the key aspects of the text, classifying them by their separate functions. On the other hand, we may attribute more to these records than simple bookkeeping without reverting to the earlier emphasis placed on Dürer's personality. The text surely goes far beyond that, even in those places where he meticulously itemises all his earnings and expenses. These jottings reveal Dürer, even before the term was

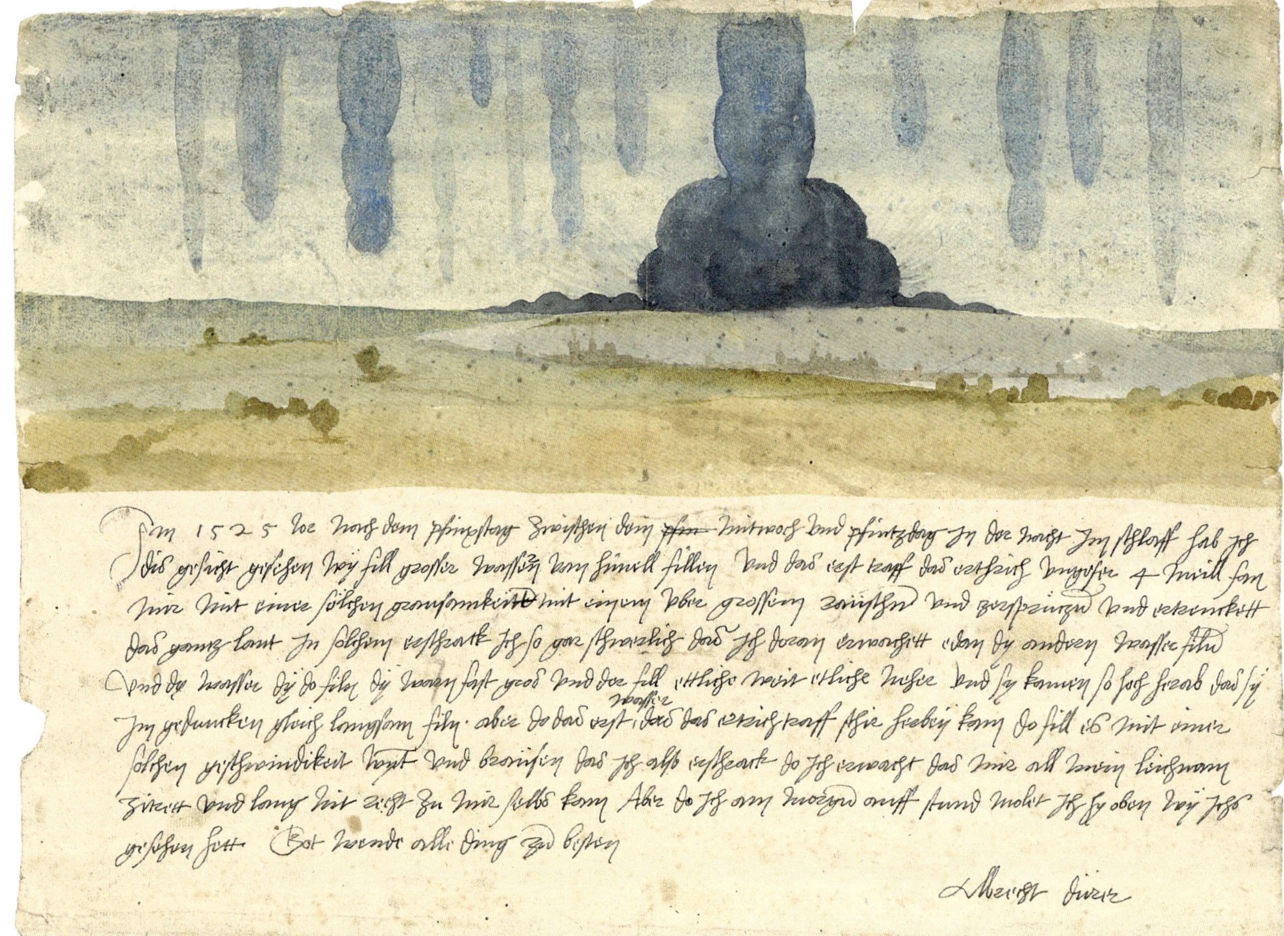

Fig. 6
ALBRECHT DÜRER
Visions of a Cloudburst, 1525
Watercolour, 47.5 × 36.5 cm
Kunsthistorisches Museum, Vienna (KK5127 [Codex])

'In Brussels I lodged, ate and drank with my Lords of Nuremberg, and they would take nothing from me for it. Likewise in Aachen I ate with them for three weeks, and they took me to Cologne and here too would accept no payment.'

coined, as *homo oeconomicus*. In this respect the journal constitutes a central category in the search for his identity: the artist as entrepreneur.[9] Indeed Sahm, who assumes that Dürer wrote the diary simply for his own use, is also aware that more can be filtered from it than bookkeeping, questioning whether the artist 'had not written at least part of it with the thought that people would be interested in his life later'. Her somewhat discouraging conclusion, however, reads: 'Where and how far such a motive resonates in the text cannot be distinguished in detail'.[10]

Dürer's Netherlandish journal only survives in two copies (cat. 14); indeed, that it was copied at all is eloquent testimony to the interest in the artist's life long after his death, a condition about which he would have speculated in his journal, the family chronicle and elsewhere. With his interest in himself and his claim to individuality, seeking recognition in his own time as much as hoping for posthumous fame, Dürer demonstrates the movement towards biographical self-representation adopted since Petrarch. The 'discovery of the individual' would become, as famously stated by Jacob Burckhardt, the signum of the Renaissance.[11] Although scholarship today no longer attributes the discovery of one's individuality exclusively to the early modern era, claiming instead that its beginnings were already evident in the Middle Ages, it is true that decisive steps were taken in the fourteenth and fifteenth centuries in the formation of written self-assertions, evolving fully in the sixteenth century. Interestingly, besides literary products it was the *libri dei conti* or account books, that expanded to include personal data, thus initiating the modern journal.[12] The fact that the humanist and poet Conrad Celtis (1459–1508) promoted self-fashioning – that is, the construction of one's own identity, fame and immortality – through his writings, among others in his *Quattuor libri amorum (Amores)* published in Nuremberg in 1502, refers directly to Dürer's circle of friends.[13] It is above all in his engagement with himself that Dürer is the equal of his humanist contemporaries.

The types of text under discussion cannot, however, be characterised as autobiographical in the modern sense: the term cannot be applied to the Renaissance, as it was established in Germany only in the eighteenth century.[14] Dürer's Netherlandish journal may therefore

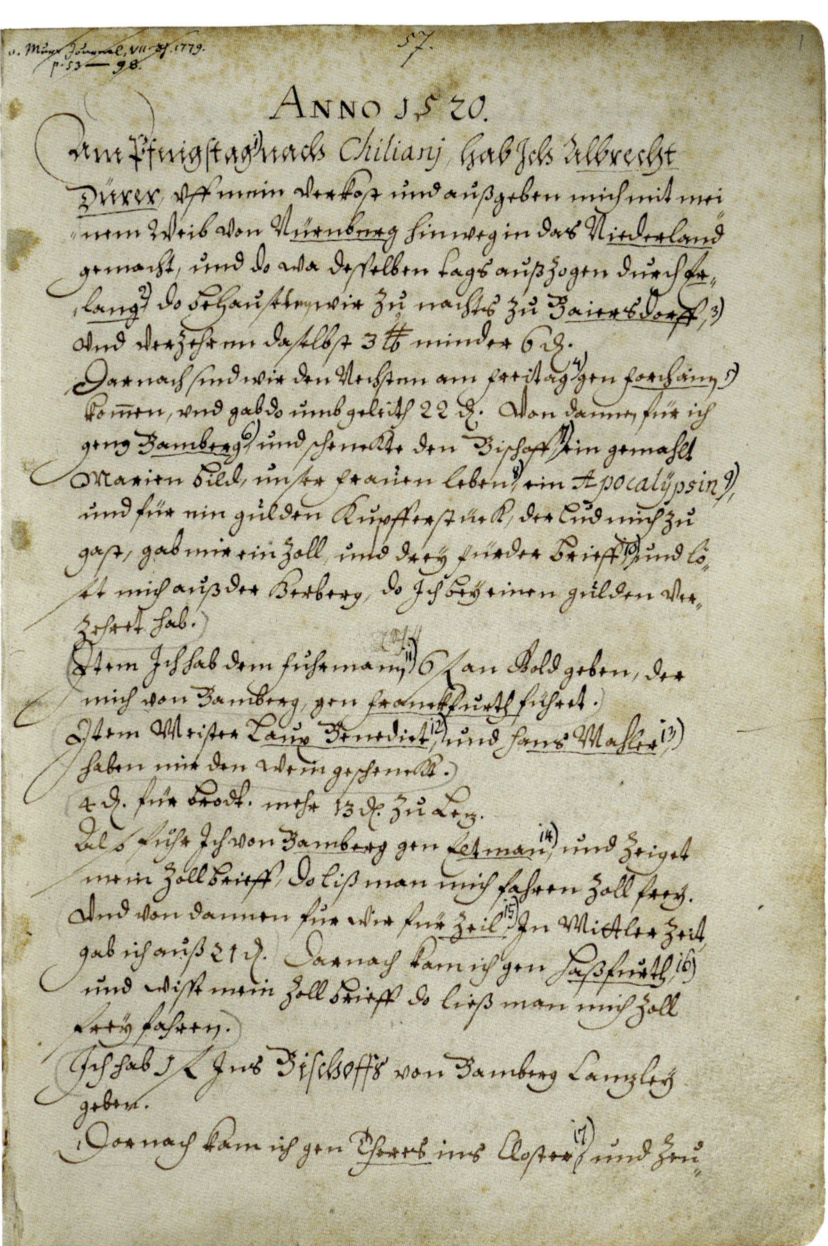
Anno 1520

14
JOHANN CHRISTOPH HAUER (?)
(1586–1660)
Copy after Albrecht Dürer's diary of the journey to the Netherlands, about 1620
Pen on paper, 30 × 20.5 cm
Staatsbibliothek, Bamberg

be understood at best as a text that represents its author's constant efforts to understand and satisfy himself, thus in effect creating himself. In doing so, the point is not whether a complete, accomplished text has been created, but rather if the text is evidence of the artist's *cura sui* – his care for himself – often in disconnected annotations or even in fragments.[15] The diary is rich in such jottings. True, these initially convey the appearance of personal checks and balances, as controlled bookkeeping, with earnings and expenses recorded in order to calculate the profits of the entire journey. That, too, is part of the journal. It is remarkable, however, that, unlike Dürer's earlier journey to Venice, no correspondence from his Netherlandish travels has survived – and indeed may never have been written. This alone would encourage us to look in the journal for more than pure housekeeping.

Several passages in the journal are concerned with Dürer's body, his physical self. Among these, for example, are the entries referring to his diet during the journey, bearing in mind that the intake of nutrients to sustain the physical body is necessary in order to continue self-fashioning. One generation later the painter Pontormo (1494–1556/7) obsessively records such details in his *Libro mio*, which primarily discusses his food intake and digestion.[16] And the self-observation of Michel de Montaigne (1533–1592) concerning his diet, recorded in his *Essais* as well as during his Italian journey in 1580–1, is still considered the fundamental text of biographical self-reflection.[17] Dürer's journal anticipates this genre, even if only as subtext. Indeed, why would posterity be interested in his text if it did not reveal the self-empowerment of an artist?

During Dürer's journey a meal frequently represents a reciprocal gift, and occasionally a testimony of honour.[18] His accounts of meals thus have added significance: 'Item: Master Bernhart, the painter, invited me and prepared such a costly meal that I can't think it could be had for 10 gulden',[19] or 'I have eaten twice with the Augustinians … Ate once more with the Augustinians … Ate again with the Augustinians'.[20] Occasionally communal meals serve as an affirmation and safeguarding of Dürer's own network: 'I dined with my Lords … Further I dined once more with my Lords of Nuremberg … Again I have twice dined with my Lords'.[21] And when he writes about their cost, or the lack thereof, his comments read like an account book, while at the same time expressing social recognition and the concern of others for his physical well being: 'In Brussels I lodged, ate and drank with my Lords of Nuremberg, and they would take nothing from me for it. Likewise in Aachen I ate with them for three weeks, and they took me to Cologne and here too would accept no payment.'[22] On other occasions, however, he was required to reciprocate: 'I had to give Leonhard Groland my large oxhorn, and to Hans Ebner I had to give my large cedarwood rosary.'[23]

In a diary entry for the city of 's-Hertogenbosch, Dürer's account of his journey, his travel impressions, intake of food and possible offerings in recognition of his status appear close together in the same space: 'On Tuesday we set off again early towards Bommel on the Maas … Bosch is an attractive town with an exceptionally beautiful church and very well fortified. There I spent 10 stuivers, even though Master Arnold paid for my meal. And the goldsmiths did me the great honour of attending me.'[24] A socio-culinary highpoint occurs in Brussels shortly before Dürer's return journey, when King Christian II (1481–1559) invites the artist to a princely banquet in the presence of Emperor Charles V as well as the ruler of the Habsburg Netherlands, Margaret of Austria: 'Note: on the Sunday before St Margaret the King of Denmark held a great banquet for the emperor, Lady Margareta and the Queen of Spain, and I was invited and dined there.'[25] The frequent combination of eating and the making of tributes is noticeable, emphasising the social demands of dining. In Mechelen Dürer records: 'There at my lodgings the painters and sculptors invited me to dinner and treated me nobly in their assembly.'[26] His experience in Antwerp is similar: 'And for the evening the retired Prefect of the city had invited me and gave a feast and showed me much honour … On Monday night Sir Lopez gave me a carnival invitation to the great banquet which lasted until two o'clock and was most extravagant [*köstlich*].'[27]

In the context of the present study, which brings together art and the realities of the artist's life, it is revealing that Dürer uses the adjective *köstlich* (delicious, precious, lavish) indiscriminately for both food and the art that he looks at. In Antwerp he notes: 'I have also been in the rich Abbey of St Michael where they have the most splendid triforium gallery chapel with traceried stone arcades, the like of which I never saw, and costly choir-stalls.'[28] In Brussels he praises a house: 'I was also in the Count of Nassau's townhouse, lavishly [*köstlich*] built and beautifully decorated.'[29] At the same time, it would not have escaped Dürer that the term *köstlich*, even if initially applied to taste, had its origin in the word *Kost* (cost), denoting value.[30] Thus by using the term he idiosyncratically gave his journal the character of an account book.

A very special function is accorded to the gifts of wine that Dürer received everywhere he went. He was greeted thus by two local painters in Bamberg: 'Item: Master Lukas Benedict and Hans, the painters, stood me wine in welcome.'[31] In Frankfurt he notes: 'Then we came to

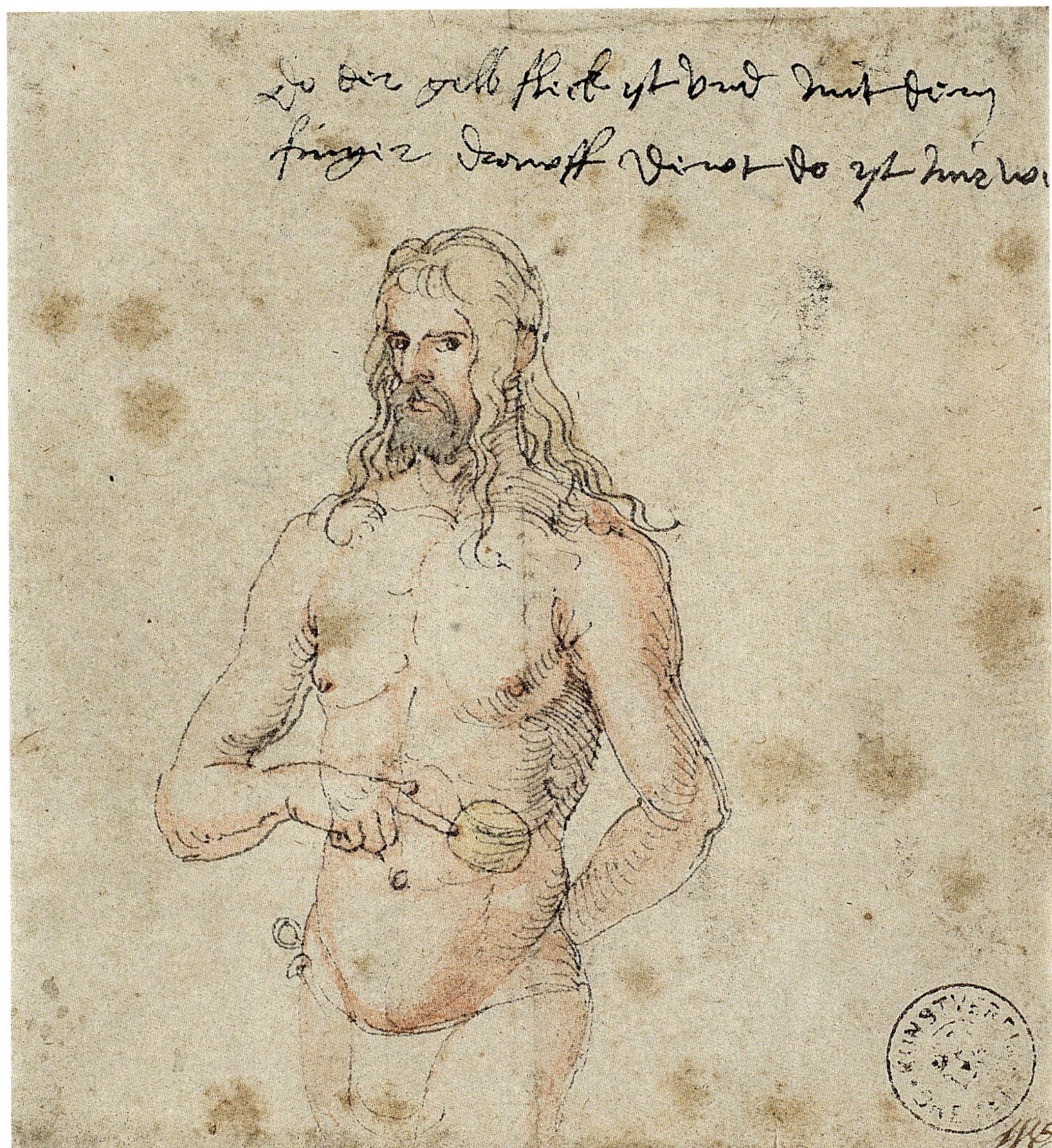

Fig. 7
ALBRECHT DÜRER
Self Portrait, III, 1509–11
Brown ink and watercolour, 11.8 × 10.8 cm
Kunsthalle Bremen (1851/50_Z)

Frankfurt and there too I showed my pass and was allowed through … Herr Jakob Heller sent wine to my lodgings.'[32] We should bear in mind, however, that in all probability these were not strongly alcoholic wines but rather lighter and lower in alcohol, drunk in place of water, which was often contaminated. It is otherwise difficult to explain the enormous amount of wine recorded in the journal – even if we include Dürer's wife, Agnes, and the maid Susanna in its consumption. Gifts of wine delivered to the artist's boat or his lodgings are mentioned again and again, while other delicacies were added to it in Antwerp: 'Item: the Portuguese factor sent a gift of wine, French and Portuguese, to my lodgings. Item: Signor Rodrigo of Portugal gave me a cask of preserved sweets of various kinds, including a box of sugar candy, two large trays of barley-sugar, marzipan, all kinds of other sweets, and quite a lot of sugar-canes just as they were harvested.'[33]

Wine was always considered a special gift, even among royalty. In an art-historical context it is significant that wine could also be presented to artists in payment for their work.[34] In Dürer's case, however, it is no longer possible to determine whether these gifts of wine were made to honour the artist, a type of compensation or simply the thoughtful provision of liquid to quench his thirst. But the meticulousness with which Dürer records the receipt of the bottles is strikingly revealing of his careful self-documentation of his own physiology. The fact that he paid special attention to his body is documented in the entry of 14 April 1521, this time in the context of threat: 'In the third week after Easter I was struck down by a high fever and drastic weakness, nausea and headache. Before, when I was in Zeeland, I suffered a mysterious illness that no one had ever heard of, and this sickness has never left me.'[35]

Fig. 8
ALBRECHT DÜRER
Self Portrait, in Awe, as Christ, 1522
Leadpoint with white heightening on green prepared paper, 41.8 × 29 cm
Kunsthalle Bremen (war loss)

It is well known that Dürer had previously created a document of his concern for his own body. In a drawing dated 1509/11, now in the Kunsthalle Bremen, he portrays himself naked but for a loincloth, pointing with his hand to the area of the spleen, with the explanation: 'Where the yellow spot is, to which I point with my finger, there it hurts' ('Do der gelb fleck ist und mit dem finger drawff dewt do ist mir we'; fig. 7).[36] In the Netherlands he may have been afflicted by the notorious Zeeland fever, ascribed to the bad air of the islands.[37] The fact that in the journal entry for 14 April 1521 he speaks of 'listlessness' ('Unlust') points to an almost psychogrammatical self-analysis in his concern. Furthermore, his reference to the illness as 'mysterious' ('wunderlich') and previously unknown to him expresses a remarkable awareness of his own singularity, as if he had been 'chosen'. This construction of oneself as an exceptional being is raised to an impressive level in a passage in the journal that can seem the crux of a drama starring Dürer, effectively declaring the artist as the saviour of himself: 'But at Arnemuiden, as I was coming into port, a serious accident happened to me. As we were approaching land and casting our mooring ropes ashore, a big ship collided with us violently, just as I was disembarking, and to escape the crush I was letting everyone else get off before me, so that only I, Georg Kötzler, two old women and the skipper with a little lad were left in the ship. When the other ship collided with us then, and I was still on board with these people and couldn't get out of the way, the thick cable snapped, and that very moment a strong gust of wind hurled our ship backwards. We all yelled for help but no one would risk coming to our rescue. The wind then started to carry us out to sea again. The skipper began to tear his hair and cry out, for his crew had all left the ship unmanned and empty. We were in fear and peril, for the wind was strong and there were not more than six of us aboard. Then I told the skipper to take heart, put his hope in God and think through what was to be done. He said, if he could just hoist the small sail, we might see whether he could try and reach land again. So all together we made a great effort and with failing strength got it halfway up and made for land again. And when the people on shore, who had given us up for lost, saw our efforts to save ourselves, they came to the rescue and we reached the land'.[38] Admittedly he speaks here of trust in God and the competence of the captain, but it is his courageous speech that initiates the favourable turn of events: although he cannot, Christ-like, calm storm and sea (Luke 8: 22–5), he presents himself as the pivotal figure who is ultimately responsible for the survival of himself and the others.

This virtually Christological role-playing corresponds to Dürer's numerous self-representations in godlike images, not only in the famous *Self Portrait* of 1500 (fig. 18) but also in his representations of Christ. In *Self Portrait in Awe* of 1522 (fig. 8), formerly in Bremen, and in other works his face appears to morph into that of Christ, or he imprints himself physiognomically into the image of God. This correlates with the idea of the artist as a second creator that was current in contemporary humanist circles.[39] What could perhaps be counted as hubris reveals itself as a devoutly religious topos that owes more to the theological thesis in which man is made in the image of God (*ad imaginem Dei*) than to vanity, thus giving him no choice but to appear with or within God's features.[40] This resemblance brings him closer both to God and to himself at the same time. We have seen that not only in Dürer's description of the miraculous rescue at sea his journal clearly crosses the boundaries of an account book. Beyond that, however, it especially articulates how he comes closer to himself, how he saves himself and how in foreign lands, where he threatens to get lost, he rediscovers his self.

1 For the biographical texts, see Sahm 2002; on the *Dream Vision*, see Böhme 1995.
2 '… die praktischen Notwendigkeiten des Daseins, Gefühle der Pietät, das Erleben einer schaufreudigen Seele … mehr als bei anderen Künstlern seiner Zeit zu schriftlichen Mitteilungen (drängten) … aus ihnen fühlen wir noch heute: er hat ein treues und warmes Herz besessen und ist ein guter Mensch gewesen': Rupprich 1956–69, vol. 1, pp. 7–8. Author's translation.
3 '… in denen sich ein höchst sympathischer Mensch fast restlos enthüllt': Wölfflin 1984, p. 11, English translation, Wölfflin 1971, p. 11.
4 Panofsky 2005, p. 10.
5 Goris and Marlier 1970, p. 8.
6 Ullmann 1994. Author's translation.
7 Sahm 2002, p. 134.
8 On this, see Jeroen Stumpel's essay in the present publication, pp. 229–39.
9 Schmid 2003.
10 '… den Text nicht doch partienweise in dem Gedanken schrieb, man würde sich später für sein Leben interessieren'; and 'Wo und wie weit ein solches Motiv im gesamten Text mitschwingt, ist im Einzelnen nicht zu entscheiden': Sahm 2002, p. 184. Author's translation.
11 Burckhardt 1860, pp. 280ff.
12 Weiand 1993.
13 Robert 2003; Schauerte 2015. I am grateful to Thomas Schauerte for kindly providing references.
14 Dickhaut 2016, p. 57.
15 Foucault 1997; Angehrn 2017.
16 Pontormo 1984; see Gründler 2015.
17 Denker 2015; see also Unverfehrt 2003.
18 See Hirschfelder 2013, pp. 118–19.
19 Ashcroft 2017, vol. 1, no. 162, p. 561.
20 Ibid., pp. 584–5.
21 Ibid., pp. 559–60.
22 Ibid., p. 565.
23 Ibid., p. 565.
24 Ibid., p. 567.
25 Ibid., p. 589.
26 Ibid., p. 584.
27 Ibid., p. 573.
28 Ibid., p. 557.
29 Ibid., p. 560.
30 Grimm 1854–60, vol. 11, cols 1876–80.
31 Ashcroft 2017, vol. 1, no. 162, p. 551.
32 Ibid., p. 552.
33 Ibid., p. 559.
34 Guasti 1887, pp. 77–8. I thank Wolf Dietrich Löhr for this reference.
35 Ashcroft 2017, vol. 1, no. 162, p. 579.
36 Bremen 2012, pp. 110–15, no. 32.
37 Unverfehrt 2007, pp. 164–5.
38 Ashcroft 2017, vol. 1, no. 162, p. 570.
39 Kopp-Schmidt 2004, pp. 1ff.
40 Belting 2013, pp. 154–6; see also Koerner 1993, pp. 45ff.

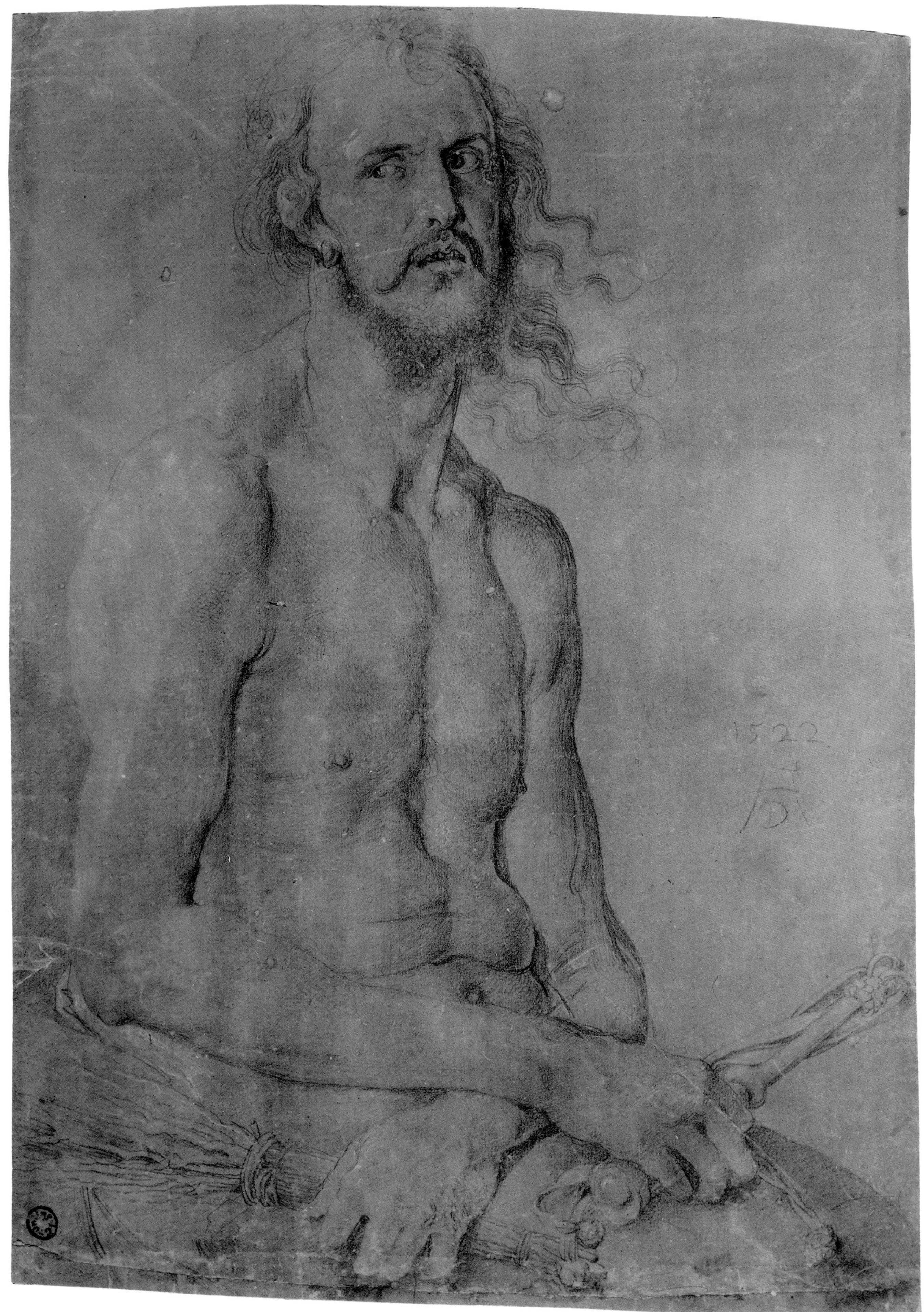
1522
AD

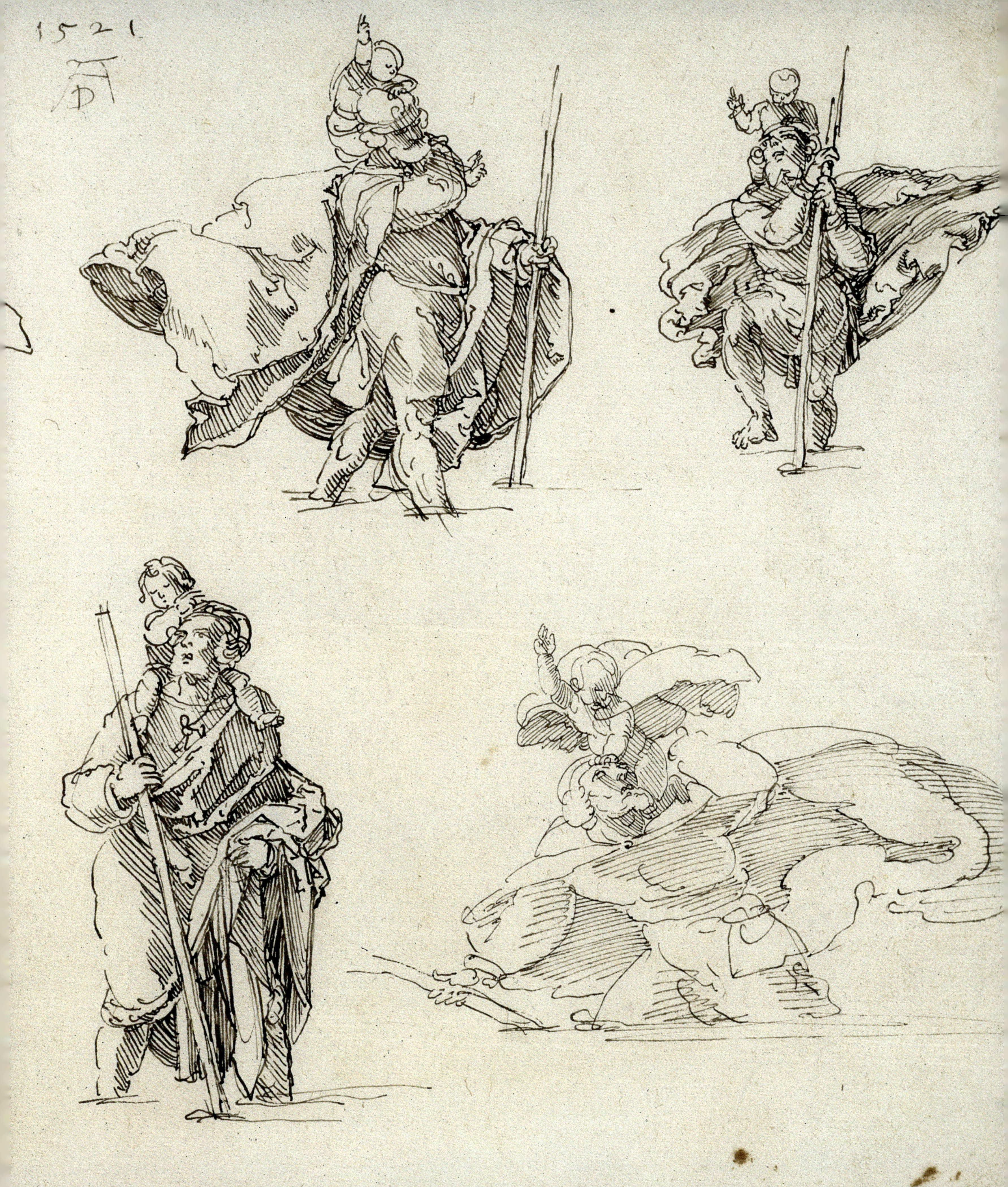
1521

JOSEPH LEO KOERNER

DÜRER IN MOTION

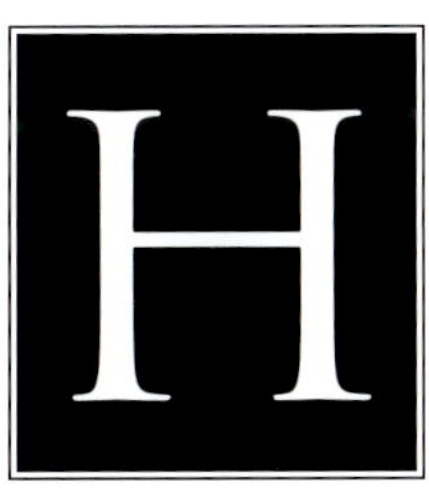

He had travelled 500 leagues by river and road from the centre of Europe to Flanders on the North Sea. Accompanied by his wife and a maid, and burdened by merchandise, his passage had been lengthened by visits to friends, relatives and dignitaries, and slowed by the many toll stations along the Main and Rhine that caused more hurried travellers to reach the coast by wagon. But this itinerary was not only about getting to a destination. It was about the journey itself. Mixing business with pleasure, stretching out for months after its chief aim was achieved, it saw the traveller entertained and entertaining at the many stops he made along the way.

They had covered vaster distances than he. A fabulous trove of artefacts, they had been hauled overland, probably from the Aztec capital of Tenochtitlan to the coast at Villa Rica (named 'Veracruz' weeks before their arrival), to be received by Hernán Cortés (1485–1547) as gifts for his king. Shipped via Cuba to Spain, they arrived at Seville on 5 November 1519, where they stood on display in the Casa de Contratación. Carted to the royal residence in Valladolid, they inspired vivid descriptions that, dispatched in letters that were translated, paraphrased, and published, broadcast news of their appearance. Already by March 1520, a garbled account had appeared in Nuremberg, four months before our traveller departed from that city, his birthplace and home.[1] Carried to Brussels, they were exhibited in the Royal Palace to celebrate Charles V's arrival to the Netherlands and Aachen. There they stopped our traveller in his path and rendered him almost speechless.

The encounter left behind a permanent trace. Recording his activities in a lively account that posterity preserved because of who he was, the traveller Albrecht Dürer put down on paper what he beheld:

> I also saw the objects which men have brought back to the king from the new Land of Gold: a sun made all of gold, a good six feet across, likewise a moon of

OPPOSITE
Detail from *Nine Studies of Saint Christopher* (cat. 17)

pure silver, of the same size, also two rooms full of those natives' armor, all manner of their weapons, military gear and missilery, amazing shields, curious costumes, bed coverings, and every kind of spectacular things for all possible uses, more worth seeing than the usual prodigies. These things are all so precious that they are valued at a hundred thousand gulden.[2]

The treasures moved the mobile artist in an unprecedented way, and for reasons he could not quite express:

> I have never in my life seen anything that gave my heart such delight as these things, for I saw in them the subtle ingeniousness [*jngenia*] of people in foreign lands. I cannot find words to describe all those things I found there.[3]

Dürer's words, even his loss for words, have long served to localise the emergence of a global perspective. Seeing strange things made by strange peoples on the ocean's once unknown other shore required conjuring not only a new world but a new image of the world. A huge book printed in Nuremberg in 1493 (Dürer himself may have helped illustrate it during his apprenticeship) expressed one last time the old landlocked world picture. The Nuremberg *Weltchronik* begins with Creation, with God separating land from sea and establishing land as the human dwelling place, and it ends with Apocalypse, when the sea will be no more (Revelation 21: 1). Its woodcut map – a two-page spread – surrounds the world with Anemoi (antique wind gods) along with the three sons of Noah who peopled the known continents (fig. 9). Fantastical monsters of medieval travel lore spill from the previous opening to decorate the margin of the map. By 1520 the sea had become a challenge rather than a limit, and the fabulous artefacts displayed in Brussels compelled the Nuremberg artist to imagine not prodigies but skilful and ingenious makers like himself. Modern readers have admired Dürer's precocious appreciation of a common humanity. After all, the gold and silver discs that delighted him vanished without a trace, probably melted down for their metals, and the items that did survive entered the Habsburg vaults as quasi-natural curiosities. At Harvard University, where I work, pre-Columbian objects are kept not in our three art museums but in an ethnological collection sharing spaces with 'natural history'.[4]

Lately, historians have tried to revise our understanding of Dürer's response. They observe that in thinking that the metallic discs depict a sun and moon, the artist forced on these alien objects his own culture's conceptual framework – Dürer spent years inventing astrological hieroglyphs for Emperor Maximilian.[5] And they take his speechless delight to be a period-typical cliché of wonderment. Much of what Dürer wrote does repeat things already reported by others from Spain: the artefacts' workmanship astonished more than did their material value, and words could not capture such astonishment. It makes a difference, though, that Dürer, the most famous European artist of his day, calls the objects 'artistic' (*künstlich*) and admires something he terms *ingenium*. This distinguishes their makers from all but the greatest of artists. As he himself wrote in 1512, artworks can only be judged by those who are good artists. Greatness is therefore known only by the great.[6]

Dürer beheld the discs with a specialist's eye. His goldsmith father, Albrecht Dürer the Elder (1427–1502), had schooled him in the arts of metalworking. This fostered the virtuosity of the younger Albrecht's first copper engravings, and it must have made him feel a kinship with goldsmiths 'in strange lands'. The elder Dürer learned these arts in far-flung places. Born in a village on the eastern march of the Kingdom of Hungary, on the contested fringes of Christian Europe, he took local goldsmith's skills to the Netherlands, where he sojourned (in the words of his son) with 'the great artists'.[7] Settling in Nuremberg in 1455, he became a master of metallurgy – Nuremberg named him the official 'weigher and tester' of minted coins.[8] The younger Dürer filtered his encounter with Aztec gold through collective experiences of travel, including his own north and south of the Alps. The New World artefacts expanded Dürer's horizons, but they sparked in him a special recognition. What he called *ingenium* was not simply some know-how that could be recognised across wide geographical distances. To those who possessed it, ingenium arrived vertically, literally through 'pourings-in' from on high (*öberen ein gissungen*) that gave the possessor a creativity 'in the image of God himself'.[9]

The convergence of Dürer and the New World gifts did not happen by chance. The artist went to the Netherlands to renew an imperial pension granted him by Maximilian. After Maximilian's death in 1519, the Nuremberg council responsible for distributing these moneys stopped paying them out. Not trusting the city to campaign on his behalf, Dürer resolved to press his case personally upon Charles V at his coronation in Aachen. Two months prior to that event, Dürer set forth from the trade capital Antwerp, where he had been fêted as an artistic hero by the city's huge community of painters, to the courtly city of Brussels. There he had his 'supplication' professionally drafted and met with

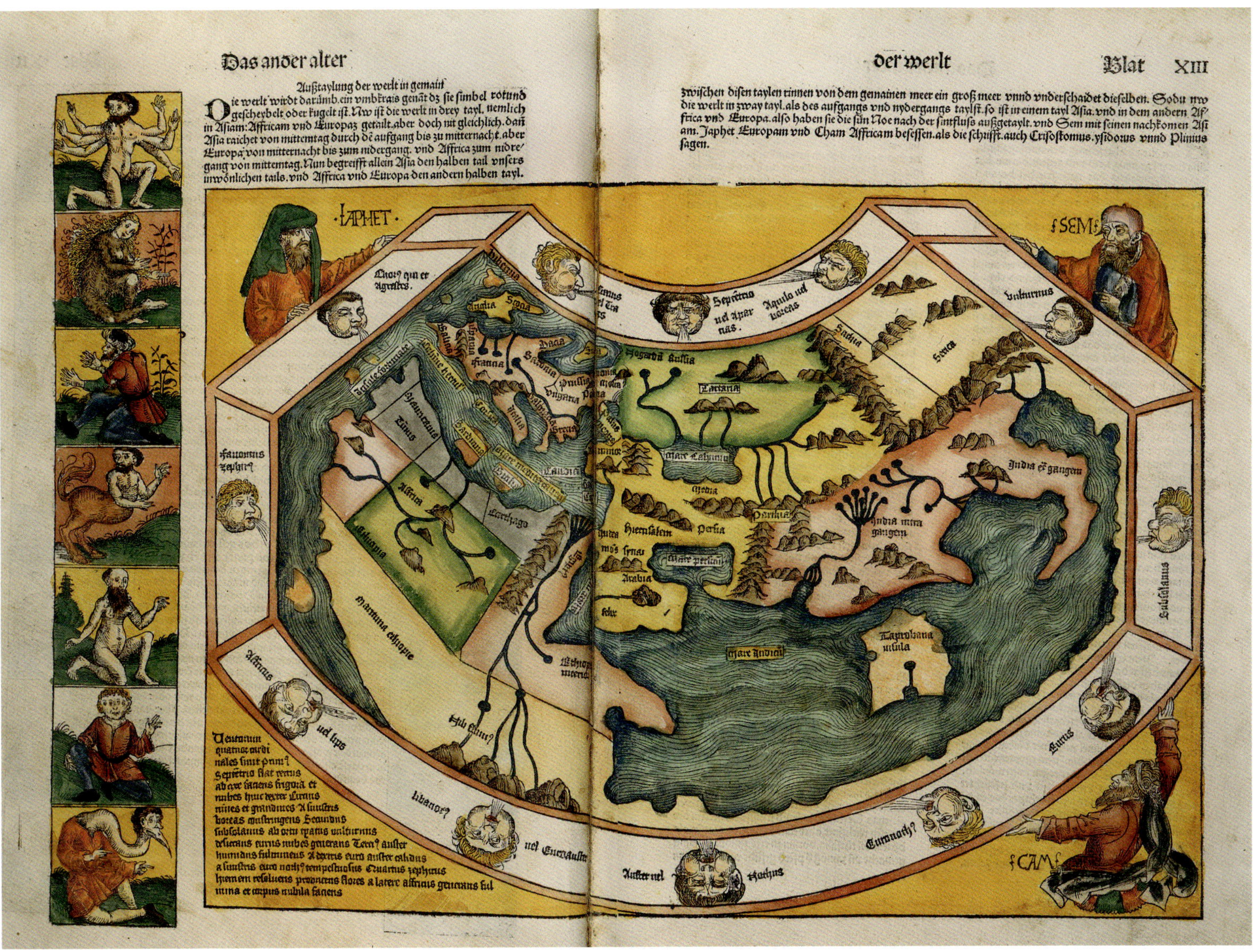

Archduchess Margaret, regent of the Habsburg Netherlands, hoping to win her favour with gifts of his art. The New World objects, for their part, had not been intended as supplications to the ruler across the sea, but Charles enlisted them in the extended ceremony of his crowning.

The coronation of the Holy Roman Emperor required certain treasures: the Imperial Crown, Sword, and Cross, all centuries old and imagined to be older still; precious vestments, also old and mostly of Sicilian manufacture; sundry sacred relics from Rome, Constantinople and the Holy Land, including the Holy Lance, believed to have pierced Christ's side; and the *Reichsapfel*, the cross-bearing orb symbolising global Christian rule. These had all been transported, via a route parallel to Dürer's, from Nuremberg, the city that permanently kept them as its most wondrous possessions.

This gathering of numinous presences from distant times and places found a divine prototype in Christ's public recognition as King of the Earth by the gift-bearing kings, or magi. Imagined as a trio on account of the Gospels' list of their gifts, and associated with the three continents, the Adoration of the Magi gave artists who pictured it a vehicle for 'exotic' display. In a 1504 panel probably painted for the Elector of Saxony Frederick the Wise, Dürer gilded his imaginative renderings of the magis' gifts (fig. 10). He may also have projected his own features on to the youthful, golden-haired second magus, who gazes sideways, past a receding stone portal (evocative of the artist's surname, which means 'door') to the African magus stationed precisely at the threshold. Dürer's painting becomes a doorway from the world's periphery to its centre, at Christ.[10]

By 1520 Adorations had become a speciality of Antwerp artists. The city's painters' workshops created these paintings through new methods of serial

Fig. 9
HARTMANN SCHEDEL (1440–1514)
Die Schedelsche Weltchronik, Nuremberg 1493, fol. 12v/13r
Hand-coloured woodcut, about 47.4 x 65.8 cm
Private collection

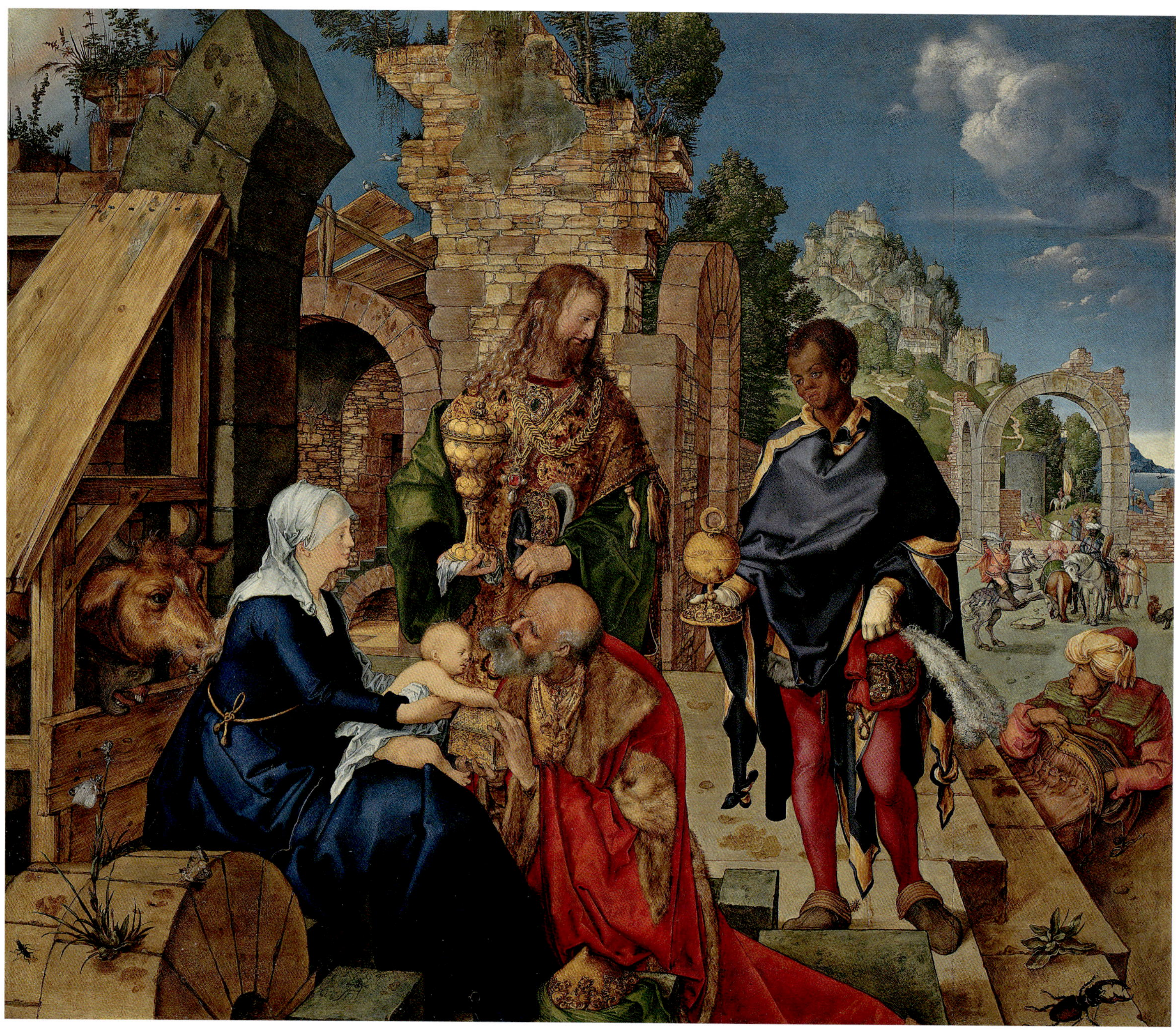

Fig. 10
ALBRECHT DÜRER
The Adoration of the Magi, 1504
Oil on wood,
99 × 113.5 cm
Gallerie degli Uffizi, Florence

production for sale on an open market. Antwerp Adorations reached out to a global clientele not only through the exoticism of their biblical subject, which involved a miraculous gathering of strangers, but also through portrayals of long-distance commerce in the form of assemblages of travellers and merchandise. In several extant panels, baggage brought by the magi appears stamped with merchant marks, like goods shipped to and from Antwerp.[11]

Soon after his return from Brazil, where he made landfall in 1500 (the first European to do so), the Portuguese explorer Pedro Álvares Cabral (1467–1520) enlisted a painter to celebrate his travels. Part of an altarpiece in Viseu, where Cabral's ancestors lay buried, the painting gives the second magus the form of a Topiniquim chieftain. Although the figure is unprecedented, the thinking behind it is not. For centuries the African magus had personified darkness at the margins coming to God and to light: the word Epiphany derives from the Greek *phaos* and *phōs* ('light').[12] Travel now revealed that there were other Others from supernumerary continents. Cabral himself appears in the guise of the wizened first magus. He presents two gifts: not just the traditional gold, here a gold coin minted with the royal Portuguese arms, but also the New World native as convert to Christ. Returned from

'I have never in my life seen anything that gave my heart such delight as these things, for I saw in them the subtle ingeniousness of people in foreign lands.'

the Antipodes, the traveller re-centres the world on Christ and Christian rule, following the motto of Henry the Navigator, 'In the name of God and gold'.[13]

On a page of a printed prayer book intended for Emperor Maximilian, Dürer sketched in pen and violet ink the image of a native of Brazil (fig. 11).[14] Dressed in a feather cloak and cap and wielding a Tupi chieftain's club, he stands in *contrapposto* on a carved spoon evocative of vernacular craft.[15] Although Dürer's other drawings for Maximilian's prayer book have at best loose connections to the texts they frame, here the relation is direct. Psalm 24 begins: 'The earth is the Lord's and the fullness thereof; the world and they who dwell in it.' Stationed between the word *habitant* ('dwell') printed beside him, and *in eo* ('in it') printed overleaf, the New World native looks in the direction of the page-turn, as if drawn into a world under the one God's dominion.

In Brussels, Dürer would experience earth's 'fullness' differently. The Aztec artefacts had probably been crafted to celebrate the rule of Moctezuma through the wind god Quetzalcoatl.[16] In Europe they were presented rather like the magi's gifts, as tributes to the Christian sovereign. Dürer did not merely witness their gathering. He belonged to it, like the goods-bearing travellers in Antwerp Adorations. At Charles V's coronation, Europe performed its identity as centre of the world, perhaps for the last time. Six months later, Dürer, in a text written into his travel accounts, lamented Luther's reported abduction and railed against the 'unchristian Papacy'.[17] Under Charles V's rule Europe split into several hostile religious confessions, while the New World became a bloodland for European aggressors. Present at the fugitive convergence of a centre that would not hold, Dürer's thinking travelled outward from Europe to the periphery, to 'humans in strange lands'.

This imaginative leap outward had been foundational to the artist's fame. When Dürer arrived in the Netherlands, his reputation preceded him. This unprecedented fame depended on what he chose to make. Before him, ambitious artists sought prestigious commissions, creating works for display in exalted locations – a church, palace, or civic space. Whether publicly or privately available, these artefacts addressed an audience limited to that one place. After Charles's coronation, Dürer spent 16 days in Cologne. Visiting the chapel of the town hall,

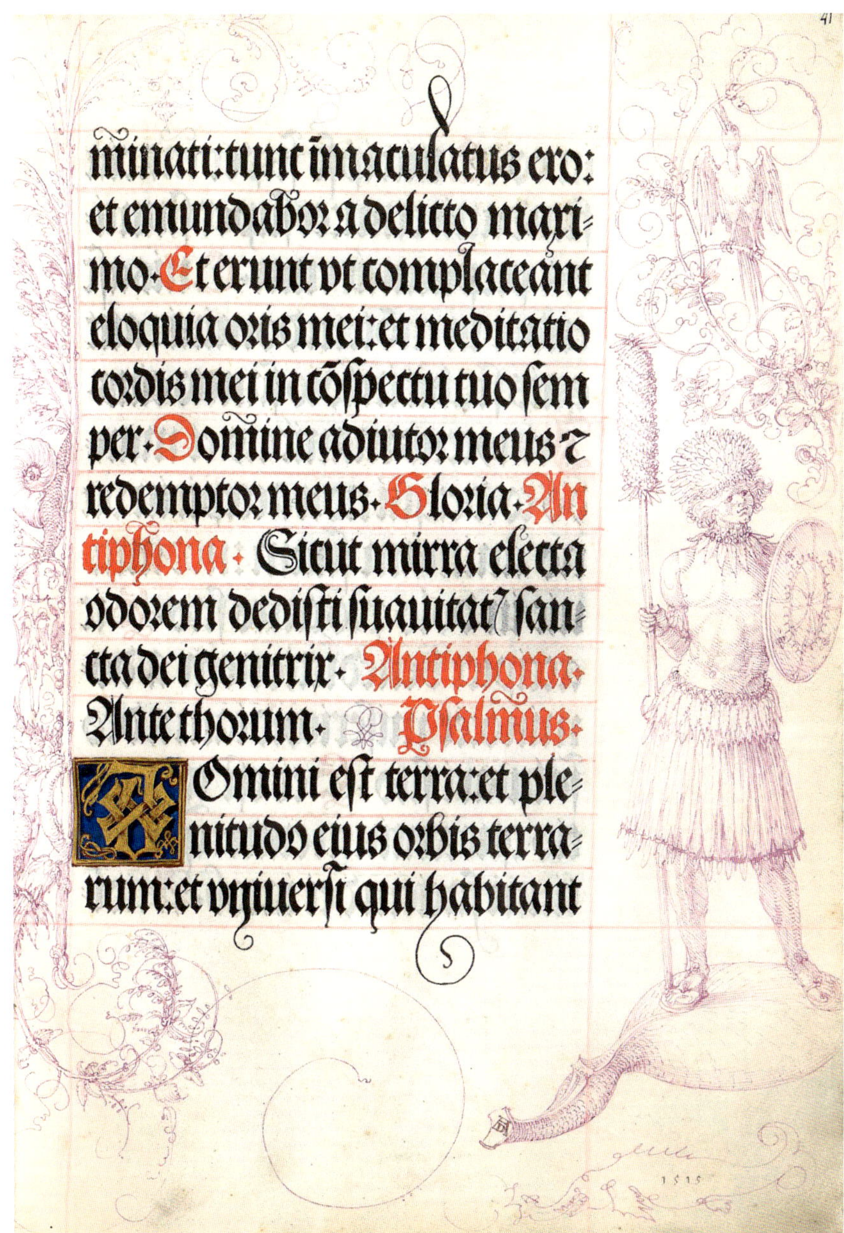
41

minati:tunc imaculatus ero:
et emundabor a delicto maxi-
mo. Et erunt ut complaceant
eloquia oris mei: et meditatio
cordis mei in cōspectu tuo sem
per. Domine adiutor meus et
redemptor meus. Gloria. An
tiphona. Sicut mirra electa
odorem dedisti suauitat[is] san
cta dei genitrix. Antiphona.
Ante thorum. Psalmus.
Domini est terra: et ple
nitudo eius orbis terra
rum: et uniuersi qui habitant

1515

Fig. 11
ALBRECHT DÜRER
Page from the *Prayer Book of Emperor Maximilian I*, 1515
Pen and violet ink on parchment, 28 × 19.5 cm
Staatsbibliothek, Munich
(fol. h3 recto)

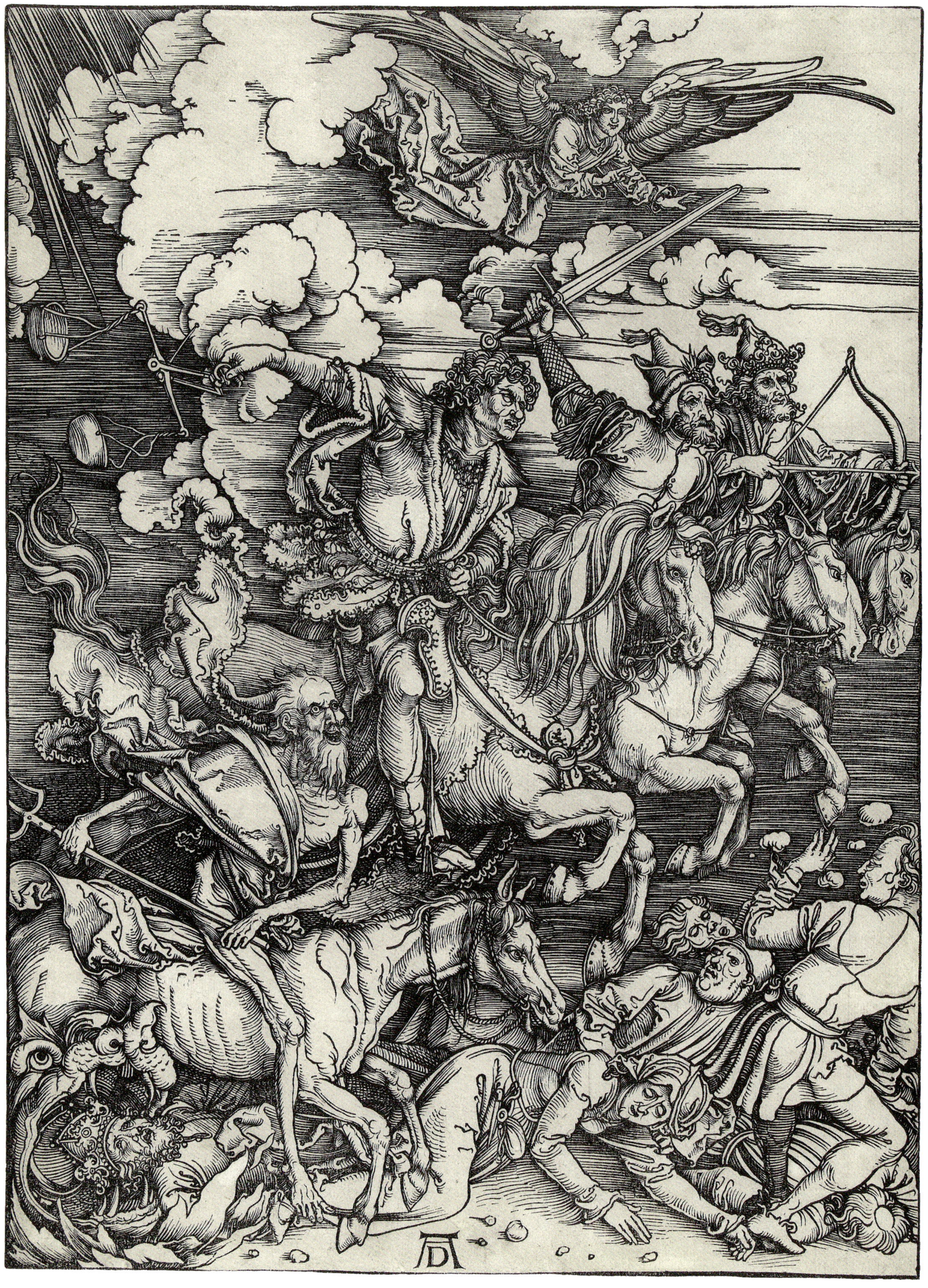

he paid to have the wings of an altarpiece by Stefan Lochner (1410–1451) opened so he could see that painter's artistry outside the timetable of its liturgical display.[18] Even in their locality, artworks were of limited access, sometimes deliberately so: altarpieces had wings so that their opening became a rare, festive occasion. The Adorations exported from Antwerp graced countless unforeseen altars, but each could address the audience where it chanced to end up. Perhaps due to his goldsmith heritage, which put him in touch with the medium of engraving, and certainly influenced by his apprenticeship with artists making woodcuts for printed books, Dürer resolved to make his name through images created and multiplied by mechanical production. Printed potentially in thousands of copies and carried far and wide by long-distance trade, these light, durable artefacts could be seen everywhere, with multiple audiences admiring the identical thing. And because Dürer thought to embed his initials into all his prints, wherever they arrived there he was, in thousands of locations.

Dürer's mental transport, in 1520, to 'humans in strange lands' reversed the thinking required in making prints. The itinerancy of prints demanded that their maker should travel imaginatively to unknown locations where they might be received. In German, popular woodcuts are sometimes called *Flugblätter* – literally 'flying pages'. This likens prints to leaves carried away by the winds of commerce or fortune. In his Netherlands journal, Dürer uses the word Fortuna to mean accident, chance, winds, a storm, or the tides of the sea. On 24 November 1520 he hears of a whale washed ashore in Zeeland by 'a great Fortuna'. He rushes to the beach but by the time he arrives, 'the Fortuna' has carried the stinking carcass away.[19] Though a disappointment here, flux is Dürer's element. An openness to change made him the ever-curious traveller his diaries show him to be. And it allowed travel to change him.

His global reach depended on more than travel, trade and print technology. It required his ability to predict what distant others want to behold. In his first major undertaking, Dürer put his bet on Christendom's most dire prediction: world catastrophe as imagined in the Book of Revelation. Published in 1498, in anticipation of the half-millennium, the 15 full-page woodcuts of the *Apocalypse with Pictures* spread through Europe a vivid image of end time. The Four Apocalyptic Horsemen trampling humanity imagine movement on an unimaginable scale while also urging the viewer-reader to turn the page (fig. 12). Mobile in their distribution, Dürer's prints visualise mobility where they arrive. One of his earliest engravings shows almost nothing but its own mode of transport. In *The Little Courier*, horse and rider gallop away, carrying paper dispatches who knows where (fig. 13). Shira Brisman has linked this stop-action scene to the conveyance of letters by the Habsburg-Taxis relay, the early postal service established by Maximilian in 1490, with Nuremberg as its centre.[20] Picturing the movement that brings it into view, *The Little Courier* is also engineered to make sense wherever it arrives. Dürer kept the meaning and purpose of prints like these open-ended, so that they could speak to a range of beholders. His dancing peasants, conspiring witches, unequal lovers, bathhouses and loitering Turks arrive with enough information to fascinate but not so much as might limit their appeal. In identifying the Aztec discs as sun and moon, Dürer performed what he imagined should happen to his artefacts in strange lands: that they only connect.

Travel and making things that travel are intertwined. In 1490 Dürer left Nuremberg to work with Martin

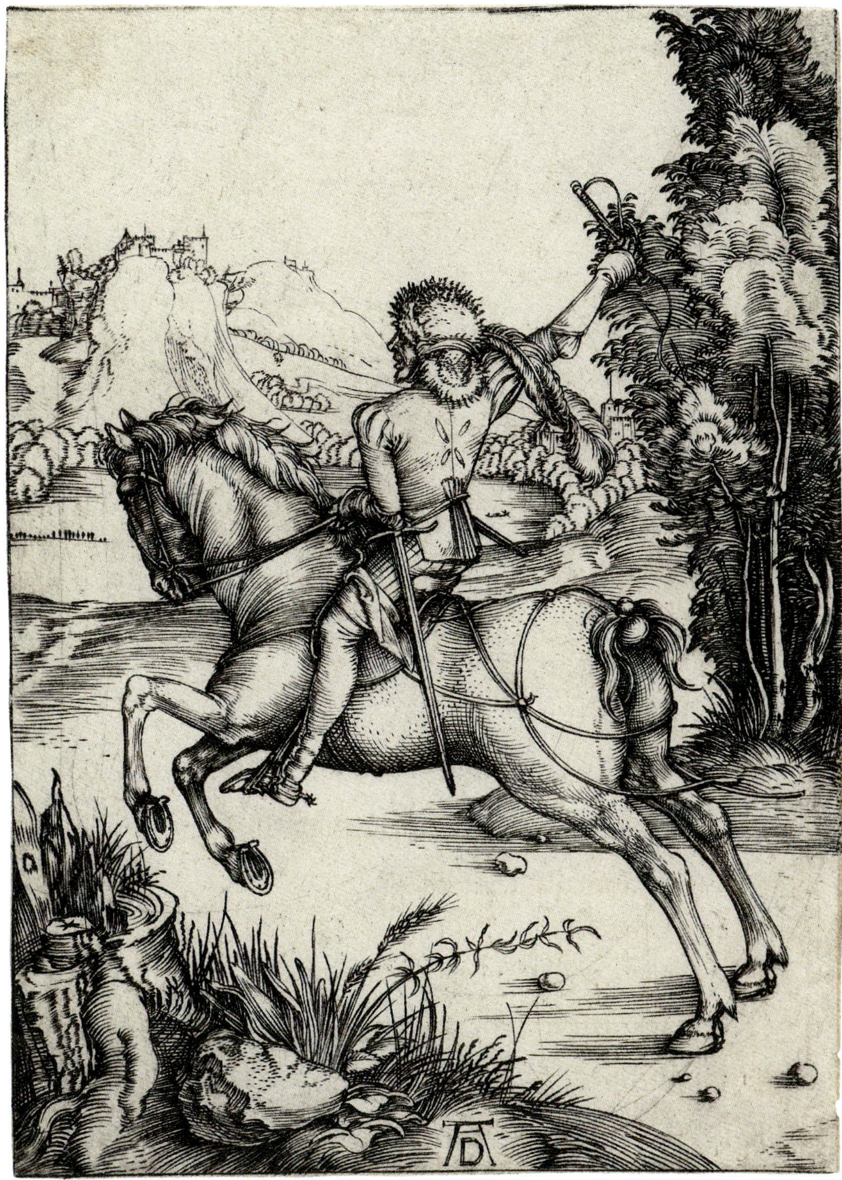

Fig. 13
ALBRECHT DÜRER
The Little Courier,
1494–8
Engraving, 10.7 × 7.6 cm
Rijksmuseum,
Amsterdam
(RP-P-OB-1246)

OPPOSITE
Fig. 12
ALBRECHT DÜRER
The Four Horsemen of the Apocalypse
(from the *Apocalypse with Pictures* series),
about 1497–8
Woodcut, 39.1 × 28.1 cm
Rijksmuseum,
Amsterdam
(RP-P-1959-193)

Schongauer,[21] a painter with roots in the goldsmith's trade whose monogrammed engravings had broadcast widely his talent and name. Dürer's first trip to Italy (1494–5) may also have been sparked by seeing Italian engravings and their radically different approach to art. The many journeys of 'the best-known artist/traveller of the Renaissance'[22] are less important for the places visited than for their effect on him. Other artists travelled widely – think of the itinerate court artists of the late Middle Ages. Only Dürer documented, expansively in words and images, how travel changed him. From Venice in 1506 he wrote, 'Here I am a gentleman, at home I am a parasite',[23] sensing how he himself had changed since his first sojourn in that city ('the things that pleased me so much eleven years ago don't please me any more'),[24] and aware of how, in Italy, attitudes towards artists were changing during the artistic rebirth or Renaissance there under way. It did not take Venice to make this artist want social mobility. Dürer's ambitions and strategies (including travel) were widely shared by Nuremberg's merchants and entrepreneurs.[25] Yet in the artist's case, mobility directly impacted the things he made.

In learned culture of Dürer's day, mobility was an ambiguous capability. In classical usage *mobilitas* referred primarily to athletic skills. Applied to mind and character, however, it had negative connotations of inconstancy and deceit.[26] Christian thinking developed this prejudice, vilifying curiosity – the wandering mind – as a cardinal sin and part cause of Eve and Adam's disobedience. Yet a mobile mind was also required for certain undertakings, such as art and architecture. Dürer was supremely mobile both mentally, in his curiosity and absorptiveness, and physically, through the sheer athleticism of his painterly marks. Newer scholarship has cautioned us not to find too much remarkable in the famous sketch the artist made of a Nuremberg housewife and a Venetian woman (fig. 14). People of the time dressed up in different clothing on different occasions, we are told, so the artist could have captured the figures without even leaving Nuremberg.[27] If only today's art history could channel Dürer's sense of wonder, for has there ever been a document of psychic and corporeal mobility more eloquent than this drawing? A large proportion of the artist's youthful drawings aimed at mastering crumpled drapery; expressive drapery dominated German sculpture, painting, and engraving of the time. And the kind of drapery that had to be mastered was the sort worn by the Nuremberg housewife: she is German as much in costume as in form, as Panofsky observed: 'Dürer contrasted the two figures as a modern art historian could contrast a Renaissance *palazzo* with a Late Gothic town house.'[28] The artist's responsiveness to difference transcends his registering different costumes and forms. Difference infiltrates his own body as the kind of pen marks his hand makes, short or long, agitated or calm. And the ability to adapt his body's movements dexterously derives from a mental dexterity that enables him to recognise the challenge that the contrast affords.

In his writings Dürer referred to manual skill as a 'freedom of hand'.[29] Such freedom needed to be practised (*geübt*) chiefly through diligent exercise of drawing. But through exposure to Italian and antique art Dürer came to realise that such freedom needed to be made obedient (*gehorsam*) through training in measurement and proportion.[30] He termed this theoretical side of artistry *kunst* and contrasted it to a practical side, termed sometimes *brauch* ('usage'), sometimes *gewalt* ('force' or 'power'), which rested in manual dexterity. His treatises on perspective and human proportion endeavoured to introduce German artists (who were masters of *brauch*) to the mysteries of *kunst*, and not just to remove errors from their work. *Kunst* boosted social mobility. It allowed artists to climb the ladder from craftsmen engaged in servile labour to practitioners of liberal or 'free' arts, which consisted in headwork, not handiwork. However, manual dexterity – 'freedom of hand' – remained vital to Dürer: his petition for an imperial pension that sent him to the Netherlands was partly justified by the fact that old age might rob him of that freedom: 'For when my eyesight fades and my hand loses its dexterity', he writes in 1520 to Georg Spalatin (1484–1545), chaplain to Frederick the Wise, 'then things won't go well with me'.[31]

Dürer demonstrated his mobile hand abundantly. On the back of a sheet showing one of the 'wise virgins' from Matthew 25, he sketched two legs (fig. 15). In fact they are two sketches of one leg: the artist's left one, observed extending from his torso. The date 1493 (pinpointing the sheet to Dürer's journeyman years) rotates the sheet 180 degrees and normalises the legs. Envisioning the drawing from the perspective of ordinary viewers, who likely never scrutinised their legs from such an angle, Dürer's rotation is one of several kinds of mobility at play in this sheet. Most obviously there is the hand–eye work of capturing a complex object from eccentric points of view. Then there is the thing that Dürer sets out to draw: a leg not quite in motion (which an image cannot show) but the same leg captured in two phases of motion, with its movement imaginable in between. That legs make humans mobile might be an accidental element in this game, but the sense of physical dislocation is deliberate. Dürer seeks to master his leg as seen from an eccentric point of view, looking down at the foot and across to the inner side of the leg. Beyond the curiosity this betrays, the experiment focuses attention on something that in ordinary experience would be unnoticed and fleeting. And then there are those strange unfinished bits at the top of legs, which make little sense unless the sheet is turned in its original orientation and we see them as limbs extending from the draughtsman's upper body, which the draughtsman himself cannot fully see.

Most of us dimly realise that the one person one cannot see in its entirety and face to face is oneself. Dürer is unique in exploring this elusive, mobile presence at the centre of human experience. The many sketched and painted likenesses he made of his person foreground the fugitive character of the 'first person' perspective. Already his earliest self portrait, drawn in silverpoint in 1484, when he was a child under his father's tutelage, finds him struggling to hide his active, mobile right hand behind a pointing gesture held stiffly by his left (fig. 16). A later sketch shows him steadying his head and gaze with his left hand as he tries to capture with his right the difficult, doubly mobile act of posing for, and drawing, himself from a mirror (fig. 17). Even his most deliberately static self portrait, the frontal, Christomorphic likeness painted to celebrate the epochal year 1500, pulsates with implied movement (fig. 18). Squeezed into the cramped confines of the portrait panel, maintaining the immobile, timeless pose of sacred icons, the artist-sitter explores with his left hand, nervously and surreptitiously, the fur of his elegant jacket while also mobilising, through the cuff of a sleeve peaking above the lower framing, the invisible but creative right hand at work painting the picture we see.

Such movement is an illusion. Dürer conveys it by making the likeness's immobility look effortful. The artist appears uncannily alive, present and immediate, down to the individual hairs on his chin. But he also seems to be holding himself still while he paints, for what must have been many days. Painting is an art of space, not time, as Lessing observed of the *Laocoön*. Yet artists have always been called upon to suggest movements, actions and events. Alberti (1404–1472), in 1435, set down rules for how to paint 'histories' where action prevails. This entailed representing bodies in *motion* within the painting, as well as effecting *emotion* in viewers standing before the painting. Moving pictures were Dürer's speciality, both in the sense of capturing movement (galloping horses, apocalyptic turmoil, serialised

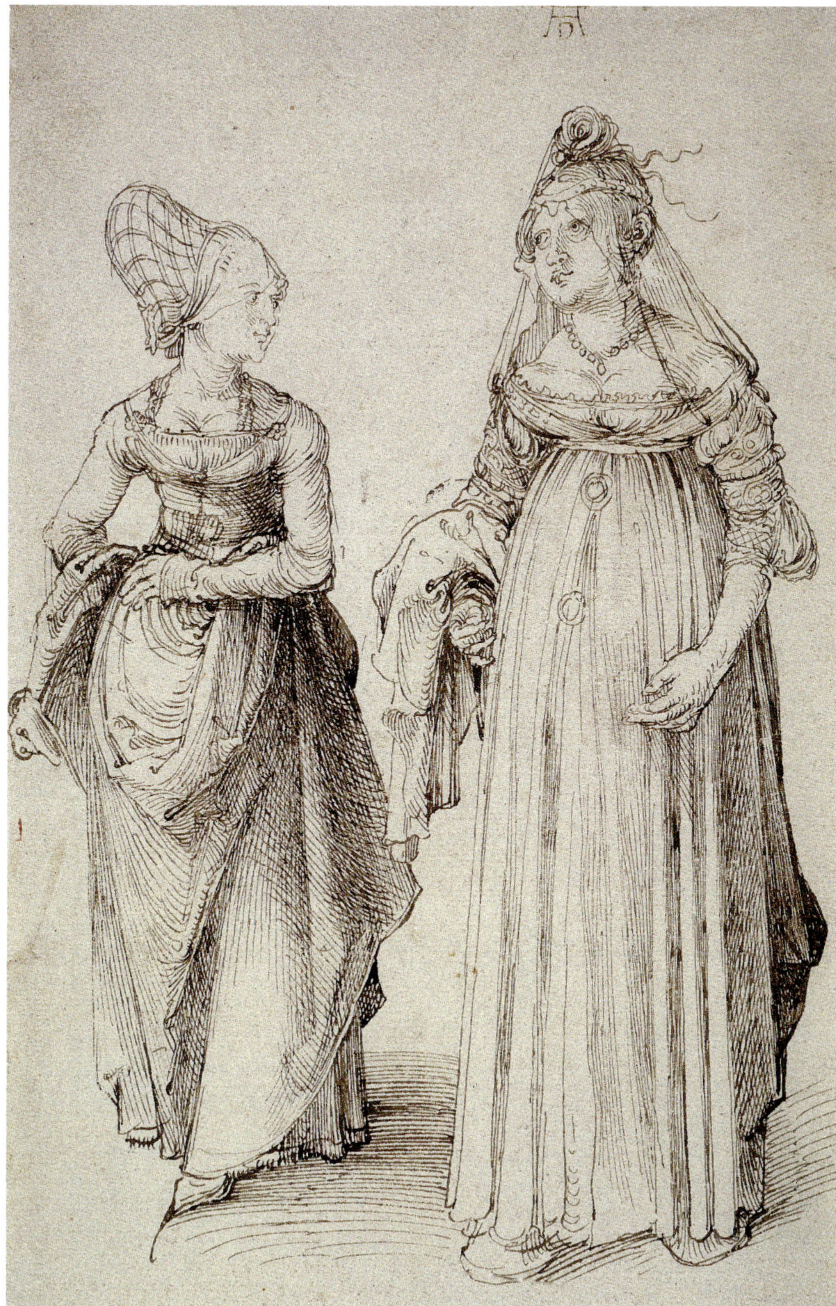

Fig. 14
ALBRECHT DÜRER
Nuremberg Housewife and Lady in Venetian Dress, about 1495
Pen and dark-grey brown ink on handmade paper, 4.5 x 15.9 cm
Städel Museum, Frankfurt am Main (696)

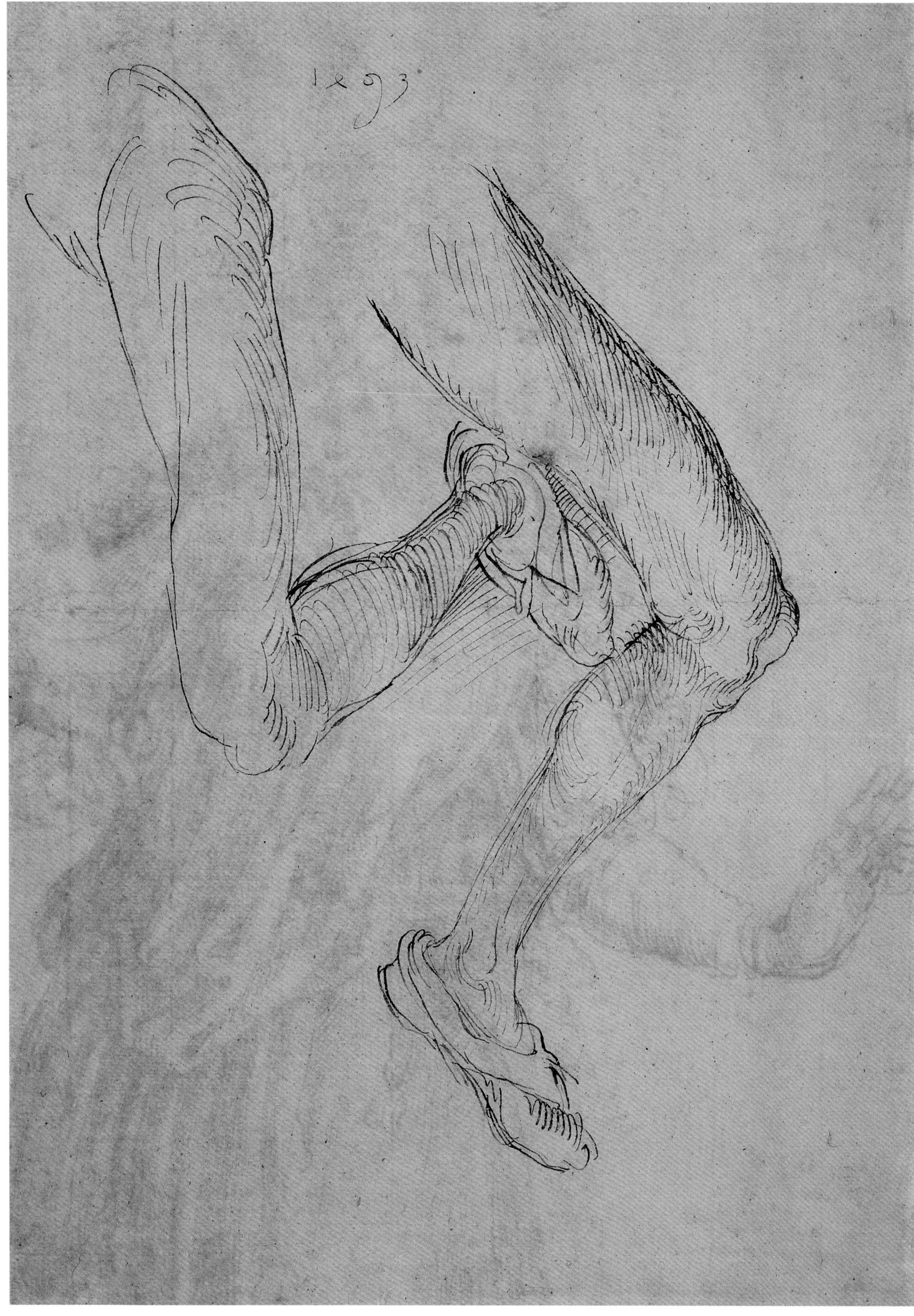

Fig. 15
ALBRECHT DÜRER
Study of a Left Leg, from Two Viewpoints, 1493
Pen and brown ink on laid paper, 29.1 × 20.2 cm
The Samuel Courtauld Trust, The Courtauld Gallery, London
(d.1978.pg.251)

histories of Christ and the Virgin and so on) and in that of moving viewers powerfully, as he felt moved in his 'heart' in Brussels.

On his fifth return to Antwerp in 1521, Dürer attended the wedding of Joachim Patinir (1480–1524), 'the good landscape painter' who 'showed him all honour'.[32] Two weeks later, probably as his marriage gift, Dürer gave Patinir '4 Christophers on grey paper heightened with white'.[33] One of these sheets probably survives in the British Museum: a highly finished *Saint Christopher* drawn in pen and black ink and white bodycolour on grey prepared ground (cat. 16).[34] More suggestive is a sheet of paper dated 1521 on which the artist has depicted nine Saint Christophers, each from a different viewpoint and in a different pose, and blasted by wind and struggling against the water's currents (cat. 17).[35] Patinir was the great pioneer of painted landscapes. He excelled in creating vast, world-embracing spaces, while for figures populating those vistas he often teamed up with other artists, such as Joos van Cleve (1485–1541) and Quinten Massys (1465/6–1530), who were better at that task. With its mighty river and picturesque setting, the Saint Christopher legend lent itself to a landscapist's art (cat. 15). Dürer's wedding present was a gift of motion. His virtuoso drawings of the saint struggling against the forces of nature would have been eminently useful. Transferring the outlines of one of Dürer's figures to a panel, Patinir could raise his own artistry by leaps and bounds.

Dürer's *Four Books on Human Proportion*, written over two decades but published posthumously in 1528, end with a discussion of movement in the human figure. The first books describe how proportioned figures should be constructed, transformed and reversed; Book IV explains how they might be variously 'bent' in order that the constructed figures can seem to move in correct and compelling ways. In the woodcut illustrations he provided, Dürer captured movement in at least three ways. First, the figures themselves bend, their bending hinged on the body's joints as the where and how of reaching, stepping, leaning and so on. Second, the artist rotates these bent figures, using what he terms 'stretched lines' to do so consistently, from one viewpoint to the next. Finally, there is the movement from construction to finished product, the clean contour drawing where 'the stretched lines have been left out'.[36] To many observers, these convoluted demonstrations are Dürer's most disappointing efforts. They seem to understand human movement not as the consequence of inner agency or even muscular action but as mere mechanical extensions into space.[37] Early on, historians linked these studies to Dürer's use of articulated artists' mannequins: one of the artist's most spectacular

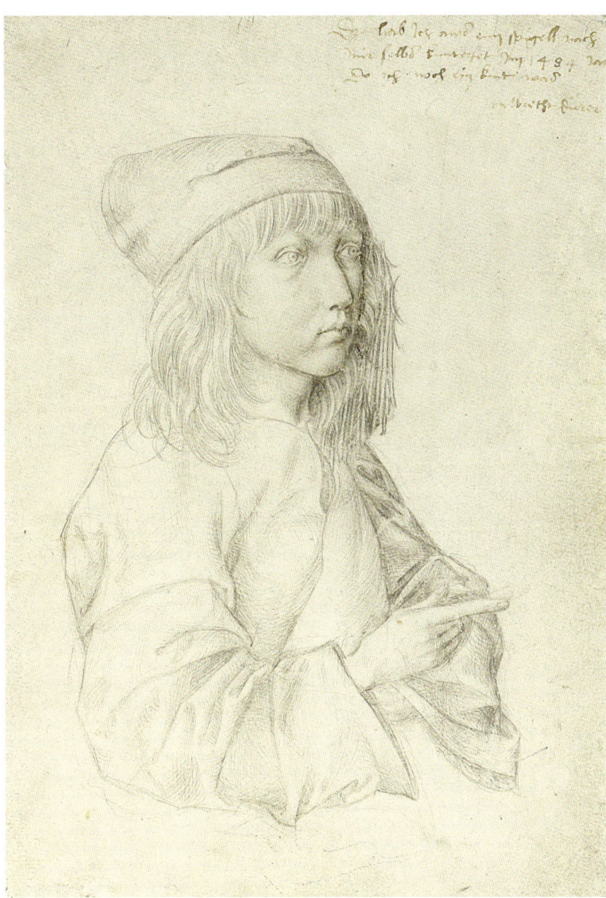

Fig. 16
ALBRECHT DÜRER
Self Portrait at the Age of 13, 1484
Silverpoint, 27.3 × 19.5 cm
The Albertina Museum, Vienna (4839)

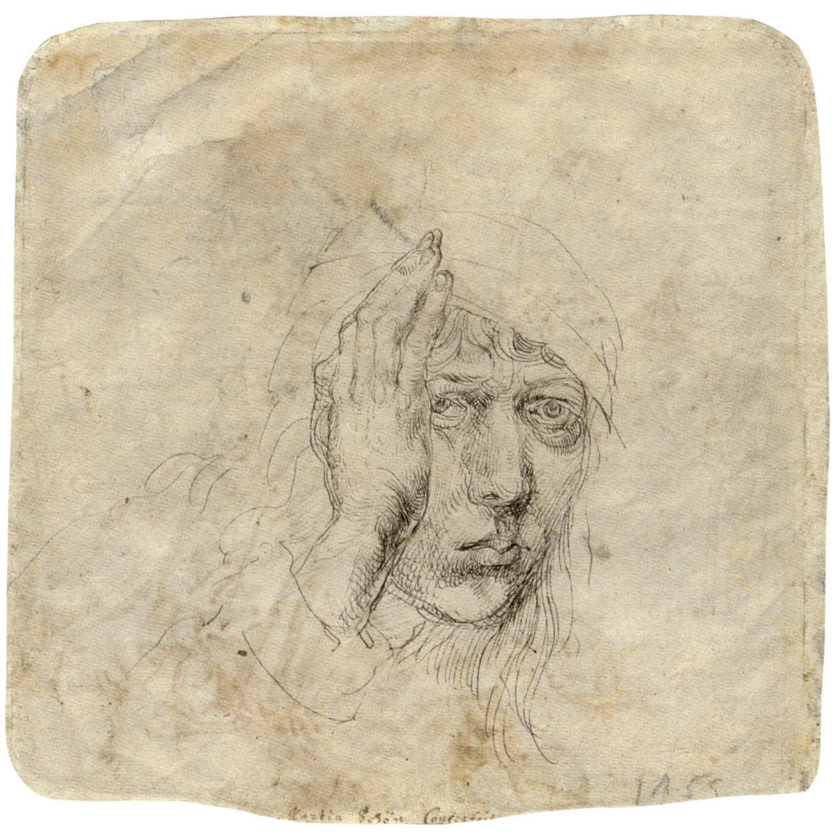

Fig. 17
ALBRECHT DÜRER
Self Portrait, about 1491–2
Pen and brown ink, 20.8 × 20.4 cm
Graphische Sammlung der Universität Erlangen-Nürnberg (H62/B 155)

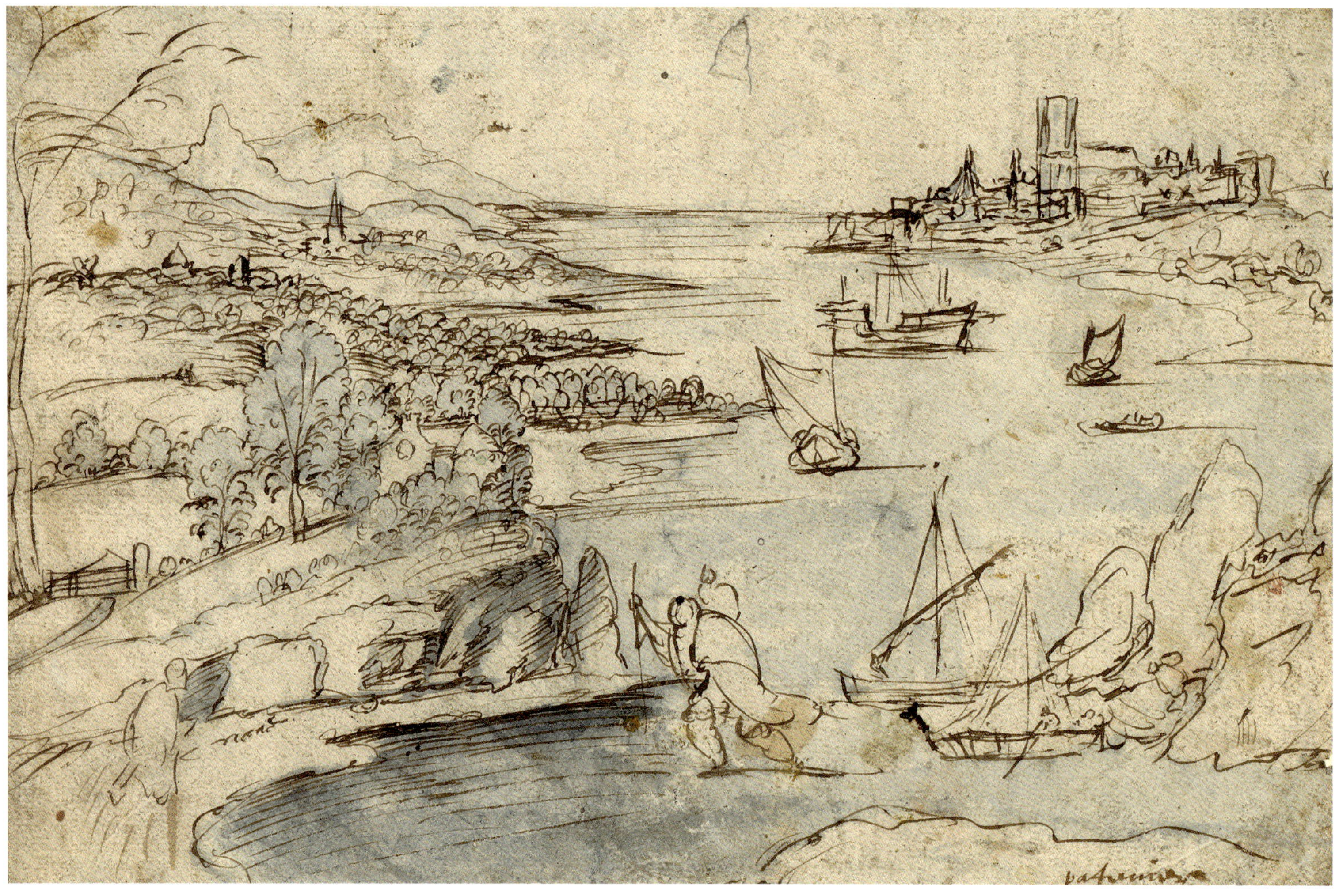

15
JOACHIM PATINIR
(1480–1524)
River Landscape with Saint Christopher, date unknown
Pen in brown ink with blue wash, 13.4 × 20 cm
Staatliche Museen zu Berlin, Kupferstichkabinett

drawings of a constructed nude features a ball-joined neck.[38] While the figures may seem robotic, their rotations evidence astonishing mobility offstage, in the mind of the artist who made and manipulated them. On the first page of his book on measurement, Dürer imagines putting a dot, or point, at the image's extensionless point of origin: 'I may in my mind throw a point high up in the air or drop it into the depths where I cannot reach it with my body.'[39] In their imagination and through their images artists can be everywhere and nowhere at once.

According to Leonardo da Vinci (1452–1519), painters are the most mobile of human beings. Receiving the ceaseless flow of images from nature that, although intense and beautiful, vanish immediately, painters ceaselessly generate new images that by contrast endure.[40] Painters can do this because they are themselves, in a special way, in a state of motion: 'The painter is moved by the real likenesses of the forms in order indeed to copy these forms.'[41] If too physically and mentally sedentary, if stuck in the same environment, or if bombarded by sensory experience but able to do nothing else but reproduce that experience, painters will only paint themselves. Leonardo's famous verdict makes Dürer's self portraits, in their restless movement elsewhere, into symptoms of a person at once turned to, and escaping from, himself.[42] Catching mobile phenomena and themselves mobile in mind and body, artists in turn move their viewers, sometimes piously, sometimes erotically, as Leonardo explained. The idea of a mobility passed from painter to the viewer was widespread in the Renaissance. It belonged to a new estimation of the artist as avatar for the human capacity for change. Artists 'change themselves beyond all human measure', wrote Leonardo Bruni (1370–1444) in his *Life of Dante and Petrarch*: 'Through their genius [*ingegno*] they are excited and aroused by a certain power' that moves them, allowing them to move others.[43]

Fig. 18
ALBRECHT DÜRER
Self portrait, 1500
Oil on lime wood panel, 67.1 × 48.9 cm
Bayerische Staatsgemäldesammlungen, Alte Pinakothek, Munich

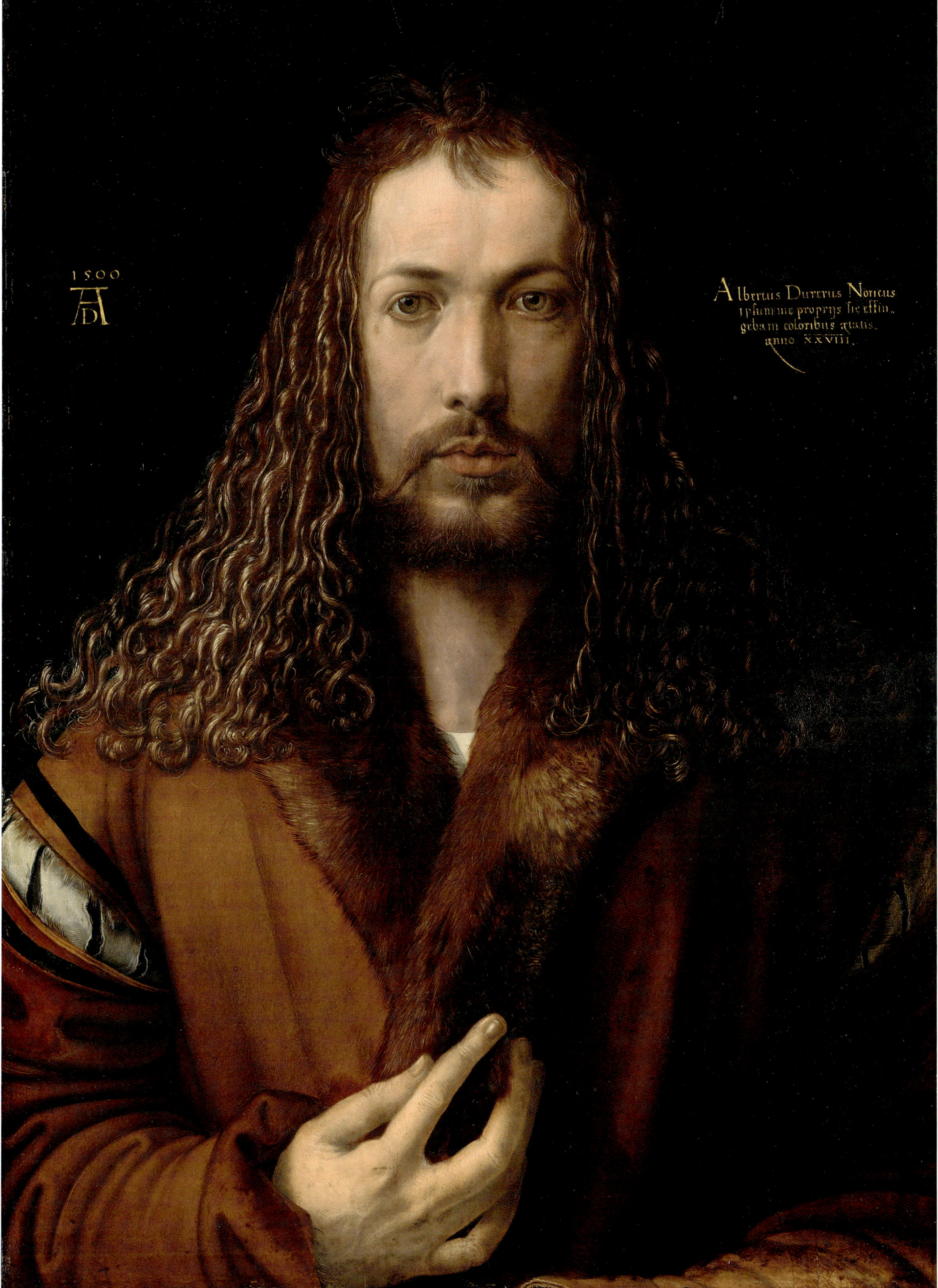
1500
AD
Albertus Durerus Noricus
ipsum me proprys sic effin-
gebam coloribus ætatis.
anno XXVIII.

16
ALBRECHT DÜRER
Saint Christopher, about 1521
Pen and black ink, heightened with white, on dark grey prepared paper, 18.6 × 14 cm
British Museum

17
ALBRECHT DÜRER
Nine Studies of Saint Christopher, 1521
Pen and black ink, 22.9 × 40.7 cm
Staatliche Museen zu Berlin, Kupferstichkabinett

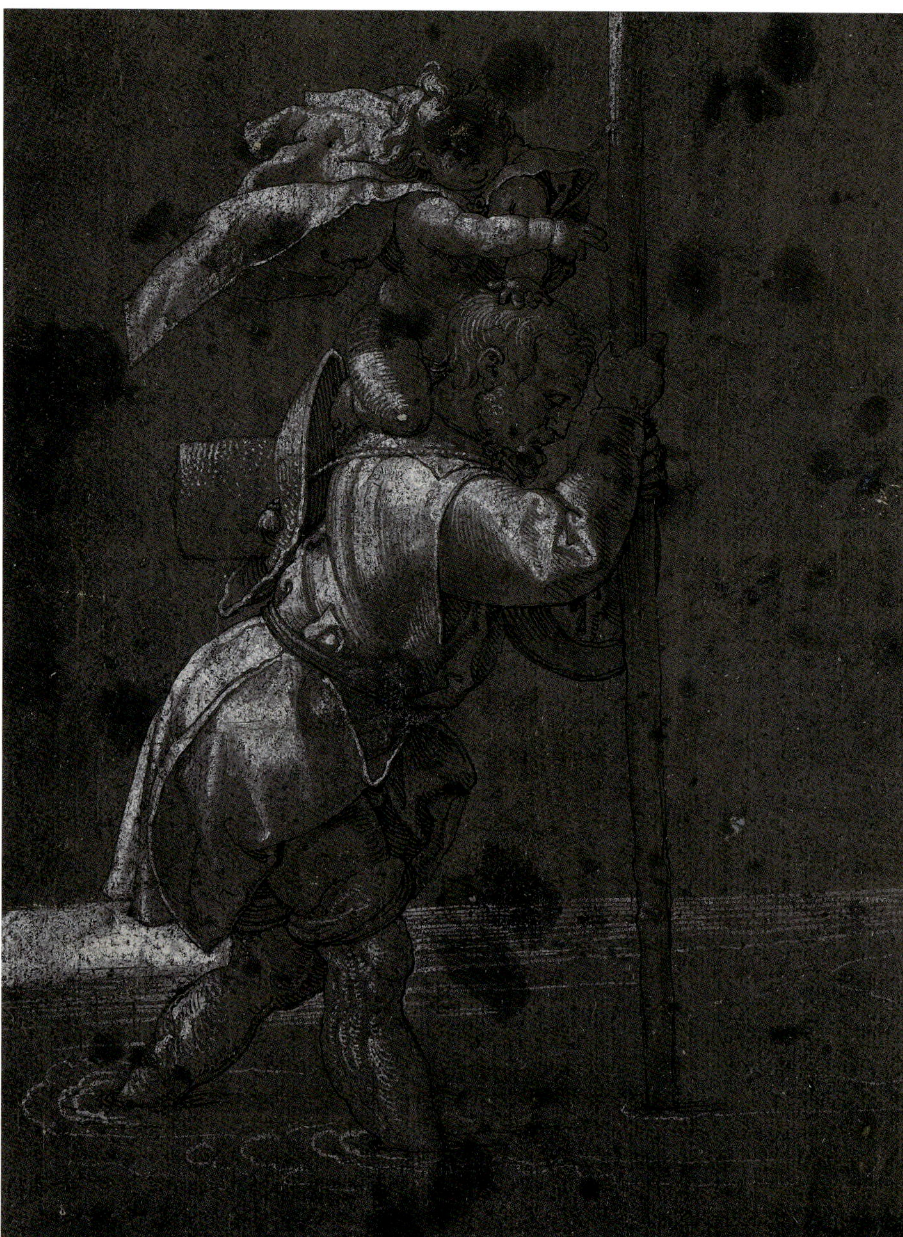

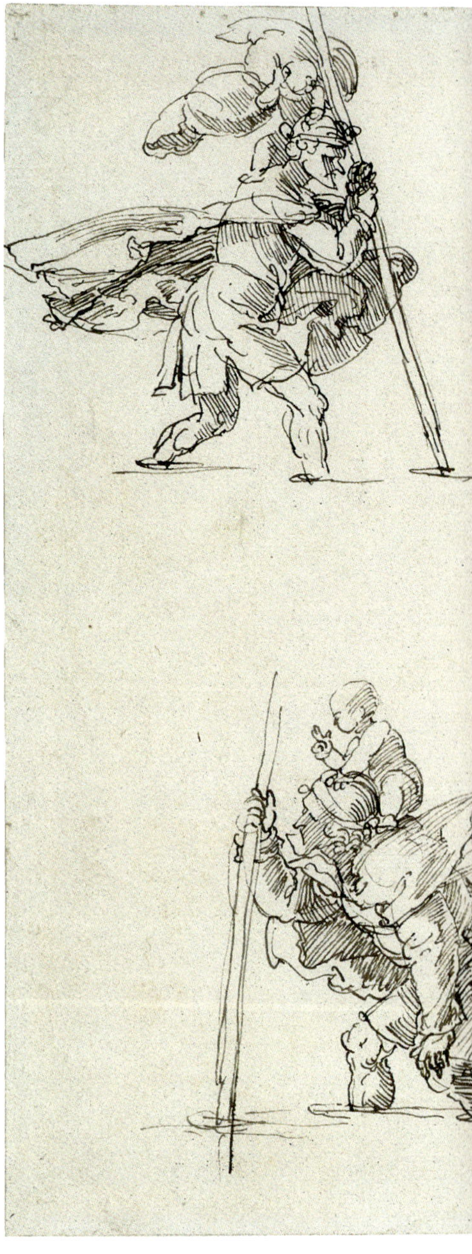

Ingenium: this was the new term for that special power which Dürer recognised, and named, in his encounter with New World artefacts in Brussels, and which allows this artist's art and travels to resonate with us 500 years later. That we know of Dürer's encounter in Brussels after all this time depends, of course, on countless contingencies. One of these is obvious, but has not been fully appreciated: this artist set his experience down on *paper*. Dürer's commitment to this relatively new material goes back to his artistic beginnings, where we find him saving, labelling and dating drawings, not only by his own hand but by others' as well – most notably Schongauer's. Taking them out of their customary circulation as designs to be kept and used in artists' workshops, Dürer preserved and archived drawings for collecting and historiographical practices that had not yet seen the light of day.[44] More momentously, Dürer's decision to bet his fortune on prints was based on his commitment to paper. The relatively cheap product of Nuremberg's state-of-the-art mills, paper had a curious staying power despite its fragility: it travels easily, stores well and compactly, and has an advantage of numbers. Out of thousands of identical sheets, some are bound to survive. The images that issued from Dürer's press, along with the papers he left behind at his death (including the original Netherlands journal), would be met by a public instructed by these 'flying pages' on what to do with them: admire them for who made them and when, hold them safe for the ages, and, in case they go missing, make copies of them, hoping that those papers will survive.

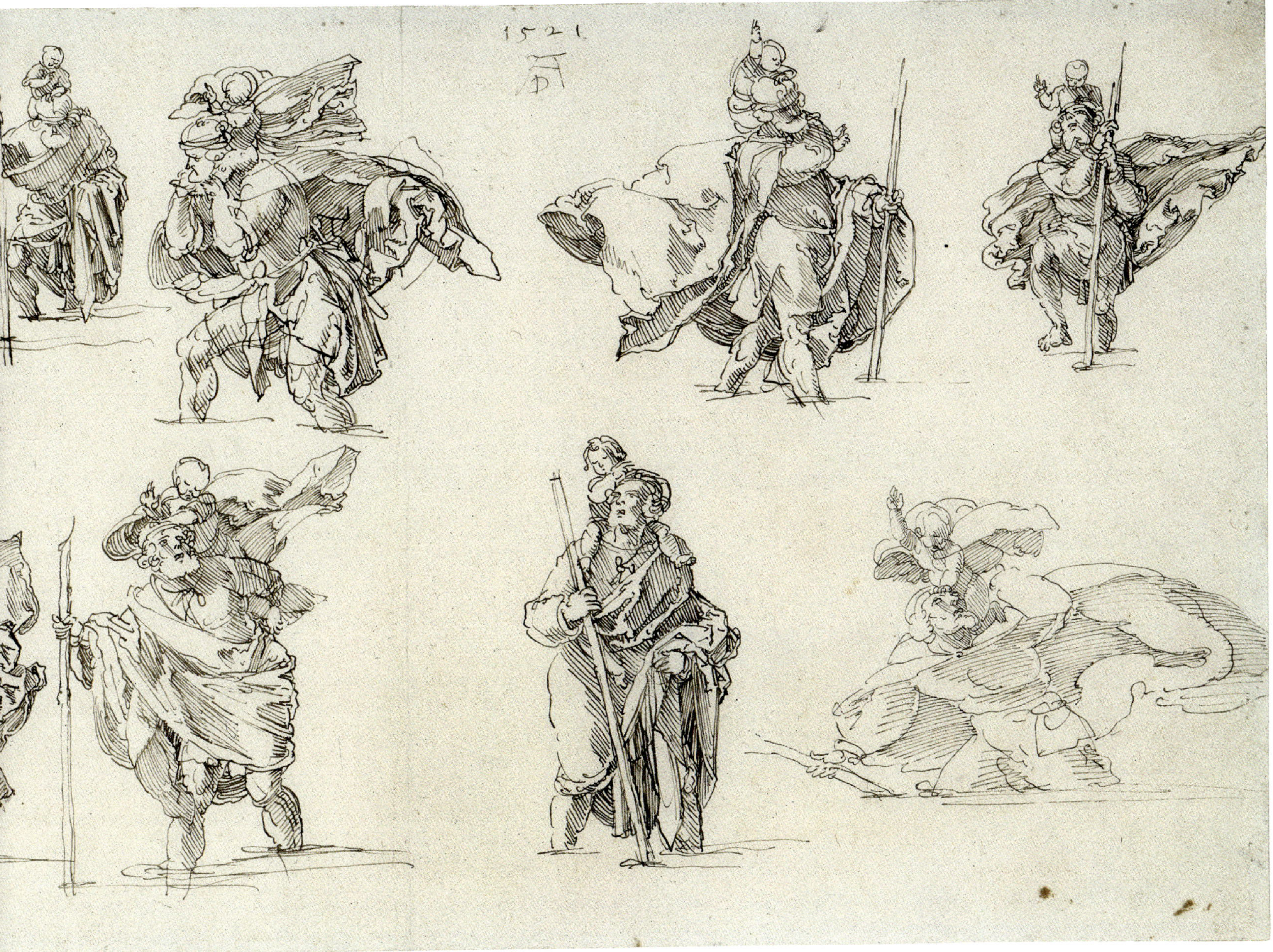

1 Saville 1920, p. 18.
2 Ashcroft 2017, vol. 1, p. 560.
3 Ibid.
4 On the refusal to categorise pre-Columbian artefacts as art, see Pasztory 1989; also Colborn 2005, p. 36.
5 Washington 1991, p. 515.
6 Ashcroft 2017, vol. 1, p. 368.
7 Ashcroft 2017, vol. 1, p. 31.
8 Mende 1983, p. 293.
9 Ashcroft 2017, vol. 1, p. 368.
10 Anzelewsky 1991, pp. 188–9 (cat. 82).
11 Vermeylen 2003, pp. 122, 124 and 161; see also Ewing 2004–5, p. 286.
12 Koerner 2010, p. 24.
13 Washington 1991, p. 152; Koerner 2010, pp. 7–17.
14 Lange-Krach 2017, vol. 1, p. 46; vol. 2, p. 89.
15 Washington 1991, p. 516; Koerner 1993, p. 59; also Cummins 2010, pp. 19–21.
16 Rupprich 1956–69, vol. 3, p. 441, citing Vienna 1959, p. xvi.
17 Ashcroft 2017, vol. 1, p. 580.
18 Ibid., p. 106 n. 170.
19 Ibid., pp. 269, 270.
20 Brisman 2016, pp. 46–51.
21 For sources and evidence, see Nuremberg 2012, pp. 29–30.
22 Washington 1991, p. 115.
23 Ashcroft 2017, vol. 1, p. 168.
24 Ibid., vol. 1, pp. 139–40.
25 Nuremberg 2012, pp. 18–36.
26 Kim 2014, p. 3.
27 Nuremberg 2012, pp. 366–7.
28 Panofsky 1955, p. 36.
29 Ashcroft 2017, vol. 2, p. 881.
30 Ibid., p. 881.
31 Ibid., vol. 1, p. 536.
32 Ibid., vol. 2, p. 579.
33 Ibid., vol. 1, p. 582.
34 Winkler 1936–9, vol. 4, no. 801; Strauss 1974, vol. 4, no. 1521/15.
35 Winkler 1936–9, vol. 4, no. 800; Strauss 1974, vol. 4, no. 1521/14.
36 A. Dürer, *Vier Bücher von menchlicher Proportion*, Nuremberg 1528, fol. Xr.
37 See criticisms in Panofsky 1915, pp. 69–72.
38 Winkler 1936–9, vol. 4, no. 930; Strauss 1974, vol. 4, no. 1526/26; on Dürer's use of mannequins, see Weixlgärtner 1903.
39 'Dann ich mag mit dem synn ein punckten hoch in lufft werffen/oder in die tyffen fellen/ da hyn jch doch mit dem leib nit reichen kan' (A. Dürer, *Unterweysung der messung mit dem zirckel und richtscheyt*, Nuremberg 1525, fol. Aii; Dürer 1977, pp. 40–1). On this sentence and its implications, see Fowler 2016, pp. 37–42.
40 Fehrenbach 2019, pp. 45–52.
41 Codex Urbinas, fol. 8v, § 19 = Ms. A, fol. 99r (about 1492), cited in Fehrenbach 2019, p. 121 n. 134.
42 Codex Urbinas, fol. 60r, § 178 (1505–10), cited in Fehrenbach 2019, p. 121 n. 136.
43 Bruno 1928, p. 59.
44 Fowler 2019, p. 84.

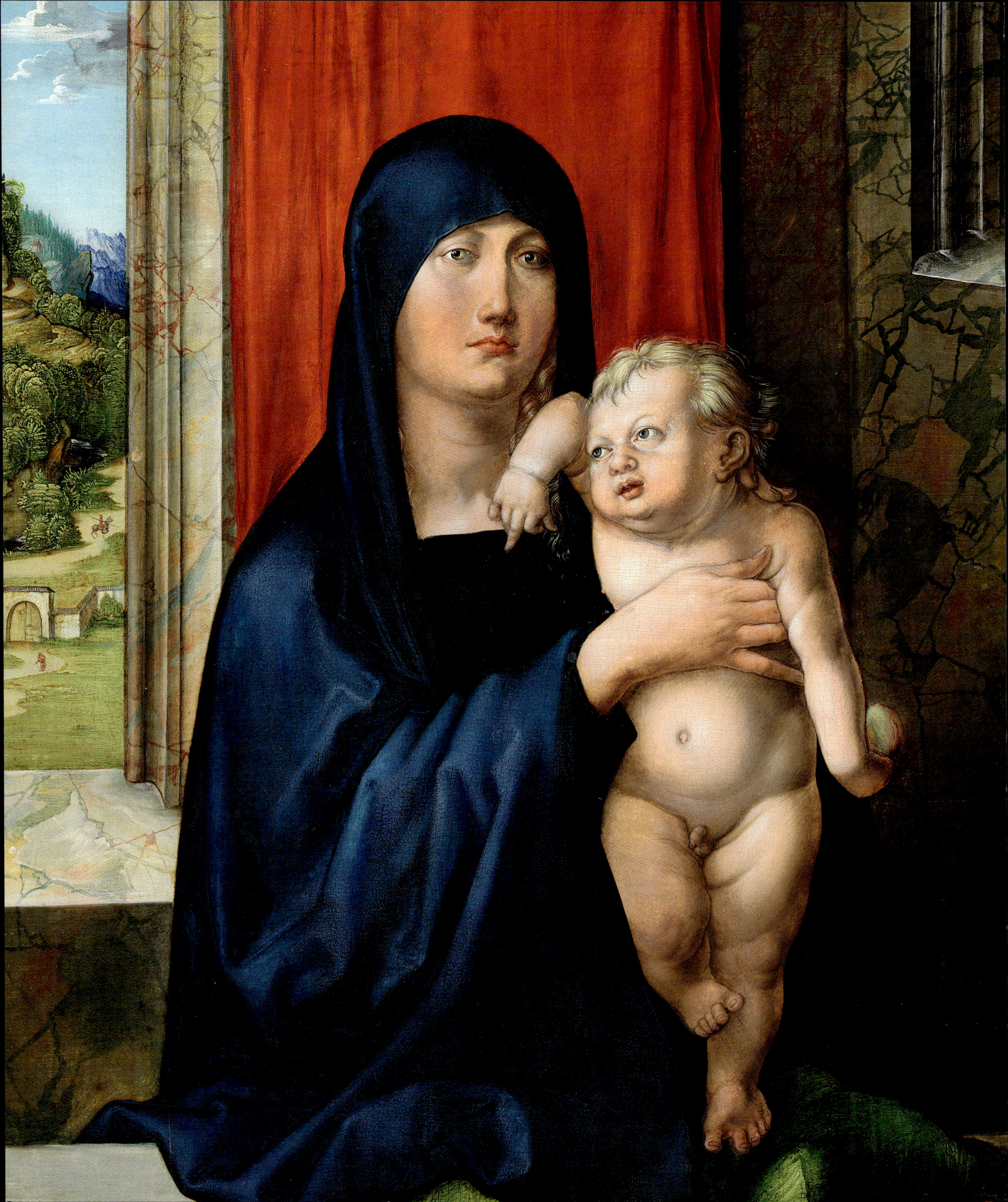

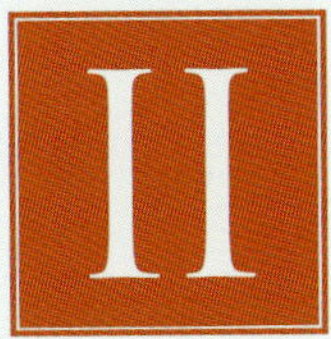

EUROPE NORTH AND SOUTH

DÜRER ENVISAGED THAT HIS CLEARLY AUTHORED PRINTS should be distributed as widely as possible throughout Europe, both north and south. He was quickly successful, with artists such as Giovanni Bellini in Venice and Jan Gossaert in the Low Countries adopting motifs from his engravings. Whereas earlier artists had relied on copies of drawings to incorporate into their work, the wide availability of prints at this time facilitated a swift exchange of motifs across Europe. Dürer himself had drawn inspiration from engravings by the Italian artist Andrea Mantegna (about 1431–1506) early in his career.

Dürer's fame as an artist in black and white was such that when he was in Venice in 1505–7 artists assumed he could not use colour, and he also records their criticism that he did not understand the now ubiquitous classical vocabulary. But he writes that his altarpiece of the *Feast of the Rose Garlands* (fig. 19) for the German Hanseatic merchants acted as a riposte to them: its brilliant, rich colour demonstrated that Dürer was an accomplished painter as well as a graphic artist. Italian-inspired motifs such as the lute-playing angel prominent in the altarpiece were absorbed into his repertoire, and still appear in his works much later in his career, for example in sketches made when visiting the Low Countries in 1520–1. The portraits he produced in Venice with their concentrated focus on the face also show Italian inspiration, but perhaps one filtered through earlier Netherlandish models. From an early date Dürer showed himself eager to understand the Italians' approach to human proportion and perspective. He records that he had tried to induce Jacopo de' Barbari to explain proportion to him in Nuremberg, but that the Italian artist refused. In turn his famous engraving of *Adam and Eve* (cat. 52) of 1504, in which he encapsulates his studies of the nude figure to date, inspired artists such as Jan Gossaert and Conrad Meit (1480–1550/1).

The revival of interest in antiquity in Italy resulted in the propagation of classical architectural and sculptural motifs that were reflected in the work of Dürer and others. On viewing the reused Roman pillars of Aachen cathedral in 1520 Dürer was able to comment that their capitals were correct according to the rules set out by the Roman author Vitruvius. The journal of his visit to the Low Countries records Dürer's admiration for the nude figure of Eve as painted by Jan van Eyck nearly a hundred years earlier in his Ghent Altarpiece, as well as his viewing of the marble *Bruges Madonna* by Michelangelo. Dürer was intensely interested in the inventions of skilled artists, irrespective of time and place. In the Low Countries he greatly admired the work of the illuminator Susanna Horenbout (about 1503–1554), as well as the ingenuity and skill of those who had created works in gold sent from Mexico. SF

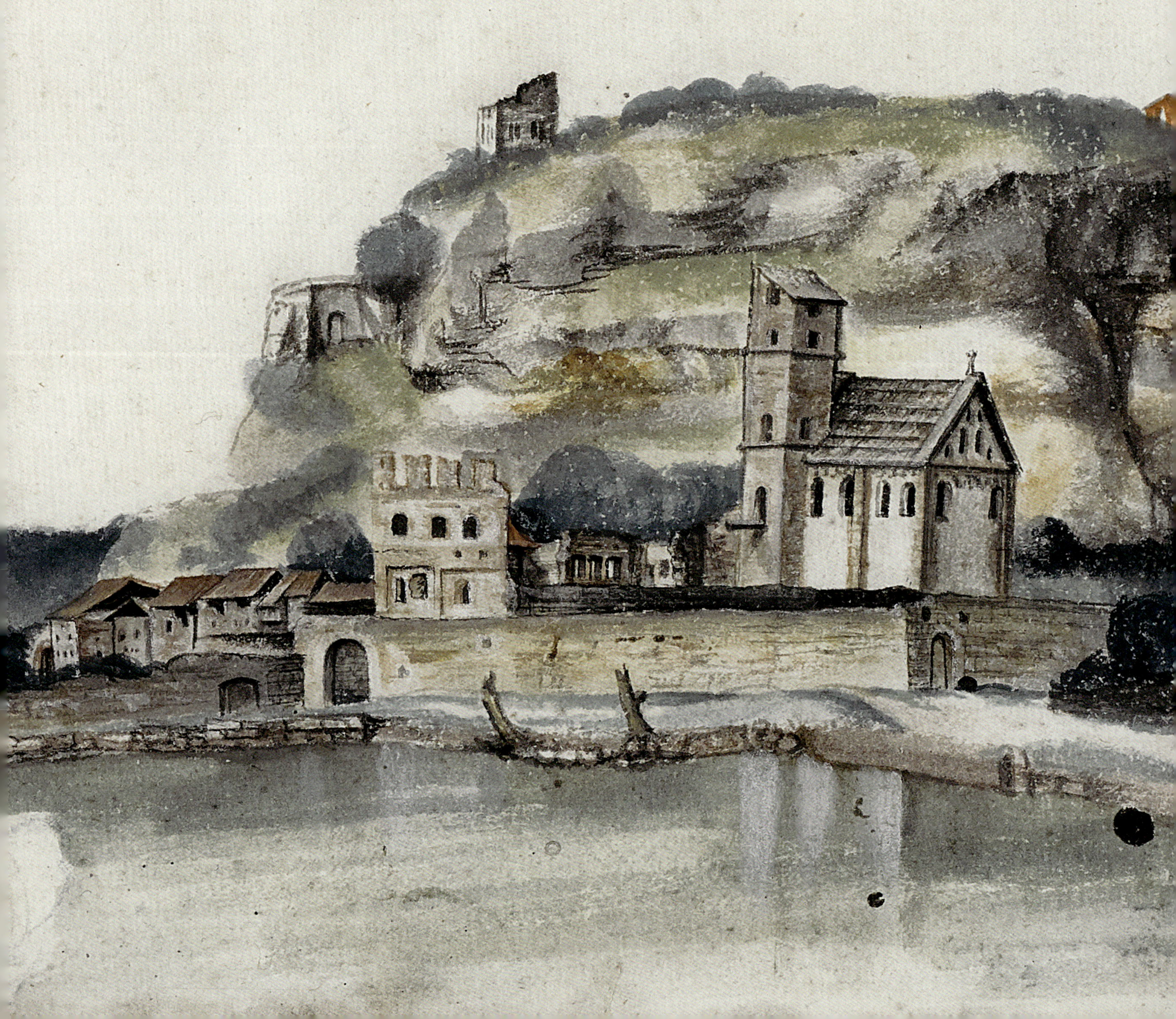
trintperg

SUSAN FOISTER

DÜRER'S EARLY JOURNEYS
FACT AND FICTION

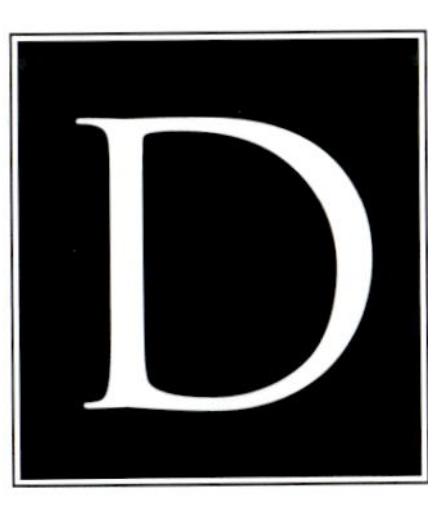

DÜRER'S NETHERLANDISH JOURNAL enumerates some of the challenges of travel in his lifetime: the necessity for obtaining permits to travel across certain territories; dealing with a great range of local currencies; the practicalities of journeying slowly on foot, by boat or on horseback in different weathers and in terrain that was sometimes physically onerous or made dangerous by those who preyed on travellers. Yet despite these challenges, many journeys were made, often long ones: it was not unusual for people to travel, and this had been the case for centuries before.

People travelled for business: there were numerous well-established trading routes throughout Europe, many passing through well-placed Nuremberg.[1] They travelled for religious reasons, particularly to go on pilgrimages. And they travelled as part of training or education: those who would become knights attached themselves to noble and courtly households, while those who were to become clerics studied at universities, an education that started to extend itself to others. In Nuremberg a tradition of travelling to study at Italian universities had begun by Dürer's lifetime.[2]

Travelling was also normal for artists in this period.[3] An artist's training, particularly in Germany, commonly included a period of travel at the end of apprenticeship, before becoming a master, a stage with which marriage was often associated: in the Krakow guild regulations a period journeying 'to practise and improve his skills before he marries' was stipulated.[4] The journeyman's quest to find a master's daughter to marry is reflected in the case of Dürer's own father, Albrecht the Elder (cat. 19), who worked for the goldsmith Hieronymus Holper (active 1435–83) in Nuremberg and married his daughter Barbara (1452–1513).[5] Artists also travelled

PREVIOUS PAGE
Detail from *Madonna and Child* (cat. 7)

OPPOSITE
Detail from *Trintperg – Dosso di Trento* (cat. 23)

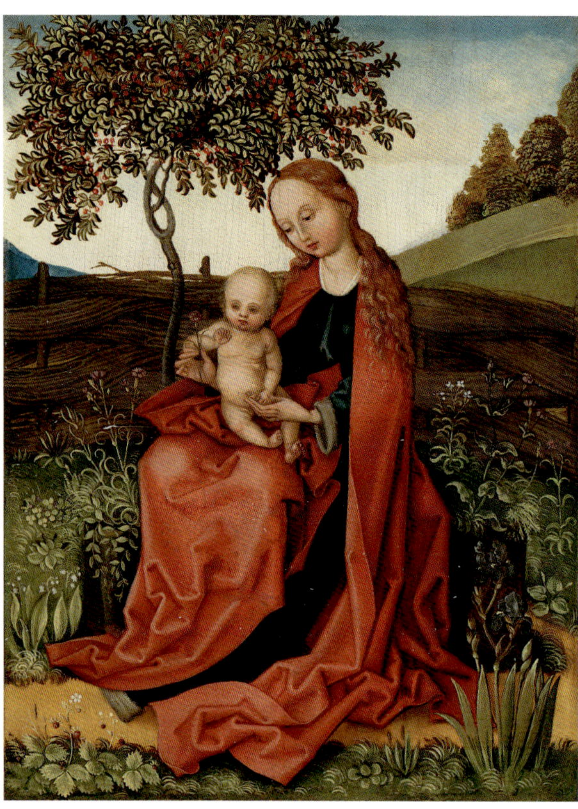

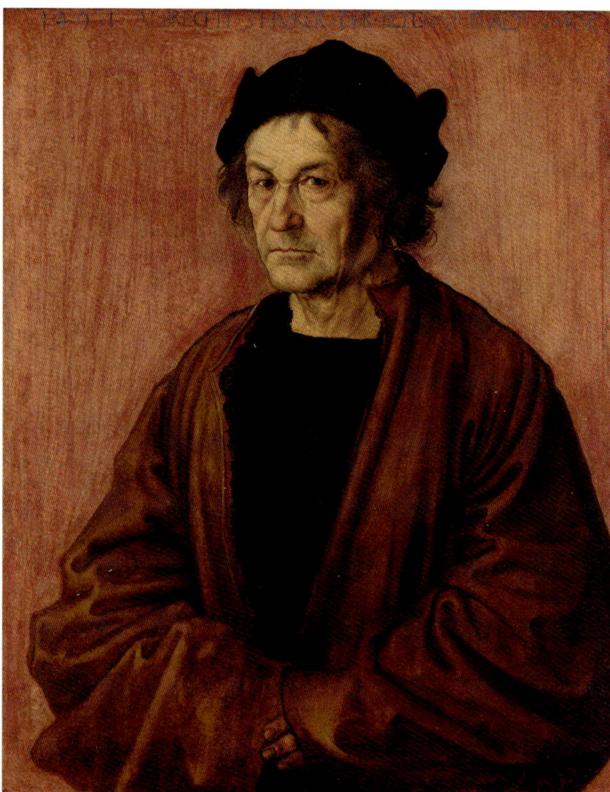

18
STYLE OF MARTIN SCHONGAUER
The Virgin and Child in a Garden, 1469–91
Oil on lime, 30.2 × 21.9 cm
The National Gallery, London

19
AFTER ALBRECHT DÜRER
The Painter's Father, 1497
Oil on lime, 51 × 40.3 cm
The National Gallery, London

for business reasons, for example to the many fairs that were becoming increasingly important for the sale of artists' outputs during Dürer's lifetime.[6] Such gatherings might also have provided occasions to see the work of others. Living in a trading centre such as Nuremberg offered opportunities to acquire material to serve as workshop patterns or source material, as well as the possibility of contacts through whom external sales might be made. Artists also sometimes migrated, or relocated in connection with specific commissions. Dürer's father came to Nuremberg from Hungary, travelling extensively in the Low Countries before settling there, and later journeyed from Nuremberg to Linz in connection with a commission from the Emperor Frederick III.[7]

Dürer documented his own life through letters, drawings and journals, exceptional survivals for this period. He provided information through the amendments he made in 1524, towards the end of his life, to the family history originally drawn up by his father, as well as through a fragment of a more personal diary or *Gedenkbuch*.[8] Aside from his own record of his journey to the Netherlands in 1520–1, he wrote letters in German from Venice in 1506 to his friend Willibald Pirckheimer in Nuremberg; paintings and drawings associated with both visits survive.[9] But for his travels in the 1490s the documentation is far less clear.

Evidence for the earliest journeys in Dürer's life can be considered in two parts: travel north of the Alps beyond Nuremberg, and travel through and putatively beyond the Alps. To take the first of these journeys, Dürer himself says in his family history that after Easter in 1490 his father sent him away for four years, returning after Whitsun in 1494.[10] This followed the completion of his apprenticeship to the painter and designer Michael Wolgemut (1434–1519). Dürer's movements evidently followed the pattern of the *Wanderjahre*, travels as a so-called 'journeyman', although these were not required in Nuremberg, freed from the traditional guild system.[11]

Where did he go? In his biography of 1604 Karel van Mander (1548–1606) asserts that Dürer made a first journey to the Low Countries as a young man, but earlier sources do not mention this.[12] Jakob Wimpfeling (1450–1528) wrote in 1505 that Dürer had studied with the painter and engraver Martin Schongauer (cat. 18); however, the German humanist Christoph Scheurl (1481–1542), writing in 1515, says he went there in 1492, too late to meet Schongauer in person, since he died on 2 February 1491, but that he met Schongauer's four brothers.[13] Although Scheurl may have wished to create a sense of historic connection between Dürer and Schongauer, there were good reasons for the artist to seek out Schongauer: his master in Nuremberg, Michael Wolgemut, designed woodcuts, but Schongauer had extended the possibilities of engraving (cat. 20). Dürer was to transform the art of printmaking, bringing woodcut closer to the sophistication of engraving as well as greatly developing the pictorial possibilities of engraving.[14] A visit could have been facilitated by Schongauer's Nuremberg connections if, as seems likely, he spent time in the workshop of the painter Hans Pleydenwurff (1420–1472) there: Wolgemut married Pleydenwurff's widow.[15] Furthermore, three drawings by Schongauer exist which are inscribed by Dürer, another being lost (cat. 21); although it has been argued these could have been obtained in Nuremberg, they have also been taken as evidence for Dürer's visit to Colmar.[16]

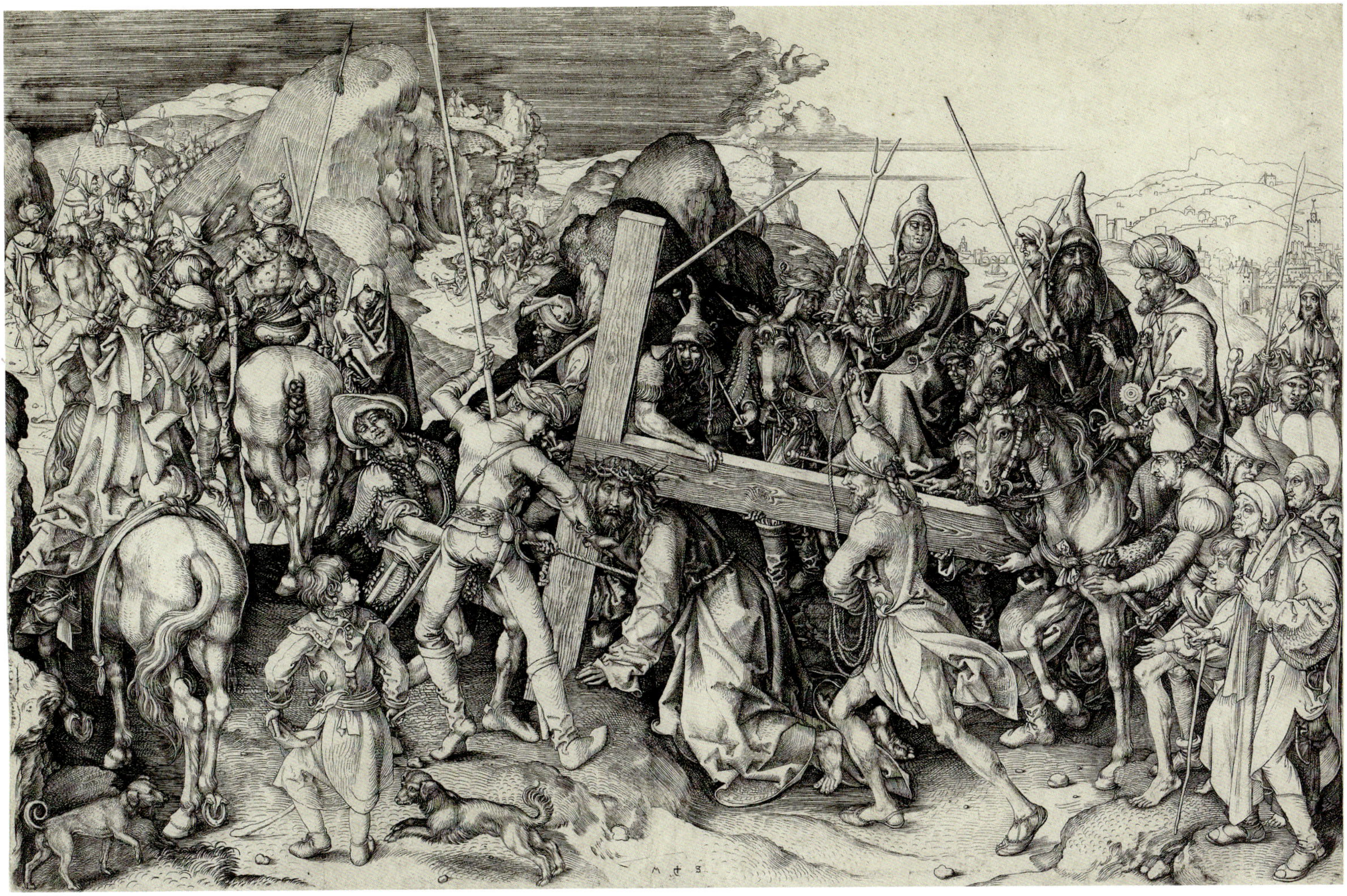

As well as visiting Colmar, Scheurl says that Dürer visited Basel.[17] It is a reasonable assumption that Basel, with its well-established book publishing industry, would be a logical place for a young aspiring printmaker to visit; but the evidence beyond Scheurl's assertion is less clear. Schongauer's brother Georg (died 1514), a goldsmith, was a citizen there, making one possible connection. Furthermore, the existence of a woodblock for a title-page woodcut of Saint Jerome published in Basel in 1492 (cat. 22), signed or inscribed on the reverse as the work of Dürer himself, has generally been agreed

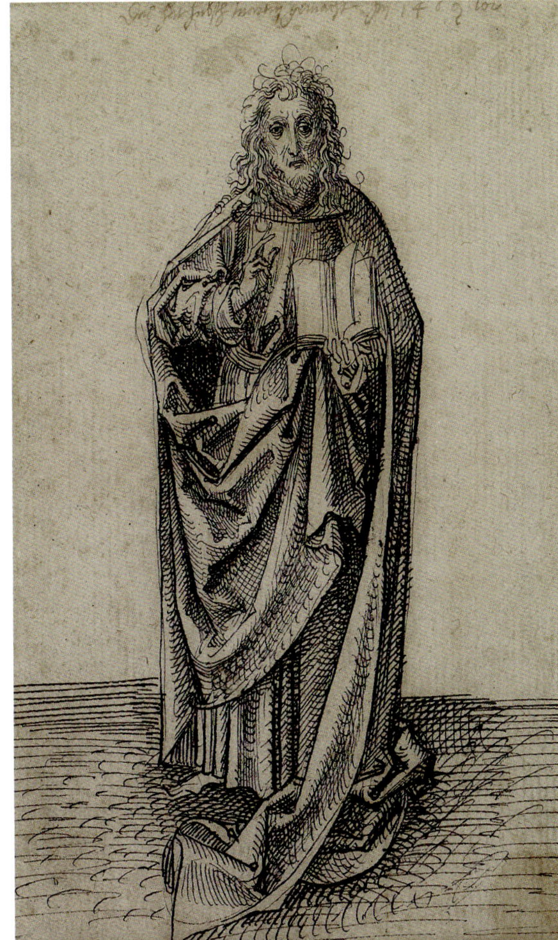

20
MARTIN SCHONGAUER
(active 1469; died 1491)
The Road to Calvary, about 1475
Engraving, 28.6 × 42.5 cm
The Syndics of the Fitzwilliam Museum, University of Cambridge

21
MARTIN SCHONGAUER
(active 1469; died 1491)
Christ as Teacher, 1469
Pen and black ink, 20.7 × 12.4 cm
British Museum

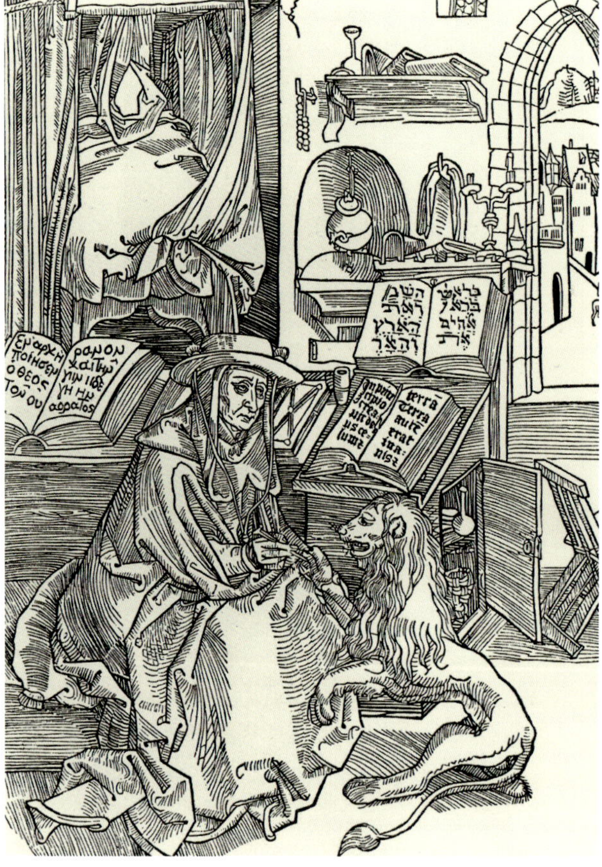

22
ALBRECHT DÜRER
Saint Jerome, 1492
From *Epistolare beati Hieronymi*, published by Nikolaus Kesler
Woodcut, 13.5 × 19.1 cm
Syndics of Cambridge University Library (Peterborough)

to provide evidence of the authorship of the woodcut and of Dürer's sojourn in the city. This in turn has led to the attribution of a series of woodcuts and drawings for woodcuts by Dürer illustrating comedies by Terence (about 186–159 BC), *Der Ritter vom Turn* (1493), part of the *Ship of Fools* (1494) and even some paintings. The extent of this work has suggested a sojourn in Basel of some time and some significance for the start of Dürer's career as a printmaker. Attributing this corpus of work to Dürer has however always been fraught with uncertainty, as apart from the evidence of the woodblock, recently questioned, the attributions are purely stylistically based.[18] But Basel seems to have had a very flexible approach to employing journeymen: regulations of 1463 stipulated they could be employed by the week, the month or the year, so Dürer's sojourn could have been a brief one.[19]

A visit to Strasbourg emerges from an entry in the Pirckheimer family inventory of 1573. This refers to portraits by Dürer of his 'master', painted in Strasbourg in 1494, and of a woman (presumably the latter's wife).[20] As the Strasbourg sculptor Niclaes Gerhaert (active 1462–1473) was working on the tomb of the Emperor Frederick III, and Dürer's father was also making work for the Emperor, it has been suggested that Dürer could well have taken advantage of this connection between Nuremberg and Strasbourg; moreover, Gerhaert's daughter Apollonia was married to Georg Schongauer.[21] It has also been assumed that Dürer's 1493 Louvre self portrait was made there, as well as drawings dated 1493.[22] Dürer probably planned his journey strategically, with reference to potential employment with painters and publishers; at Strasbourg he may also have familiarised himself with designing for stained glass. It is not clear where he went at the start of his travels between 1490 and 1492, but it has been plausibly suggested that he may have visited the publishing warehouse in Frankfurt of his godfather Anton Koberger (about 1440–1513), perhaps going back and forth, travelling via the river Main. The lack of details regarding Frankfurt and Mainz in his Netherlandish journal may suggest that he was familiar with these cities and he may also have visited Würzburg and even Cologne.[23] But there is no evidence in surviving work of such visits.

Dürer's family chronicle says that in spring 1494 he was called back by his father to Nuremberg and seven weeks later, on 7 July, he was married to Agnes, the daughter of the brassworker Hans Frey. Needing marriage in order to be allowed to operate independently under Nuremberg craft rules, Dürer was now in a position to establish himself as a painter, printmaker and even a designer of stained glass.[24] But art history suggests that he next left Nuremberg to travel to Venice. What is the evidence for this? Two documents have been interpreted as references to an earlier trip to Venice in relation to Dürer's well-documented visit of 1505–7: the first is the well-known reference, in his letter of 7 February 1506 to Willibald Pirckheimer, to the 'Ding' that pleased him 11 years earlier no longer pleasing him.[25] The second is a reference in Christoph Scheurl's *Libellus de laudibus Germaniae et ducum Saxoniae* (1508), which appears more specific: it says Dürer 'nuper in Italiam rediiset' ('recently returned to Italy'). Again, some have argued that Scheurl is not to be relied on, given that he does not mention a journey to Italy in his account of Dürer's early journeys in 1515.[26]

Although there is no reference to an earlier journey in Dürer's family chronicle, scholars have noted that there was an outbreak of plague in Nuremberg in September 1494, which would have led some to leave the city to escape it.[27] Dürer had an Innsbruck connection, which might have propelled him south. He could have stayed with one Peter Rummel, a relative of the mother of his wife, Agnes, Dürer's new marriage thus facilitating the establishment of business as an artist. The Rummel commercial connections also extended to Italy, and Agnes herself may even have accompanied her husband there.[28] What evidence for this is provided by Dürer's work? Among studies that have been associated with an

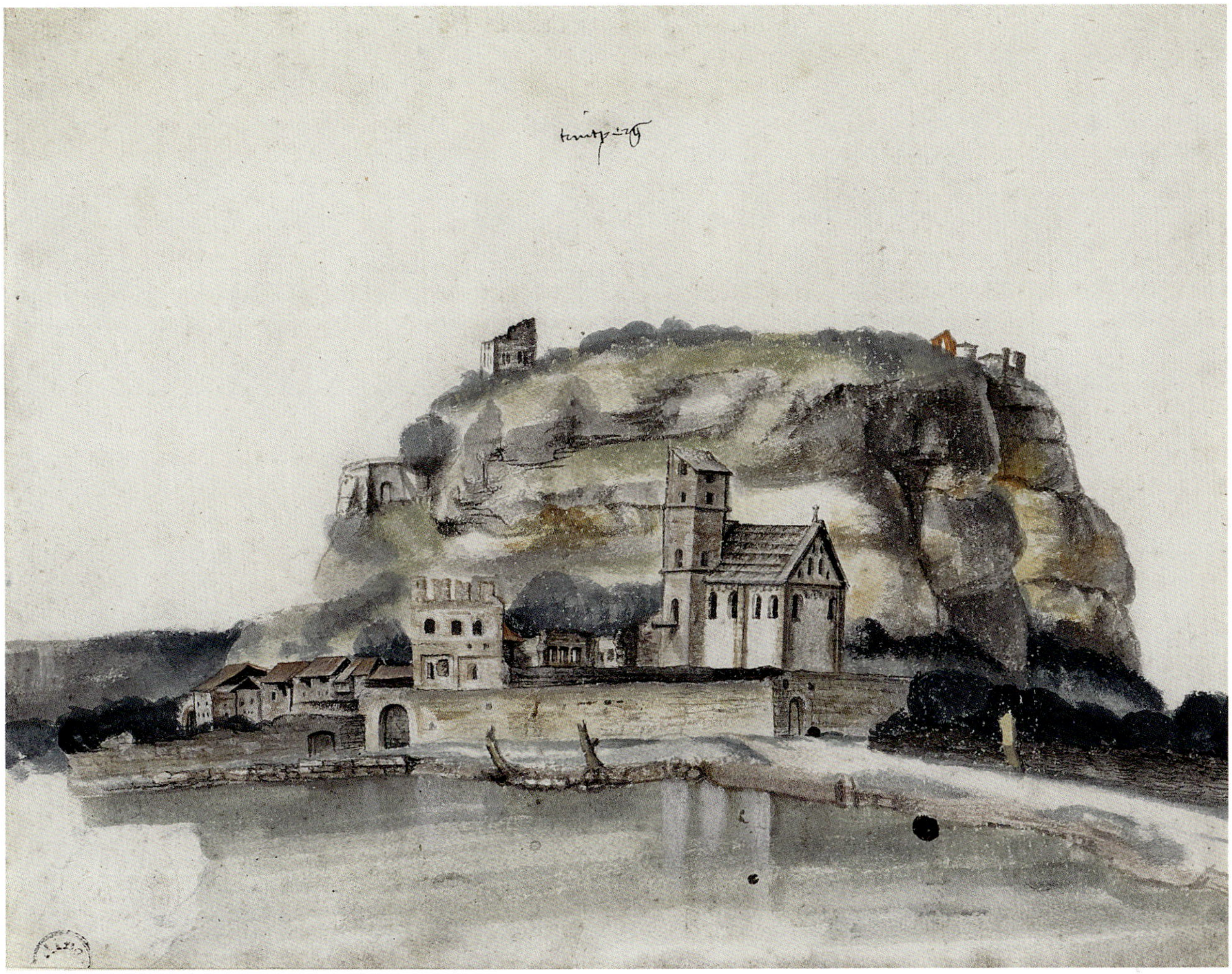

23
ALBRECHT DÜRER
Trintperg – Dosso di Trento, 1495
Watercolour and bodycolour, 17 × 21.2 cm
Kunsthalle Bremen

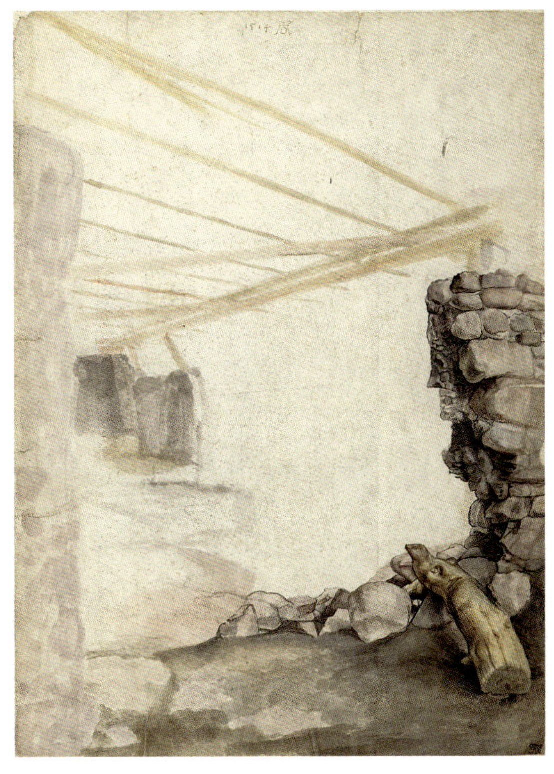

24
ALBRECHT DÜRER
Ruin of an Alpine Shelter, 1514
Metalpoint and watercolour, heightened with white, 37.2 × 26.6 cm
Veneranda Biblioteca Ambrosiana, Pinacoteca, Milan

early journey to Italy are a number of undated landscapes, some associable with specific places south of Nuremberg, including Innsbruck, Trent and Arco, and inscribed as such by Dürer himself (cats 23, 24); studies of women wearing Venetian dress (cat. 25; fig. 114); and some studies with Italian sources or references, such as drawings after Andrea Mantegna and Lorenzo di Credi (about 1458–1537) dated 1494 and 1495 respectively, as well as the study of three Turks after the 1496 Corpus Christi procession by Gentile Bellini.[29]

Consideration of these works led to the traditional view that Dürer travelled over the Alps to Venice in the mid-1490s, recording views of his surroundings on the way there and on the way back, and in Venice itself noting down the appearance of local people, sights such as a large crab and a lobster, and works of art including paintings and prints, particularly those showing the nude figure. This view has been prevalent in art history since the second half of the nineteenth century, and is ultimately based on the view of Dürer’s journeys as a form of *Bildungreise*, educational travel. A more recent and nuanced view of an artist’s travel, one also applicable to the journeys Dürer seems to have made north of the Alps, is that it was important for the artist to create and collect valuable material that he would use in his workshop, in prints and in paintings. An early journey to Venice should not be seen as an extension of the *Wanderjahre*, but rather the start of the business of being a successful artist.[30]

An alternative view recently championed by some scholars was put forward by Ephrussi in the late nineteenth century, namely that Dürer had only made a single, later visit to Venice: Katherine Crawford Luber has suggested that specific works associated with the earlier visit should be re-dated to 1505–7.[31] The argument recently put forward by Jörg Robert also ruled out a first visit to Venice but did not necessitate a re-dating of all the landscape views and other works. He proposed that Dürer’s travels in the mid-1490s were geographically limited and specifically focused, in that they did not extend beyond the borders of the Habsburg empire (which included Trent as well as Innsbruck), and that his views – rather than being picturesque or subjective impressions of his journey – were connected with the *Germania Illustrata*, a specific project of the humanist Conrad Celtis.[32] If a visit to Venice is to be ruled out, then the works traditionally associated with an early visit there must all be explained differently: Venetian dress could be seen in Innsbruck or even in Nuremberg; Dürer came by copy drawings of Italian paintings in either location; Italian prints were readily available in Nuremberg as source material; and the crustaceans were conveyed inland or even taken from sculptural models.[33]

It is clear that art history has had a strong desire since the inception of the discipline to locate Dürer at the nexus of a north–south relationship, one in which the work of a Northern artist in the early Renaissance period could only be validated through a journey to Italy and a consequent infusion of Italianate values into their art.[34] Some artists did make such a journey: Jan Gossaert in Dürer’s lifetime, later on Marten van Heemskerck (1498–1574) and Pieter Bruegel the Elder (active 1550/1; died 1569). But whereas the work of an artist such as Hans Holbein the Younger (1497/8–1543) might reflect the impact of Italian prints even if he did not travel over the Alps, Gossaert’s work was arguably not transformed by his visit to Rome; again, in the case of Bruegel, the influence of Italy is not evident in his art.[35] Similarly, Stephanie Buck has argued that we should not expect to see immediate evidence of a changed painting technique in Dürer’s work of the second half of the 1490s, but that Dürer instead absorbed influences gradually, over a long period.[36]

Dürer’s documented visit to Venice in 1505–7, as well as the evidence that exists for the earlier journey, has been framed by assumptions and expectations of an Italian epiphany. Beate Böckem has, however, suggested that Dürer visited Venice in 1505–7 primarily for commercial reasons.[37] The ten surviving letters that Dürer sent from Venice in 1506 to Willibald Pirckheimer in Nuremberg do not give any explanation for his visit, but escaping plague could have been the spur again.[38] Dürer makes reference to his major commission for the German merchants in Venice, the altarpiece of the *Feast of the Rose Garlands* (fig. 19), and to other work. His *Christ among the Doctors* (cat. 31), for which a number of studies survive (cats 29, 30), four portraits of both men and women (cats 26, 42, 44) and a number of further

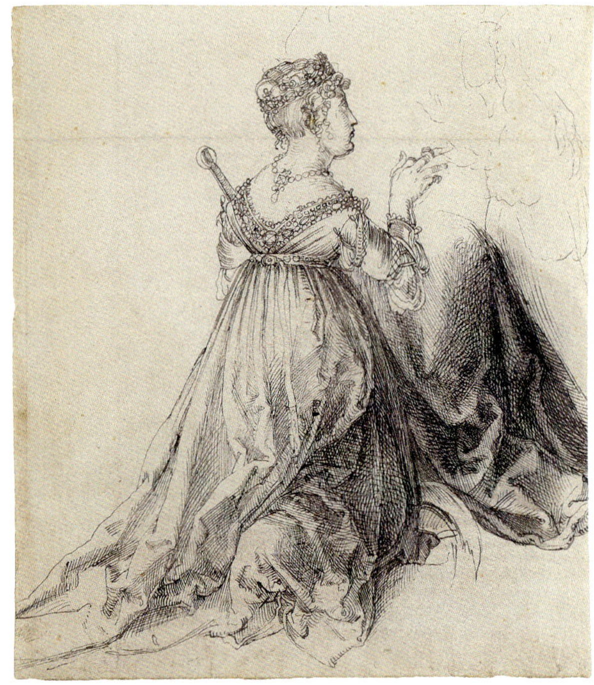

25
ALBRECHT DÜRER
Saint Catherine, about 1494
Pen and light grey ink, 23.4 × 20.1 cm
Wallraf-Richartz-Museum & Fondation Corboud, Cologne

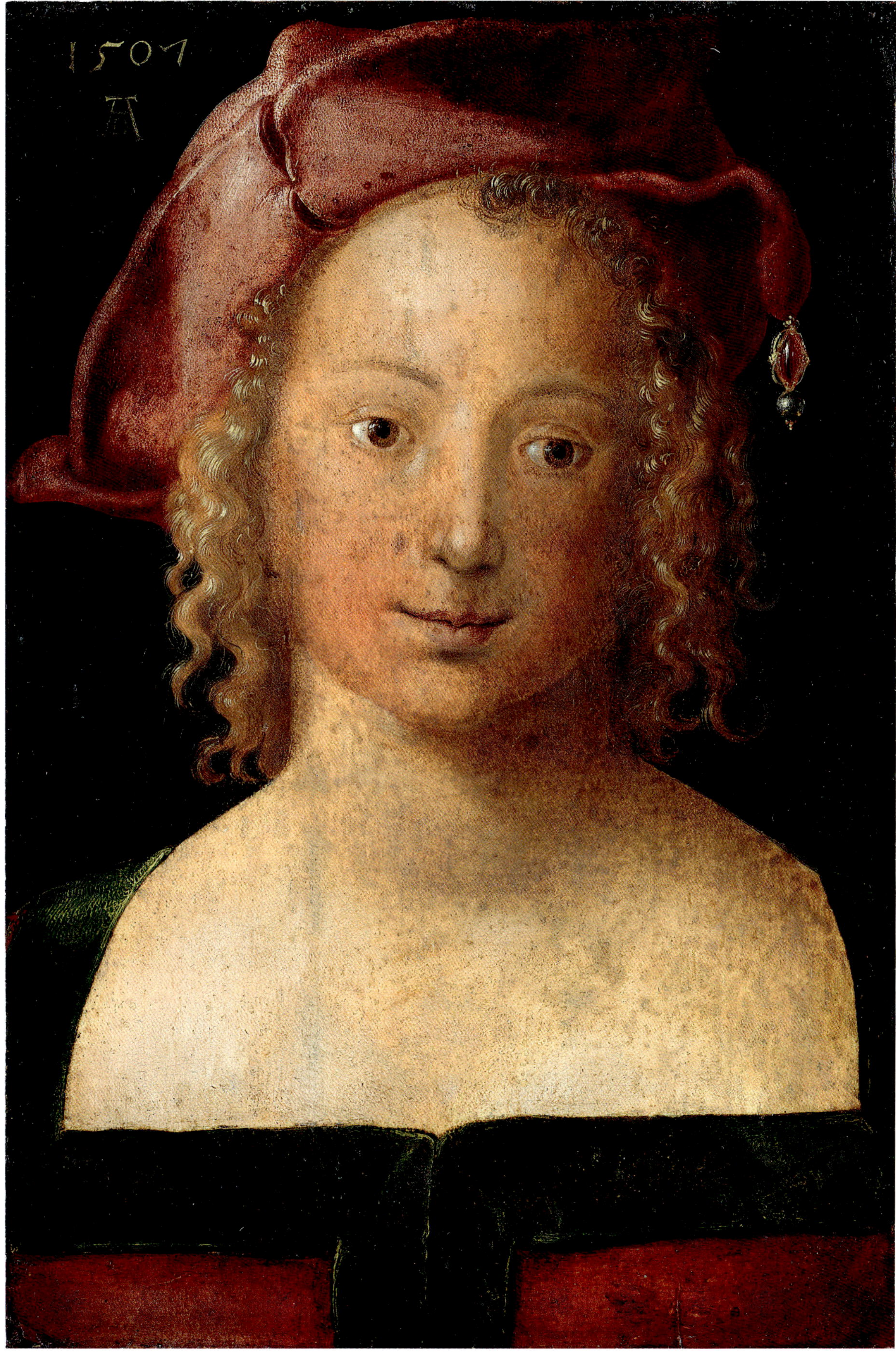

26
ALBRECHT DÜRER
Portrait of a Young Woman in a Red Beret, 1507
Parchment on panel,
32.5 × 22.3 cm
Staatliche Museen zu Berlin, Gemäldegalerie

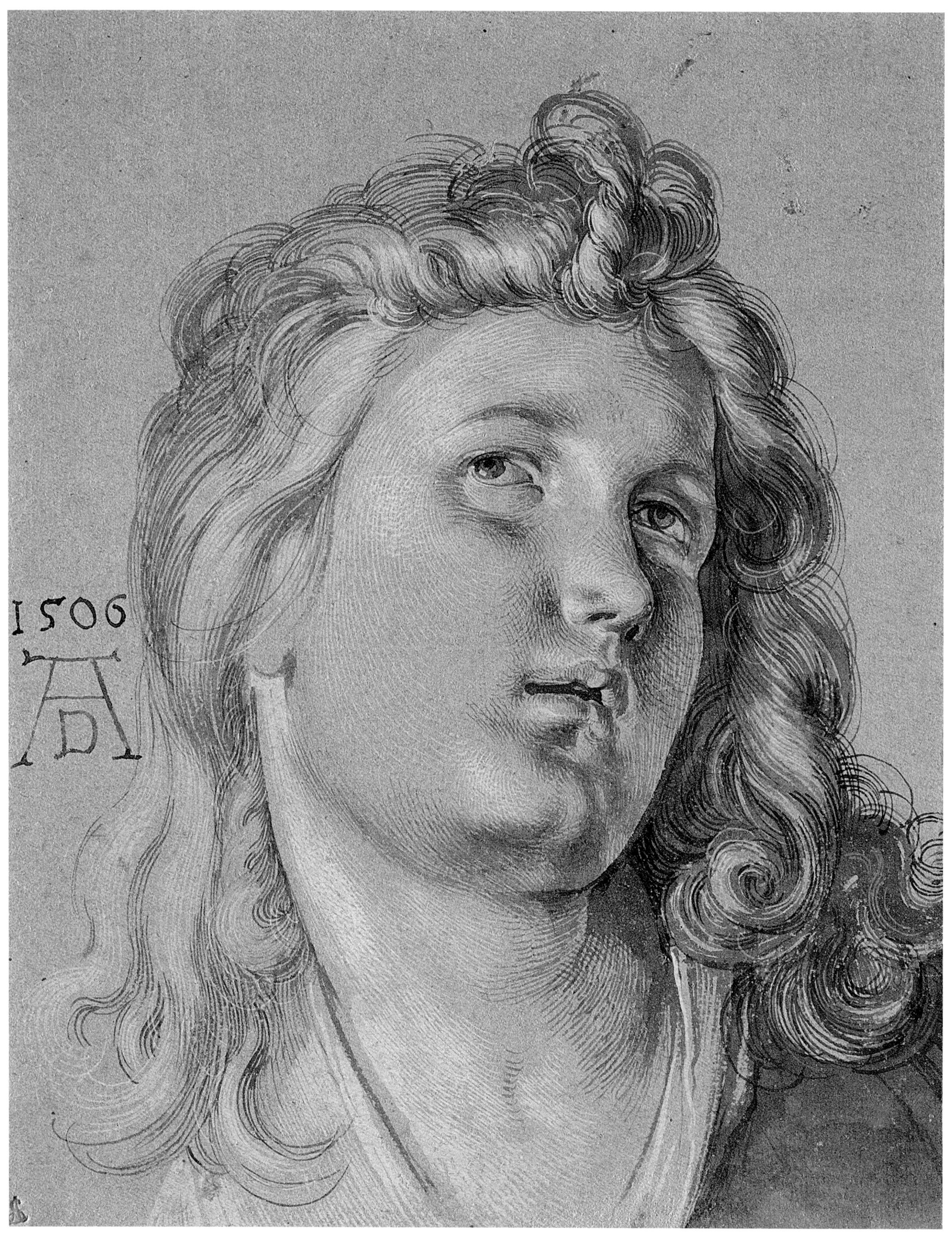
1506
AD

27
ALBRECHT DÜRER
Head of the Lute-playing Angel (study for the *Feast of the Rose Garlands*), 1506
Brush and black and grey ink, grey wash, heightened with white, on blue paper, 27 × 20.8 cm
The Albertina Museum, Vienna

Fig. 19
ALBRECHT DÜRER
Feast of the Rose Garlands, 1506
Oil on wood panel, 162 × 192 cm
National Gallery, Prague

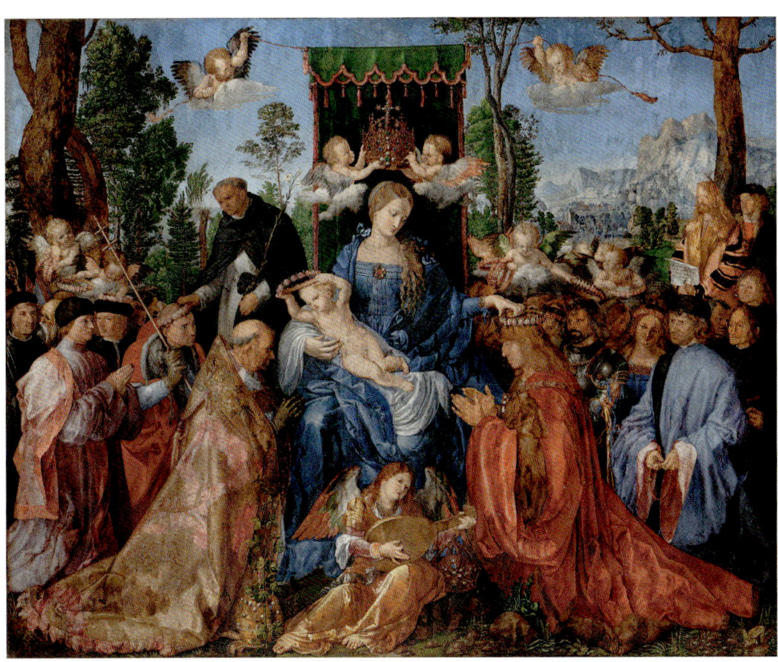

drawings of various subjects all testify to Dürer's preoccupation with his work as an artist. In his letter to Pirckheimer of 23 September 1506 he mentions his promise to make several portraits, as well as his satisfaction with the Venetian response to his painting of the Virgin: 'for all artists praise it'.[39] But his letters more frequently refer to shopping, in particular the constant search for material objects of value desired by Pirckheimer: precious stones and also items such as crane feathers used to adorn caps.[40] The outlets at Venice were strongly controlled, since the rulers felt that it was undesirable for citizens to have open access to luxury goods.[41] Dürer remarked more than once that he was advised that precious stones could be acquired in Nuremberg at a better price than in Venice.[42] Did he perhaps also seek to acquire pigments such as ultramarine, which – as opposed to precious stones – might well have been cheaper in Venice? He certainly did so later in Antwerp.[43]

The letters give a clear sense of Dürer's own commercial enterprise, including the sale of his prints.[44] But his relationship to Venetian artists is also mentioned: we are told that he is valued in Venice as an artist, whereas in

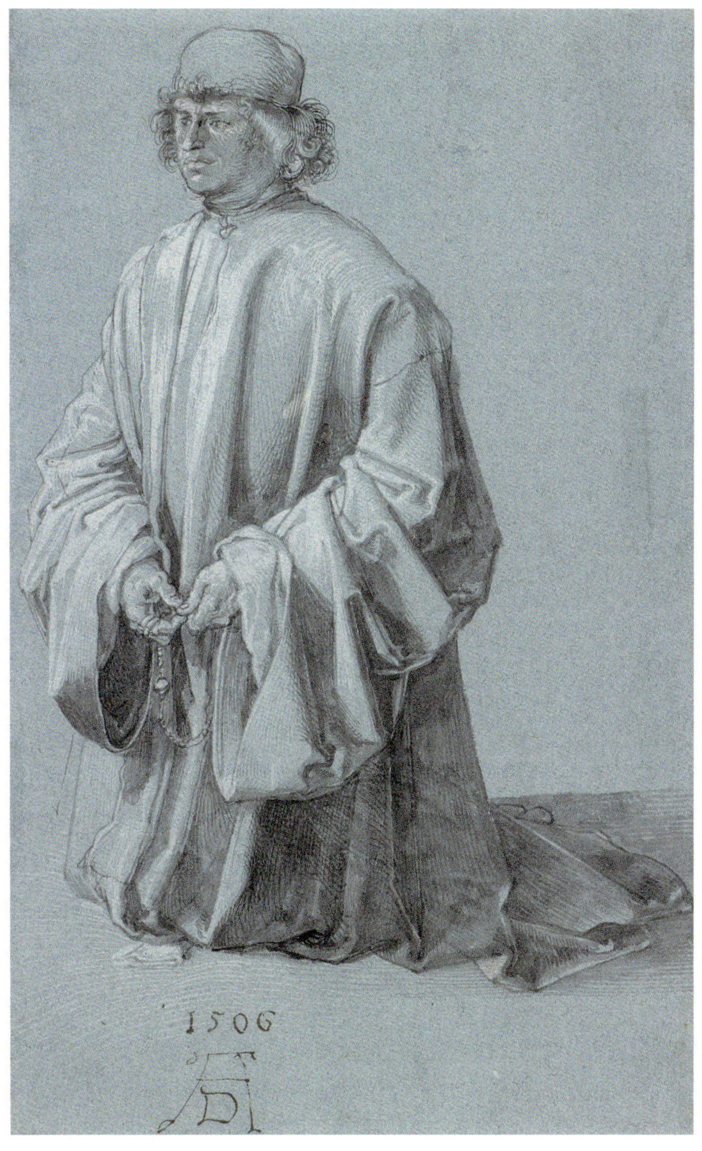

28
ALBRECHT DÜRER
Kneeling Donor, 1506
Brush and black ink and wash, with white opaque watercolour, with pen and dark ink, on blue paper, 32.4 × 19.8 cm
The Morgan Library & Museum, New York

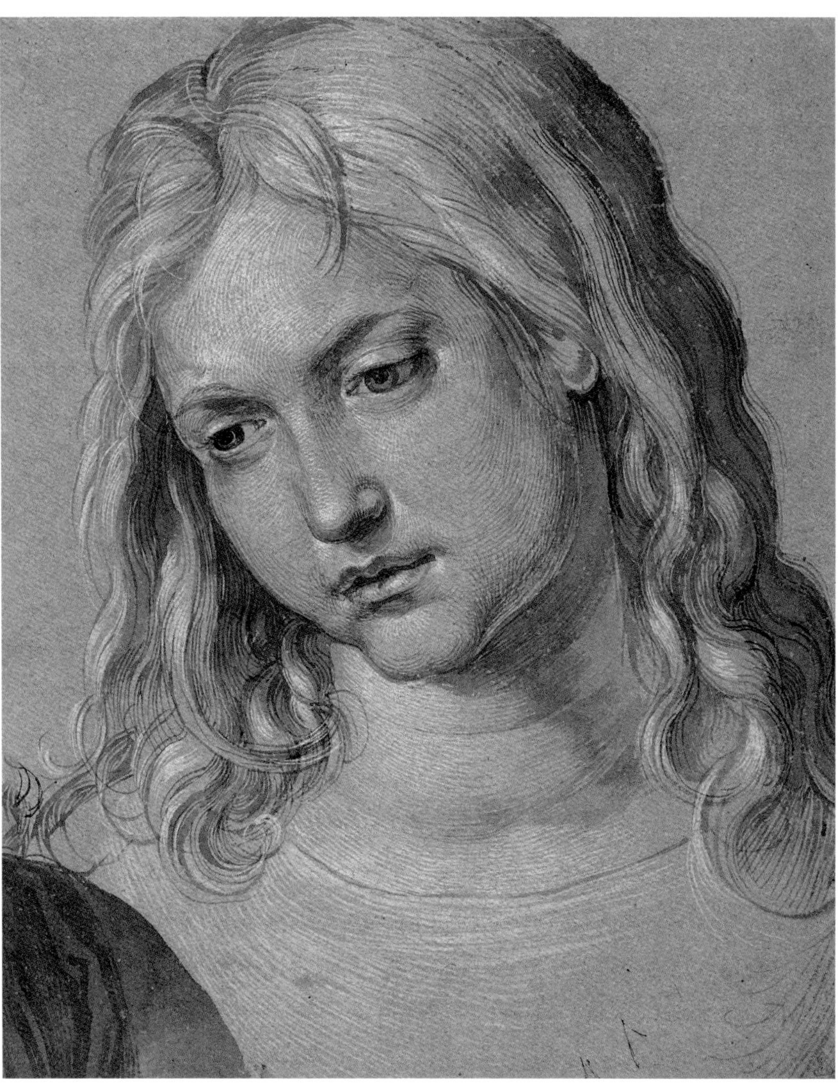

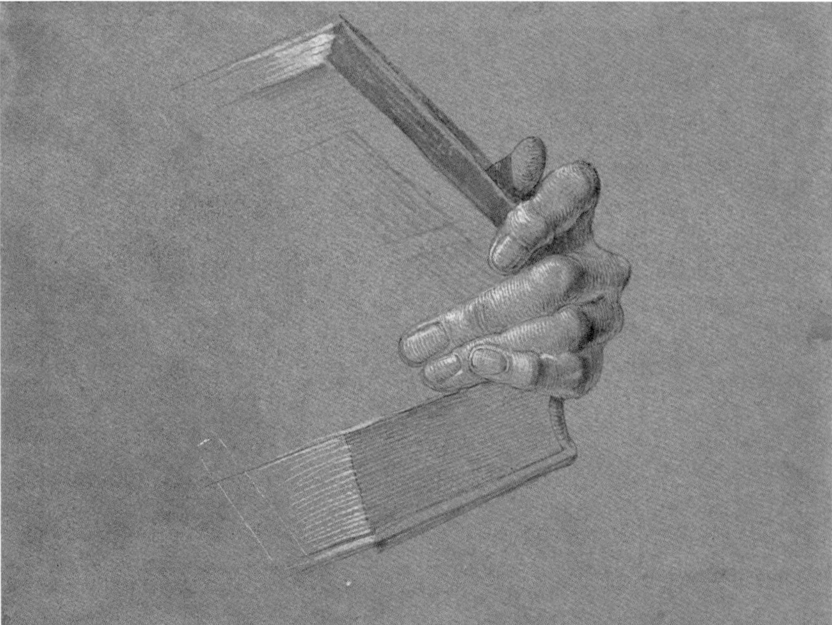

29
ALBRECHT DÜRER
Head of the 12-Year-Old Christ (study for *Christ among the Doctors*), 1506
Brush and grey ink, heightened with white on blue paper, 27.5 × 21.1 cm
The Albertina Museum, Vienna

30
ALBRECHT DÜRER
Hand with Book (study for *Christ among the Doctors*), 1506
Brush, heightened with white on light-blue paper, 19 × 25.1 cm
The Albertina Museum, Vienna

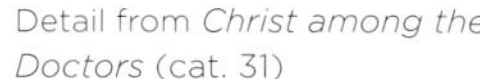

Detail from *Christ among the Doctors* (cat. 31)

Nuremberg his status is famously defined as that of a parasite, a *Schmarotzer*; that at the same time many of the Venetian artists are inhospitable to him but that he has many friends; and that Giovanni Bellini, whom he admires, has praised him.[45] Apparently hitherto unnoticed evidence of Bellini's referencing of Dürer at this time is to be found in his recently cleaned *Assassination of Saint Peter Martyr* (cat. 33): Jill Dunkerton has observed that the truncated bullock on the left was directly copied from Dürer's engraving of *The Prodigal Son* (cat. 32).[46] The impact of Dürer's art on Venice, as opposed to the impact of Italian art on Dürer, has perhaps been underestimated. It was in Venice in particular that he was able to embark on the creative artistic exchanges that travel facilitates – and that would also be a feature of his journey in 1520–1.

What Dürer does appear to have been seeking in Venice at this period other than increased funds is information on artistic theory. His studies of human proportion may have owed something to the Venetian artist Jacopo de' Barbari (cat. 35), who was in Nuremberg from 1500 for at least a year, as court painter to the Emperor Maximilian; Nuremberg scholar Hartmann Schedel (1440–1514) owned engravings by Jacopo, and the prints of both artists show some evidence of creative exchange.[47] But Dürer complains that he did not succeed in eliciting from Jacopo all the information in which he was interested, and in Venice he recorded the view that the artist was not esteemed.[48] Nevertheless, in 1521 in the Netherlands he still (unsuccessfully) asked for a book by Jacopo owned by Margaret of Austria.[49] In a letter to Pirckheimer from Venice, Dürer declared his intention to seek out information on perspective from an unnamed man in Bologna, where Scheurl records that he was welcomed by the city's artists, as he would be later in Antwerp.[50] It seems possible that Dürer was also expecting to travel to Rome in the train of the Emperor Maximilian for his coronation, but this did not take place; he recorded his concern that his agent in Rome had died and that his stock there had been lost, but there is no evidence he went there.[51]

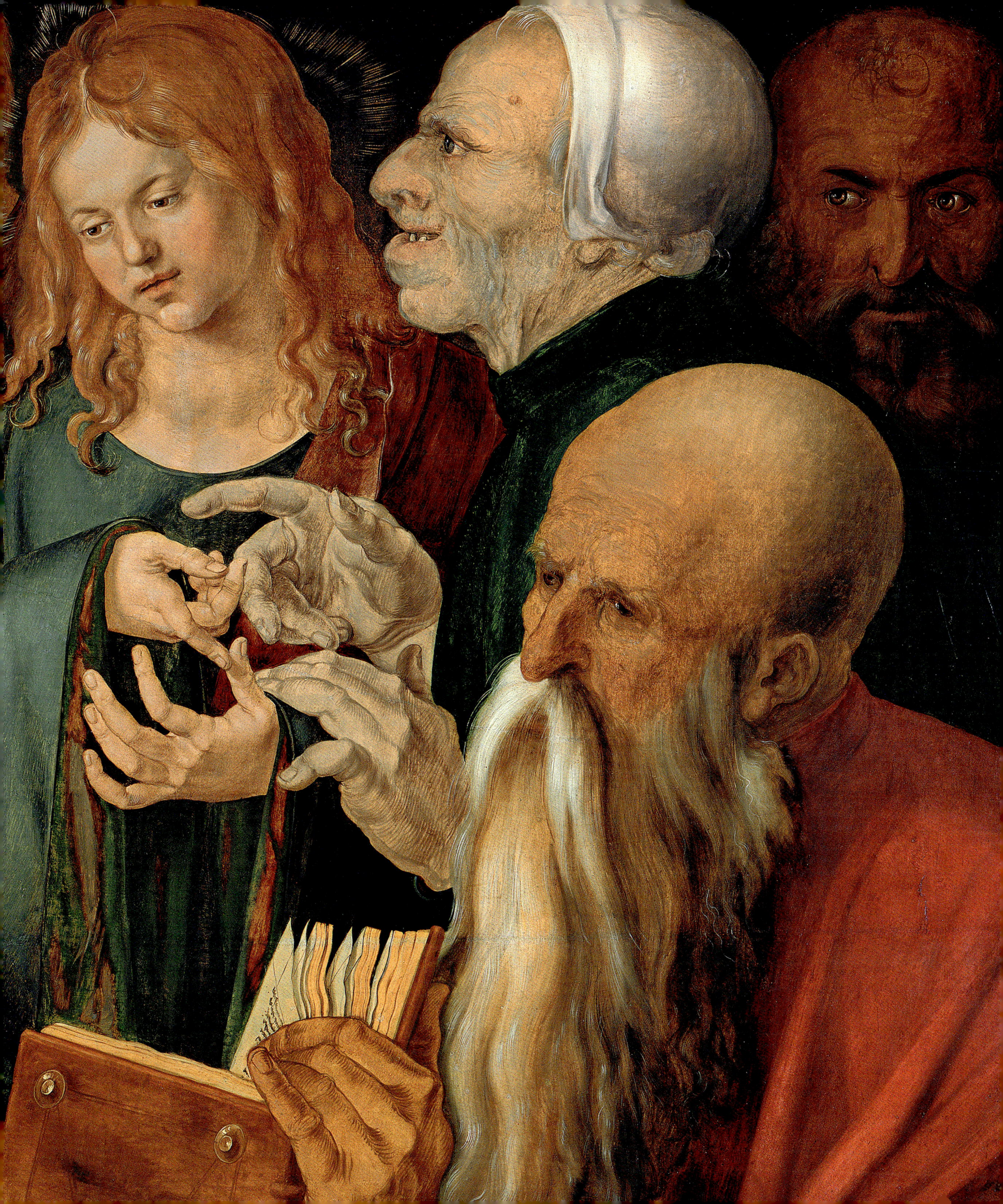

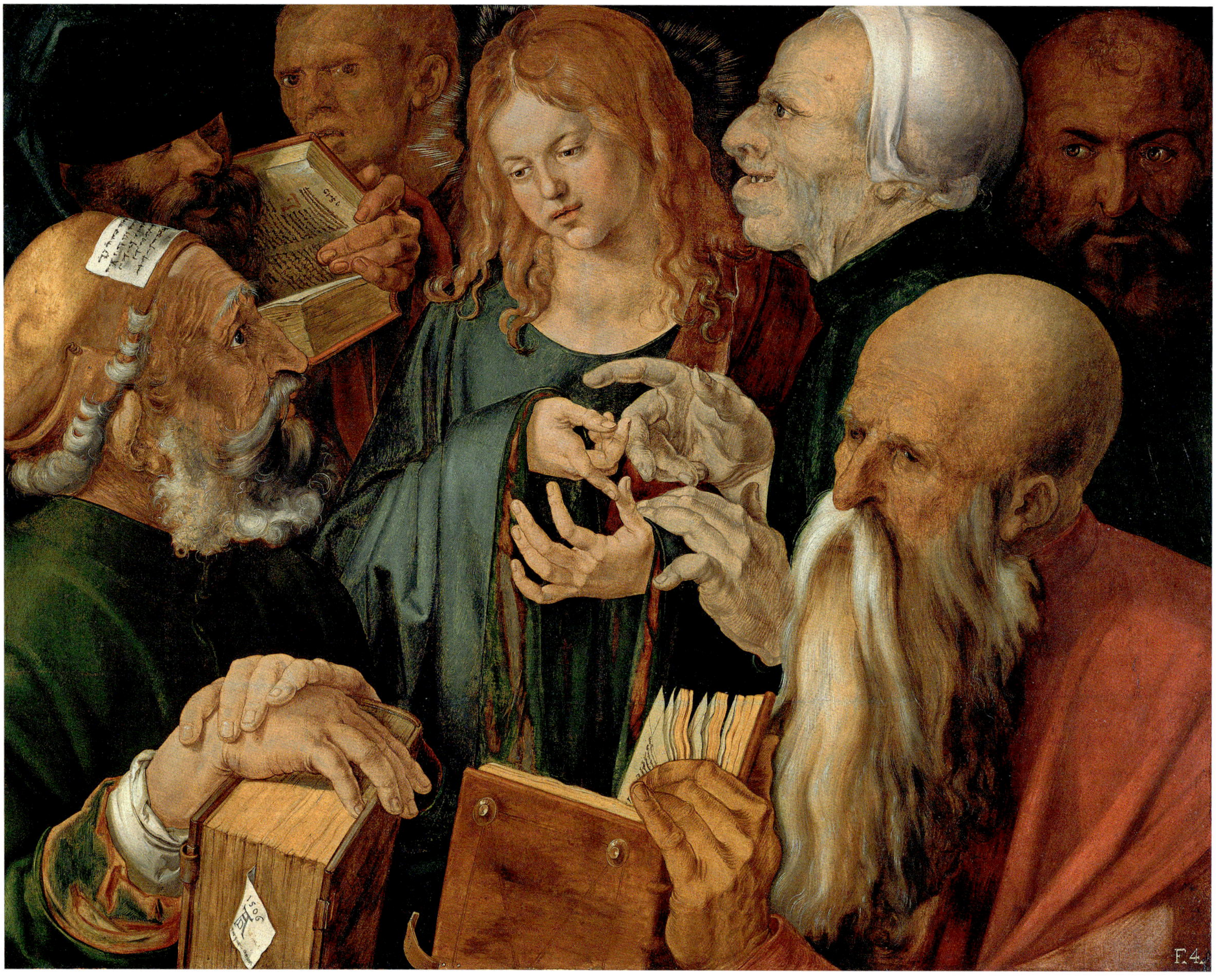

31
ALBRECHT DÜRER
Christ among the Doctors, 1506
Oil on panel,
64.3 × 80.3 cm
Museo Nacional Thyssen-Bornemisza, Madrid

There were substantial settlements of German artists in Venice in the sixteenth century but Dürer was not intending to join them permanently.[52] His apparent ambition was to create some additional income through commerce, bringing prints with him to sell in Venice – just as he did later on his journey to the Low Countries – and to build on the international distribution network he had already set up through two contracts in Nuremberg in 1497.[53] To do so he could build on the considerable and well-established trade routes between Germany and the South, particularly those established by the very important trading routes going through Nuremberg. Those seeking to emphasise the theoretical necessity for Northern artists to travel south to become validated as artists have neglected the commercial imperatives as much as the relative frequency and ease of travel. Arguments carefully dating watercolours to the autumn or spring of 1494–5, when it is proposed that Dürer first went south, have rested on the necessity for the solo traveller to avoid Alpine passes in the snowy winter – but recently it has been shown that this was a normal period of travel, with advantages over the warmer months, and that travellers usually went in groups; we know that Dürer returned from Venice in 1507 with a group of messengers.[54] Those who have studied Dürer's journeys in isolation have tended not to consider the immense amount of travel and resettlement by artists in fifteenth- and sixteenth-century Europe, in addition to the movement of works of art themselves.[55]

Finally, those contemplating Dürer's journeys as necessary to inspire and refresh his individual male genius have also underestimated the reverse side of the

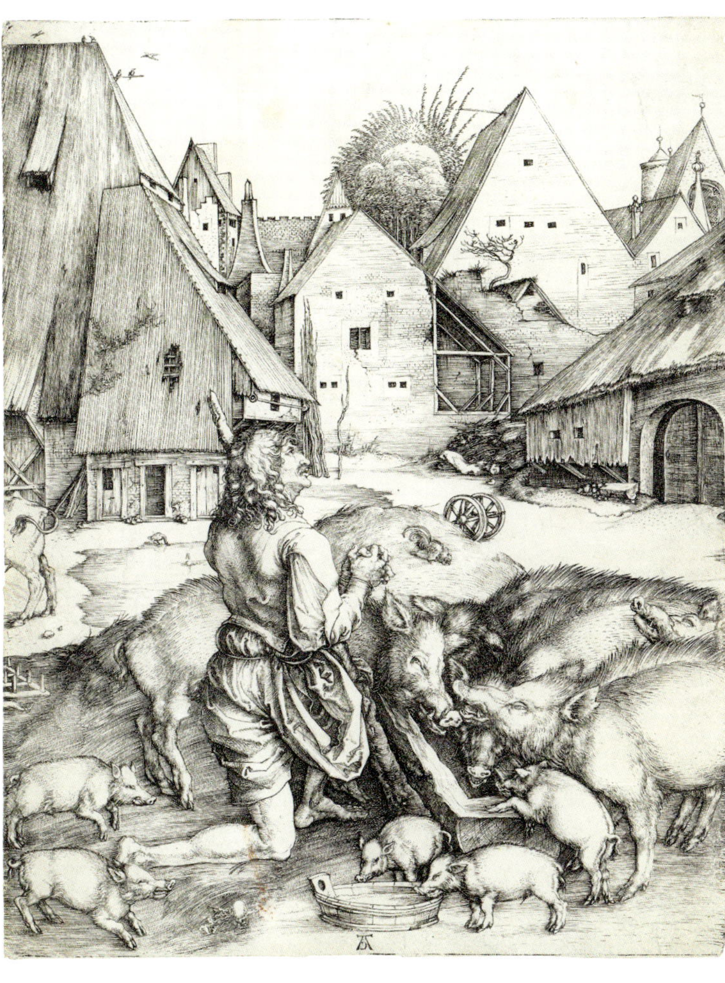

32
ALBRECHT DÜRER
The Prodigal Son, about 1496
Engraving, 24.7 × 19 cm
Victoria and Albert Museum, London

33
GIOVANNI BELLINI (about 1435–1516)
The Assassination of Saint Peter Martyr, about 1505–7
Oil on wood, 99.7 × 165.1 cm
The National Gallery, London

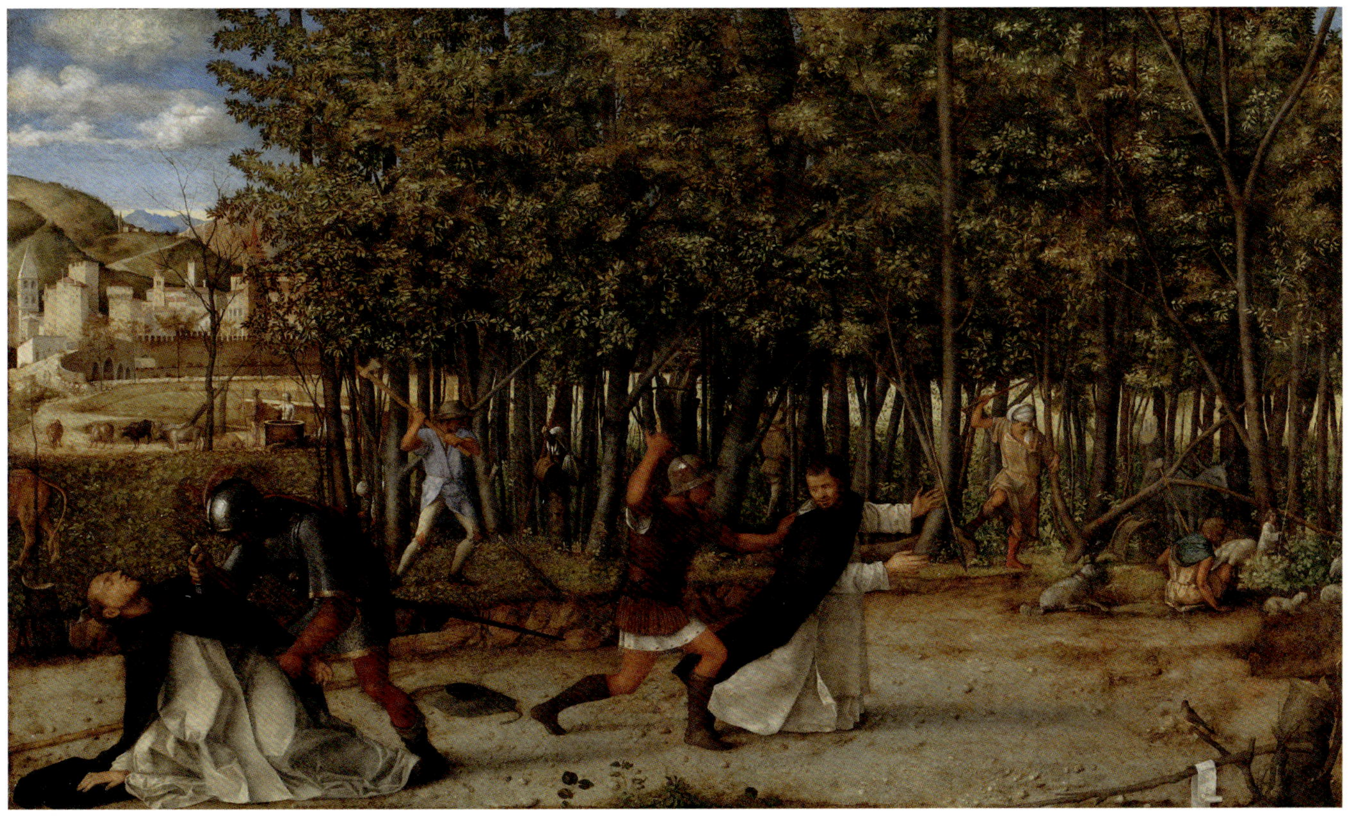

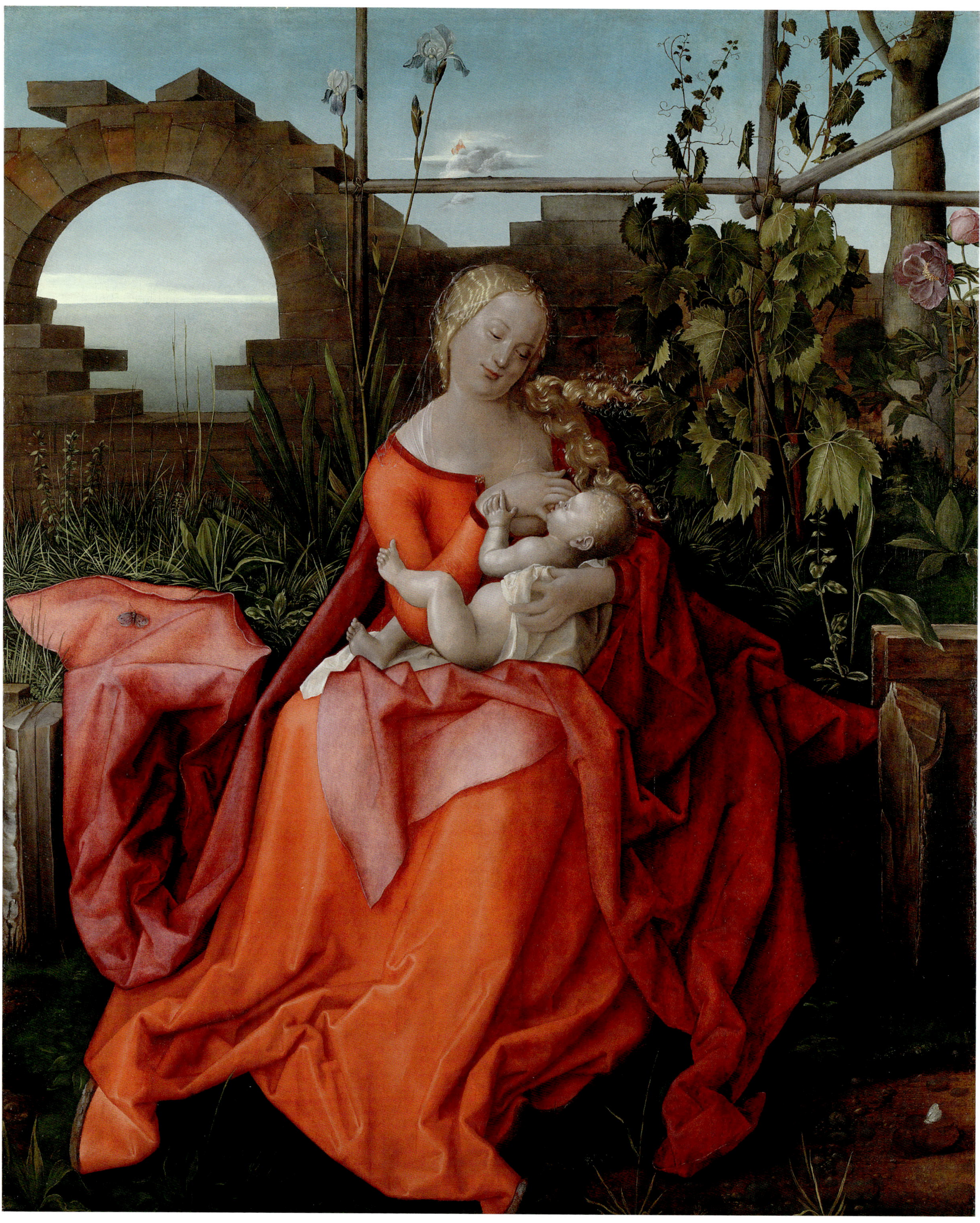

ability to travel – the support of women for the family business which allowed for this fresh injection to their joint enterprise. Wives, mothers and even daughters were involved in operating workshops, and Dürer's wife and mother were employed by him selling and marketing his prints, something common in Nuremberg and other German towns.[56] Dürer's mother, Barbara, may originally have worked in her father's goldsmith's workshop: her husband addressed her in 1492 as '*Goldschmiedin*' when he wrote to her from Linz.[57] Dürer's letters from Venice show how the business was being run in his absence by Agnes and Barbara: Agnes sold prints at the Frankfurt fair and Barbara at the Nuremberg one, and both were evidently literate.[58] Works such as the *Madonna with the Iris* (cat. 34) were also produced in his absence.[59] Although there is more than a quarter of a century between Dürer's earliest journeys and his journey to the Netherlands, they are linked by the threads of an ambitious commercial family enterprise, selling the remarkable skills of a highly innovative artist whose output, especially his printmaking, although rooted in Nuremberg, had a strong value far beyond the confines of his home town.

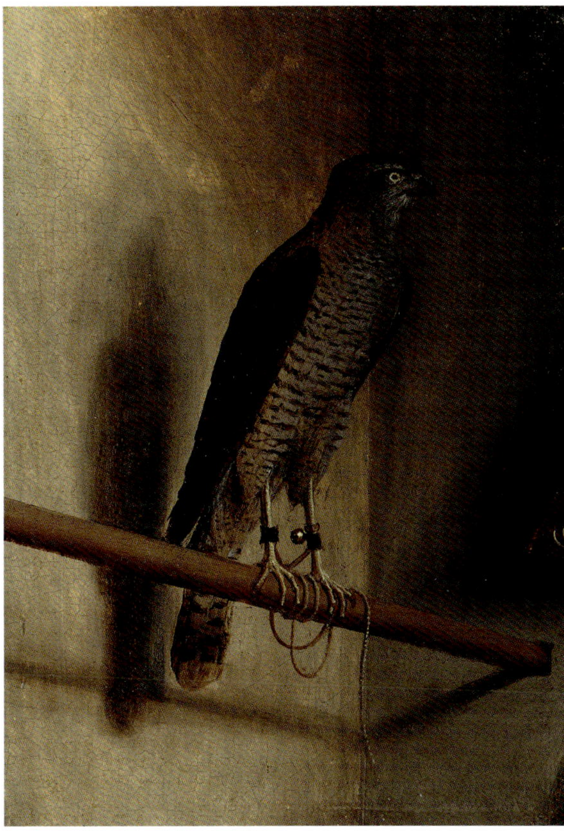

35
JACOPO DE'BARBARI
(active 1500; died 1516?)
A Sparrowhawk, 1510s
Oil on oak, 17.8 × 10.8 cm
The National Gallery, London

OPPOSITE
34
WORKSHOP OF ALBRECHT DÜRER
The Virgin and Child ('The Madonna with the Iris'), about 1500–10
Oil on lime, 149.2 × 117.2 cm
The National Gallery, London

1 Spufford 2002, pp. 352–4.
2 Evans 2004, p. 2; B. Böckem, 'The Young Dürer and Italy: Contact with Italy and the Mobility of Art and Artists around 1500', in Nuremberg 2012, pp. 52–64, at p. 59.
3 Nash 2008, pp. 105–6, 187.
4 Ibid., pp. 187–9.
5 Hutchison 1990, p. 10; S. Buck, 'Art and Nature: Dürer's Early Travel Years 1490–5', in London 2013, pp. 13–36, at p. 29.
6 Spufford 2002, p. 193; Hutchison 1990, p. 32.
7 Hutchison 1990, pp. 3–13.
8 T. Eser in Nuremberg 2012, pp. 262–3, illustrated pp. 268–9.
9 Ashcroft 2017, vol. 1, no. 29, pp. 133–74.
10 Quoted in ibid., vol. 1, p. 35; S. Buck (see note 5) in London 2013, p. 16.
11 S. Buck in London 2013, p. 29.
12 Hutchison 1990, p. 31.
13 Quoted in ibid., p. 37 and S. Buck in London 2013, pp. 16–17.
14 M. Roth, 'The Young Dürer and Drawing for a Purpose', in London 2013, pp. 73–88, at pp. 75, 79–81; on woodcut, see P. Schmidt, 'Why Woodcut? Dürer in Search of his Medium and Role', in Nuremberg 2012, pp. 146–59, esp. pp. 155–8.
15 Hutchison 1990, p. 24; S. Buck in London 2013, p. 17.
16 Rowlands 1993, vol. 1, nos 13, 14, pp. 9–10; S. Buck in London 2013, p. 17.
17 Hutchison 1990, p. 37.
18 Ibid., pp. 37–8; P. Schmidt in Nuremberg 2012 (see note 14), pp. 149–51, 424–7 and nos 112–20; T. Eser in Nuremberg 2012, pp. 540–1; see also M. Roth in London 2013 (see note 14), pp. 77–8, and S. Buck in London 2013, p. 21 n. 47.
19 Nash 2008, pp. 187–8.
20 Hutchison 1990, p. 39; M. Roth, 'Albrecht Dürer and Strasbourg', in Nuremberg 2012, pp. 39–51, at pp. 40–1.
21 Hutchison 1990, p. 38; Nuremberg 2012, pp. 276–9, no. 9; M. Roth in Nuremberg 2012, pp. 45–6.
22 Hutchison 1990, p. 39; S. Brisman, 'Sternkraut: "The Word that Unlocks" Dürer's Self-Portrait of 1493', in Nuremberg 2012, pp. 194–207; M. Roth in Nuremberg 2012. S. Buck in London 2013, p. 23, presumes two visits.
23 S. Buck in London 2013, pp. 18–20; Hutchison 1990, p. 32.
24 Wiesener Wood 1981, p. 6.
25 Ashcroft 2017, vol. 1, letter 29.2, pp. 139–42. Ashcroft translates 'Ding' as 'stuff'. Hutchison 1990, p. 43. Crawford Luber 2005, pp. 62–4, interprets this as a general observation on his shift in taste away from prints to paintings.
26 Hutchison 1990, p. 43; Crawford Luber 2005, pp. 65–7.
27 Hutchison 1990, p. 42; S. Buck in London 2013, p. 30.
28 London 2002, p. 107; Hutchison 1990, pp. 41–2, 46.
29 Evans 2004, p. 3; S. Buck in London 2013, p. 31; S. Porras, 'Dürer's Copies', in London 2013, pp. 57–72, at pp. 59–65. For the drawing after Bellini, see Rowlands 1993, vol. 1, no. 123, pp. 60–1. Crawford Luber 2005, p. 57, refers to the drawing as executed on Venetian watermarked paper.
30 S. Buck in London 2013, p. 30.
31 Crawford Luber 2005, esp. pp. 55–9, 68 and 97–104.
32 J. Robert, 'Dürer, Celtis and the Birth of Landscape Painting from the Spirit of the "Germania Ilustrata"', in Nuremberg 2012, pp. 65–77; for arguments concerning the dating of the Albertina 'View of Innsbruck', see D. Hess and T. Eser in Nuremberg 2012, pp. 402 and 543.
33 Crawford Luber 2005, pp. 58–9; S. Buck in London 2013, pp. 30–3, accepts Robert's proposal for the function of the views but argues in favour of an Italian journey.
34 See B. Böckem (note 2) in Nuremberg 2012, pp. 53–4.
35 For Holbein, see Foister 2004a, pp. 1, 180; for Gossaert, see Campbell 2014, p. 379; for Bruegel, see Campbell 2014, pp. 171–4.
36 S. Buck in London 2013, p. 31.
37 B. Böckem in Nuremberg 2012, p. 58.
38 Hutchison 1990, p. 90.
39 Ashcroft 2017, vol. 1, letter 29.9, p. 163.
40 Ibid., pp. 136, 142, 144, 146, 149, 152; see also B. Böckem in Nuremberg 2012, p. 61.
41 Welch 2005, pp. 132–3.
42 Ashcroft 2017, vol. 1, pp. 136, 144.
43 See Foister 2015, p. 207.
44 In anticipation of being paid 105 florins for the altarpiece, Dürer writes: 'I hope to put all the money by'. B. Böckem in Nuremberg 2012, p. 58; Ashcroft 2017, vol. 1, p. 137.
45 Ashcroft 2017, vol. 1, pp. 139, 147, 168.
46 J. Dunkerton, 'Cat. 10. *The Assassination of Saint Peter Martyr*, about 1505–7 (NG812)', in Spring 2018, pp. 87, 93.
47 Evans 2004, p. 3; B. Böckem in Nuremberg 2012, pp. 61–4.
48 Hutchison 1990, p. 72.
49 Ibid., p. 168.
50 Ibid., pp. 81, 95; Ashcroft 2017, vol. 1, p. 228, also p. 230 n. 2.
51 Hutchison 1990, pp. 89–90.
52 See L.C. Matthew, 'Working Abroad: Northern Artists in the Venetian Ambient' in Venice 1999, pp. 61–9.
53 London 2002, p. 106; T. Eser in Nuremberg 2012, pp. 545–6.
54 B. Böckem in Nuremberg 2012, p. 57.
55 See Foister 2015, pp. 207–8.
56 Wiesener Wood 1981, pp. 3–4; Hutchison 1990, p. 83; Nash 2008, p. 189; see also pp. 77–8; C. Schlief, 'Albrecht Dürer between Agnes Frey and Willibald Pirckheimer', in Silver and Chipps Smith 2010, pp. 185–205.
57 Hutchison 1990 p. 12; T. Eser in Nuremberg 2012, p. 277, no. 9.
58 Hutchison 1990, p. 83.
59 See Foister 2004b.

TILL-HOLGER BORCHERT

ALBRECHT DÜRER AND PORTRAIT PAINTING IN THE NETHERLANDS

IT HAS LONG BEEN ACKNOWLEDGED THAT the relevance of early Netherlandish art for Albrecht Dürer should not be understated. While the impetus he received during his stays in Venice and Italy found immediate expression in his own work, the many possible sources of inspiration he encountered on his journey through the Low Countries seem to have played a secondary role. True, his *Saint Jerome* (cat. 110)[1] marks a highpoint in the artist's painting, but the portraits he executed in 1521 while he was in the Netherlands remain comparatively beholden to tradition: they bear no trace of contemporary innovation in Netherlandish portrait painting seen in the work of Quinten Massys, Bernaert van Orley, Joos van Cleve, Jan Mostaert (active 1498; died 1552/3) or Jan Gossaert.[2]

Netherlandish portraiture, on the other hand, did receive important impulses from the Nuremberg artist. When in 1517 Quinten Massys rejuvenated the tradition of the scholar's portrait in two companion pieces celebrating the friendship between Peter Gillis (Peter Aegidius; 1486–1533) and Erasmus of Rotterdam (cats 38, 37), it was Dürer's conception of a scholar's study in his 1514 engraving *Saint Jerome in his Study* (fig. 140) that served as model. The same motif of the scholarly interior would later go on to play a foundational, if indirect, role for Bernaert van Orley, who took inspiration from Massys's portraits for his own portrait of *Doctor Georges de Zelle* in 1519.[3] Clearer reference to Dürer's Master Engravings[4] appears in van Orley's *Portrait of a Secretary of Charles V* (cat. 36), a painting probably completed shortly afterwards, which places its subject in a detailed interior still life in three-quarter view. This pictorial concept was as instructive for Gossaert's portraits of merchants as it was for those of Hans Holbein the Younger. It is likely that Dürer, who paid a visit to 'Master Bernhart'[5] on 28 August 1520 in Brussels and also drew van Orley in the same period, saw portraits of a similar nature; it is certain, however, that they made little impact.

Dürer's influence similarly holds true for the architectural elements one occasionally encounters in

OPPOSITE
Detail from *Portrait of a Young Man* (cat. 44)

RIGHT
36
BERNAERT VAN ORLEY
(1487/91–1541)
Portrait of a Secretary of Charles V, after 1519
Oil on oak panel,
54.9 × 45.6 cm
Royal Museums of Fine Arts of Belgium, Brussels

BELOW LEFT
37
QUINTEN MASSYS
(1465/6–1530)
Desiderius Erasmus, 1517
Oil on oak panel,
50.5 × 45.2 cm
The Royal Collection / HM Queen Elizabeth II

BELOW RIGHT
38
QUINTEN MASSYS
(1465/6–1530)
Portrait of Aegidius (Peter Gillis), 1517
Oil on panel,
74.5 × 53.4 cm
Longford Castle Collection

Netherlandish portraits from the first decade of the sixteenth century, as in Massys's pendant portraits of a man and a woman (cats 39, 40). Rendered in the style of classical antiquity, the ornamentation looks on the one hand to Italian decorative elements that had made their way into works by Hans Memling (active 1465; died 1494) and Gerard David (active 1484; died 1523) by the end of the fifteenth century in the form of garlands and festoons. In this respect too, however, Dürer's depiction of architecture in his woodcut series of the *Life of the Virgin* provided the Netherlands with models in addition to the Italian works.[6] Ultimately, examining Netherlandish portraits and those Dürer painted while in the Low Countries for any reciprocal effect comes up against the issue that the former cannot always be dated with certainty, leaving it unclear whether they were in fact created after Dürer's trip. Still, even if one is led to this conclusion on the basis of style, the portraits of Massys, Gossaert and van Cleve are of no significant importance to the Nuremberg artist. The subtle play with different levels of reality that Massys evokes in his twin portraits (cats 39, 40) through the use of fictive Italianate frames, for example,

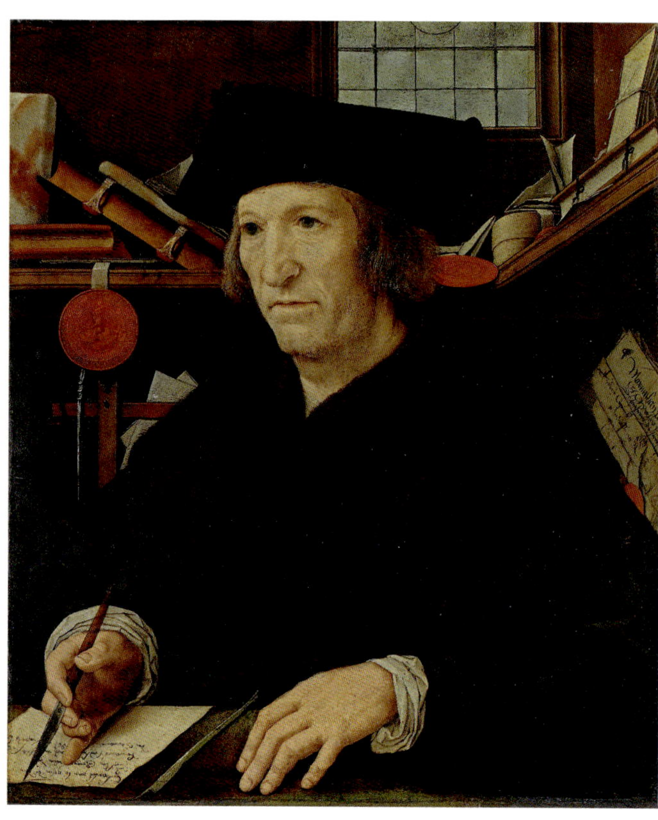

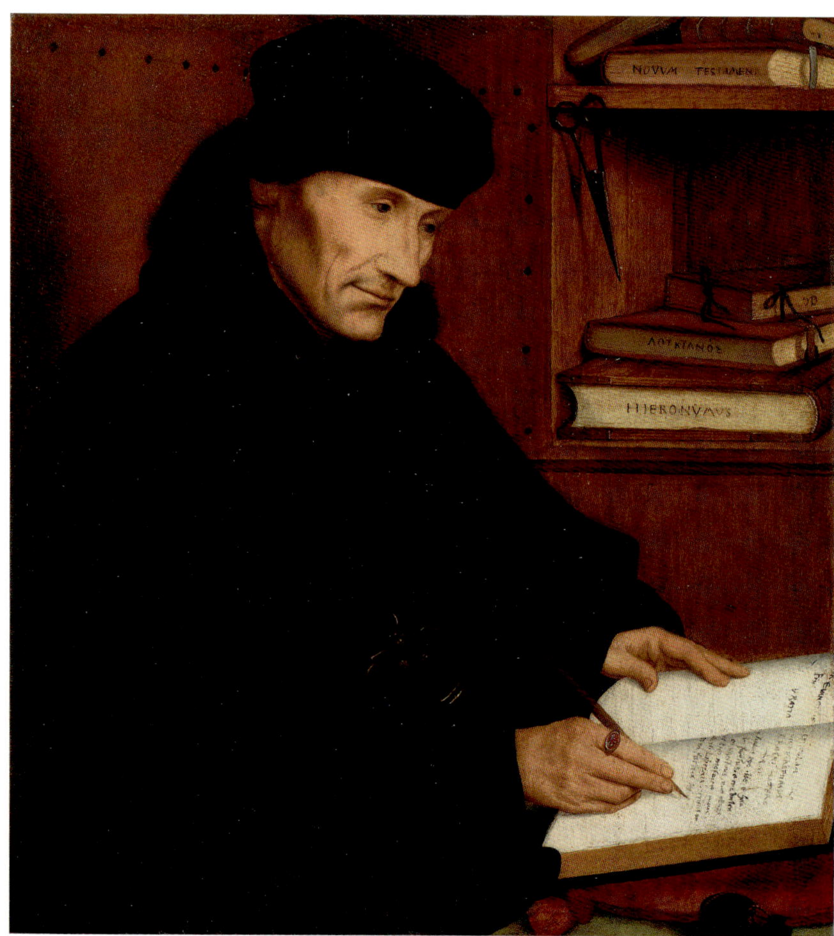

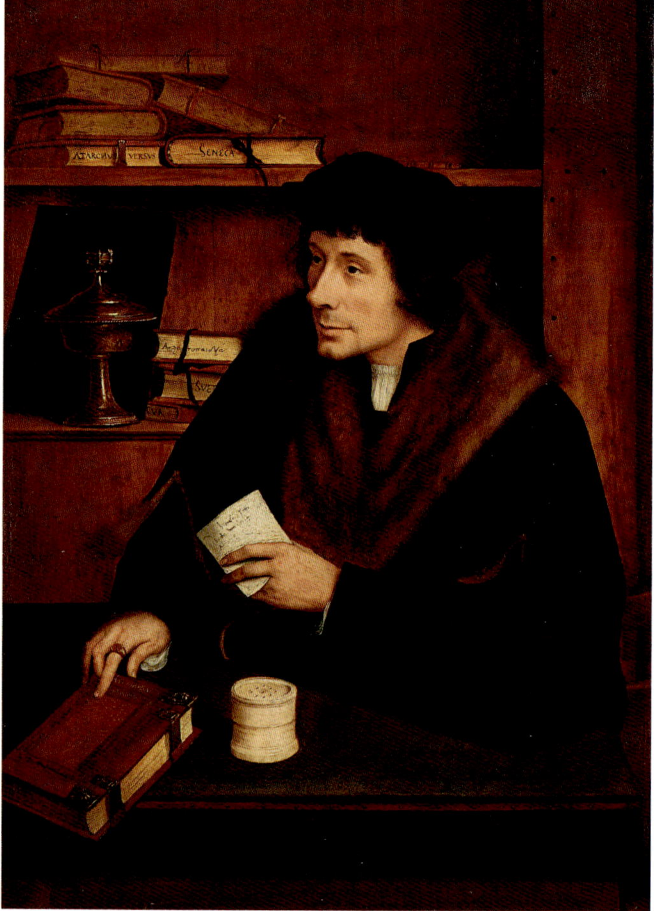

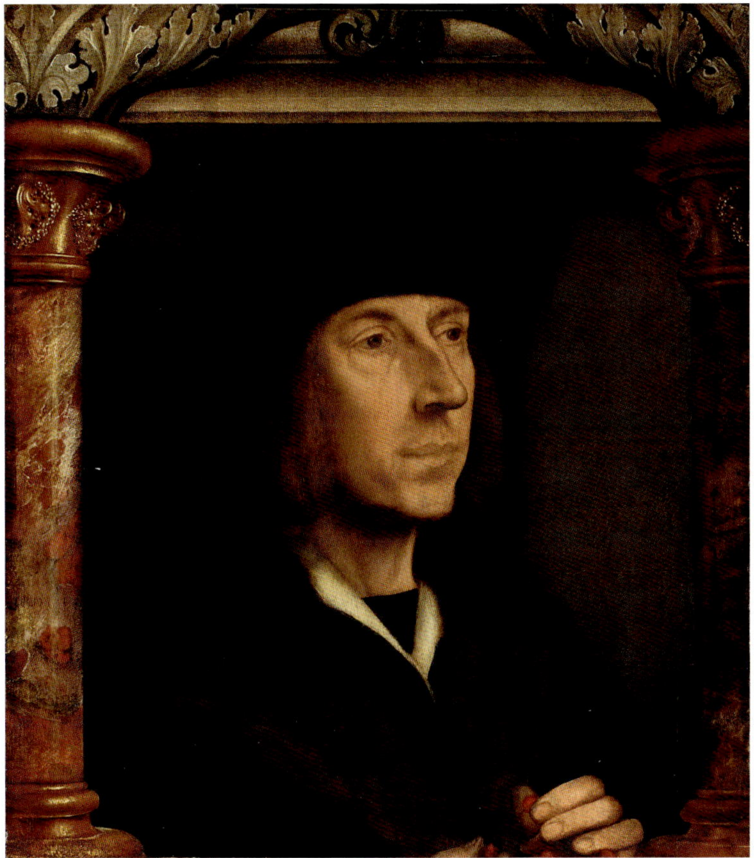

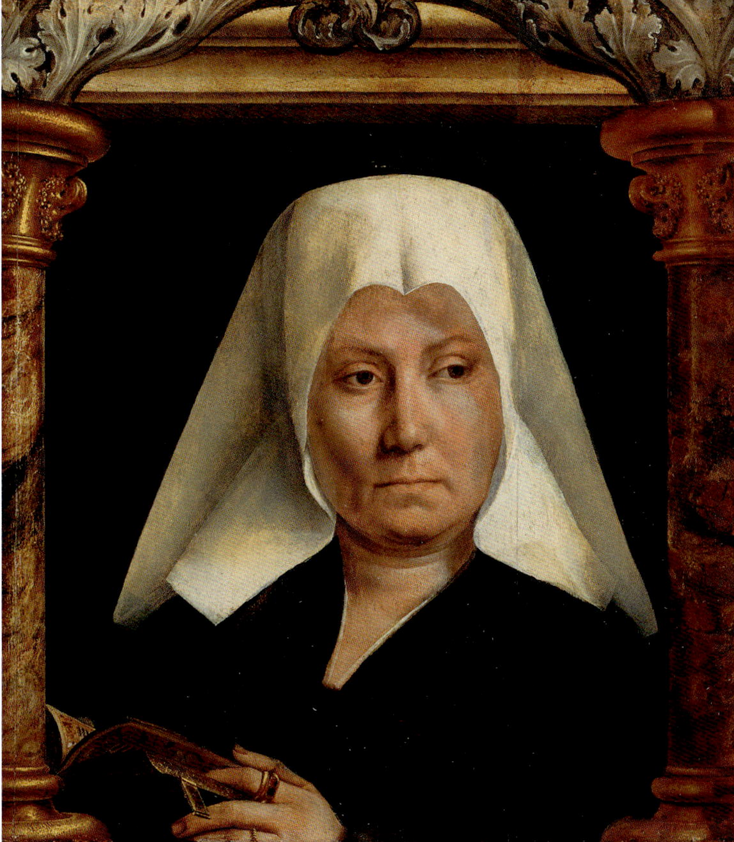

39
QUINTEN MASSYS
(1465/6–1530)
Portrait of a Man with a Rosary, about 1520
Oil on oak panel,
48.2 × 41.9 cm
Private collection,
Antwerp

40
QUINTEN MASSYS
(1465/6–1530)
Portrait of a Woman,
about 1520
Oil on oak panel,
48.3 × 43.2 cm
The Metropolitan
Museum of Art,
New York

which are then underscored by *trompe-l'œil* elements and cast shadows, is altogether foreign to Dürer's work in the genre.

In order to understand why Dürer did not situate himself alongside his Netherlandish contemporaries in the portraits he painted while in the Netherlands, it is essential to consider the work made before his departure. Paradoxically, his seemingly hesitant attitude is linked to the fact that the self-aware artist visited the Netherlands at the height of his career.[7] Other experiences had already shaped him. Dürer had been given an opportunity to engage with Netherlandish art before, as a youth in Nuremberg. Panel paintings from the Netherlands had been in circulation throughout Europe since the mid-fifteenth century, with the compositions of Flemish masters finding remarkably rapid dissemination via prints and drawn reproductions. At the time, the influence of Netherlandish art made itself felt not only across France, the Iberian Peninsula and Italy, but also within the Holy Roman Empire, particularly in its large trading cities. Prized for their technical perfection and original imagery, Flemish panel paintings provided models and inspiration for local workshops along the Rhine – in Cologne, Strasbourg and Basel – as well as in the trading centres of Upper Germany, like Ulm and Augsburg.[8]

Nuremberg proved no exception in this regard. By 1457 at the latest, with the successful relocation of Hans Pleydenwurff's workshop to the city, individual motifs and entire compositions of Netherlandish origin had become familiar sights there. It is worth recalling here that until the mid-century – representative portraits of potentates notwithstanding – the painted individual portrait and its pendant were largely unknown in the territories of the Holy Roman Empire, and only began to appear and develop here in the final third of the century. In these works, early German portraitists drew without exception on forms common to the Burgundian Netherlands from the 1430s and 1440s. The German portrait was largely Netherlandish in character from the outset.[9]

One of the first examples from Franconia comes in Hans Pleydenwurff's *Portrait of Count Georg von Löwenstein* (fig. 21). Painted in 1456 as the right wing of a memorial diptych, the portrait depicts the aged canon of Bamberg against a dark blue background, prayer book in hand. The painting's form owes a clear debt to portraits by Jan van Eyck and Rogier van der Weyden (about 1399–1464), albeit without achieving the realistic detail of either.[10] Dürer's teacher Michael Wolgemut, who took over Pleydenwurff's workshop in 1473 after the latter's death the previous year, was also active as a

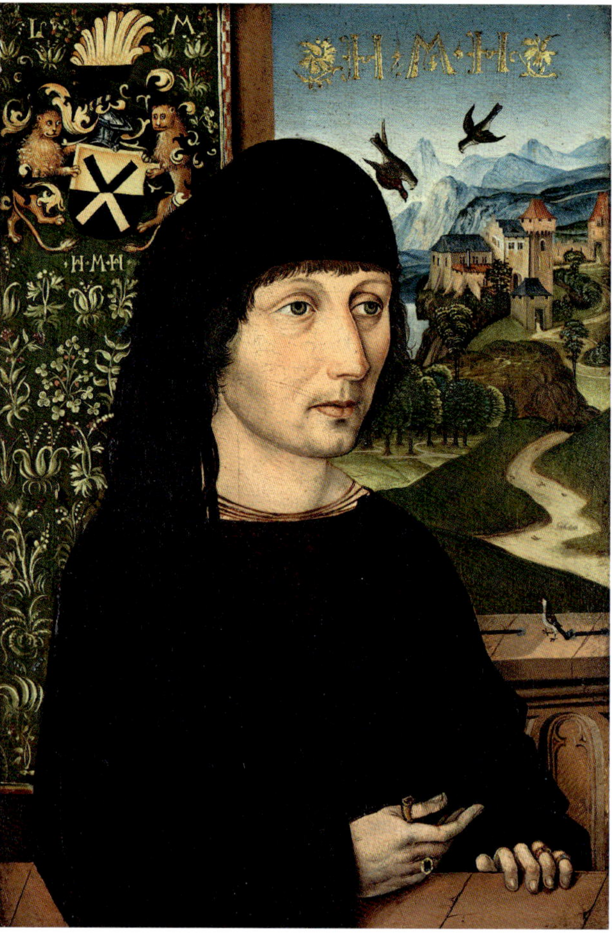

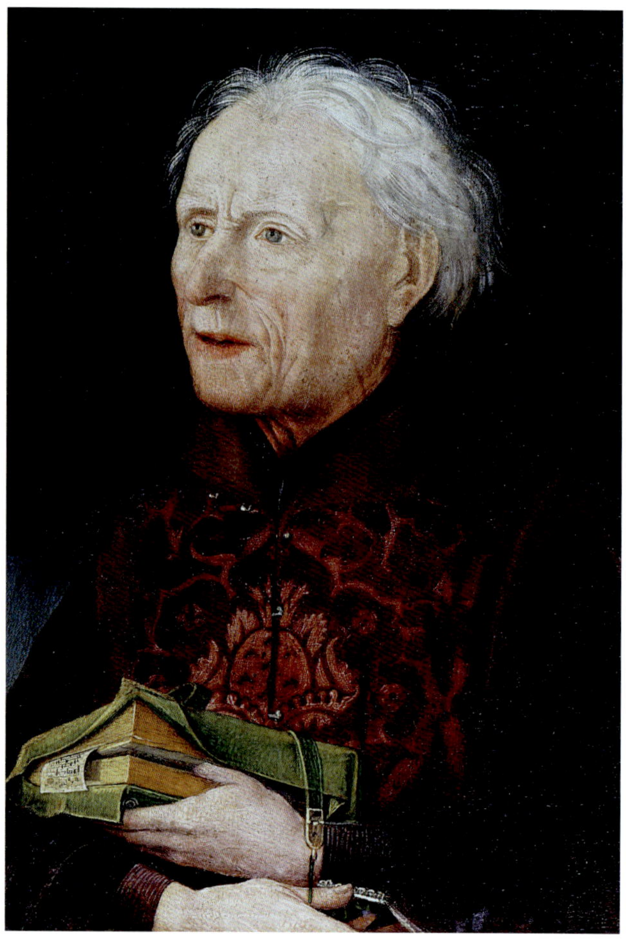

Fig. 20
MICHAEL WOLGEMUT (1434–1519)
Portrait of Levinus Memminger, about 1485
Oil on panel, 33.7 × 22.9 cm
Museo Nacional Thyssen-Bornemisza, Madrid

Fig. 21
HANS PLEYDENWURFF (about 1420–1472)
Portrait of Count Georg von Löwenstein, 1456
Oil on parchment glued on limewood, 33.3 × 24.5 cm
Germanisches Nationalmuseum, Nuremberg

portraitist. While most of his subjects appear against a neutral background, his 1485 *Portrait of Levinus Memminger* (fig. 20) shows the Nuremberg judge seated by a window revealing a landscape in the background. Wolgemut drew here on a pictorial concept that had long been included in the repertoire of Netherlandish portraits; Dirk Bouts (1400?–1475) introduced the motif of a window with a landscape view to portrait painting in 1462, and the following decade saw Memling situate his portraits of Bruges merchants entirely before a landscape,[11] a combination that he and his contemporaries realised to particular effect. Although landscapes gave way increasingly to neutral backgrounds in sixteenth-century Netherlandish portraiture, portraits set against spectacular landscapes can still be found into the 1540s, such as in the work of Quinten Massys[12] and especially of Jan Mostaert, whose *Portrait of Joost van Bronckhorst* (fig. 22) from the early 1520s is exemplary in this regard.

It took only a few years for the 'Netherlandish' motif to spread throughout Germany, making its way eastwards via Cologne and the central Rhine region to appear in Bavaria in the portraiture of the early 1480s, and shortly thereafter in Franconia. In its pairing of window and landscape, Wolgemut's *Portrait of Levinus Memminger* was thus part of a trend.[13]

In the course of his apprenticeship at the Wolgemut/Pleydenwurff workshop between 1486 and 1490, Dürer was exposed to examples of the Netherlandish pictorial tradition. A portrait of his father from 1490 (fig. 23)[14] originally envisioned a window opening out onto a landscape, although the artist ultimately decided in favour of a neutral background in keeping with the older tradition of southern German portraits.[15] Still, in the quality of his painterly execution and naturalistic reproduction of lines in the face and cloth surfaces, Dürer approximates the realism of earlier Flemish portraits much more closely than his master. It remains unclear whether the artist was in this way seeking to impress his father, who had visited the Low Countries as an apprentice goldsmith.

There is much that points to Dürer encountering many more works by Netherlandish masters, or those who had trained in the Netherlands, during his journeyman travels.[16] His first Italian journey, which brought him to Venice in 1494, proved at any rate formative. Scholars frequently describe the influence that Venetian art exercised on Dürer. Yet it is often overlooked that

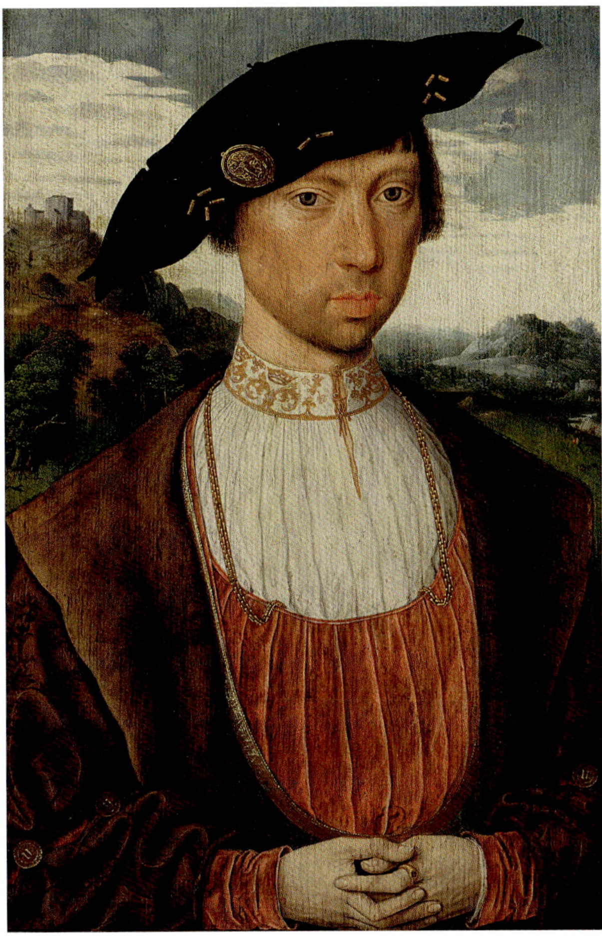

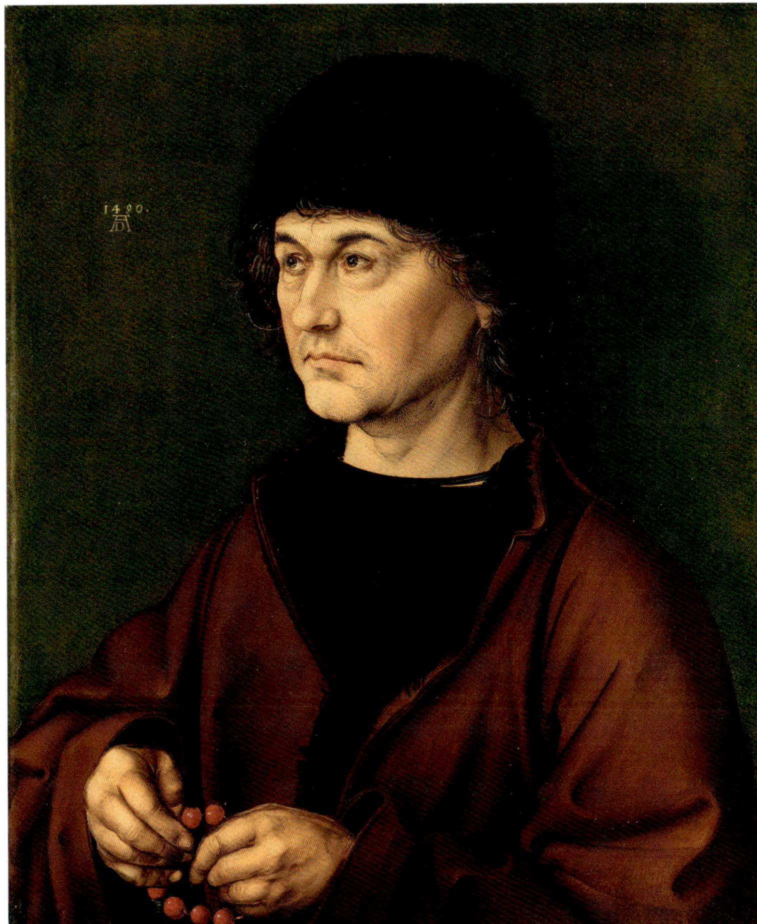

Fig. 22
JAN MOSTAERT
(active 1498; died 1552/3)
Portrait of Joost van Bronckhorst, about 1520
Oil on oak, 43.5 × 28.7 cm
Musée Petit Palais, Paris

Fig. 23
ALBRECHT DÜRER
The Painter's Father, 1490
Oil on wood, 47.5 × 39.5 cm
Gallerie degli Uffizi, Florence

Dürer during his stay in Venice might also have encountered portraits by Memling and other Netherlandish artists, whose conception of portraiture was of pivotal importance for the work of Antonello da Messina (active 1456; died 1479), Jacometto Veneziano (1472–1497) and Giovanni Bellini, among others.[17]

If Dürer's *Self Portrait* of 1493[18] still looked to portraits of Nuremberg patricians such as Jakob Elsner's 1486 painting of Konrad Imhof,[19] his *Self Portrait* of 1498 (fig. 24)[20] attests not only to his mimetic skill, as shown in his treatment of various fabrics, but also to his pride as an artist. It is not only the extravagant clothing or the cape draped casually about him that communicate his attitude; it is also his right arm leaning on the balustrade, his folded hands, and finally his gaze, which is directed out beyond the painting. The artist makes conscious use of the window motif to reveal the landscape spread out below, as seen from a room in a tower.[21] The care with which the painting has been arranged demonstrated to contemporaries that in Dürer they had a painter who was at least the equal of the Netherlandish masters. In this way he hoped to establish himself as the leading portraitist in Nuremberg.[22]

Shortly before this, Dürer had created portraits on *Tüchlein* – supple cloth that allowed paintings largely intended for private use to be created relatively quickly – including a double portrait of two young women.[23] He conceives of the two portraits in a wholly different manner: the portrait now held in Frankfurt[24] shows a devout female figure with downcast eyes, while its Berlin pendant[25] gives a markedly secular impression, showing a young woman with arms folded, regarding the viewer from an interior with a landscape view. The Berlin painting fulfils all the criteria of an independent portrait, and a comparison of formal motifs may even lead one to see it as a precursor to Dürer's self portrait today held in Madrid.[26] Granted, the Madrid self portrait was painted on a wooden surface, assuring its permanent role as an aide-mémoire.

Dürer's efforts to establish himself as a portraitist brought him the commissions he sought. In a distinguishing trait, the artist looked to realise the wishes and expectations of his illustrious clientele on an individual basis, instead of relying on common tropes; when commissioned to paint members of the Tucher Family in 1499, for example, Dürer modified the relationship between landscape and portrait. His two

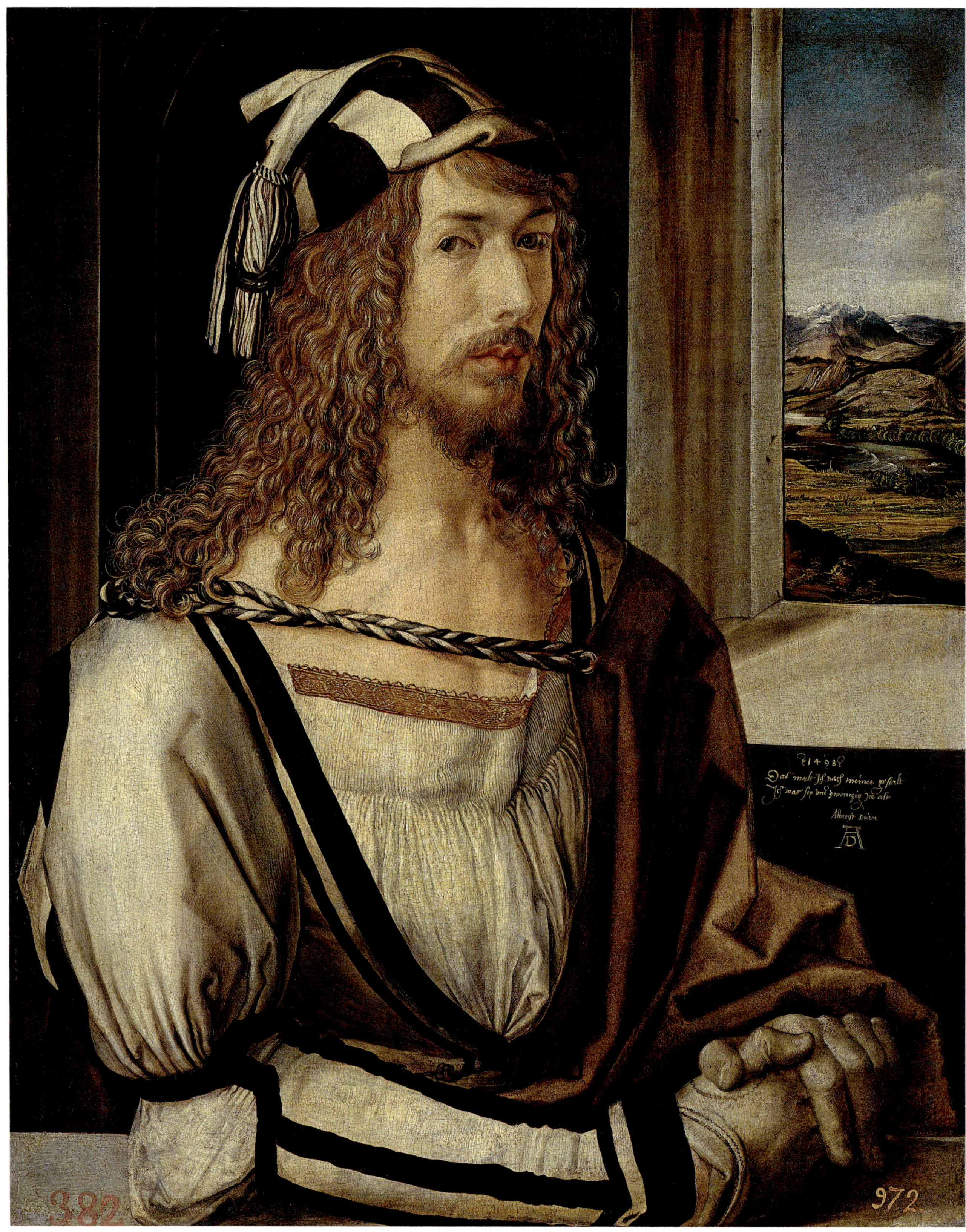

Fig. 24
ALBRECHT DÜRER
Self Portrait, 1498
Oil on panel, 52 × 41 cm
Museo Nacional del Prado,
Madrid

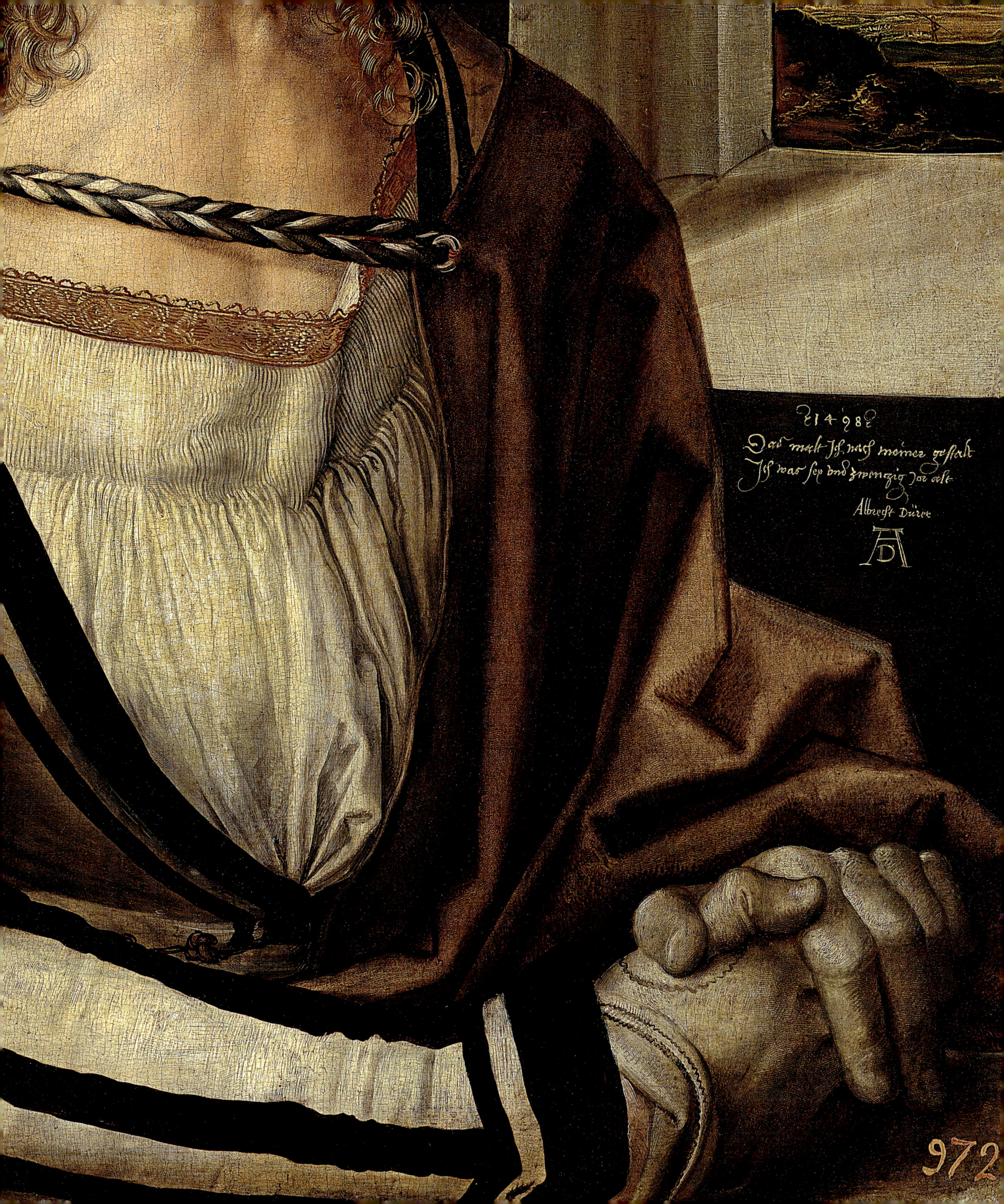
1498
Das malt Ich nach meiner gestalt
Ich was sex und zwenzig Jor alt
Albrecht Dürer
AD
972

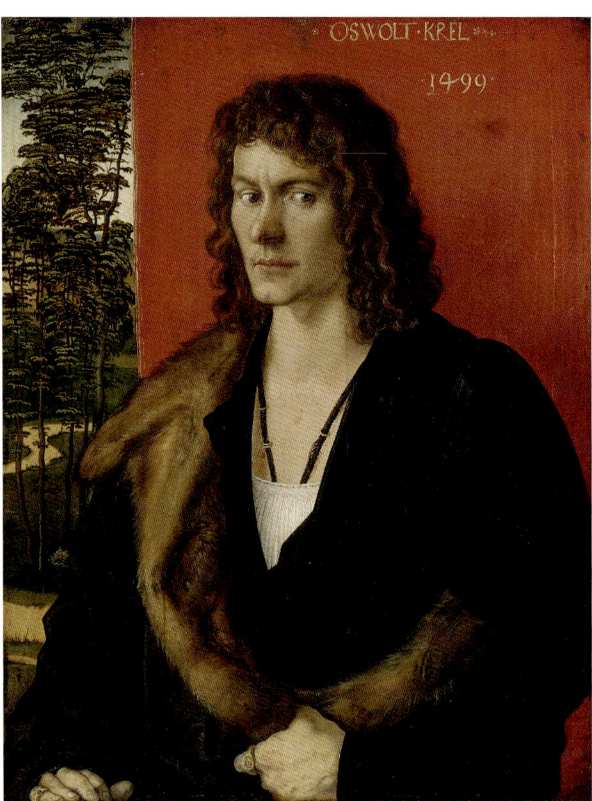

Fig. 25
ALBRECHT DÜRER
Portrait of Oswolt Krel, 1499
Oil on lime, 49.7 × 38.9 cm
Bayerische Staatsgemäldesammlungen, Munich

close-up portraits of the brothers Nikolaus and Hans Tucher each make up one half of a diptych; their respective wives, Elsbeth and Felicitas, form the pendants, both shown turning to their right, towards the husband. The portrait of Elsbeth Tucher now held in Kassel[27] and its missing pendant were conceived of in the same manner as the portraits of Hans and Felicitas, preserved in Weimar:[28] both brothers are depicted at bust length in three-quarter view; behind each a cloth of honour hangs before a balustrade that gives out onto a sweeping landscape continued to the viewer's right in the mirroring portrait of their wives. Formally considered and with a view to their reduced format, the Tucher portraits recall Memling's diptych of an elderly married couple, as well as side wings of devotional diptychs and triptychs from Flanders. The motif of a background landscape set behind a simple balustrade was characteristic of Memling's portraiture in his final years, work that found its way into Franconia by the mid-1480s and was now taken up anew by Dürer.[29] The Tucher portraits, in any event, reveal the recent influence of Netherlandish art and its formal language.

Dürer's portraiture from before 1500 reveals a remarkable spectrum of pictorial approaches that was at the time without parallel in the Netherlands, Germany or Italy. The artist not only brought the range of his clients' personalities to bear in his portraits, but he adopted different formal strategies to suit the portraits' intended functions. In a painting dating from the same year as his Tucher portraits, he deviates significantly from their design in his *Portrait of Oswolt Krel* (fig. 25).[30] A Nuremberg member of the Great Ravensburg Trading Society, Oswald Krell (1460–1534) is shown half-length, turned to the viewer's left in three-quarter view and set against a monochrome red hanging. One hand grips the fur pelt draped across his shoulder, the other rests on the edge of the picture. In place of the balustrade motif common to Netherlandish portraits Dürer chooses to show his client in half-length,[31] exchanging the close-up view of the Tucher portraits – which focused on their sitters' physiognomy – for a more distanced view that takes in the upper half of Krell's body, and makes use of the subject's posture in addition to the facial expression to communicate personality. Krell's imposing figure, which self-consciously encourages the gaze of the viewer, may well bear a connection to Dürer's self portrait of the previous year: the impression of nonchalance in the latter painting suited the merchant's taste and likely prompted the contract. The narrow strip of landscape directly to the left of the red panel, which shows the course of a river edged with trees, is a novelty – without parallel in this form even in the Netherlands. Meanwhile, Dürer's omission of any architectural details creates an ambiguous relationship between interior and landscape; it is only the hint of a shadow against the red background that gives the impression of enclosed space.

A three-quarter view shown at bust-length, at times expanded to half-length; a balustrade that coincides with the edge of the picture upon which, alternatively, hands or arms are brought to rest; lastly, a monochrome background with a landscape view: such were the set pieces of early Netherlandish portraiture that Dürer included in his own portraits prior to his second Italian journey.

Dürer's view of the portrait changed during his second stay in Italy. This shift was due in no small part to a commission that now also brought him recognition as a painter in Venice, the *Feast of the Rose Garlands* (fig. 19).[32] Dürer drafted numerous studies and sketches of portraits in the course of preparing the work commissioned for San Bartolomeo, the church of German merchants in Venice, at the same time undertaking an intensive study of the portrait as a painting genre. Those he created while in Venice anticipated principles of his future work in the genre, and in their close attention to the face remained exemplary even for those made during his journey through the Low Countries. The artist's Venetian portraits are of a relatively small size and focus, usually from a slightly elevated standpoint, on the subject's face, which stands out in contrast against a neutral background. Lighting is used to enhance the three-dimensionality of the sitter. Dürer consistently makes do without arms or hands in the portraits, not to mention background landscapes. While this aspect reveals the influence of the late portraits of Giovanni Bellini, an artist whom Dürer greatly admired, he did have to consider first and foremost the taste of his German clients, who may well have come to him to have their portraits painted, but had taken to the painting of Venice as regards taste.

Dürer's portrait of Burkhard of Speyer (cat. 42)[33] shows how the artist looked to Venetian portraiture when selecting his palette for the flesh tones and hair and sharply outlining the sitter's facial features. The deep concentration on his face lends its physiognomy a particularly sculptural effect. His prominent chin, full lips and nose dominate the sitter's appearance, which seems in this regard to serve as a predecessor to Dürer's portrait of Bernhard von Reesen (cat. 43) of 1521.[34] As in the portrait of Speyer, it is the head that occupies by far the largest part of the painting surface; the same is true of his two portraits of Venetian women now in Vienna and Berlin.[35] The artist seems to have designed the one today preserved in Vienna, dated 1505 and composed of subtle layers of glaze, especially on the basis of his own study of proportion.[36]

Among Dürer's Venetian portraits, his depiction of a young man, now in Genoa, dated 1506 (cat. 44)[37] occupies a special place. The format is larger, while the posture of the subject, who confidently looks out past the frame, sets the manner of representation apart. In its monumentality the portrait is more reminiscent of Lorenzo Lotto (about 1480–1556/7) than Bellini.

Dürer's continued fidelity to this form of portraiture even after his return to Nuremberg – as becomes apparent in his *Portrait of a Young Man* of 1507, today in Vienna[38] – may be explained by the fact that such concentration on the face was consistent with his own work process, which proceeded from a meticulous sketch of the portrait to the finished painting. It is above all in his portrait sketches that Dürer emulated the type of Venetian portraiture, as in a charcoal drawing of an African man likely created around this time,[39] or two bust-length charcoal drawings of two sisters, which date from 1515 and are today held in Berlin.[40] In similar fashion, format and medium notwithstanding, the many drawings in which Dürer portrayed his friends, hosts and encounters throughout his travels in the Netherlands adhered to strategies previously worked out in Venice.

He suffered no shortage of commissions after his return from Italy, although portraits appear only as isolated instances. A number of sheets mostly executed in charcoal show the artist to have made portraits and character studies during this period too, however, with members of his family often standing in as models.[41] In 1516 he completed his *Portrait of a Clergyman* on parchment, setting the figure against a green background, turned slightly to the left.[42] The portrait resembles his *Portrait of a Young Man* (cat. 44) of ten years earlier, executed while Dürer was still in Venice. The year 1516 also saw Dürer complete his portrait of 82-year-old Michael Wolgemut,[43] in this case not by commission, but at the artist's own initiative.[44] The painting shows the elderly man in three-quarter view, turned towards the right of the viewer, against a green background and wearing a simple head covering. The face – depicted from a slightly elevated perspective that includes only the throat and shoulders – occupies nearly the entire pictorial surface; the resulting concentration on the subject's physiognomy lends the portrait an immediacy that in turn recalls Dürer's Venetian work.

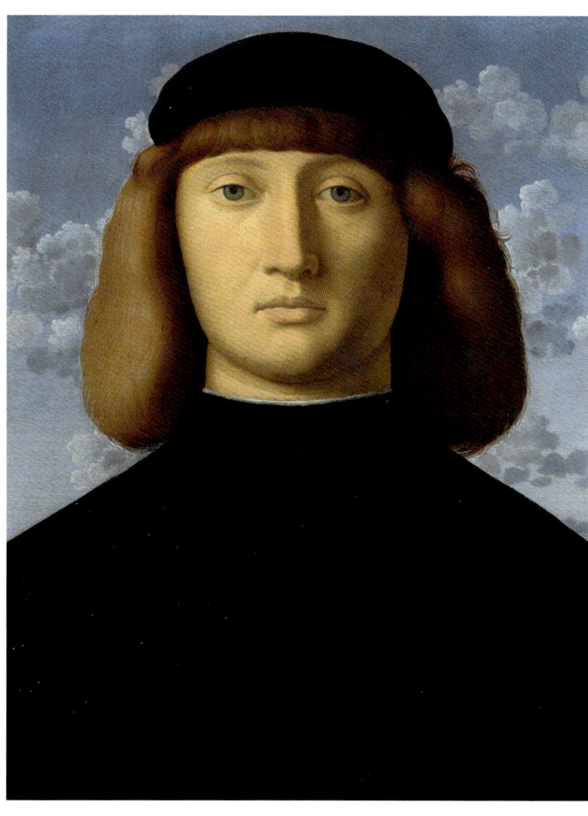

41
VINCENZO CATENA
(active 1506–31)
Portrait of a Young Man,
probably about 1510
Oil on wood,
30.5 × 23.5 cm
The National Gallery,
London

Be that as it may, the portraits Dürer created after his return from Venice were completed under the shadow of graphic works such as the *Small Passion*, his Master Engravings and large-scale projects commissioned by Emperor Maximilian.[45]

This changed in the summer of 1518, when as an official representative for the city of Nuremberg the artist was invited to attend the Imperial Diet summoned in Augsburg, at which the elite and full entourage of the

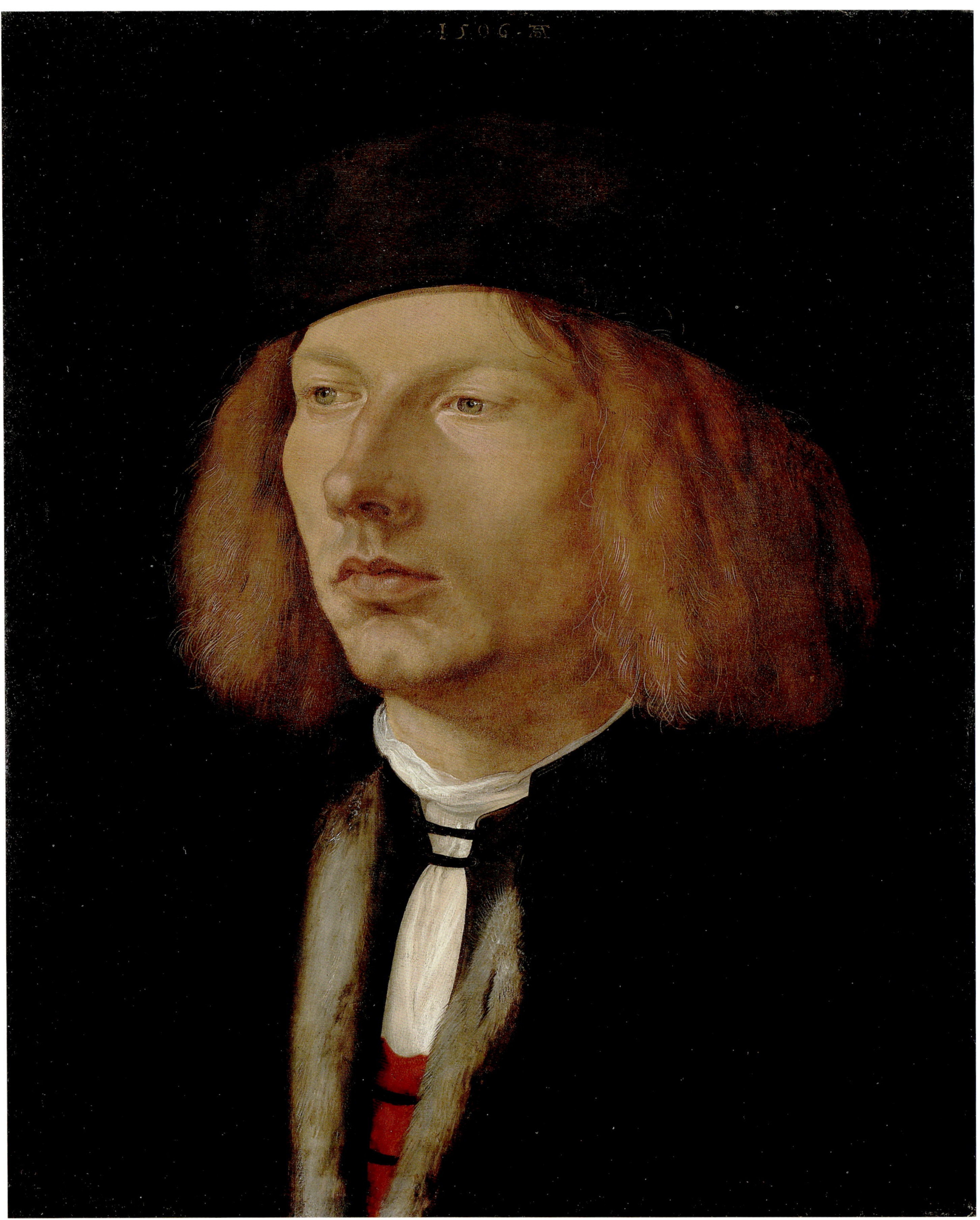

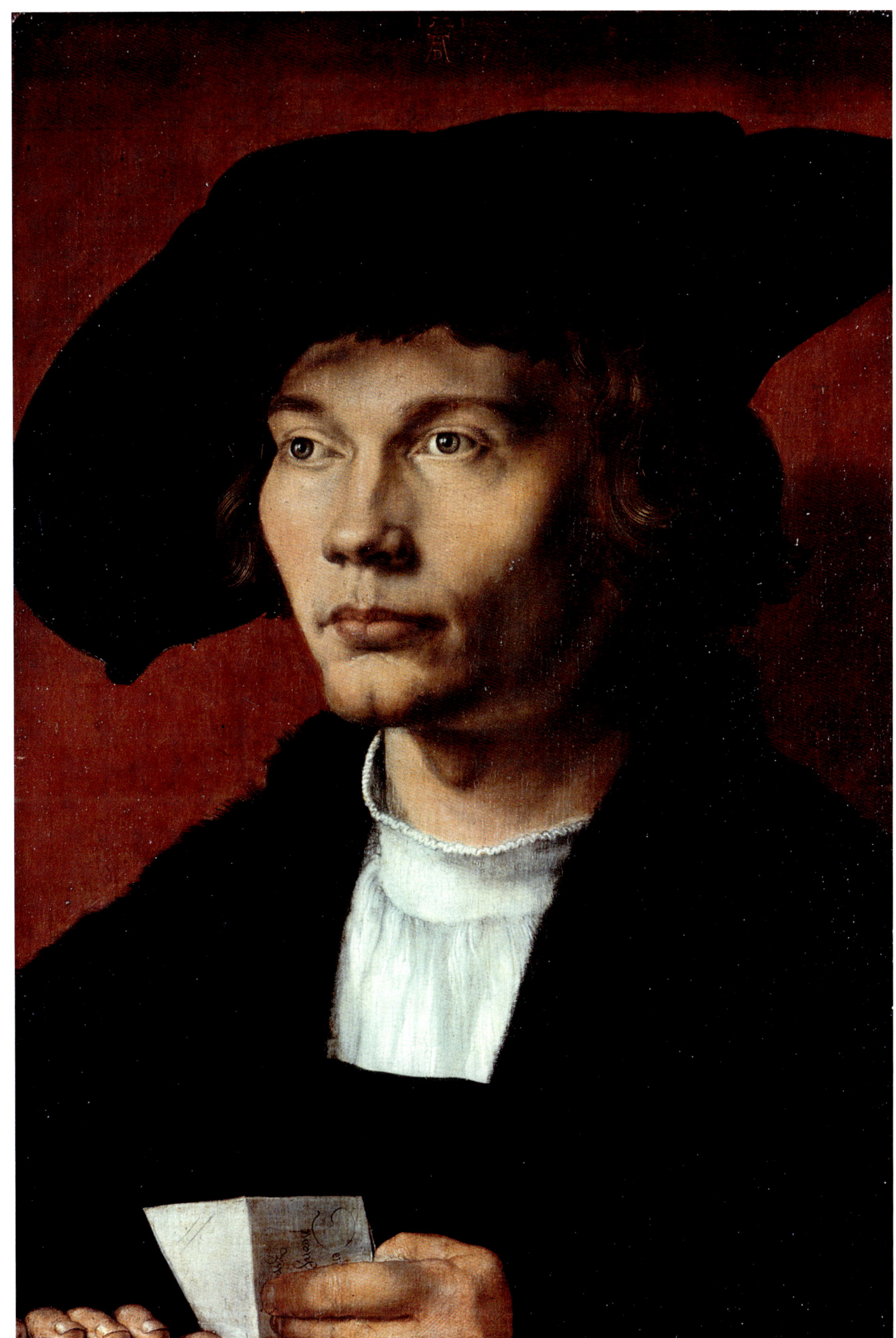

RIGHT
43
ALBRECHT DÜRER
Bernhard von Reesen, 1521
Oil on oak, 45.5 × 31.5 cm
Gemäldegalerie Alte Meister,
Staatliche Kunstsammlungen
Dresden

OPPOSITE
42
ALBRECHT DÜRER
Burkhard of Speyer, 1506
Oil on panel, 31.7 × 26 cm
The Royal Collection /
HM Queen Elizabeth II

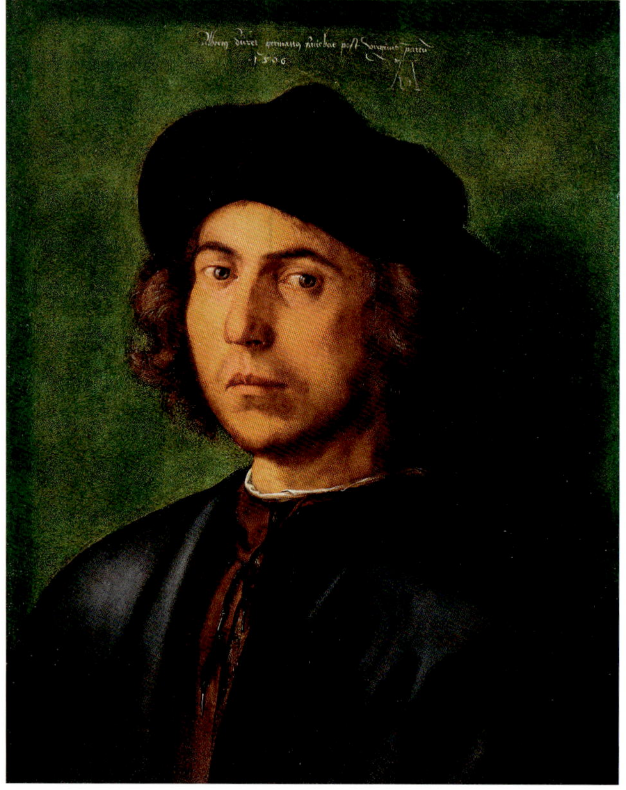

44
ALBRECHT DÜRER
Portrait of a Young Man, 1506
Oil on panel, 46 × 35 cm
Musei di Strada Nuova-Palazzo Rosso, Genoa

Holy Roman Empire would be present. The summit gave Dürer the opportunity both to obtain commissions from significant personages and to draw the portraits of various participants.[46] It is in all likelihood the Diet in Augsburg to which we owe the sketch for a portrait of Jakob Fugger now held in Berlin.[47] The sheet shows the Augsburg financier and patron in three-quarter view, turned towards the left. The brisk, expert linework in charcoal applied to the subject's face and clothing, and the black background, recall, on the one hand, the black backgrounds of the artist's drawn portraits from 1515;[48] in its precision, however, it also anticipates sketches for portraits that Dürer would realise during his journey through the Netherlands. The sketch for Jakob Fugger's portrait is pricked around the contours, a method commonly used to assist in transferring the outlines of a sketch to the surface to be painted; it therefore presumably served as the model for a painting lost in the original but preserved in a workshop version.[49]

The highest-ranking figure Dürer portrayed in Augsburg was the Emperor Maximilian himself. His sketch of Maximilian (fig. 26), hastily carried out in charcoal and coloured chalk, speaks to the narrow window of time that the artist and his subject had at their disposal.[50] Limited to bust-length, in just a few strokes the drawing suggests the emperor's brocaded mantel, shirt collar and the chain of his chivalric order. Dürer concentrates on the sitter's face, which is shown in three-quarter view, turned towards the left. Despite its narrow focus, the drawing captures the complex personality of the emperor in all its dignity and served as the basis for a woodcut that has survived in numerous versions (cat. 5). One version – the first state portrait ever realised in the medium of woodcut – shows the emperor against a white background, a second against a black background. A Latin inscription identifies the subject of the print but the sovereign's regalia is conspicuous by its absence: Maximilian wears only the collar of the chivalric order over which he presided, the Habsburg Order of the Golden Fleece, and a medallion of the Virgin Mary on his beret as a token of piety.

After the monarch passed away a few months later, in January 1519, the woodcut, probably published while he was still alive, unexpectedly took on the function of a quasi-official memorial portrait. Given the altered context, the print's omission of the sovereign's regalia, and consequent emphasis on the person of the emperor rather than his office, proved problematic. When at the instigation of Jakob Fugger Dürer then received a commission to paint a portrait of Maximilian as a gift for the emperor's grandson and successor, Emperor Charles V, the artist reviewed the fitness of his representation for this new context.

A *Tüchlein*, or painting on canvas (using a glue medium), today preserved in Nuremberg with the portrait of the emperor – a preliminary study for Dürer's client – bears an inscription on parchment that states Maximilian's titles and his years of birth and death on what was originally a green background.[51] Maximilian, now in half-length, wears the resplendent collar of the Order of the Golden Fleece, a red mantle and a broad fur shoulder cape; he holds a pomegranate in both hands. The latter motif, introduced especially for a study drawing from 1519, alludes not only to the *globus cruciger* – the orb topped with a cross symbolising Christianity's dominion over the world – and the resurrection, but also serves as one of Maximilian's emblems. Dürer would have been aware of this both from his work on the monumental woodcut of the Triumphal Arch, in which the symbol appears, and the interpretations of humanist cartographer Johannes Stabius (1450–1522).[52] To the left of the sovereign's head the painter has reproduced the Habsburg coat of arms, encircled by the collar of the Order of the Golden Fleece and surmounted by the imperial crown. Thus the portrait attests to the imperial status of the deceased and pays tribute to his His Majesty, especially as the dynastic progenitor of the house of Habsburg-Burgundy.

The pictorial concepts on display in the Nuremberg *Tüchlein* were developed further in a panel painting of painstaking design now in Vienna (fig. 27). The

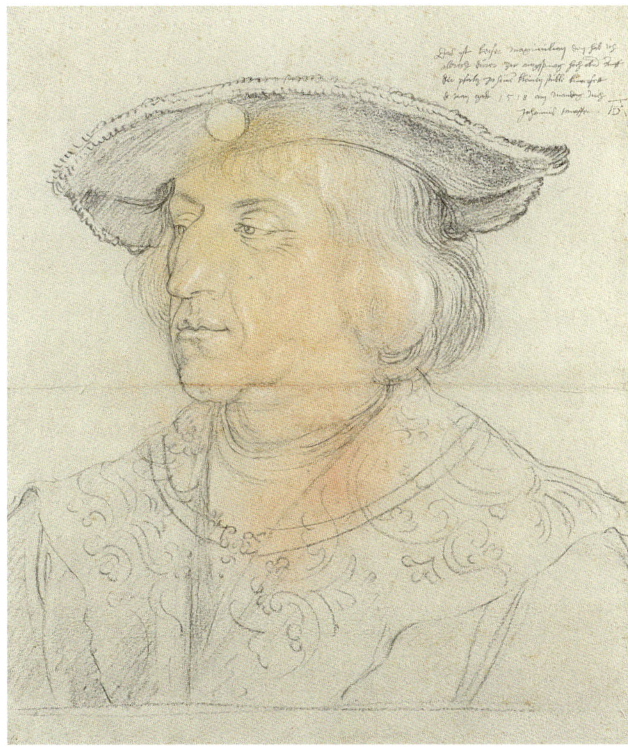

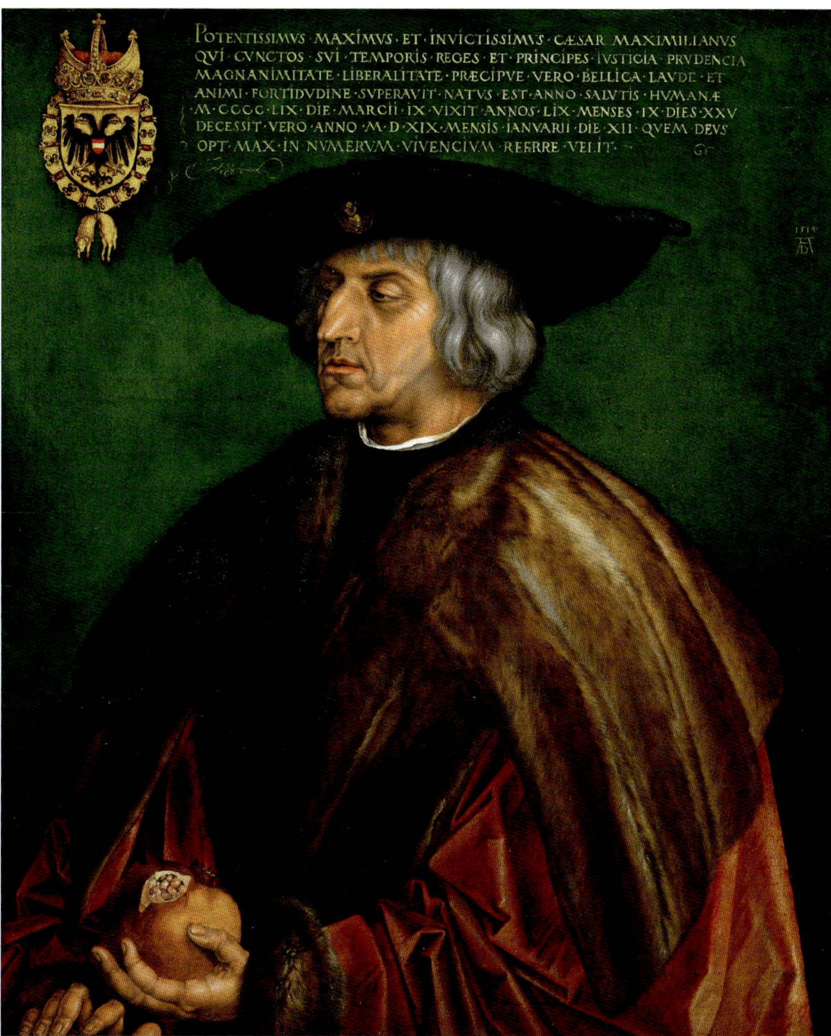

Fig. 26
ALBRECHT DÜRER
Portrait of Maximilian I, 1518
Charcoal, red chalk, heightened with white chalk, 38.1 × 31.9 cm
The Albertina Museum, Vienna (4852)

Fig. 27
ALBRECHT DÜRER
Portrait of Emperor Maximilian I, 1519
Oil on linden wood, 74 × 62 cm
Kunsthistorisches Museum, Vienna

various alterations Dürer undertook largely concerned the appropriate representation of his subject and the painting's function as a portrait of the deceased emperor: a collar no longer adorns the figure, but the Burgundian Order of the Golden Fleece still encircles the Habsburg coat of arms, while the imperial crown rests atop the motif as before. The coat of arms, which had taken up a relatively large amount of pictorial space on the *Tüchlein*, is reduced in size, now smaller than the sitter's head. The German inscription has been replaced with a carefully lettered dedication in Latin, written in capitals directly on the green background. Finally, in his most significant modification Dürer adapts an informal gesture in the Nuremberg *Tüchlein* to suit the picture's new purpose: the emperor no longer holds the opened pomegranate in both hands but presents it with the left, his left arm and the fingers of his right hand now resting against an imaginary balustrade that coincides with the lower edge of the painting. As with the portraits he painted after returning to Nuremberg from his travels as a journeyman and his first Italian trip, Dürer once again looks to early Netherlandish portrait types to find a fitting solution for the intended memorialising function of the state portrait.[53]

The commission of the emperor's posthumous portrait must have given Dürer cause to consider every conceivable aspect of what makes a portrait appropriate, and to arrive at decisions only after careful consideration. This explains his surprise when during his visit to Mechelen, Margaret of Austria expressed disapproval of a portrait of the emperor intended as a gift to her.[54]

Between his depiction of the emperor and other portraits commissioned at the Augsburg Imperial Diet, the genre took on a new relevance for Dürer and would continue to occupy him in the Netherlands. The artist's stay in Antwerp and his visits to Bruges, Ghent and other cities allowed him to engage with portraiture at the level of form and content alike, and to make a systematic study of the panels of Netherlandish masters from the fifteenth century as well as those of his contemporaries. A majority of the drawings that Dürer references in his journal are portraits of his hosts, friends

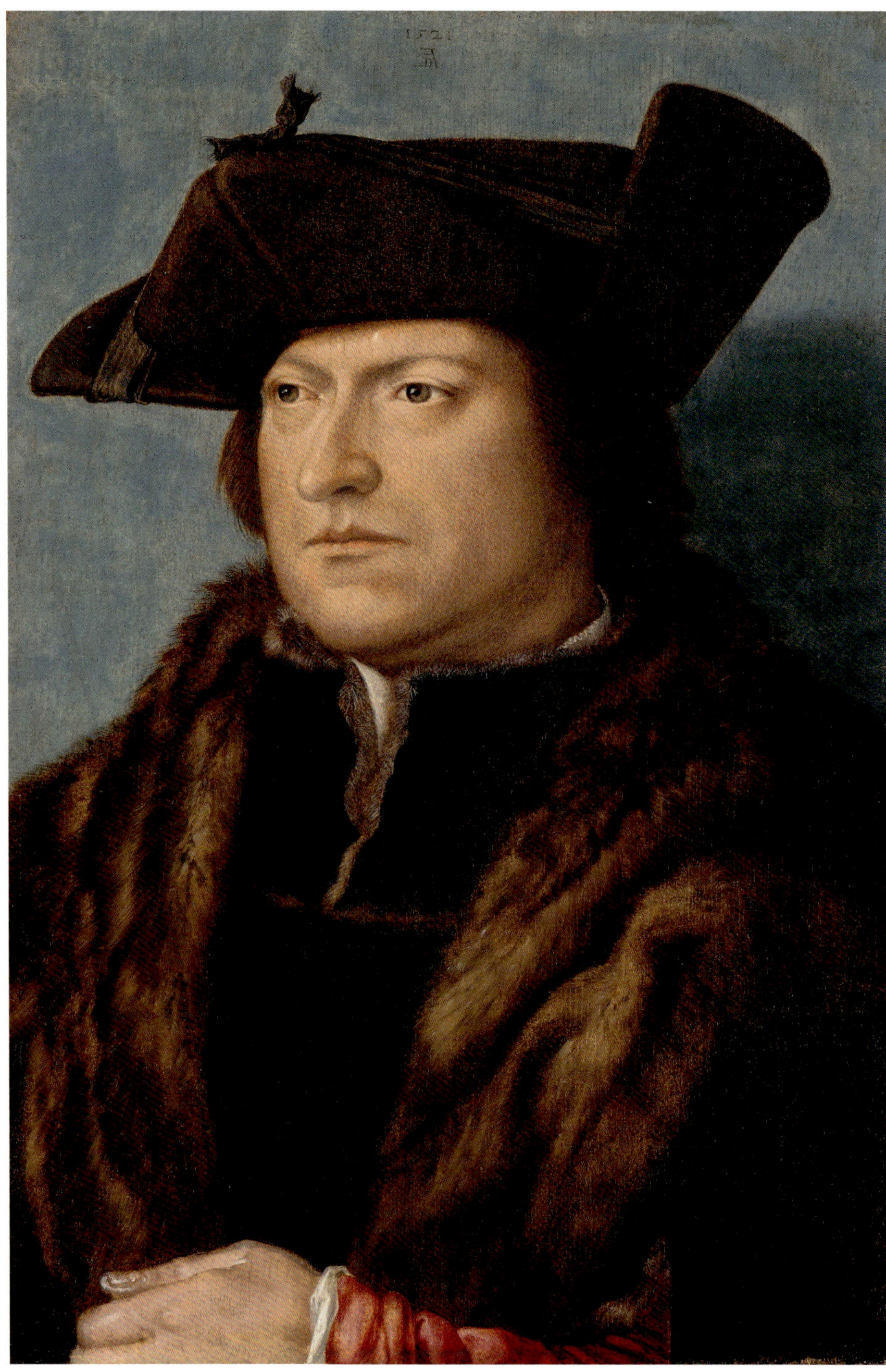

Fig. 28
ALBRECHT DÜRER
Rodrigo Fernandes de Almada, 1521
Oil on oak, 50.6 × 32.9 cm
Isabella Stewart Gardner Museum, Boston, Massachusetts

or acquaintances, a concrete illustration of the high regard in which he held the genre.

Dürer prepared at least 109 portrait drawings during his travels through the Netherlands. While they attest to the artist's virtuosic handling of quill, pen, charcoal and brush, the drawings also give an impression of the compositional diversity that characterised his portraits. The spectrum ranges from variations on the three-quarter view to frontal views, and rough studies of heads to bust-length portraits worked out in great detail.[55]

By comparison, one is hard-pressed to find a similar range of expressive forms in the three panel portraits that have survived from this period. Instead, these paintings should be seen as a further development of Dürer's return to traditional, earlier portrait forms, a process that originated in his work on the portrait of the emperor. Furthermore, those commissioning portraits from Dürer – such figures as the Portuguese trading representative Rodrigo Fernandes de Almada (fig. 28) or Bernhard von Reesen (1491–1521), a

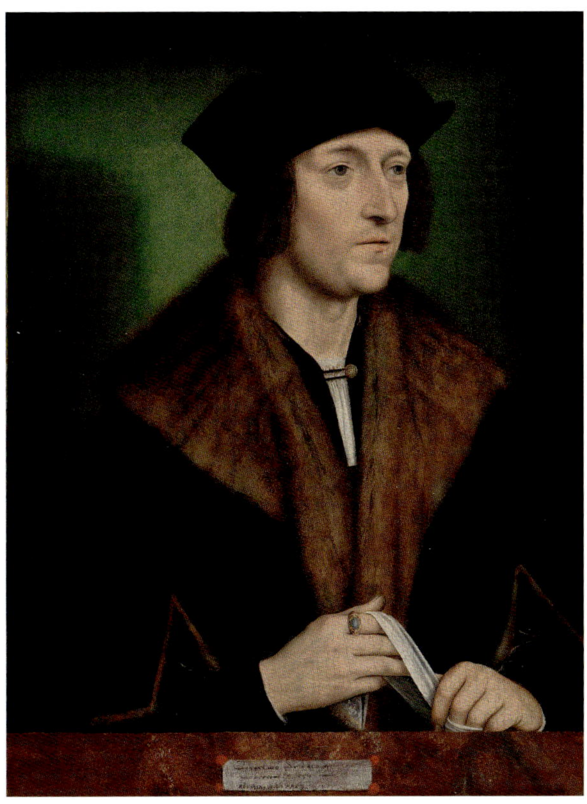

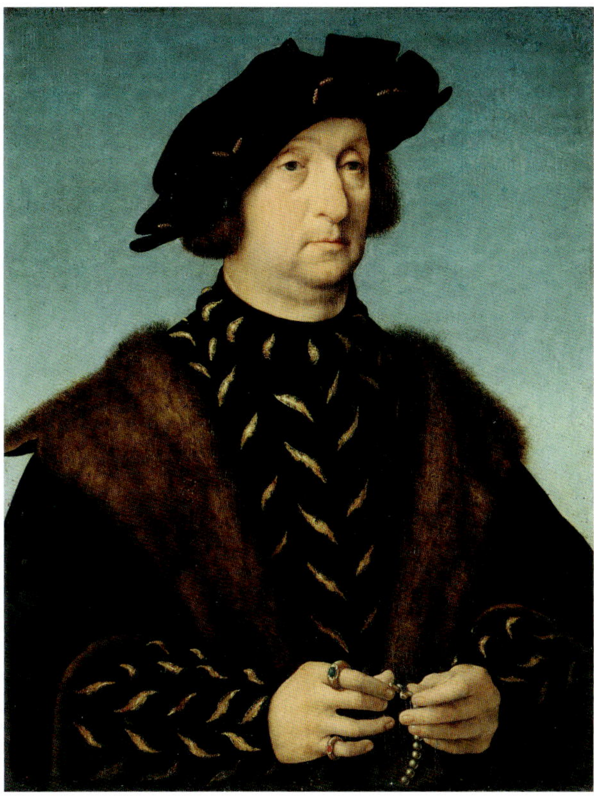

Fig 29
QUINTEN MASSYS
(1465/6–1530)
Portrait of a Portuguese Merchant, 1517
Oil on oak, 65 × 51 cm
Staatliche Kunsthalle Karlsruhe

Fig. 30
JOOS VAN CLEVE
(1485–1541)
Portrait of a Man, about 1520
Oil on oak, 43.5 × 33 cm
Gemäldegalerie Kassel

merchant from the Hanseatic city of Danzig (cat. 43) – looked to their home of the Netherlands not only in their choice of clothing and manners, but also for forms of pictorial representation. It comes as little surprise, then, that Dürer would consciously seek out earlier Netherlandish models with reference to execution as well as form.

This was certainly the case with Rodrigo Fernandes de Almada, with whom Dürer regularly interacted socially and whose hospitality he enjoyed. Such encounters would have left the artist with no doubt as to the tastes of the educated Portuguese merchant. As part of his preparation for the portrait, Dürer completed a detailed brush drawing in black and white on violet-grounded paper (fig. 114) before leaving for Ghent and Bruges in late March 1521.[56] In doing so the artist made use of a technique he had employed in a series of painstaking study drawings for the Jerome panel, similarly destined for his Portuguese client. It remains unclear in this case whether Dürer had not been able to locate coloured paper in Antwerp, or was instead consciously making use of a technique of chiaroscuro drawing common in the Netherlands since Hugo van der Goes and the Antwerp mannerist Jan de Beer (died 1527/8), and still present in the work of Jan Gossaert.[57] It is noteworthy that the drawing of de Almada today housed in Berlin depicts its subject at bust-length, while the painting in Boston (fig. 28) focuses on his facial features and now shows his hand resting on the lower edge of the picture. De Almada is set against a light background, his shadow falling visibly to the right. The combination of the close-up view and the positioning of the hands is new in Dürer's work, as are the conspicuous cast shadows and the depth of field they suggest. The artist clearly draws inspiration from Netherlandish models in this case, thus inscribing himself into local tradition.

It may be revealing in this connection to make a comparison with a 1517 portrait of another Portuguese merchant (fig. 29), traditionally attributed to Quinten Massys. The sitter is depicted in half-length against a green background; the sense of spatial depth that derives from the shadows cast by the subject's figure and the frame is strengthened by the positioning of the hands, which play with a ribbon. Typical of portraits produced in Antwerp at the time, the painting's underlying concept appears elsewhere in Massys's paintings and especially in the work of Joos van Cleve (fig. 30), and recalls Dürer's portraits from before his second Italian journey – his inclusion of the entire upper body in the portrait of his father, for example (cat. 19). In the work attributed to Massys the Portuguese merchant's torso is shown nearly in full; by contrast, Dürer's portrait of Alamada includes only a segment, focusing instead on the face. De Almada's arm, lying along the edge of the picture, appears disembodied and has in fact been heavily painted over, although it was probably included in the original design.

Fig. 31
MICHAEL SITTOW
(1568/9–1525/6)
Man with a Rosary,
about 1521
Oil on oak,
33.6 × 22.8 cm
Het Noordbrabants
Museum,
's-Hertogenbosch

Another portrait presumably dating from around the same time, *Man with a Rosary* (fig. 31) by Michael Sittow, bears closer resemblance to Dürer's portrait of de Almada, offering points of comparison beyond the elaborate design of the fur collar and the subject's clothing. As with Dürer, Sittow depicts his elderly subject against a neutral background with cast shadows; between his hands he holds a rosary, while his left arm (admittedly a passage that has been revised in Dürer) similarly rests on the edge of the painting. The key difference lies in the positioning of the head, which turns towards the viewer in Sittow but not in Dürer, accounting in no small part for the stronger impression of monumentality and distance achieved in Dürer's portrait of Rodrigo Fernandes de Almada.

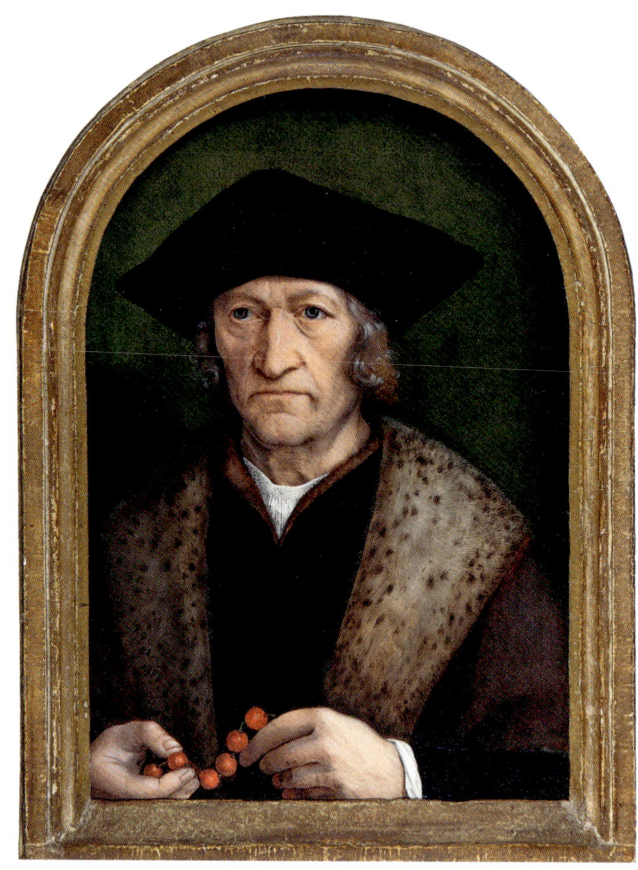

Dürer's recourse to Netherlandish models becomes much clearer in his portrait of Bernhard von Reesen (cat. 43), preserved today in Dresden. Thanks to the journal Dürer kept while in the Netherlands, we know that von Reesen belonged to a circle of German merchants with whom the artist and his wife kept in regular contact while they were in Antwerp. Dürer may have met and drawn the trader from the Hanseatic city of Danzig as early as December 1520, during his trip to Zeeland in Bergen op Zoom, where he noted 'Note: Did portraits of young Bernhard of Breßlen [and others]…'.[58] The drawing likely served as the basis for the painted portrait, completed in March 1521. Von Reesen paid Dürer eight florins for the painting; the artist's wife and maid also received gifts of money.[59]

The bust portrait shows the merchant in three-quarter view turned to the viewer's left; this time the artist has selected a red background. Here, too, the face is depicted from close up and once again Dürer rests the subject's hands on the edge of the picture. It is not difficult here to detect deliberate reference to a trope in portraiture that reached back far into the fifteenth century – one with which Dürer was familiar from his youth and which never fell entirely out of fashion in the Netherlands, also appearing in the portraits of Massys, van Cleve and Jan Mostaert (cat. 45). It can be traced back to Jan van Eyck, who expanded the motif of hands in his portraits to include pieces of writing, rings and other objects.[60]

In his hands von Reesen holds a folded document, a piece of correspondence addressed to 'pernh … zw …' according to the inscription, probably intended as an allusion to the sitter's extensive business ventures and aiding his identification. Dürer not only draws on earlier motifs in this case, however: his use of light also takes its cue from earlier models of Netherlandish

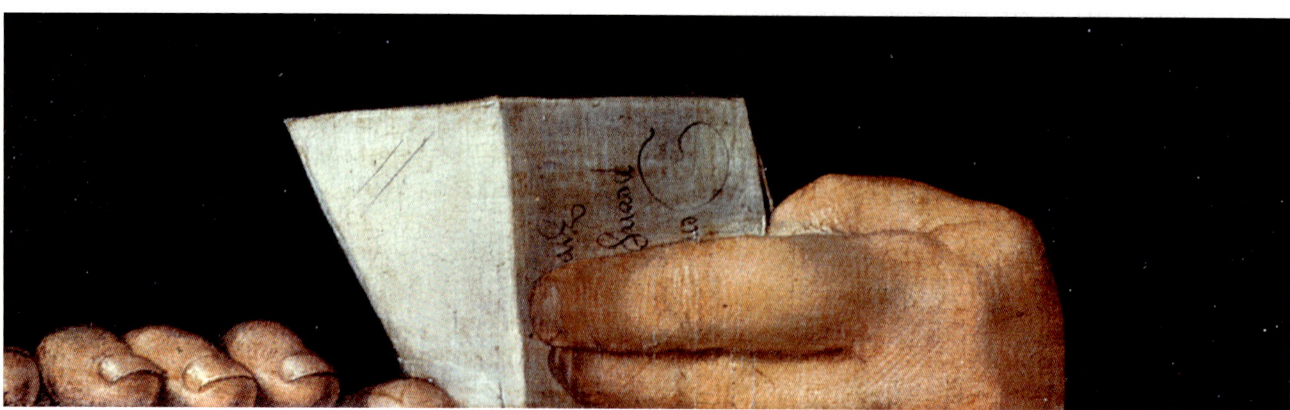

Detail from *Bernhard von Reesen* (cat. 43)

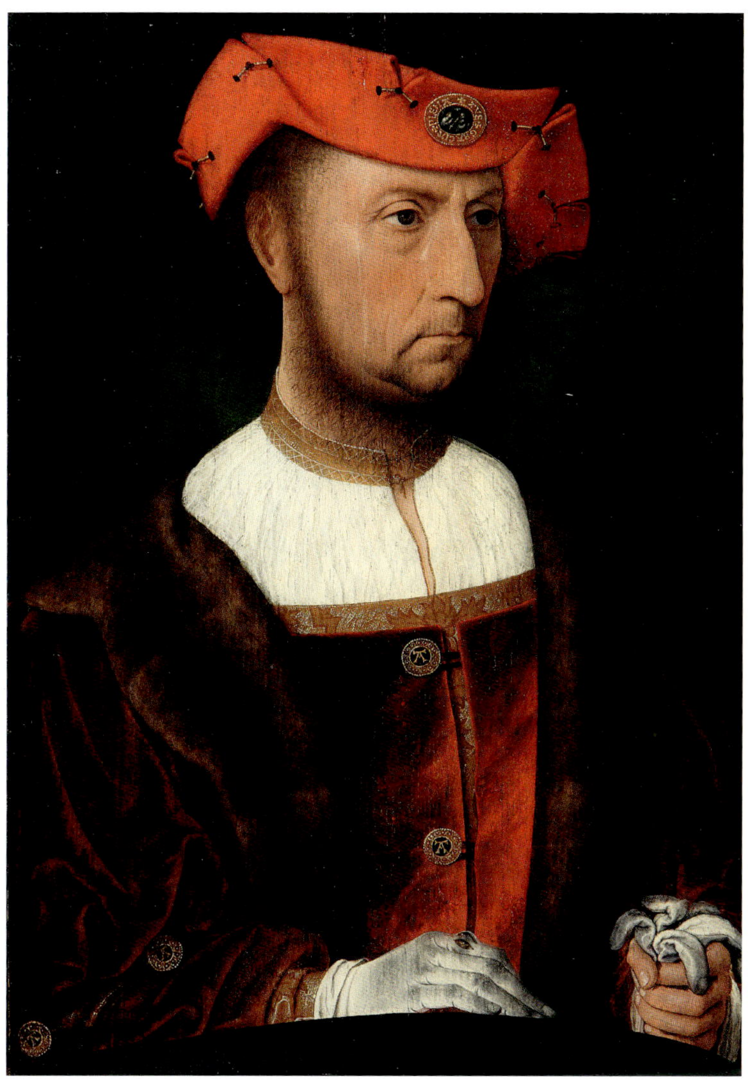

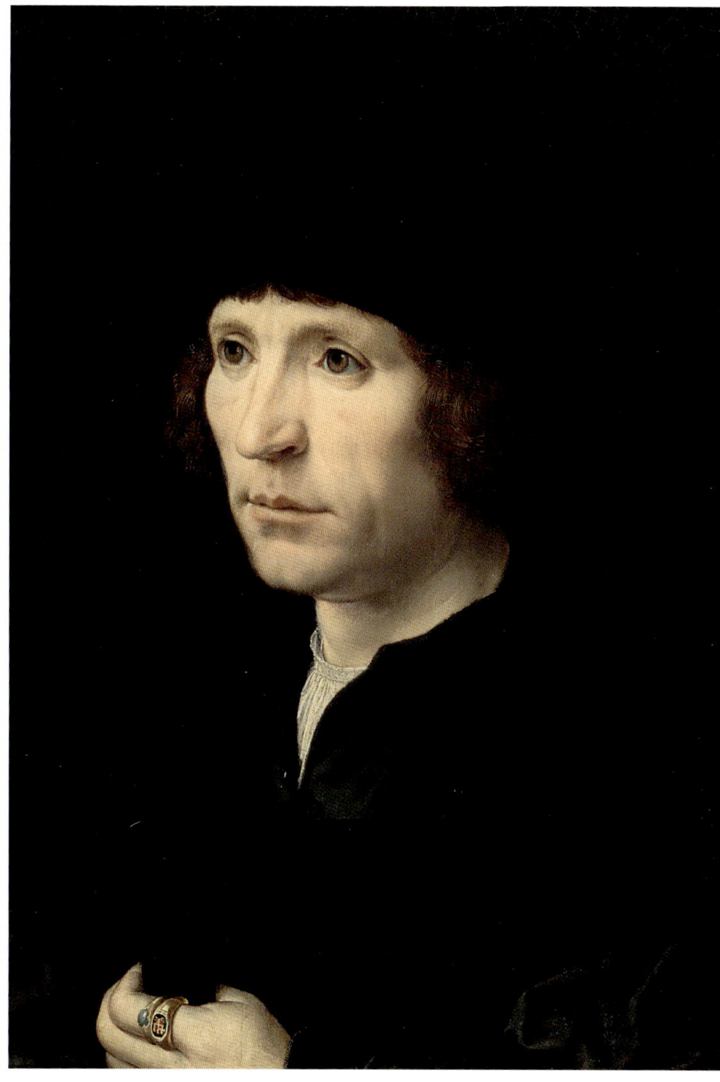

painting. The strong contrast that defines this portrait is perhaps not only caused by the fact that Dürer executed its preparatory sketch in charcoal, but also attests to his engagement with van Eyck and his contemporaries. Light was a leading element of design within Netherlandish portrait panels of the fifteenth century, enhancing their sculptural effect and with it their much-vaunted life-like quality. Dürer had ample opportunity to study portraits of the past while in Antwerp or on one of his excursions to Flanders and Brabant. His trips to Bruges and Ghent were important in this regard, although the first of these was after the completion of the von Reesen portrait in April 1521. Dürer visited the donor panels of the Ghent Altarpiece and saw the portraits of van Eyck and his wife preserved in the chapel of the Bruges painters' guild, as well as the portrait of the goldsmith Jan de Leeuw, probably in the same location.[61]

The traditional character of Dürer's portrait of von Reesen becomes apparent when compared with a contemporaneous portrait of a man painted by Jan Gossaert, today in Vienna (fig. 32). Dürer's painting is only marginally larger than Gossaert's. The green background of the latter has darkened dramatically over time, causing the subject to stand out in greater contrast than was originally intended. The two works resemble one another in the clothing worn by each subject, but also in the position of the sitter's left arm. Even so, Gossaert's depiction has a less static quality, a difference that derives largely from the artist's perspective: he looks down from above at his model, whose head is tilted slightly upward. While the left arm is placed at the edge of the image, in the Gossaert portrait – unlike Dürer's – the man seems to rest his hand on his chest. In this way Gossaert's portrait implies movement and achieves a dynamic effect, while Dürer's portrait of Bernhard von Reesen retains a fixed and thus timeless quality (cat. 43).

A close-up face depicted in combination with hands holding a scroll resting on the edge of the picture similarly characterise a work by Dürer probably dating from 1521, a portrait of a man today in the Prado,

45
JAN MOSTAERT
(active 1498; died 1552/3)
Portrait of a Man,
about 1520
Oil on oak,
44.6 x 30.9 cm
Staatliche Museen zu Berlin, Gemäldegalerie

Fig. 32
JAN GOSSAERT
(active 1508; died 1532)
Portrait of a Man,
about 1520–5
Oil on oak,
40 x 27.5 cm
Kunsthistorisches Museum, Vienna

'I have taken much trouble to paint a very faithful oil-colour portrait of Lorenz Sterk, the Treasurer. I gave it to him as a gift, and in response he gave me 20 gulden and Susanna a 1 gulden gratuity.'

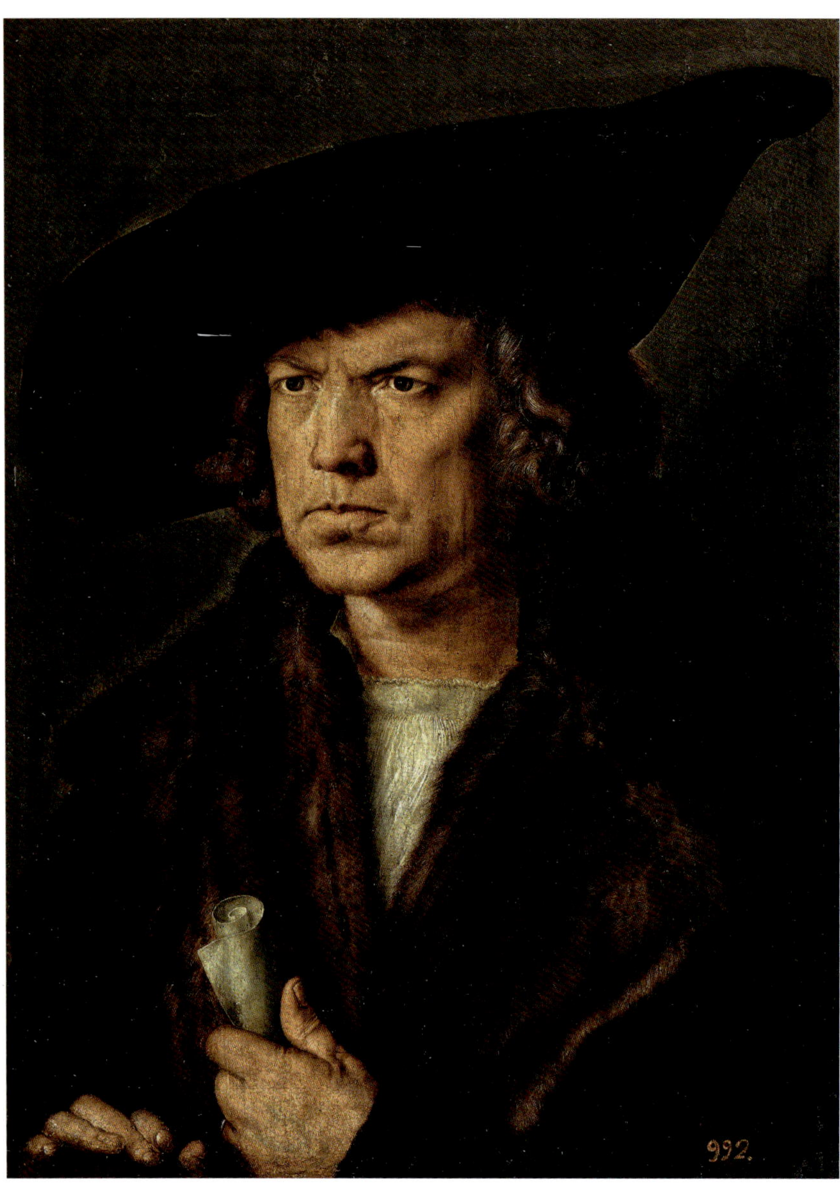

46
ALBRECHT DÜRER
Portrait of a Man, 1521
Oil on oak, 50 × 36 cm
Museo Nacional del Prado, Madrid

Madrid (cat. 46).[62] The subject, no longer young, is shown against a neutral background; he wears a black mantel with a broad fur collar over a pleated shirt, his head covered by a broad hat. Despite the stern appearance of the sitter, the Madrid portrait startles with its vivacious quality, inviting the viewer to imagine the personality of the man depicted. The actual identity of the subject is subject to debate; the use of Baltic oak as a painting surface challenges the hypothesis that Dürer created the painting after his stay in the Netherlands.[63] There are multiple references in Dürer's journal to recipients of portrait panels who might theoretically be associated with the painting. One possibility that can be ruled out is Lazarus Ravensburger, who received a portrait from Dürer towards the end of 1520, to which the artist anyway attributed little value.[64] Nor can the portrait drawing of Ravensburger today preserved in Berlin (cat. 90)[65] be reconciled with the painting, and the subject's identification as Jobst Plankfelt, Dürer's innkeeper in Antwerp, does not hold up on closer inspection. Plankfelt did receive portraits of himself and his wife from Dürer in 1521, valued at 31 florins and intended in part-payment for Dürer's lodging and hospitality.[66] However, the artist's *Portrait of Jobst Plankfelt* of 1520 (cat. 88)[67] today in Frankfurt – with an inscription at the top identifying Plankfelt as its subject – reveals a much younger man than the sitter in the Madrid portrait. One possible subject is Lorenz Sterk, from 1514 to 1525 the chief tax collector for the Duchy of Brabant in the districts of Antwerp, Lier and Herentals, whom Dürer portrayed in May 1521: 'I have taken much trouble to paint a very faithful oil-colour portrait of Lorenz Sterk, the Treasurer. I gave it to him as a gift, and in response he gave me 20 gulden and Susanna a 1 gulden gratuity.'[68] Yet the identification is by no means conclusive.

The Prado portrait captivates with the sculptural presence of the face, which is achieved through the careful use of light and impresses upon the viewer the wilful character and energetic gaze of the subject, qualities that are emphasised by his dark headwear. In this regard Dürer's painting bears some resemblance to Gossaert's likeness of a man from a double portrait now in the National Gallery, London (cat. 47), although this assumes an almost anecdotal quality when compared

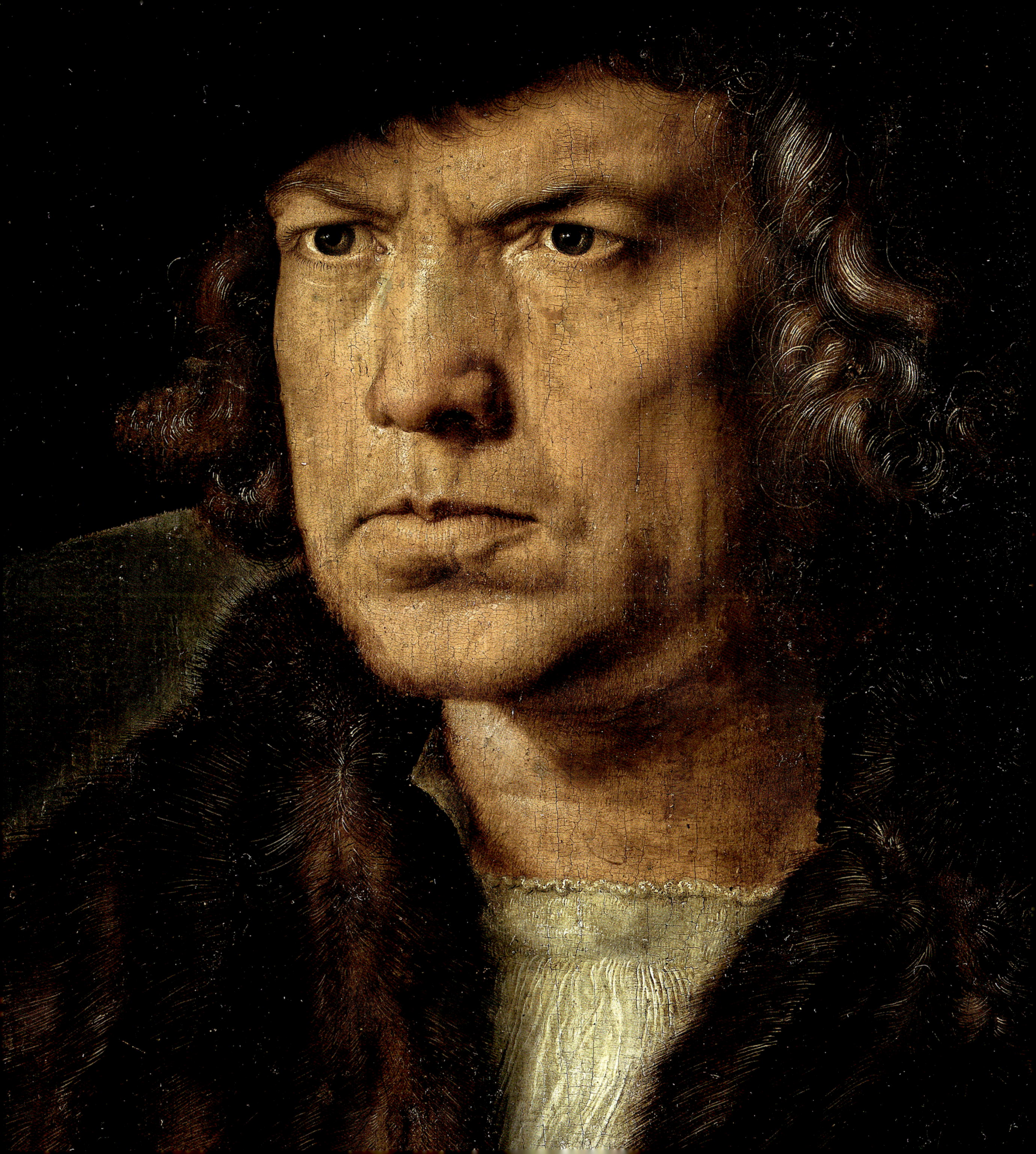

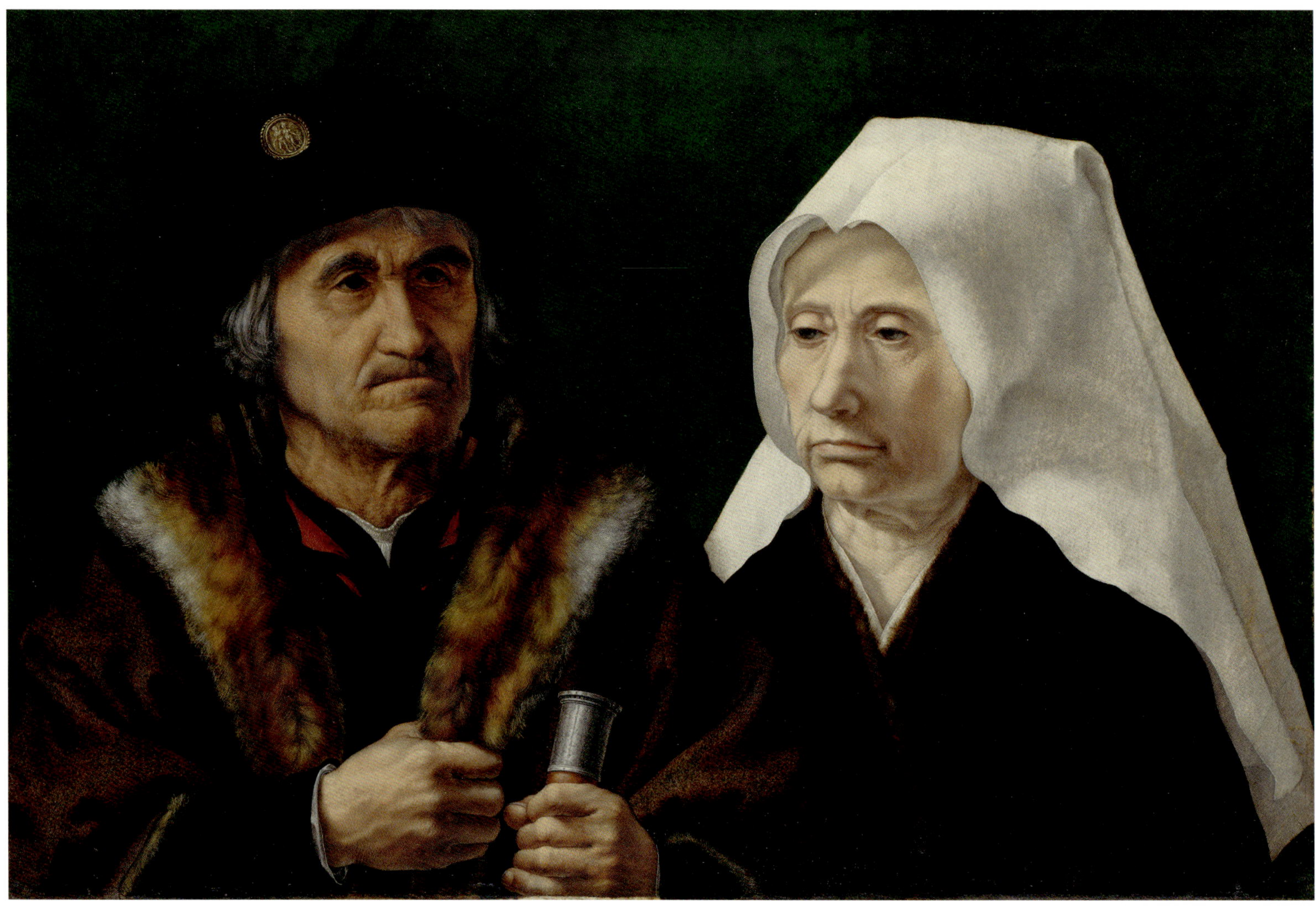

47
JAN GOSSAERT
(active 1508;
died 1532)
An Elderly Couple,
about 1520
Oil on parchment
laid down on canvas,
48.1 × 69.2 cm
The National Gallery,
London

with Dürer's strict composition. Once again, his painterly execution exhibits a meticulous aspect that is otherwise uncharacteristic of the artist, and which on the whole distinguishes his paintings from the time of his travels through the Low Countries.[69]

Without question, such careful attention on Dürer's part was the result of his determination that his work should meet, perhaps even exceed the expectations that arose from the recognition he received as an artist while in the Netherlands. This involved, as a matter of course, applying the standards of craftsmanship and painting technique then in use among leading painters in Antwerp, Brussels and elsewhere in the Netherlands. One possible explanation for the occasional use Dürer made of painting apprentices from the workshops of masters he befriended is his desire to conform to local practice.[70] His portrait of a *Bearded Man in a Red Cap* (fig. 33) is an exception: it is a *Tüchlein* now in the Louvre, which bears the date 1520 above the artist's monogram and which – though it is not mentioned in his journal – may thus be associated with his trip to the Netherlands.[71] Yet it is not clear whether this is a portrait or whether the sitter is an invented character, nor is the dating verified as authentic. The rendition of the head recalls the artist's *Portrait of Michael Wolgemut*, and may be of an earlier date.

Dürer would certainly have made a precise study of contemporary portraits in Antwerp and other cities in the Netherlands, where as a celebrated artist he enjoyed a months-long opportunity to study early art and to acquaint himself with the painting of his Flemish contemporaries. Viewing works by Sittow, Massys (fig. 31, cats 39, 40) or Joos van Cleve (fig. 30), for example, may well have provided inspiration in conceptualising his fur collars. By contrast, Dürer remained unimpressed with an incipient transformation then occurring in Netherlandish portraits, one that evolved from the interiors and still-life arrangements of Bernaert van Orley, Quinten Massys, Joos van Cleve and Jan Gossaert into a true blossoming in Flemish Renaissance portraiture in the following decade. While his Master Engravings and his Antwerp portrait of Saint Jerome contributed in no small measure to the

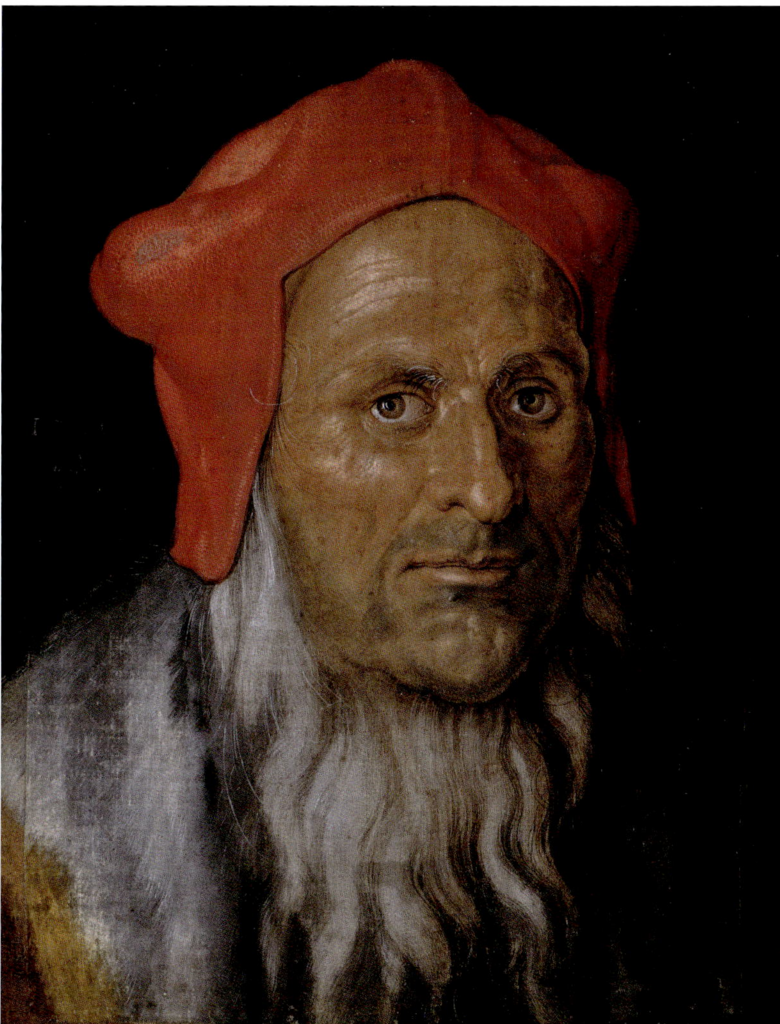

Fig. 33
ALBRECHT DÜRER
Bearded Man in a Red Cap, 1520
Gouache, oil and black ink,
40 × 30.3 cm
Musée du Louvre, Paris

development of the Flemish portrait, as a portrait painter himself, Dürer kept his distance.

Setting Dürer's portraits alongside those of his Netherlandish contemporaries reveals a comparatively austere and static body of work, one that stands, furthermore, in sharp contrast to the lively portrait drawings the artist created on his visit to the Low Countries. At first glance, their formulaic nature would seem to make the portrait panels a brief episode within Dürer's career. Appearances may also be deceptive. Even if the portraits Dürer painted after his return to Nuremberg reject the subtle colouring of the early masters in favour of greater graphic orientation, and purposefully place greater limits on their range of focus, it is precisely in this shift that one can recognise an ongoing effort on Dürer's part to develop a timeless and classical appearance for his portraits. This found its origins at the Imperial Diet in Augsburg, to continue in the Netherlands and again with the artist's return to Nuremberg. While this aspiration appears in his painted portraits, it is also clearly evident in his printed portraits. These are themselves connected with Dürer's artistic interest in the portrait as a genre that can be traced back to his Augsburg portrait of the emperor.

An engraving of 1524 with the portrait of Willibald Pirckheimer shows Dürer's friend behind a tablet, which is inscribed with an admonishing epitaph contrasting the transience of the body to the eternity of the spirit. Another engraving, from 1526, bearing the likeness of Erasmus of Rotterdam (cat. 94) finds the renowned humanist in his study amidst his papers; behind him an inscription calls attention to the portrait's origin in another likeness, and reminds the viewer that the figure of the humanist is best disclosed in his writings. Such printed portraits reveal a profound, humanistically inclined concern with decorum in the genre that would have consequences for their painted counterparts.

Dürer's *Portrait of Jakob Muffel* (fig. 34)[72] of 1526 can be regarded as a further step towards reducing the portrait to the classical portrait bust. The painting is reminiscent of portraits from his journey to the Netherlands, among other things in the posture, gaze and the cast shadows, even if Dürer now, as after his

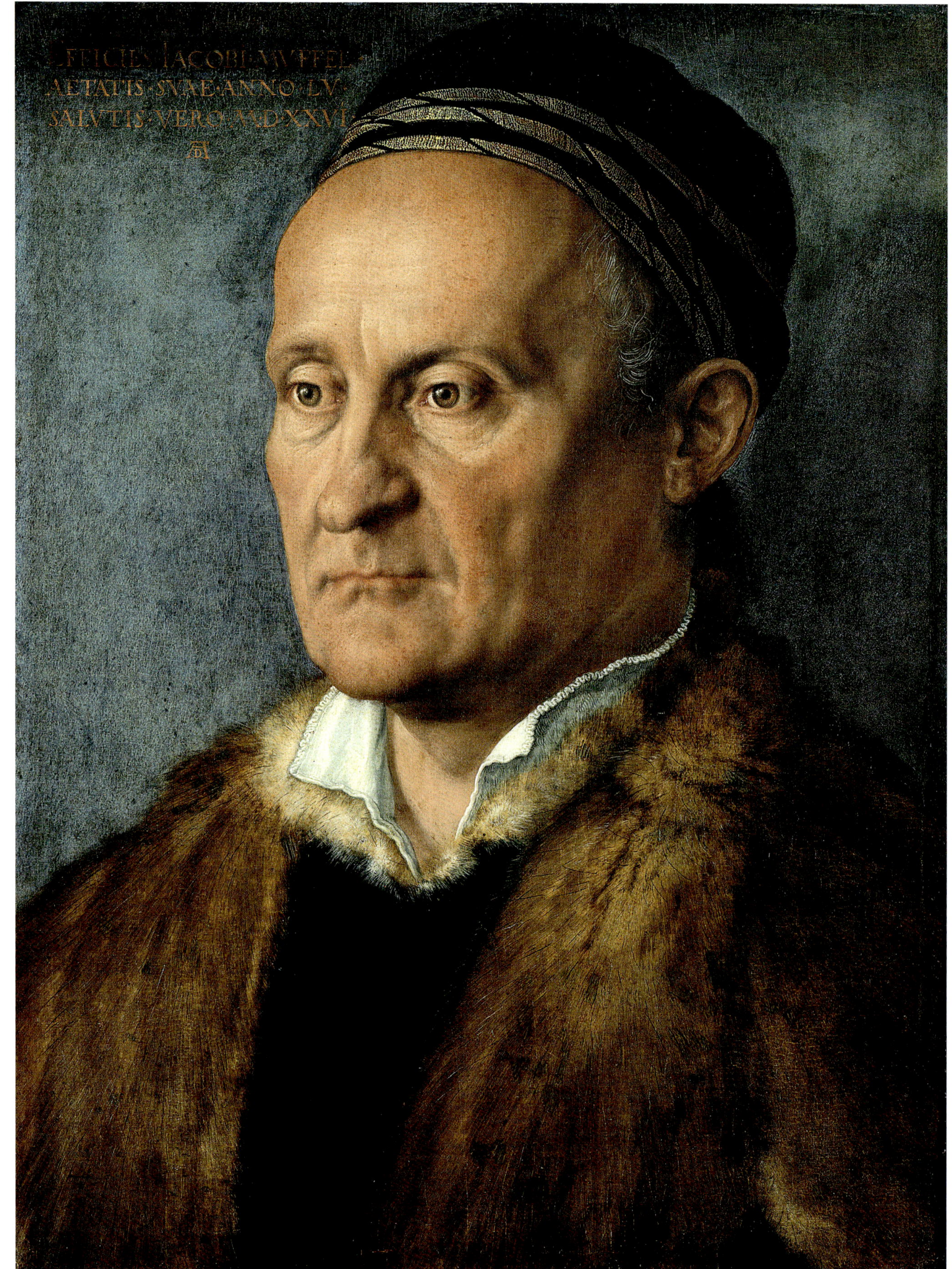

Fig. 34
ALBRECHT DÜRER
Portrait of Jakob Muffel, 1526
Oil on canvas, 48 × 36 cm
Staatliche Museen zu Berlin, Gemäldegalerie

Fig. 35
ALBRECHT DÜRER
Portrait of Hieronymus Holzschuher, 1526
Oil on lime, 51 × 37 cm
Staatliche Museen zu Berlin, Gemäldegalerie

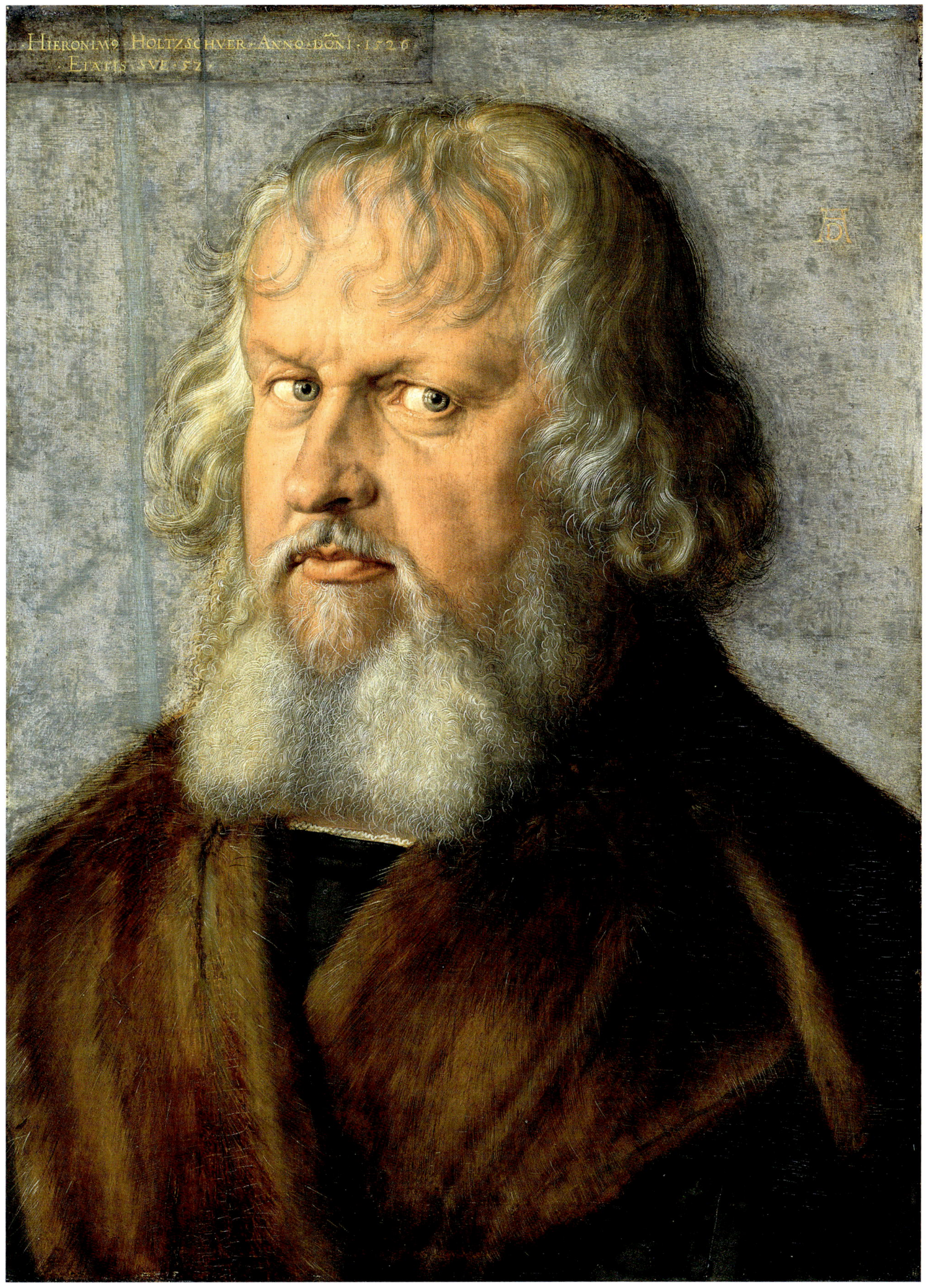
HIERONIMVS HOLTZSCHVER · ANNO · DÕNI · 1526
· ETATIS SVE · 57 ·

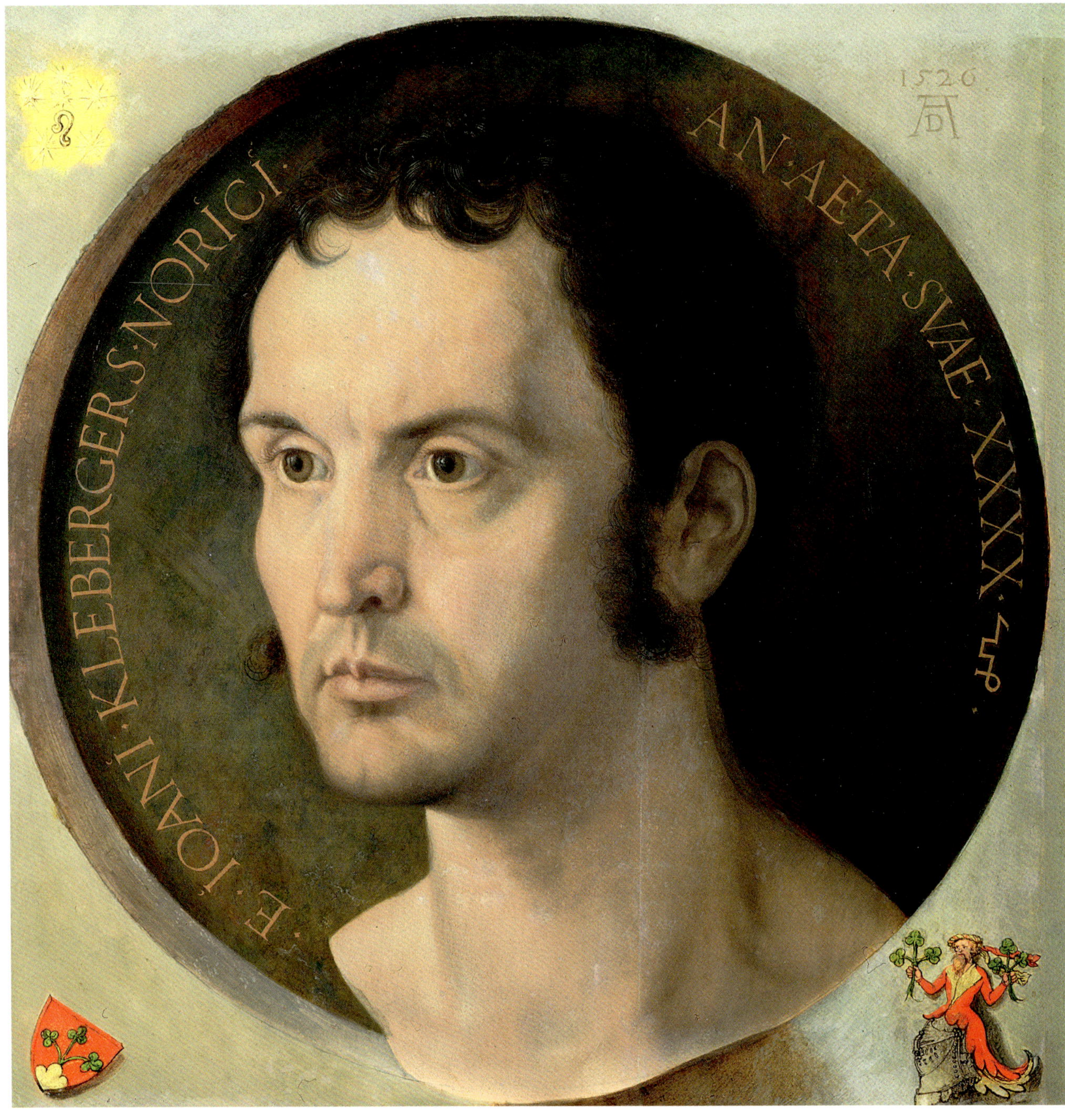

Fig. 36
ALBRECHT DÜRER
Portrait of Johannes Kleberger, 1526
Oil on lime,
36.5 × 36.5 cm
Kunsthistorisches Museum, Vienna

second trip to Italy, foregoes the hands as a pictorial motif. In another painting from the same year, his *Portrait of Hieronymus Holzschuher* (fig. 35),[73] the subject looks out at the viewer while the shadow falling directly behind his head suggests an almost claustrophobic confinement of the pictorial space. Yet in its form the portrait continues the line of development outlined here towards an ever more classical type of portrait. In this regard there is a touch of irony to the fact that it should of all works be the *Portrait of Johannes Kleberger* (fig. 36)[74] that marks the end of Dürer's career as a portrait painter, a painting in which an exceptionally ambitious businessman is set in frame on a feigned medallion and depicted as a portrait bust incarnate. Despite their conscious use of traditional forms, when considered from the perspective of such a trajectory Dürer's portraits from his journey through the Netherlands represent an important milestone in the development of this renowned Nuremberg artist's portraiture.

1 Anzelewsky 1991, vol. 1, no. 162.
2 Kathke 1997, pp. 59–68.
3 See V. Bücken, 'Bernard van Orley. De kunstenaar en zijn artistieke milieu', in Brussels 2019, pp. 29–36, at pp. 30–4.
4 Durer's three large prints known as the *Meisterstiche* or Master Engravings are *The Knight Death and the Devil* (1513), *Melancholia I* (1514) and *Saint Jerome in his Study* (1514).
5 Ashcroft 2017, vol. 1, no. 162, p. 561.
6 Held 1931, pp. 112–26; D. Eichberger, 'Dürer and the Netherlands: Patterns of Exchange and Mutual Admiration', in Silver and Chipps Smith 2010, pp. 149–65, at pp. 158–62.
7 Friedländer 1921, p. 176.
8 Bruges 2010, *passim*.
9 S. Kemperdick, 'Die Gestalt der Menschen nach ihrem Tod bewahren. Bildnismalerei des 15. und 16. Jahrhunderts in Deutschland, Frankreich und den Niederlanden', in Basel 2006, pp. 19–38, at pp. 19–25; K. Schütz, 'Das Unsichtbare sichtbar machen. Deutsche Porträts um 1500', in Vienna and Munich 2011, pp. 13–19, at pp. 15–17.
10 Hess, Hirschfelder, and von Baum 2019, vol. 1, pp. 337–49; Nuremberg 2019, pp. 161–4; Suckale 2009, esp. pp. 103–212; D. Hirschfelder, 'Hans Pleydenwurff und seine Bedeutung für das Schaffen Wolgemuts', in ibid., pp. 37–45, at pp. 42–4; M. Teget-Welz, 'Albrecht Dürer. Die Lehrjahre bei Michael Wolgemut', in ibid., pp. 143–51.
11 On Wolgemut, see Lübbeke 1991, pp. 192–95 and Nuremberg 2019, pp. 264–5. On Bouts, see Campbell 1998, pp. 46–51. On Memling, see Madrid, Bruges and New York 2005; Kemperdick in Basel 2006, pp. 24–5; Schmidt 2018, p. 158, no. 5.
12 Silver 1984, pp. 165–6, 237–40 (cats 61, 64–5).
13 Buchner 1953, pp. 122–52; P. Nuttall, 'Hans Memling und das europäische Portrait der Renaissance', in Madrid, Bruges and New York 2005, p. 91; Basel 2006, pp. 48–51; Schmidt 2018, pp. 92–8; Nuremberg 2019, pp. 263–7.
14 Anzelewsky 1991, vol. 1, no. 2.
15 D. Hirschfelder, 'Dürers frühe Privat- und Auftragsbildnisse zwischen Tradition und Innovation', in Nuremberg 2012, pp. 102–6.
16 S. Buck, 'Art and Nature: Dürer's Early Travel Years, 1490–95', in London 2013, pp. 13–35, at pp. 19–20, conjectures that Dürer passed through the central Rhine region and Cologne.
17 In this context, see Susan Foister's article in the present volume, pp. 61–75; B. Aikema, 'The Lure of the North: Netherlandish Art in Venetian Collections', in Venice 1999, pp. 82–91, at pp. 84–9.
18 Anzelewsky 1991, vol. 1, no. 10.
19 Buchner 1953, pp. 140–1, no. 157; Dülberg 1990, pp. 191–2, no. 48; Schmidt 2018, pp. 163–4, no. 7.
20 Anzelewsky 1991, vol. 1, no. 49.
21 In Memling, too, one looks down onto a landscape: Madrid, Bruges and New York 2005, nos 15, 18, 23.
22 Eser 2011, 166–72.
23 If Dürer did in fact complete his Berlin portrait of Frederick the Wise during the latter's stay in Nuremberg in April 1496, the *Tüchlein* marks the beginning of the artist's career as a portraitist and must be considered a precursor to the Madrid self portrait. See L. Silver, 'Civic Courtship: Albrecht Dürer, the Saxon Duke, and the Emperor', in Silver and Chipps Smith 2010, pp. 130–48, at pp. 131–2. The date is anything but certain, however, and was fixed most recently at around 1500. On the portraits of the young women see Frankfurt, Leipzig and Berlin 2006, *passim*.
24 Anzelewsky 1991, vol. 1, no. 45.
25 Ibid., no. 46.
26 Ibid., no. 49.
27 Ibid., no. 63.
28 Ibid., nos 60–2.
29 See Memling's wedding portrait, his Benedetto Portinari triptych – in which the landscape continues across all the panels – and his portrait of a donor in the Thyssen-Bornemisza museum (see Madrid, Bruges and New York 2005, pp. 118–19, 143, 145, nos 5, 25). Memling's portraits served as a model for a wedding portrait of Berthold and Christina Tucher completed in 1484 by a successor to Pleydenwurff, a painting with which Dürer and his patrons were familiar (Buchner 1953, pp. 176–8, no. 200). Schmidt 2018, pp. 92–8, 213–20, nos 25–7.
30 Anzelewsky 1991, vol. 1, no. 56.
31 Goldberg, Heimberg and Schawe 1998, pp. 237–59; K. Schütz, 'Gestalt und Geist. Albrecht Dürer als Porträtist', in Vienna and Munich 2011, pp. 79–84, at p. 79; Schmidt 2018, p. 209, no. 24.
32 Anzelewsky 1991, vol. 1, no. 93.
33 Ibid., no. 97.
34 Ibid., no. 163.
35 Ibid., nos 92, 95.
36 Kunsthistorisches Museum, Gemäldegalerie, Vienna, inv. GG 6440 (Anzelewsky 1991, vol 1, no. 92).
37 Anzelewsky 1991, vol. 1, no. 96.
38 Ibid., nos 99–101. C. Metzger in Vienna and Munich 2011, p. 89, no. 41.
39 Winkler 1936–9, vol. 2, no. 431. M.L. Sternath in Vienna 2003, pp. 386–97, no. 127.
40 Winkler 1936–9, vol. 2, nos 361, 362. H. Mielke in Basel and Berlin 1997, pp. 154–5, no. 10.27; M.L. Sternath in Vienna 2003, pp. 482–3, no. 169.
41 Dürer now took to sketching portraits in charcoal, as with the portrait of his mother (Winkler 1936–9, vol. 3, no. 559).
42 Anzelewsky 1991, vol. 1, no. 133.
43 Ibid., no. 132.
44 Löcher 1997, pp. 210–12; Goldberg, Heimberg and Schawe 1998, pp. 417–29; M. Teget-Welz in Nuremberg 2019, pp. 155–7, no. 1.
45 Schauerte 2001, pp. 87–104; Vienna 2003, pp. 448–68; Vienna 2012, pp. 258–9; Vienna 2019, pp. 386–91.
46 On Dürer's portrait drawings, see Peter van den Brink's article in the present volume, pp. 205–25.
47 Winkler 1936–9, vol. 3, no. 571.
48 Ibid., nos 563–6.
49 Anzelewsky 1991, vol. 1, no. 143. In this connection see M. Roth in Berlin 2006, pp. 164–5, no. 108. On the painting's attribution, see Goldberg, Heimberg and Schawe 1998, pp. 463–9, and E. Michels in Vienna 2012, p. 322.
50 Silver 2008, pp. 211–14; F. Polleroß, 'Tradition und Innovation. Kaiser Maximilian I. im Porträt', in Vienna 2012, p. 110; Vienna 2012, pp. 292–4; C. Metzger in Vienna 2019, pp. 380–5, no. 173.
51 Löcher 1997, pp. 213–16.
52 Ibid., p. 214; Vienna 2003, p. 474; Silver 2008, pp. 211–12 n. 145.
53 Vienna 2003, pp. 470–4; Silver 2008, pp. 211–14; Vienna 2019, pp. 380–3.
54 Ashcroft 2017, vol. 1, no. 162, p. 584. See Dagmar Eichberger's article in the present volume, pp. 119–27.
55 See Peter van den Brink's article in the present volume, pp. 205–25.
56 Ashcroft 2017, vol. 1, no. 162, p. 577.
57 On the de Almada drawing (Winkler 1936–9, vol. 3, no. 813), see H. Mielke in Anzelewsky and Mielke 1984, pp. 108–9, no. 105; Düsseldorf 1991, pp. 106–7, no. 41; M. Roth in Berlin 2006, pp. 150–1, no. 94; Koreny 2008, pp. 334–5. On the drawings of the Antwerp Mannerists, see P. van den Brink in Antwerp and Maastricht 2005, nos 30–8, 43–5, 47–56, 59–61, 63, as well as van den Brink 2006 and D. Ewing, P. van den Brink and C. Scailliérez in Paris 2017, nos 6, 9–12, 15, 17–19, 24. On Jan Gossaert, see especially S. Alsteens in New York and London 2010, nos 64, 70, 84, 94–7. On Jan de Beer, see Ewing 2016, pp. 89–127, nos 29–31, 34, 36, 37, 39; Ewing 2016, no. C9; P. van den Brink in Birmingham 2019, nos 5–7; P. van den Brink, 'In Pursuit of the Individual Hand: Jan de Beer as a Draughtsman', in ibid., pp. 27–32.
58 Ashcroft 2017, vol. 1, no. 162, p. 571.
59 Ashcroft 2017, vol. 1, no. 162, p. 576.
60 Friedländer 1921, p. 180; Koreny 2008, pp. 334–5.
61 Ashcroft 2017, vol. 1, no. 162, pp. 577–8. On Dürer's stay in Bruges, see T.-H. Borchert, 'Die Entdeckung der Brügger Malerei', in Bruges 1998, pp. 15–21, at p. 15. On van Eyck's panels in the chapel of the Bruges painters' guild, see Hindriks 2019, pp. 178–83. The goldsmith Marc de Glasere, with whom Dürer stayed while in Bruges, may have facilitated the artist seeing the works by van Eyck outside a public context. On the possible guild context for the portrait of Jan de Leeuw, see Borchert 2012, pp. 220–1; for Bruges sources regarding the person of Marc de Glasere, see Muylaert 2011–12, pp. 164–6.
62 Anzelewsky 1991, vol. 1, no. 165.
63 See ibid., vol. 1, pp. 262–3, no. 165; M. Sellink in Bruges 2010, no. 238; J. Zaunbauer in Vienna 2019, p. 402.
64 Ashcroft 2017, vol. 1, no. 162, p. 572. Dürer estimates the value of the portrait – 'a portrait head on the small panel' – at 6 stuivers, thus only a fraction of the sum he was paid for his portrait of Bernhard von Reesen (8 florins = 160 stuivers). In this case the portrait is more likely to have been a drawing.
65 Winkler 1936–9, vol. 3, no. 774.
66 Ashcroft 2017, vol. 1, no. 162, pp. 580, 586.
67 Winkler 1936–9, vol. 4, no. 747.
68 Ashcroft 2017, vol. 1, no. 162, p. 580. The price exceeds that of the von Reesen portrait by such a margin as to justify doubts raised as to whether the Madrid panel is in fact the portrait of Lorenz Sterk that Dürer mentions.
69 Koreny 2008, pp. 336–7; Vienna 2019, p. 402.
70 Ashcroft 2017, vol. 1, no. 162, p. 557.
71 Anzelewsky 1991, vol. 1, no. 148.
72 Ibid., no. 178.
73 Ibid., no. 179.
74 Ibid., no. 182.

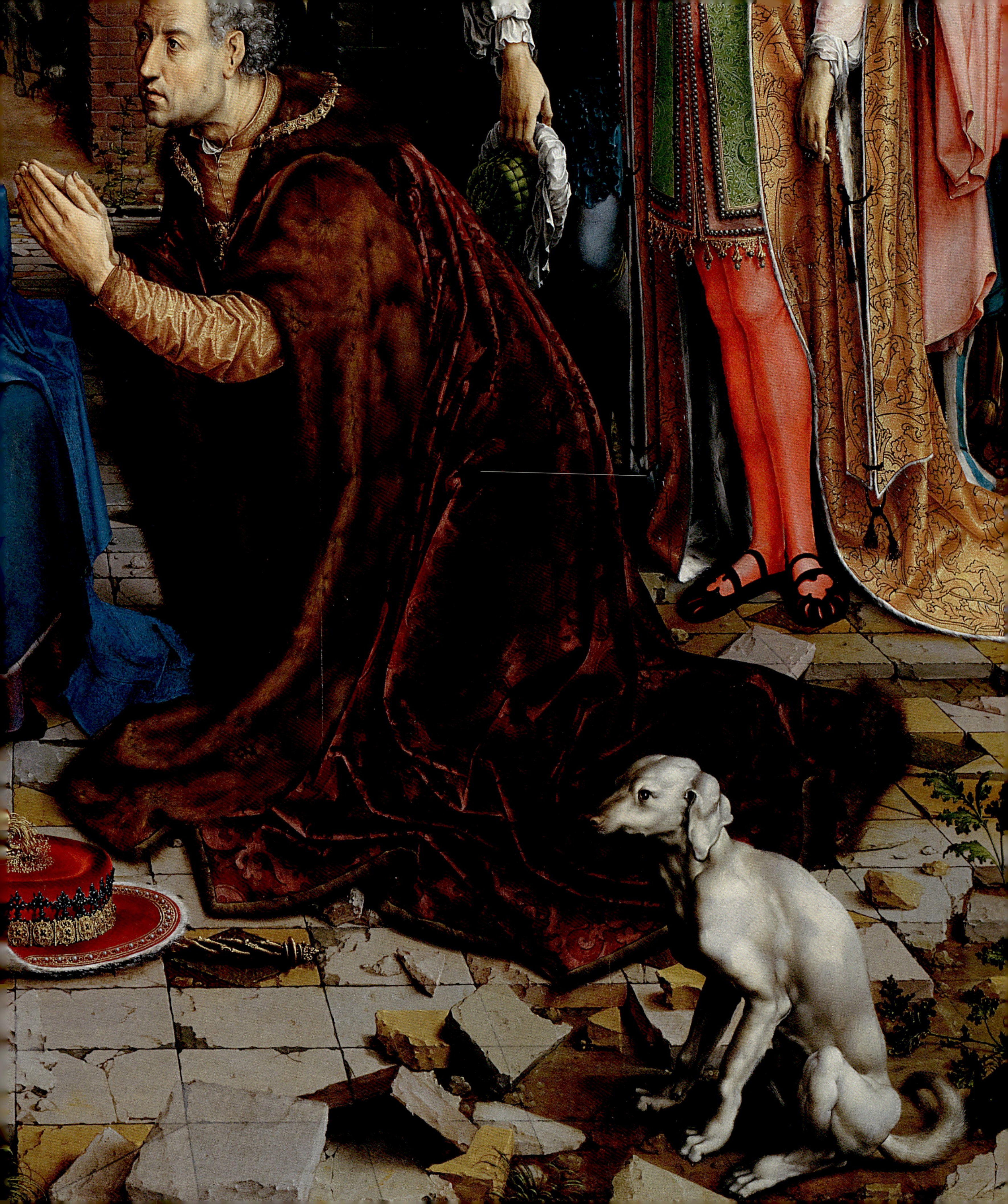

LARRY SILVER

DÜRER AND GOSSAERT

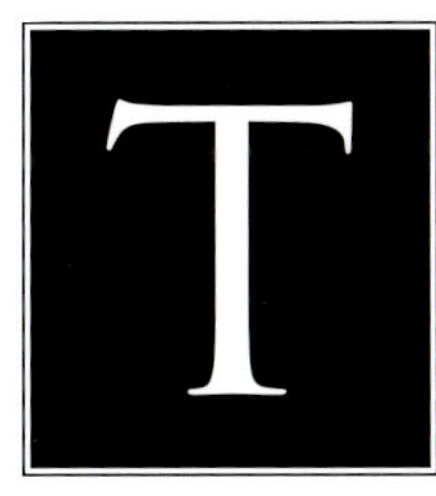

HE MANY ARTISTS OF THE MAJOR port metropolis of Antwerp welcomed Albrecht Dürer as a conquering hero when he visited their city in 1520–1. Of course, many of these individuals were already quite familiar with Dürer's more public art through his widely circulated prints, which he brought with him and distributed widely in Antwerp.[1] But their encounter in person with the celebrity artist from Nuremberg, in an atmosphere of 'exchange and mutual admiration', also marked a watershed experience for Netherlandish art-making and sparked a lasting influence for some leading individual artists in Antwerp.[2] Conspicuously absent from these interactions was Jan Gossaert (also known as Mabuse), whose large Middelburg Altarpiece (lost in a 1568 fire) Dürer clearly admired: 'in the [Middelburg] Abbey Jan Gossaert has painted a great altar panel, not as good in terms of the modelling of the heads as in its use of colour.'[3] In fact Gossaert's painting is the only contemporary work by any Flemish master that Dürer even mentions in his journal, alongside his passing references to older paintings, including the famous Ghent Altarpiece by Jan van Eyck.[4] Gossaert's own fame, particularly through this masterwork, must by the time of Dürer's visit already have been well assured in order to attract that kind of unique attention and commentary.

Both the pictorial ambition of Gossaert, the artist from Maubeuge, as well as Dürer's hint of personal rivalry with this lone contemporary are clearly signalled through his appreciative yet also critical remark. Indeed, Dürer surely appreciated the degree to which the forms of the figures in Gossaert's altarpiece echoed his own, although 'great' in this case chiefly points to the massive size of the painting. However, Dürer the critic still manages to find some fault in the rendering of Gossaert's own active, robust figures. We can also measure Dürer's admiration in the light of his own frustrated earlier remarks in letters about his own laborious effort on the Heller Altarpiece (1507–9, also lost). Certainly he could appreciate Gossaert's effort expended on the Middelburg

OPPOSITE
JAN GOSSAERT, detail from *The Adoration of the Kings* (cat. 49)

painting, particularly in relation to colour. Writing to his patron in the summer of 1509, he lamented:

> I put all my skill into it, as you will see, and it's painted with the finest colours I was able to get. It is underpainted, overpainted, and fine-finished with good quality ultramarine, five or six times over … I am sure nobody will criticise it, unless to annoy me. And I firmly believe it will please you. No one shall ever be able to persuade me again to paint a picture involving so much work … So I shall get back to my engraving – and if I'd done that all this time, I'd be 1000 fl. richer today.[5]

Across his own career, Albrecht Dürer was primarily known as a graphic artist, one who enjoyed European-wide fame for his virtuoso prints, both engravings and woodcuts; by contrast, Gossaert, his younger potential rival in Middelburg, was best known as a painter and draughtsman. Moreover, as we shall see, Gossaert engaged intensively with the art of Dürer, especially after the German's visit in 1520–1. Of all the Netherlandish artists of his time, Jan Gossaert was the one most thoroughly steeped in the Renaissance idiom of powerful and beautiful bodies.[6] For his muscular figures, whether of Jesus or of newly adopted classical mythological subjects, and for his preternaturally full-bodied ideals of the Virgin and Child, Gossaert demonstrably depended on Dürer models, chiefly based on his widespread medium of prints – before, during and, especially, after Dürer's trip to the Netherlands in 1520–1.

Enrolled in the Antwerp guild in 1503, Gossaert soon attracted the courtly patronage of Philip of Burgundy (1464–1524), illegitimate son of Philip the Good (1396–1467), Admiral of Zeeland, and after 1517 Bishop of Utrecht until his death. Philip's influence on the artist was formative early: Gossaert had already travelled with Philip in 1508 to Rome, where he received early exposure to the same classical roots as Dürer's own figures.[7] Additionally, Philip's patronage included commissions from Gossaert for a number of mythological subjects, with erotic interactions between Olympian gods with perfectly formed bodies.[8]

Reinforcing Dürer's influence in the wake of his 1521 visit, according to Karel van Mander in 1604, Gossaert also met Lucas van Leyden in person, when the North Netherlandish artist visited Middelburg, possibly in 1526–7. Van Mander states that

> When Lucas was 33 years old he had the urge to visit the painters of Zeeland, Flanders, and Brabant … Arriving in Middelburg, he took pleasure in studying the works of the industrious and artistic Jan de Mabuse, who was living there at the time and had executed various works there.[9]

Since Lucas's precise year of birth is unknown, and van Mander was writing some eight decades later, the year in which the artists met cannot be determined with any certainty.[10] Like Dürer, Lucas himself was already renowned as a printmaker of both engravings and woodcuts in the nearby Northern Netherlands, and his art was also strongly shaped by Dürer models. Lucas's prints also would have been readily available to Gossaert well before the two artists actually met.

Across his career, Gossaert's own art oscillates between his use of two opposing models. On the one hand he draws upon art of the previous century in the Low Countries, especially that of Jan van Eyck and Rogier van der Weyden. For example, Gossaert literally copied the main holy figures from van Eyck's Ghent Altarpiece and he also emulated Rogier's devotional diptychs with donors and holy figures painted against monochrome backgrounds.[11] Yet for his alternative, Renaissance figural ambitions Gossaert instead emulated Dürer and other Italianate imagery of his own era, including sculpture by Conrad Meit at the court of Regent Margaret of Austria in nearby Mechelen.[12]

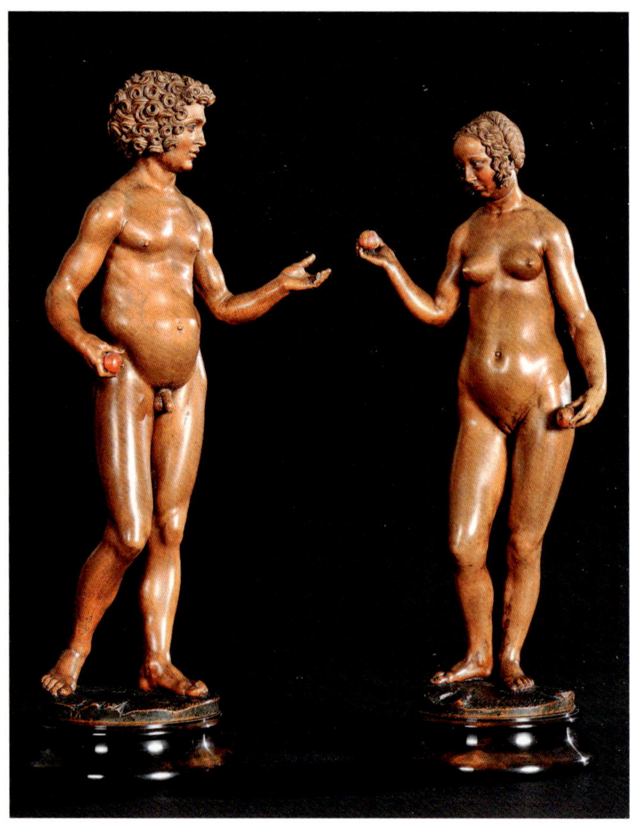

48
CONRAD MEIT
(1480–1550/1)
Adam and Eve, 1515
Glazed boxwood,
Adam: 36 × 15.8 × 9 cm;
Eve: 33.7 × 14.5 × 5.3 cm
Stiftung Schloss
Friedenstein Gotha

'in the [Middelburg] Abbey Jan Gossart has painted a great altar panel, not as good in terms of the modelling of the heads as in its use of colour.'

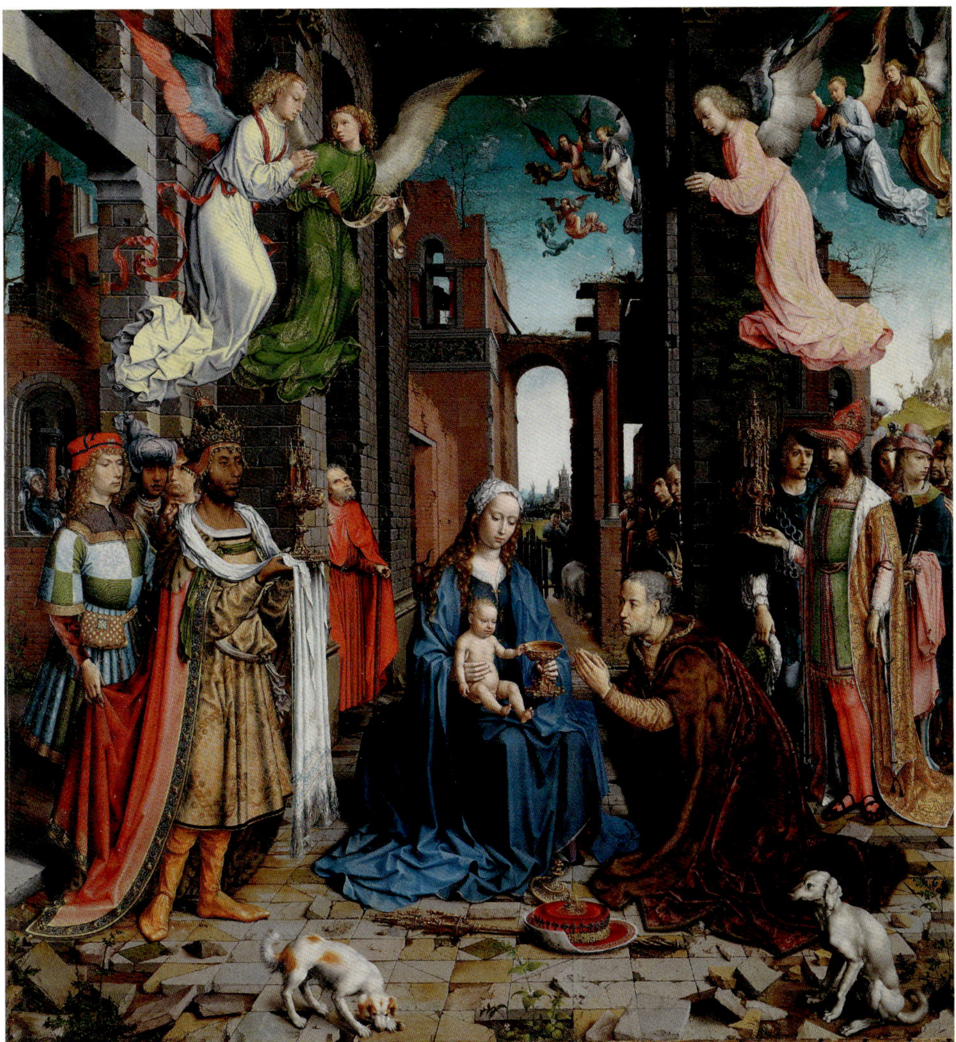

49
JAN GOSSAERT
(active 1508; died 1532)
The Adoration of the Kings,
1510–15
Oil on oak, 179.8 × 163.2 cm
The National Gallery, London

Fig. 37
HUGO VAN DER GOES
(active 1467; died 1482)
The Adoration of the Magi (for the Montforte Altarpiece), about 1470
Oil on oak, 147 × 242 cm
Staatliche Museen zu Berlin, Gemäldegalerie

Gossaert's interest in Dürer actually began early, in both drawings and paintings. He began by chiefly using individual figures and motifs derived from Dürer prints. One remarkable early large-scale painting even combines Gossaert's careful emulation of Early Netherlandish models with inclusion of a single new motif, derived from a noted Dürer engraving. His *Adoration of the Kings* (cat. 49) was almost certainly completed after his 1508 trip to Rome but still based on a major fifteenth-century work of the same subject by Hugo van der Goes, the Montforte Altarpiece of about 1470 (fig. 37). Into the lower right corner Gossaert inserted a distinctive, additional hunting dog, which enhances the splendour of the three kings' entourage. The hound closely derives from Dürer's undated but meticulous turn-of-the-century engraving, *Saint Eustace* (cat. 50), in which the saint is startled into

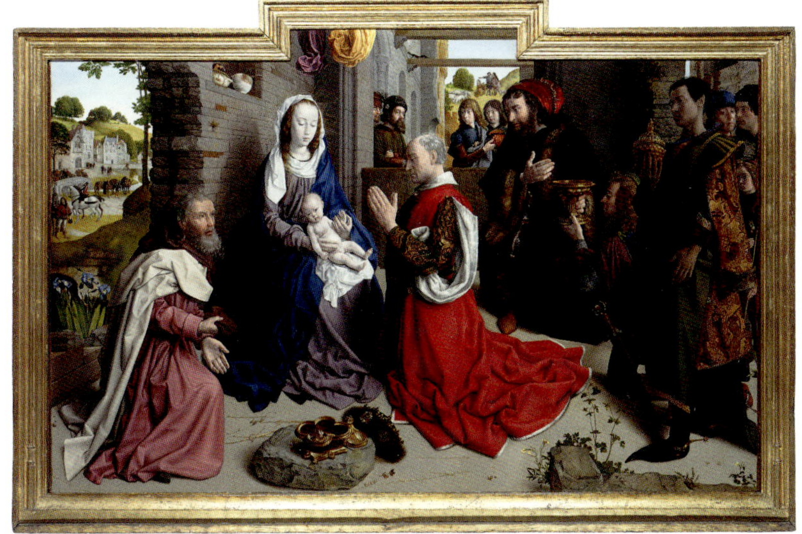

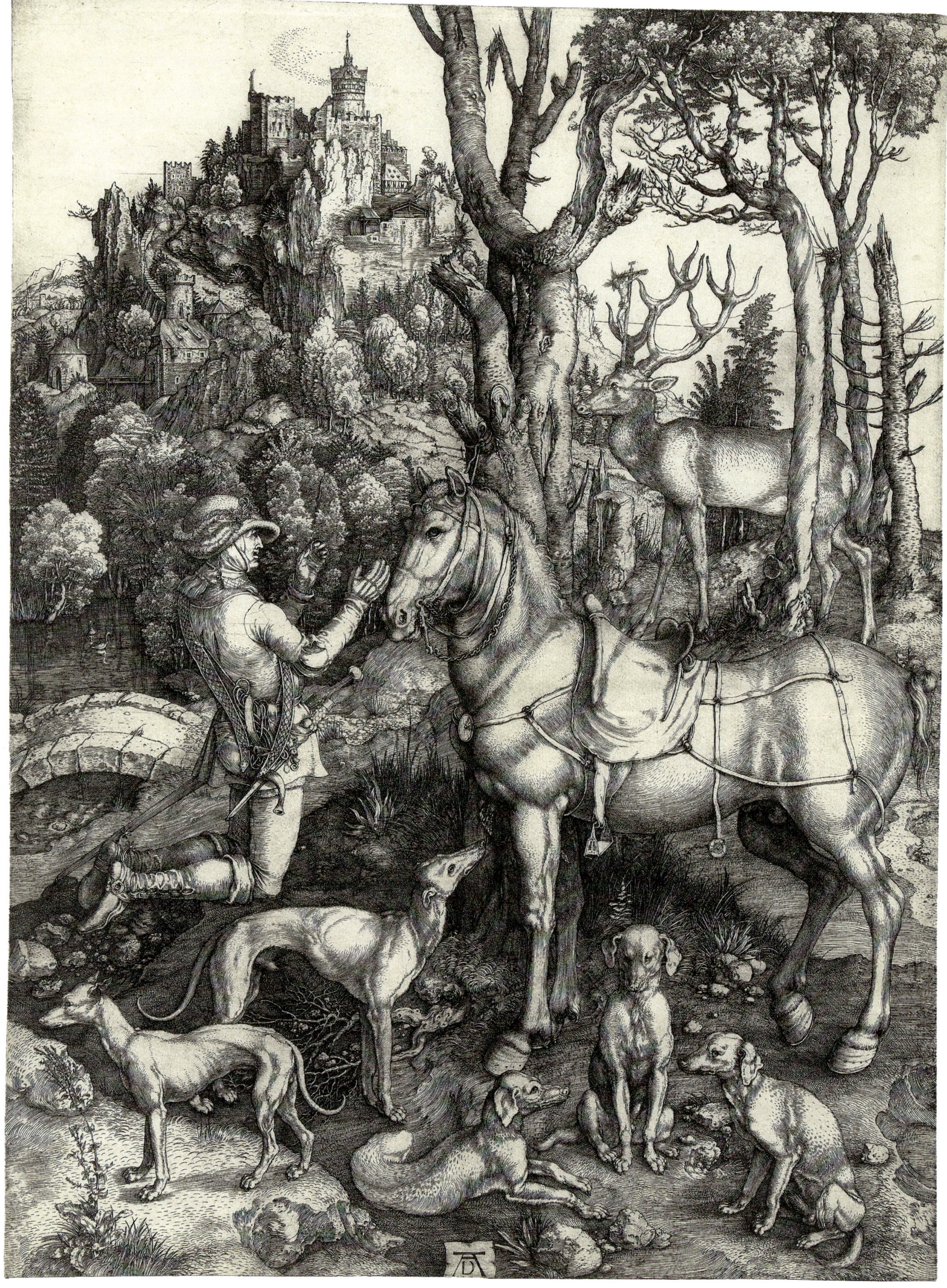

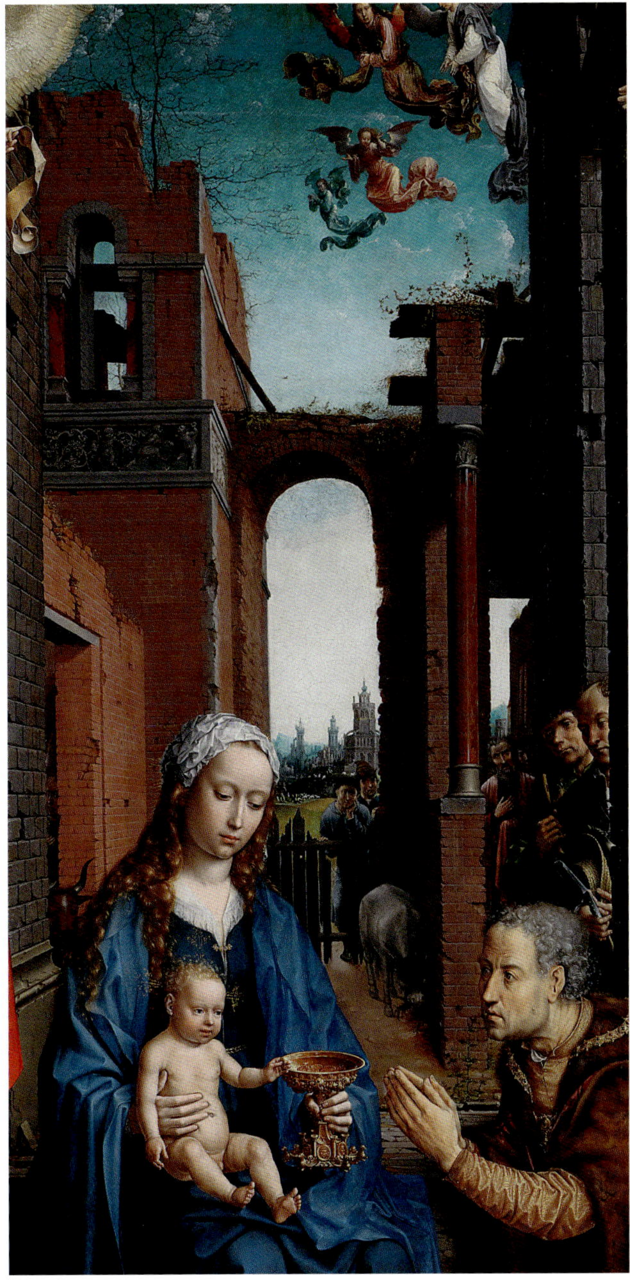

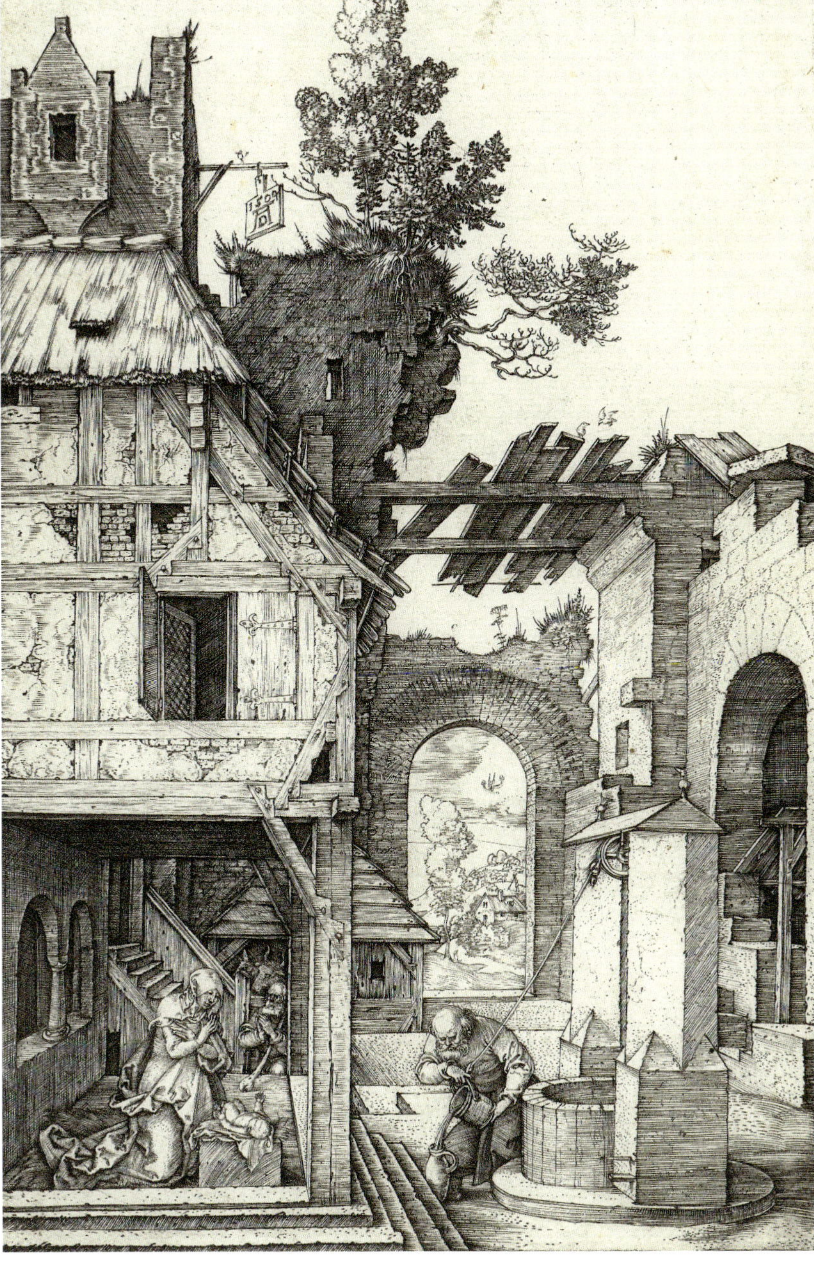

an epiphany and conversion, falling to his knees while on a hunt with his dogs after beholding a crucifix between the horns of a stag, his quarry.[13] Although the hound is only an accessory figure within Gossaert's richly detailed panel, this corner motif shows him attending closely to a Dürer source at a formative stage of his career. Moreover, the sharply receding centralised perspective of the ruined setting remains unique for Gossaert. This construction derives directly from another Dürer print: a bold experiment with deep linear recession in his 1504 *Nativity* engraving (fig. 38).

Also early in his career, Gossaert had derived heroic nude figural types from Dürer, especially in a small painted panel (cat. 51) that closely copies Dürer's 1504

OPPOSITE
50
ALBRECHT DÜRER
Saint Eustace, about 1499–1503
Engraving, 35.9 × 26.1 cm
Rijksmuseum, Amsterdam

ABOVE
JAN GOSSAERT
Details from *The Adoration of the Kings* (cat. 49)

Fig. 38
ALBRECHT DÜRER
Nativity, 1504
Engraving, 17.7 × 12 cm
Rijksmuseum, Amsterdam
(RP-P-OB-1157)

Adam and Eve engraving (cat. 52).[14] A few years later Gossaert painted a close variation on Dürer's recent 1510 *Adam and Eve* woodcut from the *Small Passion* (fig. 39) to form the exterior wings of his Malvagna Triptych of about 1513–15 (fig. 40).[15] While he reversed the direction of the two full-bodied figures, Gossaert closely copies their intertwined, erotic pose, as Eve holds up the fateful apple and Adam reaches up to pluck one of his own. During the 1520s Gossaert would later explore ideal nudes in both drawings and paintings of the First Parents and the Fall, expanding on these early lessons that he had learned from Dürer, as well as from Dürer-influenced woodcuts of the Fall by Hans Baldung Grien (1484/5–1545), which further expand upon both the physicality and the eroticism of that theme.[16]

Stijn Alsteens has further revealed how Gossaert's early works on paper rework details from Dürer's prints, chiefly as motifs of figures, of curly-haired males in profile, or of compositional spaces.[17] For one such setting, Alsteens convincingly compares the basic arrangement of figures and setting in Gossaert's early pen drawing, *The Mystic Marriage of Saint Catherine* of about 1503–8 (Statens Museum for Kunst, Copenhagen),[18] demonstrating its development – allowing for slight reversals, especially of the Virgin and Child – from Dürer's almost contemporary woodcut of about 1502,

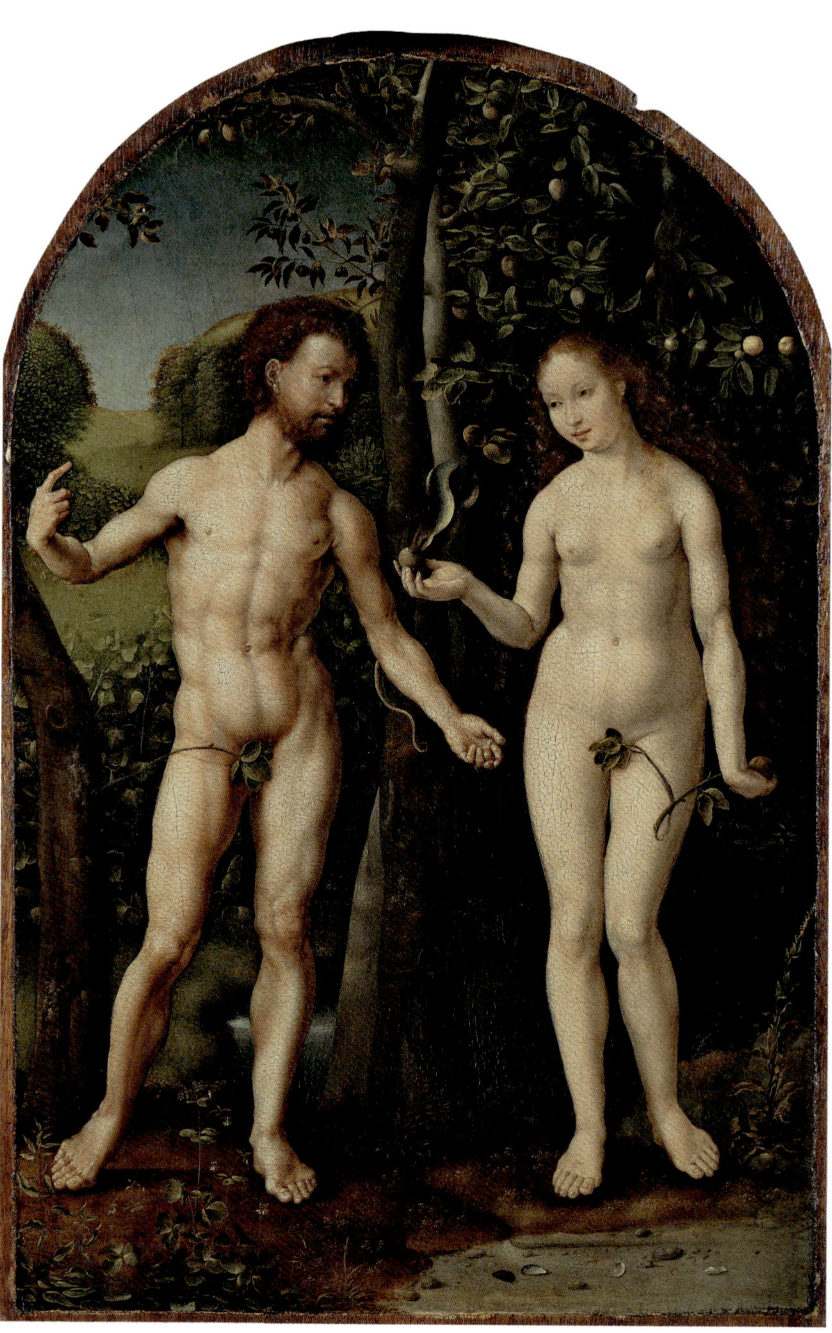

51
JAN GOSSAERT
(active 1508; died 1532)
Adam and Eve, about 1507–8
Oil on board, 56.5 × 37 cm
Museo Nacional Thyssen-Bornemisza, Madrid

OPPOSITE
52
ALBRECHT DÜRER
Adam and Eve, 1504
Engraving, 25.1 × 19.2 cm
Rijksmuseum, Amsterdam

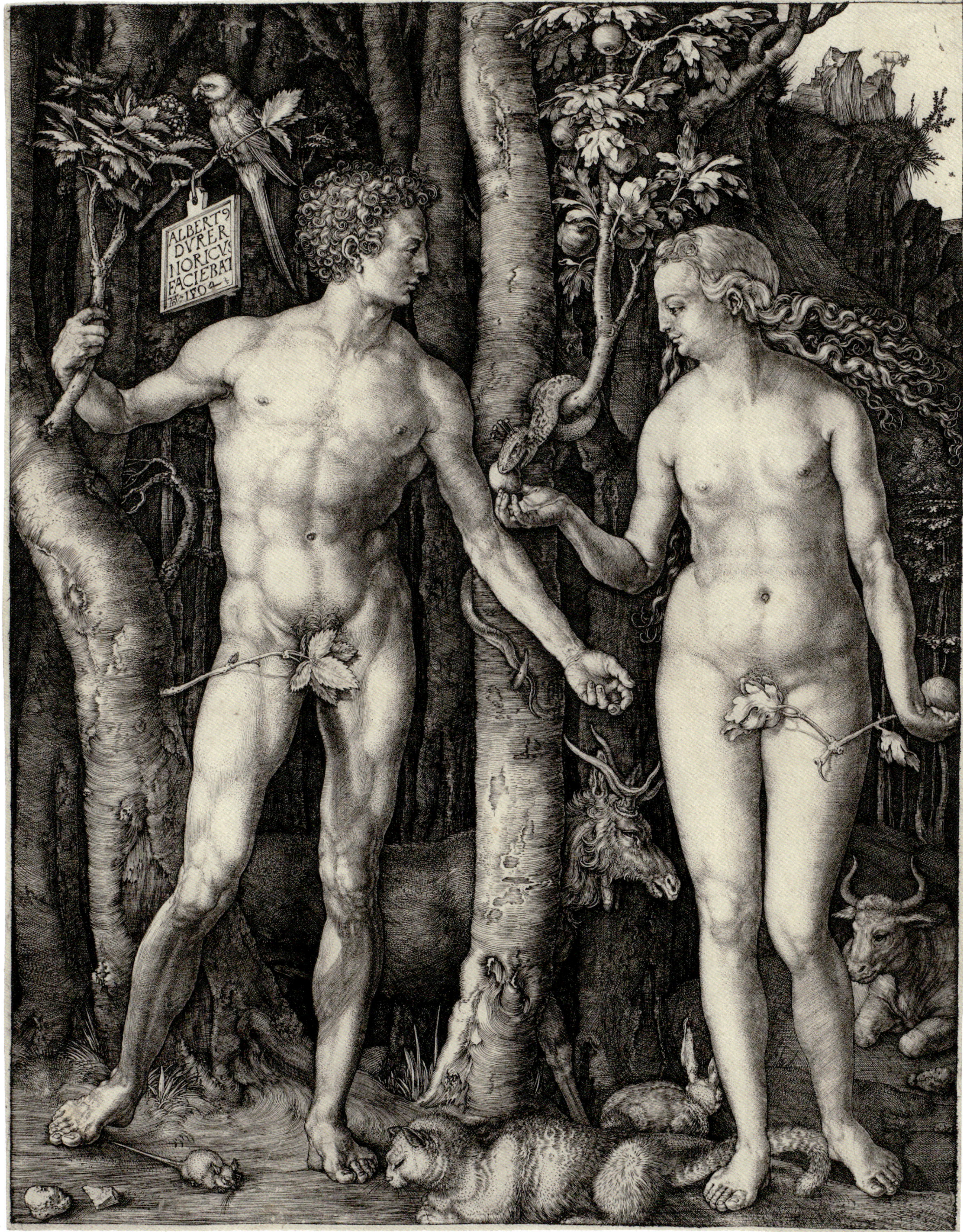
ALBERTꝰ
DVRER
NORICVS
FACIEBAT
AD 1504

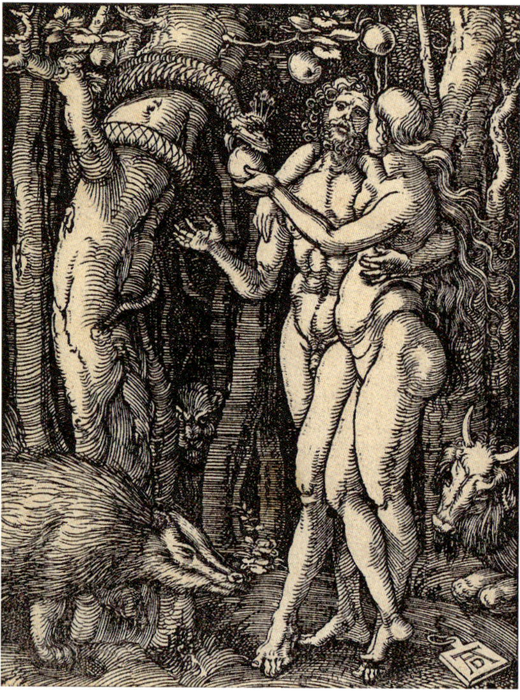

Fig. 39
ALBRECHT DÜRER
Adam and Eve, from the *Small Passion*, about 1510
Woodcut, 12.8 × 9.8 cm
The Metropolitan Museum of Art, New York. The George Khuner Collection, Gift of Mrs George Khuner, 1975 (1975.653.23)

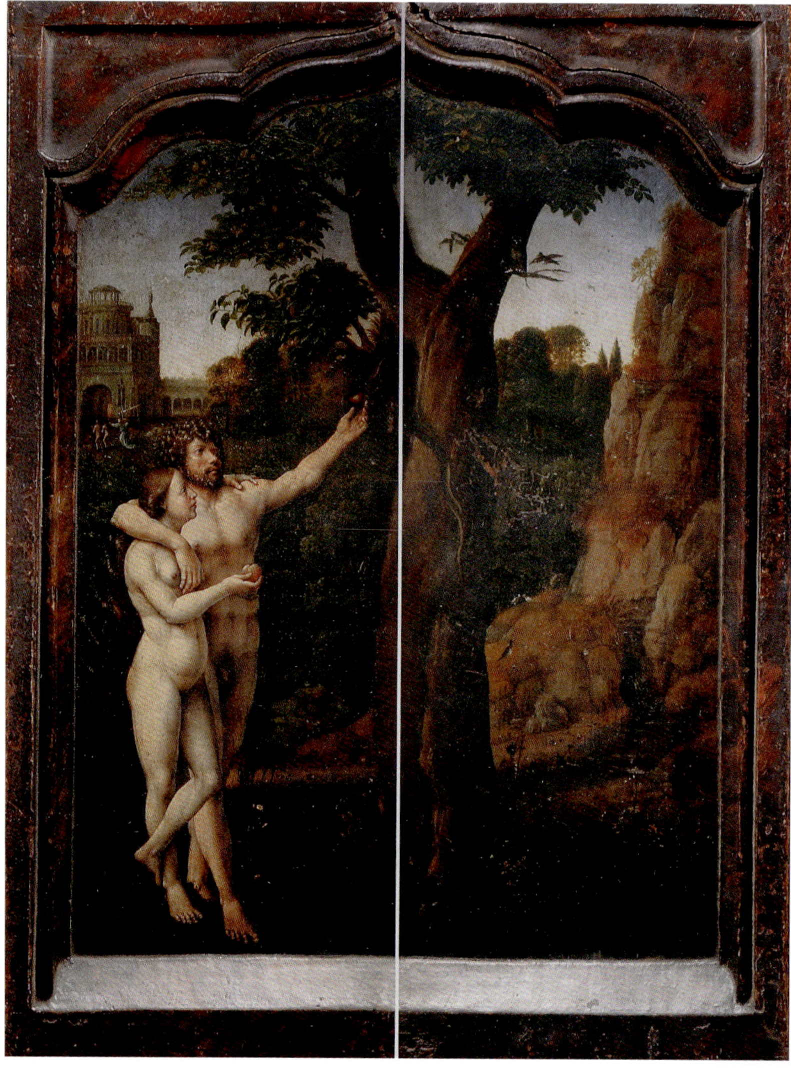

Fig. 40
JAN GOSSAERT
(active 1508; died 1532)
The Fall of Men, from the Malvagna Triptych, about 1513–15
Oil on panel,
45 × 17 cm, each wing
Galleria Interdisciplinare Regionale della Sicilia di Palazzo Abatellis, Palermo

The Glorification of the Virgin, from his Life of the Virgin series. Most of Gossaert's early drawings, however, are much closer to local trends in contemporary Antwerp painting, especially the movement known as 'Antwerp Mannerism'.[19]

That trend in Gossaert's output changed dramatically in the wake of the watershed years of 1520–1. Thereafter, more consistently influenced by Dürer, he drew extensively upon the distinctive full bodies and broad faces of Dürer's Madonna and Child images. Gossaert was particularly inspired by Dürer's recent, mature prints of the holy figures produced in the 1510s, closer in the time to Dürer's own trip to the Low Countries, including: *Virgin and Child under a Tree* of 1513 (fig. 41); *The Virgin and Child crowned by Two Angels* of 1518; and *The Virgin nursing the Christ Child* of 1519 (fig. 42).[20] Thus a significant Dürer influence, especially for Madonna and Child imagery, was readily available when Gossaert set out during the 1520s to paint his own numerous versions of those same holy figures in tender intimacy. Gossaert's nursing *Virgin and Child,* now in Münster, provides a good measure of how much he derived from Dürer's models, particularly the 1518 *Virgin and Child crowned by Two Angels*.[21] Like Dürer, Gossaert shows the Virgin bare-headed, her flowing, centrally parted hair framing her fleshy oval face. She tilts her head towards the curly-haired Christ Child, whose chubby, rounded body suggests an infantile power that Gossaert would elsewhere amplify into firm muscularity. Both figures are pale-skinned, redolent of their purity and perfection even in painted colours. Without any signs of their heavenly status, such as haloes or accompanying angels, Gossaert's robust half-length figures, captured in a physical moment of maternal intimacy, are signalled as sacred chiefly through the Latin prayer inscribed on the original frame. Basing his imagery of holy figures on their perfect human bodies, and taking his cue from Dürer models, Gossaert largely eliminated traditional signs and symbols of their heavenly transcendence.

Gossaert painted another tender vision of the holy figures, this time at full length, in his *Saint Luke drawing the Virgin* of about 1520–2 (fig. 45). Here again he incorporated elements from several engravings by Dürer on the theme of the apocalyptic Virgin in the Sun, especially his 1514 *Virgin and Child on a Crescent Moon* (fig. 44).[22] Dürer represents the Virgin wearing only a cape, without the crown and sceptre of his own more conventional reprise of the same subject in 1516.[23] In his Vienna painting Gossaert in turn adopts Dürer's linear graphics of radiant haloes, fashioning a golden glow with surrounding clouds behind the visionary figures to underscore their supernatural nature. Moreover, here he

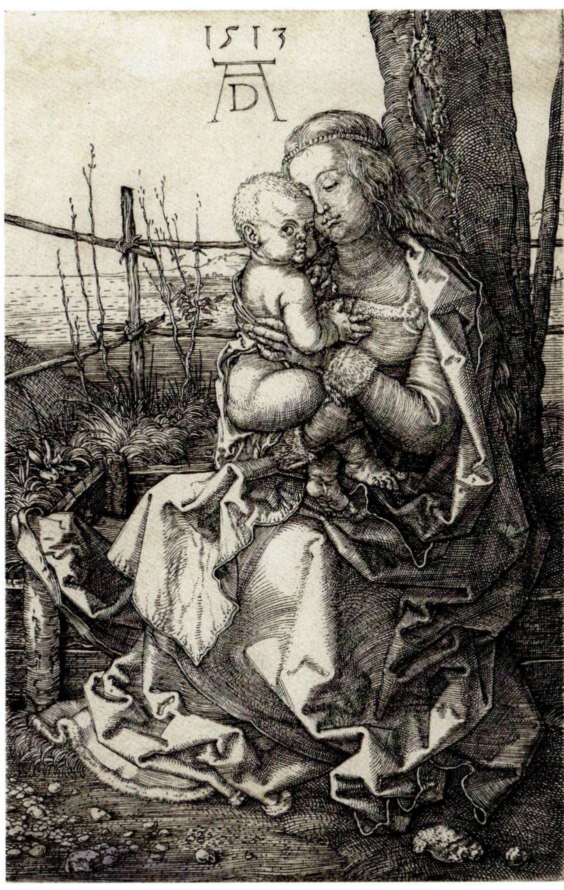

Fig. 41
ALBRECHT DÜRER
Virgin and Child under a Tree, 1513
Engraving, 11.8 × 7.6 cm
Städtische Sammlung Aachen,
Suermondt-Ludwig-Museum (DK 1830)

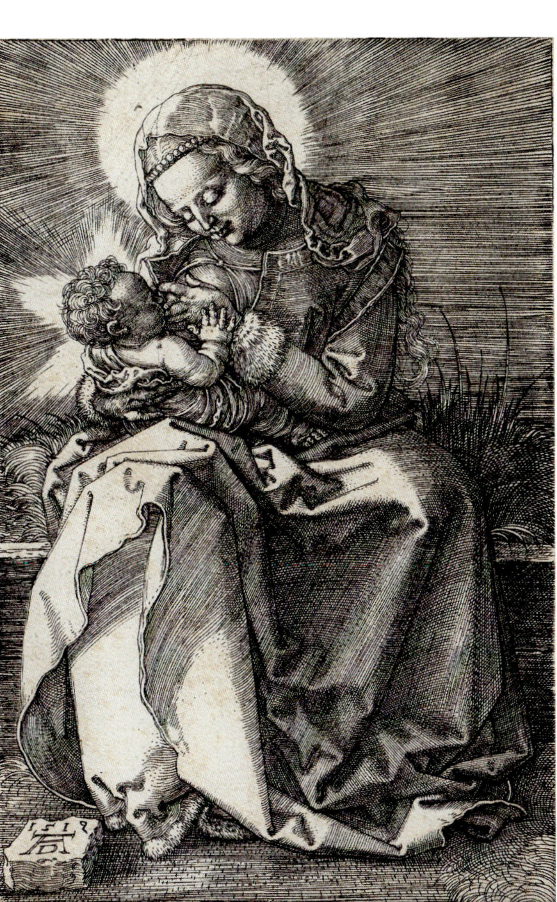

Fig. 42
ALBRECHT DÜRER
The Virgin nursing the Christ Child, 1519
Engraving, 11.8 × 7.6 cm
Städtische Sammlung Aachen,
Suermondt-Ludwig-Museum (DK 695)

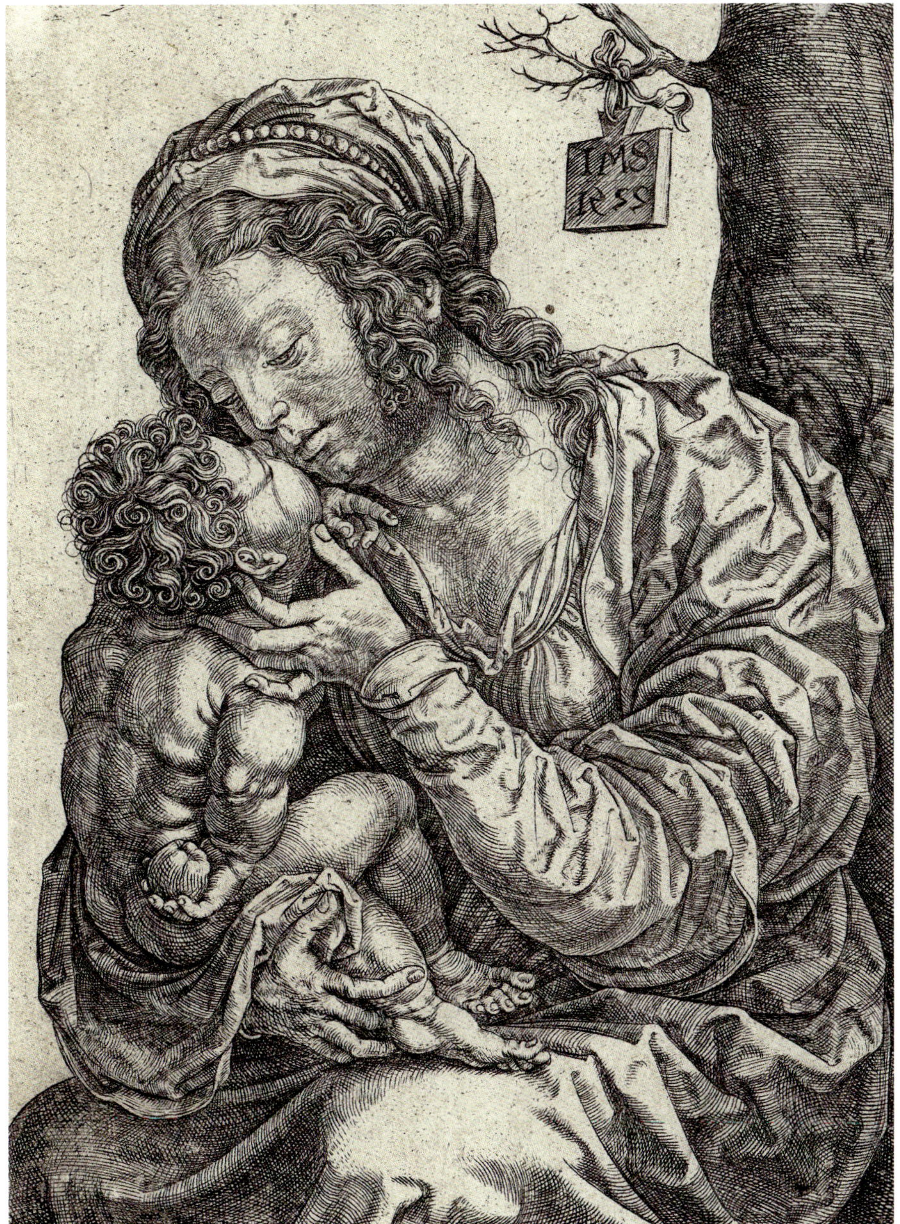

Fig. 43
JAN GOSSAERT
(active 1508; died 1532)
Virgin and Child, 1522
Engraving, 12 × 8.7 cm
Rijksmuseum, Amsterdam
(RP-P-OB-2144)

Fig. 44
ALBRECHT DÜRER
Virgin and Child on a Crescent Moon, 1514
Engraving, 12.1 × 7.6 cm
Suermondt Ludwig Museum, Aachen
(DK 1831)

Fig. 45
JAN GOSSAERT
(active 1508; died 1532)
Saint Luke drawing the Virgin, about 1520–2
Oil on oak, 110.5 × 83.5 cm
Kunsthistorisches Museum, Vienna

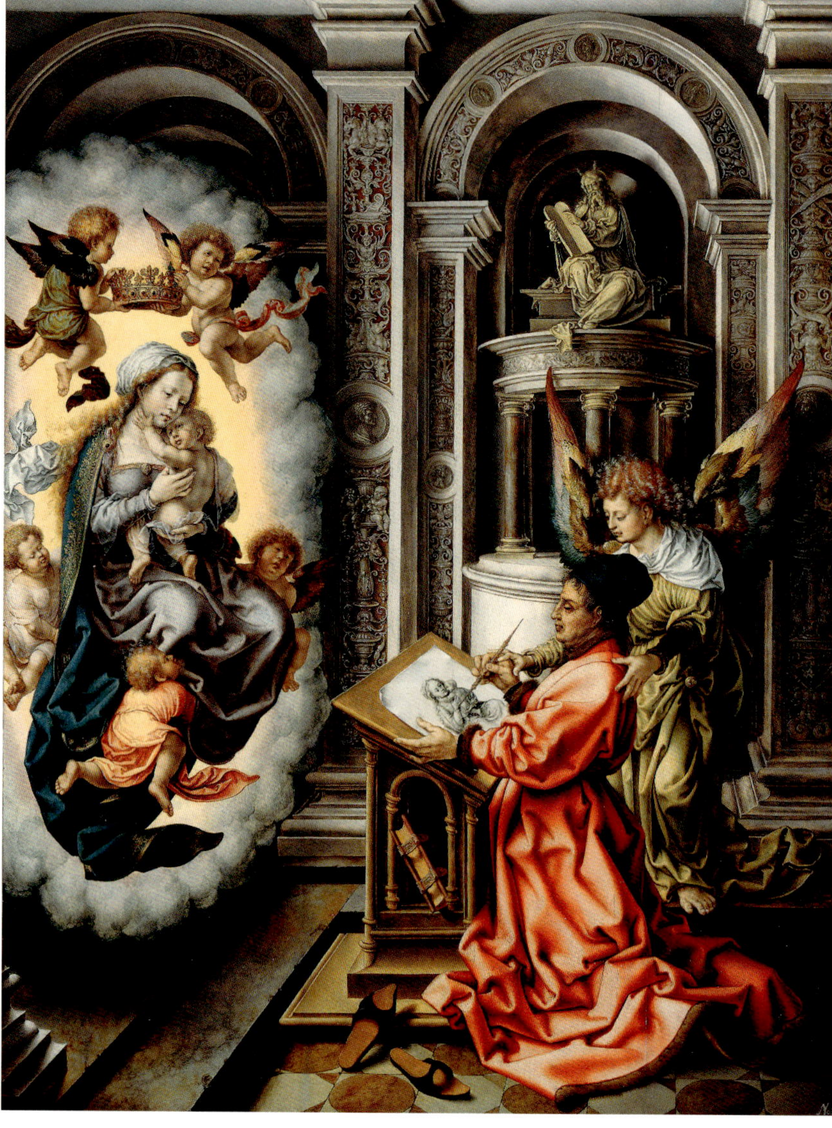

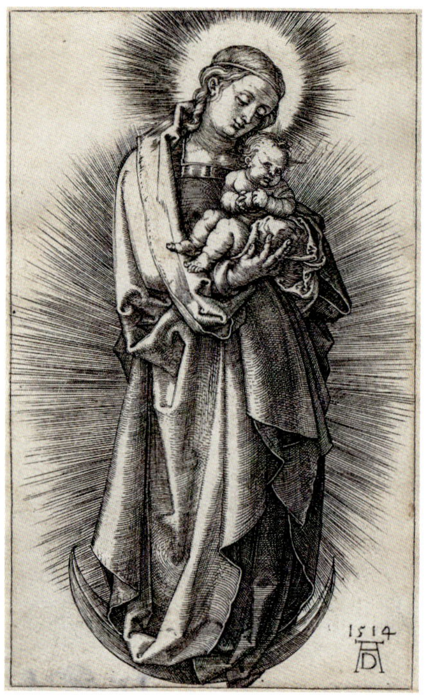

intensifies the other external markers of their heavenly status outside the clouds, including a hovering pair of cherubs bearing a crown over the head of the Virgin to signal her regal status despite her apparent humility; another trio of angels supports her from below, still within the hovering cloud. Comparison of the faces by both artists shows the extent to which Gossaert has truly adopted, even enhanced, the full bodies and the tender posture of the Christ Child nestling in his mother's arms.

If Gossaert's Virgin and Child imagery converges with the models derived from Dürer prints, the younger artist, who had never before produced any prints of his own, now turned suddenly to printmaking in the immediate wake of Dürer's trip to Antwerp.[24] Even more strikingly, Gossaert made his own print adaptation of a Dürer subject in a dated engraving of 1522: the Virgin and Child beneath a tree (fig. 43) derives from Dürer's 1513 engraving of the subject (fig. 41), whereas the intimacy of Gossaert's figures echoes Dürer's 1519 *Virgin nursing the Christ Child* (fig. 42). He freely adopts Dürer's distinctive pictorial branding by including a tablet with the date and his own monogram (here 'IMS', for 'Ioannes Malbodius Sculpsit') hanging from a branch. Once again, his two half-length holy figures beside the tree trunk bear no signs of their divinity. Their broad faces and robust bodies, even fuller than those in the Münster painting, are even more intense in their intimacy, as they converge in a maternal kiss and a gentle chuck of the Christ Child's chin, in what would otherwise depict an erotic exchange between adults.[25] The halting linear execution of this engraving further suggests that it was an experiment by Gossaert, and not a comfortable one for the newcomer to printmaking. Around the same time he made another sketchy engraving, without any background, showing the buxom Madonna enfolding a Herculean Christ Child under her sheltering mantle, a thick cascade of folds extending across the bottom of the print.[26] These dated works from the early 1520s strongly suggest that Gossaert's turn to Dürer stemmed directly from a fuller exposure to his prints in the wake of the German artist's immediate presence in Antwerp, Middelburg and Mechelen. Dürer's journal records innumerable exchanges of artworks and his own widespread local distribution of his prints across the Netherlands during his visit.

Similarly, Gossaert's *Mocking of Christ* etching of about 1525 (fig. 47) is also based upon the physically perfect image of the seated Man of Sorrows, closely borrowed from Dürer's two Woodcut Passion title pages. In particular, this muscular Jesus wearing a crown of thorns is confronted by an ugly tormentor raising a reed as a mock sceptre (interpreted by Gossaert as a bulrush), echoing the title page of Dürer's *Large Passion* of 1511 (fig. 46).[27] Moreover, the novel technique of etching, recently developed by other German artists during the 1510s and used by Dürer himself, among others,[28] enabled Gossaert, a non-specialist printmaker in the Netherlands, to produce his own print by drawing directly on a plate coated with a ground and then dipped in acid. Gossaert and his workshop also produced painted variants of this print composition. In his 1527 *The Mocking of Christ,* now in Budapest (fig. 49), for example, a heckler holds a reed as Jesus is mocked by a group of grotesque tormentors below him. The large, isolated subject of *Christ on the Cold Stone* (fig. 48) faces the viewer, holding his head in hand in distress, reminiscent of the melancholic pose made famous by Dürer's 1514 engraving *Melancholia I* (cat. 116).[29]

Gossaert returned to the theme of Adam and Eve in both painting and drawing during the 1520s. He now showed the First Parents interacting far more intensely, often with an explicit erotic charge, as Eve's naked body also reinforces her temptation with the apple by the serpent. In the two painted versions Adam seems hesitant to follow her lead, whereas in the drawings the figures are already intimate, with intricately intertwined bodies.[30] The figure of Adam has the same muscular nude body, derived from Dürer, as Christ on the Cold Stone (similarly, the curls on his head derive from the types borrowed from Dürer for Gossaert's early drawings).[31] Eve's face again echoes the Dürer Madonna types.

A final arena in which Gossaert emulated Dürer was in the German artist's lifelong fascination, also shared by Philip of Burgundy, with muscular classical mythological figures, such as Hercules. Many of Gossaert's nude mythological narratives carried the same erotic charge, also including an admonitory nod (like Adam and Eve) to the late medieval tradition of the Power of Women,

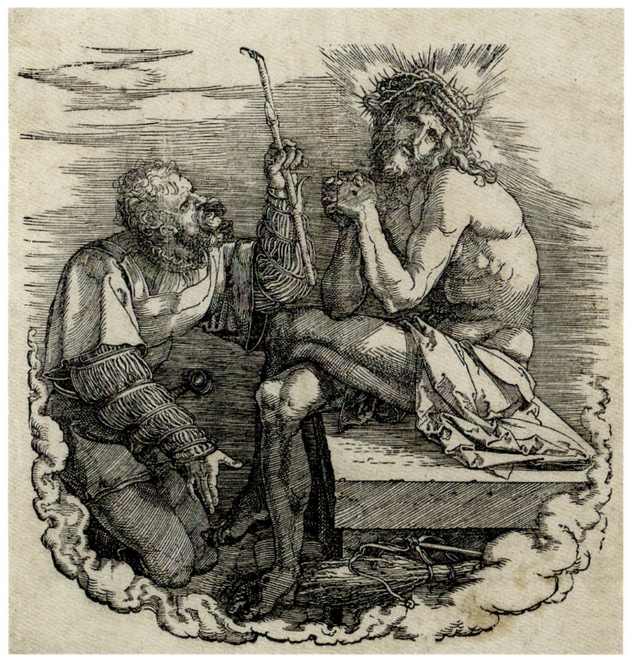

ABOVE
Fig. 46
ALBRECHT DÜRER
The Mocking of Christ
(from the *Large Passion*, title page), 1511
Woodcut, 22 × 20.2 cm
Städtische Sammlung Aachen, Suermondt-Ludwig-Museum
(DK 627)

BELOW
Fig. 47
JAN GOSSAERT
(active 1508; died 1532)
The Mocking of Christ, about 1525
Iron etching, 20 × 14.9 cm
Rijksmuseum, Amsterdam
(RP-P-1972-198)

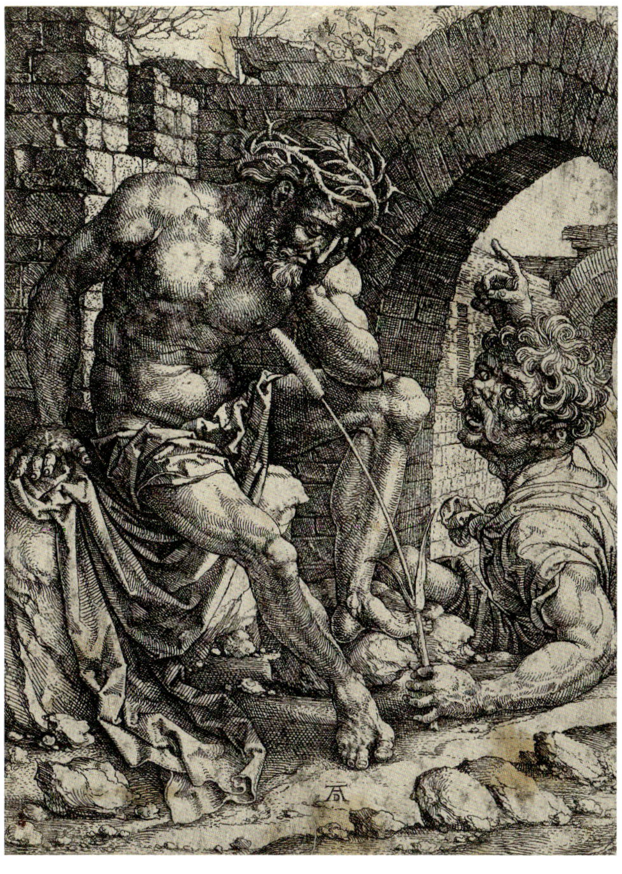

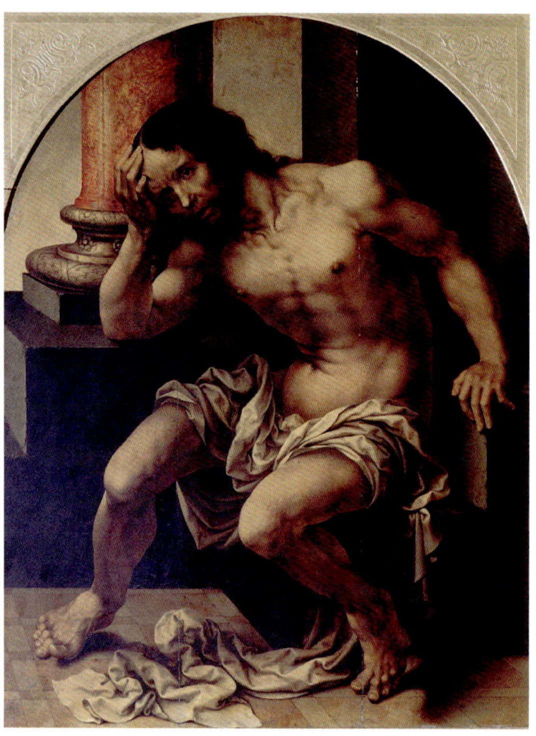

Fig. 48
JAN GOSSAERT (active 1508; died 1532)
Christ on the Cold Stone, about 1530
Oil on panel, 112 × 84 cm
Real Colegio del Corpus Christi, Valencia

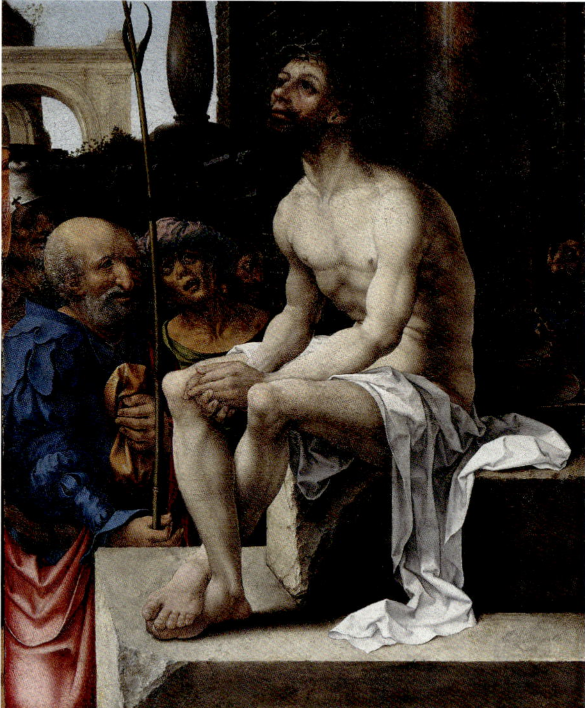

Fig. 49
JAN GOSSAERT (active 1508; died 1532)
The Mocking of Christ, 1527
Oil on oak, 51 × 40.3 cm
Szépművészeti Múzeum, Budapest

whose beauty overcomes any masculine strength or reason. After his painting *Neptune and Amphitrite* of 1516 (Gemäldegalerie, Berlin) and other mythical figures painted for Philip of Burgundy,[32] during his later printmaking phase in the 1520s Gossaert again readily took up the same depiction of physically powerful bodies. He is credited with a final, undated etching of two classical nudes, *Hercules and Deianira*, sitting side by side and impassive, without the erotic entanglement of bodies, in contrast to his small, earlier panel painting of the same pair (Barber Institute, Birmingham) of 1517.[33] Even though the two figures in the etching display body types characteristic of Gossaert's style, the repetitive, patterned linework here remains ineffective as modelling because of its very density and flattened, uniform linear background.

Gossaert also seems to have learned one important printmaking lesson for his final works – namely, that following German precedents of Lucas Cranach (1472–1553), Hans Burgkmair (1473–1531) and Dürer himself, he operated as a designer who did not cut his own blocks, which thus enabled the artist to achieve full artistic animation of his figures in woodcuts. Thus Gossaert was inspired to produce a woodcut of the violent attack of *Cain and Abel*, including his placement of the powerful figures before a well-developed rocky landscape. This was followed by his ultimate image of classical nude eroticism and asserted male dominance, the woodcut *Hercules and Deianira* (fig. 50).[34] In a twisting pose, here the lusty male, in profile with a conqueror's laurel wreath, attempts to mount his mate within a classical porch setting.[35]

With this print, combined with his erotic Adam and Eve paintings and drawings, the Flemish master has fully absorbed and emulated his German progenitor in media, figures and content, making his own distinctive contribution to a Netherlandish Renaissance art.

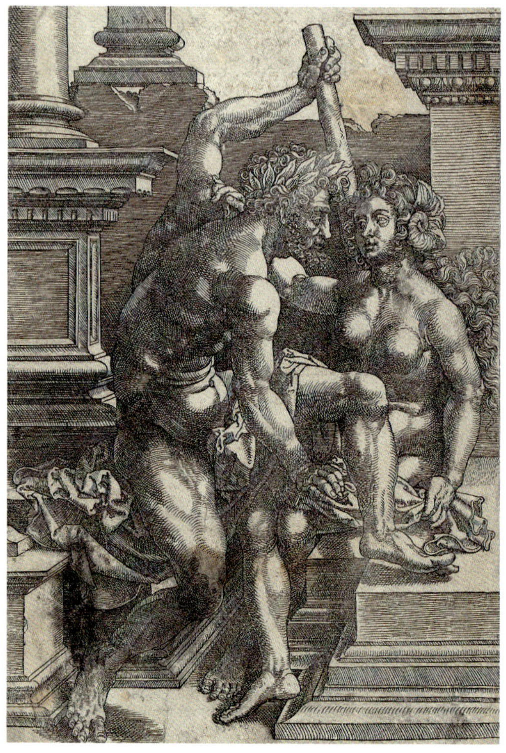

Fig. 50
AFTER JAN GOSSAERT
Hercules and Deianira, about 1530
Woodcut, 25.8 × 17.1 cm
Rijksmuseum, Amsterdam (RP-P-1912-361)

1 J.L. Koerner, 'Albrecht Dürer: A Sixteenth-Century *Influenza*', in London 2002, pp. 18–38; Brisman 2016. See also the essay by Joseph Koerner in the present volume, pp. 43–57.

2 The *fons et origo* of all later studies is Held 1931, esp. pp. 79–133. It should be noted that for Held, 'influence' often extends to the earlier adoption of Dürer imagery and motifs from his widespread print distribution rather than from specific contact with the artist or his art during his travels in the Netherlands. See also Brussels 1977; D. Eichberger, 'Dürer and the Netherlands: Patterns of Exchange and Mutual Admiration', in Silver and Chipps Smith 2010, pp. 149–65. Dagmar Eichberger compiled a list of the artists (both from Antwerp itself and the wider Netherlands) who are referenced in Dürer's journal of his travels. This list includes Lucas van Leyden (see the essay by Peter van den Brink in the present volume, pp. 205–25), Joachim Patinir and Dirk Vellert, as well as Jan Provoost, Bernaert van Orley, sculptor Conrad Meit (see the essay by Dagmar Eichberger, pp. 119–27), sculptor Jean Mone, plus Mark de Glassere and goldsmith Jan of Brussels, both unknown today. Dürer also visited the house of Antwerp's leading painter, Quinten Massys, but in his records he does not even mention Joos van Cleve (for the latter's *Saint Jerome* images, see the essay by Maximiliaan Martens and Astrid Harth in the present volume, pp. 253–65).

3 On Dürer's diary of his journey to the Netherlands, see Goris and Marlier 1971, esp. pp. 17–36, and p. 78 for the Gossaert quote; also now in English with commentary, Ashcroft 2017, vol. 1, pp. 545–638, esp. p. 570 n. 203. On Gossaert and the Middelburg Altarpiece, see A. Koopstra, 'The Middelburg Altarpiece', in Weidema and Koopstra 2012, pp. 153–64. Here Koopstra argues with earlier scholars that echoes of Gossaert's lost work appear in his surviving *Deposition* (Hermitage, St Petersburg). According to Peter van den Brink, Dürer may also have left a small pen drawing copy after Gossaert's Middelburg *Deposition* (cat. 11): see p. 27 in the present volume.

4 Dürer wrote of van Eyck: 'Then I looked at the altar of St John's [now St Bavo's, Ghent], which is highly precious and skilfully painted, and quite especially Eve, Mary and God the Father are very good' (Ashcroft 2017, vol. 1, p. 578 n. 298). According to Nash 2008, p. 36, this is 'our first comment by a northern artist on a northern work of art'.

5 Ashcroft 2017, vol. 1, pp. 224–5, letter 47.8.

6 New York and London 2010, esp. S. Schrader, 'Gossart's Mythological Nudes and the Shape of Philip of Burgundy's Erotic Identity', in ibid., pp. 57–67.

7 S. Schrader, 'Drawing for Diplomacy: Gossart's Sojourn in Rome', in ibid., pp. 45–55.

8 A handy touchstone on the Dürer precedent of nude bodies is Thomas Schauerte in Osnabrück 2003. For his classical nudes, see Bonnet 2001.

9 Mander 1604 (1994), fol. 214r.

10 Miedema 1994–2002, vol. 3, p. 28, discusses the basis of assigning that date to their shared time. In light of their apparent contact, it is worth noting that Lucas's massive *Last Judgement* altarpiece (Museum De Lakenhal, Leiden) of 1526–7 shows resurrected nude bodies closely akin to those of both Dürer and Gossaert, so their contact apparently occurred before then; see C. Vogelaar in Leiden 2011, pp. 321–2.

11 On the Netherlandish tradition as a model in general, see Silver 1987; Mensger 2002, pp. 33–55. For the copy (carefully traced) after the Ghent Altarpiece, see M. Ainsworth in New York and London 2010, pp. 213–17, no. 29, associating this work with Margaret of Austria's tomb complex at Brou and dating it around 1525–30. Also on Gossaert's use of the earlier diptychs, Washington and Antwerp 2006, to be compared to his own Carondelet Diptych (1517; Louvre, Paris). See also Mensger 2002, pp. 45–51, and M. Ainsworth in New York and London 2010, pp. 245–9, no. 40.

12 On the artist's use of heroic nudes for both religious and mythological paintings, see Silver 1986; Lehmann 2002; S. Schrader in New York and London 2010 (see note 6); M. Ainsworth, 'The Painter Gossart in his Artistic Milieu', in New York and London 2010, pp. 9–29, at pp. 16–18; Bass 2016, pp. 6–21. Conrad Meit, 'the fine stone carver' according to Dürer, closely emulated Dürer's famous 1504 *Adam and Eve* engraving in three dimensions (cat. 48). On Meit as a visual source, see D. Eichberger in the present volume, pp. 119–27; see also J.L. Burk in Munich 2006, pp. 68–71, no. 1, and pp. 80–4, no. 4. Dürer mentions meeting Meit on three occasions ('whose equal I have never seen, who serves the king's daughter Lady Margareta ... the sculptor from Mechelen'): Ashcroft 2017, vol. 1, pp. 559, 560, 582.

13 M. Ainsworth in New York and London 2010, pp. 145–50, no. 8; Campbell 2010 documents the painting as an altarpiece for the Chapel of Our Lady in the abbey church of St Adrian at Geraardsbergen, near Brussels, and identifies the patron as Daniel van Boechout (died about 1526), who is buried in that chapel.

14 M. Ainsworth in New York and London 2010, pp. 114–17, no. 1.

15 Ibid., pp. 131–9, no. 6. The Malvagna Triptych is noteworthy (according to Ainsworth) for Gossaert's collaboration with the archaising Bruges painter Gerard David; in any case, Gossaert closely emulated David in the central figures of Virgin and Child.

16 For nudes by Hans Baldung Grien in relation to Dürer, both for Adam and Eve as well as eroticised witches, see Frankfurt 2007, *passim*.

17 S. Alsteens, 'Gossart as a Draftsman', in New York and London 2010, pp. 89–103, esp. pp. 89 n. 17, 93 n. 38, fig. 95, and ibid., pp. 318–23, 328, 342–4, 346–8, nos 69–71, 75, 82, 84.

18 S. Alsteens in New York and London 2010, pp. 318–20, no. 69.

19 Antwerp and Maastricht 2005; Ewing 2016.

20 Other examples are *The Madonna with the Pear* (1511; B. 41), *The Virgin on the Crescent Moon* (1514; B. 33) and *The Madonna by the Wall* (1514; B. 40).

21 *The Virgin and Child crowned by Two Angels* (1518; B. 39). M. Ainsworth in New York and London 2010, pp. 158–9, no. 11; signed on the frame.

22 For the iconography of this imagery – a vision from Revelation 12: 1–5, usually interpreted as prefiguring the Virgin birth and the triumph of Christ over Satan – see Silver 2009, pp. 289–315.

23 *Virgin with Sceptre and Crown of Start* (1516; B. 32).

24 N. Orenstein, 'Gossart and Printmaking', in New York and London 2010, pp. 105–12; ibid., pp. 408–14, nos 112–14.

25 Steinberg 1983, pp. 1–3, 110–15. This kind of tender intimacy between Madonna and Child, usually depicted with innovative Leonardesque body types, also appears in works by Massys (Berlin, Paris, and the lost but often copied *Madonna of the Cherries*) in the later 1520s; see Silver 1984, pp. 78–80. But it also derived from Byzantine icons of Madonna and Child, as transmitted by way of early Netherlandish painters, such as Dirk Bouts; see M. Ainsworth, 'Á la façon grèce: The Encounter of Northern Renaissance Artists with Byzantine Icons', in New York 2004, pp. 578–93, and ibid., nos 345–55.

26 N. Orenstein in New York and London 2010, pp. 410–11, no. 113; a related painting by Gossaert of the same motif at half-length, about 1520, survives in one original (Musées Royaux, Brussels): M. Ainsworth in New York and London 2010, pp. 154–7, no. 10, and numerous copies.

27 N. Orenstein in New York and London 2010, pp. 412–14, no. 114, also notes Italian print models as another possible source for the musculature of the body of Christ. For the motif itself, see Osten 1935; M. Merback, 'The Man of Sorrows in Northern Europe', in Puglisi and Barcham 2013, pp. 77–116, particularly the melancholic Christ, pp. 106–10.

28 Landau and Parshall 1994, pp. 323–36; L. Silver and M. Cole, 'Fluid Boundaries: Formations of the Painter-Etcher', in Philadelphia 2006, pp. 5–35; also S. Dackerman, 'Dürer's Etchings: Printed Drawings?', in ibid., pp. 37–51; N. Orenstein, 'Tentative Beginnings: Etching in the Netherlands from 1520 to 1550', in New York 2019, pp. 65–80, at pp. 78–80, no. 30 for Gossaert's *Mocking of Christ*. Freyda Spira, 'Expanding Discourses in German Etching', in New York 2019, p. 93, notes that the first German treatise on etching was published in Nuremberg in 1531, only after the death of Dürer.

29 Real Colegio de Corpus Christi, Valencia. See M. Ainsworth in New York and London 2010, pp. 207–12, nos 27–8.

30 Silver 1986, pp. 2–8; M. Ainsworth in New York and London 2010, pp. 118–22, nos 2–3 (paintings); S. Alsteens in New York and London 2010, pp. 308–18, nos 64–8 (drawings, including copies after lost Gossaerts). Unlike Alsteens, I regard no. 68 as an original drawing by Gossaert, if rubbed, and not a copy. On Eve as the progenitor of the Power of Women theme (subject of two woodcut series by Lucas van Leyden), see Bleyerveld 2000.

31 See S. Alsteens in New York and London 2010 (note 17 above).

32 S. Schrader in New York and London 2010 (see note 6) and M. Ainsworth in ibid., pp. 217–35, nos 30–5; Bass 2016, pp. 80–102, on the significance of Hercules imagery for Gossaert's patron. For Neptune, see ibid., pp. 58–73.

33 N. Orenstein in New York and London 2010, pp. 417–18, no. 116, suggests that the figures might be by Gossaert himself but that the faces and hair were finished by a lesser, second hand, perhaps even at a later date. For the Birmingham painting, see ibid., pp. 221–3, no. 31.

34 See Carroll 1989 on how such mythological scenes reaffirmed the masculine prerogatives of absolute rulers. In the denouement of this story, however, Deianira inadvertently brings about the death of the mortal hero Hercules, thus warning the informed male observer of the dangers of lust.

35 N. Orenstein in New York and London 2010, pp. 418–23, nos 117–18. In the *Cain and Abel*, Lucas van Leyden's versions of the same theme exerted real influence on Gossaert.

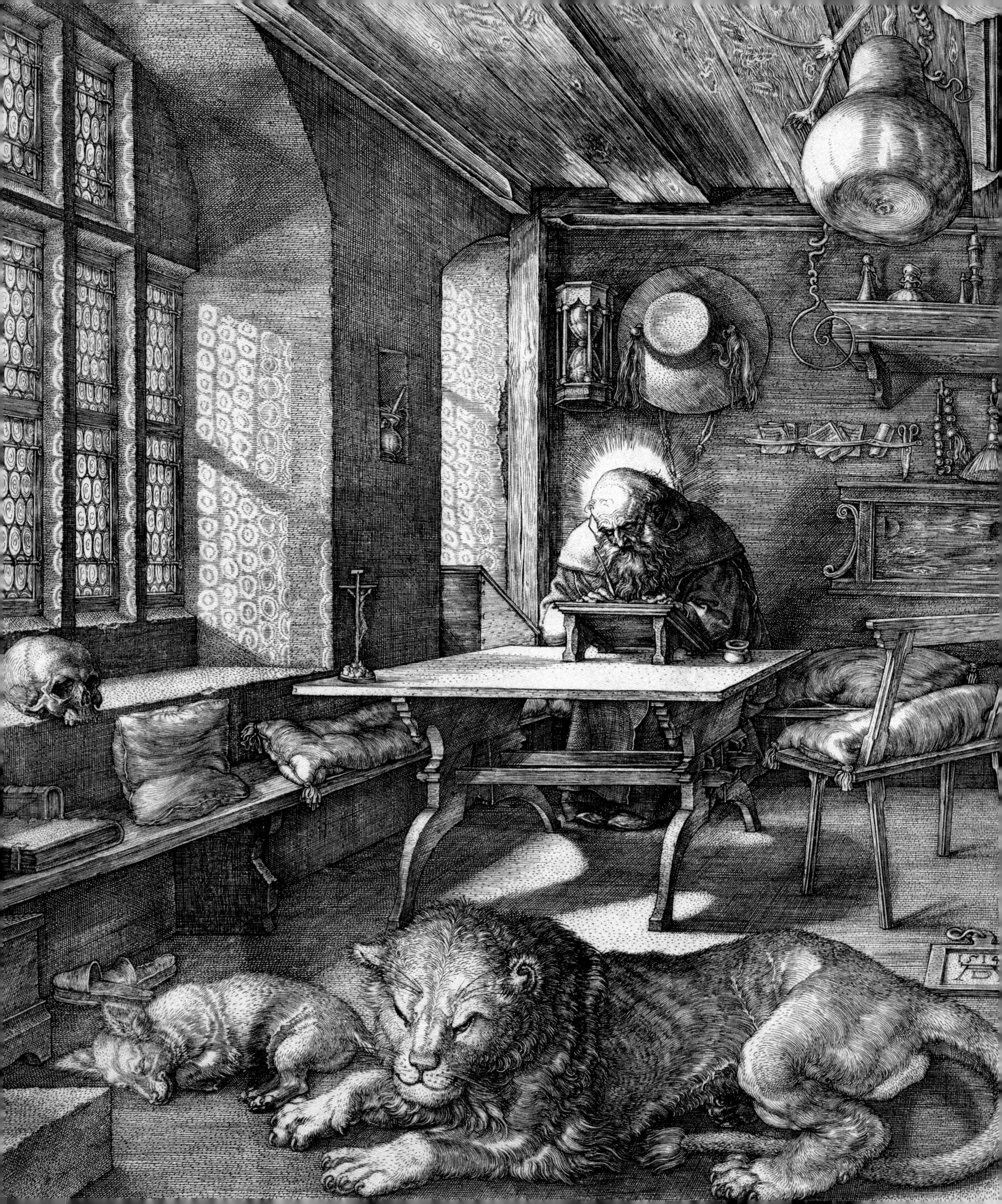

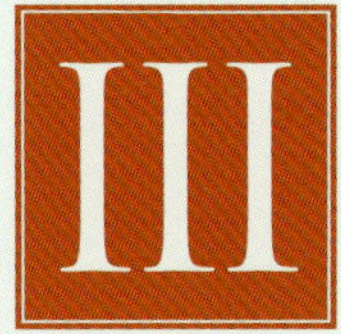

COURT AND CITY

MANY ARTISTS IN FIFTEENTH- AND SIXTEENTH-CENTURY Europe worked at the courts of the rulers, or aspired to do so, valuing the salaries and security provided as well as the ability to operate outside the stringent regulations of the town and city guilds. Dürer's path was that of the artist-entrepreneur: he aimed to be primarily a print-maker, of an extraordinarily innovative kind, and his projects to publish books of his woodcuts allowed him to create his own market. But as well as selling his prints, the meticulous records of his travel journal to the Low Countries in 1520–1 show how he used gifts of prints to curry favour and enable access to the powerful. On different occasions he presented a complete set of all of his prints to the ruler of the Low Countries, Margaret of Austria, as well as his large engraving of *Saint Jerome in his Study* (fig. 140), and a set of his *Passion* engravings; he also gave a set of the latter to Jean de Marnix (1483–1532), Margaret's treasurer. A set of his 'best prints' went to the exiled ruler King Christian II of Denmark, who was living at her court.

The city of Nuremberg was an exception in doing without the usual craft guilds: instead regulation was provided directly by the city council itself. In this way the city was more open than most to those coming to work and trade there from outside its boundaries, such as Dürer's father. But Nuremberg was also an imperial city, subject only to the Emperor Maximilian: Dürer himself received a pension from the Emperor, which he had arranged to have paid by the city of Nuremberg. In 1518 Dürer joined a party from Nuremberg that attended the Imperial Diet or assembly at Augsburg, making a portrait of Maximilian in black chalk, as well as those of other dignitaries. The drawing would be used as a basis for two painted portraits of the Emperor and a woodcut.

When Maximilian died in 1519 he was succeeded by his son Charles V, whose coronation in Aachen Dürer attended the following year with the intention to have his imperial pension renewed. Maximilian's own marriage to Mary of Burgundy and those arranged for his children had resulted in a vast European empire, including present-day Germany, Spain, Austria and the Low Countries. Maximilian's widowed daughter, Margaret of Austria, was an important collector and patron of the arts in her own right. Dürer's gifts of prints and a portrait of her father aimed to win her favour, but his journal contrasts her evident lack of enthusiasm for his work with the summons he later received from King Christian II of Denmark to attend a banquet at Brussels and to take his portrait there. SF

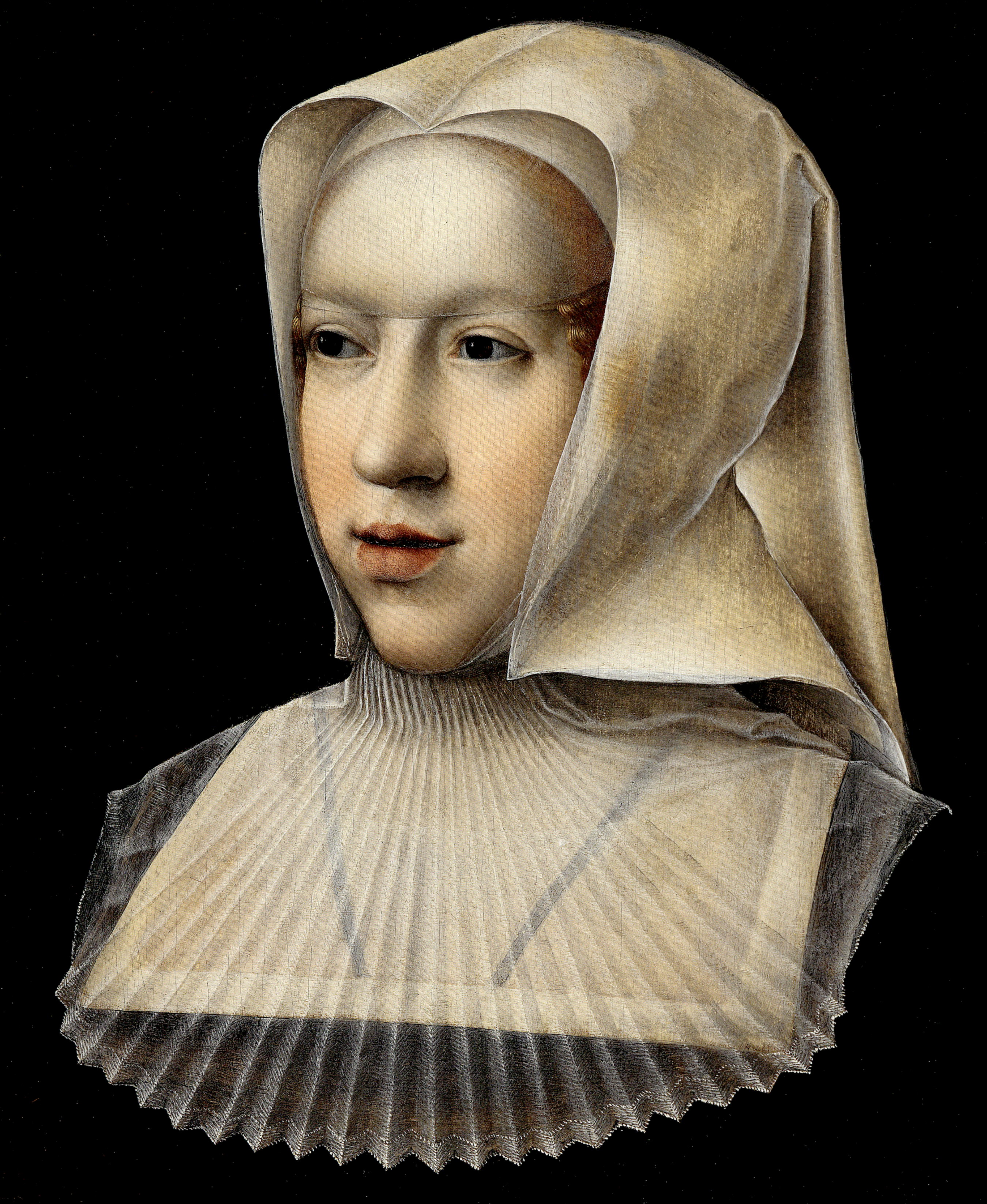

DAGMAR EICHBERGER

ART AND ENTREPRENEURSHIP
DÜRER'S ENCOUNTERS WITH MARGARET OF AUSTRIA AND HIS NETWORK AT THE IMPERIAL COURT

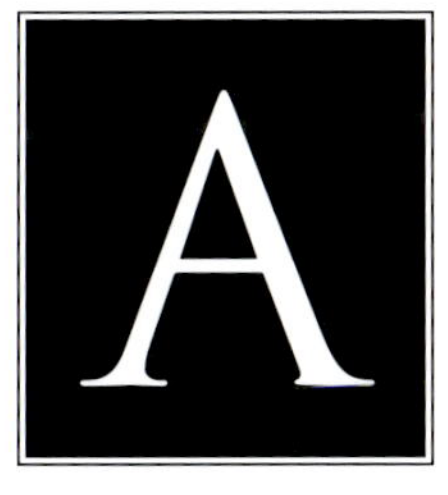

RTISTS OF ALBRECHT DÜRER'S DISTINCTION were not only outstanding draughtsmen and masters of their craft but also possessed keen business acumen, concerning themselves with the marketing and distribution of their works. In the process they developed close networks of contacts that would become useful in their endeavours. Dürer's encounters with Margaret of Austria, Regent of the Netherlands (cat. 57), are a particularly good example of this phenomenon. However, as important as his contact with the Emperor's proxy was, Dürer's relationship with Margaret's highest-ranking court officials and those of her nephew, Charles V (cat. 54), was equally significant. Due to their positions at court, the administrators and artists that Albrecht Dürer met on his journey enjoyed direct access to the decision-makers of the day, thus enabling them to intercede on Dürer's behalf.

Dürer's contact with the Archduchess Margaret of Austria was especially important because she was able to act as an intermediary in his financial affairs. He had been indirectly in contact with her five years before his Netherlandish journey, through her father, Maximilian I (1459–1519; fig. 52). In January 1515 the Holy Roman Emperor had corresponded with his daughter about the design of a Triumphal Arch (fig. 51), even sending a painted model to her in Mechelen and asking for her comments and alterations:[1]

> Furthermore, we have sent you a painted image of the Triumphal Arch which we had made so that you correct, augment or reduce what seems to you good, appropriate and meaningful. We ask you to send us the corrections and improvements as soon as possible

PREVIOUS PAGE
Detail from *Saint Jerome in his Study* (fig. 140)

OPPOSITE
Detail from *Portrait of Margaret of Austria* (cat. 57)

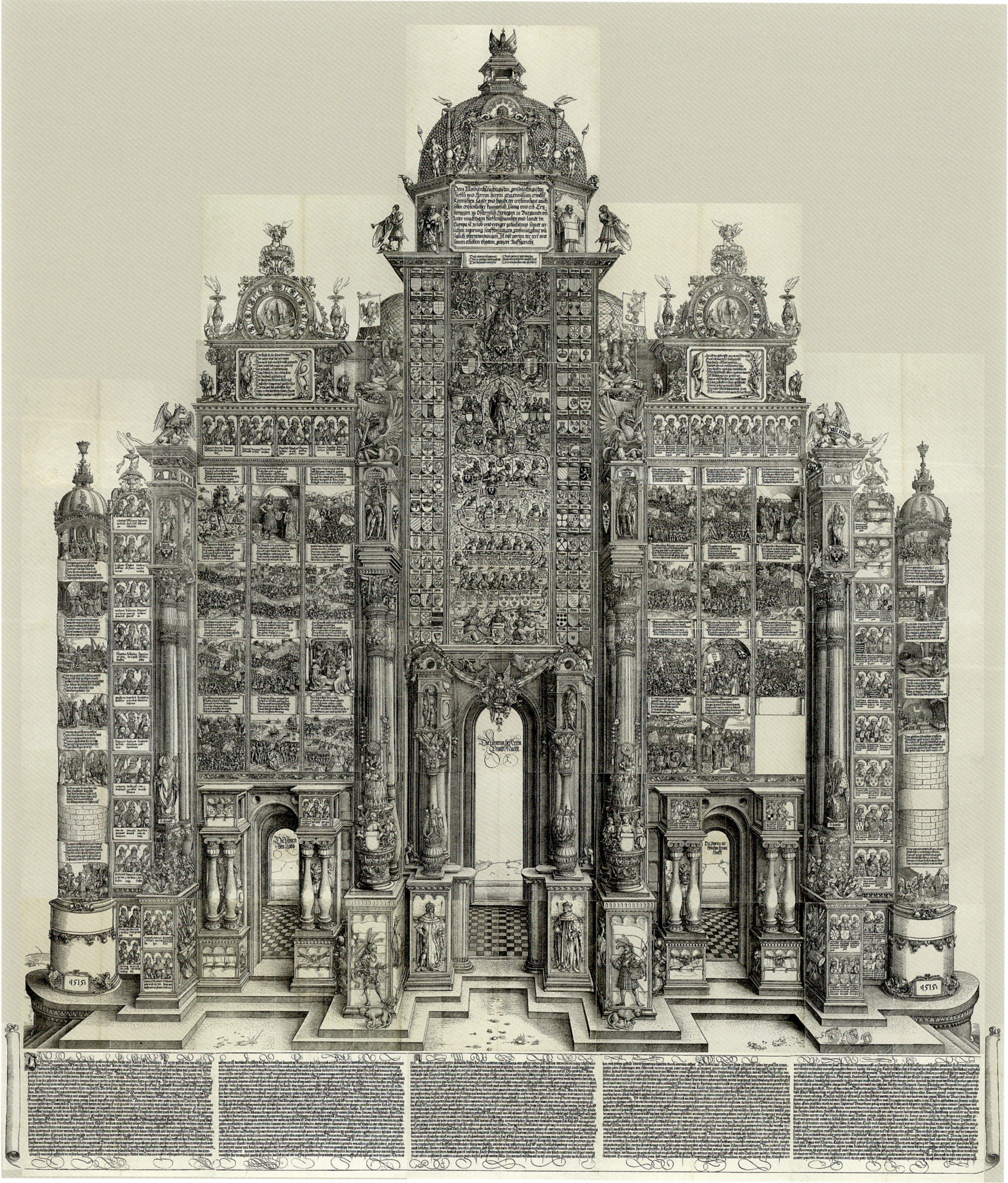
1515
1515

> so that we are informed about what in your opinion should be done and have them executed and enhanced in a beautiful and magnificent design to our and your eternal glory.[2]

A little later Margaret received a copy of the giant woodcut, which she subsequently stored in a leather box in her library. Dürer met the Regent of the Netherlands three times in total: his first, brief contact with her was a few weeks after his arrival in the Burgundian-Habsburg Netherlands in Brussels in August 1520. Almost ten months later, after the issue of his pension had been satisfactorily resolved, Dürer visited her in her Mechelen residence, taking the opportunity to inspect her collection. Their third and last meeting was at the banquet given by King Christian II of Denmark (cat. 53) in Brussels in July 1521. Besides these three personal encounters, Dürer writes regularly about Margaret in his diary, since on the one hand he was in close contact with many of her artists and court officials, and on the other, as Maximilian's daughter, she played an important part in the artist's life. There is no doubt that Dürer concerned himself more with Margaret of Austria during his Netherlandish journey than he did with Maximilian's successor, Charles V (cat. 54).

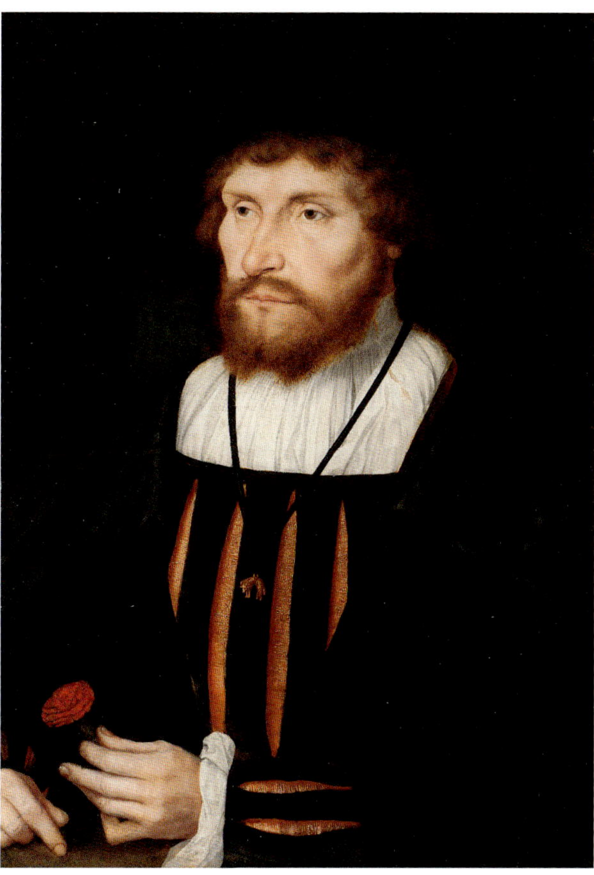

OPPOSITE
Fig. 51
ALBRECHT DÜRER AND WORKSHOP, WITH ALBRECHT ALTDORFER (about 1480–1538)
The Triumphal Arch or The Arch of Maximilian I, 1515
Woodcut, 36 sheets, each 45.7 × 62.2 cm
The Metropolitan Museum of Art, New York. Harris Brisbane Dick Fund (1928 28.82.7–.42)

LEFT
53
QUINTEN MASSYS (1465/6–1530)
Portrait of King Christian II of Denmark, 1522
Oil on paper glued to a thin oak board, 38.5 × 32 cm
Archbishopric Olomouc

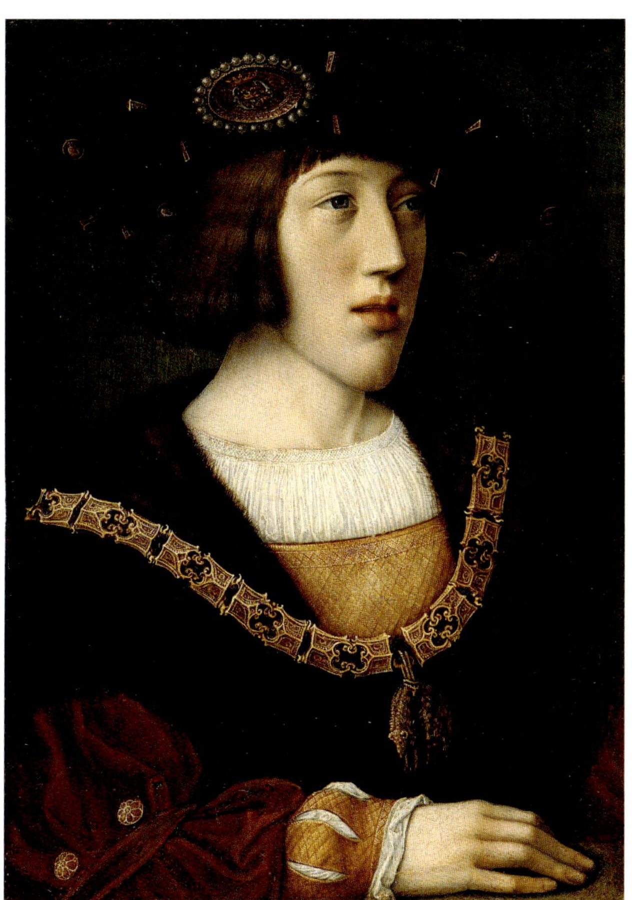

54
BERNAERT VAN ORLEY (active 1515; died 1541)
Portrait of Charles V, 1516
Oil on oak panel, 37 × 26.5 cm
The Royal Monastery of Brou, Bourg-en-Bresse, on loan from the Musée du Louvre, Paris

THE FIRST ENCOUNTER WITH MARGARET OF AUSTRIA IN BRUSSELS

In Brussels it was Margaret who took the initiative to contact Dürer in August 1520. As recorded by the artist in his journal, she summoned him to meet her, conceivably in the Coudenberg Palace, promising him to intercede on his behalf with Charles V. Dürer was favourably surprised by this meeting: 'Item: Madonna Margareta has sent word to me in Brussels and promised me she will put my case to King Charles and has shown herself extremely friendly towards me'.[3] On this occasion Dürer presented the Regent with his engraved *Passion* in gratitude for her efforts. He repeated this gesture with greater magnanimity a little later, in order to consolidate the connection. At the end of September 1520, as recorded in his journal, he gave her copies of his whole graphic output, valued at 30 guilders. In addition, he had produced two drawings on parchment specifically for Margaret, which he had executed 'with complete diligence and "utmost care"'.[4] The exceptional extent of his efforts demonstrate that this contact was of particular importance to him. Furthermore, he designed a house for Margaret's personal physician, possibly Jehan Marie de Bonisiis, for which he was paid 10 guilders. Earlier he had presented the physician with an engraving of *Saint Jerome*.[5]

Even before his first encounter with Margaret of Austria, Dürer took advantage of the courtly network, using his artworks as means of payment. To begin with he had dined with Jakob Banisius, secretary to Emperor Maximilian I and friend of Willibald Pirckheimer, presenting him with the engraved *Passion*.[6] A few days later he gave Banisius further artworks as gifts – a painted Veronica and six engravings – and subsequently drew his portrait in chalk.[7] Together with Banisius and his secretary, Erasmus Strenberger (1483–1558), Dürer discussed the petition that was to be submitted to Charles V for signature and which Strenberger prepared in duplicate.[8] In gratitude the artist presented him with eight engravings worth 7 guilders each. Dürer did not have to wait long for the confirmation of his annual pension by Charles, which occurred only two months later, on 4 November 1520, in Cologne.[9]

During Dürer's first visit to Brussels, Margrave Johann of Brandenburg-Ansbach, chamberlain and travel companion of Charles V, received an engraved *Passion* as a gift, together with the wish that he would remember the artist when he contemplated it.[10] Dürer also made a portrait in chalk of Jean de Marnix, Margaret's treasurer and a member of her privy council.[11] He met further members of her inner circle at the end of August at a banquet given by his painter colleague Bernaert van Orley, including Jehan de Metenye, Charles V's steward, and Gillis (?) van Busleyden, the city treasurer.[12] At this point Dürer also mentions Richard Contault, Margaret's keeper of her collection (*garde-joyaux*), whom he portrayed at van Orley's banquet.[13] He met Contault's assistant, the chamberlain Etienne Lullier, in Aachen a few months later (on 23 October 1520), when he presented him with three pieces of art.[14]

THE VISIT TO THE COURT OF SAVOY IN MECHELEN

Dürer's second meeting with Margaret of Austria took place seven months after their encounter in Brussels, after the confirmation of his imperial life annuity. At this point the 50-year-old artist was free from worry about his annual income of 100 guilders. From Thursday 6 June 1521 he and his wife, Agnes, spent two days travelling from Antwerp to the nearby town of Mechelen.[15] His journal records the warm reception he received from the town's painters and sculptors, who organised a banquet at the inn where he was staying, 'Zum Guldenen Haupt'. He subsequently describes his sightseeing programme, which was typical for his various visits to cities in the Netherlands.[16] This naturally included a visit to the Court of Savoy, Margaret of Austria's residence, as previously undertaken and recorded in his travel journal by the Italian Antonio de Beatis.[17] Dürer's account reveals that he was received twice at court.

Research on Dürer's journey to the Netherlands has directed most attention to the episode in which Margaret rejected the artist's gift. In the journal entry for 6 June 1521 Dürer notes: 'I also visited Lady Margareta and showed her my Emperor and wanted to present it to her, but she disliked it so much that I took it away with me again'.[18] Scholarly discussion initially focused on the question of whether the gift was a painted portrait or a black-and-white woodcut of Emperor Maximilian.[19] For logistical reasons a large-scale panel or canvas painting seems unlikely, thus pointing in favour of a woodcut. The latest research has shown that Dürer produced a hand-coloured woodcut with gold leaf during Maximilian's lifetime (fig. 52).[20] Such a luxury edition would have been an appropriate gift for the Regent of the Netherlands, who had already received the artist's entire printed oeuvre. After this rejection, shortly before his departure to Brussels and Nuremberg, Dürer exchanged his portrait of the Emperor in Antwerp for a piece of white cloth from England.[21]

There may have been many reasons why Margaret did not accept Dürer's gift. His reaction necessarily reflects his point of view – his honour as internationally acclaimed artist was wounded, especially as he had embarked on a new artistic path with his coloured woodcut portrait. But Margaret already had three portraits of Maximilian in her collection: two oil paintings by Joos van Cleve and another by Bernhard Strigel (1461–1528).[22] Accepting a further gift would have required monetary compensation on Margaret's part, something she might have wanted to avoid. This negative experience did not, however, prevent the 'German Apelles' from visiting Margaret again the following day, 7 June. She apparently considered Dürer sufficiently important to give him a personal tour of her art collection, including the large library and her personal living quarters.[23] The art objects about which he writes with great admiration were located in Margaret's state bedroom and adjoining study. His description does not specify whether he entered the separate room on the ground floor that also held part of her collection. Among others, he mentions seeing works by Juan de Flandes, Michel Sittow (1468/9–1525/6), Jan van Eyck and Jacopo de' Barbari, Margaret's Italian court painter who had died five years earlier.[24] He writes:

> On Friday Lady Margareta showed me all her beautiful pieces. Among them I found forty small oil-painted panels whose equals for quality and precision I have never seen before. There I saw also other good things, works by Jan and by Jacopo the

'I also visited Lady Margareta and showed her my Emperor and wanted to present it to her, but she disliked it so much that I took it away with me again.'

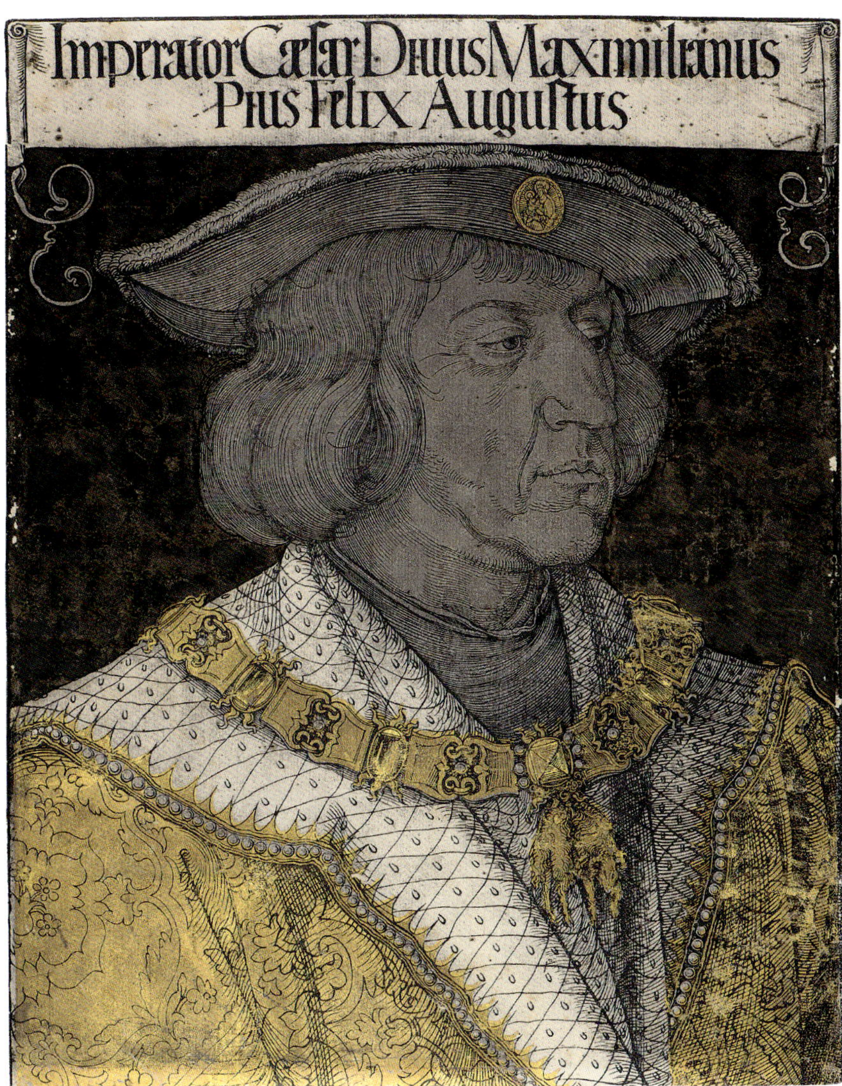

Fig. 52
ALBRECHT DÜRER
Portrait of Emperor Maximilian I,
about 1519
Woodcut from two plates (black, gold), hand-coloured,
41.5 cm × 32.3 cm
Stiftung Schloss Friedenstein, Gotha (8,26)

> Italian. I asked my lady for Master Jacopo's little book, but she said she had promised it to her own painter. Many other precious things I saw too, and a very valuable library.[25]

Among Margaret's most precious paintings in the state bedroom were the small panels by Juan de Flandes (cat. 55) and Michel Sittow, which came from the altar-piece of Queen Isabella of Castile,[26] as well as Jan van Eyck's *Arnolfini Portrait* (fig. 53)[27] and a version of his *Madonna at the Fountain*. When Dürer tried to acquire Jacopo de' Barbari's sketchbook, which was of special interest to him, his request was denied with the argument that it had already been promised to Margaret's court painter, Bernaert van Orley. Like Dürer, who was greatly interested in the Italian Renaissance, van Orley would have been eager to own the Italian sketchbook.[28] Dürer was fascinated by Jacopo de' Barbari's theoretical abilities, and had already mentioned 'Master Jacopo' in a letter from Venice to Pirckheimer.[29] His interest had motivated him to access works by Raphael: in October 1520 he had paid the Italian painter and architect Tommaso Vincidor to acquire objects from the estate of Raphael, who had died in Rome six months earlier.[30]

In a journal entry for 29 June 1521, towards the end of his stay in the Netherlands, Dürer takes stock of his expenses and earnings. Taking everything into account, his expenses exceed his income. Margaret's

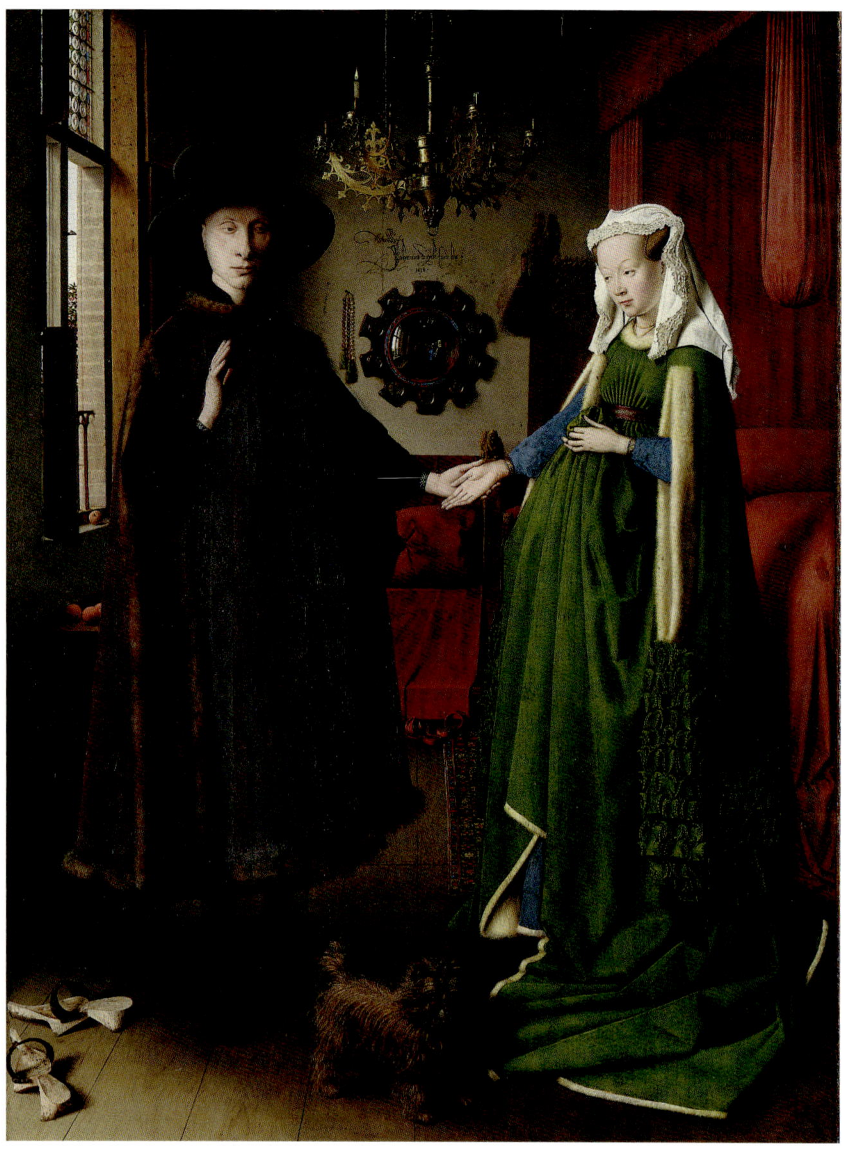

Fig. 53
JAN VAN EYCK
(active 1422; died 1441)
Portrait of Giovanni Arnolfini and his Wife, 1434
Oil on oak, 82.2 × 60 cm
The National Gallery, London

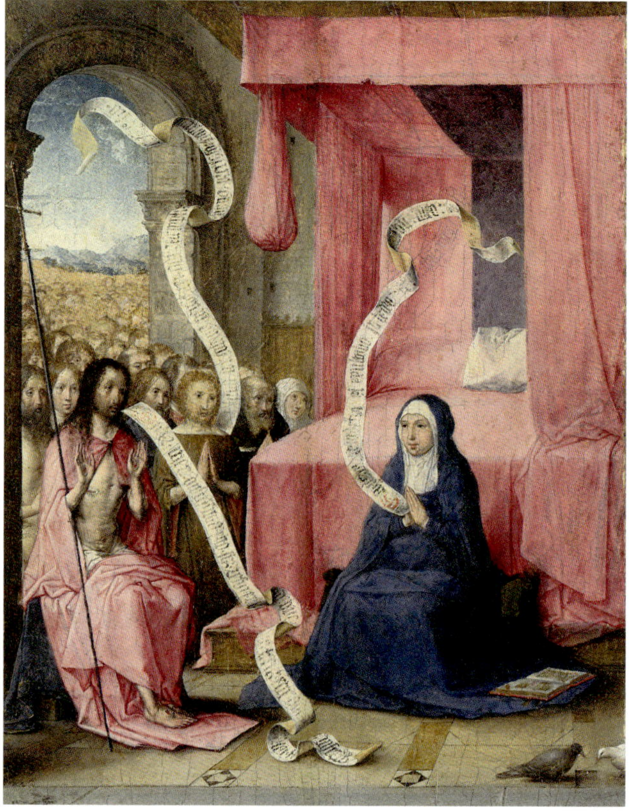

55
JUAN DE FLANDES (active from 1496; died 1519)
Christ appearing to the Virgin with the Redeemed of the Old Testament, about 1499–1500
Oil on oak, 21.2 × 15.4 cm
The National Gallery, London

behaviour towards him remained a source of concern, for in his view she did not adequately compensate him for his gifts:

> In all I have done, in my living expenses, sales and other dealings in the Netherlands, in all my relationships whether with higher or lower classes of people, I have lost out, and quite especially with Lady Margareta who in return for what I presented to her and made for her has given me nothing.[31]

The third and last meeting with Margaret of Austria occurred rather incidentally. On 2 July 1521 King Christian II of Denmark summoned the artist to Antwerp to draw his portrait (fig. 54). The artist complied with the wish immediately, at the same time drawing the royal envoy Anton von Metz.[32] At Christian's request Dürer accompanied him to Brussels the following day to attend a banquet in his honour organised by Charles V and Margaret of Austria. On 7 July Christian reciprocated with a banquet for Charles and Margaret, at which Dürer was a guest,[33] an honour of which he must have been especially proud. Shortly afterwards he painted the portrait of the Danish king in oil on panel, acquiring a protective case for which he was generously remunerated with 30 guilders.

DÜRER'S CONTACTS WITH PAINTERS AND SCULPTORS AT COURT

Dürer's travel journal reveals that he had direct contact with at least 17 court officials of Margaret of Austria or Charles V, whose good will he persistently sought. Initially he concentrated on those with the rank of chamberlain or councillor, such as Johann of Brandenburg-Ansbach, Jakob Banisius, Gillis van Busleyden, Jehan de Meteyne and Jean de Marnix. Richard Contault and Margaret's personal physician also belong to this circle.

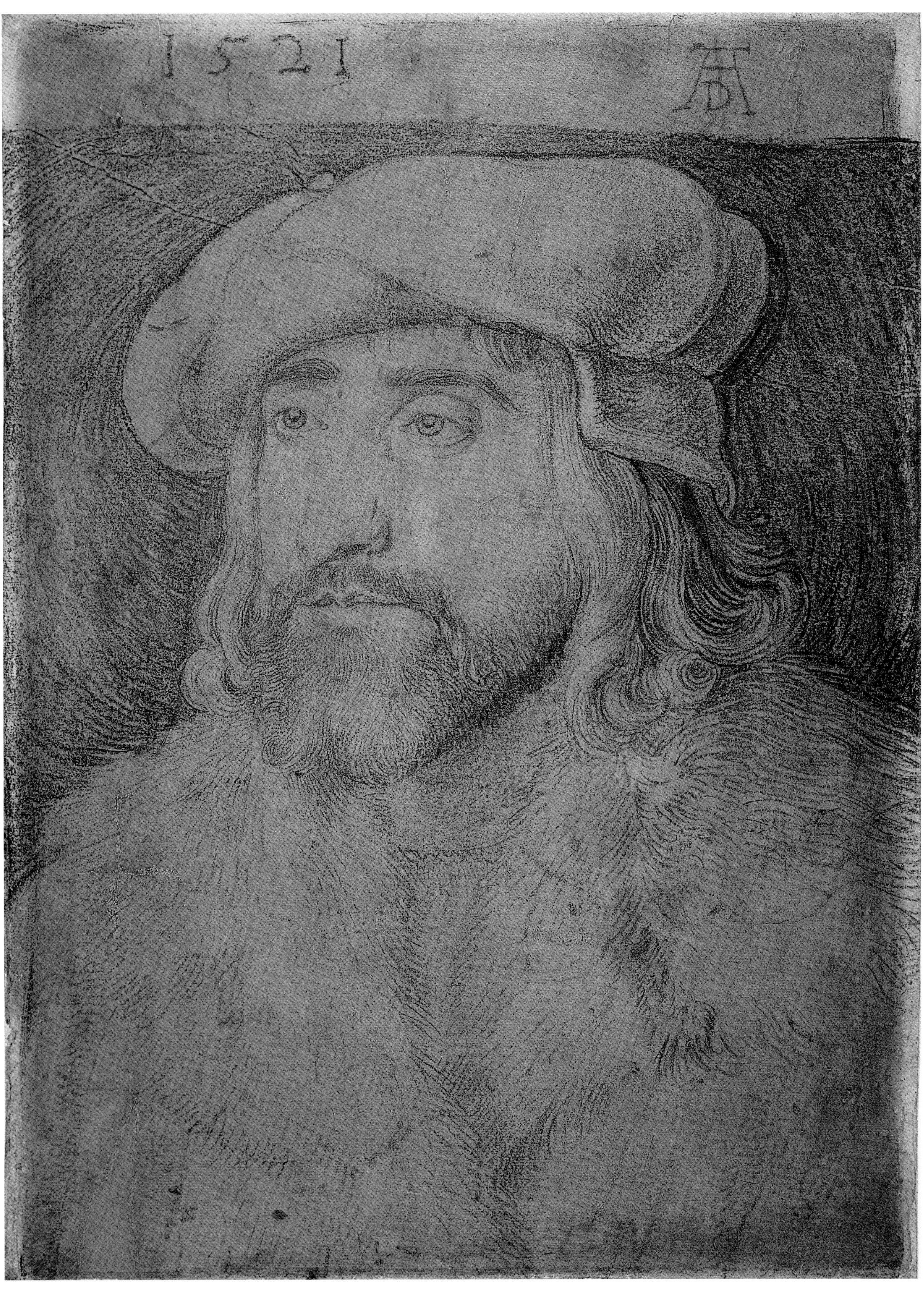

Fig. 54
ALBRECHT DÜRER
Portrait of a Man, possibly King Christian II of Denmark, 1521
Black chalk on paper, 39.9 × 28.7 cm
British Museum (SL,5218.48)

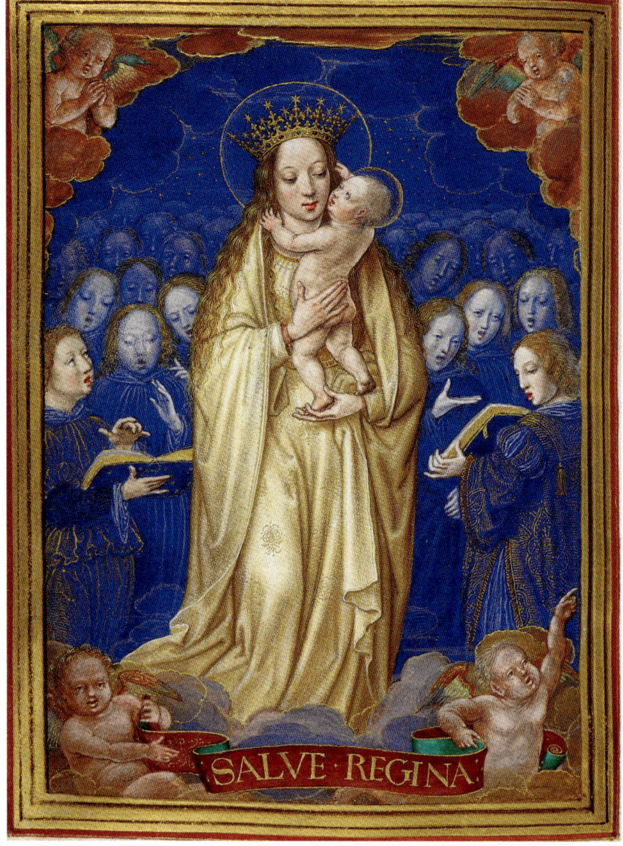

56
GERARD HORENBOUT
The Virgin Mary as Queen of Heaven holding the Christ Child, from the *Sforza Hours*, about 1519–21
Tempera on parchment, 13 × 10 cm
The British Library

In the second half of his stay in the Netherlands, Dürer turned his attention more to court artists who, as his creative peers, must have been of special interest to him. While Dürer no doubt had contact with many municipal artists from Antwerp, Brussels, Ghent and Bruges,[34] the focus here is on artists in the service of Margaret of Austria or Charles V.

In 1521 Dürer met twice with Jean Mone (1485/90–1549/50), imperial sculptor from Metz. In his notes he praises Mone as a 'skilled marble-sculptor' ('guten marmelstain hauer'), emphasising that he was trained in Italy.[35] Around Shrovetide 1521 he drew a portrait in chalk of 'the French sculptor' ('franczoß bildhauer') in Antwerp. Shortly before his departure there was a last exchange of gifts, when Dürer presented the much-valued Mone a complete set of his printed works.[36] Unlike the often strategically motivated gifts of his prints in 1520, we can detect here a true appreciation of his artist colleague.

Dürer's contact was even closer with Conrat Meit, Margaret's court sculptor, who lived with his wife in Mechelen. Here the initiative was clearly taken by Dürer, who had a high opinion of Meit: '… the fine stone-carver called Master Konrad, whose equal I have never seen'.[37] On 19 August 1520 he arranged for the German royal usher Gilles von Apfenauwe to deliver seven engravings to Meit; a few days later, on 26 August 1520, he and Meit met in Mechelen. On the way to Brussels Dürer invited the sculptor, together with an unidentified artist, to dine with him.[38] They met again in Brussels, where Dürer was invited by Meit to dine with him and the Nuremberg councillors. On this occasion he portrayed Meit, as well as his wife, Berthelmine le Paige, and Johannes Lamparter, son of Dr Gregor Lamparter (1453–1523), an imperial councillor.[39] Nine months later, on 20 May 1521, the two met once more in Antwerp, where Dürer received Meit as his guest.[40] Six days after that Meit presented him with a gift, a precious knife, or possibly a set of knives ('schöne barr messer'), a special gesture of friendship.[41] The last time Dürer and Meit met was in Mechelen. The otherwise parsimonious Dürer did not refrain from inviting his colleague twice to dine with him. At one of his encounters with Meit he drew the sculptor in chalk – as well as Margaret's chamberlain, Etienne Lullier.[42] Presumably Lullier was present when Dürer visited Margaret in her palace.

The third court artist for whom Dürer had great respect was Bernaert van Orley, whose workshop was in Brussels, suggesting that the meetings recorded by Dürer took place in that city.[43] Van Orley's generous invitation during Dürer's first visit has been mentioned already. The Nuremberg artist describes his painter colleague as 'Master Bernhard, Lady Margareta's painter' ('maister Bernhart, der fraw Margarethae mahler'),[44] again revealing that van Orley's closeness to the court was an important factor for him.

Another of Dürer's acquaintances from Margaret of Austria's circle of artists and craftsmen is her goldsmith, Marc de Glasere ('Master Mark'/'meister Marx'). Dürer met him twice, at the beginning and the end of his journey. In September 1520 de Glasere was one of the court officials whose company the German artist sought. Initially he was presented with a copy of Dürer's engraved *Passion*; in addition, he purchased further prints to the value of 3 guilders.[45] In May 1521 Dürer met de Glasere a second time in Antwerp, where he made a portrait drawing of him.[46] Dürer was also in contact with an Italian goldsmith working in Antwerp, Stefano Capello, who produced several works *à l'antique* for Margaret but was not permanently employed at court. In November 1520 Capello presented Dürer with a cedarwood rosary, whereupon the latter reciprocated by drawing his portrait.[47] A somewhat different case is that of the Ghent miniaturist

Gerard Horenbout (1465–1541; cat. 56), who, after many years in the service of the Regent, decided to move to the English court of Henry VIII (1491–1547), taking his family with him.[48] Dürer's meeting with Horenbout and his 18-year-old daughter, Susanna, took place in Antwerp in May 1521, shortly before their move to England. On that occasion Dürer purchased a Salvator Mundi miniature made by Susanna for 1 guilder,[49] not without expressing great surprise that a woman was capable of producing such a work.

Dürer was an artist who understood the combination of urban milieu with courtly society, feeling at home in both worlds.[50] In order to retain his annual pension, he had to travel to the Netherlands to make a personal petition to the court officials of Margaret of Austria and Charles V. Over the months he developed close relationships with the international court artists van Orley, Mone, Meit and de Glasere, going beyond mere business dealings. His participation at the celebrations of the coronation of Charles V in Aachen and Cologne, as well as the courtly festivities in Brussels, illustrates how close Dürer had come to the leading rulers of the day in the course of a single year. His mission was ultimately crowned by success and he was able to return to his home town with many new impressions and experiences.

57
BERNAERT VAN ORLEY
(active 1515; died 1541)
Portrait of Margaret of Austria, about 1518
Oil on wood, 37 × 27 cm
The Royal Monastery of Brou,
Bourg-en-Bresse

1 Eichberger 2002, p. 149 n. 16.
2 'Nous nous avons puis aucun temps envoyé en painture la porte d'honneur que avons faite et conceute à celle fin que la corrigiez, augmentez ou diminuez de ce que vous sembleroit y estre bon, propice et duysable. Si vous requérons de rechief nous mander la correction et amendement que sur ce il vous semblera estre à faire, pour en aprez avoir eu iceluy vostre adviz. La faire mectre et rédiger en belle et ample forme, telle que à perpétuité elle devra demourer pour nostre et vostre perpétuelle gloire': Le Glay 1839, p. 341: no. 634 (18 January 1516), pp. 339–42 and no. 661 (17 February 1518), p. 374. Author's translation.
3 Ashcroft 2017, vol. 1, no. 162, p. 560; Unverfehrt 2007, p. 64.
4 Ashcroft 2017, vol. 1, no. 162, p. 563.
5 Ibid., pp. 562–3. On the identification of the physician, see Unverfehrt 2007, p. 82.
6 Ashcroft 2017, vol. 1, no. 162, p. 559.
7 Ibid., p. 562.
8 Ibid., p. 560. For letters 33 and 34, see Rupprich 1956–69, vol. 1, pp. 88–90; Unverfehrt 2007, p. 64; Ashcroft 2017, vol. 1, nos 165.1 and 165.2, pp. 639–2. Letter 34 (Ashcroft no. 165.2) is today in the Germanisches Nationalmuseum, Nuremberg.
9 Ashcroft 2017, vol. 1, nos 165.3 and 165.4, pp. 642–4.
10 '… that he might remember me …', ibid., no. 162, p. 560.
11 Ibid., p. 560.
12 Ibid., p. 561; Unverfehrt 2007, pp. 61–2.
13 Rupprich identifies this person as Jean de Marnix: Rupprich 1956–69, vol. 1, pp. 155–6 n. 206. For Contault and Lullier, see Eichberger 2002, pp. 8–9.
14 '… presented three prints': Ashcroft 2017, vol. 1, no. 162, p. 565.
15 Ibid., p. 584.
16 D. Eichberger, 'Dürer and the Netherlands: Patterns of Exchange and Mutual Admiration', in Silver and Chipps Smith 2010, *passim*.
17 Eichberger 2002, pp. 127–8.
18 Ashcroft 2017, vol. 1, no. 162, p. 584.
19 Here opinions differ. Rupprich speaks of a painted portrait (either the oil painting on canvas now in Nuremberg or the oil on panel now in Vienna), Unverfehrt introduces into the discussion a silver dedication medal, rejecting the possibility of a woodcut: see Rupprich 1956–69, vol. 1, p. 200 n. 673; Ashcroft 2017, vol. 1, pp. 625–6, no. 363; Unverfehrt 2007, p. 182. See also Hirschfelder 2013, p. 121.
20 C. Metzger, 'Maximilian I', in Augsburg 2019, pp. 276–8.
21 Ashcroft 2017, vol. 1, no. 162, p. 587.
22 Eichberger 2014, pp. 100–14.
23 Eichberger 2002, pp. 237, 365–7.
24 Ibid., pp. 86, 107–8.
25 Ashcroft 2017, vol. 1, no. 162, p. 584.
26 Eichberger 2002, pp. 234–48; Ishikawa 2004; Weniger 2011, pp. 25–38.
27 Campbell 1998, pp. 174–211.
28 Unverfehrt 2007, p. 183.
29 Letter by Albrecht Dürer to Willibald Pirckheimer, 7 February 1506. Ashcroft 2017, vol. 1, no. 29.2, p. 140.
30 Ashcroft 2017, vol. 1, no. 162, pp. 563–4.
31 Ibid., p. 586.
32 See the essay by Peter van den Brink in the present publication, pp. 205–25.
33 Ashcroft 2017, vol. 1, no. 162, p. 589.
34 D. Eichberger in Silver and Chipps Smith 2010 (see note 16), *passim*.
35 Ashcroft 2017, vol. 1, no. 162, p. 575.
36 Ibid., p. 586.
37 Ibid., p. 559.
38 Ibid., p. 559.
39 Ibid., p. 560.
40 Ibid., p. 582.
41 Ibid., p. 583; I. Eaves in Augsburg 2019, pp. 250–1, no. 46.
42 Ashcroft 2017, vol. 1, no. 162, p. 584.
43 Galand 2013; Brussels 2019.
44 Ashcroft 2017, vol. 1, no. 162, p. 561.
45 Ibid., pp. 562, 580.
46 Ibid., p. 580.
47 Ibid., p. 569; Eichberger 2002, p. 259.
48 Campbell and Foister 1986, pp. 719–27.
49 Ashcroft 2017, vol. 1, no. 162, p. 583.
50 Eichberger, Lorentz and Tacke 2017.

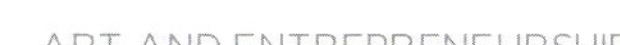

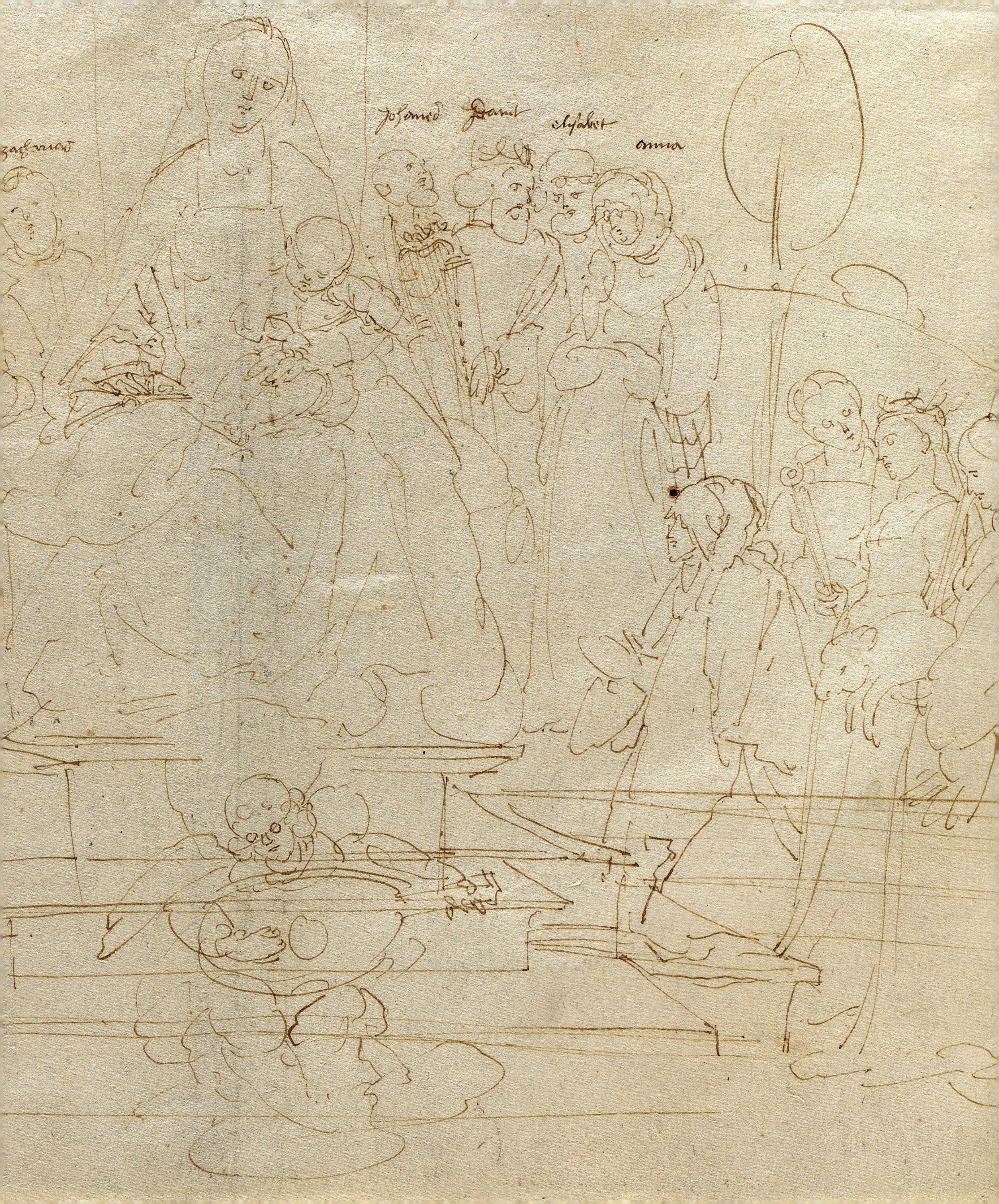
zacharias
Johannes
Dauit
elysabet
anna

STIJN ALSTEENS

DÜRER'S *VIRGIN AND CHILD WITH SAINTS* OF 1521–2 AN ARCHDUCAL COMMISSION?

In addition to the substantial corpus of drawings that Albrecht Dürer made during his stay in the Netherlands – first and foremost the impressive series of portrait drawings in chalk and the delicate sketchbook sheets in silverpoint – art history has been able to recover his preoccupation in the years 1521 and 1522 with a project of larger scope and ambition. To quote two scholars, among many others: it could have been 'his most important painting', 'the greatest painting of his whole career', while another somewhat dramatically called the fact that it never seems to have been realised 'perhaps the greatest tragedy of Dürer's fate as an artist'.[1] Fedja Anzelewsky, who thought the painting would have become 'one of the most important altarpieces north of the Alps', was probably right in assuming that, had it been executed, it 'would have left traces in the form of copies and imitations'.[2] The only traces it did leave are to be found in a group of drawings by Dürer related to the project, which, although discussed together since the early twentieth century,[3] warrant a fresh examination on the ground of their quality, their iconography and sources, and their variety, and because of the interesting question surrounding the work's possible patron or dedicatee.

That Dürer lavished particular attention on the project and prepared it 'with the utmost effort'[4] may be clear from the number of surviving drawings. If these can be taken as a measure, they place it squarely alongside some of his largest works, notably the *Rosenkranzfest* (*Feast of the Rose Garlands*) in Prague of 1506, and the Heller Altarpiece, commissioned for the Dominican church in Frankfurt and completed in 1509. Around twenty related autograph drawings are known for both pictures.[5] Twenty sheets, now all in public collections, can also be associated with the project that concerns us here. What distinguishes the latter drawings from the ones related to the earlier pictures is their variety, which offers an unprecedented insight in the range of sketches and studies Dürer would make in preparation for a complex composition, 'its internal history'.[6] 'Never before in studies for a painting', wrote Friedrich Winkler, 'had his genius expressed itself so imaginatively and in

OPPOSITE
Detail from *Virgin and Child Enthroned, Fourteen Saints, a Female Donor and Music-making Angels* (cat. 63)

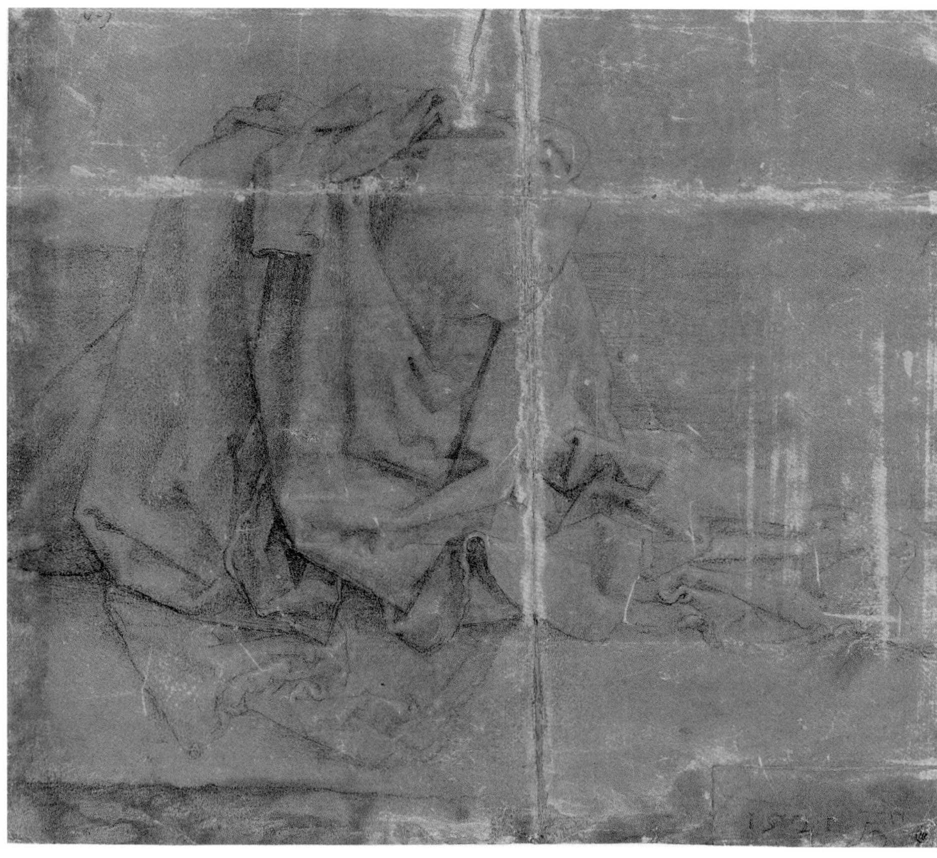

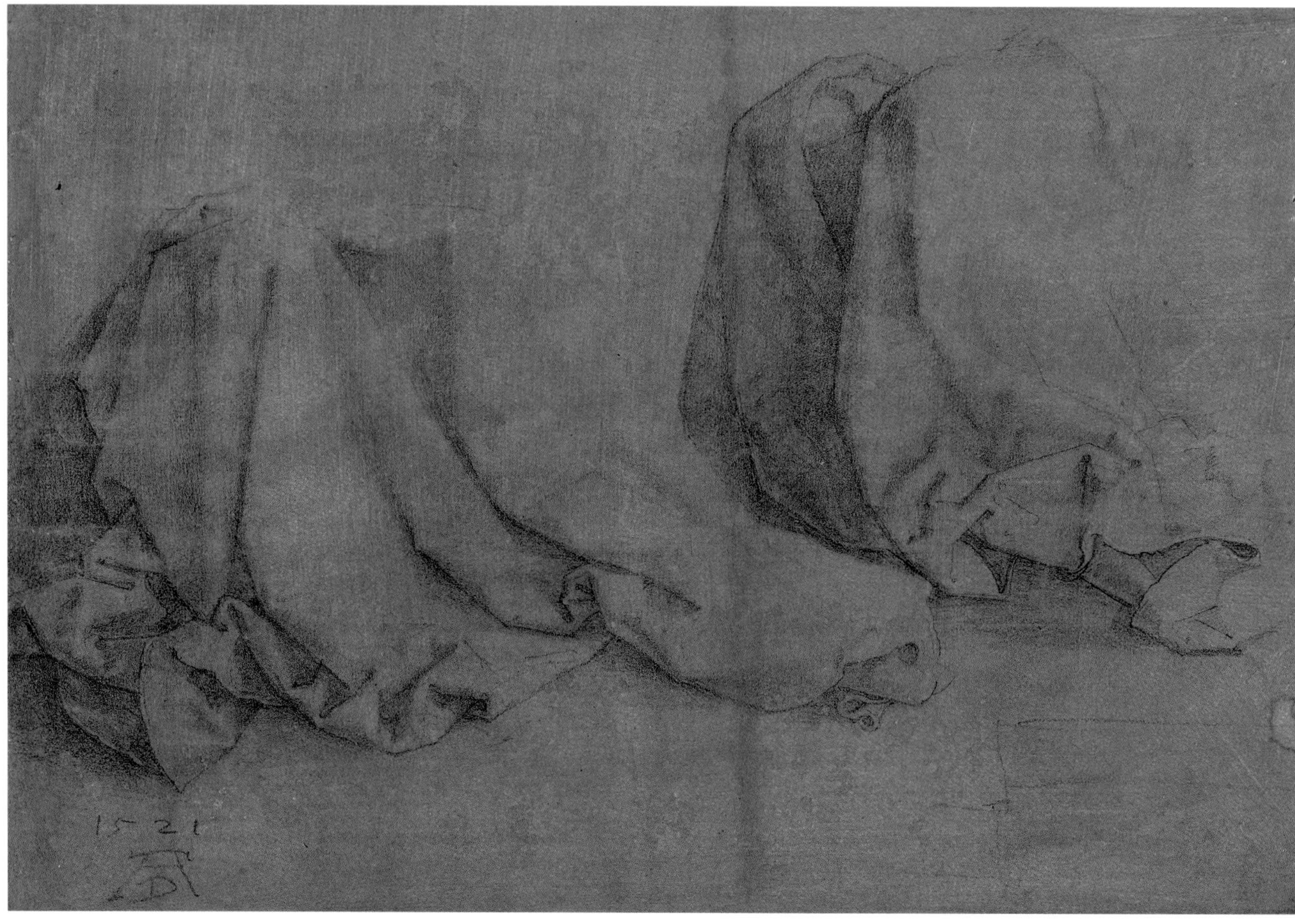

Fig. 55
ALBRECHT DÜRER
Drapery Study, 1521
Metalpoint heightened with white, on blue-green grounded paper, 27. × 30.3 cm
Germanisches Nationalmuseum, Nuremberg (Hz 5489)

58
ALBRECHT DÜRER
Two Drapery Studies, 1521
Metalpoint on green prepared paper, 29.6 × 41.3 cm
Hamburger Kunsthalle, Kupferstichkabinett

such a varied manner, so grandly and concisely, and so varied in technique.'[7]

The drawings include the highly finished sheets on coloured ground, comparable to the celebrated studies of heads, hands and feet for the two earlier paintings. Five of these are drapery studies – two in Berlin, one each in Hamburg and Nuremberg (cat. 58; fig. 55) and one in Bremen (fig. 56, recovered after the Second World War), all executed on prepared paper, some heightened with white.[8] To these can be added no fewer than seven head studies in the same technique: three of women now in the Louvre (fig. 57), in Berlin (fig. 59) and the Biblioteca Ambrosiana in Milan (cat. 60),[9] a weathered head of an old man at the British Museum (cat. 61),[10] one of an angel formerly in Bremen (fig. 58)[11] and two more of a young woman, apparently after the same model, now in the Lehman collection at the Metropolitan Museum of Art and in the Louvre (fig. 60; cat. 62).[12] The latter sheet contains a quietly masterful study of clasped hands. Depicting a woman in an elaborate headdress are a further two grisailles at the Museo Correr in Venice and formerly in Bremen (figs 61, 62).[13] In addition, a detailed drawing in pen and ink, a study of music-making angels, survives at the Metropolitan Museum of Art (cat. 59).[14]

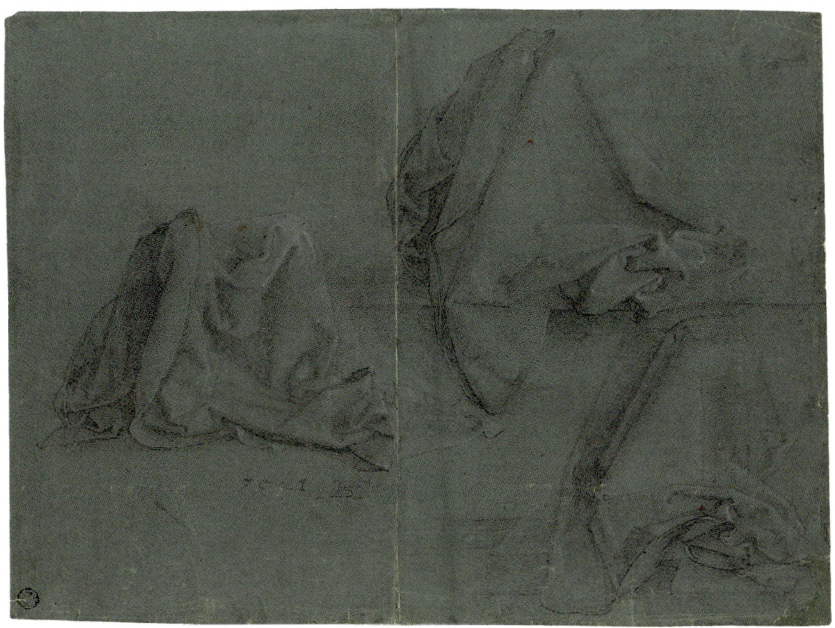

Fig. 56
ALBRECHT DÜRER
Drapery Studies, 1521
Black chalk, heightened with white on green prepared paper, 31.5 × 41.8 cm
Kunsthalle Bremen (Kl 17)

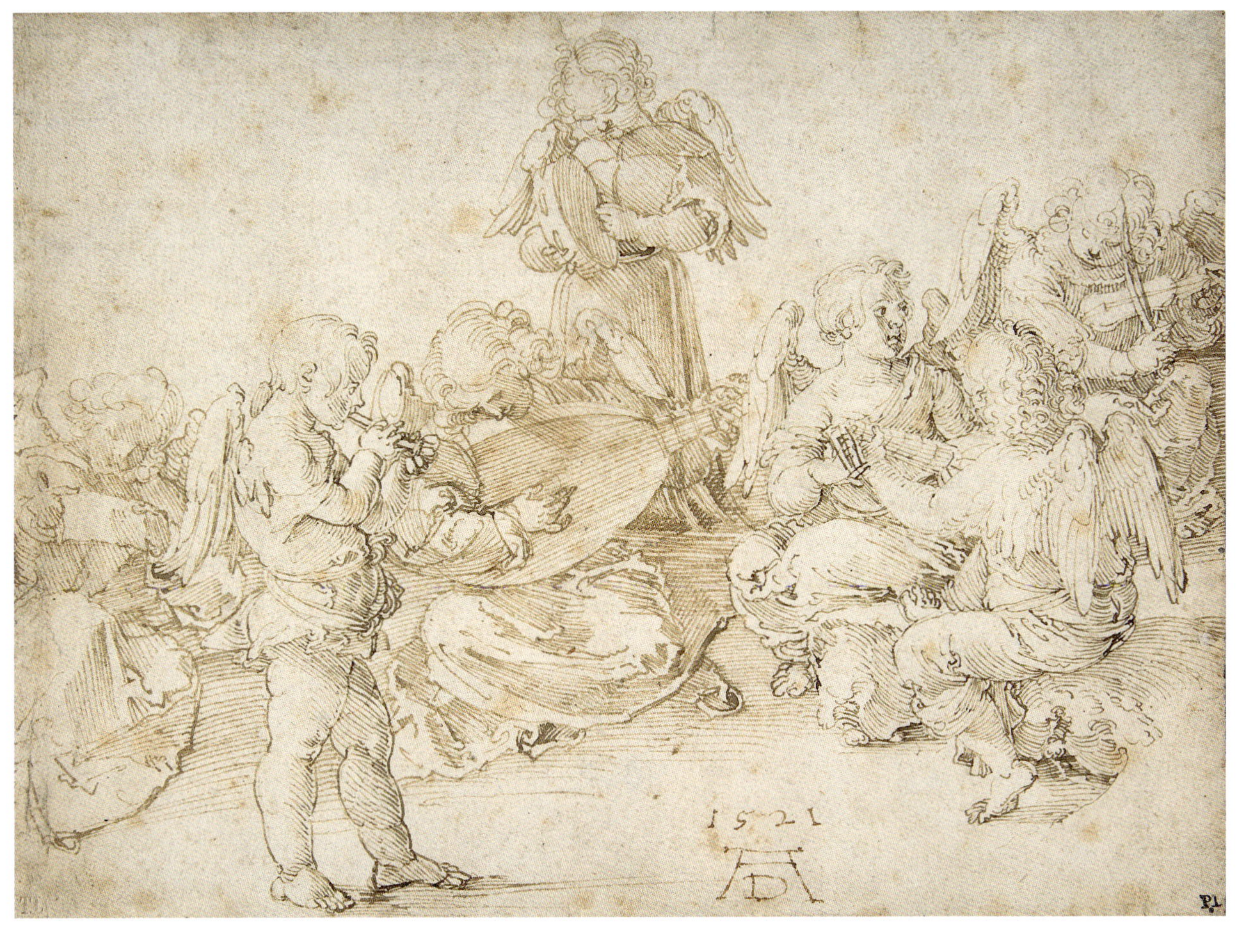

59
ALBRECHT DÜRER
Music-making Angels, 1521
Pen and brown ink, 16.9 × 22.3 cm
The Metropolitan Museum of Art, New York

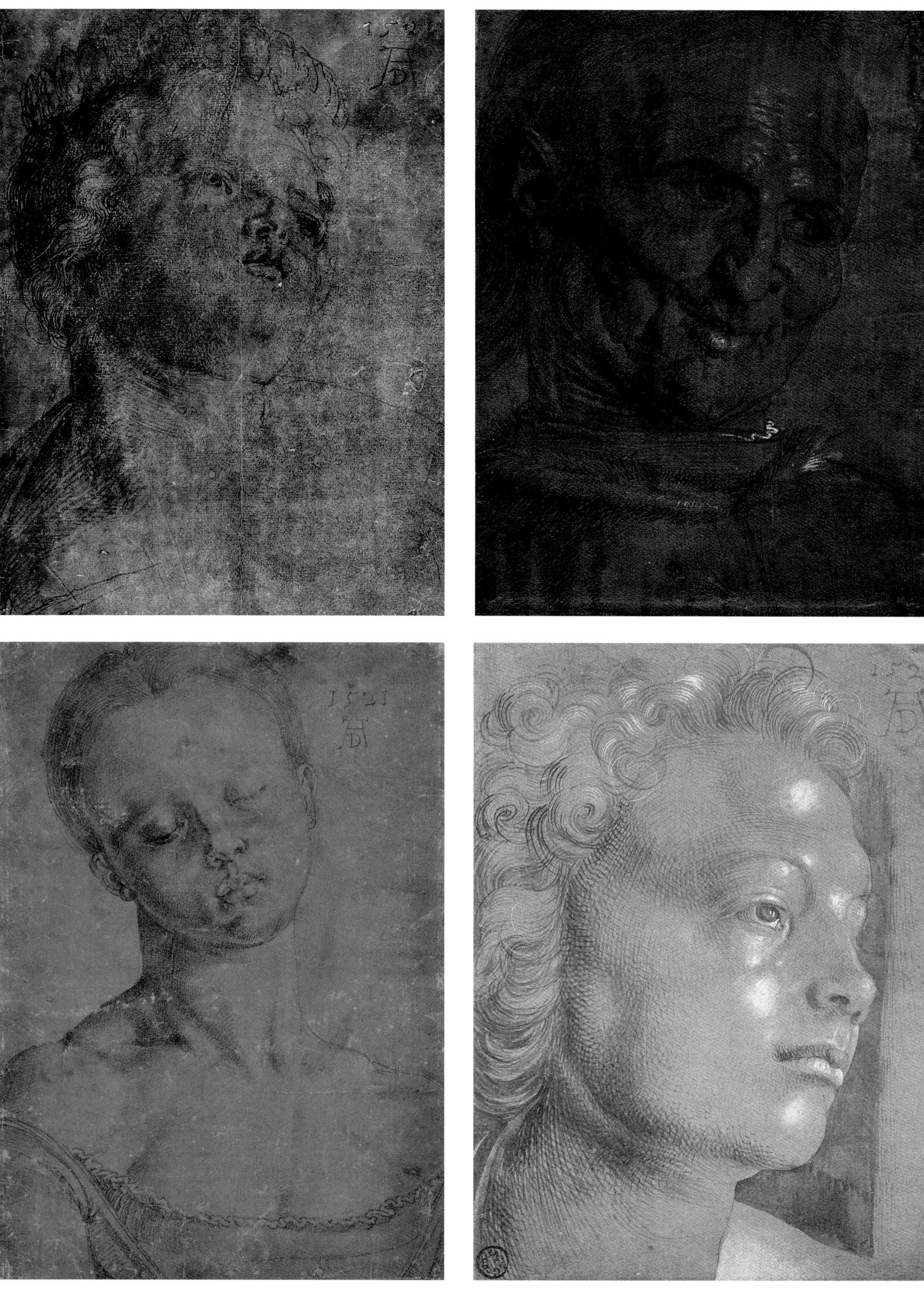
1521
1521
1521

OPPOSITE
TOP LEFT
60
ALBRECHT DÜRER
Saint Catherine, 1521
Black chalk on green grounded paper, 26.6 × 19.7 cm
Veneranda Biblioteca Ambrosiana, Pinacoteca, Milan

TOP RIGHT
61
ALBRECHT DÜRER
Saint Joseph, 1521
Leadpoint heightened with white on dark-grey prepared paper
20.7 × 18.3 cm
British Museum

BOTTOM LEFT
Fig. 57
ALBRECHT DÜRER
Saint Barbara, 1521
Black chalk on green grounded paper, 41.7 × 28.6 cm
Musée du Louvre, Paris (18590)

BOTTOM RIGHT
Fig. 58
ALBRECHT DÜRER
Head of an Angel, 1521
Brush in black and white on grey paper, 21.8 × 15.4 cm
Kunsthalle Bremen (war loss, Kl 13)

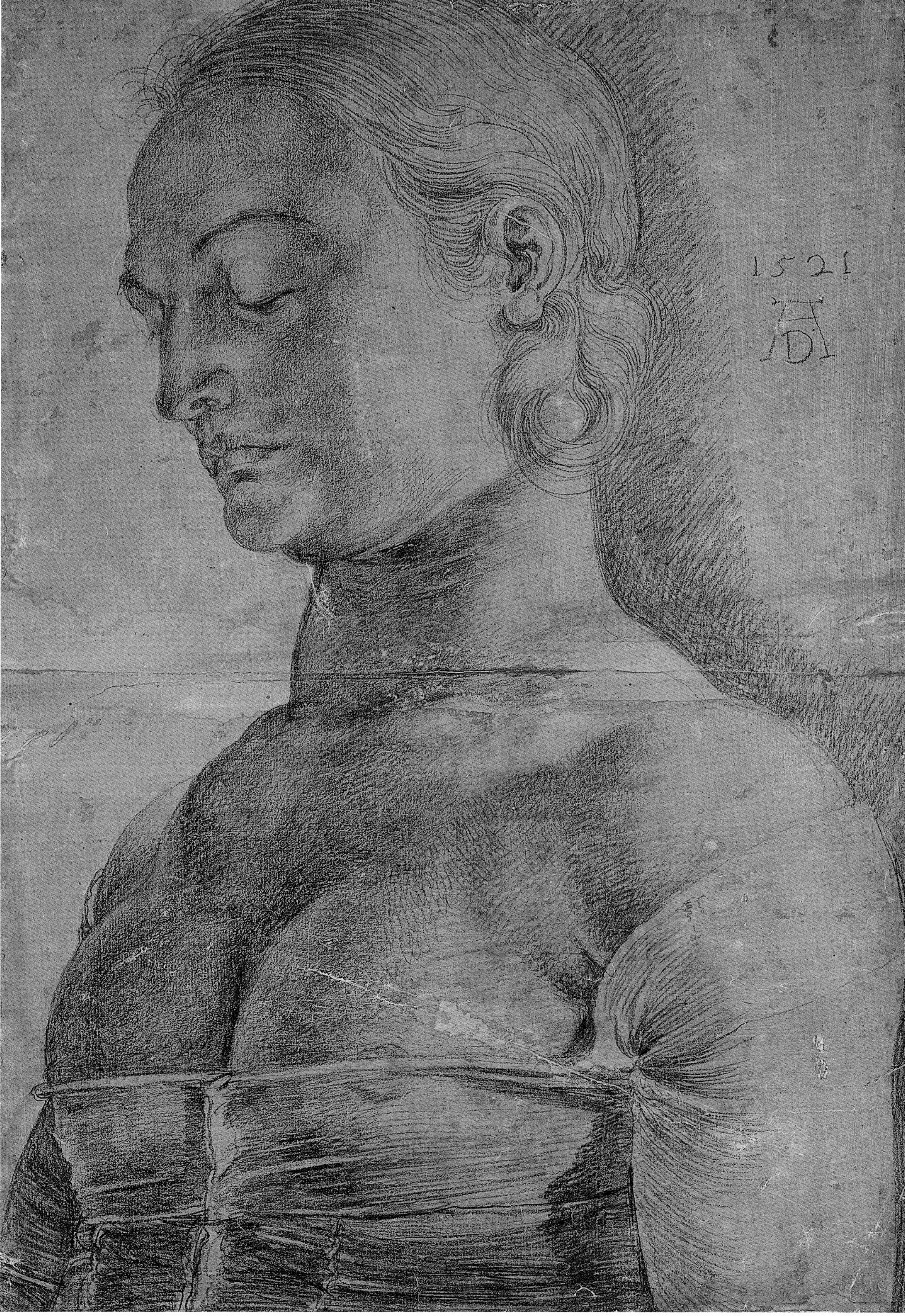

Fig. 59
ALBRECHT DÜRER
Saint Apollonia, 1521
Black chalk on green prepared paper, 41.4 × 28.8 cm
Staatliche Museen zu Berlin, Kupferstichkabinett (KdZ 1527)

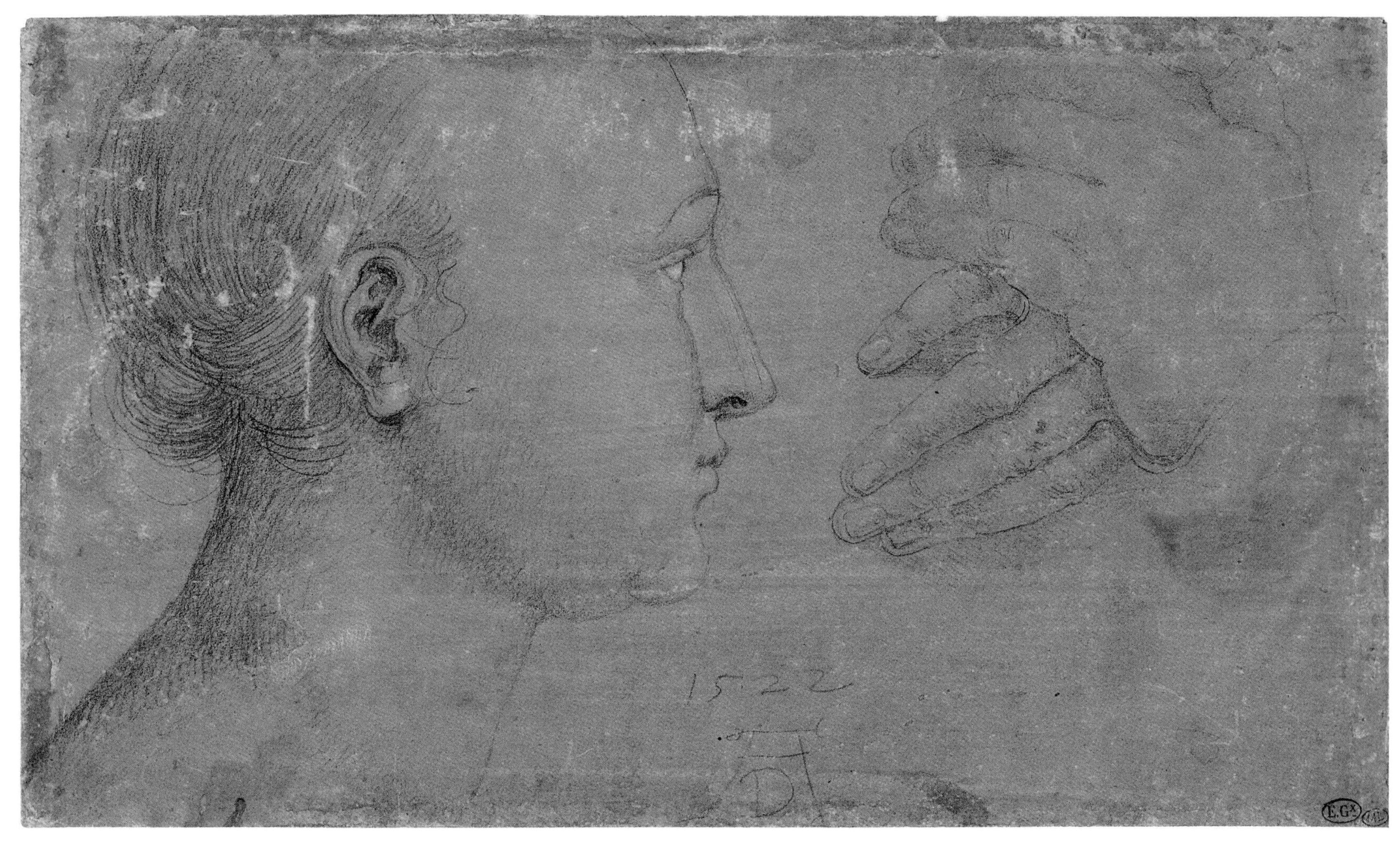

62
ALBRECHT DÜRER
Head of a Woman and Study of Two Hands, 1522
Black chalk heightened with white on green prepared paper, 17.5 × 29 cm
Musée du Louvre, Paris

Fig. 61
ALBRECHT DÜRER
Saint Anne, 1522
Brush in black, white and grey, 39.9 × 28.7 cm
Museo Correr, Venice
(8222)

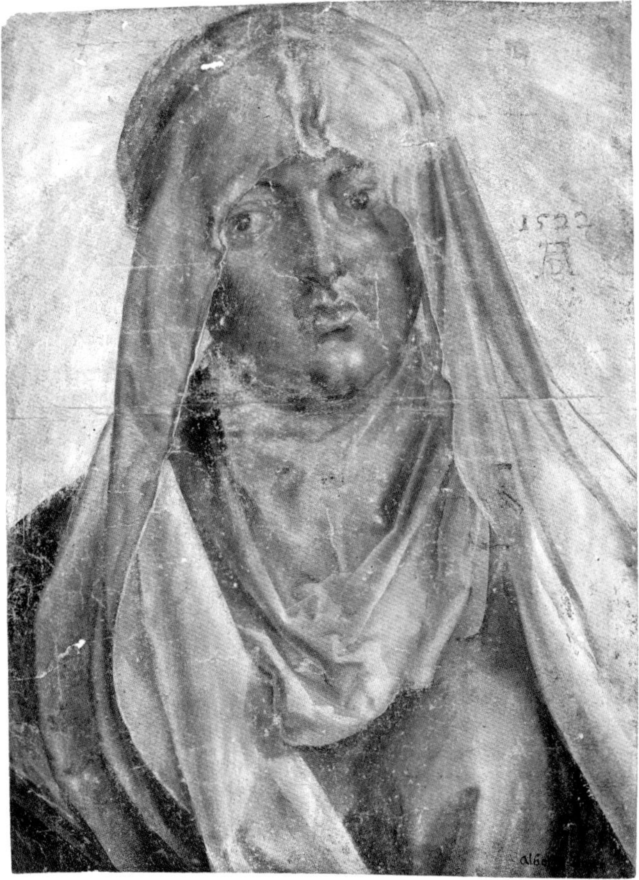

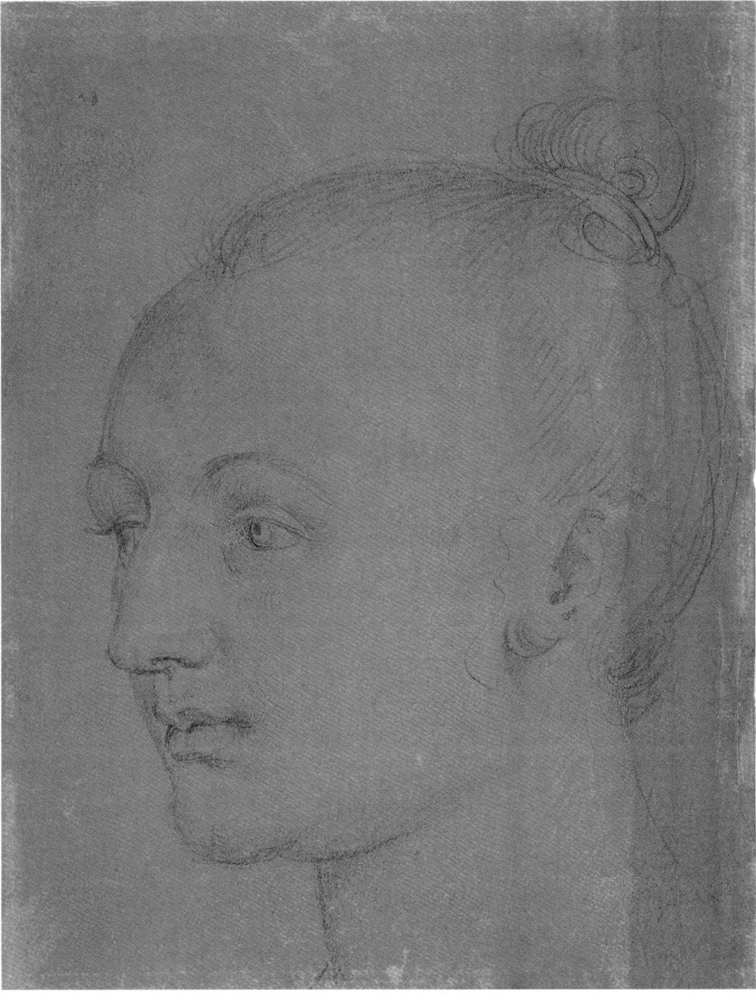

Fig. 60
ALBRECHT DÜRER
Head of a Woman facing Left, 1521
Black chalk highlighted with white chalk (abraded) on green prepared paper, 20 × 15.1 cm
The Metropolitan Museum of Art, New York. Robert Lehman Collection, 1975 (1975.1.85)

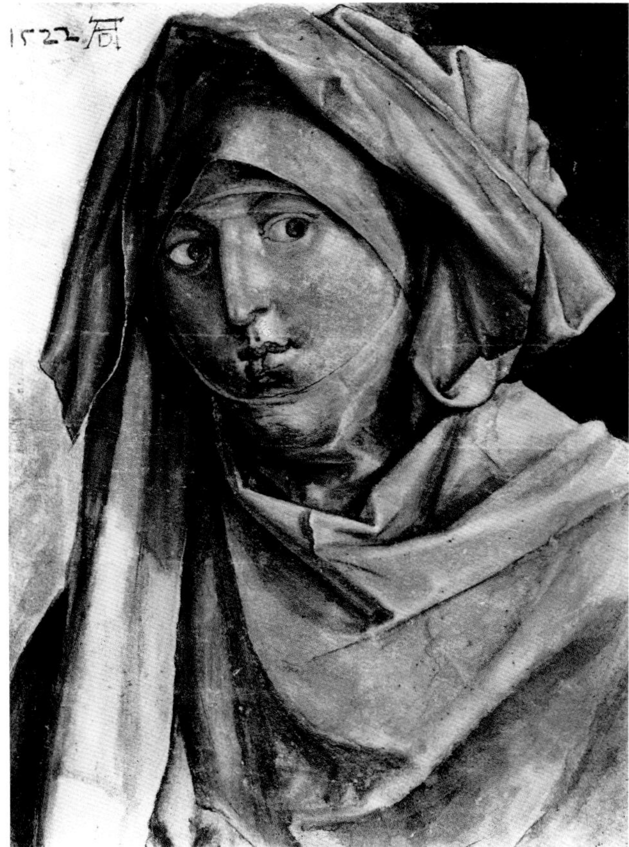

Fig. 62
ALBRECHT DÜRER
Saint Anne, 1522
Brush in black, white and grey on paper partly prepared with black wash, 39.8 × 30.3 cm
Kunsthalle Bremen
(war loss, Kl 15)

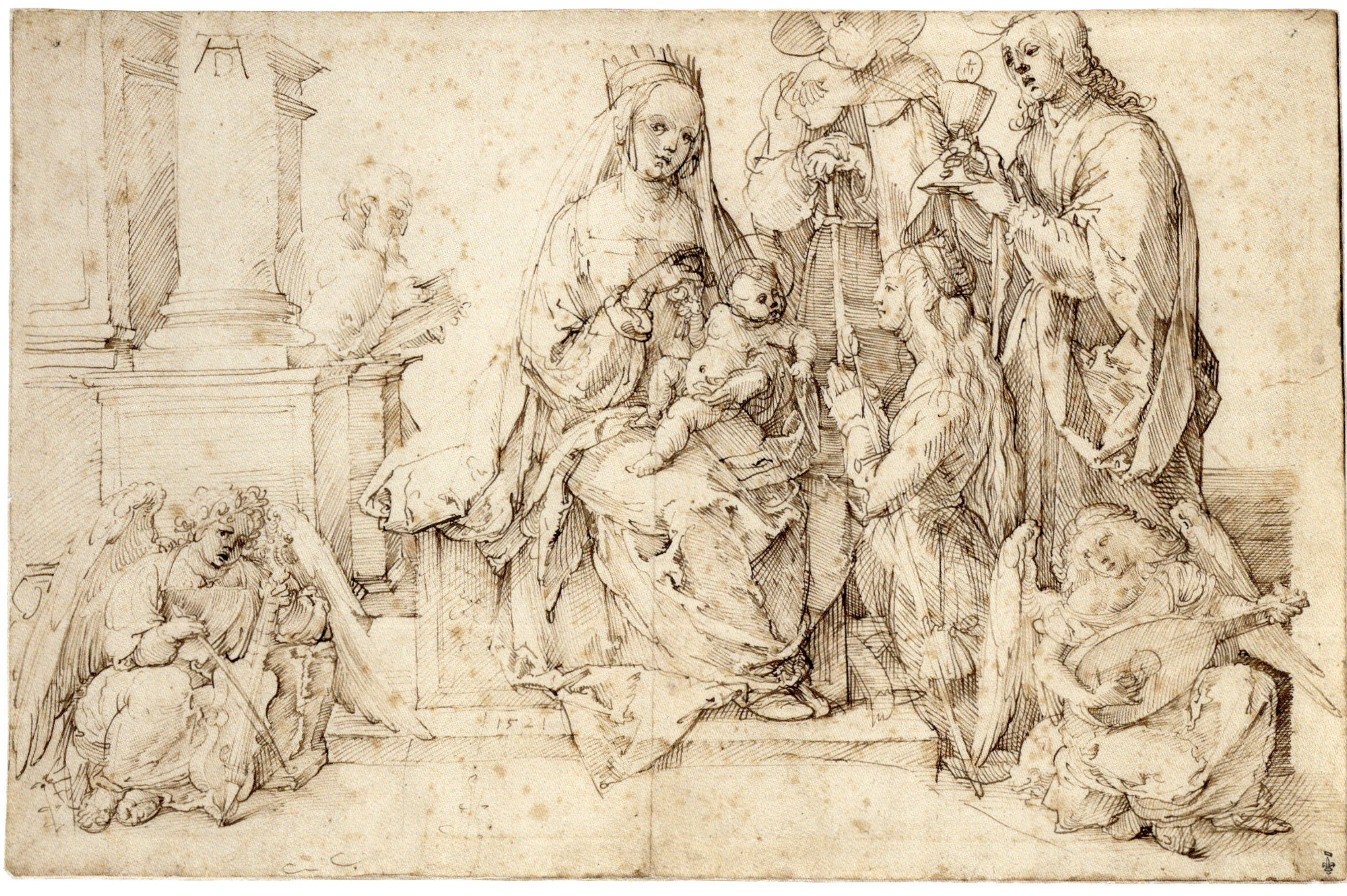

Fig. 63
ALBRECHT DÜRER
Virgin and Child, Joseph, Saints Catherine and James and Music-making Angels, 1521
Pen and brown ink, 25 × 39 cm
Musée Condé, Chantilly (DE889)

It is, however, in a group of compositional pen studies that the drawings related to the project under discussion are most unique – nothing similar survives for either the *Rosenkranzfest* or the Heller Altarpiece, or indeed for almost any of Dürer's other great projects – in painting or print. Three of these studies are among the treasures brought together by the collector and painter Léon Bonnat (1833–1922) and now in Bayonne (figs 64, 65, 66), one is in the Louvre (cat. 63) and one, the most detailed of the five, at the Musée Condé in Chantilly (fig. 63).[15] No less important for a reconstruction of the development of the composition are two copies of a lost original (cat. 64).[16] It is these drawings that allow us to form a precise idea of the project's scope, to follow Dürer's evolving thoughts about the composition, clarify its iconography and identify certain influences that may have shaped it. And it is thanks to them that art historians, starting with Friedrich Lippmann in the late nineteenth century, were able to connect to the project many of the previously mentioned studies of heads and draperies.[17]

The compositional studies make immediately clear that the painting was to depict a gathering of saints around the enthroned Virgin and Child. Ernst Heidrich called it the *Grosses Altarbild*; Emil Waldmann and later Erwin Panofsky a *sacra conversazione*, the kind of sacred conversation piece popular in Italian art from the fifteenth century on; Friedrich Winkler referred to it as the *Grosses Marienbild*.[18] I will title it simply *Virgin and Child with Saints.* In its earliest versions it would not have been unlike the *Rosenkranzfest*, even if the Virgin in that painting is adored not by saints (although she is accompanied by one, standing next to her throne) but by a group of accurately portrayed men, led by Pope Julius II and Emperor Maximilian I and including Dürer himself. No donor appears in the drawing in Chantilly, dated 1521 (fig. 63), but in the more elaborate groupings of the sketch at the Louvre (cat. 63) and one of the sheets in Bayonne (fig. 64), which must both date to the same year, a kneeling woman joins the group of saints at right and can be identified as the painting's *donatrix*.

There can be little doubt that the drawing in Chantilly (fig. 63), which combines a Holy Family with a Mystical Marriage of Saint Catherine, preceded all others: its asymmetrical grouping of the figures and the limited number of saints – only Catherine,

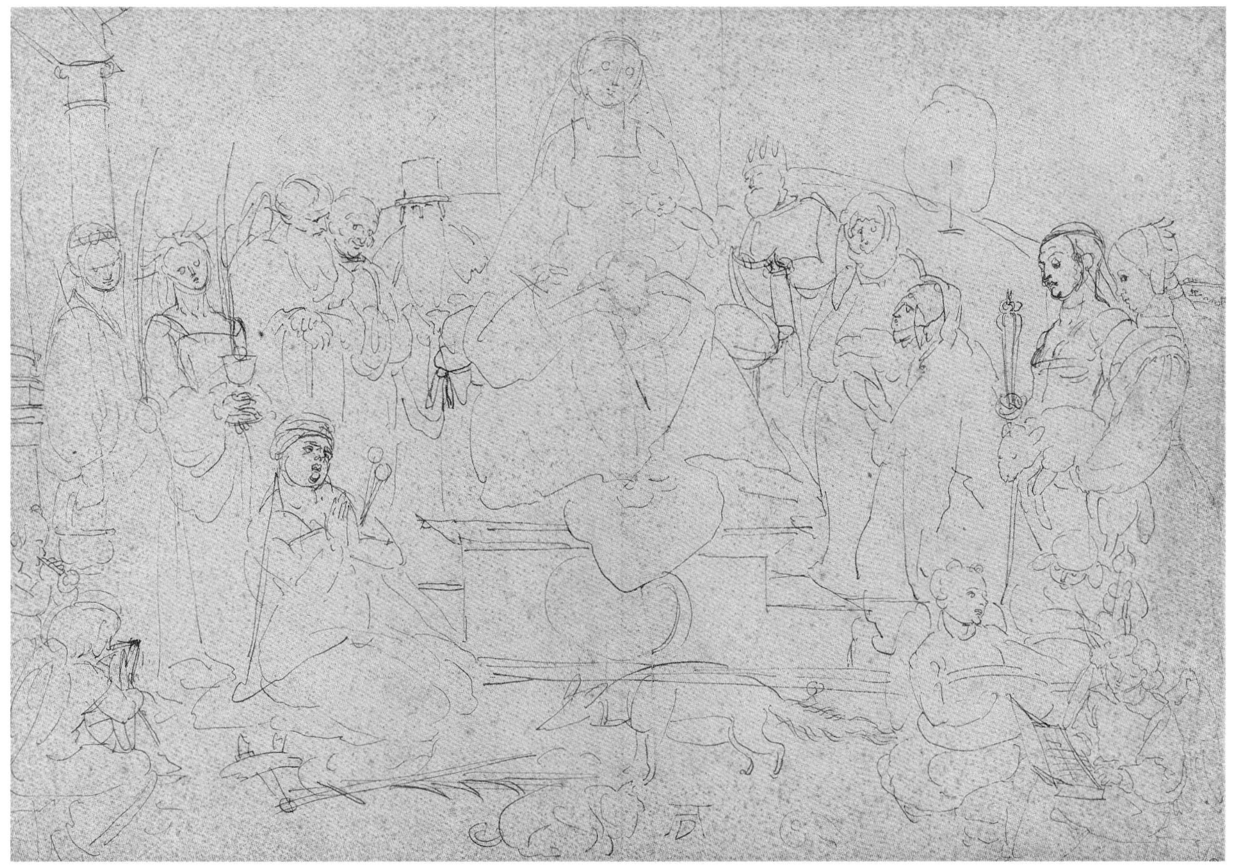

Fig. 64
ALBRECHT DÜRER
Virgin and Child Enthroned, Fourteen Saints, a Female Donor and Music-making Angels, 1521
Pen and brown ink, 31.6 × 44.5 cm
Musée Bonnat-Helleu, Bayonne (1505)

BELOW LEFT
Fig. 65
ALBRECHT DÜRER
Virgin and Child, Eight Saints and Music-making Angels, 1522
Pen and brown ink, 26.3 × 22.8 cm
Musée Bonnat-Helleu, Bayonne (1506)

BELOW RIGHT
Fig. 66
ALBRECHT DÜRER
Virgin and Child Enthroned, Eight Saints and Music-making Angels, 1522
Pen and brown ink, 40.1 × 30.7 cm
Musée Bonnat-Helleu, Bayonne (1504)

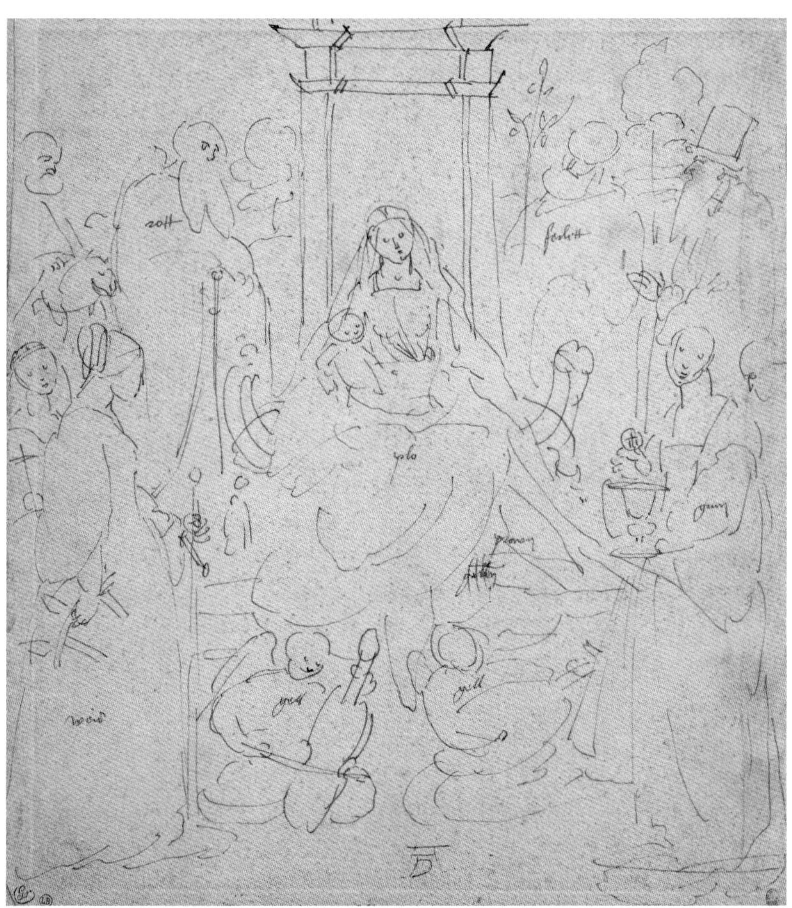

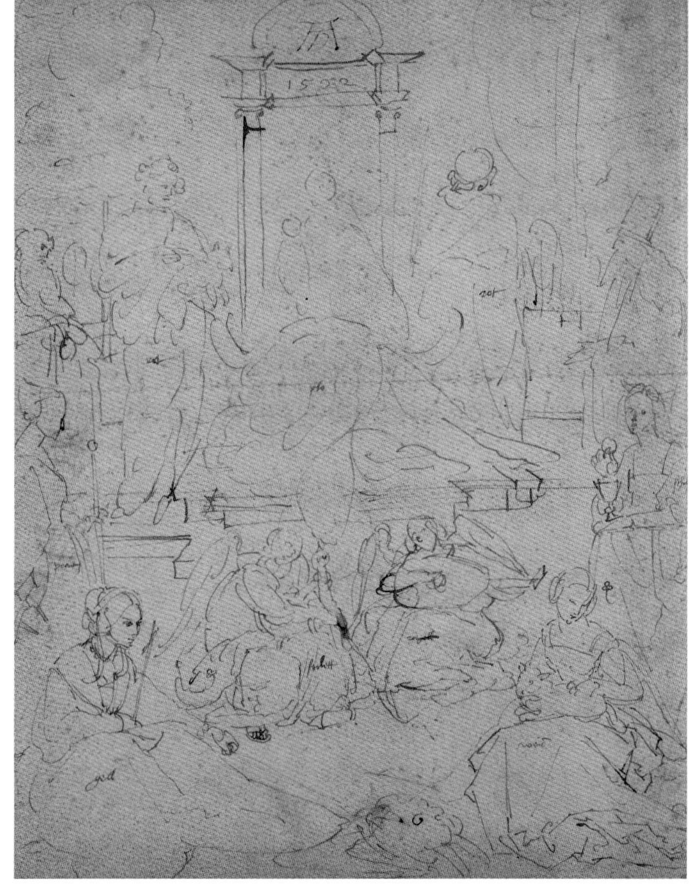

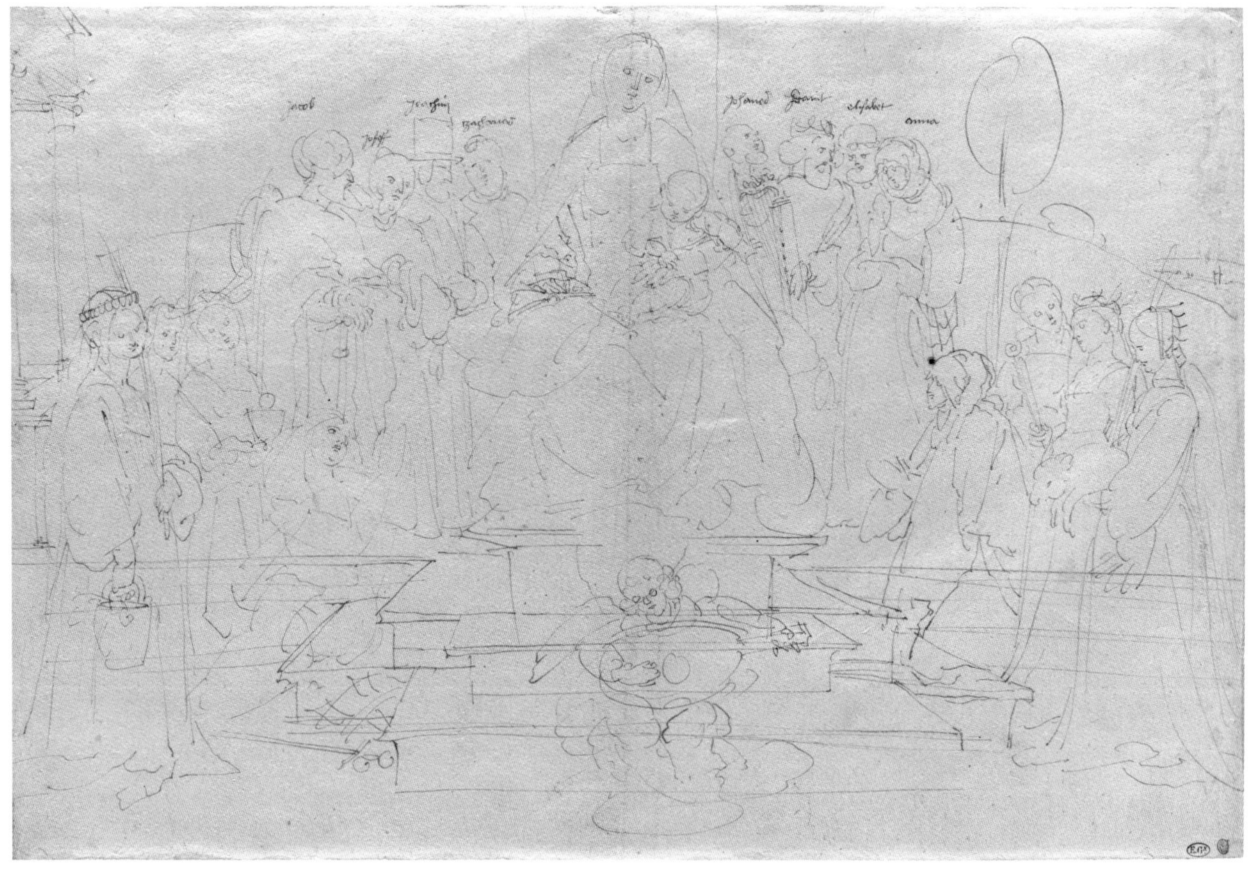

63
ALBRECHT DÜRER
Virgin and Child Enthroned, Fourteen Saints, a Female Donor and Music-making Angels, 1521–2
Pen and brown ink,
31.2 × 44.5 cm
Musée du Louvre, Paris

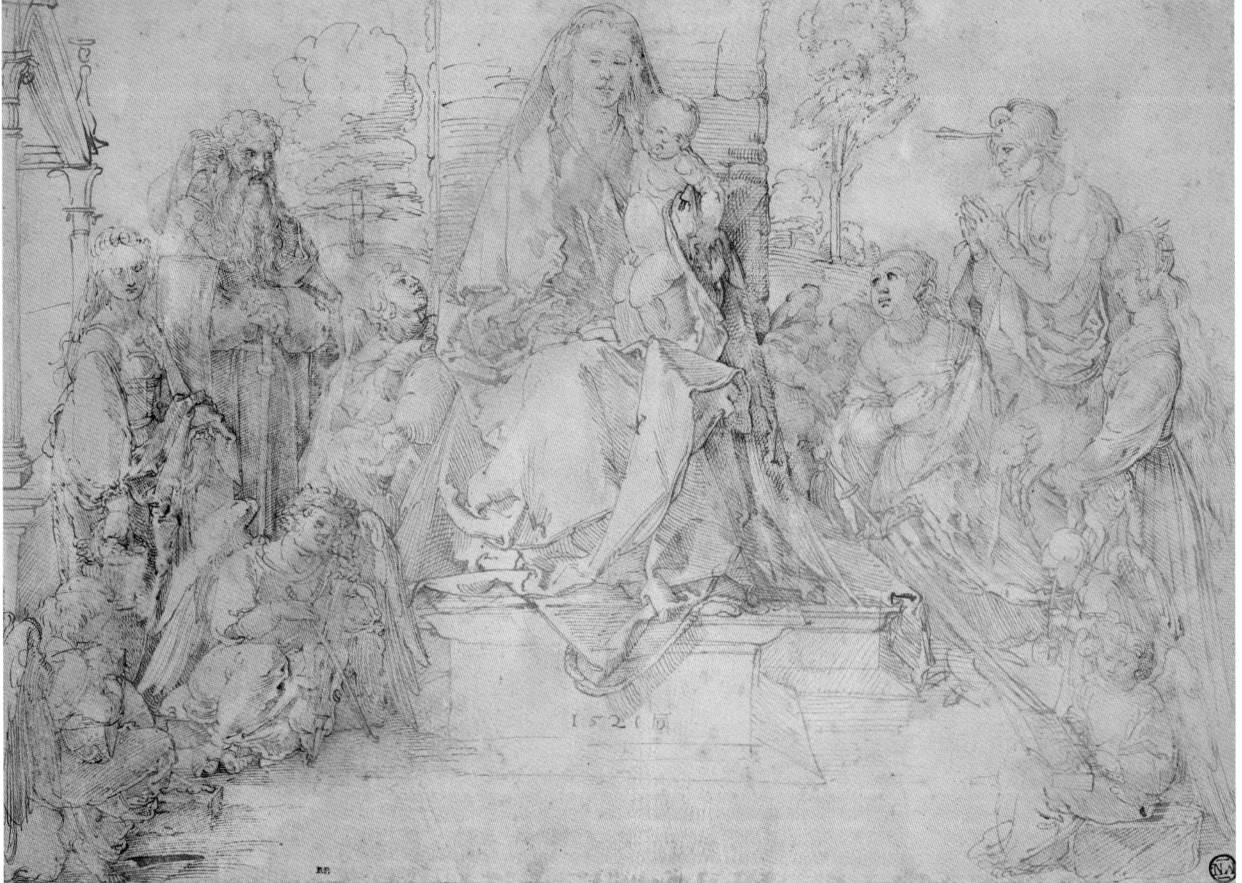

64
AFTER ALBRECHT DÜRER
Virgin and Child Enthroned, Six Saints and Music-making Angels, 1521
Pen and brown ink,
31.6 × 43.8 cm
Musée du Louvre, Paris

James and John the Evangelist, in addition to Joseph in the left background – set it apart from the others. A major transformation of the composition took place between the Chantilly drawing and the one only known from the two copies (cat. 64): while the architectural elements at left are greatly reduced, the composition as a whole has gained in monumentality and complexity – traits that would remain evident in all successive sketches. Saints Catherine and James have remained, and Saints Dorothea (with flowers in her hair and her basket) and Agnes (with her lamb) make their appearance, as well as Saint Sebastian. He is no longer included in the two following sketches, the horizontal drawings in the Louvre and in Bayonne (cat. 63 and fig. 64), but the total number of saints is greatly expanded – and conveniently identified in the former. The Bayonne drawing includes slightly fewer saints (ten) but is no less monumental than the sheet in the Louvre (which has 14, plus King David), and it can be considered Dürer's final version of the horizontal variant of the composition, to which the surviving head studies can be most closely related.

In all these drawings, angels playing music occupy the foreground. (In addition, the Bayonne drawing has a dog and a chained fox, a quotation from Dürer's own celebrated watercolour of *The Virgin with a Multitude of Animals* in Vienna).[19] The pair of angels in the sketch at Chantilly (fig. 63) – one left, one right – has doubled in the copies after the lost sketch (cat. 64), while the original in the Louvre has only one (cat. 63), and the horizontal sketch in Bayonne has five (fig. 64). No fewer than seven are grouped together in the Metropolitan Museum of Art's drawing of 1521 (cat. 59), which comes closest to the Bayonne sketch; here the flute player can be found back at left, next to a lutenist not dissimilar to the one at right in the New York sheet, but in reverse. Moreover, the group of three angels, with variations in pose and instruments, is clearly related to the three at right in the Bayonne composition, which was likely made after Dürer had worked on the New York study and decided to break up the group of angels, perhaps because he felt they would occupy too much of the foreground.

The Louvre's compositional sketch is extensively inscribed with the names of the saints, most of which are also included in the first Bayonne sketch. Five of these saints can be related to large head studies on prepared ground: from left to right, thoughtful Saint Barbara (fig. 57), recognisable in both sketches by her chalice; supplicative Saint Catherine (cat. 60), who corresponds neatly to the kneeling woman looking up at left, with the broken wheel and the sword of her martyrdom at her feet; the broadly smiling Joseph (cat. 61); the formidable Saint Apollonia (fig. 59), perhaps the most beautiful and famous of all the drawings for the series, identified in the sketches by the tongs with which her teeth were pulled; and an angel looking up (fig. 58), so similar to one of the music-making angels at right in the Bayonne drawing that it must have been made as a preparatory study for that figure. The remaining drawings can also, with more or less certainty be connected to individual figures in the compositional sketches. The five drapery studies (see cat. 58; figs 55, 56) are, as one might expect, more loosely connected with the sketches, but the date on them, 1521, establishes at the very least a chronological proximity to the *Virgin and Child with Saints.* Furthermore, the use of prepared paper so similar to that used for the head studies makes it all the more plausible that they were conceived with the figure of the Virgin Mary or one of the kneeling figures in mind.[20]

Taken all together, the three compositional sketches and the numerous individual studies indicate just how far advanced Dürer was with his project and how thoroughly he felt he needed to prepare it. Most of this activity appears to have taken place in 1521, the date found on a good number of the drawings discussed above, alongside Dürer's monogram. But that at least some were executed after his return to Nuremberg is not only evident from watermarks,[21] but also suggested by the fact that four are dated the following year: the study of a head and hands in the Louvre (cat. 62); the grisailles in Venice and formerly in Bremen (figs 61, 62); and another compositional sketch in Bayonne (fig. 66). The latter drawing, together with an undated second one in the same collection made at the same time (fig. 65), documents a major change in Dürer's mind: the horizontal composition has now become a vertical one, with far fewer figures attending to the Virgin and Child, and those remaining arranged in a different way and taking different poses. The female donor has disappeared, but in the dated drawing a new saint is introduced: Margaret, seated in the left foreground with the dragon or demon she conquered given the exact form of a walrus Dürer sketched in the Netherlands (fig. 112). These changes show that Dürer kept generating ideas for the painting – or, one could argue, was still struggling to find its right format. During the process the artist remained focused on the final realisation of his explorations, adding colour notes to both sketches, which are absent from the horizontal ones. The new compositions group the figures in a more circular way and give more prominence to the architecture of the Virgin's throne.

One could almost think Dürer had abandoned the 'horizontal' project altogether, starting the vertical one with a tabula rasa. However, many connections exist between the two groups of compositional sketches, notably the central position of the enthroned Virgin, the music-making angels and some of the saints. Saint Barbara, for instance, simply seems to have changed sides, taking her chalice with her and becoming her own mirror-image. Saint James, identified with an inscription in the Louvre drawing (cat. 63) and in the same pose in both that drawing and the related compositional study in Bayonne (fig. 64), is closely comparable to the similarly bearded man also on the Virgin's right-hand side, his hands resting on his staff (figs 65, 66). The close connection between the horizontal and vertical studies is illustrated by the drawing of a female head and hands at the Louvre (cat. 62). While the hands are easily recognisable as those of Saint James in all drawings, the study of the head of a young woman in profile looking to the right does not relate to any of the female saints in the horizontal compositions – but it can be connected with the now standing Saint Catherine in the two vertical drawings in Bayonne. The undated drawing in the same technique in the Metropolitan Museum of Art (fig. 60) does not correspond to any of the saints but may have been made after the same young model, or, if done from memory, presents the same features and hairstyle.

Distinguished by their technique from both the compositional sketches and the studies of heads and draperies discussed above are the two grisailles in Venice and formerly in Bremen (figs 61, 62). Like a celebrated grisaille in the Albertina dated 1519 (fig. 67), they are executed in brush and black, grey and white on a grey ground. All three examples represent Saint Anne; the example in Vienna is even directly connected – and probably preparatory – to a figure representing her in a painting in the Metropolitan Museum of Art (fig. 68).[22] The two grisailles linked to the *Virgin and Child with Saints* are related to the figure in the horizontal sketches identified as Saint Anne, the Virgin's mother, in the Louvre sheet (cat. 61), where she stands close to the kneeling female donor. Anne's elaborate headdress is the main subject of the grisailles: the technique is marvellously adapted to the purpose of studying the intricate folds and complex play of light and shadow. The position of her head in the horizontal compositional sketches is not as precisely defined as that of some of the other saints, but the Bayonne sketch in particular, in which Anne seems to face the viewer, comes close to the Bremen grisaille.

That some of the drawings for the *Virgin and Child with Saints* date from 1522, when Dürer had certainly returned to Nuremberg, has raised the question of whether or not all drawings, including those dated 1521, were made after his sojourn in the Netherlands. Compositionally, the sketches – and most clearly the vertical ones – go back to the type of Venetian *sacre conversazioni*, such as one from around 1490 by Alvise Vivarini, formerly in Berlin – the kind of altarpieces that Dürer admired on his trips to Venice (fig. 70).[23] Venetian influences were already evident in his horizontal sketches, especially in the music-making angels, which are such a common feature in Venetian altarpieces. In fact, one of the angels in the Metropolitan Museum of Art drawing seems to be directly inspired by Vivarini's flute-player at left. One wonders what kind of copies, unknown to us today, Dürer must have made during his time in Italy to record works of art that inspired him. Such copies would have served him during the rest of his career. For example, a lute-playing angel is common to both the *Rosenkranzfest* of 1506 and works from later periods in his career, as in a drawing in Hamburg depicting the Virgin and Child seated on a grassy bank and accompanied by an angel playing the lute – or the superb pen drawing at Windsor Castle of 1519 (fig. 69; cat. 65).[24]

But even some of the earliest scholars commenting on the *Virgin and Child with Saints* project have pointed out that the compositions, in particular the horizontal ones, are also influenced by Netherlandish paintings. Dürer, who in his journal records numerous works of art he admired in Antwerp and beyond, must have studied these works not only with his eyes but also by drawing copies after them.[25] A sheet from the silverpoint sketch-book, formerly in Bremen, seems to be one of the rare extant examples of this practice by the artist.[26] While only the model for the young woman looking down at left may have been identified (see below), most scholars agree that the crowned woman in profile at right, too, must have been based on a Netherlandish model. The latter is strongly reminiscent of the kneeling Saint Catherine in the compositional sketch in Chantilly, the Saint Agnes (with the lamb) at right in the horizontal sketches and (in reverse) Saint Catherine at left in the vertical ones. And it is easy to imagine the serene face of the study at left being a source of inspiration for that of the Virgin.

More importantly, the Virgin's face points to a probable source for Dürer's composition in its horizontal iteration. Among the works that Dürer may have copied in the study of the woman looking down is the large panel now in Rouen by Gerard David.[27] Presented in 1509 by the artist to the Carmelites of Sion in Bruges, the magnificent assembly of female saints around the Virgin and Child flanked by music-making

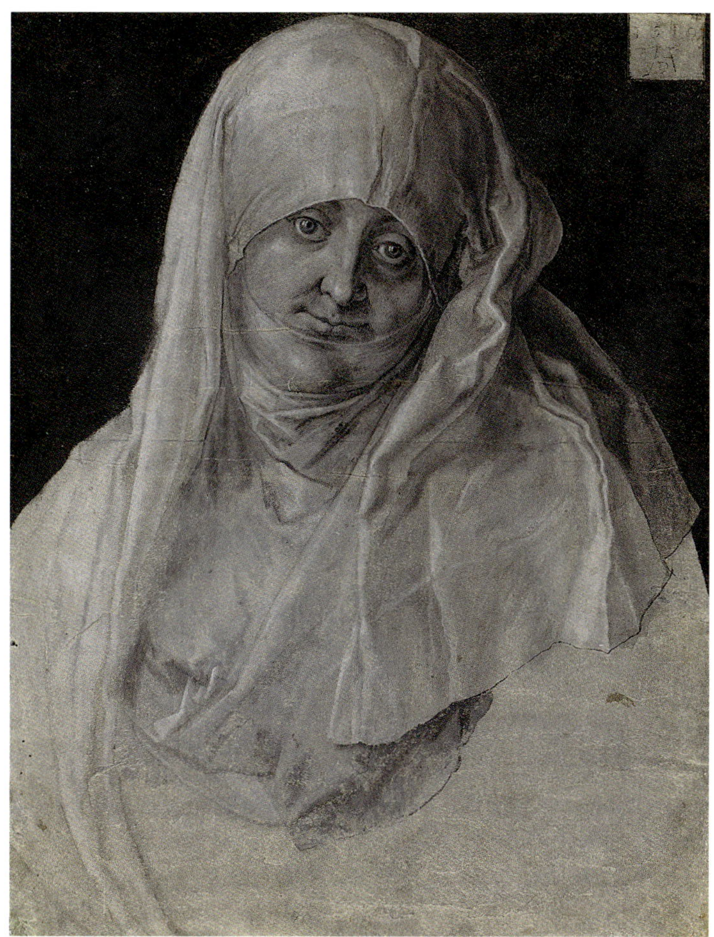

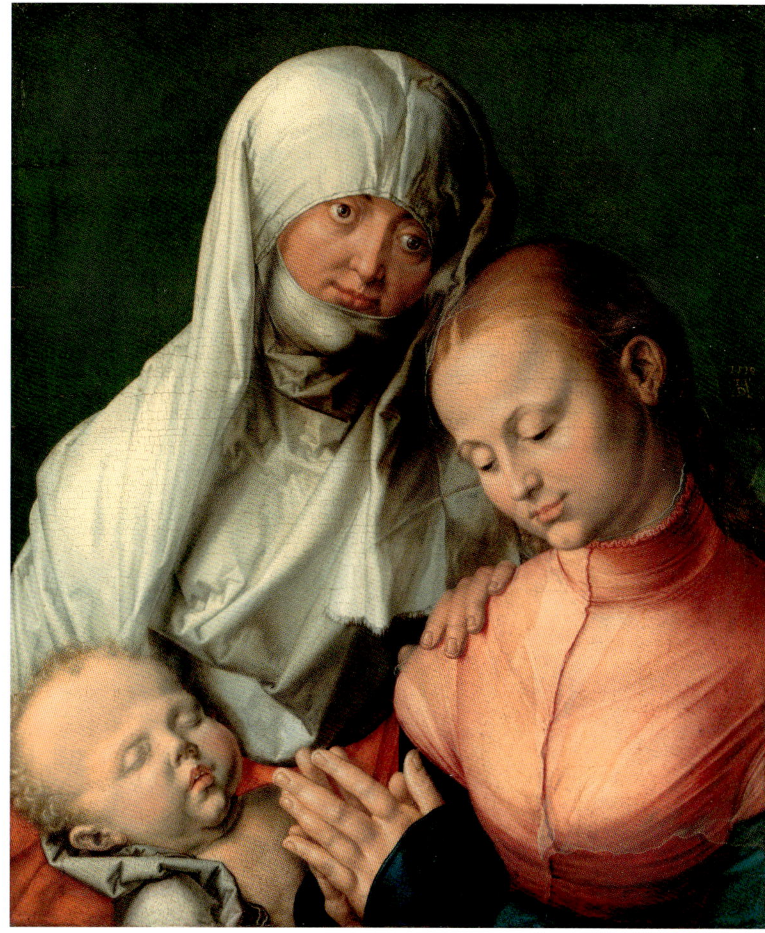

angels is rooted in fifteenth-century models but 'bold in every way, even unprecedented in northern art'.[28] Although Dürer does not single out the painting among those he saw when visiting Bruges in early April 1521, it seems highly likely it was among 'all the fine paintings of which they have an abundance there' that his hosts took him to see.[29] It is without doubt the kind of work Dürer had in mind when he was developing the composition of the *Virgin and Child with Saints*, trying to emulate it but also surpass it by infusing it with the artistic experiences of a lifetime.[30] The inspiration taken from David's example may not have been only formal, but also iconographical, since at least three of the less familiar saints included by Dürer – Dorothea, Apollonia and Agnes – are also among those depicted by David.[31]

He could, of course, have carried such inspiration back to Germany, most likely in the form of studies such as the one from the silverpoint sketchbook discussed above, and only started working on the project there. Matthias Mende has suggested that the fact that not even an allusion is made to the *Virgin and Child with Saints* in Dürer's otherwise detailed journal must be seen as an indication that he did not work on it before returning to Nuremberg, and even there 'hardly before the end of the year'.[32] He proposes that the painting may have been commissioned for the Tucher family, and suggests that the presence of the female donor may have to do with the death in 1520 of Magdalena Stromer, wife and mother to the men who made the family business flourish. While more convincing than an earlier suggestion, already refuted by Winkler, that the painting was a commission for the church of St Peter in Riga,[33] Mende's hypothesis does not offer a satisfactory explanation for the obsession with which Dürer seems to have worked, nor for the lavishness of the projected painting, which can only be compared to that of the *Rosenkranzfest* and seems rather out of league for a Nuremberg merchant family. It also leaves unexplained why none of the men of the locally prominent family, but only a (deceased) woman should have been included in the painting, against all customs in German painting of the time.

An argument in favour of an earlier starting date of the project, while Dürer was still in the Netherlands, is provided by the first of the compositional sketches, that in Chantilly (fig. 63). The watermark in the fairly large sheet (25 × 39 cm) on which it was made – a salient unicorn with mane and dashes on the horn – is found with great frequency in paper used in the third decade

Fig. 67
ALBRECHT DÜRER
Saint Anne, 1519
Brush and grey, black and white ink on grey grounded paper, partly blackened by a later hand (?), 39.5 × 29.2 cm
The Albertina Museum, Vienna (3160)

Fig. 68
ALBRECHT DÜRER
Virgin and Child with Saint Anne, 1519
Oil on linden, 60 × 49.8 cm
The Metropolitan Museum of Art, New York. Bequest of Benjamin Altman

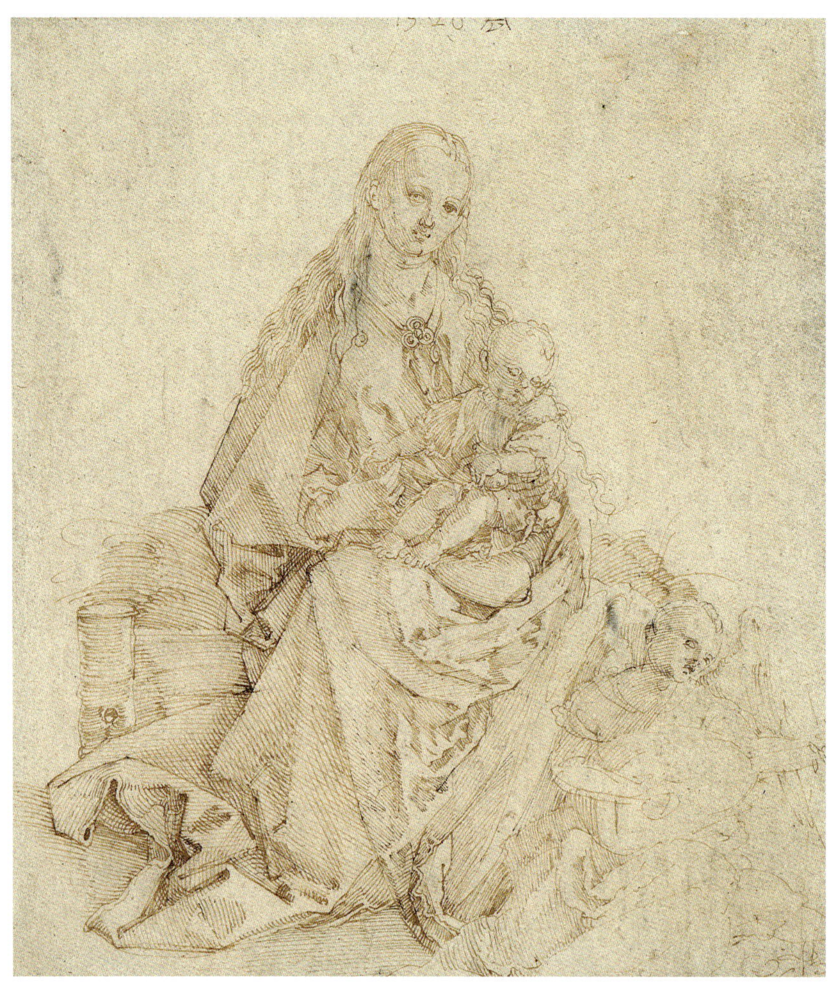

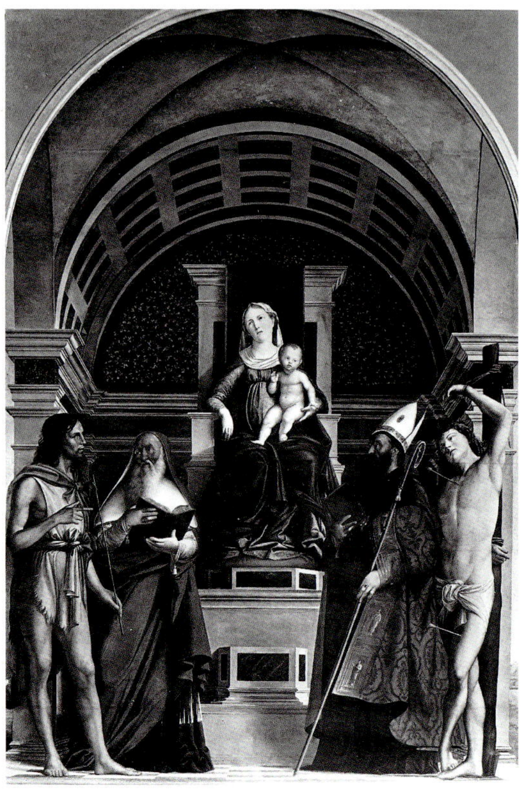

Fig. 69
ALBRECHT DÜRER
Virgin and Child with Music-making Angel, 1520
Pen and brown ink, 24.2 × 20.6 cm
Hamburger Kunsthalle, Hamburg (23001)

Fig. 70
ALVISE VIVARINI
(before 1475–1503/5)
Virgin and Child Enthroned with Six Saints ('Pala di Belluno'), about .1490
Oil on panel, 385 × 231 cm
Staatliche Museen zu Berlin, Gemäldegalerie (war loss, 38)

of the century in both the northern and southern Netherlands, including Antwerp, Brussels and Mechelen.[34] Although that drawing does not yet include the female donor, she does appear in the following two horizontal sketches, and it must at least be explored whether no woman resident in the Netherlands could feature as the donor of such an ambitious work. That such a donor would have had to be of the highest rank is evident from the rarity of works with single female donors, that is, without husband or male counterpart. Where they appear, in paintings or manuscripts, they are usually of royal birth.[35]

In my catalogue of early German drawings at the Metropolitan Museum of Art, I ventured to suggest – in a footnote and in cautious terms – that the patron may have been a woman of greater renown than those suggested before, who had become a widow in 1504 and who on her own continued to pursue an ambitious activity as a collector of works of art, while also being a devout Christian with a particular veneration for the Virgin.[36] The patron I had in mind was Archduchess Margaret of Austria, aunt of Charles V and governess of the Netherlands during Dürer's time there, whom he personally met and whose favour he tried to win. Not only was she of the highest birth, she was also occasionally portrayed in the context of a religious painting, as for instance in Bernaert van Orley's *Crucifixion* in Rotterdam, the central panel of an incomplete triptych, in which she appears in the guise of Caritas (fig. 71).[37] The summarily drawn face in Dürer's two horizontal sketches offers no help in identifying her, but the hood of Netherlandish type and the widow's dress worn by the kneeling donor corresponds to those worn by Margaret in paintings from the time, including van Orley's *Crucifixion* and the famous likeness, datable to 1518 or shortly after and known in several versions (cat. 57), by the same artist and his workshop.[38]

It is true that no commission from Margaret is mentioned anywhere in Dürer's journal, which does discuss at some length his interactions with the archduchess during his two visits to Mechelen. But surely no journal, not even one as meticulous as Dürer's, records every event or turn of conversation. Perhaps one should

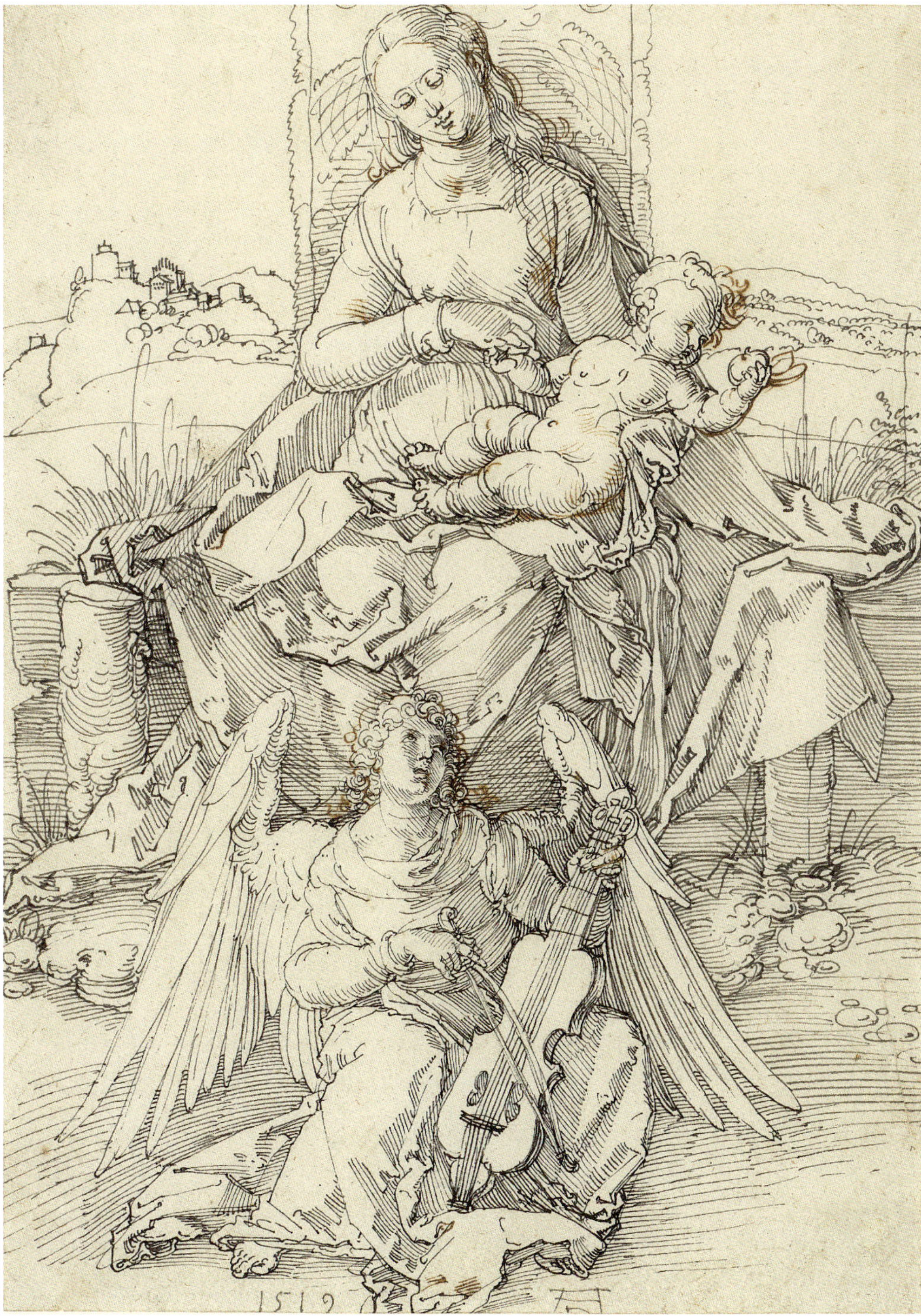

65
ALBRECHT DÜRER
Virgin and Child Seated in a Landscape with an Angel playing the Violin, 1519
Pen and black ink, with revisions in brown ink, 30.3 × 21.2 cm
The Royal Collection / HM Queen Elizabeth II

not imagine that the painting was a direct commission from Margaret but rather a project that Dürer devised to ingratiate himself with a figure of power who was also a distinguished and highly discerning patron of the arts. Both of his visits to her in Mechelen show his preoccupation with securing her and Charles V's favour and patronage. In the journal he is pleased to note in August 1520 that 'she will put my case to King Charles' and 'has shown herself extremely friendly towards me', while adding, in his characteristically punctilious manner, that he offers her and her adviser Jean de Marnix a copy of his *Engraved Passion*.[39] During the second visit, in June 1521, Margaret generously shows him 'all her beautiful pieces', which greatly impress the artist. But a portrait of the emperor that he had shown her the day before – perhaps most likely a hand-coloured woodcut representing her father, emperor Maximilian – Margaret 'disliked so much … that I took it away with me again'.[40]

If the *Virgin and Child with Saints* was not a true commission but perhaps an initiative of the artist,[41]

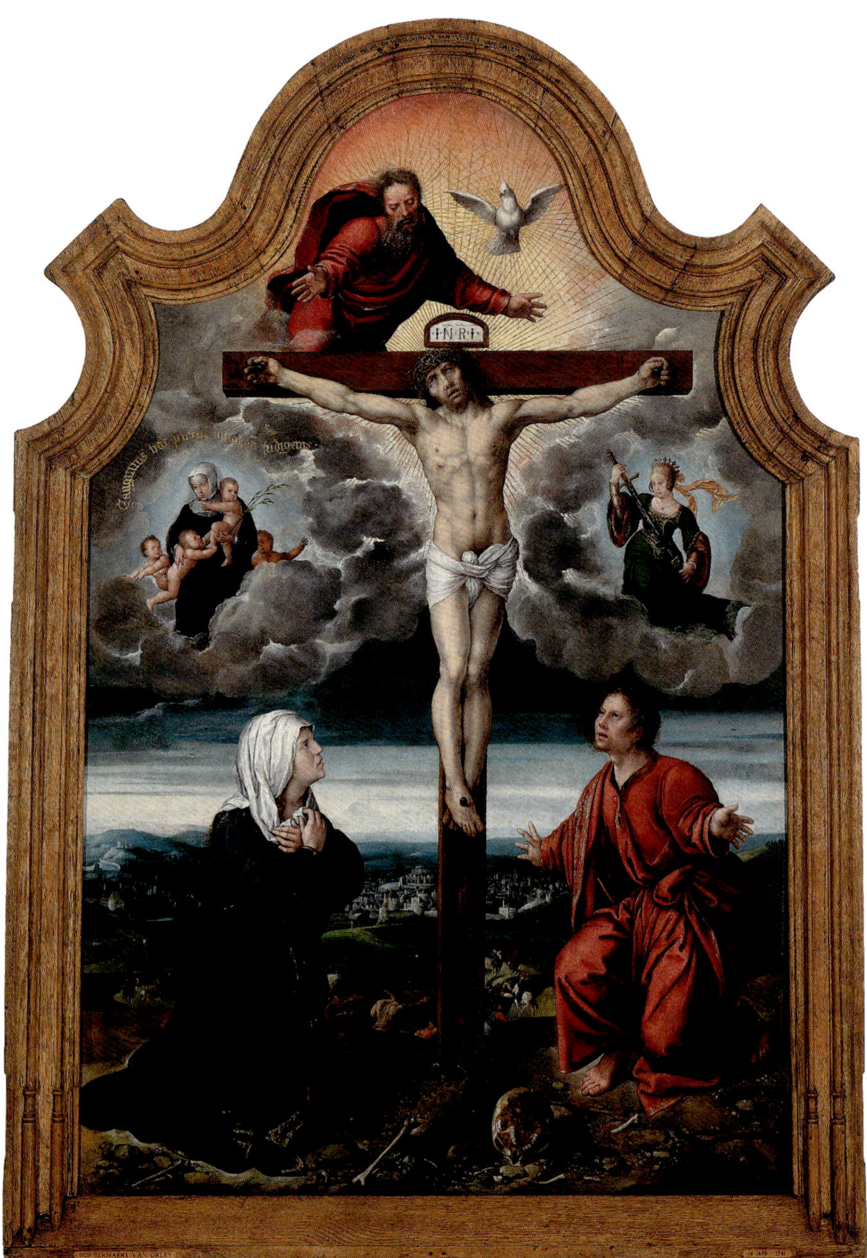

Fig. 71
BERNAERT VAN ORLEY (1487/91–1541)
The Crucified Christ between the Virgin Mary and Saint John the Evangelist, about 1525
Oil on panel, 140 × 91 cm
Museum Boijmans Van Beuningen, Rotterdam

this could also explain why its iconography and format shifted so dramatically from its first, fairly simple iteration in the drawing in Chantilly, over the two horizontal compositions in Paris and Bayonne (the only ones in which the kneeling patron is included) to the two vertical ones in Bayonne, when the project had more purely become a homage to Venetian predecessors. In the words of Erwin Panofsky, 'Giovanni Bellini has ultimately prevailed over Gerard David and Quinten Massys'.[42] Indeed, Dürer's return to Nuremberg – and perhaps also a sense of discouragement after his last visit to the archducal court – may have prompted the change in composition, away from his Netherlandish models, and the elimination of the patron. Concluding his journal, Dürer voices his disillusion unambiguously when he writes that, 'in all I have done … in the Netherlands, I have lost out, and quite especially with Lady Margareta who in return for what I presented to her and made for her [für das ich ihr geschenckt und gemacht hab] has given me nothing'.[43] (Note his distinction between presents and what he says he produced specifically for her.) Back in Nuremberg, did he hope that he could 'recycle' the work already done and find a new patron – perhaps a church – to which he might offer the painting? It will probably never be possible to clarify fully the context of one of Dürer's most ambitious projects, but as demonstrated above, there certainly is sufficient evidence to suggest that it had its roots in the trip of 1520–1 and in his immersion in the artistic, and perhaps also the political life of the Burgundian Netherlands.

For various assistance during the writing of this essay, the author is grateful to Peter van den Brink, as well as Piero Boccardo, Till-Holger Borchert, Hans Buijs, Emma Capron, Mathieu Deldicque, Maïtena Horiot-Ortega, Margherita Priarone and Ken Soehner.

1 Wölfflin 1908 (1984), p. 299; White 1971, p. 197; and Waldmann 1920, p. 53.
2 Anzelewsky 1991, vol. 1, pp. 53–4; Erwin Panofsky (1945, vol. 1, pp. 232–3) proposes that the two monumental panels with three apostles and Saint Mark in Munich (Bayerische Staatsgemäldesammlungen, Alte Pinakothek, invs 540, 545; see Anzelewsky 1991, vol. 1, nos 183–4 and vol. 2, figs 185–90) were intended as side wings of the *Virgin and Child with Saints*, but this suggestion has long been refuted (see Anzelewsky 1991, p. 283).
3 Lorenz 1904, pp. 63–9, 73–4; Heidrich 1906, pp. 139–52, 206–9; Flechsig 1928–31, vol. 2, pp. 245–54; Winkler 1936–9, vol. 4, pp. 46–56; Panofsky 1955, pp. 223, 224–9; Winkler 1957, pp. 319–23.
4 Winkler 1936–9, vol. 4, p. 46.
5 For the *Rosenkranzfest* at the Národní Galerie v Praze (inv. O 1552), see Anzelewsky 1991, vol. 1, no. 93 and vol. 2, figs 104–9; and Prague 2006. For the related drawings, see Winkler 1936–9, vol. 2, nos 380–401; Strauss 1974, vol. 2, nos 1506/9–1506/30; J. Zaunbauer and C. Metzger in Vienna 2019, pp. 264–79. For Dürer's lost contribution to the Heller Altarpiece, see Anzelewsky 1991, vol. 1, nos 107–16, figs 97, 99, and vol. 2, fig. 135. For the related drawings, see Winkler 1936–9, vol. 2, nos 448–65; Strauss 1974, vol. 2, nos 1508/1–1508/19; C. Metzger in Vienna 2019, pp. 302–15. The comparison of the *Rosenkranzfest* and the Heller Altarpiece was previously made in Winkler 1936–9, vol. 4, p. 46.
6 Panofsky 1955, p. 225.
7 Winkler 1936–9, vol. 4, p. 47.
8 Kupferstichkabinett, Staatliche Museen zu Berlin, invs KdZ 39 and 41 (Winkler 1936–9, vol. 4, nos 843, 844; Strauss 1974, vol. 4, nos 1521/88, 1521/89); Hamburger Kunsthalle, inv. 23004 (Winkler 1936–9, vol. 4, no. 841; Strauss 1974, vol. 4, no. 1521/86; Prange 2007, [vol. 1], no. 297, vol. 2); Germanisches Nationalmuseum, Nuremberg, inv. Hz 5489 (Winkler 1936–9, vol. 4, no. 842; Strauss 1974, vol. 4, no. 1521/87); Kunsthalle Bremen, inv. Kl 17 (Winkler 1936–9, vol. 4, no. 840; Strauss 1974, vol. 4, no. 1521/85; A. Röver-Kann in Bremen 2012, no. 42).
9 Département des arts graphiques, Musée du Louvre, Paris, inv. 18590 (Winkler 1936–9, vol. 4, no. 845; Strauss 1974, vol. 4, no. 1521/92); Kupferstichkabinett, Staatliche Museen zu Berlin, inv. KdZ 1527 (Winkler 1936–9, vol. 4, no. 846; Strauss 1974, vol. 4, no. 1521/93; M. Roth in Berlin 2006, no. 100); Biblioteca Ambrosiana, Milan, inv. F.246 inf. 27 (Winkler 1936–9, vol. 4, no. 847; Strauss 1974, vol. 4, no. 1521/96).
10 Department of Prints and Drawings, British Museum, London, inv. SL,5218.42 (Winkler 1936–9, vol. 4, no. 848; Strauss 1974, vol. 4, no. 1521/95).
11 Kunsthalle Bremen, inv. Kl 13, lost during the Second World War (Winkler 1936–9, vol. 4, no. 849; Strauss 1974, vol. 4, nos 1521/94, 1521/61; A. Röver-Kann in Bremen 2012, no. 42).
12 Robert Lehman Collection, Metropolitan Museum of Art, New York, inv. 1975.1.859 (Winkler 1936–9, vol. 4, no. 850; Strauss 1974, vol. 4, no. 1522/4; S. Alsteens in New York 2012, no. 11); Musée du Louvre, Paris, inv. R.F. 1080 (Winkler 1936–9, vol. 4, no. 857; Strauss 1974, vol. 4, no. 1522/3). A refined pen study of an old bearded man in the Universitätsbibliothek Erlangen (inv. B 158), in the past identified by some as a study for Saint James in the drawing reproduced here as cat. 64, is now no longer accepted as autograph (Winkler 1936–9, vol. 4, nos 851, as by Dürer; Strauss 1974, vol. 4, no. 1521/97, as by Dürer; I. Brahms in Dickel 2014, no. 86, as possibly a later imitation).
13 Museo Correr, Venice (Winkler 1936–9, vol. 4, no. 853; Strauss 1974, vol. 4, no. 1522/5); Kunsthalle Bremen, inv. Kl 15, lost during the Second World War (Winkler 1936–9, vol. 4, no. 854; Strauss 1974, vol. 4, no. 1522/6; A. Röver-Kann in Bremen 2012, no. 43).
14 Metropolitan Museum of Art, New York, inv. 61.257 (Winkler 1936–9, vol. 4, no. 836; Strauss 1974, vol. 4, no. 1521/84; S. Alsteens in New York 2012, no. 10). An old copy is at the Département des arts graphiques, Musée du Louvre, Paris, inv. 18633 (S. Alsteens in New York 2012, p. 25, under no. 10).
15 Musée Bonnat-Helleu, Bayonne, invs 1505, 1504, 1506 (Winkler 1936–9, vol. 4, nos 839, 855, 856; Strauss 1974, vol. 4, nos 1521/91, 1522/1, 1522/2); Département des arts graphiques, Musée du Louvre, Paris, inv. R.F. 1079 (Winkler 1936–9, vol. 4, no. 838; Strauss 1974, vol. 4, no. 1521/83); Musée Condé, Chantilly, inv. 889 (311) (Winkler 1936–9, vol. 4, no. 837; Strauss 1974, vol. 4, no. 1521/81; Mandrella 1999, no. 11).
16 Département des arts graphiques, Musée du Louvre, Paris, inv. 19604 (Strauss 1974, vol. 4, no. 1521/82). The second copy is at the Palazzo Rosso, Genoa, inv. D2207 (ibid., p. 216).
17 Lippmann 1883–1929, vol. 4, pp. 6–7, under nos 362–4.
18 Heidrich 1906, p. 139; Waldmann 1933, p. 48; Winkler 1936–9, vol. 4, p. 46; Panofsky [1943] 1945, vol. 2, p. 81.
19 The Albertina Museum, Vienna, inv. 3066 (Winkler 1936–9, vol. 2, no. 296; Strauss 1974, vol. 2, no. 1503/22).
20 In spite of most of the literature on these drawings, where they are described as executed in black chalk, the drapery studies seem rather to have been drawn in metalpoint on paper prepared in green or dark violet (as already suggested by Alice Strobel in Strobel and Koschatzky 1971, p. 394, under no. 130). The technique was established for the Hamburg sheet by Georg Dietz, as reported by P. Prange in Prange 2007, [vol. 1], p. 153, under no. 297.
21 See note 34 below.
22 Metropolitan Museum of Art, New York, inv. 14.40.633 (Anzelewsky 1991, vol. 1, no. 147, vol. 2, pl. 174; J.P. Waterman in Ainsworth and Waterman 2013, no. 25).
23 Gemäldegalerie, Staatliche Museen zu Berlin, inv. 38, destroyed in 1945 (Steer 1982, no. 8, fig. 29; Michaelis 1995, no. 38).
24 Hamburger Kunsthalle, inv. 23001 (Winkler 1936–9, vol. 4, no. 537; Strauss 1974, vol. 4, no. 1520/40; P. Roettig in Prange 2007, vol. 1, no. 295, vol. 2); Royal Collection, inv. RCIN 912180 (Winkler 1936–9, vol. 3, no. 536; Strauss 1974, vol. 3, no. 1519/13). A connection between the Hamburg drawing and the *Virgin and Child with Saints* was suggested in Tietze and Tietze-Conrat 1938, vol. 2, p. 30, under no. 843.
25 D. Eichberger, 'Dürer and the Netherlands: Patterns of Exchange and Mutual Admiration', in Silver and Chipps Smith 2010, pp. 155–65, at p. 155; Schauerte 2012, p. 212. See also the suggestion in van den Brink 2020.
26 Kunsthalle Bremen, inv. Kl 9, lost during the Second World War (Winkler 1936–9, vol. 4, nos 782, 783; Strauss 1974, vol. 4, no. 1521/46; A. Röver-Kann in Bremen 2012, no. 41).
27 Musée des Beaux-Arts, Rouen, inv. 1803.4 (Ainsworth 1998, pp. 73–87, fig. 79; Bakhuÿs and Coudert 2010, in particular Philippe Lorentz's essay, '*Fait et donné par maître Gheraert David:* la Vierge de l'Immaculée Conception parmi les vierges', pp. 17–39).
28 Ibid., p. 73.
29 Ashcroft 2017, vol. 1, p. 575.
30 The connection between David's painting and Dürer's composition was previously made in Strauss 1974, vol. 4, p. 2148, under no. 1521/83 ('almost certainly inspired by Gerard David's "Madonna with Twelve Female Saints"'). Panofsky (1955, p. 228) saw a (less convincing) relationship with Quinten Massys's *Holy Kinship* of 1509 in the Royal Museums of Fine Arts of Belgium, Brussels, inv. 2784 (Silver 1984, no. 10, pls 1, 6–10).
31 P. Lorentz in Bakhuÿs and Coudert 2010, pp. 25–6.
32 M. Mende in Vienna 2003, p. 530, under no. 189: 'kaum vor Jahresende'. See also M. Roth in Berlin 2006, p. 156, under no. 100.
33 Busch 1931, pp. 32–64. Winkler (1957, p. 320) suggests, without further arguments, that the patron could be from the milieu of Portuguese merchants in Antwerp.
34 For numerous similar watermarks, see the Piccard Watermark Collection at the Landesarchiv Baden-Württemberg, Hauptstaatsarchiv Stuttgart (www.piccard-online.de, accessed November 2019), nos 124442 (Trier, 1519), 124445 (Brussels, 1529), 124490 (Ghent, 1531–2), 124495 (Kessel, 1533), 124496, 124542 (Arnhem 1531), 124547 (Koblenz, 1528), among others. The importance of the watermark in locating the place of creation of the drawing was already stressed in Mandrella 1999, p. 62, under no. 11. For an additional argument based on Dürer's use of paper, see Winkler 1957, p. 320. Some of the other drawings, such as the drapery studies and *Saint Apollonia* in Berlin (figs 55, 56, 59, cat. 58), were made on paper with a watermark – a high crown – commonly found in his prints, indicating that they date from after Dürer's return to Nuremberg (H. Mielke in Anzelewsky and Mielke 1984, nos 109, 110, 112).
35 Pearson 2005, *passim*. For manuscripts, see the examples discussed in Hand 2013, pp. 35, 108, 113, 118, 121, 123, 134, 174, figs 1.1, 3.3, 3.4, 3.7, 3.9, 3.13, 4.1; and in Brown 2018. Among the Netherlandish exceptions are a small group of devotional paintings painted by Cornelis Engebrechtsz (about 1462–1527) and his workshop for the nuns at the wealthy convent of Mariënpoel, near Leiden (C. Vogelaar and J.P. Filedt Kok in Leiden 2011, pp. 28–9, 33, nos 8, 12; Filedt Kok, Gibson and Bruijnen 2014, pp. 119, 121, 127, 131, cats 11, 17, 36, Rej. 12, figs 110, 120, 123).
36 S. Alsteens in New York 2012, p. 27 n. 14, under nos 10–11.
37 Museum Boijmans Van Beuningen, Rotterdam, inv. 1629 (Véronique Bücken in Brussels 2019, no. 38). For Margaret's patronage, see, among others, D. Eichberger, 'Margaret of Austria: A Princess with Ambition and Political Insight', in Mechelen 2005, pp. 48–55, and Pearson 2005, *passim*.
38 A. Galand in Brussels 2019, nos 30, 31. For Dürer's interest in Netherlandish costume, see D. Eichberger in Silver and Chipps Smith 2010, pp. 155–6.
39 Ashcroft 2017, vol. 1, p. 560. For the *Engraved Passion*, see A. Scherbaum in Schoch, Mende and Scherbaum 2001–4, vol. 1, pp. 125–8, nos 45–60.
40 Ashcroft 2017, vol. 1, p. 584. For a discussion of what portrait this may be, see ibid., pp. 625–6 n. 363; and K. Schütz in Vienna 2012, p. 294.
41 This possibility was previously suggested in Romdahl 1928, p. 26.
42 Panofsky 1955, p. 229.
43 Ashcroft 2017, vol. 1, p. 586; Rupprich 1956–69, vol. 1, pp. 175–6.

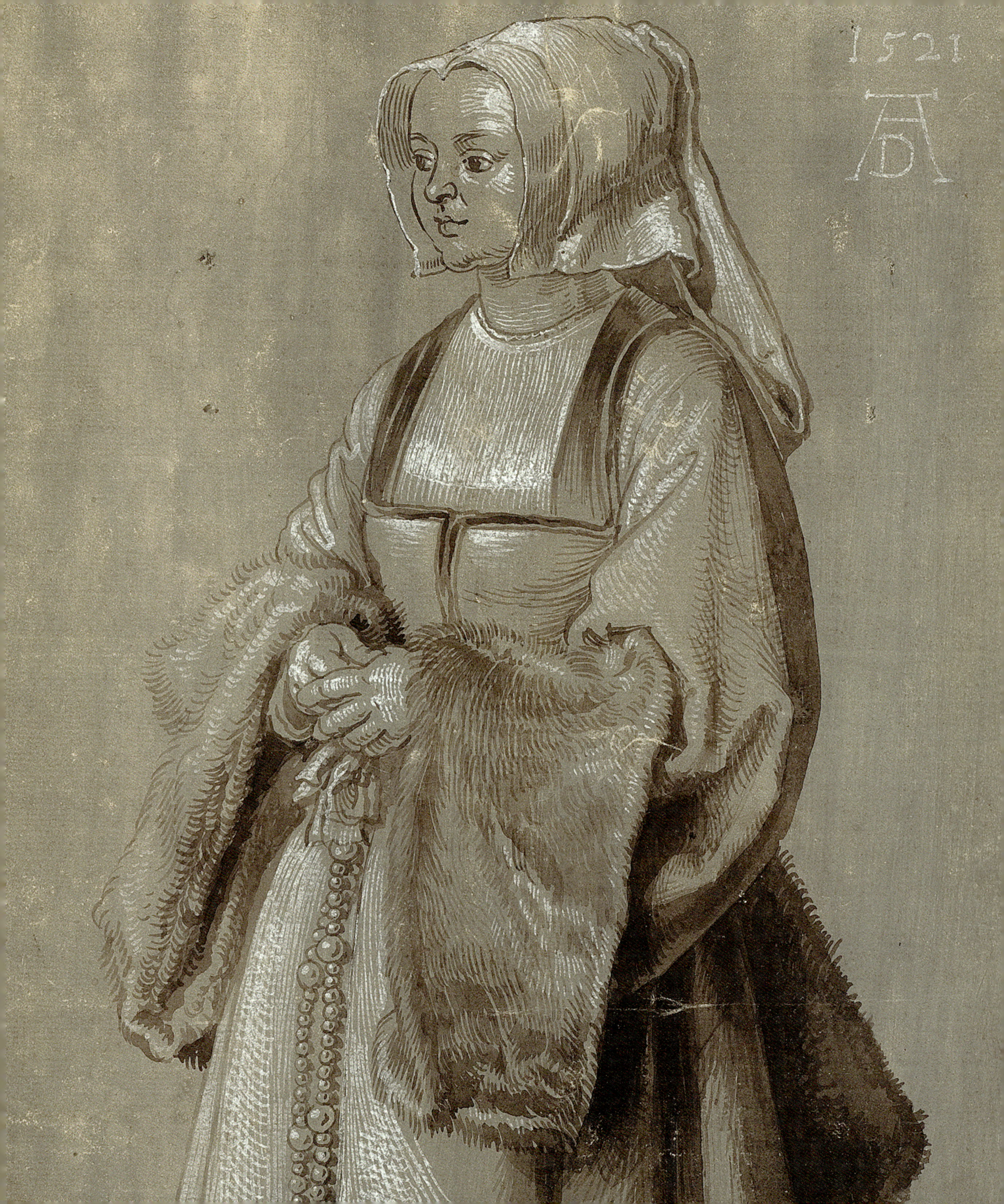
1521
AD

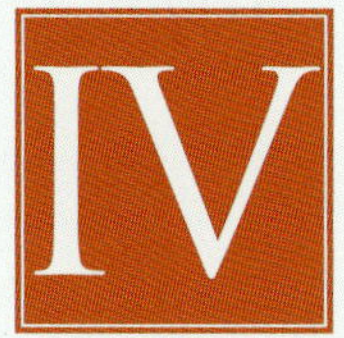

THE VISUAL LEGACY OF THE NETHERLANDISH JOURNEY

THE NUMBER AND RANGE OF DRAWINGS BY DÜRER that survive are exceptional and testify both to the preservation of his legacy by his family and others in Nuremberg, and the eagerness of collectors to acquire them in the decades after his death. Those from his visit to the Low Countries in 1520–1 include sketches serving as working material as well as large, finished drawings that could be sold or given away; the evidence provided by his travel journal demonstrates some of the ways in which Dürer used his drawings, and assists in the understanding of some of the works which remain today.

By the sixteenth century drawings were usually made on paper, although Dürer used parchment on a few occasions, such as the study of a lion used for his early small painting of Saint Jerome. In Venice he discovered the rich blue *carta azzurra*, which he used for very detailed and strongly three-dimensional studies worked up on this mid-tone using a brush with black ink and white highlighting. Later he gave some of the sheets he used in Nuremberg a green coating to use in a similar way. His first extremely precise self portrait (fig. 16), made at the age of 13, was drawn with a metalpoint stylus, leaving its oxidised trace on prepared paper: this was not a medium that lent itself to correction but Dürer continued to use it on occasion throughout his career. He frequently used ink and pen or brush in drawing compositions, sometimes quickly and roughly in outline, or else in much greater detail, using hatching to render shadows. He also employed charcoal or black chalk in extremely swift, impressionistic renderings that capture, for example, the extremes of facial expression. Some drawings use watercolour to add precision or occasionally to suggest the quickly fading light of a sunset.

Traditionally artists had assembled drawings as models for all manner of aspects of their painted compositions, for example figures in differing poses, distinctive buildings or townscapes. Frequently these were copies of drawings by other artists. As well as providing an important source for compositional models via his prints, Dürer himself made drawings for his associates in Nuremberg. When he was in the Low Countries he provided model drawings of Saint Christopher for the artist Joachim Patinir to use in his painting. Patinir was primarily a landscape painter who often relied on collaborators for the figures in his subjects. Dürer's own drawings would have served as important reference material for his practice: landscape studies such as those he made in the Alps and in and around Nuremberg; studies of women in local dress, sketches of the human body including his own; rough and evolving compositional ideas, as well as finished studies reflecting his most elaborate paintings. SF

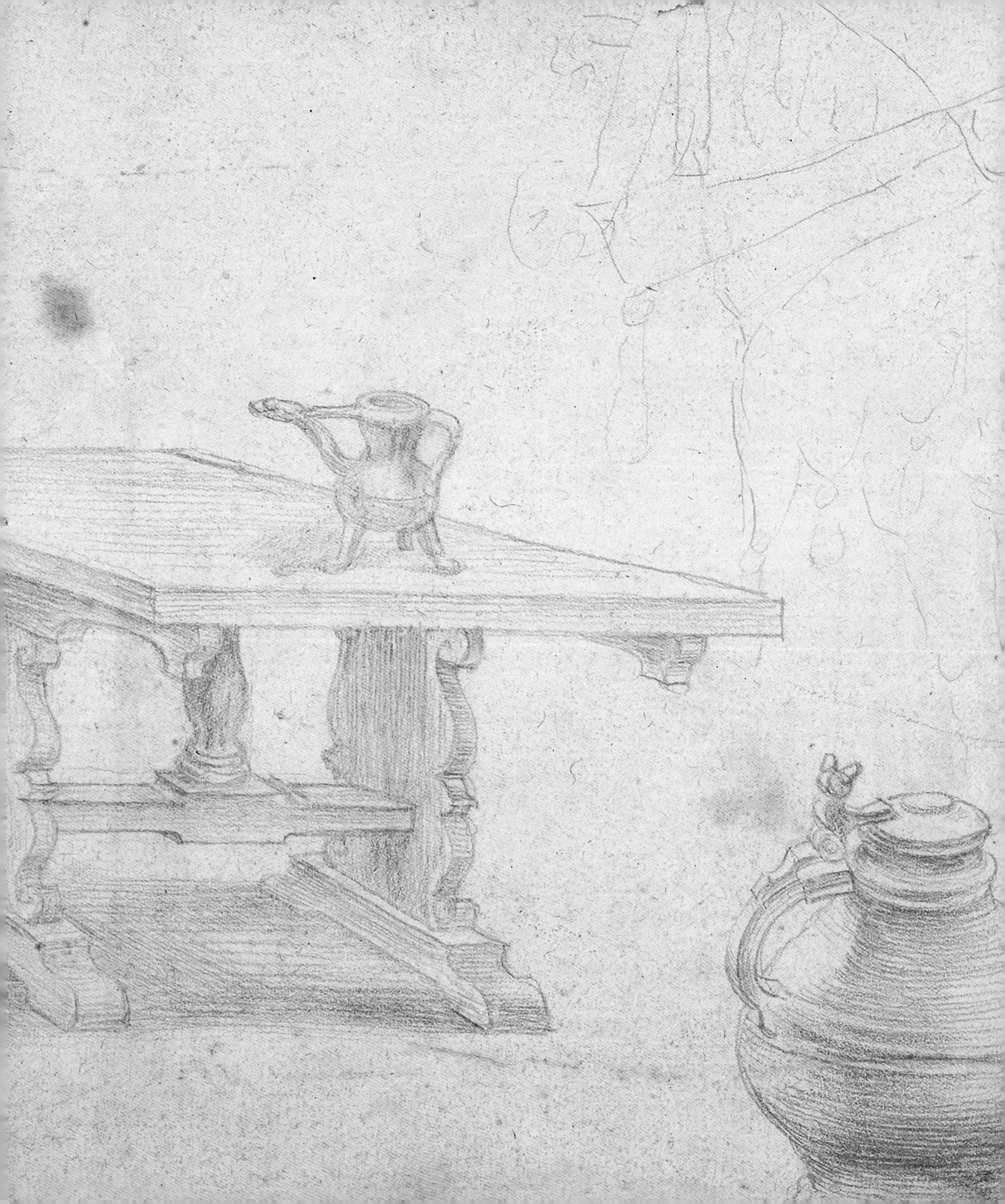

CHRISTOF METZGER

IMAGE AND ITINERARY
DÜRER'S DRAWINGS FROM HIS TRAVELS THROUGH THE NETHERLANDS

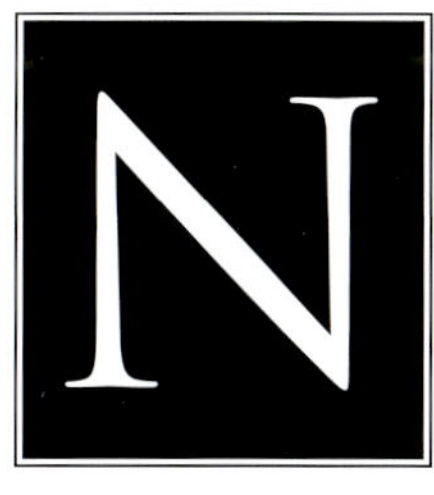

No other stretch in the life of Albrecht Dürer – nor that of any other artist, or virtually any figure of the era for that matter – was the subject of such concentrated and meticulous documentation, written or visual. Kept in a journal that today is preserved only in the form of two copies and two page-fragments thought to be original, Dürer's record of his travels through the Low Countries begins promptly on Thursday, 12 July 1520, with a report on his, his wife Agnes, and their maid Susanna's initial progress northward via Erlangen to the village of Baiersdorf and towards the Main river – the water route they would use to hasten the journey. His remark that they spent '3 pounds less 6 pence'[1] in Baiersdorf on provisions for the trip illustrates the journal's simultaneous status as a notebook, log and housekeeping journal. Dürer used it to balance expenditure and income; record his travel itinerary; mark special occasions, noteworthy sights and important meetings; and catalogue a number of the works he created during the trip.[2] The latter includes several paintings, mostly portraits,[3] and a considerable number of works on paper. Friedrich Winkler and Walter L. Strauss each list around a hundred surviving sheets in their catalogues raisonnés,[4] by slightly varying standards still calling for critical appraisal.

PREVIOUS PAGE
Detail from *Young Woman in Netherlandish Dress* (cat. 73)

OPPOSITE
Detail from *A Table and Jugs and a Slight Sketch of a Horse in Trappings* (cat. 66)

DRAWING ON DEMAND

The journal itself mentions some 140 drawings created during the trip; the number of works that go unmentioned can hardly be guessed at, let alone the actual rate of loss. One reason for this is that Dürer gave away no small number of drawings while travelling, most of which have since become untraceable. One reads time and again in the journal about drawings, generally portraits, given to the subject as a tip, or on a quid pro quo basis in exchange for services rendered. The first instance comes in Antwerp in early August 1520, when Dürer notes '... my landlord I have also drawn a likeness of, that is Jobst Plankfelt' (cat. 88), to whom it was worth a branch of white coral.[5] When that September Dürer drew the family coat of arms on a wood block for one of the von Rogendorf brothers – Wilhelm (1481–1541) or Wolfgang (1483–1540) – compensation was settled in kind, in the form of seven ells of velvet.[6] Hard currency was also welcome: in August 1520 Hans Pfaffrot, a representative of Portuguese trading interests, agreed to pay one Philip's gulden for a portrait of himself in charcoal – a sum with the same purchasing power as the two gulden of the unknown Italian gentleman Dürer sketched later that year, in early October.[7] In each case the fee Dürer received for the incidental favour filled out the travel purse by a week's budget.[8] The artist also recorded – for himself as well as posterity – the offence taken when such devotion was lacking, as with the six misers who Dürer portrayed a month earlier in Brussels, who failed to honour the arrangement.[9] As with Hans Lieber's offer of one gulden for his portrait in charcoal, there are also recorded episodes in which, for whatever reason, the artist turns down payment from the recipient.[10]

From the time of Dürer's fourth stay in Antwerp, following his trip to Zeeland in December 1520, these mainly chalk or charcoal portraits (fig. 72) were pasted on wooden panels and may have been outfitted with frames,[11] signalling that they approximated the autonomous status, if not the material value, of a painted portrait.[12] There is even evidence that Dürer's drawings were considered valuable enough to be accepted as gifts of honour in their own right. In September 1520 vice-chancellor of the Holy Roman Empire Nikolaus Ziegler (died 1531) – who shortly afterwards played a key role in confirming Dürer's imperial privileges – received 'a *Deposition from the Cross*, worth 3 gulden'.[13]

Finally, there were numerous commissions that the illustrious guest received. Early on during his stay in Antwerp we learn of 'a sketch design with colour washes', Dürer's terminology for a pen-and-ink drawing with watercolour, created especially for a group of unnamed painters.[14] Was this a sort of sample work by which he either sought, or was obliged to provide proof of his ability to the local artist class? Reference is made to other *Visierungen*, or sketches intended for eventual execution in a different medium,[15] including goldsmith's work,[16] weapon ornamentation,[17] 'designs for a masque' around the time of Carnival,[18] multiple instances of coats of arms to be completed in woodcut,[19] façade decoration,[20] and in one case even for an entire estate.[21] This final sketch was so elaborate that Dürer did not want to let it go for less than 10 gulden. 'Drawing on demand' played no minor role in boosting Dürer's travel funds.

Fig. 72
ALBRECHT DÜRER
Portrait of a Man, 1520–1
Charcoal and brown chalk, 37 × 27.6 cm
British Museum (5218-52)

DRAWING FOR STOCK

All this may be well documented in Dürer's travel journal; the drawings themselves, however, have been lost virtually without exception. Still, the works that Dürer kept for himself from the trip, and which later found their place within his repertoire of workshop motifs, may have come down to us in essence. Some of it can be linked to Dürer's notes; other works, to which no economic value was initially attached, cannot. At one point Dürer mentions 'two Dutch costume studies also in black and white on grey paper', by which he doubtlessly refers to the two sheets held respectively at the National Gallery of Art in Washington (cat. 73) and Vienna's Albertina Museum (fig. 99).[22] Two depictions of the Agony in the Garden (forming part of a larger cycle of the Life of Christ ultimately completed in 1524 in Nuremberg) came around the same time, of which at least one bearing the date 1521 has survived (fig. 130).[23]

Oddly enough, with the exception of the Middelburg Altarpiece by Jan Gossaert, not a single work of art for which Dürer expresses admiration in his journal also finds visual representation. By comparison, his first trip to Italy in 1494–5 offers multiple instances of such depictions, among them detailed studies of the work of Lorenzo di Credi and Gentile Bellini.[24] And in cases where Dürer did sketch what he saw, a lack of relevant written references persists – as with the statuette of a female pleurante at the tomb of Isabella of Bourbon at St Michael's Abbey in Antwerp (fig. 93) although two visits to the church are documented[25] or what may have been the sculpture of an enthroned bishop.[26] Both are found in the *Silberstiftzeichenbuch*, a drawing book executed in silverpoint that Dürer kept throughout his trip. By contrast, much of what strikes us today as outlandish or noteworthy goes unmentioned, as with the Irish or Livonian costumes,[27] or the stunning chiaroscuro studies dating from around the time of the *Saint Jerome* that Dürer painted for Rodrigo Fernandes de Almada between January and March 1521 (cat. 110).[28] The fact

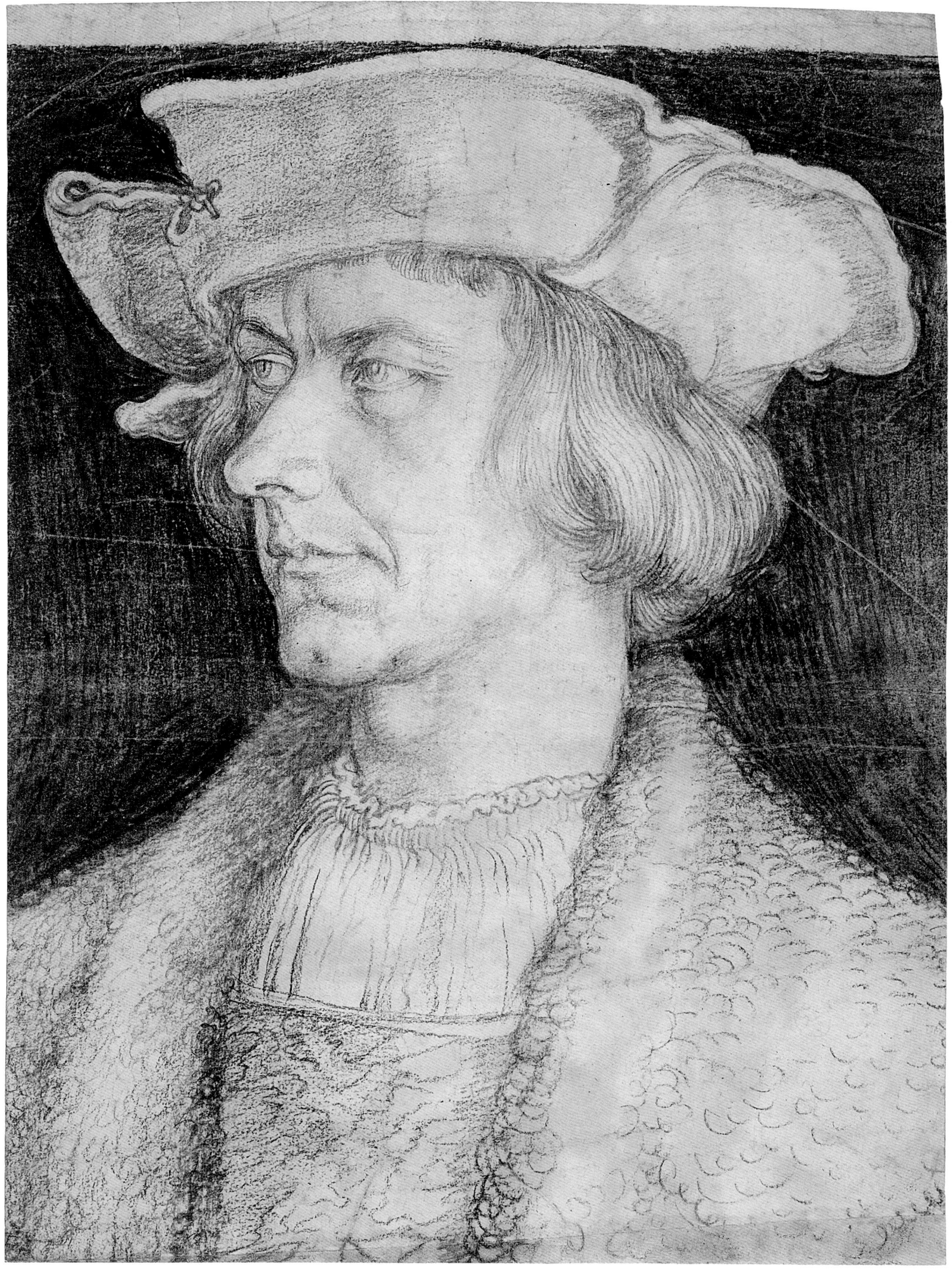

that Dürer took advantage of his visit to Brussels to view the Raphael cartoons without leaving any immediate traces in word or image is mystifying.[29]

One further note as regards technique and material: in the Netherlands, Dürer's preferred media were charcoal and black chalk, silverpoint when working in his drawing book or on loose sheets,[30] pen, 'black and white on grey paper', that is, on paper that had been primed,[31] and 'colour washes'.[32] By the latter he may have been referring to a coloured, water-based painting medium. Expenditure on 'red chalk' or 'the colour they get from bricks' is listed on multiple occasions,[33] though not a single drawing corresponding to this medium still exists today. By his own account, Dürer acquired most of these and other materials wherever he happened to be.[34] This included paper (aside from the sheets from the so-called pen-and-ink sketchbook), as both watermarks and his expenses from October and November 1520 can attest.[35] Dürer continued to use papers he acquired during his travels once he returned to Nuremberg until shortly before his death.[36]

THE SILVERPOINT DRAWING BOOK

In addition to creating numerous drawings on loose sheets, Dürer worked in two different books throughout his journey, neither of which has come down to us in their entirety. Of the renowned silverpoint drawing book – its highly balanced design and perfection in detail in most of the drawings making the term 'sketchbook' a misnomer – 15 leaves have been preserved, mostly used on both sides and measuring approximately 13 × 19 cm, the narrow dimensions of the landscape octavo format. The book was likely composed of four quires obtained from twice folding then trimming the edges of four double folio sheets. The paper used was of a truly high quality, while generous block trimming of the narrow booklet eliminated watermarks and left the refined quality of the pink grounding uninterrupted by any irregularities in the structure of the paper itself. The double-sided preparation of the paper and Dürer's subtle drawing technique further prevented any bleed-through from the verso to the recto side of the sheet. The book block would definitely have been bound by thread. Despite intensive research, there is still some uncertainty regarding the status of front and back pages, not to mention the original sequence of all pages in their entirety.[37]

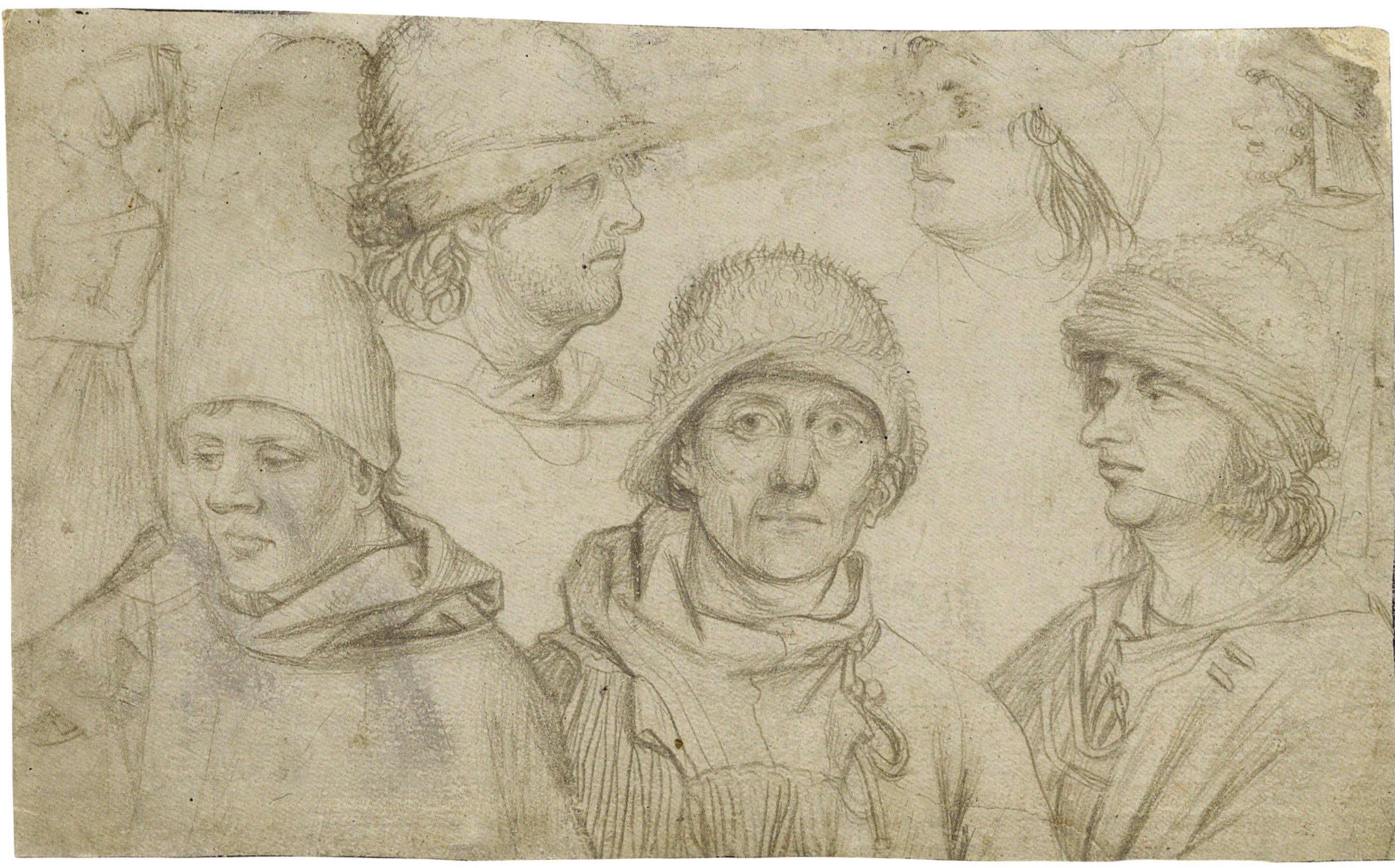

Fig. 73
LOWER RHINE OR NETHERLANDISH ARTIST
Six Male Heads and a Woman in Profile, about 1480
Silverpoint, 11.8 × 19.1 cm
Kunstmuseum Basel (1966.168)

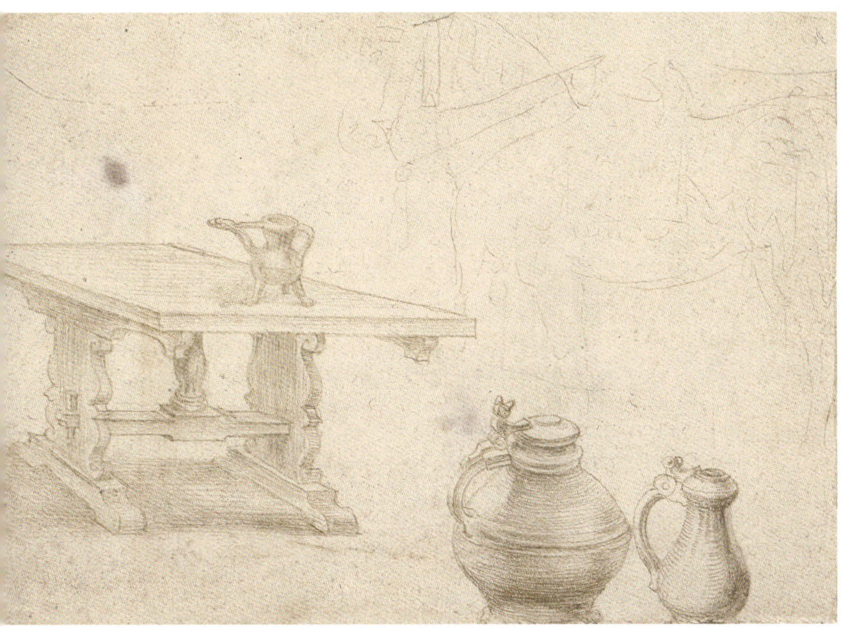

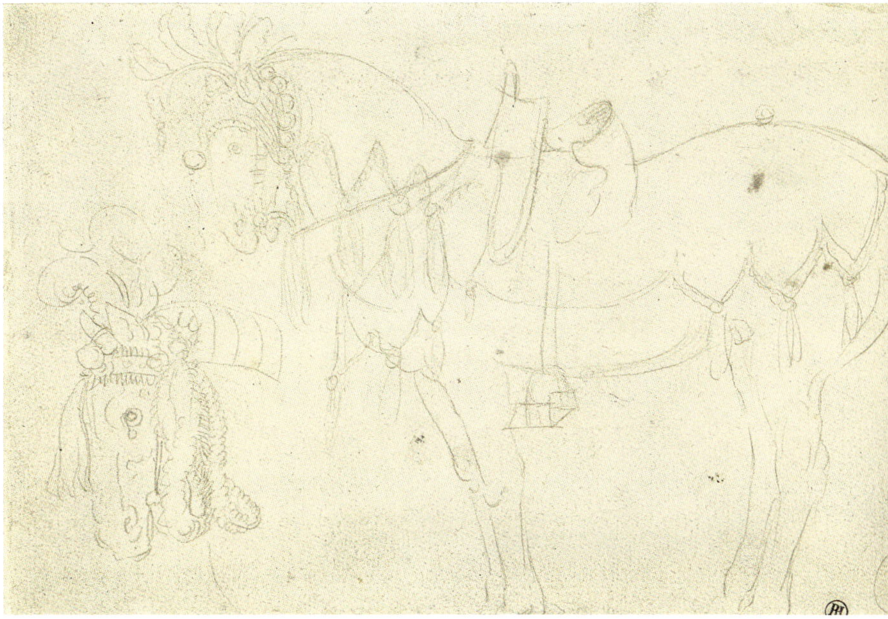

66
ALBRECHT DÜRER
A Table and Jugs and a Slight Sketch of a Horse in Trappings, 1520
Silverpoint on pale pink prepared paper, 11.5 × 16.7 cm
British Museum

Fig. 74
ALBRECHT DÜRER
Horse in Trappings – Head of a Horse, 1520
Silverpoint on pale pink prepared paper, 12.5 × 18 cm
Germanisches Nationalmuseum, Nuremberg (Hz5488 recto)

It seems that Dürer acquired the silverpoint drawing book in the autumn of 1520 and filled it through his return trip in July 1521. The booklet occupies a unique place in the artist's oeuvre, if not in technique then in a formal aesthetic sense, in which it likely takes its cues from the customs of Antwerp artists. Fragments from an anonymous drawing book dating from the 1480s that is either of the Lower Rhine Valley or the Netherlands in origin bear a great similarity in format and conception, giving us a clear picture of the local standard. The three leaves from the volume preserved in their entirety, alongside individual sheet fragments, present a combination of figure and landscape studies; image motifs composed in the moment, such as the pattern of a brocade fabric; and – most notably – a series of portrait-style busts arranged side by side (fig. 73).[38] The artist made somewhat haphazard use of the landscape format, with the depictions on the sheet preserved at the Albertina Museum revealing extensive erasure. When compared to Dürer's sheets, many of the older master's drawings far transcend the category of purely sketched material in their quality of draughtsmanship and compositional harmony, and can thus essentially be discussed as studies or works in progress. One does, of course, also find spontaneous, quickly rendered motifs in Dürer's drawing book on more than one occasion, generally on the verso side, although two depictions – the head of a lion in profile and a horse saddled with a magnificent harness – have been worked out in detail on what is presumably the facing page (see figs 94, 95; cat. 66; fig. 74).[39]

Fifteen sheets from the silverpoint drawing book have survived, the sixteenth of which would complete the four quires supposed for the volume and can be inferred indirectly. Scenery known to have come from the drawing book appears in the background of the *Crucifixion in Outline*, a partially completed copperplate engraving in which Giulia Bartrum rightly recognises an elaborate counterfeit from the Antwerp workshop of Hieronymus Cock (pp. 267–76). To the left we spy the Gertrudiskerk in Bergen op Zoom as Dürer had rendered it in December 1520 (cat. 115; figs 154, 155),[40] although here the engraver has added an imposing tower built on a polygonal ground plan, with upwardly tapering storeys flanked by pillars leading up to the penultimate floor. On the top storey of the tower is a clock, over which a cornice with pinnacles supports a sheer spire crowned by a lantern (see fig. 75 and detail on p. 156). The structure shown is undoubtedly 'Langer Jan' or 'Long Jan', the tower built in the second half of the fourteenth century for Middelburg's abbey. The building has retained its late medieval aspect to this day, even if the exterior was adapted to suit contemporary fashion following a fire in 1568. Dürer writes at length about visiting the abbey, concluding his section on Middelburg by noting that 'altogether the town made a delightful subject for drawing'.[41]

Another drawing, which has been severely marred by improper mounting that has yet to be fully removed, and which has therefore received little attention so far in research on Dürer, comes on the reverse side of the double portrait of Paulus Topler (1456–1544) and Martin Pfinzing (1490–1552) from Aachen (fig. 84).[42] Painstaking examination and the digital manipulation of photographic stills taken under both normal and UV light have revealed a view of a *Bohlenstube*, a fully

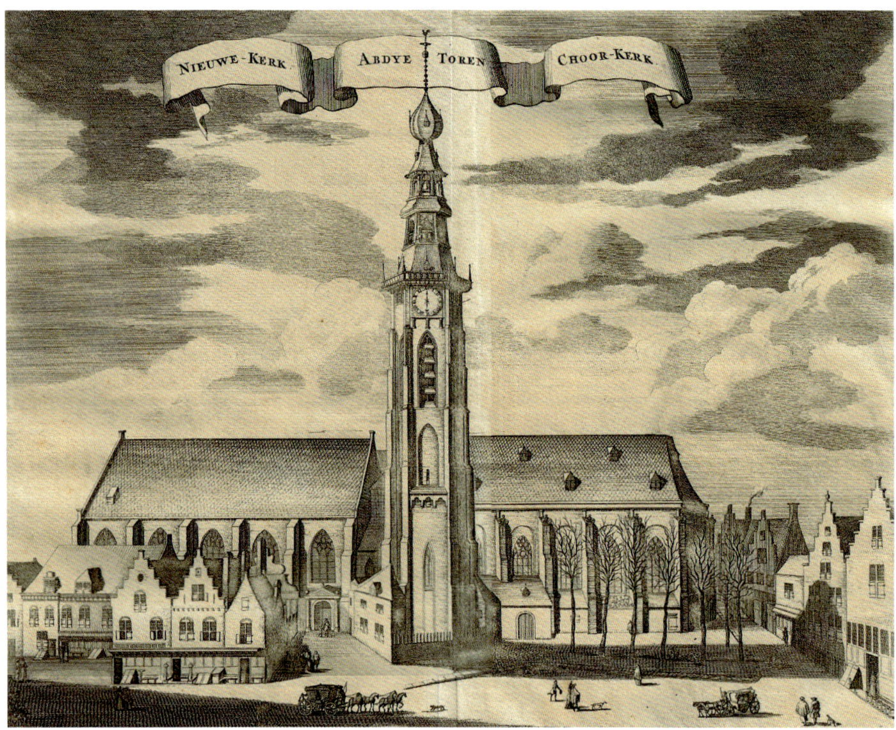

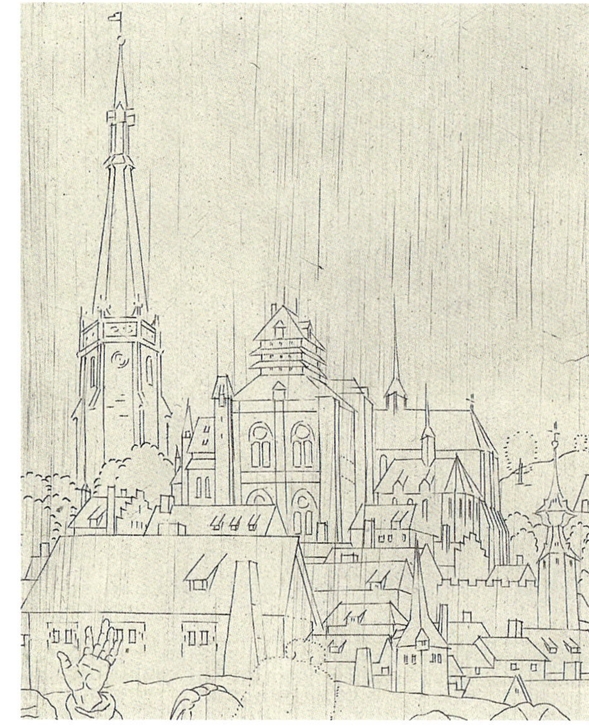

Fig. 75
NETHERLANDISH ENGRAVER
Middelburg Abbey, from Mattheus Smallegange, *Nieuwe Cronyk van Zeeland, Middelburg*, 1696
Engraving and etching,
27.6 × 33.8 cm
Rijksmuseum, Amsterdam
(RP-P-AO-15-121)

ABOVE RIGHT
Detail from *Crucifixion in Outline* (cat. 115)

timbered and panelled room in late Gothic manner featuring an impressive exposed fireplace along the left wall (fig. 76).[43] The formerly facing page is probably the sheet featuring the depiction of an andiron and a chest with a heavy iron lock (cat. 67), whose reverse side shows a table with gable edges and various jugs, all probably from the same parlour (cat. 66).[44] This leads one to speculate whether Dürer may have been present to document the rampant gambling at the public house 'Zum Spiegel' (The Mirror), which he evidently visited on more than one occasion.[45]

THE JOURNAL

Research is now unanimous in the view that, in addition to the silverpoint drawing book Dürer had a second booklet, albeit one in which he drew exclusively in pen and ink. This group was put together by Friedrich Winkler and includes portraits as well as several quickly executed head and figure studies.[46] Those sheets that have not been trimmed all retain a uniform upright format as quarter folio leaves, measuring approximately 16 × 10.5 cm. Owing to their thinness, Dürer used the sheets on one side only, and in some cases they reveal binding traces along the left edge. The drawings also accounted for the sheets' narrowing towards the stitched fold, as can be seen from the hatching ending before the left edge of the sheet in his portrait of Jobst Plankfelt, or the contour lines running right along where the fold would have been in the portrait of a goldsmith from Mechelen (fig. 116).[47] The upper corner of five different sheets – *A Man with an Oar* (cat. 75), *Portrait of Arnold Rucker of Seligenstadt, sleeping* (fig. 105), *The Imperial Captain Felix Hungersperg* (cat. 87), *Lady from Brussels* (cat. 89) and the *Descent from the Cross* from Middelburg after Jan Gossaert (cat. 11)[48] – all bear the remains of a quarter of a high crown watermark.[49] This is the mark of a South German paper brand that Dürer used frequently, which indicates that he did not acquire the paper locally. The surviving sheets, then, must come from a thread-bound booklet in octavo format that Dürer would have brought with him from Nuremberg. The binding suggests at least two quires of eight sheets each, or 16 drawings, leading one to assume greater losses overall.

The vast majority of dated drawings come from the beginning of Dürer's trip; a single depiction has been preserved from his return trip in July 1521, a Virgin[50] bearing the inscription 'made on river Rhine' (cat. 76). Other works that can be correlated with his travel itinerary include the *Descent from the Cross*, created in Middelburg in December 1520; the sheet fragment with Saint Veronica's cloth (fig. 77) of September 1520 or January/February 1521; and the *Praying Woman in Netherlandish Church Dress* of May 1521, housed in Bremen's Kunsthalle.[51] It is striking that in the case of three figures – Jobst Plankfelt, Felix Hungersperg (cat. 87) and Hans Pfaffrot (fig. 115)[52] – the journal refers to other portraits of the same subject in the same timeframe, which were however expressly handed over to the sitters. This suggests that Dürer's pen-and-ink drawings were preliminary studies for, or more likely

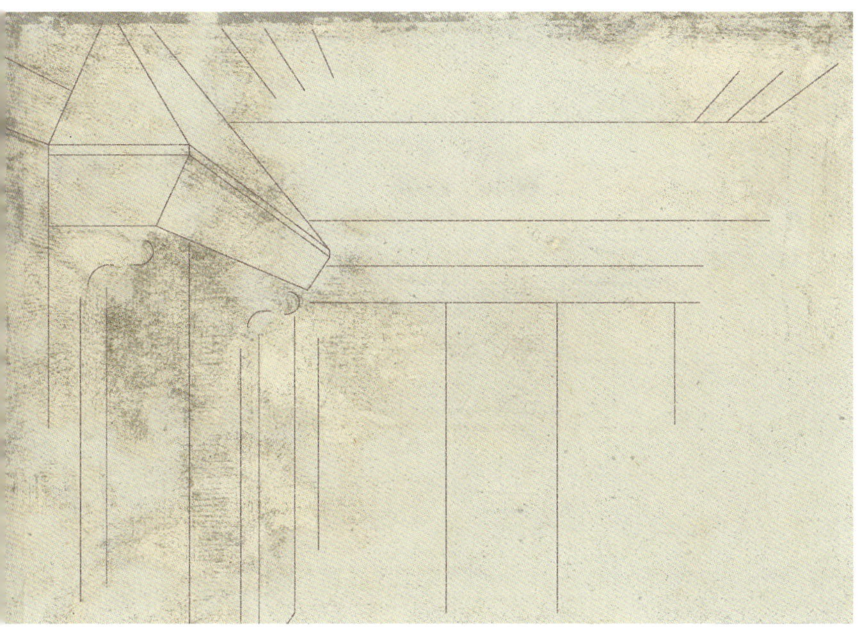

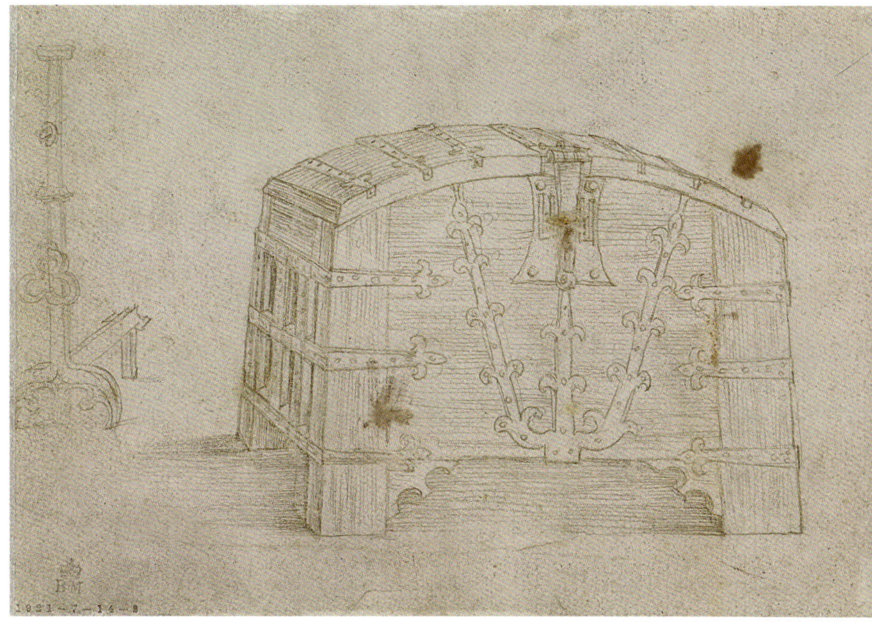

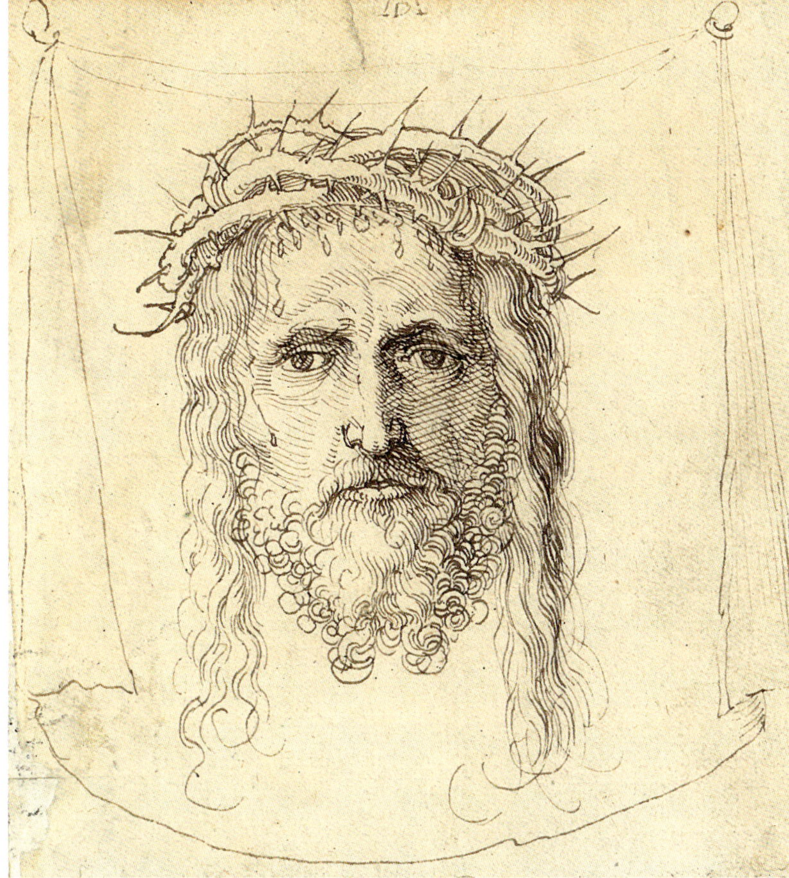

Fig. 76
ALBRECHT DÜRER
Room in a guesthouse in Aachen, 1520, reconstruction by Christof Metzger
Silverpoint on pale pink prepared paper, 12.8 × 18.8 cm
Staatliche Museen zu Berlin, Kupferstichkabinett
(KdZ 4179 verso)

67
ALBRECHT DÜRER
A Chest and a Firedog, 1520
Silverpoint on pink prepared paper, 11.5 × 16.7 cm
British Museum

Fig. 77
ALBRECHT DÜRER
Veronica's Sudarium, about 1520–1
Pen and brown ink, 11.8 × 10.6 cm
The Albertina Museum, Vienna
(3132)

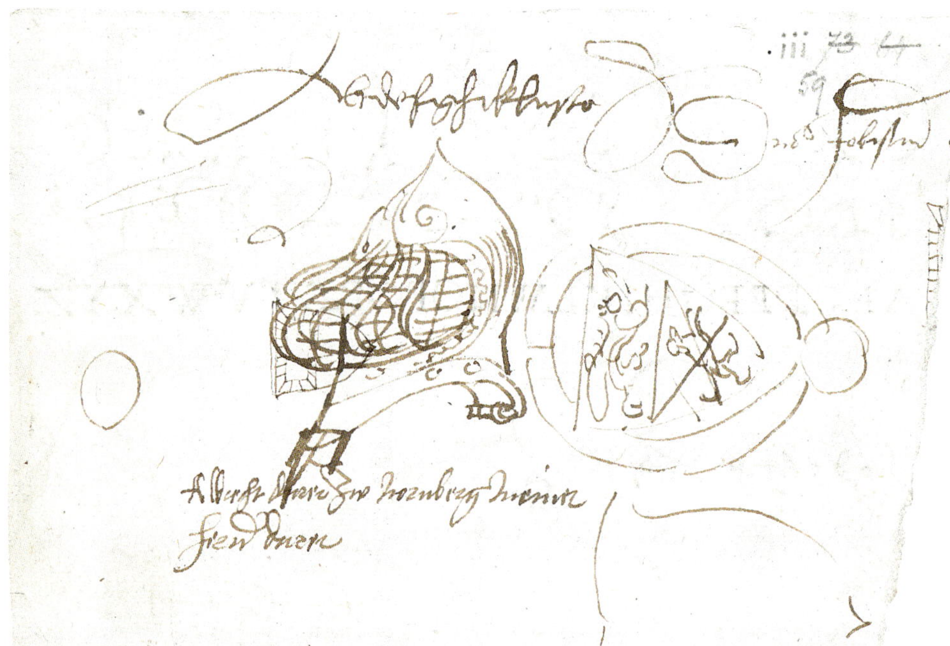

Fig. 78
ALBRECHT DÜRER
Sketches for Lorenz Staiber's Coat-of-Arms, page from the journal, Cologne, November 1520 or Antwerp January–February 1521
Pen and brown ink, 6.2 × max. 9 cm
The British Library (Add MS 5229, fol. 59 recto)

visual documentation of, such gifts which the artist may have been recording in miniature for his own stock.[53]

The same practice is evident in the silverpoint drawing book. In addition to his portrait in front of the turret of the van Lier court in Antwerp, Lazarus Ravensburger (cat. 90) received a second charcoal or chalk version executed on a 'small panel'.[54] Similarly, Art Praun (Aert Bruyn) is portrayed once alongside his wife in black chalk, then again in 'a further sketch of him with the metalpoint', by which Dürer is certainly referring to the likeness of a man set in front of the Krahnenberg outside Andernach but drawn earlier 'in Antwerp'.[55]

Much like its counterpart in silverpoint, the so-called pen-and-ink sketchbook can be seen as a sort of visual accompaniment to Dürer's journal. The journal itself apparently contained drawings as well, of which only two seem to have been preserved. First is a sheet that research has shown to be a journal excerpt containing two patterns for a woman's cloak from the Netherlands (cat. 6). To this may be added a second in the same album in London, which shows two drafts of the coat of arms of Lorenz Staiber, in preparation for an eventual woodcut (fig. 78).[56] As these are rather rough sketches, not fully realised drawings, the verso has also been used. Finally, a third depiction that has since gone missing is mentioned in Dürer's travel journal: the sketch of 'a fishbone, so huge' on display in Brussels – the rib of a whale from its description – 'and shaped as I have sketched here'.[57]

The sheet with the two cloak patterns measures 14.5 × 10 cm, although it shows considerable fraying along the top, right and bottom edges and is thus somewhat reduced from its original size. Approximately 5 mm of the facing page has been preserved at left, with binding marks running along the fold, which has since been flattened. The fragment with the Staiber coat of arms, measuring 6 × 9 cm, may be the upper or lower half of a horizontally divided sheet. Dürer's journal was thus in octavo format,[58] making it very likely that the sheets with the group of pen drawings are also remnants from this journal – possibly a quire reserved especially for this purpose. Dürer had previously kept such a compendium, or 'notebook' as he described it, on his second sojourn in Venice between 1505 and 1507, which in all likelihood combined records of the day's events with visual motifs.[59] Notably, while Dürer repeatedly refers to work in the silverpoint drawing book,[60] a pendant in pen and ink is never discussed.

Dürer may have removed single pages himself while travelling, which may explain gaps and some of the other lapses in continuity in the present text.[61] While our picture of its subsequent fate remains so far incomplete, making such considerations unverifiable, the statement by the owner of the Bamberg copy, Hans Albrecht von Derschau (1755–1824), that the journal had been burned during the Napoleonic Wars in the vicinity of Nuremberg merits greater consideration.[62]

THE PROVENANCE OF THE NETHERLANDS RECORDS

This in turn raises the question of how the records from Dürer's Netherlandish trip were preserved to the extent that they were. There is no question the drawings and the work in the silverpoint drawing book were incorporated into the artist's workshop repertoire following his return, apart from any sheets given away on the trip. This latter

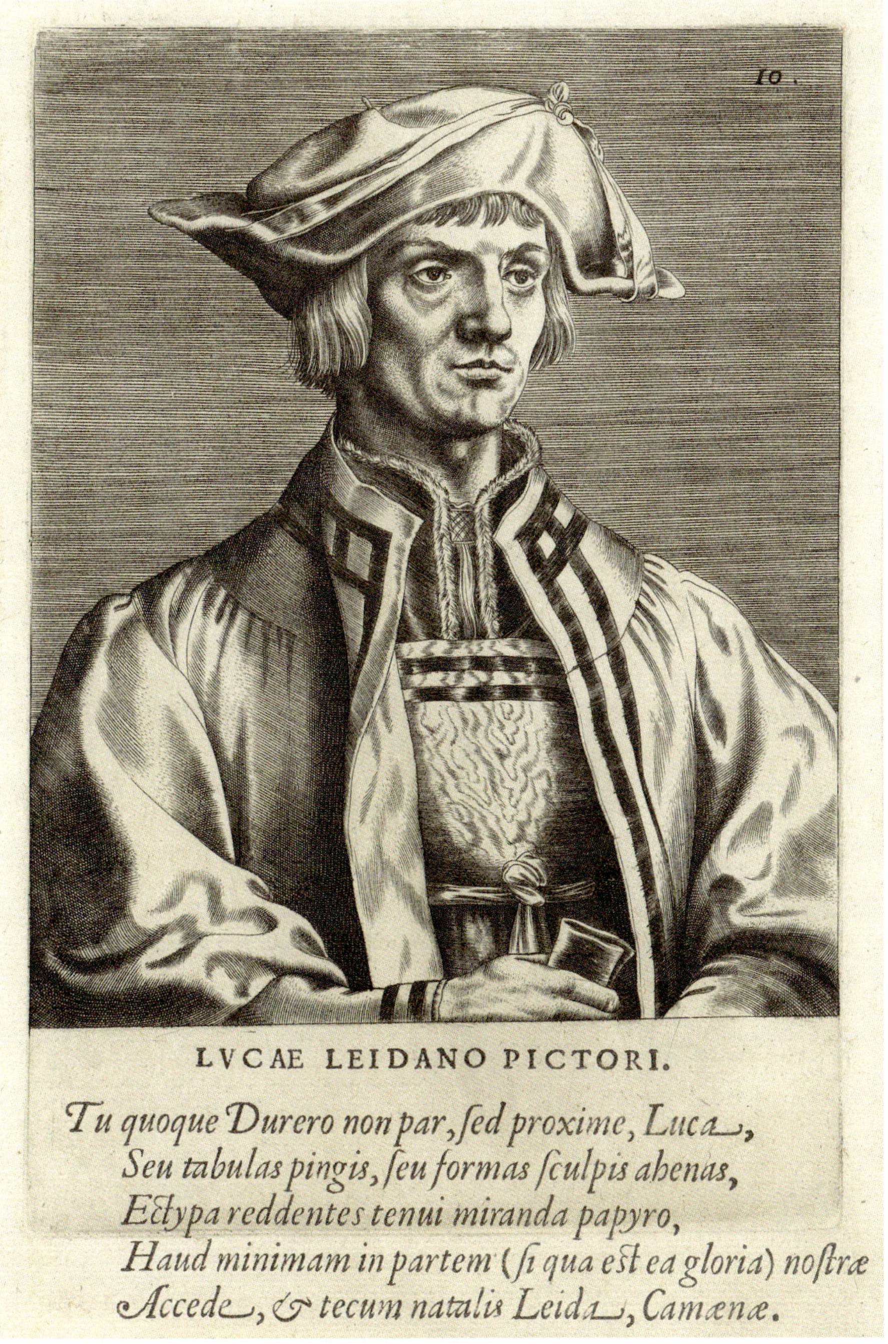

Fig. 79
ATTRIBUTED TO JAN WIERIX (1539–1620)
AFTER ALBRECHT DÜRER
Portrait of Lucas van Leyden, in *Pictorum Aliquot Celebrium Germaniae Inferiores Effigies, Antwerp*, 1572
Engraving and letterpress, 19 × 12.8 cm
Rijksmuseum, Amsterdam
(RP-P-1907-602)

group includes the *Portrait of Lucas van Leyden* (fig. 118),[63] of which it can demonstrably, if indirectly, be shown that it was still present in the Netherlands in the late sixteenth century, by way of an engraved copy in Hieronymus Cock's *Pictorum Aliquot Celebrium Germaniae Inferioris Effigies* (*Effigies of Some Celebrated Painters of Lower Germany*), published in Antwerp in 1572 (fig. 79). The same compendium contains portraits of Bernaert van Orley and Joachim Patinir that may themselves have been based on drawings of Dürer's which were still on hand at the time but have since been lost. A copy also exists of what is presumably a portrait of Jan Provoost (cat. 92),[64] etched and monogrammed in the late sixteenth century by 'AP', who was active in the Netherlands. Finally, we know of another etching created around 1600 after the second portrait of Lucas van Leyden, as it is known (fig. 126).[65] This last drawing has the longest traceable history in the Netherlands, present in various collections in Amsterdam from the early eighteenth century until 1833. Most of the drawings, however, came back to Nuremberg with Dürer, where they were integrated into his workshop stock according to strict criteria.[66] The chiaroscuro sheet showing Agnes with a Netherlandish headdress (fig. 100)

Fig. 80
ALBRECHT DÜRER
Portrait of Endres Dürer, 1514
Silverpoint on bluish white primed paper, 29.6 × 21 cm
The Albertina Museum, Vienna (3137)

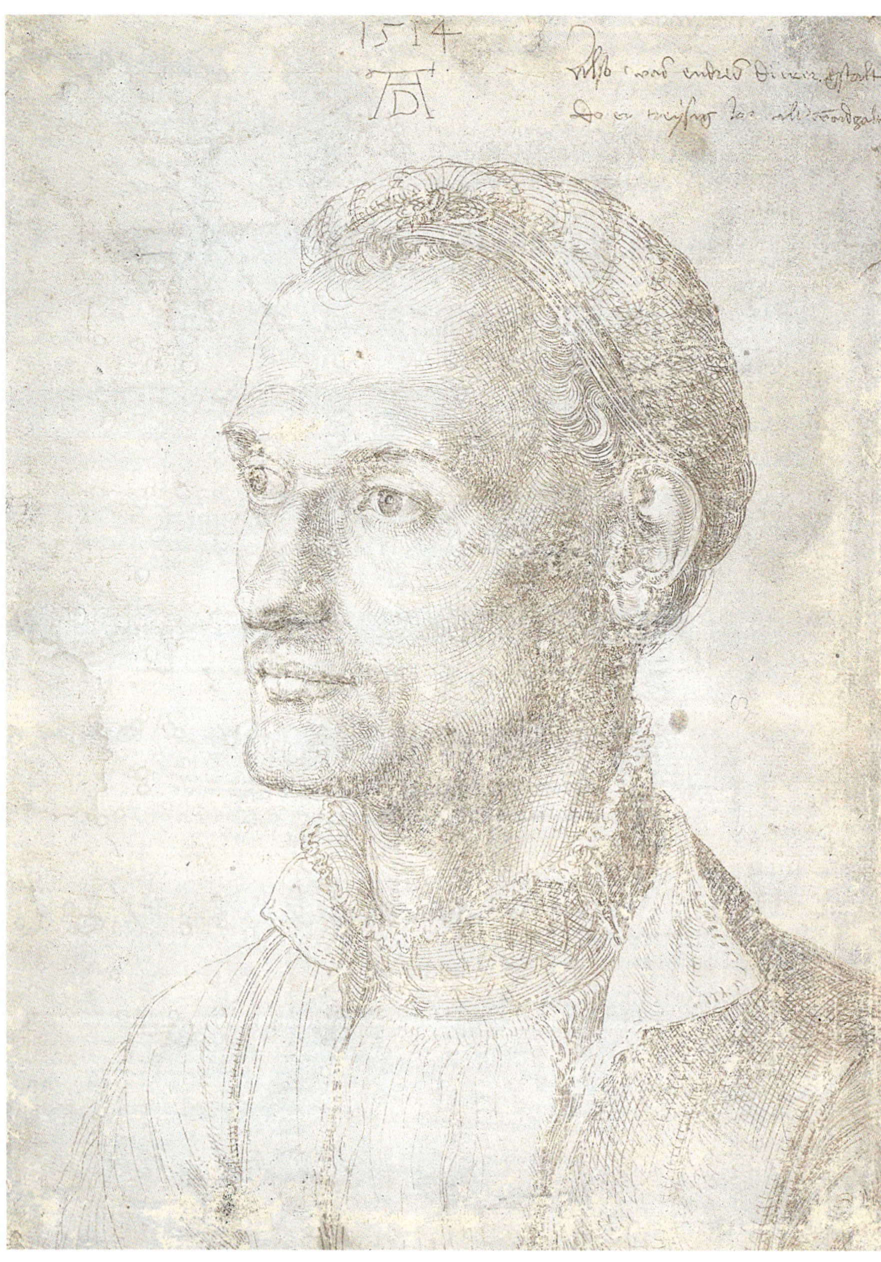

thus finds its place among other family portraits, while the watercolours depicting Irish warriors and the Livonian women (cat. 74; fig. 101)[67] were evidently grouped with earlier studies of Nuremberg costumes.[68] We owe such detailed knowledge to the subsequent fate of the drawings from Dürer's estate, which were kept in the artist's original arrangement well beyond his death – in large part up until 1800.

In addition to any cash and property in hand, in April 1528 Dürer's newly turned widow, Agnes, took possession of the artist's drawings, manuscripts and printing plates. After her death in 1539 the artistic work was inherited by the artist's brother, Endres (fig. 80), so that his claims resulting from the Albrecht's inheritance were settled. Larger sales followed, and upon Endres's death in 1555 the valuable estate passed to his widow, Ursula (died 1560). In 1557 'all paintings and drawings'[69] were transferred to the Nuremberg merchant Willibald Imhoff (1519–1580), who from the 1550s assembled a collection of the artist's work that soon became one of the largest and most significant to date.

At the time of his death, Imhoff's art collection (preserved in his *Kunstkammer* or art collection) encompassed more than twenty paintings associated with Dürer's name, a number of volumes featuring the artist's printed works and the coveted *Kunstbuch* ('Art Book'), which brought together more than a hundred of his most important drawings and watercolours.[70] Among others, the *Kunstbuch* contained portraits of Dürer's family, including the aforementioned portrait of Agnes;

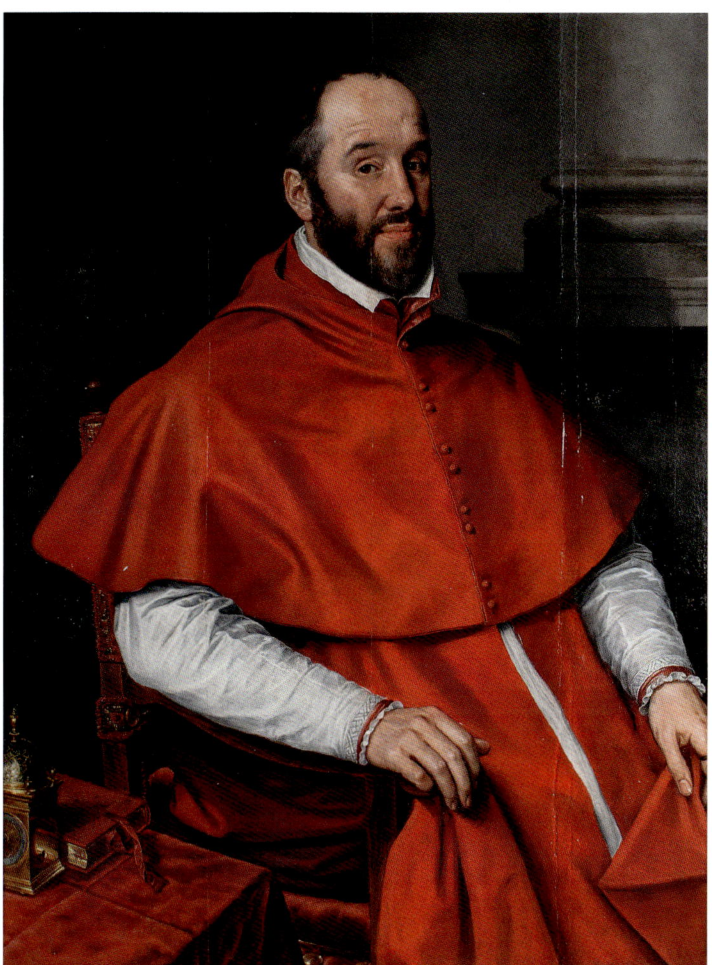

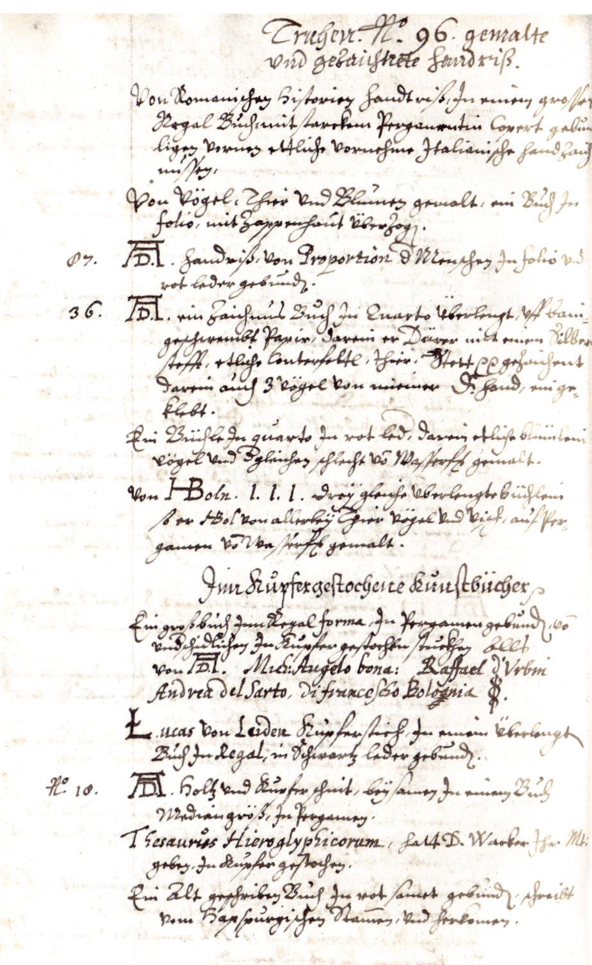

Truhen: No. 96. gemalte vnd gezaichnete handriß.

Jnn Kupfergestochene Kunstbücher

chiaroscuro studies of heads and hands from the time of his second trip to Venice and works in preparation for the Heller Altarpiece. These were supplemented by the Berlin version of the portrait of a 93-year-old man,[71] although not the other sheets associated with Jerome; and the studies of costumes and regional dress, including watercolours from the Netherlands. While other works from the Netherlands were absent, the book otherwise contained the majority of the artist's earlier drawings from the period before his first Italian journey, as well as nearly all of his of animal and plant studies. Such classification criteria doubtless reflect a system that dates back to Dürer himself.

A dramatic decline in the fortunes of the Imhoff trading house, however, soon saw the family forced to sell the valuable work to Rudolf II, a fanatical Dürer collector (fig. 82). While the Holy Roman Emperor's initial interest lay chiefly in seven paintings, Imhoff's widow, Anna, also made the *Kunstbuch* over to him. At the turn of the year 1588/9 the precious item entered the emperor's Prague art collections. It seems likely that the second source for the emperor's collection also derived from sales by Endres and Ursula Dürer. In 1589 Rudolf II secured 'a folio' with more than two hundred drawings by Dürer from the estate of Cardinal Antoine Perrenot de Granvelle (fig. 81). Granvelle could only have acquired this set en masse, while attending the Diet of Nuremberg in the spring of 1543.

Much less is known about the contents of the Granvelle album than about the Imhoff *Kunstbuch*. The only note of some use refers to 'drawings of all manner of places' and drawings 'made with charcoal':[72] Rudolf II's holdings did in fact include both landscape watercolours as well as portraits in charcoal and chalk, which are scarcely represented in the Imhoff collection. Other possible components of the Granvelle collection that can be traced back to the imperial collection include a later group of chiaroscuro drawings executed in metalpoint and chalk, works completed in the context of the *sacra conversazione*[73] and the bulk of drawings from the Netherlands, including the sheets removed from the journal. Rudolf II may also have acquired the silverpoint drawing book from Granvelle's estate. While no reference to this exists in the surviving documentation, in the 1560s the drawing book would have been available to the Antwerp workshop of Hieronymous Cock (as Giulia Bartrum plausibly concludes, pp. 275–6), along with

Fig. 81
WILLEM KEY
(1516–1568)
Portrait of Cardinal Antoine Perrenot de Granvelle, 1561
Oil on panel,
114 × 88 cm
Klassik Stiftung
Weimar (G 1164)

Fig. 82
DANIEL FRÖSCHL
(1563–1613)
Inventory of the *Kunstkammer* of Emperor Rudolf II in Prague, 1607
Liechtenstein. The Princely Collections, Vaduz–Vienna
(HS 130, fol. 381 verso)

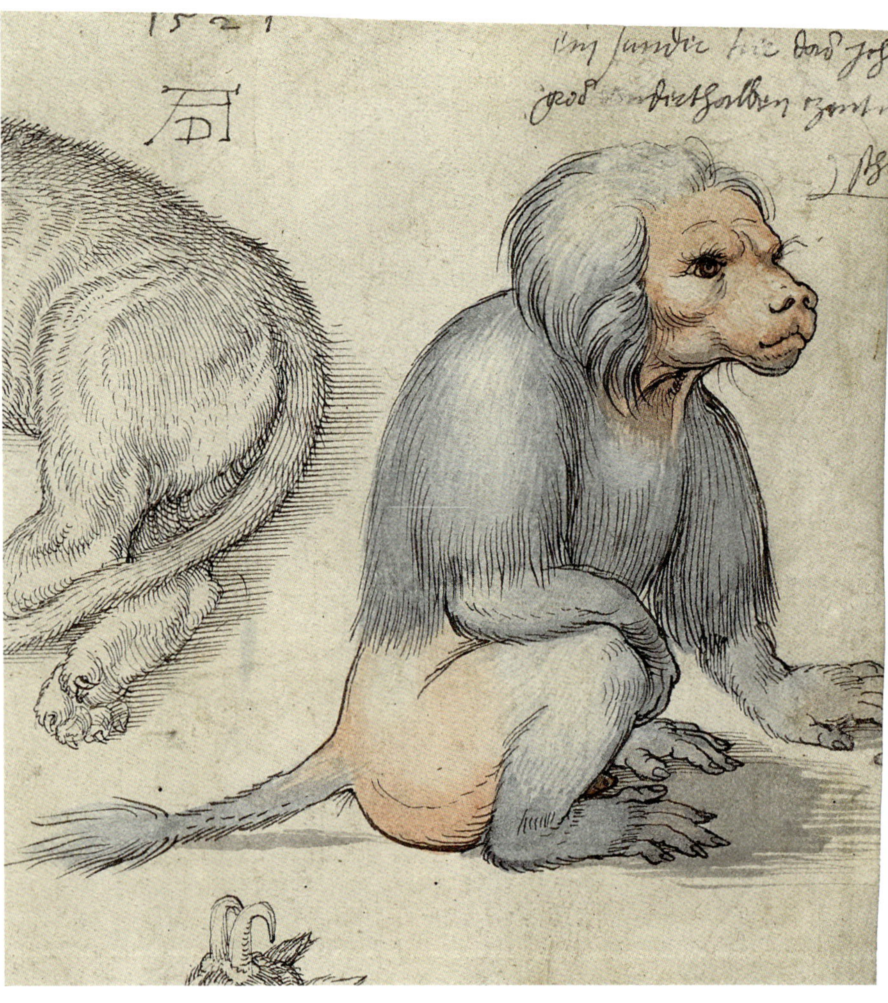

Detail from *Sketches of Animals and Landscapes* (cat. 85)

other works of the same provenance or from around the time that Granvelle resided in Brussels.

So it was that Prague came to house the largest collection of Dürer's drawings assembled since the artist's death, which included nearly the entire yield of his travels through the Low Countries. Dürer's 'best drawings, sketches and portraits'[74] were pasted into two richly adorned albums for a total of 371 'original drawings by Albrecht Dürer',[75] according to an inventory of the volumes compiled in 1783 and subsequently transferred to Vienna's court library. The silverpoint drawing book was preserved separately and is described in Rudolf II's inventory from 1607/11 as 'a drawing book in quarto, landscape format, on paper grounded with bone meal, in which Dürer has drawn several portraits, animals and city views in silverpoint, in which also three birds are pasted by my [Daniel Fröschl's] hand'.[76]

Before turning to the subsequent fate of these collections, two further groups of drawings from the Netherlands are worth considering. The Uffizi Gallery in Florence owns a small number of works – the portrait of an African woman and three sheets from the *Oblong Passion* – that can be traced back to 1673.[77] The sheet with studies of landscapes and animals (cat. 85) was also separated from the main stock at an early point, and served as the basis for a number of precise replicas made by Giovanna Garzoni (1600–1670), a miniaturist active in Naples, Florence and Rome during the seventeenth century (fig. 83).[78] The fact that Dürer's inscription for the baboon was itself copied in counterfeit quality implies the presence of the original. Garzoni had lived in Florence since 1642 and counted the Medici among her patrons and supporters, giving rise to the suspicion that she may have found the sheet in their collection. The precious works may have come from the imperial collections in Prague, where the remaining depictions of the Passion were found among the Granvelle group and likely came to Florence in 1628, after Grand Duke Ferdinando de' Medici (1610–1670) and his brother Giancarlo (1611–1663) had visited their uncle Ferdinand II in Prague and received a host of spectacular gifts from the emperor to mark the occasion. These included copies

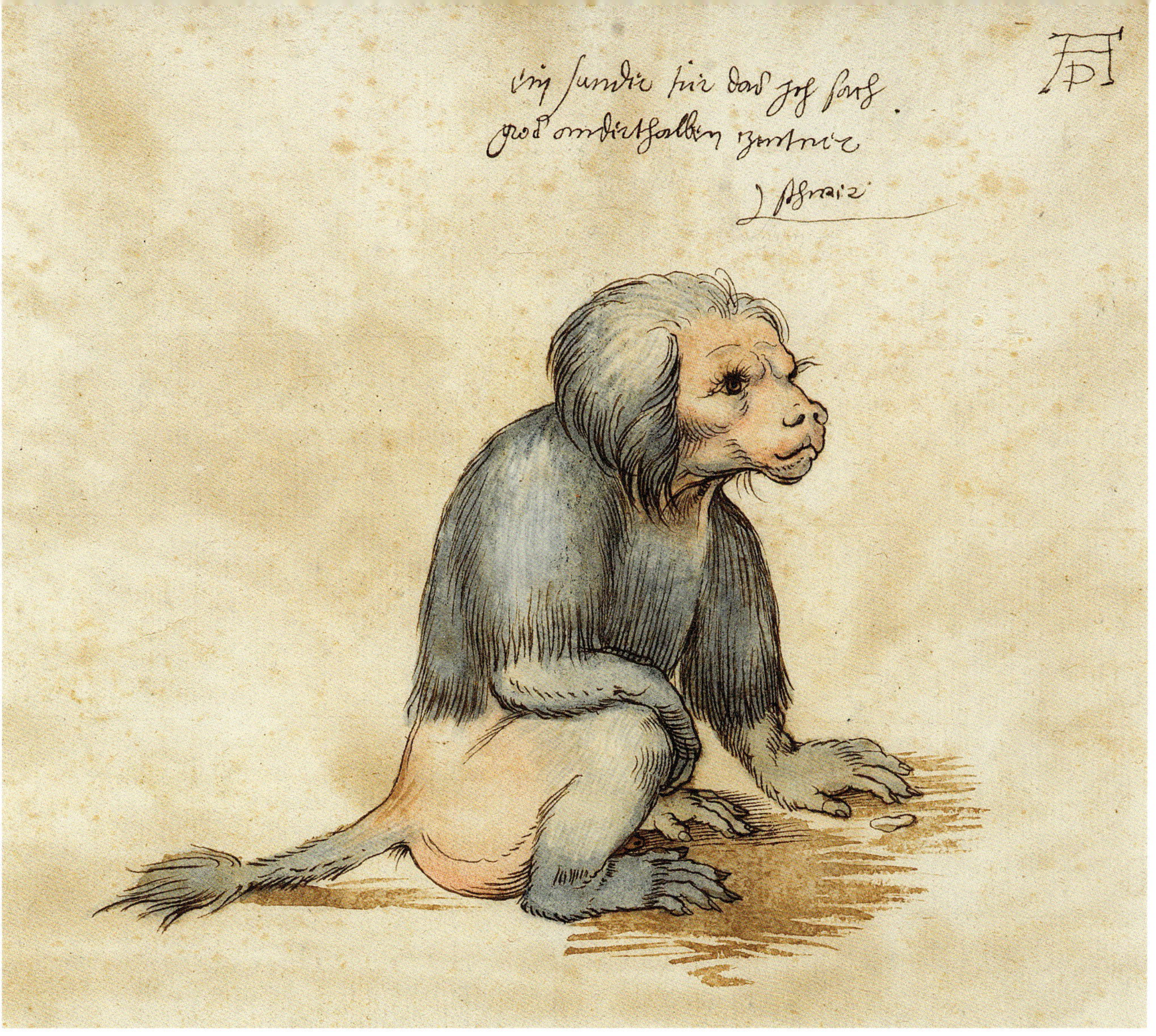

Fig. 83
GIOVANNA GARZONI
(1600–1670)
AFTER ALBRECHT DÜRER
A Baboon, about 1642
Pen and brown ink,
watercolour,
15.8 × 17.7 cm
Accademia Nazionale di
San Luca (rz33_043688
and rz33_043692)

of Dürer's *Adam and Eve*, as well as the *Large Mount Calvary* attributed to the latter.[79]

After Prague, the largest collection of Dürer's works was assembled by the Irish naturalist, botanist and physician Sir Hans Sloane (1660–1753), who made it over as a bequest to the British nation upon his death. The collection specifically concerns a volume in the British Museum originally containing some two hundred drawings that has since largely been broken up (and of which only about half were by Dürer's hand), as well as manuscripts with notes and drawings preserved today in the British Library.[80] The British Museum album included six sheets from Dürer's journey to the Netherlands, among them a depiction of a walrus (fig. 112), multiple portraits and two chiaroscuro drawings of children's heads in the style of the studies for the *Crucifixion in Outline* (cat. 115). The latter two figures do not appear in Cock's engraving, however, which weighs in favour of the whole Sloane complex having been separated from the main body of Dürer's estate at an early point, or at least prior to 1560.

Bound uniformly in black, and each album bearing Dürer's monogram as well as the year '1637' in gold print, the Sloane volumes also carry a short title in Dutch: 'Teekeningen [Drawings] 1637' for illustrated volumes, and 'Schriften [Writings] 1637' for manuscripts on art theory. These were likely assembled by Pieter Spiering van Silvercroon (1594/96–1652), who had risen to wealth as a businessman and to prominence as an art collector.[81] We learn from Joachim von Sandrart that Spiering's collection encompassed 'a great number of fine hand sketches' of Dürer's.[82] The chief source for Spiering's own holdings may have been Gommer Spranger (1577–1637) or his estate. Spranger was a nephew of Bartholomäus Spranger (1546–1611), court painter to Rudolf II; Gommer died in 1637 in Amsterdam, where the remnants of his estate came up for auction the following year. These included no fewer than 33 woodblocks and three copperplates by Dürer, as well as the artist's own corrected proof of his *Treatise on Measurement*.[83] According to a handwritten note on its flyleaf, Bartholomäus Spranger had acquired the copy of the treatise, along with a number of 'Houtplaten' or wood blocks, in 1580. It seems likely, then, that a majority of the works demonstrably present in the Netherlands in 1637 belonged to the legacy of Bartholomäus and Gommer Spranger.

The trail leading back from the Dürer collection in London to the artist's workshop is also relatively quick to trace. When Ursula Dürer died in September 1560, her will included the names of two nieces, one named Regina whose husband was Hieronymus Alnpeck, likely a goldsmith in Prague. We now know that in 1560 Alnpeck applied to Nuremberg City Council for an exemption from the taxes on his wife's inheritance. The scope and value of Albrecht Dürer's estate had decreased considerably since the artist's death: there is mention of copperplates, woodblocks and a number of leaves having been removed. Most of the copperplates, and the drawings in their entirety, had gone missing in the meantime. Alnpeck's conclusion is that the estimated value of 600 gulden calculated for the estate at the time of Dürer's death should be reduced to 500.[84] While there is no reference to drawings or manuscripts in this case, they may well have held no interest for the artist's heirs, who were clearly preoccupied with the estate's commercial exploitation – as opposed to the printing plates, which could still produce copies.

To return to the treasures of the imperial collection: after a period of total neglect following its transfer to Vienna in 1631, the body of work resurfaced once more in 1796. At this time the Duke of Saxe-Teschen, Albert Casimir (1738–1822), managed to acquire a considerable portion – the entire contents of one volume – for his collection, later the Albertina Museum in Vienna. A second part was acquired by a syndicate of traders and collectors during the French occupation of Vienna in 1809. The principal beneficiaries of the sell-off were Prince Henryk Ludwik Lubomirski (1777–1850); Joseph Daniel Böhm (1794–1865), Director of the Academy of Engraving at the Imperial and Royal Central Mint in Vienna; the Vienna art dealer Josef Grünling (1785–1845), whose stock went to Bremen's Kunsthalle in 1852; and especially Dominique-Vivant Denon (1747–1825) and the military governor of Vienna at the time, Antoine-François Andréossy (1761–1828).

With this, however, the fate was finally sealed of a collection that had remained self-contained over centuries, as the volumes from Rudolf's collection retained Dürer's original order only in part, and the sheets from the artist's trip to the Netherlands were distributed throughout both volumes by a system that remains obscure. The silverpoint drawing book was divided between Denon, who acquired the largest share, Grünling and Böhm. Denon ultimately acquired some forty sheets, including nearly all the full studies for the *sacra conversazione*; Andréossy for his part was chiefly interested in the large-format portraits and costume studies. Before his death, the majority of Andréossy's sixty or so drawings went to the British portraitist Thomas Lawrence (1769–1830), who also possessed several sheets that came from Denon. When the works by Dürer and Titian from Lawrence's collection came up for auction at Samuel Woodburn's of London in 1836, the catalogue noted regarding the origin of the sheets that these could be largely 'the spoils of the late war' that had fallen to General Andréossy after Vienna's surrender.[85] Almost the entire trade in Dürer drawings in the nineteenth and twentieth centuries would ultimately derive from these sources,[86] seeing Dürer off on his greatest expedition yet – into the world.

1 Ashcroft 2017, vol. 1, no. 162, p. 551.
2 For a highly informative account of the book's character and function see Sahm 2002, pp. 133–84, esp. pp. 134–7 for terminology.
3 See Anzelewsky 1991, nos 150–69, as well as the concise survey in Unverfehrt 2007, p. 210, with references to the written part.
4 Winkler 1936–9, vol. 4, nos 744–835; Strauss 1974, vol. 4, nos 1520/6–47, 1521/1–60. See also the survey in Unverfehrt 2007, pp. 207–10. See the author's appendix on the National Gallery website for a systematic overview and survey of the core group, encompassing works that have been verified as coming from Dürer's trip either by journal entries, monograms or dating, or again on the basis of stylistic or technical analysis.
5 Ashcroft 2017, vol. 1, no. 162, p. 556. On the drawn portraits, see also Hirschfelder 2013, as well as Peter van den Brink's article in the present publication, pp. 205–25. The author, moreover, has his discussion and exchange with Peter van den Brink to thank for many of the insights in this article.
6 Ashcroft 2017, vol. 1, no. 162, p. 562. On the Rogendorf coat of arms, see also note 19 below.
7 Ashcroft 2017, vol. 1, no. 162, pp. 557, 564.
8 See Gert Unverfehrt's debit and credit summary in Unverfehrt 2007, pp. 224–5.
9 Ashcroft 2017, vol. 1, no. 162, p. 561.
10 Ibid., p. 578.
11 During his fourth stay in Antwerp from December 1520 to early April 1521, these included Lazarus Ravensburger, the 'Portuguese factor's servant', as well as 'the new factor', Ashcroft 2017, vol. 1, no. 162, p. 572. During his sixth stay, from early June to early July 1521, Dürer depicted 'Master Jakob' and the wife of Bernhart Stecher, Ashcroft 2017, vol. 1, no. 162, pp. 584–5.
12 The price for an oil portrait ranged from 8 to 30 gulden. See Ashcroft 2017, vol. 1, no. 162, pp. 576 ('Bernhard von Resten': 8 Gulden), 589 (Christian II of Denmark: 30 gulden).
13 Ashcroft 2017, vol. 1, no. 162, p. 563.
14 Ibid., p. 557.
15 For the term *Visierung*, see Jörg Kölderer's invoice for Emperor Maximilian I. In this context works on paper for which nothing further was intended either took the verb malen, to paint, or abmalen, to reproduce. See Schönherr 1884, pp. xxviii–xxix, Reg. 831 (1507 März 30).

16 During his first stay in Antwerp in August 1520, Dürer mentions work 'for the goldsmiths', then again in May 1521 for 'Jan, the goldsmith from Brussels'. Ashcroft 2017, vol. 1, no. 162, pp. 559, 583.

17 Among others, while in Antwerp in May 1521 Dürer refers to three sword hilts for Tommaso Bombelli, the paymaster of Archduchess Margaret. Ibid., p. 583.

18 In February 1521, during his fourth stay in Antwerp for the family of Fuggers' managing director, and again for Tommaso Bombelli, mentioned in note 17 above. Ibid., p. 573.

19 During his second stay in Antwerp from autumn until early November 1520 for the brothers Wilhelm and Wolfgang von Rogendorf (ibid., pp. 561–2), and in early 1521 for Lorenz Staiber (ibid., pp. 566; 573). See the three woodcuts with the coat of arms for Rogendorf and Staiber from Meder 1932, nos 290, 293; Schoch, Mende and Scherbaum 2001–4, vol. 2, nos 253–5. In this connection, Dürer's note in late May 1521 that 'for the Englishman I did his coat of arms in colour and he paid me 1 gulden' also deserves mention: the first depiction of the Mount of Olives held in Frankfurt shows a sketch on the reverse side with details on the colouring, Ashcroft 2017, vol. 1, no. 162, p. 583.

20 In March 1521 Dürer sketched 'a design, drawn in pen and tinted', in other words a pen-and-ink drawing with watercolour, a façade painting for Tommaso Bombelli, ibid., p. 576.

21 During his second stay in Antwerp in September 1520, for the physician of Margaret of Austria, ibid., p. 563.

22 Strauss 1974, vol. 4, nos 1521/23, 1521/24; see Ashcroft 2017, vol. 1, no. 162, p. 583.

23 Strauss 1974, vol. 4, no. 1521/20; see Ashcroft 2017, vol. 1, no. 162, p. 583. A list of pertinent sheets is published on the National Gallery website (see note 4 above). Strauss 1974, vol. 4, nos 1523/14, 1524/4 and 1524/5 all came about after the trip. In this context see Christof Metzger in Vienna 2019, pp. 437–45, as well as Dana Cowen's article in the present publication, pp. 241–51.

24 Strauss 1974, vol. 1, nos 1495/3, 1495/12, probably also 1495/13 and 1495/20.

25 Ashcroft 2017, vol. 1, no. 162, pp. 557, 559.

26 Strauss 1974, vol. 4, nos 1520/24, 1521/10.

27 Ibid., nos 1521/36–1521/39.

28 Drawings: Strauss 1974, vol. 4, nos 1521/2–1521/7. Paintings: Anzelewsky 1991, no. 162; on the paintings see also Ashcroft 2017, vol. 1, no. 162, p. 576.

29 For more in this context see also London 2010, especially M. Evans, 'The Impact of the Cartoons', pp. 48–53, and Arnold Nesselrath's essay in the present publication, pp. 165–83.

30 See e.g. Ashcroft 2017, vol. 1, no. 162, pp. 575, 578–9, 585.

31 Ibid., pp. 577, 582–3.

32 Ibid., pp. 557, 576.

33 Ibid., p. 563.

34 See e.g. ibid., pp. 555 (ink), 556 ('… three small panels, plus 4 stuivers for white ground for preparing them'), 562 (anthracite and black chalk), 567–9 (parchment, chestnut brown, black chalk), 573 (brushes). On the panels acquired for mounting drawn portraits see p. 152 above.

35 On the watermarks, see the National Gallery website (note 4 above); image in Strauss 1974, vol. 6, pp. 3273–94. On paper purchases, Ashcroft 2017, vol. 1, no. 162, pp. 565, 569.

36 This applies in particular to the Flemish paper bearing a coat of arms with lilies and attached letter 'B', of which Dürer made repeated use while in the Netherlands and continued to use until 1527. See the listing in Strauss 1974, vol. 6, p. 3281.

37 The sequence favoured by the author is: fol. 1r: blank (endpaper); 1v: Strauss 1974, vol. 4, no. 1520/22; 2r: ibid., no. 1520/19; 2v: timber board parlour (see main text pp. 155–6); 3r–v: ibid., no. 1521/43–2; 4r–v: ibid., no. 1521/44–5; 5r–v: ibid., no. 1520/20–1; 6r–v: ibid., no. 1520/23–4; 7r–v: ibid., no. 1520/35–6; 8r–v: ibid., no. 1520/29–30; 9r–v: ibid., no. 1520/32–1; 10r or v: the abbey church of Middelburg (lost, see main text p. 155); 11r–v: ibid., no. 1520/33–4; 12r–v: ibid., no. 1521/10–11; 13r–v: ibid., no. 1521/12–60; 14r–v: ibid., no. 1521/13–57; 15r–v: ibid., no. 1521/46–25; 16r: ibid., no. 1521/59; 16v: blank (endpaper). On the silverpoint drawing book, see also Arnold Nesselrath's essay in the present publication, pp. 165–83; on the other portraits in silverpoint, see Peter van den Brink's essay, pp. 205–25.

38 Kunstmuseum, Basel, inv. 1966.168; Musée du Louvre, Paris, inv. 20678; the Albertina Museum, Vienna, inv. 7788.

39 The lion: Strauss 1974, vol. 4, nos 1521/11 and 1521/12; the horse: ibid., nos 1521/42 and 1521/44.

40 Ibid., no. 1520/30.

41 Ashcroft 2017, vol. 1, no. 162, p. 570.

42 Verso from Strauss 1974, vol. 4, no. 1520/19. See also Anzelewsky and Mielke 1984, pp. 97–8, under no. 94 ('remnants of thick lines in silverpoint', 'architectural image'), fig. appendix VII.

43 My thanks to Georg Dietz und Michael Roth (Staatliche Museen zu Berlin, Kupferstichkabinett) for a number of productive conversations.

44 Strauss 1974, vol. 4, nos 1521/42 and 1521/43.

45 Ashcroft 2017, vol. 1, no. 162, pp. 564–5.

46 See the National Gallery website (note 4 above), which includes the sheets I have excluded from this group.

47 Strauss 1974, vol. 4, nos 1520/8, 1520/9. In this context see Stephanie Buck in Frankfurt 2003, pp. 102–3, no. 29 with n. 1.

48 Strauss 1974, vol. 4, nos 1520/6, 1520/7, 1520/10, 1520/13, and vol. 2, no. 1504/43. Regarding the identification and interpretation of this last sheet, I follow the plausible explanation Peter van den Brink will advance in a separate publication. See van den Brink 2020.

49 See image in Strauss 1974, vol. 6, p. 3285.

50 Ibid., vol. 4, no. 1521/58.

51 Ibid., vol. 2, no. 1504/43, vol. 6, nos XW.608, XW.601; for *Saint Veronica's Cloth/Veronica's Sudarium* see Ashcroft 2017, vol. 1, no. 162, pp. 570, 562 ('… a good painted *Face of Saint Veronica* …'), 573, ('… another oil painting of Holy Veronica …'), 583.

52 Strauss 1974, vol. 4, nos 1520/8, 1520/10, 1520/11; see Ashcroft 2017, vol. 1, no. 162, pp. 556–7.

53 On Dürer's workshop holdings as a testament to the artist's accomplishment and talent, see C. Metzger, 'Dürer, the Draftsman', in Vienna 2019, pp. 36–49. See also Peter van den Brink's essay in the present publication, pp. 205–25.

54 Strauss 1974, vol. 4, no. 1520/35 (silverpoint version); see Ashcroft 2017, vol. 1, no. 162, p. 572.

55 Strauss, 1974–82, vol. 4, no. 1521/60; see Ashcroft 2017, vol. 1, no. 162, p. 585.

56 Strauss 1974, vol. 4, nos 1520/44, 1520/26. On the first version, see Ashcroft 2017, vol. 1, no. 162, pp. 558–9, 561; on the second see ibid., pp. 566, 573. On the woodcuts created between 1520 and 1521, see Meder 1932, no. 293 or Schoch, Mende and Scherbaum 2001–4, vol. 2, nos 254, 255.

57 Ashcroft 2017, vol. 1, no. 162, p. 560.

58 Calculating for the most economical use results in a total minimum length of 50 pages.

59 See Dürer's letter to Willibald Pirckheimer of 25 April 1506 (Royal Society, London, inv. MM/20/59); Ashcroft 2017, vol. 1, no. 162, pp. 149–50.

60 Ibid., pp. 564, 569.

61 See Sahm 2002, p. 141 n. 34 (missing payment for board at Plankfelt's), p. 144 (missing delivery to Nuremberg), p. 147 n. 66 (Dürer draws Erasmus of Rotterdam 'again', although an earlier sitting is not mentioned). Felix Lautenschlager is also portrayed 'another time' (Ashcroft: 'a second portrait …') in August 1520, without Dürer mentioning the first occasion. See Ashcroft 2017, vol. 1, no. 162, p. 556.

62 Thomas Frognall Dibdin, *A Bibliographical Antiquarian and Picturesque Tour in France and Germany*, London 1829, p. 442.

63 Strauss 1974, vol. 4, no. 1521/26. Greater detail on these and other printed works mentioned below can be found on the National Gallery website (see note 4 above).

64 Ibid., no. 1520/42. Traditionally identified as Sebastian Brant (1457–1521). Here I follow Peter van den Brink's reinterpretation, with some caution.

65 Ibid., no. 1521/30.

66 On the following facts and considerations, see in greater detail C. Metzger in Vienna 2019, pp. 36–9, 50–67 and 466–79.

67 Strauss 1974, vol. 4, nos 1521/1, 1521/36–1521/39.

68 Ibid., vol. 2, nos 1500/3, 1500/5–1500/7, vol. 4, no. 1527/3.

69 Metzger in Vienna 2019, appendix 2 (Dürer on Paper in the Habsburg Collections), doc. 1.

70 On the content and sequence of the art book, see the 1588 inventory, published and commented on by C. Metzger in Vienna 2019, appendix 1 (catalogue of Willibald Imhoff's Art Book, 1588).

71 Staatliche Museen zu Berlin, Kupferstichkabinett (inv. KdZ 15307). Strauss 1974, vol. 4, no. 1521/2.

72 C. Metzger in Vienna 2019, appendix 2, doc. 17.

73 See the essays by Stijn Alsteens (pp. 129–45) and Giulia Bartrum (pp. 267–76) in the present publication.

74 C. Metzger in Vienna 2019, appendix 2, doc. 22.

75 Ibid., appendix 2, doc. 67.

76 Ibid., appendix 2, doc. 24. The inventory's author, miniaturist Daniel Fröschl, had been active at the Prague court since 1603 and in 1607 was named 'antiquarius' of the imperial collections. The page he mentions here has since gone missing.

77 Strauss 1974, vol. 4, nos 1521/8, 1520/37, 1520/38, 1521/17.

78 Ibid., no. 1521/40. See the essay by Sarvenaz Ayooghi and Heidrun Lange-Krach in the present volume, pp. 185–203.

79 Swoboda 2009, p. 106.

80 British Museum, London, Codex Sloane 5218; British Library, London, Codices Sloane 5228, 5229, 5230, 5231. For a summary account of these volumes, see Rowlands 1993.

81 In this context, see Veldman 2015–16.

82 J. von Sandrart, *Teutsche Academie der Edlen Bau-, Bild- und Mahlerey-Künste*, vol. 1, Nuremberg 1675, p. 225. Sandrart in turn draws his knowledge of the Spiering collection from Karel van Mander.

83 Bayerische Staatsbibliothek, Munich, inv. Sign. 4° L. impr. c. n. mss. 119. On this see Schauerte 2006.

84 See C. Metzger in Vienna 2019, p. 56.

85 *A Catalogue of One Hundred Original Drawings by Albert Durer and Titian Vecelli, collected by Sir Thomas Lawrence*, London 1836, p. 8: 'The major part of the choice drawings by this master, described in the present atalogue, were the spoils of the late war. They came into the hands of Gen. Andreossi soon after the capture of the city of Vienna: the condition of them is truly surprising.'

86 See C. Metzger in Vienna 2019, appendix 3 ('Dürer Drawings from the Imperial Collections in Prague and Vienna').

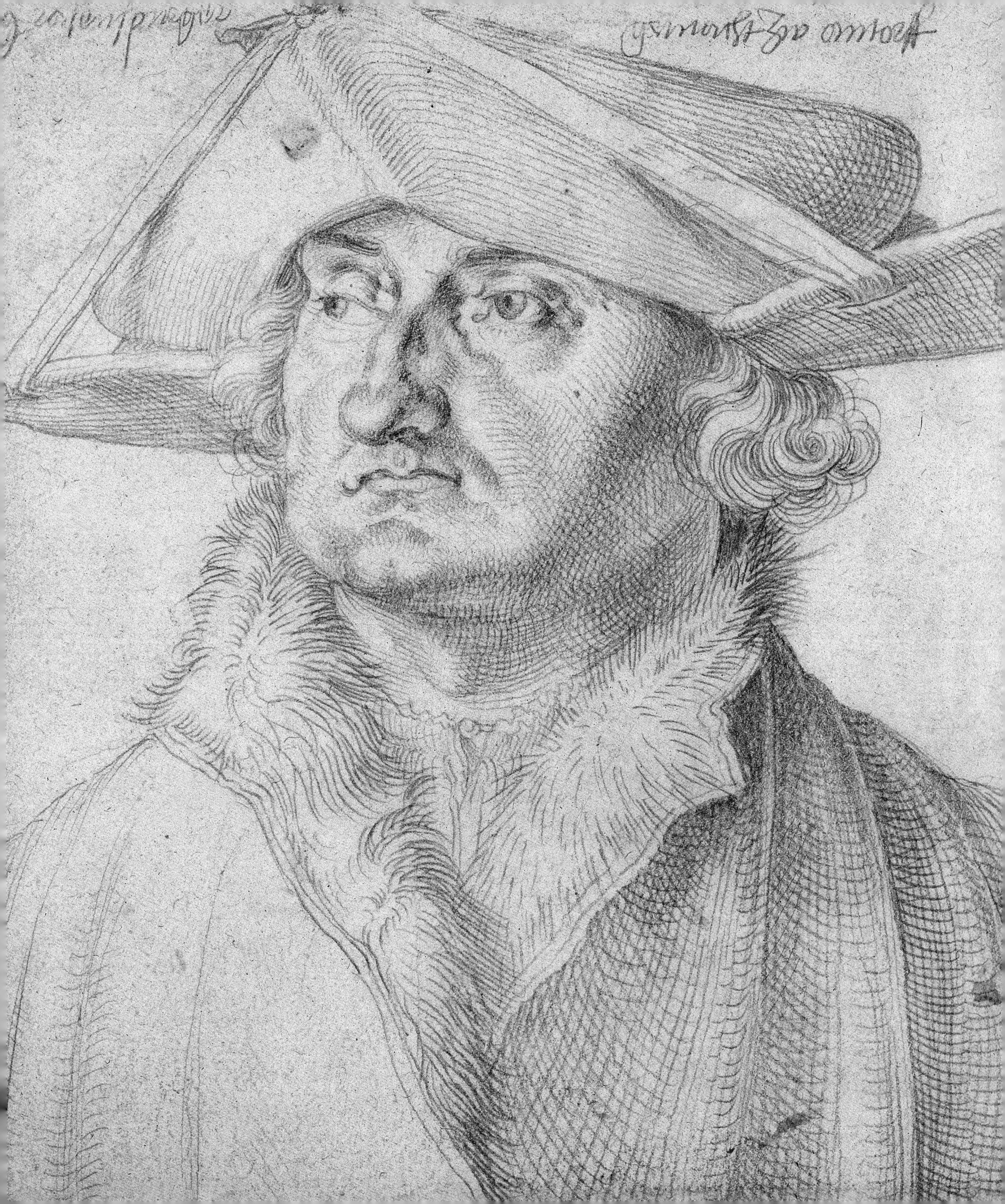

ARNOLD NESSELRATH

ALBRECHT DÜRER'S SILVERPOINT SKETCHBOOK

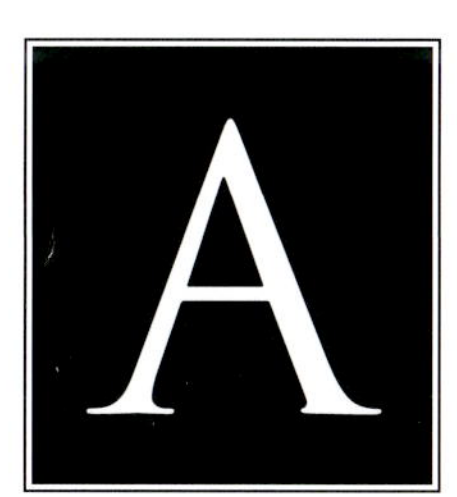

LBRECHT DÜRER'S SILVERPOINT SKETCHBOOK was a typical sketchbook.[1] Although it was a carefully prepared item, the artist drew quite spontaneously into the subtle booklet, collecting chance impressions or capturing subjects of particular interest; choosing and casually assembling motifs according to personal criteria; and annotating drawings where he thought necessary. As has often been noted, the silverpoint sketchbook thus forms a visual counterpart to Dürer's Netherlandish journal. It is not currently possible to determine how many pages the sketchbook originally contained.[2] In its diversity it is the most immediate and personal visual testimony of Dürer's journey to the Netherlands, touching on aspects that extend beyond his other drawings and artworks and become all the more evocative when set within their context. Page by page, the course of the sketchbook's creation reveals the enduring creative presence of an artist continuously making spontaneous adjustments to an otherwise coherent approach when arraying portraits, adding landscape or cityscape backgrounds, allowing motifs both small and large to draw his enthusiasm, getting swept up in animals and their movements, or simply conveying the inspiration he drew from everyday objects. The absolute confidence with which he implemented, then developed aesthetic decisions in his work impresses; the sketchbook shows no signs whatsoever of elements' correction or removal, which would have left behind significant traces in a medium like silverpoint drawing.

THE MEDIUM

Since all pages of such a volume must be specially prepared for the traces left by the silver stylus to appear on the page at all, Dürer's choice of technique implies that central elements of artistic realisation and formal design were decided well before any actual drawings were put to paper. Such a book was likely bought ready-made and bound, thus avoiding the laborious effort that went into preparing such an object. Consistent technical results from an analysis of the pages, their coating and

OPPOSITE
Detail from *Lazarus Ravensburger and the Tower of the House of Mayor Arnold van Liere in Antwerp* (cat. 90)

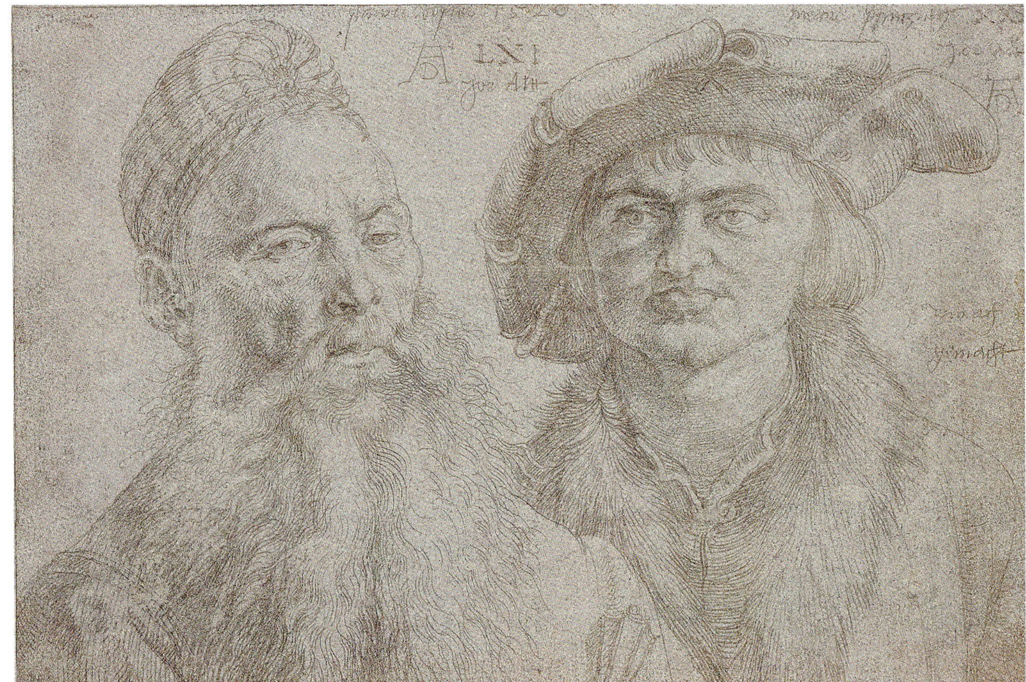

Fig. 84
ALBRECHT DÜRER
Paulus Topler and Martin Pfinzing in Aachen, 1520
Silverpoint on white grounded paper,
12.8 × 18.8 cm
Staatliche Museen zu Berlin, Kupferstichkabinett
(KdZ 4179 recto)

Fig. 85
ALBRECHT DÜRER
Interior of a room in Aachen, 1520,
photography with transmitted light by Annette T. Keller in collaboration with Georg Josef Dietz. It reveals the drawing underneath the backing paper as well as the latter's varying thickness in its different areas due to an earlier unsuccessful attempt to lift it.
Silverpoint on white grounded paper,
12.8 × 18.8 cm
Staatliche Museen zu Berlin, Kupferstichkabinett
(KdZ 4179 verso)

the metal of the stylus speak in favour of Dürer using a ready-made product.[3] This means that if the silverpoint sketchbook were in fact packed in his luggage when he set out from Nuremberg on 12 July 1520, Dürer could have intended it only for special occasions. Notably, no drawings from the sketchbook pertaining to the early part of the journey seem to exist and, if one goes by the references in his travel journal, cautiously heeding the growing evidence for the sketchbook's reconstruction, Dürer in fact only began to draw in it in Aachen after 7 October – on a special occasion, that is. In this case he could just as easily have bought the silverpoint sketchbook in Aachen, an idea that may have come to him there.[4]

Other examples of ready-made and bound drawing books that used a silverpoint stylus as a latch have been preserved, among them one that belonged to Hans Cranach (1513–1537). Cranach's father, Lucas Cranach the Elder, had the 42-page silverpoint book prepared in

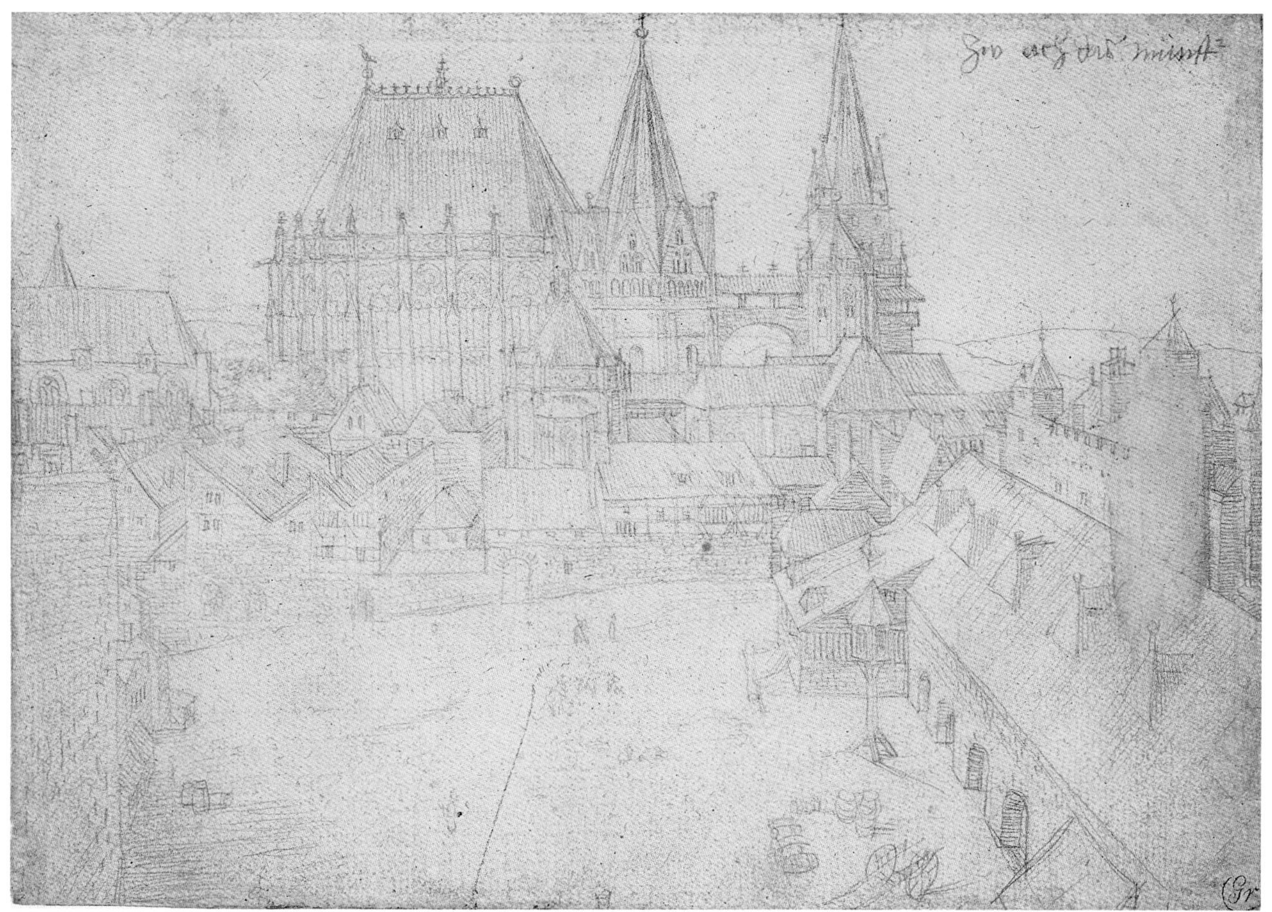

Fig. 86
ALBRECHT DÜRER
The Cathedral at Aachen,
1520
Silverpoint on pale pink
prepared paper,
12.6 × 17.4 cm
British Museum
(1895,0915.982)

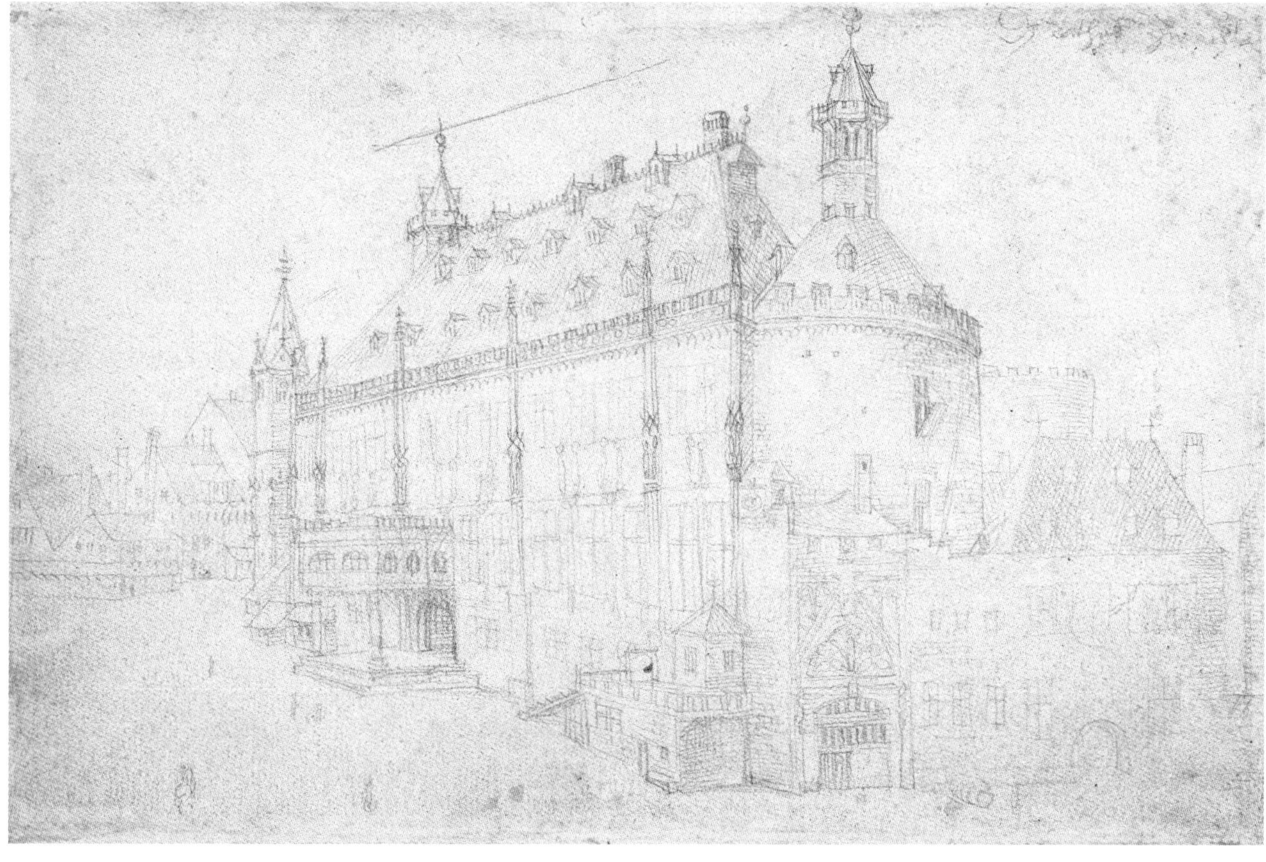

Fig. 87
ALBRECHT DÜRER
The Town Hall in Aachen,
1520
Silverpoint on ivory-
coloured prepared paper,
12.8 × 19 cm
Musée Condé, Chantilly
(DE893 recto)

1536 in anticipation of his beloved son's journey to Italy – one from which he sadly did not return.[5] Hans Baldung Grien's silverpoint album, on the other hand, comprising more than a hundred drawings on 75 folios and today preserved in Karlsruhe, was assembled later by a collector who bound together fragments from five different sketchbooks;[6] the artist himself never used the volume in this form. In spite of the fact, or rather because it was assembled from various sketchbooks, this particular object does give an impression of what was available on the market. Using the drawing tool, or what is possibly the original silver stylus, as a convenient closure or locking bar, was likely common practice.[7]

Dürer's familiarity with the silverpoint technique from early childhood and through his father's instruction has been stressed time and again. Indeed, his earliest preserved drawing, *Self Portrait at the Age of 13* (fig. 16), is in silverpoint.[8] The technique reappears throughout different phases of Dürer's career with varying frequency; before his departure for the Netherlands he had shown less engagement with the medium for some time, so the renewed focus is further evidence that a conscious artistic intention lay behind the choice. Silverpoint was a particularly popular technique in the Netherlands, with artists like Jan van Eyck and Rogier van der Weyden – two figures whose paintings held particular interest for Dürer during his trip – making great contributions to the medium.[9] It is difficult to say whether drawings by them were also in circulation at the time.

JOURNAL AND SKETCHBOOK

Most of what we know about the silverpoint sketchbook comes from Dürer himself; first of all that it was in fact a bound 'Büchlein' as he calls it, or small book. This fact is no longer apparent from the preserved folios, which have all been trimmed and bear no traces or edge punctures from previous binding, nor any smudged corners from turning pages.[10] It is through Dürer's own records that the sketchbook can be identified with an entry in the inventory from 1607–11 of Emperor Rudolph II's *Kunstkammer*, or art collection, and its provenance traced over the centuries with relative accuracy. Up until the time the inventory was taken, the sketchbook was documented as a single coherent item. After Rudolph's death in 1612 it was probably cut up while still in Prague, before its eventual transfer to Vienna.

Sources do not disclose how many folios the sketchbook originally contained; certainly more than the 15 preserved today. The book is described as a quarto format, meaning that it consisted of a number of bundled sections of sheets called quires, each comprising four folios – eight pages altogether, that is. The sketchbook may have held more than four such sections,[11] as 16 folios would have made for a very thin booklet. Browsing even the few existing pages and addressing the individual drawn motifs grants the impression of a stream of pictures that seems without end.[12] Nonetheless, any effort to determine the true scale of the sketchbook ultimately runs up against a lack of evidence.

At times the notes Dürer made in his sketchbook overlap helpfully with his journal entries, allowing the drawings to be correlated to his descriptions. He has recorded the succession of events for himself in this way so he might reconstruct them later. Otherwise, the notes in Dürer's journal offer little in terms of further insight into his depictions or portraits. Some pointers can be used to determine a few exact dates, and these also help one perceive the course that compositions took on a single page or across two facing pages, that is, how the sketchbook developed. The information in the journal entries is not sufficiently coherent to infer any missing folios; even a sentence as unequivocal as 'I drew portraits of Paulus Topler and Martin Pfinzing in my little sketchbook'[13] does not imply a double portrait of Dürer's two Nuremberg compatriots, as a look at the preserved sketchbook page (fig. 84) shows. As the juncture between the two figures reveals, both images were drawn on the same page within a few days of one another, if not on the same day, but in any case independently.[14]

This oft-cited sentence of Dürer's may mark the start of the silverpoint sketchbook following his arrival in Aachen on 7 October 1520. Yet when he subsequently refers to his view of the cathedral at Aachen (fig. 86)[15] and the portrait of Caspar Sturm[16] – 'I sketched the Church of Our Lady with its surroundings. I did Sturm's portrait'[17] – he neither explicitly mentions the small sketchbook in which they feature so prominently nor indicates their technique. Nevertheless, Dürer's note can be taken in a literal sense: he climbed up to the roof of the town hall to include the buildings that surrounded the cathedral when capturing the view.[18]

In addition to an entire series of motifs that he names in his journal as having completed in his silverpoint sketchbook, Dürer also executed loose sheets using the same technique. When he writes that he 'made a charcoal likeness of Köpfinger's sister-in-law in Aachen, and another with metalpoint',[19] explicitly mentioning the different techniques, he may well mean a sheet much like the impressive large-format silverpoint portrait of Katharina (fig. 119), the 20-year-old servant to the Portuguese Factor João Brandão, although this portrait

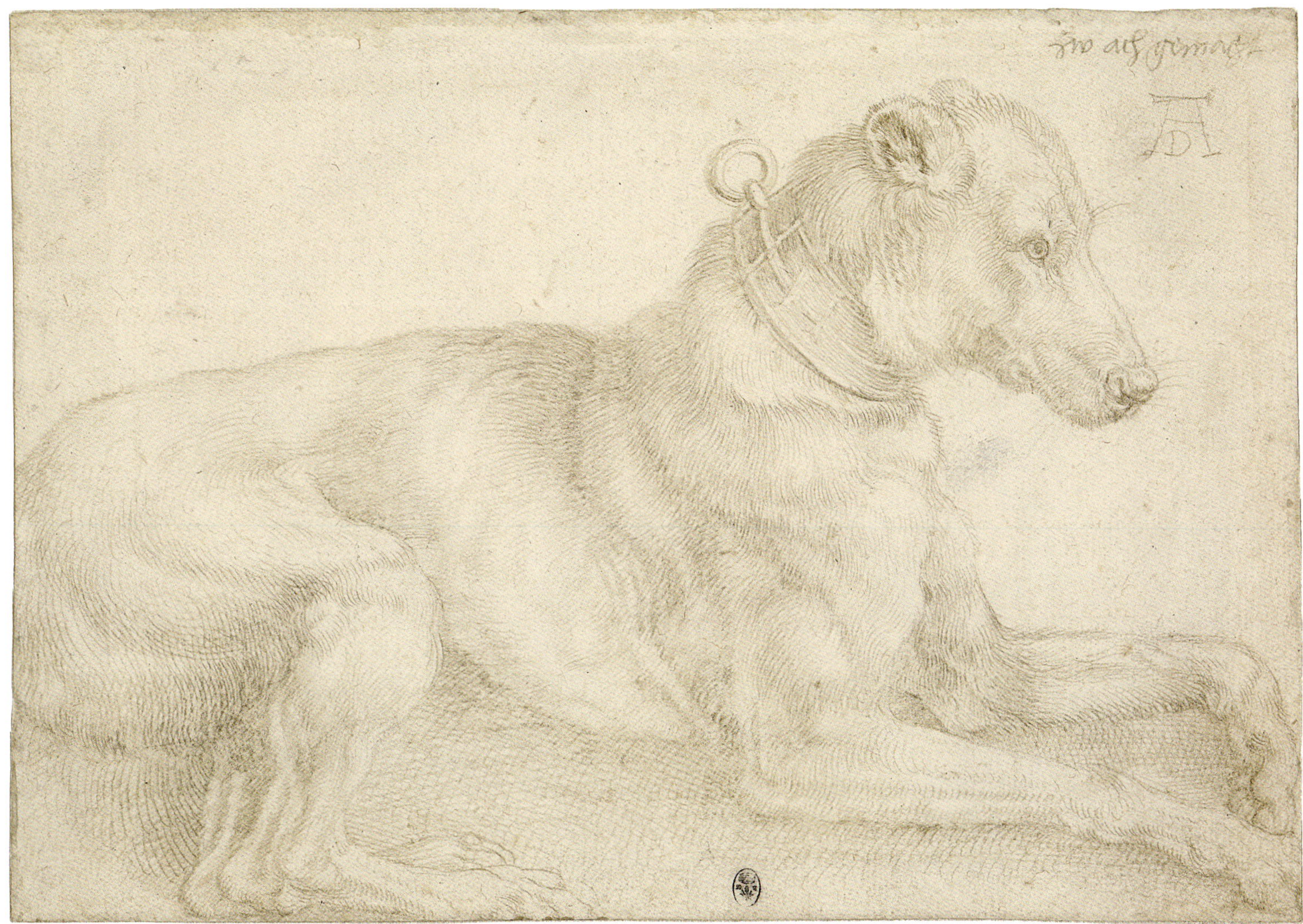

was created much later.[20] Dürer also writes of Katharina that 'I did … a silverpoint likeness of his Moorish woman'.[21] In neither case does he mention the sketchbook. Copies of the dog he drew in Aachen (fig. 88)[22] and the lions he drew in Ghent[23] – all drawn with a stylus of lead or another metal and which may have been realised by different artists, but likely date from the sixteenth century – tell only what is already known. Nevertheless, they provide clear evidence of the extent to which a number of the pages from the silverpoint sketchbook were trimmed.

Dürer's journal and silverpoint sketchbook are complementary documents, conveying distinct atmospheric inflections through two media – text and image respectively – that both incorporate artistic dimensions. The everyday objects and ornamental details that appear in the sketchbook (cats 66, 67)[24] provide a visual equivalent to the notes Dürer makes of his daily routine: the invitations, doctor's visits, or incidents such as the theft of his wife Agnes's handbag.

Fig. 88
ALBRECHT DÜRER
A Dog resting, 1520
Silverpoint on pale pink prepared paper, 12.8 × 18 cm
British Museum (1848,1125.3 recto)

THE STRUCTURE OF THE SKETCHBOOK

Too much remains speculative to reconstruct the complete folio sequence convincingly; not even the number of folios can be determined with certainty. The sketchbook's quarto format, however, means that it must have contained an even number of pages and at least one folio more than has been preserved (for a total of 16 leaves, or 32 pages). The few documentary statements that do exist, however, when combined with a handful of technical observations and considerations of content, afford quite a clear view into the dynamics of the circumstances in which Dürer employed the silverpoint

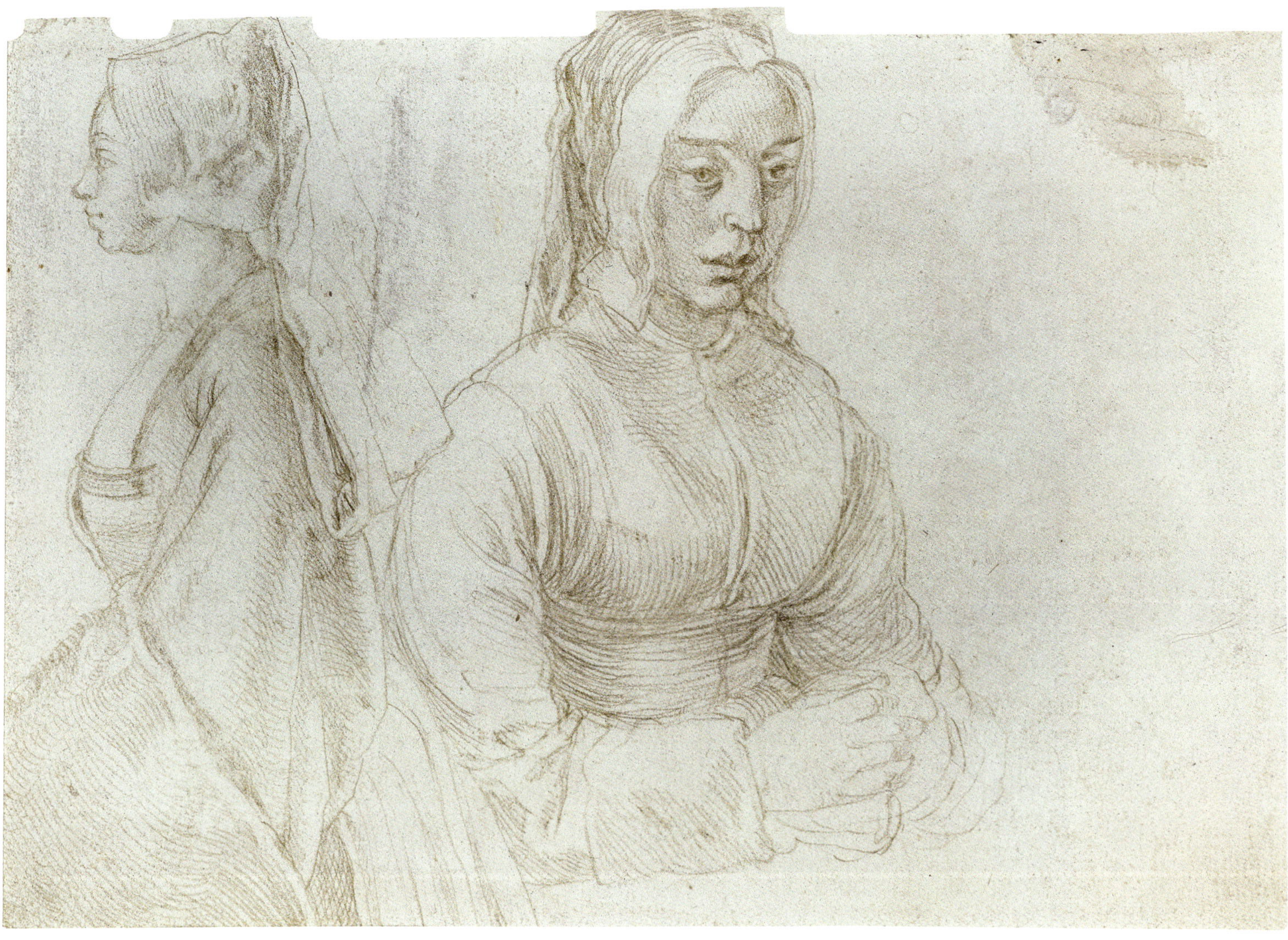

68
ALBRECHT DÜRER
Two Young Women in Netherlandish Costume, 1520–1
Silverpoint on ivory-coloured prepared paper,
12.4 × 17.1 cm
Staatliche Museen zu Berlin, Kupferstichkabinett

sketchbook and how he worked in it. This in turn allows for a particular proximity to the artist and his creation. The mention that Aachen's Paulus Topler and Martin Pfinzing (fig. 84) receive in Dürer's journal and the two striking monograms that appear beside their portraits have understandably led to that sheet being considered the first; otherwise only the Aachen dog (fig. 88) is monogrammed.[25]

The verso of the two portraits also contains an elaborate drawing, although it is not visible because the sheet was at some point glued to a support and an earlier, unknown attempt to uncover the verso was evidently abandoned due to the delicacy of the material. Earlier considerations had seen 'a beam … which closes off a door and a window at the top' and an 'architectural representation.'[26] In the meantime, several different spectral photographs employed to make the image visible have confirmed previous observations and allowed for improved legibility (fig. 85).[27] The drawing under the backing paper exists – the traces of silverpoint are not fragments torn off from the surface of a facing page, as with the two girls on the drawing in Berlin.[28] The architecture represented bears a similar complexity to the view of the Groote Kerk church in Bergen op Zoom; this is suggested by, among other things, the minute pattern of the wall structure as formed by the brickwork or narrowly paralleled joints. Two upright rectangular openings previously taken for a door and window can be clearly made out, positioned fairly centrally in the wall that runs parallel to the picture surface. At left a niche or a door nearly covers the entire height of the wall; at right a window begins in the middle and reaches to the top. The room is covered by a ceiling of beams or planks. The structure at left in front of the foreshortened wall looks like a fireplace, which reaches the full height of the room with a hood in the form of a pyramid at top. The interior has several parallels among rooms that Dürer drew in the decade surrounding the representation; a comparable foreshortened fireplace in front of a wall with analogous hatching appears on a

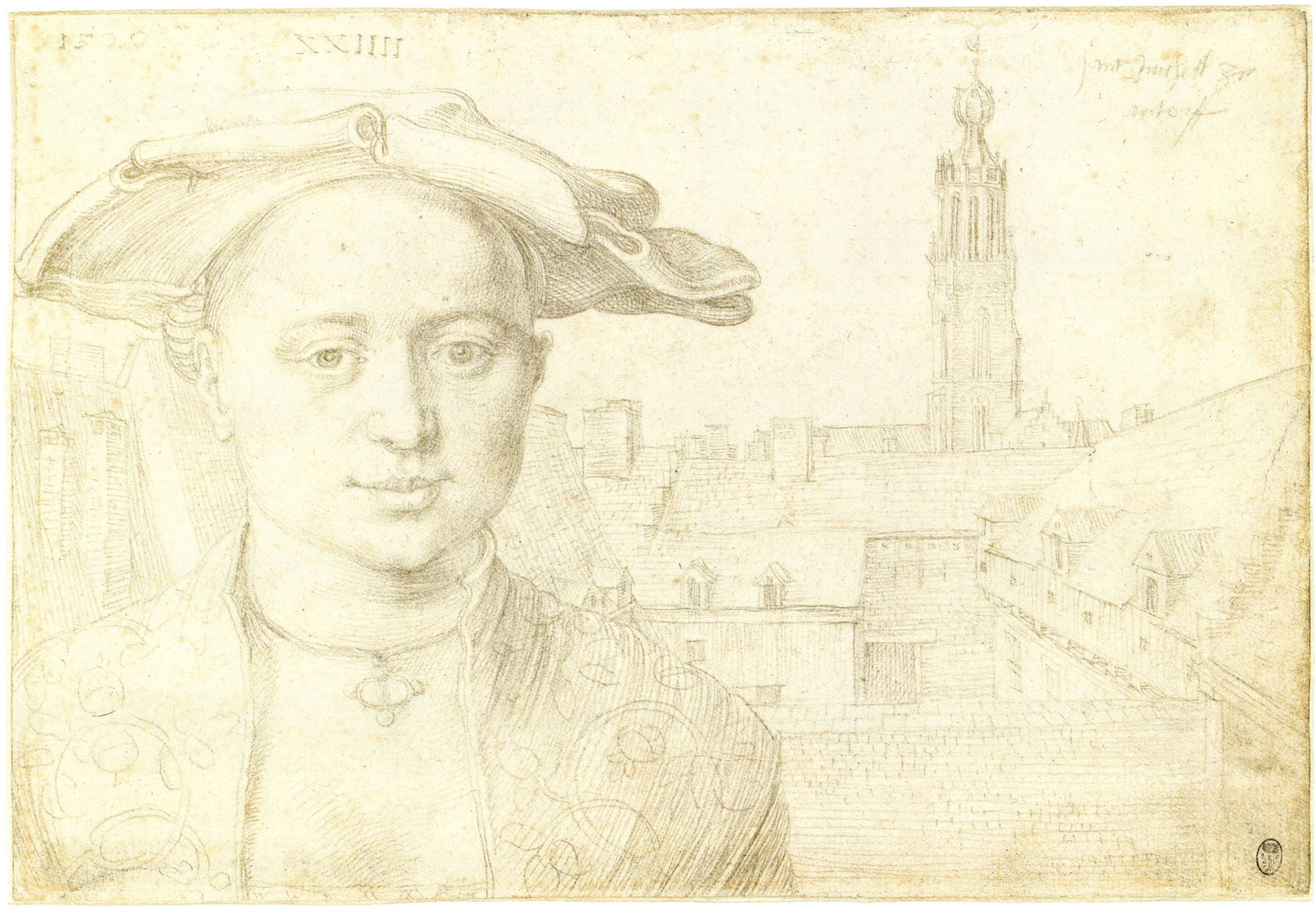

drawing dating about five years before the verso of the first folio in the silverpoint sketchbook.[29] Dürer arranged window and door openings as well as the planks of the roof in parallel fashion in his *Nativity*, dated 1514.[30] Finally, *Saint Jerome*, which is sometimes dated after Dürer's Netherlandish journey, is situated within similar walls and underneath a similar timber ceiling.[31] The interior in the sketchbook was almost certainly a room in Aachen, since the drawing comes amidst the pages drawn in Aachen; it contains, however, no hint regarding a specific location or function for that matter, or why Dürer documented it.[32]

On the right-hand side of the sheet containing the portrait of Caspar Sturm, one can make out the tab of a garment or something similar beneath the landscape that belongs to a drawing from the facing page continued over the fold.[33] It follows that the page with Sturm's portrait was created as a verso in the sketchbook; since the tab does not belong to any preserved motifs, however, the folio in question is clearly missing. This means further that *The Town Hall in Aachen* (fig. 87) was drawn on a recto and preceded the portrait of Caspar Sturm, at least in its position within the sketchbook.[34] While Dürer does not mention every drawing in his 'booklet', the chronology of the ones to which he does refer appears to be reliable, meaning that *The Cathedral at Aachen* (fig. 86) likely preceded the view of the town hall, and thus either faced it as its pendant or was drawn on the preceding recto. Further information may emerge in the future from the reverse of the sheet, which at present is still covered.[35]

Furthermore, the two young females in Netherlandish dress (cat. 68)[36] and the elegantly dressed *Portrait of a 24-Year-Old Man with a View of St Michael's Abbey in Antwerp* (fig. 89)[37] were obviously on sheets that were originally facing, and lay on top of one another when the sketchbook was closed. At some point the two sheets stuck together in one small spot; the second page was damaged when the book was opened, with the upper right of the facing page showing torn-off remnants of its

Fig. 89
ALBRECHT DÜRER
Portrait of a 24-Year-Old Man with a View of St Michael's Abbey in Antwerp, 1520
Silverpoint on ivory-coloured prepared paper, 13 × 19 cm
Musée Condé, Chantilly (DE892 recto)

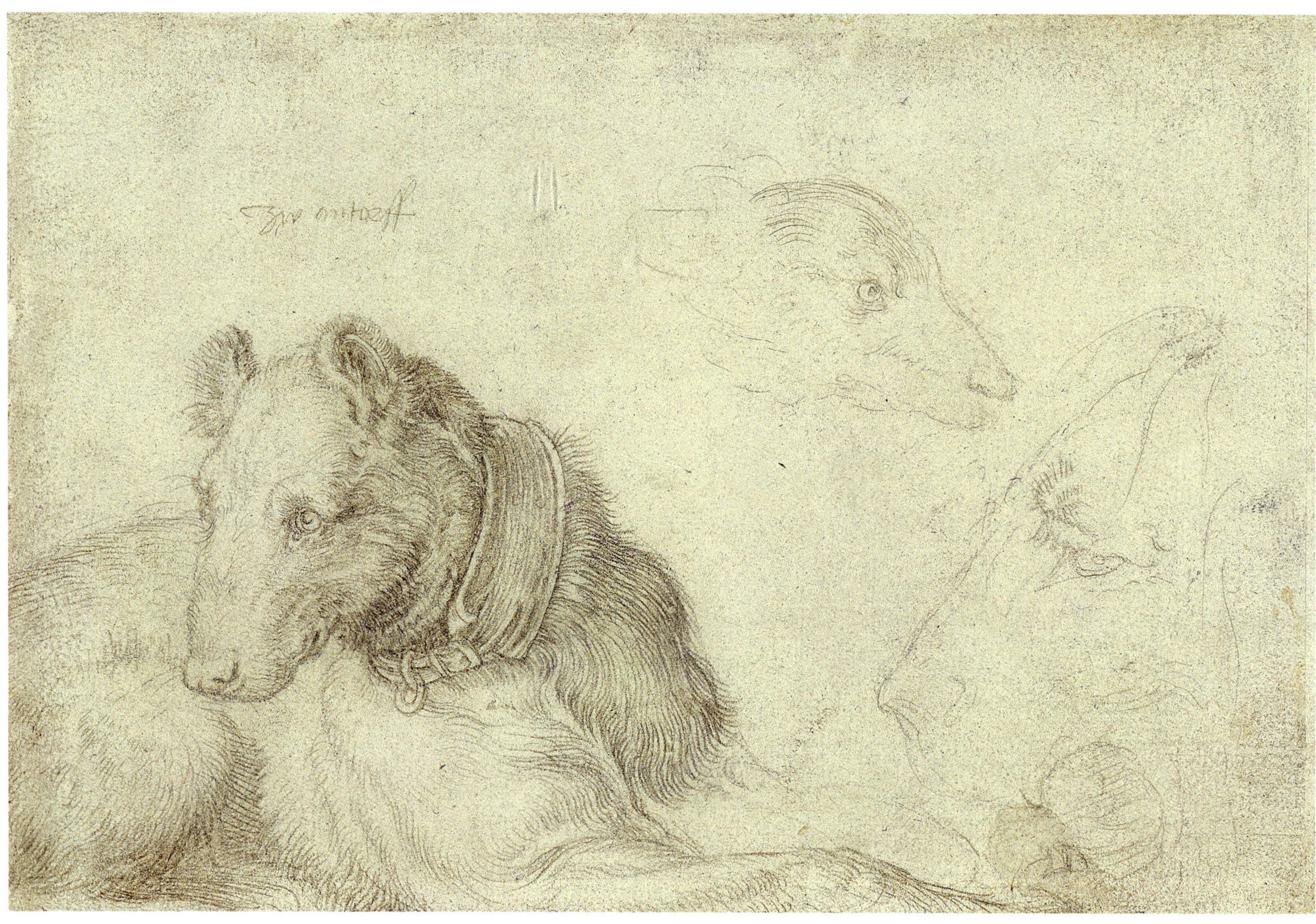

Fig. 90
ALBRECHT DÜRER
Dog lying down, with Additional Contour Sketches and a Lion's Head, 1521
Silverpoint and brown ink on white grounded paper, 12.7 × 18.4 cm
Staatliche Museen zu Berlin, Kupferstichkabinett (KdZ 34 verso)

surface. This most likely happened while the sketchbook was in its original state.

With few exceptions – *Two Castles* (fig. 96),[38] *Sitting Bishop and Portrait of a Man with a Fur Cap*[39] and two studies of a seated lion in the Ghent Zoo (fig. 94) among them[40] – Dürer usually began drawing on the left side of the page, then later added a second motif, sometimes after a good deal of time had passed. A lapse of at least two weeks thus occurs between his portrait of a man from Antwerp, which is dated 1521 and was drawn at the latest before his departure on 3 July, and the view of the Krahnenberg near Andernach, which he passed by during his journey after 15 July (fig. 91).[41] A longer stretch of time, as many as two months, lies between the portrait of Markus Ulstett (1494–1556) – inscribed 'Marx Ulstat' – which was drawn in Zeeland before 14 December 1520, and *The Beautiful Young Woman of Antwerp* of 1521 (cat. 69).[42] As with the drawings of the *Woman from Bergen and Girl from Goes*,[43] the division between the two *en face* representations is very clear and in each case the later drawing accommodates the earlier one.[44] The left one of the girls in Netherlandish costume (cat. 68) and the statuette from the tomb of Isabella of Bourbon (fig. 93)[45] reveal just how frugal Dürer's calculations were: at points he began his drawing so far to the left that he scarcely covered half of the page. He would also later add the landscapes and detailed views to serve as backdrops for portraits, yielding gratifying compositions such as *Caspar Sturm before a River Landscape*, but especially the *Portrait of a 24-Year-Old Man with a View of St Michael's Abbey in Antwerp* (fig. 89) and the *Portrait of a Man from Antwerp* from 1521 with a view of Krahnenberg near Andernach (fig. 91), in which the landscape is continued on both sides of the portrait.

Unfortunately, no obvious clues exist as to whether Dürer filled the pages of his 'booklet' regularly or irregularly, successively or intermittently. He may not always have taken the same approach, as aesthetic criteria were often the deciding factor. The more he began to use half-pages and fill gaps left next to previous motifs, the more irregularly parts of the pages are composed.

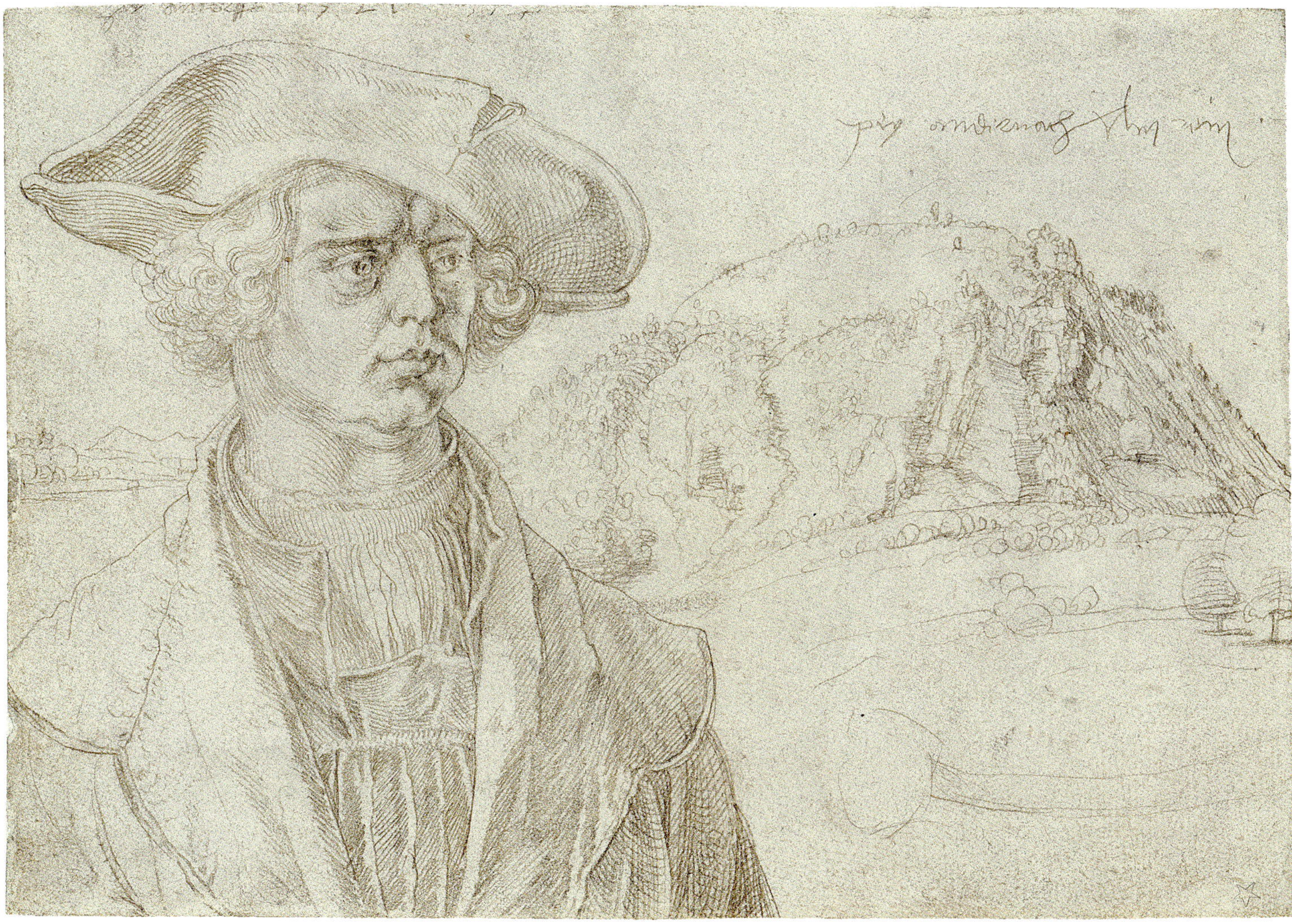

Certain distinct sections can nonetheless be made out, offering potential insight into his working style. The pages he drew while travelling in Zeeland, for example, are the most homogeneous group in terms of their technique, content and preservation, and suggest that Dürer drew them successively during his outbound journey. Five are preserved: the city view of Bergen op Zoom (fig. 162);[46] the 'maid and old woman'[47] in the house of his host Jan de Haas; a young woman from Bergen, next to whom Dürer added 'a girl wearing her folk costume' a few days later at the next stop on his journey in Goes;[48] and finally the choir of the Groote Kerk in Bergen op Zoom (cat. 70).[49] On the other side of this last sheet is the aforementioned portrait of Markus Ulstett, whom Dürer had 'portrayed at sea' (cat. 69) according to the inscription, probably during his travels by ship in Zeeland – following his first visit to Bergen op Zoom, that is. If an entire folio leaf, recto and verso, is not missing somewhere in between, it is likely that the drawings in the sketchbook from the artist's trip to Zeeland have been preserved in their entirety. There is little reason to divide the drawings from the Zeeland trip into outbound and return journeys, as Dürer drew the portraits of women in Bergen op Zoom and Goes on the outbound journey and seems also to have drawn the views of Bergen during this stay. In that case, the group would begin with the city view of Bergen op Zoom, a verso whose recto showed the 24-year-old man (fig. 89). The girls in Netherlandish costume (cat. 68) stand opposite this latter portrait so that the portrait of 'that great man'[50] Lazarus Ravensburger (cat. 90),[51] drawn in Antwerp during his first meeting with Dürer in November 1520, comes on their recto.

If the pages from the journey to Zeeland form a coherent group in the sketchbook, the same is probably true of the drawings from Aachen, as the journal suggests, and according to the sequence described above – albeit with the aforementioned gaps that owe to conservational conditions and losses, such as the other side of the drawing of Aachen cathedral and the missing pendant to the portrait of Caspar Sturm. Upon his return to Antwerp from the coronation of Charles V,

Fig. 91
ALBRECHT DÜRER
Portrait of a Man from Antwerp and View of Andernach, 1521
Silverpoint on white grounded paper, 12.1 × 17.1 cm
Staatliche Museen zu Berlin, Kupferstichkabinett (KdZ 33 verso)

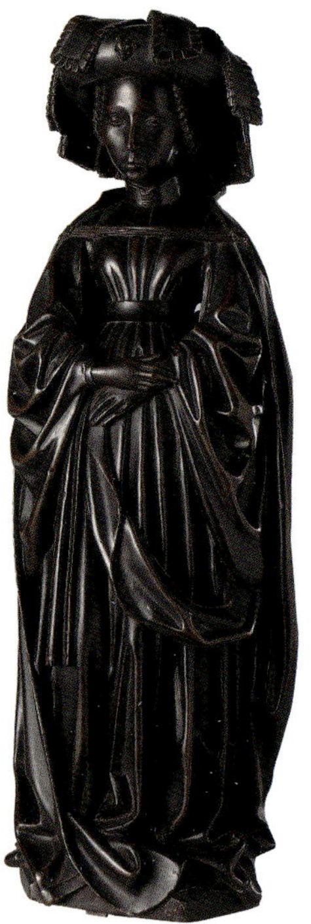

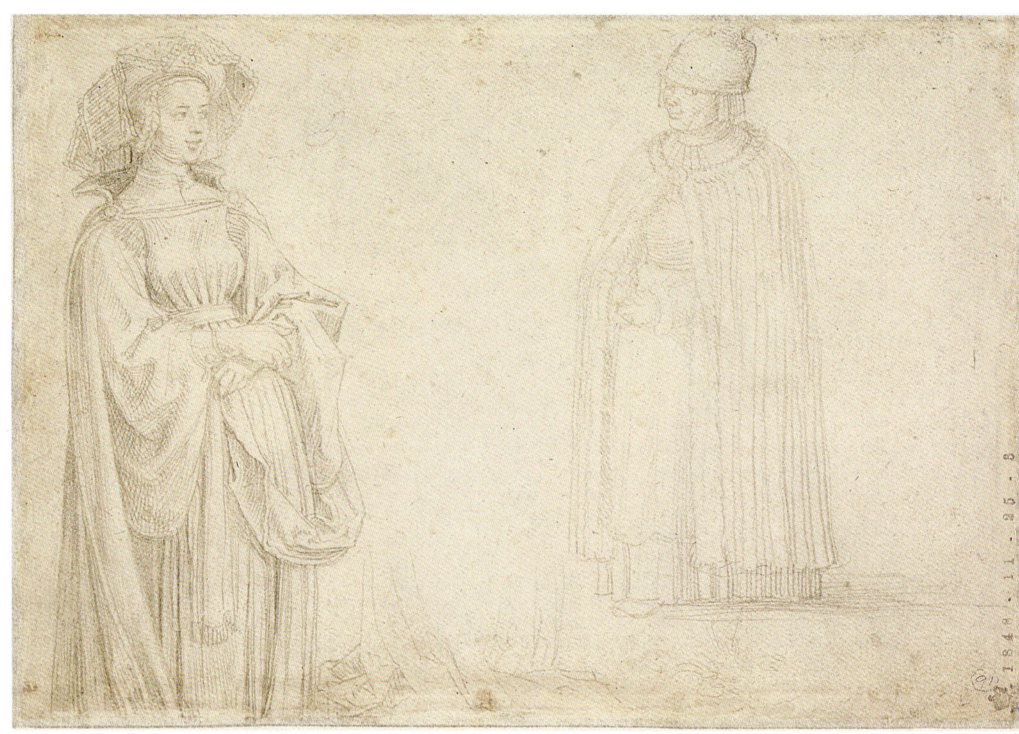

Fig. 92
JAN BORMAN II (active about 1479–1520) and RENIER VAN THIENEN (active 1465–98)
Pleurant from the Tomb of Isabella of Bourbon, in St Michael's Abbey, Antwerp, about 1475
Bronze,
58 × 20.5 × 12.5 cm
Rijksmuseum, Amsterdam

Fig. 93
ALBRECHT DÜRER
A Copy after a Pleurant from Isabella of Bourbon's Tomb in the Abbey of St Michael in Antwerp and a Study of a Woman from Burgenland, 1520–1
Silverpoint on pale pink grounded paper, 12.8 × 18 cm
British Museum (1848,1125.3 verso)

Dürer continued on the verso of the final drawing he made in Aachen of the dog with a drawing of the bronze statuette created by Jan Borman II (active about 1479–1520) and Renier van Thienen (active 1465–98) for the tomb of Isabella of Bourbon in St Michael's Abbey (figs 92, 93).

The seven leaves that remain cannot be arranged without further ado, as there is no well-founded means of telling at what point they might have been incorporated.[52] All seem to have been created after Dürer's journey to Zeeland. A more ample time-frame is conceivable only for the two pages that show magnificently groomed and saddled horses fit for a parade or a procession (cat. 66; fig. 74).[53] While Charles V's entrance into Antwerp on 23 September 1520 seems a questionable date for their creation – if the 'booklet' did indeed begin with the portraits of Paulus Topler and Martin Pfinzing in Aachen – the coronation celebrations in Aachen cannot be definitively ruled out. Dürer would have had subsequent opportunity to see horses involved in such stately processions, especially later and up until his final visit to Brussels, where he was present for the meeting of Christian II and Charles V.[54] The subject was very familiar to Dürer through his intensive design work for the triumphal procession of Emperor Maximilian two years before.[55] The artist must have taken down various observations during one of the numerous festivities he attended, since the horses in the sketchbook do not have riders, the saddles and stirrups are empty and the individually drawn horse head reveals a different ornamental bridle.

On 10 April 1521, seeing the lion at the Ghent zoo fascinated Dürer sufficiently for him to promptly create four drawings, in the most intense exploration of a single motif in the entire sketchbook.[56] The spontaneous execution and the inscription 'zw gent' (at Ghent) suggest that he first drew a single image of the animal (fig. 95)[57] before creating a double view, regardless of which sheet it was on (fig. 94),[58] since one can imagine the two pages either facing or following one after another, or at the very least in close proximity. The arrangement of the lion drawings in the book may, however, not correspond to the order in which they were done, especially if they originally faced each other. The head of the lion added next to the Antwerp dog (fig. 90)[59] could have been sketched on an earlier page where Dürer still found space, and independently of the other two folios.

The heterogeneous nature of the motifs on the seven outstanding sheets also makes their context quite difficult to determine, something that is especially the case with everyday objects such as a table, jugs or chests (cats 66, 67). The same holds true for drawings that Dürer himself annotated with a date, such as the portrait of *The Beautiful Young Woman of Antwerp* (cat. 69) or the *Man from Antwerp* of 1521 (fig. 91), both of which were added to an earlier page. Of the 32 pages that we can be sure existed, at least three full pages and two half-pages – those next to the *Mortar on a Mounting*[60] and the *Man from Antwerp* (fig. 91) – were blank when Dürer left Antwerp. This number does not include the unknown

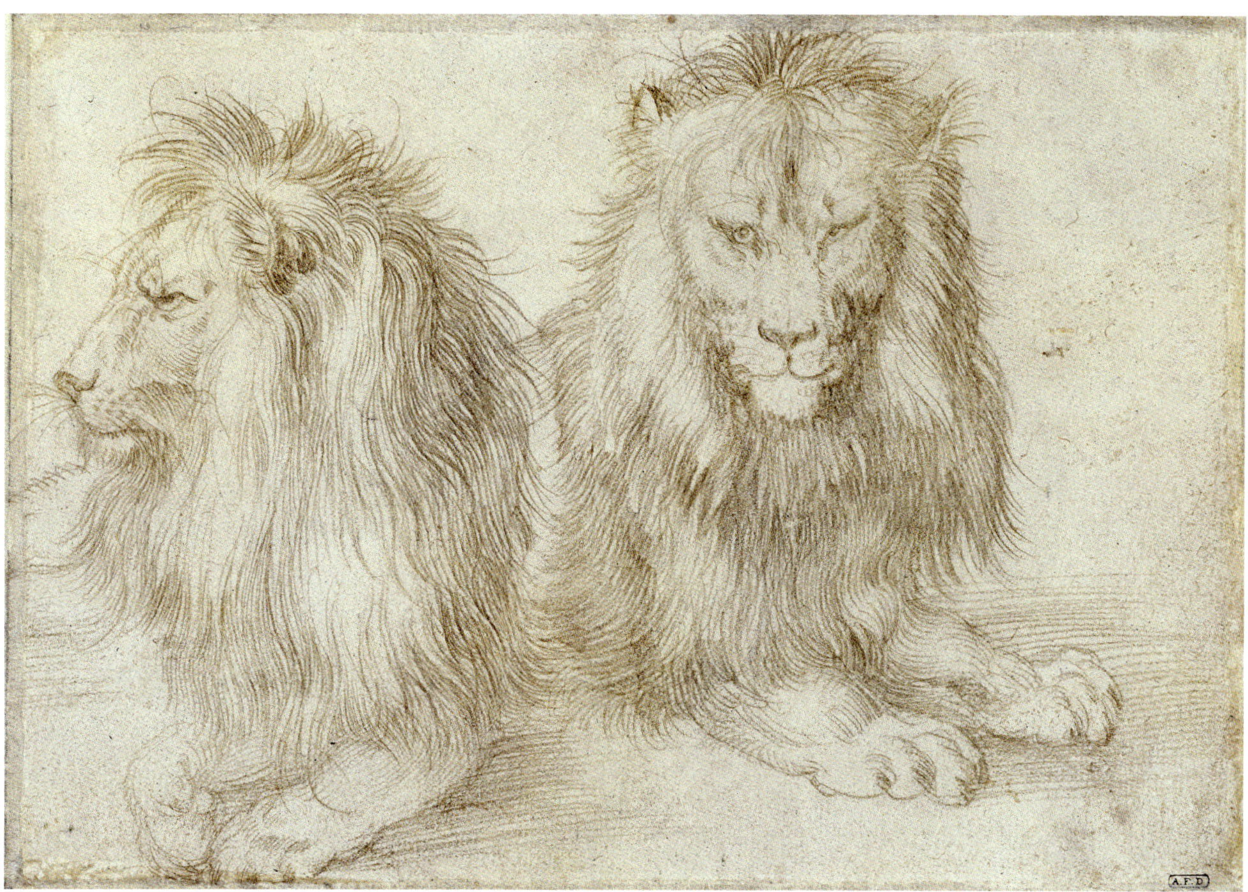

Fig. 94
ALBRECHT DÜRER
Two Studies of a Lion in Ghent Zoo, 1521
Silverpoint on white grounded paper, 12.1 × 17.1 cm
Staatliche Museen zu Berlin, Kupferstichkabinett (KdZ 33 verso)

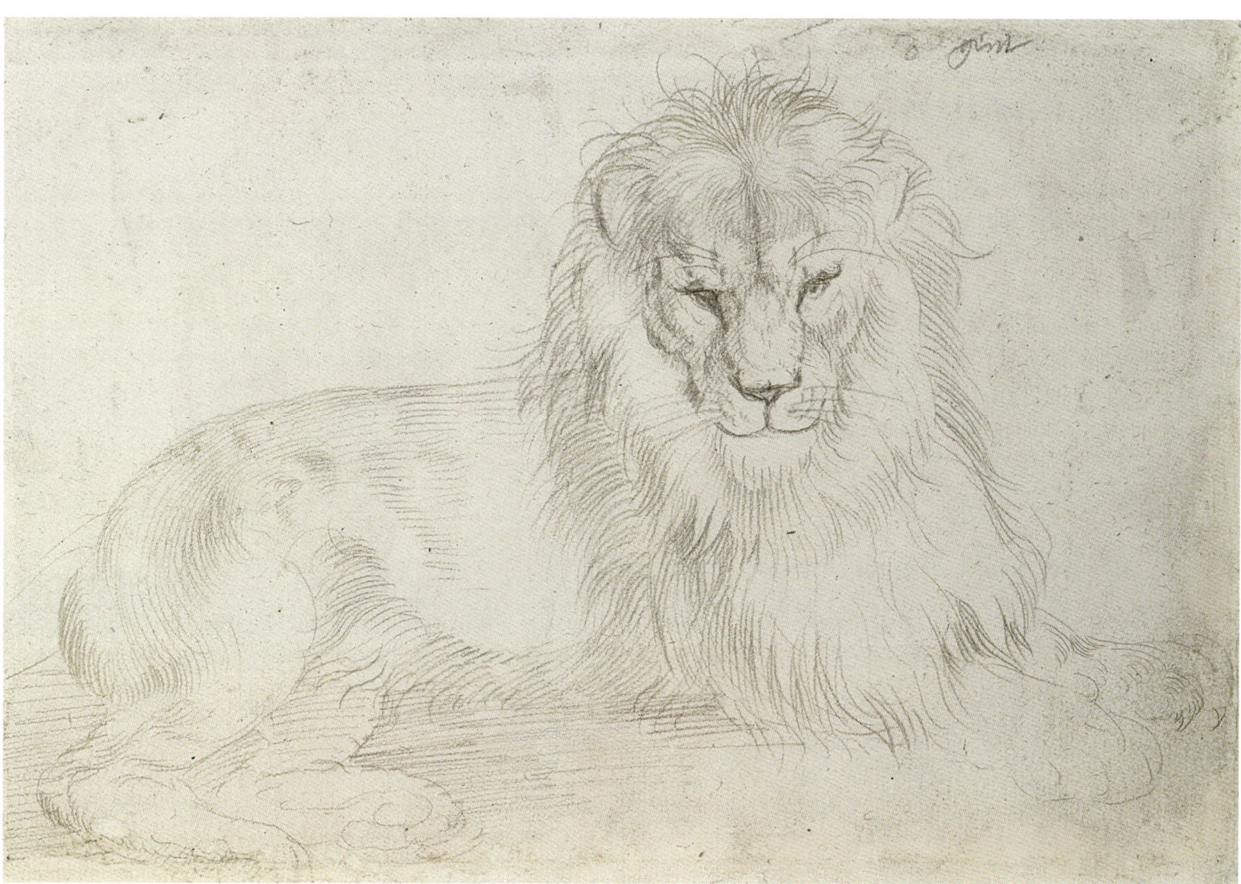

Fig. 95
ALBRECHT DÜRER
A Lion in Ghent Zoo, 1521
Silverpoint on white prepared paper, 13.5 × 19.6 cm
The Albertina Museum, Vienna (22385 verso)

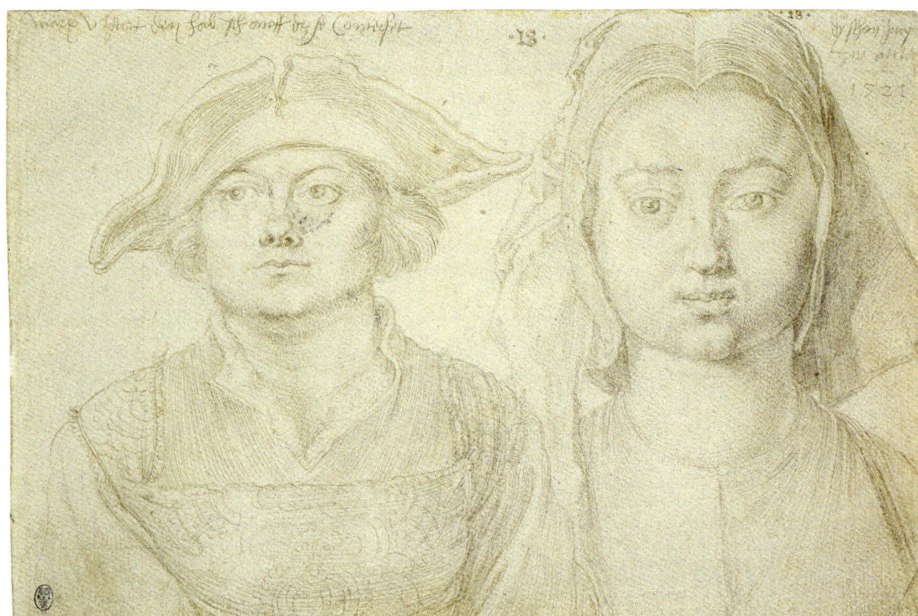

69
ALBRECHT DÜRER
Marx Ulstat; The Beautiful Young Woman of Antwerp, 1520–1
Silverpoint on ivory-coloured prepared paper, 12.9 × 18.8 cm
Städel Museum, Frankfurt am Main

reverse sides to *The Cathedral at Aachen* (fig. 86) or *Two Castles* (fig. 96), both of which are today laid down onto backing paper, nor for that matter the missing folio facing *Caspar Sturm*. In addition to the half-page view of the Krahnenberg near Andernach (fig. 91), at least two of the empty pages were filled in two stages, namely with his portrait of the girl from Cologne and the intimate portrait of his wife, Agnes, on the Rhine as they passed Boppard aboard ship (fig. 117),[61] followed by the aforementioned *Two Castles*. Both the view 'at Andernach on the Rhine' and the two female portraits come on the other sides of the two sheets Dürer used for his lion studies in Ghent on 10 April 1521, in which case he seems to have returned to these blank spaces three months later, before continuing on to fill the final pages in the sketchbook. The sequence, especially of the later drawings, grows less and less consistent with their chronology over time, as their arrangement came increasingly to depend on the space available.

In the sheet depicting two castles on the Rhine (fig. 96), the castle at right – unlike the one on the left – is drawn not from below (that is, from a boat) but rather from the hill opposite. Unfortunately the polygonal keep of the fortress at right is not enough to clearly identify it as Lahneck Castle;[62] nevertheless, the subject matter means that it may have been drawn on its own page prior to the portrait of Agnes, which itself takes up an empty half-page. The castle added at left, however, Rheinfels Castle above Sankt Goar, must have been drawn after the portrait of Agnes, since it lies south of Boppard. If the reverse side of the page with the castles is in fact empty, Rheinfels Castle may represent the final drawing Dürer made in the silverpoint sketchbook.

Regardless of how many pages it may have had in total, Dürer's sketchbook still contained at least three empty sheets when he arrived in Nuremberg: Daniel Fröschl, the author of the 1607–11 inventory, would hardly have glued the three 'birds' he mentions in his entry for the sketchbook over original drawings by Dürer.[63] Determining whether it is not actually drawings but possibly adhesive marks that are on the other sides of *The Cathedral at Aachen* (fig. 86)[64] and the *Two Castles* (fig. 96) – something that is unfortunately not possible in the case of the lost folio opposite the portrait of Caspar Sturm – would be important evidence in favour of Dürer's sketchbook containing only 32 pages.[65]

THE SILVERPOINT SKETCHBOOK IN THE CONTEXT OF DÜRER'S JOURNEY

While Dürer's journal entries begin with his departure from Nuremberg 'on the Thursday after Saint Kilian's day',[66] his visual documentation (as far as it has been preserved) begins at a comparatively late date, perhaps even after his arrival in Antwerp. No convincing account of the portrait of the sleeping Master Arnold of Seligenstadt (fig. 105)[67] exists; while he is clearly identified by Dürer's inscription on the sheet, no evidence is available whether the artist made this drawing when passing by the German town at the beginning of his journey or whether he met the sitter later in the Netherlands. Therefore, it remains difficult to determine how much Dürer drew during the early part of his journey. This adds a particular consideration to the notion that Durer began his silverpoint sketchbook in Aachen and could be a general indication of his artistic production during his journey. On the other hand, the sketchbook documents Dürer's travels through the Netherlands almost up to the end of his journey along the Rhine – much longer than the journal, which ended in Cologne. Dürer seems to have brought his sketchbook along on most occasions, if only for spontaneous drawings of greater or lesser coherence in various contexts. Of the larger stops along his trip, no drawings are preserved from Bruges – where he certainly had the sketchbook with him as he used it in Ghent, the second stop on the same trip – Mechelen and, most importantly Brussels, unless any of the unplaceable sketches were executed there. The sketchbook seems to have been Dürer's personal *vade mecum*, at once a comprehensive art object given life by the artist's travels and at which he toiled constantly, and which ran like a silver thread through the works he produced along the way.

One of the sketchbook's most impressive sheets shows a view of the choir of St Gertrudis in Bergen op Zoom (cat. 70). The architectural representation is neither an orthogonal elevation nor a carefully prepared perspectival construction, both of which Dürer mastered.[68] Rather, it is an analytically rendered view that captures the building in all its architectural complexity and conveys its monumental character despite the small format of the sheet. The tectonic structure – manifest in the polygon of the choir, the unfinished construction with the four crossing pillars that jut upwards, and the set-up how the surrounding buildings and simple walls, which themselves do not necessarily belong to the church, are staggered into the depth – required concentrated analysis on the part of the draughtsman in order to comprehend the spatial arrangement stretching upward before him. The network of joints between the bricks of the building, which are drawn less regularly than they appear in context, seem almost to vibrate, lending a provisional, unplanned and fragmentary quality to the structures. The subtle shading Dürer achieves by varying his drawing technique makes the volumes pulsate. In the case of the wall closest to the viewer, for example, Dürer seems to have suppressed the line left by the silver stylus with his thumb – he did not erase it or rub it out because of the primer – leaving the centre window clearly recognisable as such, but gently receding from view in the bright light. The tectonics of the building convey an atmosphere of utter calm, interrupted only by the lone bricklayer working on the smallest building in the picture at bottom right, a Beckett-like *Endgame* of the building ruin that found its endpoint one and a half centuries later. The view Dürer shows no longer exists today.

If everything in the view from Bergen op Zoom turns on a monumental stillness in the layered arrangement of building material, the double head of the Antwerp dog (fig. 90) effects a gentle movement,[69] employing a cross-fading technique akin to Futurist Giacomo Balla's in his *Dynamism of a Dog on a Leash*, even if Balla sought to express speed in a much more frantic manner.[70] In the overlap of head and body, the wavy neck and the play of light on the fur, Dürer generates volume and depth much as he does in the architectural depiction. The second head, sketched roughly yet positioned naturally in relation to the dog's body, gives the figure a majestic and sensitive appearance that resembles a silhouette in its two-dimensional aspect – and avoids the danger of creating a multi-headed Cerberus. In this way the dog's profile, when combined with its monumental treatment, implies that it might sit up on the page.

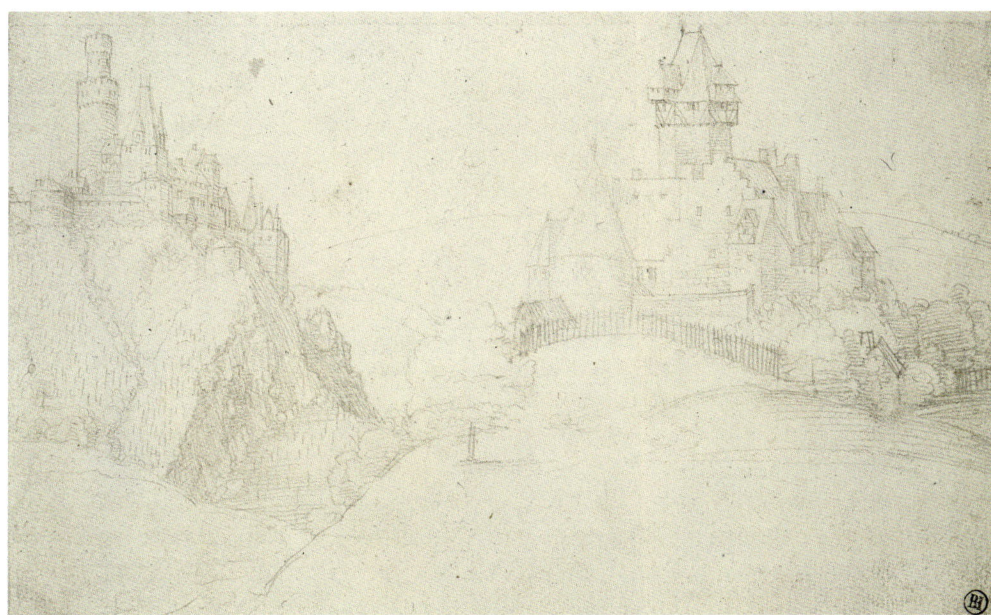

Fig. 96
ALBRECHT DÜRER
Two Castles, Burg Rheinfels near Sankt Goar (left) and an Unidentified Castle (right), 1521
Silverpoint on ivory-coloured grounded paper, 11 × 17.8 cm
Germanisches Nationalmuseum, Nuremberg (Hz 5487)

In a similar vein, Dürer's studies of the lion in Ghent come in three different poses, although the sketches are not linked to each other. His interest was such that one note in his diary mentions several lions, only one of which he drew explicitly: 'Next I saw the lions and drew one with the silverpoint'.[71] The three drawings (figs 94 95),[72] as well as a fourth (fig. 90)[73] showing only a view of the head in profile, are all of the same animal. Dürer thus devoted a significant amount of space to the lion, which provided greater inspiration than the van Eyck brothers' Ghent Altarpiece.

The silverpoint sketchbook appears in concert with other drawing media, such as black chalk or pen and ink, on Dürer's travels through the Low Countries, differentiating the artist's production and asking to be set in relation to them. As opposed to the nine landscapes in the small sketchbook, only two further large detailed views have been preserved otherwise from the whole journey. Here the compositional methods resulting from the tight confines of the sketchbook's pages find creative application in the larger format. Furthermore, the minute dimensions of the sketchbook, at approximately 12 × 18 cm, make it appear dainty next to the almost monumental charcoal drawings, which are up to four and a half times as large.

The pen-and-ink drawings form the most heterogeneous group in every respect, with the question of whether some were drawn in a sketchbook – thus implying the existence of a second, alternate sketchbook – remaining unresolved. The silverpoint sketchbook evidently does not contain copies of drawings Dürer made using other techniques, as the artist seems to have kept fairly accurate records of parallel drawings, and he does not mention copying pages that he sold or gave away. At most he alludes to drawing a subject twice, but never identical replicas. The woman in Burgenlandish dress, the so-called Turkish woman or 'bürgin' (fig. 104), offers an example of how such iterations of pen-and-ink drawings looked.[74] Dürer's second versions differ greatly from sketchbooks prepared by copyists that were widespread in Italy, such as the Codex Escurialensis or the Fossombronne Sketchbook,[75] or the drawn copies that Pieter Saenredam (1597–1665) later created in the Netherlands.[76]

Dürer also brought his sketchbook with him on excursions to see the old masters, as shown in the head of a Virgin which he copied after a painting by a Flemish master,[77] probably from the period between Dirk Bouts (around 1405–1475) and Gerard David (active 1484; died 1523). In this context it is remarkable that neither the silverpoint sketchbook nor any other preserved sheets contain any copies of works by Hans Memling, Hugo van der Goes or Rogier van der Weyden, not to mention the Ghent Altarpiece by the brothers Jan and Hubert van Eyck, which Dürer had viewed and commented on in detail.[78] At best, the tiles (*Two Hands holding a Puppy; Tiled Floor Patterns*) with their foreshortened perspective, might have been taken from paintings, especially by Memling.[79]

Finally, several topics that were important to Dürer are missing from the silverpoint sketchbook. As long as it is unclear whether the relevant pages have been lost or he never took up the subjects in it to begin with, several aspects of the sketchbook's character remain open. Dürer was greatly fascinated by the treasures of Moctezuma, for example, yet we do not know of a single visual reaction to them.[80] These may be missing because he saw them during an initial brief stay in Brussels and may not have had the sketchbook with him.

It is even more striking that Dürer's patent interest in his contemporary Italian colleagues finds no visual expression. A visit to Michelangelo's *Bruges Madonna* is mentioned only in his journal.[81] While he comments and reflects on the group's subtle sculptural qualities, even thinking erroneously that it was made of alabaster, it did not seem to inspire a visual reaction in him, perhaps because the chapel was simply too dark.

By the same token, it is a source of constant wonder that there are no written or drawn traces of Dürer's visit to Pieter van Aelst's tapestry workshop in Brussels, despite a lively back and forth with the 'Polonier' Tommaso Vincidor, a former close collaborator of Raphael's from Bologna. Dürer had cultivated an intensive exchange of drawings and paintings with Raphael during the latter's lifetime, and now learning about Raphael's fate made note of his unexpected death, which had occurred a little over five months previously. Dürer was eager to exchange a set of Raphael's prints for his own, with Vincidor's support, and otherwise took interest in Raphael's artistic legacy concerning the members of his workshop.[82] Raphael's coloured cartoons for the tapestries of the Sistine Chapel, 10 to 16 of the most important tempera paintings made by the artist's own hand and by members of his workshop, could be seen in Pieter van Aelst's manufactory; Vincidor had come to Flanders expressly to supervise their translation into picture tapestries. This monumental painting cycle is sometimes even considered more significant than the frescoes in the Vatican's Raphael Rooms. Contrary to previous assumptions that they had been cut into strips,[83] the cartoons, which originally measured up to 353 × 542 cm, were still fully intact at the time. They were not used as a template for the original series of tapestries commissioned by Pope Leo X,

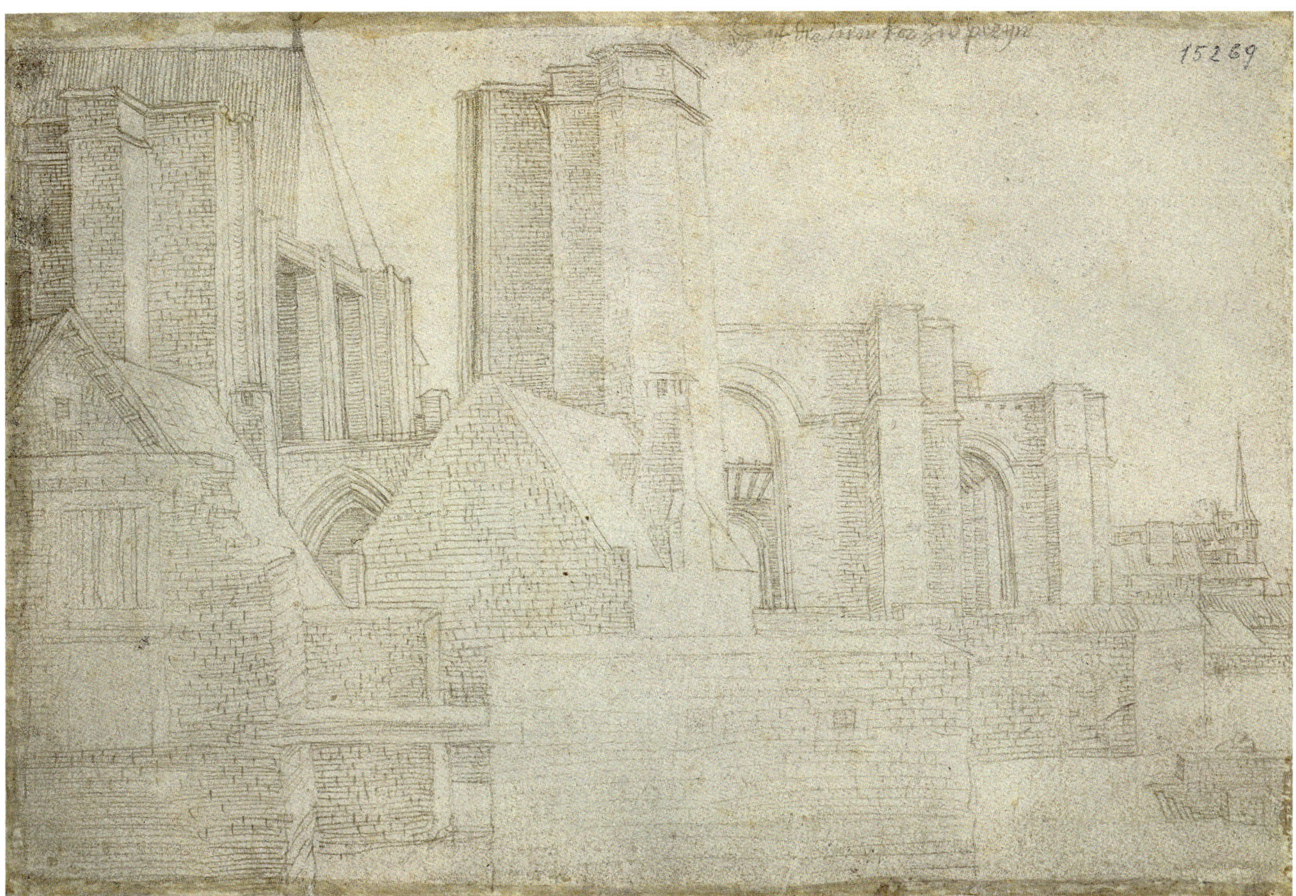

70
ALBRECHT DÜRER
The New Choir of St Gertrudis, the So-called Groote Kerk, in Bergen op Zoom, 1520–1
Silverpoint on ivory-coloured prepared paper, 12.9 × 18.8 cm
Städel Museum, Frankfurt am Main

as believed until recently: copies were made instead. It was only two decades later that the originals were used for further series and cut up.[84]

Aside from Vincidor, Bernaert van Orley, whom Dürer had already met on his first trip to Brussels, was also very involved in tapestry production and had close ties with Pieter van Aelst.[85] Dürer's return to take up work again on his copperplate engravings of the *Twelve Apostles* – a series he may first have suspended after the set of Raphael's published by Marcantonio Raimondi (about 1470/82–1527/34) had begun to circulate north of the Alps once Lucas van Leyden's earlier series went out of print – and especially his two famous later panels of the *Four Apostles*, have often raised the question of whether his close relationships to Vincidor and van Orley did not in fact bring him into contact with Raphael's paintings. It would be equally unusual if he had seen them without noting so in either word or image, as if he did not see them at all. To date there is no evidence pointing in either direction.[86]

Parallel to the silverpoint sketchbook, the drawn material of Dürer's that has been preserved reflects Raphael's strong presence in Flanders. *The Temptation of Saint Anthony* (cat. 71), a work in leadpoint bearing the year 1521 and Dürer's monogram, has always been considered unusual in Dürer's oeuvre.[87] More than five times the size of a page in the silverpoint sketchbook, bringing it within the vicinity of Dürer's large-scale charcoal drawings, it transforms the associative, synoptic compositions that are a constant hallmark of the sketchbook into a creative method, in this case resulting in an iconographic invention. An aged, bearded man shown at left in the foreground sinks to his knees, turned outward. Filling nearly the entire height of the drawing, the man holds a staff in his left hand that extends diagonally to the sheet's lower right corner, such that the figure takes up nearly the entire lower left triangle of the image, in monumental fashion. The delicate figure of a naked woman standing upright occupies the empty triangular half at the upper right of the page, separated from the hermit both by the mound of earth onto which he lowers himself, as well as the fact that she is the same height as the hermit despite her upright position, giving the impression that she stands some distance away – or seems quietly to draw near, suggesting the theme of temptation. It is often suggested, albeit somewhat vaguely and generally, that a statue of Venus from antiquity was used as a model for the female figure. The only classical sculpture of this typology with this specific form of drapery known at the time, however,

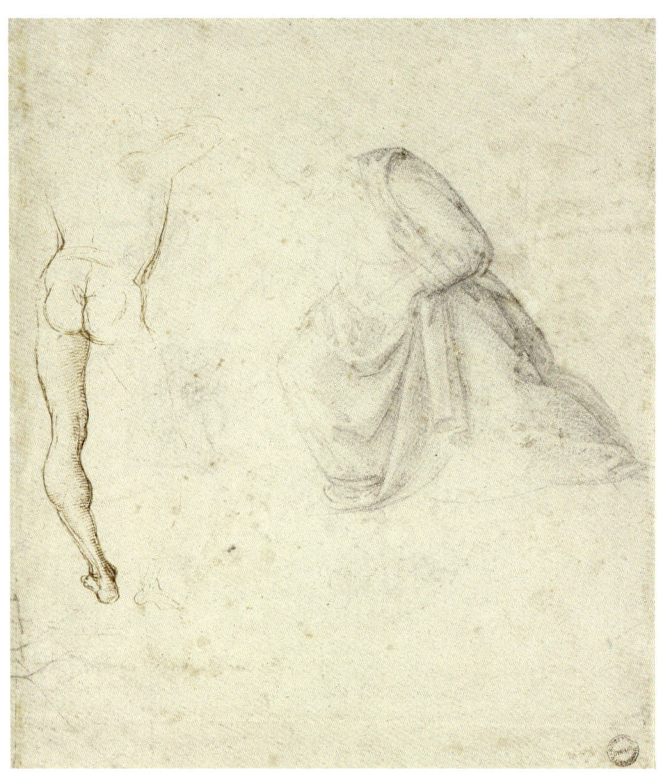

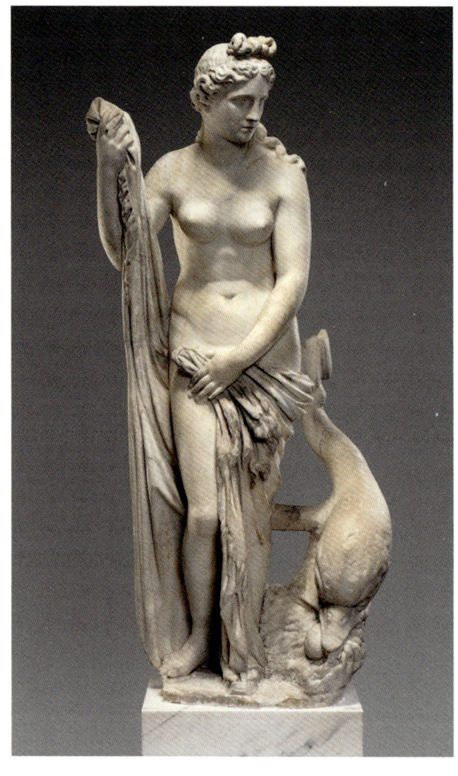

Fig. 97
RAPHAEL
(1483–1520)
Back View of a Standing Man, after Signorelli; Drapery of a Kneeling Figure, about 1499–1502
Pen and brown ink with grey-black chalk on white paper, 25.4 × 21.6 cm
The Ashmolean Museum, University of Oxford (WA1846.145)

Fig. 98
Venus Mazarin, Roman, second century AD
Marble, height 184 cm
The J. Paul Getty Museum, Los Angeles, California

is the *Venus Mazarin* (fig. 98), which owes its name to its presumed provenance from the collection of Cardinal Mazarin. Around 1509 it was excavated or turned up otherwise in distant Rome.[88] All three known early drawings after this statue,[89] two of which came from Raphel's inner circle, reveal that this *Venus pudica* was missing her head and right arm at the time. Dürer's drawing shows them fully present, however, and furthermore does not bear a resemblance to classical antiquity, but in the hairstyle and lax hand position is rather German in appearance.

The sweeping gesture and imposing size of Saint Anthony also lend the hermit a foreign air. A comparison with the study for God the Father in Raphael's *Creation of Eve* (fig. 97) is remarkable:[90] although this reference is not as specific as the statue of the *Venus Mazarin*, it is at least typological. The motifs combined in the *Temptation of Saint Anthony* suggest that the practice of copying – already current in Rome in the fifteenth century and pursued by artists drawing from ancient monuments who were motivated by an interest in precise reproduction as well as the study of the antiquarian knowledge – was likely brought to Flanders or propagated there by artists such as Tommaso Vincidor. About 15 years after the *Temptation of Saint Anthony*, 'Anonymus Mantovanus A', a Flemish contemporary of Marten van Heemskerck's who is unfortunately yet to be identified, was among the most diligent copyists reproducing drawings of Roman antiquities and contemporary Italian creations, and it is through his efforts that many of the drawings after monuments from classical antiquity produced in Raphael's immediate circle are known today.[91] Because the artworks that Dürer and Raphael gave to one another were of high artistic quality, and because very few of them exist and virtually nothing is known about the timing or the extent of the exchange, somewhat of a mythical aura clings to the interaction between the two masters up to the present day. The *Temptation of Saint Anthony* may be a posthumous development in Dürer's acquaintance with Raphael after the latter's death, and via a member of the Italian master's workshop.[92]

A majority of the sheets that have come down to us from Dürer's journey through the Netherlands are drawings that were either intended for presentation or fair copies, monumental or contracted portraits, and detailed views or commissioned projects. Even the everyday objects and animals that made their way into the silverpoint sketchbook appear carefully arranged. The same applies to Dürer's technique: everything is finely and tidily rendered. Yet as the candlesticks, the coats of arms and the chandeliers featuring female busts on the back of the *Christ on the Mount of Olives* housed today in Frankfurt show, he also produced spontaneous, explorative sketches.[93]

A fragment in Rotterdam, that today measures just 11 × 9 cm and is composed of three patches, may represent another such mixed working sheet. Two

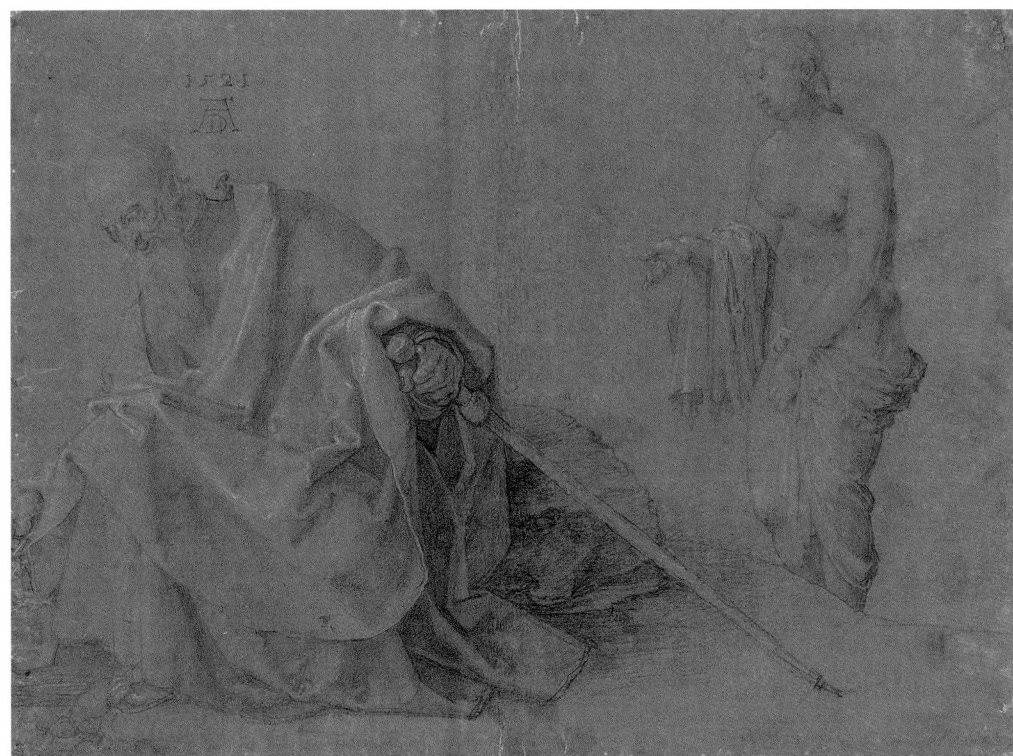

71
ALBRECHT DÜRER
The Temptation of Saint Anthony, 1521
Leadpoint with white heightening on green prepared paper,
31.6 × 42.6 cm
The Albertina Museum, Vienna

corners attached to a triangle to make it square appear originally to have come from the same sheet, and still show traces of a black chalk drawing on the obverse.[94] Two inscriptions contemporaneous with the sheet's creation, one in German and one in Italian, and references to the Flemish and Italian environments in which Dürer moved in Antwerp, give the fragment a direct bearing on the topics under discussion here. What is today the back of the sheet shows four boats lying propped up on the beach, drawn in pen and ink. The lower right corner contains German handwriting very similar to Dürer's, with the attribution 'albrecht', although this is not necessarily signed in the artist's own hand. The drawing itself is of very high quality; the understanding of the boats' staggered arrangement and the complex 'architecture' of their built forms is familiar to us from the perceptive eye that took in the church view at Bergen op Zoom. The linework along the hulls of the front boats, the slight undulation of the ropes and tackle and the complex spatial arrangement of the boats all bear very close resemblance to Dürer's famous *Port in Antwerp near the Scheldepoort* (fig. 108),[95] so the drawing may well be his.

The male portrait on the front of the sheet was originally of great intensity but has since received substantial damage, with extensive rubbing that makes it difficult to assess. Its significance lies in the aforementioned Italian inscription (which, although added later, was still contemporary), written in pen and ink in a different calligraphy from the verso: '[..]o[.]rto [..]n[.]pt/di joachimo / patenir'.

Dürer himself notes that he 'drew Master Joachim with the silverpoint and then did a second portrait for him too'.[96] It is not possible to decide from the available evidence whether both portraits were of Patinir and whether one of them was a silverpoint drawing in the sketchbook. Neither can be identified with the Rotterdam portrait in any event, which was done in black chalk.[97] Dürer's interest in Patinir was sufficiently great that Adrian Herbouts (died 1546), legal advisor and secretary of Antwerp, gave him a painting by Patinir representing the flight of Lot and his daughters from the destruction of Sodom and Gomorrah (cat. 72).[98] Patinir, as we know, also invited Dürer to his wedding. At present the relationship between the Rotterdam portrait and those by Dürer has to remain open. There have been two attempts to identify Patinir's physiognomy, one in another black chalk drawing by Dürer that is missing today,[99] and the second in a copperplate engraving that appeared more than fifty years later and is said to be based on a drawing of Dürer's, unfortunately also missing.[100] Both of the figures depicted are quite distinct from the Rotterdam image and from each other. Patinir's age – he was 40 at the time – does not contradict any of the three identifications. Although the sitter and the attribution of the Rotterdam fragment remain unresolved for the time being, it still provides a host of details about the colourful environment in which artists coming from a variety of cultural backgrounds participated in Antwerp at the time.

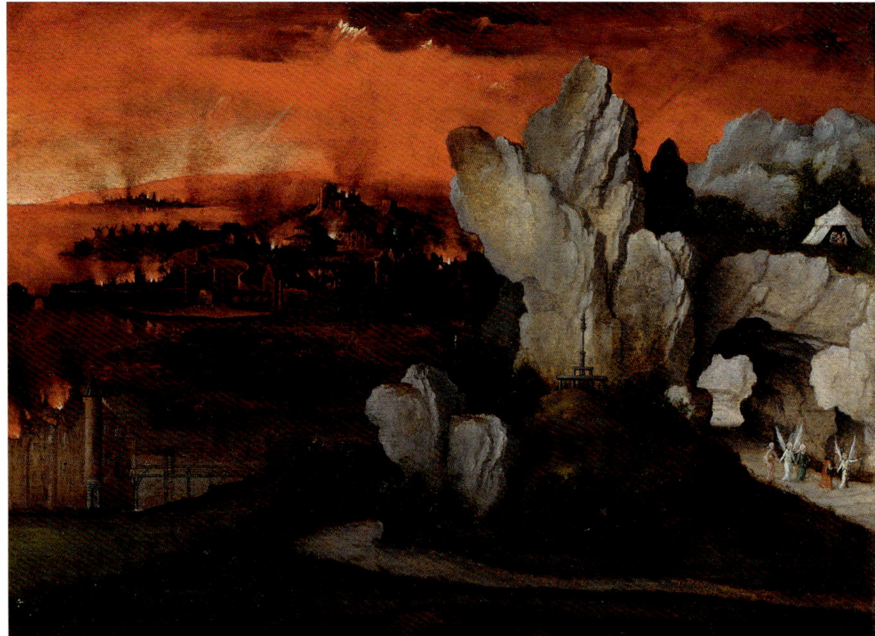

72
JOACHIM PATINIR
(1480–1524)
Landscape with the Destruction of Sodom and Gomorrah, about 1520
Oil on panel, 22.5 × 30 cm
Museum Boijmans Van Beuningen, Rotterdam

Although Dürer travelled to Aachen and the Netherlands on his own initiative, we know a great deal about his trip when compared to the life of his friend Raphael, who held an official position at the Papal Court in Rome. In this sense, it seems telling that of all questions the crucial one of whether Dürer saw Raphael's cartoons for the Sistine Chapel tapestries in Pieter van Aelst's then world-famous weaving workshop should go unanswered. Amidst the broad array of material of Dürer's that has been preserved, the silverpoint sketchbook represents a homogeneous group, which itself sheds light on a wide range of aspects. The great deal that remains to be discovered in turn points to the sheer wealth of connections arising from intellectual, economic and cultural exchange, and reveals the cultural resources that the Nuremberg artist sought out in his dialogue with Portuguese, Italian and Flemish artists, patrons and merchants from Flanders to Zeeland – and even the beguiling world of Moctezuma's Mexico. In doing so, he set a benchmark for our own globalised society.

I would like to thank Peter van den Brink and Eva Dalvai in particular for many thought-provoking discussions.

1 Nesselrath 1986, pp. 120–2; Nesselrath 2014, pp. 13, 15 and 45–6, fig. 4.
2 Winkler 1936–9, vol. 4, pp. 761–87; Goris and Marlier 1970, pp. 111–29, 188–9; Strauss 1974, vol. 4, pp. 1940–51, 1960–75, 2016–23, 2044–5, 2076–85, 2096–7, 2100–3; Unverfehrt 2007, pp. 207–8.
3 Reiche et al. 2002; Reiche et al. 2004. While this essay follows these scientific articles, the technical descriptions in the captions retain the data and wording provided by the various collections. The once uniform colours of the various sheets may have changed in their tones inconsistently over time under different conditions of conservation or they might have been photographed differently.
4 G. Bartrum, 'Silverpoint Drawings by German and Swiss Renaissance Artists', in Washington and London 2015, pp. 63–99, at p. 71.
5 Kupferstichkabinett, Niedersächsische Landesgalerie, Hanover, inv. Z 4. Plagemann 2002.
6 For a possible distinction between a sketchbook and an album, see Nesselrath 1986, pp. 89–93.
7 Staatliche Kunsthalle, Karlsruhe, inv. VIII 1062. E. Allgaier in Karlsruhe 2007, no. 47; K. Schenck, 'Drawings Under Scrutiny: The Materials and Techniques of Metalpoint', in Washington and London 2015, pp. 9–23, at p. 10, fig. 1; G. Bartrum in ibid., pp. 71–2, 96–7, 280; R. Honold and D. Schäfer in Karlsruhe 2019, pp. 270–81, cats 121, 122.
8 Albertina, Vienna, inv. 4839. London 2002, pp. 79–80, nos 1–2; H. Widauer in Vienna 2003, pp. 116–17, cat. 1; J. Zaunbauer and C. Metzger in Vienna 2019, pp. 74–8 and 446, cat. 2.
9 J.O. Hand, 'Masters of Silverpoint in the Netherlandish Renaissance', in Washington and London 2015, pp. 25–62.
10 See Nesselrath 1986 on the typology of sketchbooks; for their physical composition in particular, see pp. 129–30.
11 On provenance, see Christof Metzger (pp. 149–63) and Giulia Bartrum (pp. 267–76) in the present publication. See also Vienna 2019, pp. 60 and 475, doc. 24.
12 Panofsky (1955) 1971, pp. 214–16.
13 Ashcroft 2017, vol. 1, no. 162, p. 564.
14 Kupferstichkabinett, Berlin, inv. KdZ 4179. Winkler 1936–9, vol. 4, no. 761. H. Mielke in Anzelewsky and Mielke 1984, pp. 97–8, no. 94.
15 British Museum, London, inv. 1895,0915.982. Winkler 1936–9, vol. 4, no. 763; London 2002, pp. 207–8, cat. 151; G. Bartrum in Washington and London 2015, pp. 71, 90 and 279, panel 29.
16 Musée Condé, Chantilly, inv. 893 (316)v. Winkler 1936–9, vol. 4, no. 765; Chantilly 1999, pp. 52–4, no. 8v.
17 Ashcroft 2017, vol. 1, no. 162, p. 564.
18 Ibid., p. 564.
19 Ibid., p. 565.
20 Fig. 120 (p. 216 below). Winkler 1936–9, vol. 4, no. 818; G. Bartrum in Washington and London 2015, pp. 71–2, fig. 9.
21 Ashcroft 2017, vol. 1, no. 162, p. 577.
22 Szépművészeti Múzeum, Budapest, inv. K. 58.1231. Achilles 1986, p. 250. Since the provenance of the sheet has not been clarified, a discussion of its date and attribution, thus far to Hans Hoffmann, does not add any further information to our present context.
23 Germanisches Nationalmuseum, Graphische Sammlung, Nuremberg, inv. Hz 5493. Zink 1968, no. 76; Koreny 1985, p. 164 n. 1.
24 British Museum, London, inv. 1921,0714.2r and v. Winkler 1936–9, vol. 4, nos 784, 785; G. Bartrum in Washington and London 2015, pp. 71, 93–4, 279. Germanisches Nationalmuseum, Nuremberg, inv. Hz 5488v. Winkler 1936–9, vol. 4, no. 787; Strauss 1974, vol. 4, pp. 2076–9.
25 British Museum, London, inv. 1848,1125.3r. Winkler 1936–9, vol. 4, no. 767; G. Bartrum in London 2002, p. 208, no. 152; G. Bartrum in Washington and London 2015, pp. 71, 91, 279. The additional monogram that Georg Dietz proposes on the verso of the portraits of Topler and Pfinzing requires further discussion.
26 H. Mielke in Anzelewsky and Mielke 1984, pp. 97–8, appendix fig. VII
27 The results of the analysis, conducted by Georg Josef Dietz and Annette Keller, will be published and explained in an appendix to the German edition of

this catalogue. I am grateful to them for providing me with their interpretation of the material. Dagmar Korbacher and Michael Roth have kindly allowed this research, generously funded by Peter van den Brink and the Suermondt Museum der Stadt Aachen. All have contributed to the scholarly as well as organisational success of the enterprise.

28 See note 36.

29 British Museum, London, inv. SL,5218.133. Winkler 1936–9, vol. 4, no. 644; Rowlands 1993, p. 90, pl. 129.

30 Albertina, Vienna, inv. 3136. Winkler 1936–9, vol. 4, no. 581.

31 Kupferstichkabinett, Berlin, inv. KdZ 4443. Winkler 1936–9, vol. 4, no. 589; H. Mielke in Anzelewsky and Mielke 1984, pp. 67–8, no. 66.

32 After our research had started, Christof Metzger attempted his own reconstruction, relying on what is known at present and the available documentation. He was quick in sharing his thoughts with our group in Berlin and Aachen. His position, like ours, confirms Hans Mielke's ideas. His hypothesis that the interior shows the local inn, 'Zum Spiegel' (The Mirror), currently lacks sufficient evidence, which holds implications for the sequence he proposes in reconstructing the pages of the sketchbook. Further arguments are needed to attribute the chest and the firedog to the same room and connect the dressed-up horse with the festivities in Aachen. The group of drawings from Aachen seem more defined and less heterogeneous, occasional and sketchy than drawings for the proposed following pages. However, my arguments are not sufficient, yet, to abandon Metzger's suggestion completely.

33 Chantilly 1999, p. 54.

34 Musée Condé, Chantilly, inv. 893 (316)r. Winkler 1936–9, vol. 4, no. 764; Chantilly 1999, pp. 52–4, no. 8r.

35 The delicate material does not allow, at least with current restoration techniques, the backing paper to be lifted. I would like to thank Giulia Bartrum for her extensive attempts to determine whether the other side of the folio is empty and therefore whether it was mounted at some past date without any concern. If this is indeed the case, it is quite noticeable that Dürer left a whole page free so early on in the sketchbook. It remains open to speculation whether this is because he did not want to interrupt the Aachen section in the sketchbook at the later stage.

36 Kupferstichkabinett, Berlin, inv. KdZ 35v. Winkler 1936–9, vol. 4, no. 775; H. Mielke in Anzelewsky and Mielke 1984, pp. 99–100, no. 95v.

37 Musée Condé, Chantilly, inv. 892 (315)r. Winkler 1936–9, vol. 4, no. 769; H. Mielke in Anzelewsky and Mielke 1984, p. 100; Chantilly 1999, pp. 55–7, no. 9r.

38 Germanisches Nationalmuseum, Nuremberg, inv. Hz 5487. Winkler 1936–9, vol. 4, no. 762; Zink 1968, p. 92, no. 67; Nuremberg 1971, p. 312, no. 585; Burger 2019.

39 Kupferstichkabinett, Berlin, inv. KdZ 34r. Winkler 1936–9, vol. 4, no. 776. H. Mielke in Anzelewsky and Mielke 1984, pp. 100–1, no. 96r.

40 Kupferstichkabinett, Berlin, inv. KdZ 33v. Winkler 1936–9, vol. 4, no. 779; H. Mielke in Anzelewsky and Mielke 1984, pp. 102–3, no. 97v.

41 Kupferstichkabinett, Berlin, inv. KdZ 33r. Winkler 1936–9, vol. 4, no. 778; H. Mielke in Anzelewsky and Mielke 1984, pp. 101–2, no. 97r.

42 Städel Museum, Frankfurt, inv. 15269r. Winkler 1936–9, vol. 4, no. 773; Frankfurt 2003, pp. 104–7, no. 31r (linking a diary entry dated 11 February back to the drawing); Löcher 2004.

43 Musée Condé, Chantilly, inv. 891 (314)r and v. Chantilly 1999, pp. 58–9, no. 10.

44 About 12 years later, Maerten van Heemskerck created similar joints between the drawings on the pages of his sketchbook to make the best use of the space. See, for example, some pages in the first Heemskerck sketchbook in Berlin, most clearly on fols 13v and 41v (Bartsch 2019, pp. 326–7, 363). Such economic efficiency in displaying the single drawings on the page is, on the other hand, less common with a more relaxed approach, as found for example in the contemporary sketchbooks of Italian draughtsmen.

45 British Museum, London, inv. 1848,1125.3v. Winkler 1936–9, vol. 4, no. 766; London 2002, p. 208, no. 152; G. Bartrum in Washington and London 2015, pp. 92, 279.

46 Musée Condé, Chantilly, inv. 892 (315)v. Winkler 1936–9, vol. 4, no. 768; Chantilly 1999, pp. 55–7, no. 9v.

47 Ashcroft 2017, vol. 1, no. 162, p. 569.

48 Ibid., p. 169.

49 Städel Museum, Frankfurt, inv. 15269v. Winkler 1936–9, vol. 4, no. 772; Frankfurt 2003, pp. 104–7, no. 31v.

50 Ashcroft 2017, vol. 1, no. 162, p. 569.

51 Kupferstichkabinett, Berlin, inv. KdZ 35r. Winkler 1936–9, vol. no. 4, 774; H. Mielke in Anzelewsky nd Mielke 1984, p. 99, no. 95r.

52 No one has yet examined the paper structure of the individual sheets. It remains to be determined whether this would allow the quires to be reconstructed.

53 Germanisches Nationalmuseum, Nuremberg, inv. Hz 5488r. Winkler 1936–9, vol. 4, no. 786; Strauss 1974, vol. 4, pp. 2080–1. British Museum, London, inv. 1921,714.2. Winkler 1936–9, vol. 4, no. 785; Strauss 1974, vol. 4, pp. 2076–7; Rowlands 1993, vol. 1, pp. 99–100, vol. 2, plate 146 above, no. 218r.

54 Ashcroft 2017, vol. 1, no. 162, p. 589.

55 Winkler 1936–9, vol. 3, pp. 690–9.

56 Ashcroft 2017, vol. 1, no. 162, p. 578.

57 Albertina, Vienna, inv. 22385v. Winkler 1936–9, vol. 4, no. 781; M. Mende in Vienna 2003, pp. 496–8, no. 174.

58 See note 40.

59 Kupferstichkabinett, Berlin, inv. KdZ 34v. Winkler 1936–9, vol. 4, no. 777; H. Mielke in Anzelewsky and Mielke 1984, p. 101, no. 96v.

60 Formerly Kunsthalle, Bremen, inv. Kl 9 (lost during the Second World War). Bremen 2012, pp. 144–6, 192, no. 41.

61 Albertina, Vienna, inv. 22385r. Winkler 1936–9, vol. 4, no. 780; M. Mende in Vienna 2003, pp. 496–8, no. 174; J. Zaunbauer in Vienna 2019, pp. 402–6, 410, 412–13 and p. 463, cat. 188.

62 The proposal that the castle is Virnsberg Castle in Franken (Burger 2019) remains unconvincing, as the drawing was made before the view of Rheinfels Castle on the left half of the page.

63 Vienna 2019, p. 463 and p. 475, doc. 24.

64 Additionally, even cursory research focusing on adhesive marks could yield interesting insights for the entire sketchbook. Even if the three birds were drawn on one sheet, the tests are meaningful in other ways. Within the context of this article, however, these hypotheses must not be too elaborate .

65 I would like to thank Giulia Bartrum for her help and the special new analysis she had carried out.

66 Ashcroft 2017, vol. 1, p. 551.

67 Musée Bonnat, Bayonne, inv. 1514. Winkler 1936–9, vol. 4, no. 752. Cf. also Rupprich's (1956, p. 189) consideration and the resulting dating of the drawing.

68 Nesselrath 2011a, p. 247; Nesselrath 2014, pp. 144–6, fig. 204, pp. 206–7.

69 See note 54.

70 Albright Knox Art Gallery Collection, Buffalo, inv. 1964:16.

71 Ashcroft 2017, vol. 1, no. 162, p. 578.

72 See note 40.

73 See note 59.

74 Biblioteca Ambrosiana, Milan, inv. F. 264 inf. 5. Winkler 1936–9, vol. 4, no. 751; British Museum, London, inv. 1848,1125.3. Winkler 1936–9, vol. 4, no. 766; Rowlands 1993, vol. 1, p. 99, no. 217v; see also the contribution by Sarvenaz Ayooghi and Heidrun Lange-Krach in the present publication, pp. 185–203.

75 Nesselrath 1986, pp. 126–7, 133–4, 143–4; Nesselrath 1993a, pp. 15–18, figs 42–3, 83–6; Nesselrath 2014, pp. 124–9.

76 Bartsch 2019, pp. 141–55, 478–9, cat. 223 and pp. 480–1, cat. 227.

77 Formerly Kunsthalle, Bremen, inv. Kl 9 (lost during the Second World War); Winkler 1936–9, vol. 4, no. 782; Salzmann 1991, pp. 50 and 52, no. 165; Bremen 2012, pp. 144–6, 192, no. 41r.

78 Ashcroft 2017, vol. 1, no. 162, p. 578.

79 Germanisches Nationalmuseum, Nuremberg, inv. 5488r. Winkler 1936–9, vol. 4, pp. 22–3. See also note 24 above for the verso.

80 Ashcroft 2017, vol. 1, no. 162, p. 560.

81 Ibid., p. 577.

82 Ibid., pp. 563, 564, 579, 589; Nesselrath 1993b; Nesselrath 2011b, pp. 81–2.

83 Shearman 1972, p. 139.

84 Nesselrath 2019, pp. 320–3; Nesselrath 2020b, pp. 109–16.

85 Ashcroft 2017, vol. 1, p. 561; Shearman 1972, pp. 144–5; Bücken 2019, pp. 51–60.

86 Sulzberger 1959; Nesselrath 2020a.

87 Albertina, Vienna, inv. 3171. Winkler 1936–9, vol. 4, no. 884; Strauss 1974, vol. 4, pp. 1521–68.

88 J. Paul Getty Museum, Malibu, inv. 54.AA.11. Bober and Rubinstein 2010, p. 66, no. 15.

89 Ashmolean Museum, Oxford, inv. WA1846.261r; Albertina, Vienna, inv. 36046v; Szépművészeti Múzeum, Budapest, inv. 2551. V. Farinella in Rome and Florence 2020, p. 313, no. VII.7.

90 Ashmolean Museum, Oxford, inv. WA 1846.145. Oxford 2017, pp. 74–5, no. 2.

91 Nesselrath 1993a, pp. 54–7, 66; Nesselrath 2014, pp. 102–3, 133–44; Mattei 2019.

92 Nesselrath 2020a, pp. 182–4, figs 6–7. See also Hans Mielke's remarks (in Anzelewsky and Mielke 1984, p. 117) and van den Brink 2020, pp. 112–13, on Raphael's *Canigiani Madonna*, also a pre-Roman work by the artist like the drawing in Oxford and the painting in Città di Castello.

93 Städel Museum, Frankfurt, inv. 695. Frankfurt 2003, pp. 108–10, no. 32.

94 Museum Boijmans Van Beuningen, Rotterdam, inv. N 194. The sheet is unpublished; only a detailed catalogue entry by Judith Niessen exists in the museum's digital catalogue of Dutch drawings of the fifteenth and sixteenth centuries, with a current attribution to an unknown artist. An old attribution to Joachim Patinir is noted. My thanks to Albert Elen for his kind help and for allowing me to study the sheet.

95 Albertina, Vienna, inv. 3165. Winkler 1936–9, vol. 4, no. 821; M. Mende in Vienna 2003, pp. 488–9, no. 170.

96 Ashcroft 2017, vol. 1, no. 162, p. 579. The German *stefft* has been translated directly as 'silver-point'. For a discussion of the identification of Joachim Patinir's likeness see the essay by Peter van den Brink in the present publication, pp. 205–25.

97 Dürer's pen-and-ink drawing in the Kupferstichkabinett, Berlin, inv. KdZ 4670 (see note 91 above) also has a black chalk drawing on the verso (H. Mielke in Anzelewsky and Mielke 1984, pp. 116–17, fig. VIII).

98 Museum Boijmans Van Beuningen, Rotterdam, inv. 2312. Frankfurt 2013, pp. 346–7, no. 14.5.

99 Formerly in Weimar, Winkler 1936–9, vol. 4, pp. 35–6, no. 811; Goris and Marlier 1970, pp. 24–7.

100 Winkler 1936–9, vol. 4, pp. 35–6 and plate II, lower left. The curious hat on the engraving as well as the possible preparatory drawing (Herzog Anton Ulrich-Museum, Braunschweig, inv. Z 1289) may be inspired by a fur cap worn by the portrait on the right in the *Sitting Bishop and Portrait of a Man with a Fur Cap* in the silverpoint sketchbook.

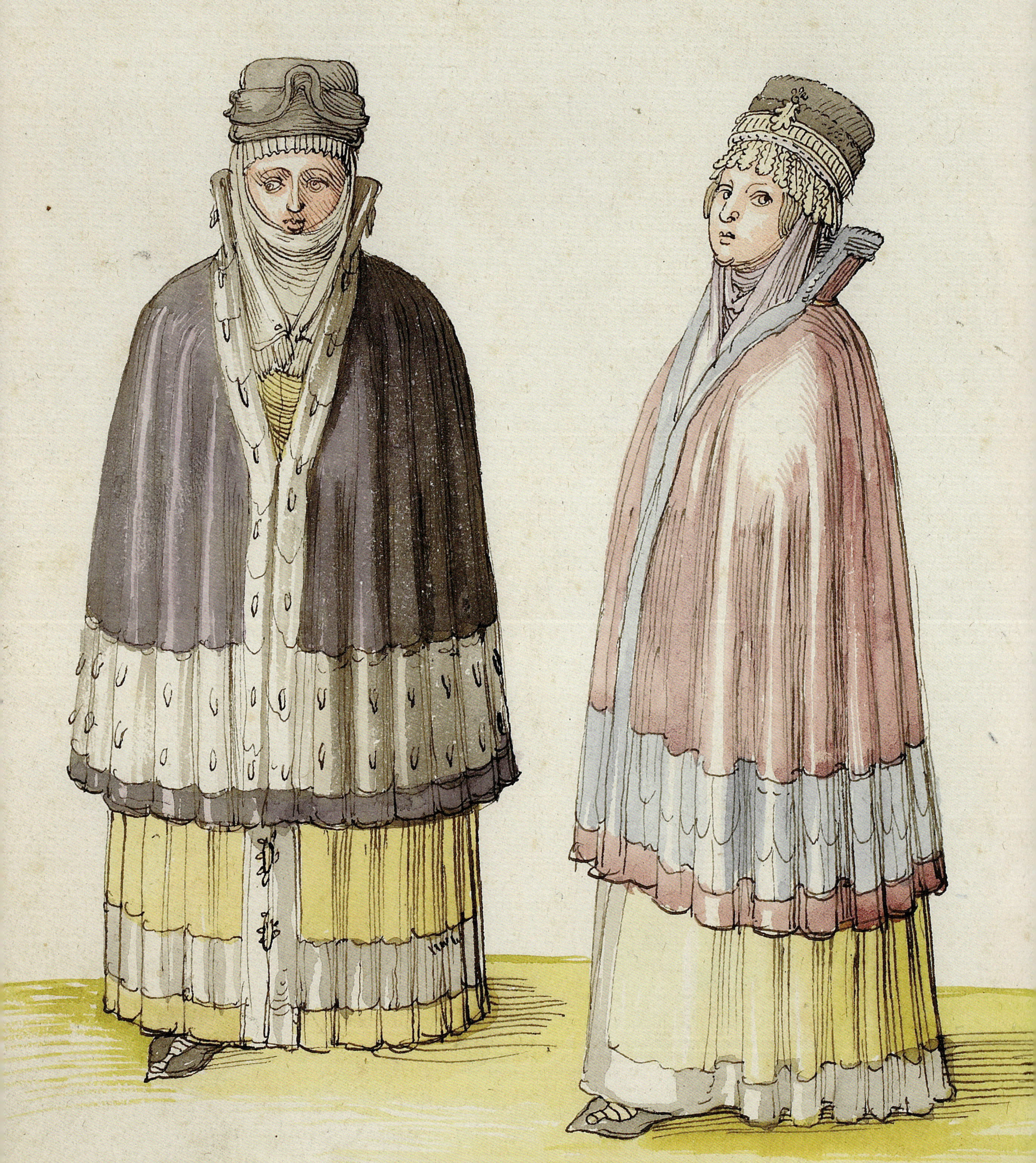

SARVENAZ AYOOGHI AND HEIDRUN LANGE-KRACH

IMPRESSIONS FROM A JOURNEY
DÜRER'S OUTLOOK ON PEOPLE, LANDSCAPES AND ANIMALS

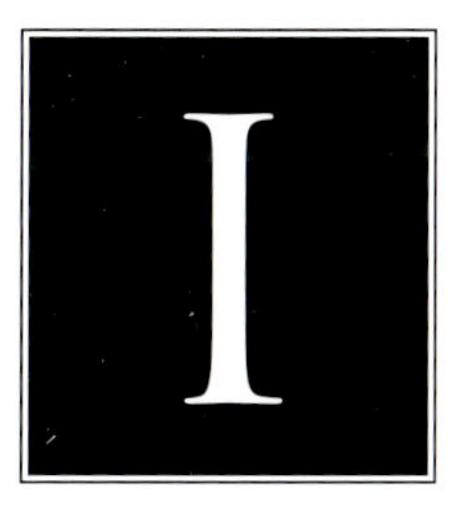

IT WAS NOT ONLY AS A CAPABLE BUSINESSMAN and renowned artist at the height of his career that Albrecht Dürer struck out northward in the direction of the Netherlands; it was also as a tourist receptive to the world around him, who sought to absorb the foreign environments and cultures, picturesque landscapes and unfamiliar animals he encountered with a curious eye. Dürer paired work and pleasure throughout the journey, gathering new impressions and drawing inspiration from any number of motifs and objects. At the time Antwerp, Dürer's residence of choice on the trip, was a gateway to the world; the metropolis and its neighbouring cities offered a spectacular array of new impulses that found reflection in the artist's numerous studies and sketches. Two earlier trips to Venice had left him with a particular fondness for the Alpine region, with landscape watercolours and depictions of clothing and costumes typical of the region occupying an increasingly prominent position within his repertoire of motifs. Dürer had also prepared a series of four drawings of women's garments typical of his own home town of Nuremberg in 1500–1, each serving as an instance of the city's dress code.[1] He adhered to the dress regulations of the time, which around 1500 was part of the classification of social hierarchies.

One of the artist's first approaches to the world of dress comes in a pen-and-ink drawing today held in Frankfurt, which sets a Venetian woman alongside a Nuremberg housewife (fig. 14).[2] Dating from 1495, the drawing is a study contrasting dress codes for women from southern Germany with those from Venice. Depicted with loose curls, a low-cut neckline and chopines, or *zoccoli* in Italian (platform shoes usually made of wood or cork worn by women to indicate social status), and wearing a dress girdled under the breast in the fashion of the day, the Venetian cuts a smaller, daintier figure than her rather earthy Nuremberg counterpart, who is shown with bonnet, bodice, and apron.[3] Commonly attributed to Dürer's first Venetian trip, the sheet has often been discussed in terms of a comparison between German and Italian culture.[4] Counter to this interpretation, Thomas Eser has cited

OPPOSITE
Detail from *Two Livonian Women* (cat. 74)

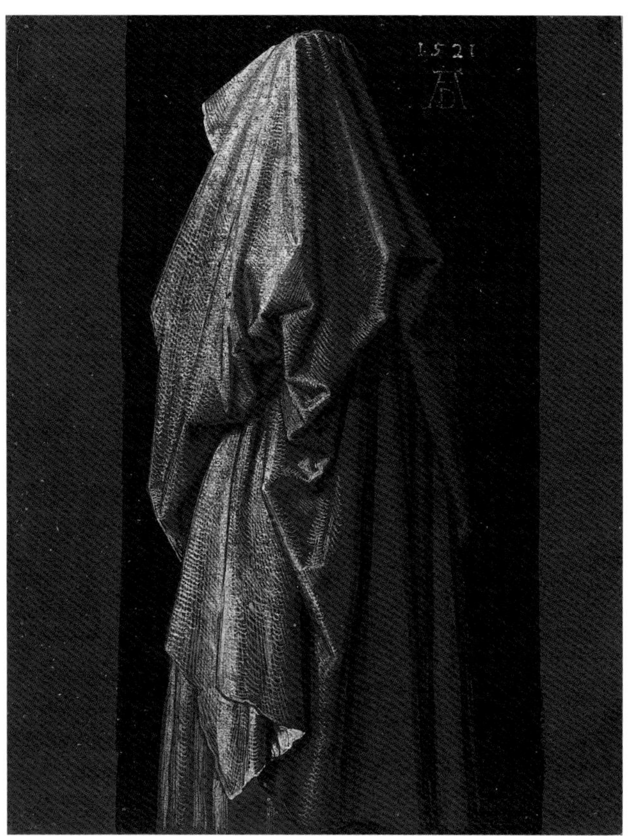

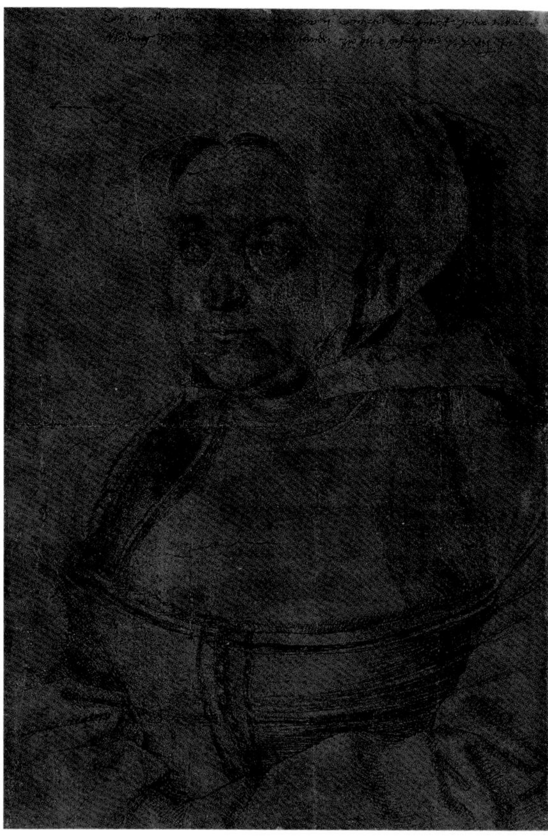

Fig. 99
ALBRECHT DÜRER
A Woman in Netherlandish Dress, seen from the Back, 1521
Brush in black, heightened with white on grey-violet grounded paper, 28 × 21.1 cm
The Albertina Museum, Vienna (3174)

Fig. 100
ALBRECHT DÜRER
Agnes Dürer in Netherlandish Dress, 1521
Brown metalpoint on grey-violet paper, 40.7 × 27.1 cm
Staatliche Museen zu Berlin, Kupferstichkabinett (KdZ 36)

correspondence from Bianca Maria Sforza (1472–1510) – originally of the Milanese nobility, and later brought to Innsbruck as Empress of the Holy Roman Empire – who, along with other ladies of the court, would try on various national costumes, at times reaching for the German wardrobe, at times for the Italian.[5] By Eser's account, Dürer would thus have had any number of opportunities to observe and engage with Italian fashion outside Italy itself. Christof Metzger has in turn amended this supposition with an unassuming but highly significant detail – that of the chopines. Aside from making their wearer taller, the shoes were intended to protect the clothing from getting dirty – while themselves remaining hidden from sight beneath the long gowns worn at the time.[6] Dürer, then, must have been aware of this concealed 'accessory', which he could only have discovered on site, as it were.[7] In time, clothing would enter the foreground of his work as a motif in its own right, with the female subject coming to play a secondary role. One of the contexts in which this process can be observed is provided by the studies of garments and regional dress that Dürer prepared during his journey through the Low Countries.

CLOTHING, REGIONAL DRESS AND COSTUME

During his fifth stay in Antwerp, Dürer notes in his journal that he 'drew two Dutch costume studies also in black and white on grey paper'.[8] Scholars have speculated as to whether the passage refers to the *Young Woman in Netherlandish Dress* (cat. 73), now in the National Gallery in Washington, and the garment study in back view in Vienna (fig. 99).[9] The speculation is due in part to the vague nature of the description, which does not necessarily refer to either work; it remains unclear in this case whether Dürer's 'costume studies' are actually studies or works of his own invention. Eser, at least, detects a degree of refinement far surpassing a rough study in its quality of execution.[10] In the garment study now in Vienna, Dürer concentrates on a cloth that has been pulled up and over the head of a figure who is turned away from the viewer, making use of chiaroscuro and a black background to virtuosic three-dimensional effect. The drawing ultimately served as the basis for Dürer's depiction of the woman on the far right of his *Entombment* now in the Germanisches Nationalmuseum, Nuremberg (fig. 133).[11]

The *Young Woman in Netherlandish Dress* in Washington, by contrast, bears the artist's monogram as well as the year (1521) and gives the impression of a standalone image, probably intended as part of a series on women's regional dress, or a cultural exploration building on his depictions of women from Nuremberg (cat. 73).[12] Dürer shows an obvious interest in the structure and composition of the sumptuous garment, devoting particular attention to details such as its fur lining and square bodice, as well as the rosary that hangs

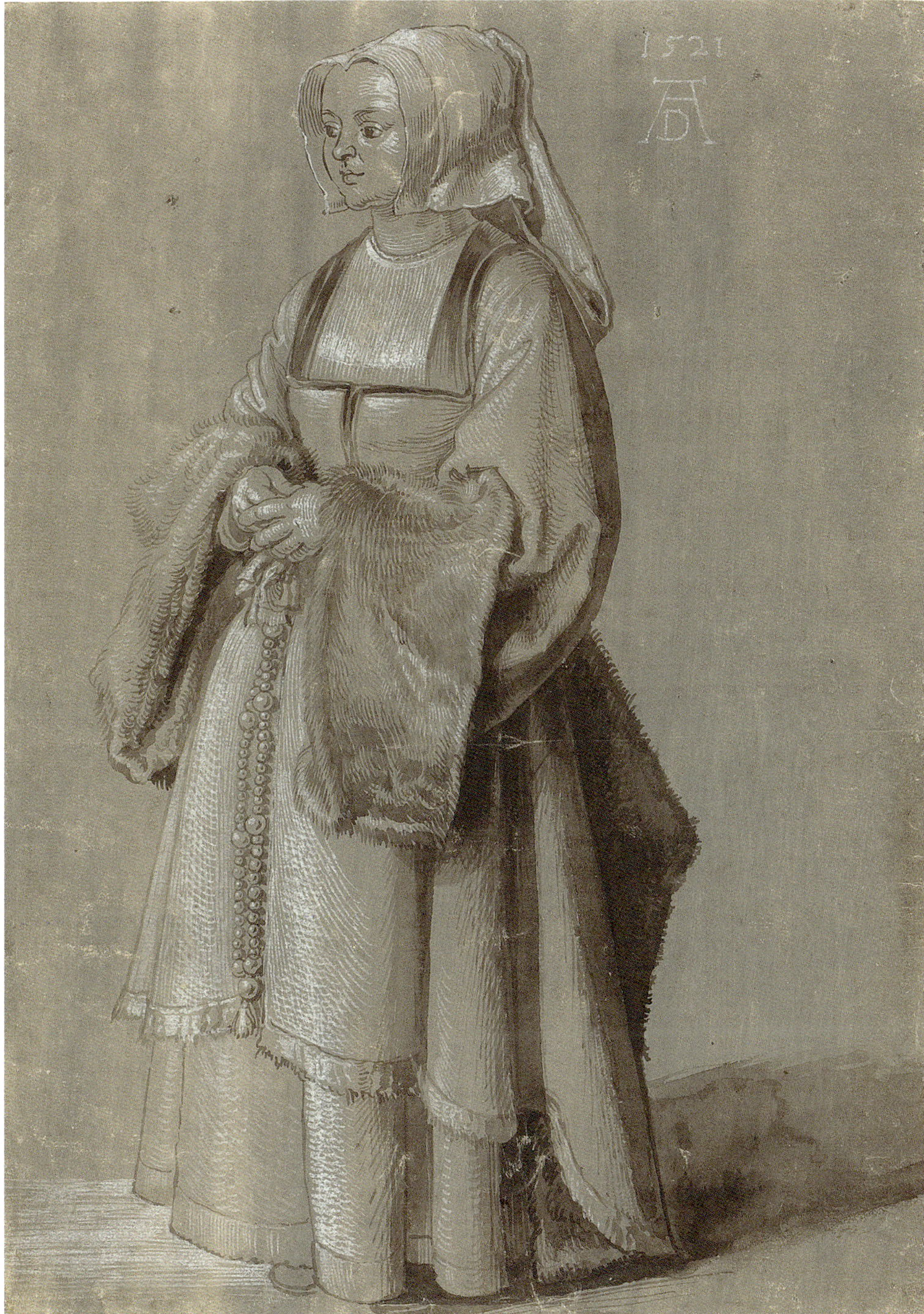

73
ALBRECHT DÜRER
Young Woman in Netherlandish Dress, 1521
Brush and brown and white ink on grey-violet prepared paper, 28.3 × 19.8 cm
National Gallery of Art, Washington

loosely from the subject's hands. The head covering is typical of the region and appears in other drawn likenesses by Dürer, in particular the portrait of his wife Agnes in Netherlandish clothing (fig. 100),[13] the *Lady from Brussels* (cat. 89), probably Berthelmine le Paige or his silverpoint drawing *The Beautiful Young Woman of Antwerp* (cat. 69). Unlike the women depicted in his studies of Nuremberg costumes, the face of the sturdy young woman in the Washington drawing has been the source of some debate, even if her doll-like, almost wooden features speak against a drawing from life.[14] Still, certain similarities in physiognomy – the fullness of the face, the mouth, the chin and the striking eye – cannot be entirely discounted, leaving *The Beautiful Young Woman of Antwerp* as one possible template for the *Young Woman in Netherlandish Dress.* The former is mentioned twice in Dürer's notes, on 1 January 1521 and again on 11 February 1521 (or contemporaneously to the drawing from Washington) – as the fiancée of Gerhard Bombelli and the daughter of Sebastian the city procurator.[15]

Nowadays the drawings' titles contain the term *Tracht*, denoting traditional or regional dress, although

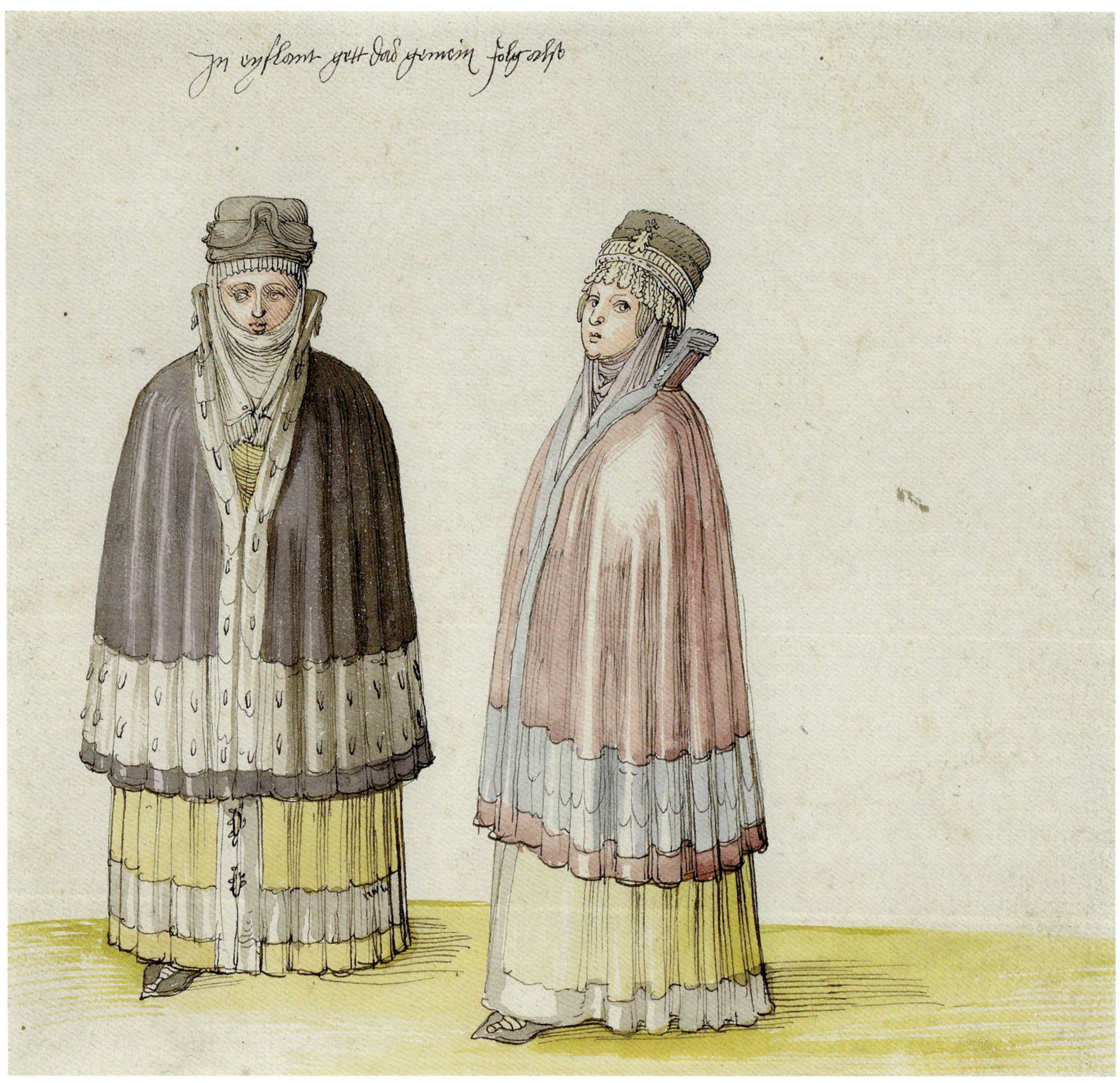

74
ALBRECHT DÜRER
Two Livonian Women, 1521
Pen and brown ink, watercolour, 18.4 × 19.5 cm
Musée du Louvre, Paris

the word does not appear once in his journal, where his descriptions refer either to 'dress' ('klaidung') or 'dressed' ('beklaidet') as the case may be, usually linked to the modifiers 'lordly' ('herrlich') or 'lavish' ('köstlich'). Observing a procession through Antwerp, for example, he notes 'a whole company of notable people, in lordly and costly dress'.[16] Moreover, he continues, 'In this company there also rode boys and maidens, most pretty and dressed exceedingly finely according to the custom of many different lands'.[17] In a similar vein, the inscription on the drawing of his wife reads 'This likeness of his wife in Netherlandish costume was drawn by Albrecht Dürer at Antwerp in the year 1521'.[18]

The etymology for *Tracht* explains its likely distinction from the more general term for dress or clothing, *Kleidung*. Coming from the Old High German *draht*(*a*) or the Middle High German *traht*(*e*), *Tracht* derives from tragen, the verb 'to wear', and was understood originally in the sense of 'that which is worn'.[19] While *Kleidung* had long served as a distinguishing mark for social status, during the fifteenth century the lines between the urban patrician class and the nobility blurred increasingly,[20] giving rise to dress codes intended to make class differences visible. Especially with the growing textile trade, luxurious clothing became a 'strategic tool of social ascendancy for the merchant class'.[21] By the sixteenth century it was no longer the cut of the clothing that distinguished class but the quality of the material: velvet, brocade, silk or damask long remained the exclusive preserve of the nobility and upper classes, while strict regulations prescribed materials such as linen, hemp or coarse cotton for the lower social strata.[22] It was out of these dress codes that the term *Tracht* developed, a term used today in a narrower sense with reference to traditional, historical or regional fashion.

Of all Dürer's work featuring such fashion, his portraits of women from Livonia (cat. 72; fig. 101) doubtless rank among the most intriguing and unusual. Shown in national costume, the women are depicted as representatives of a foreign and distant culture who must have captured the curious artist's imagination. As with his depiction of women's *Tracht* from Nuremberg, and again with his *Irish Warriors and Peasants*,[23] the Livonian women are drawn in coloured pen-and-ink. They were initially thought to be Icelandic, until in 1931 the Baltic German historian Nicolaus Busch was correctly able to place them geographically, based on their inscriptions – albeit with the explanation that Dürer had visited the Baltic region himself and had seen and drawn the costumes from life.[24] Subsequent research has questioned whether Dürer ever travelled to Livonia, considering it much more plausible either that he would have seen the colourful designs in the multicultural trading metropolis of Antwerp or copied them from one of the costume books in circulation at the time. Jean Michel Massing even considers it possible that Dürer may have encountered drawn models for his *Irish Warriors and Peasants* while in Antwerp, as the inn of his host, Jobst Plankfelt, was located on Wolstraat, which was also called Engelsche Straat since it mainly housed English merchants.[25] While no definite reuse of Dürer's studies of Livonian or Irish dress has been identified to date, the drawings nonetheless served as templates for subsequent costume books. In the German-speaking world, Dürer's figures first appear to the last detail in Hans Weigel's costume book from 1577,[26] albeit in reverse order.[27] They

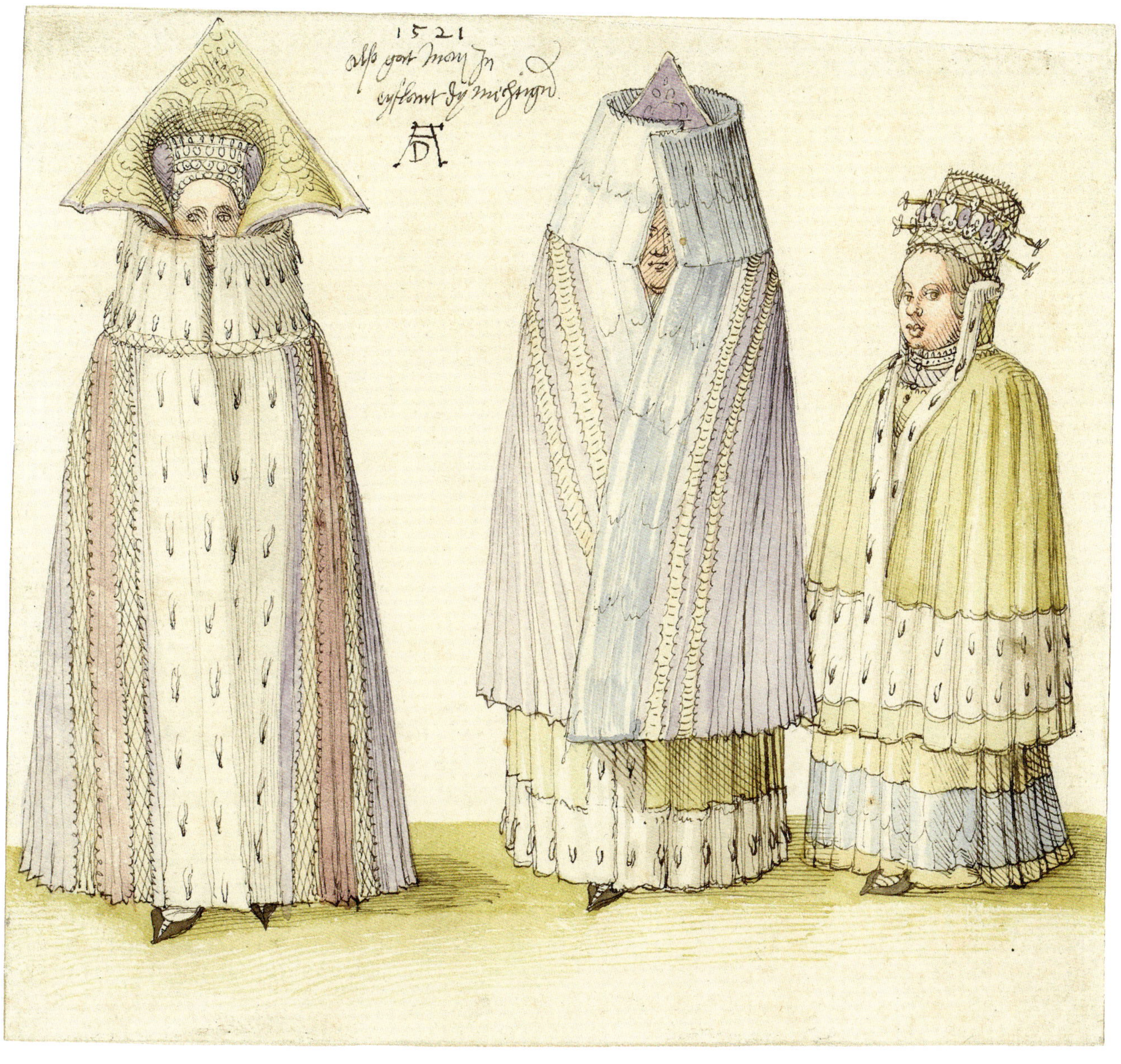

Fig. 101
ALBRECHT DÜRER
Three Livonian Women in Winter Dress, 1521
Pen and brown ink, watercolour, 18.3 × 195 cm
Musée du Louvre, Paris

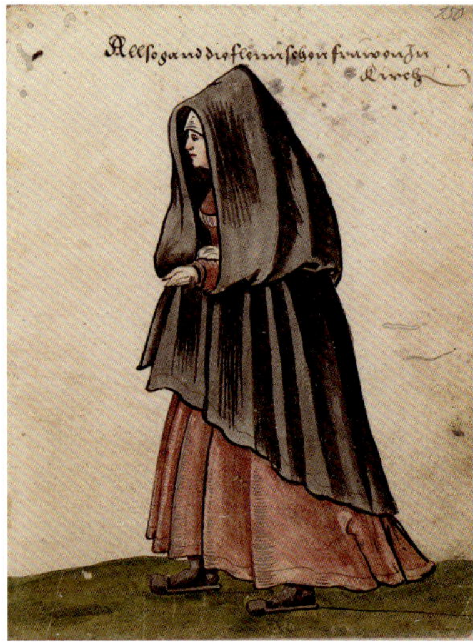

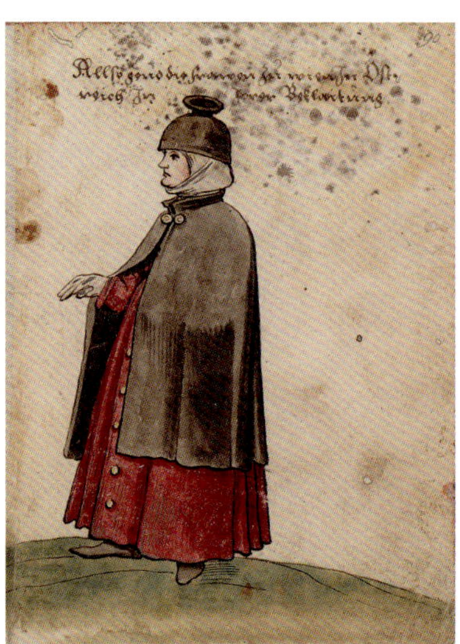

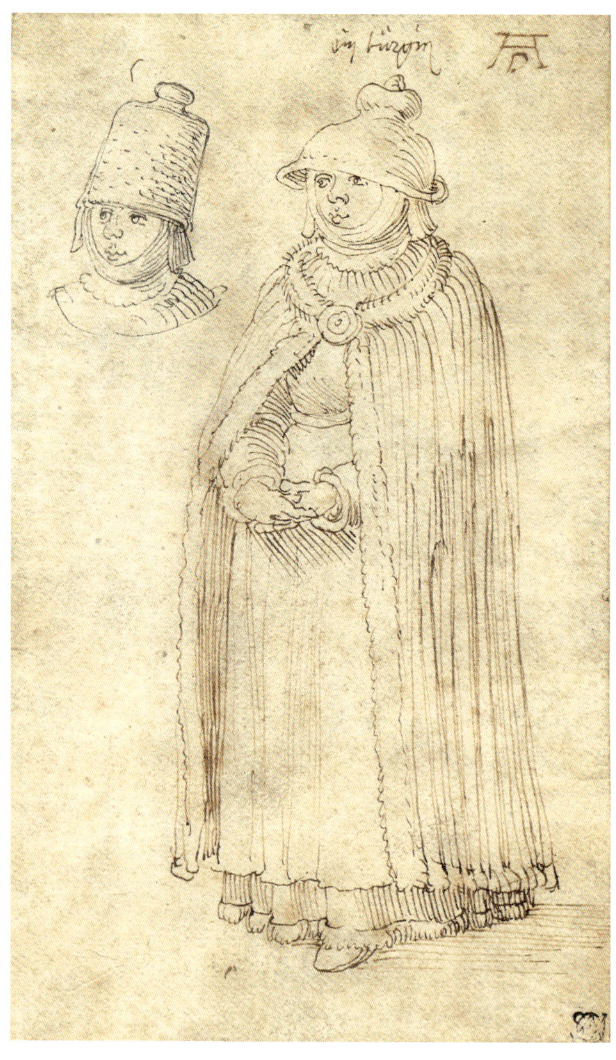

Figs 102, 103
CHRISTOPH WEIDITZ (1500–1559)
Pages from costume book, about 1530–40
Germanisches Nationalmuseum, Nuremberg (Hs22474 fol 90r and 150r)

Fig. 104
ALBRECHT DÜRER
Two Studies of Women from Burgenland, about 1520–1
Pen and dark-brown ink, 18.1 × 10.7 cm
Veneranda Biblioteca Ambrosiana, Pinacoteca, Milan

turn up again in Jost Amman's book from 1588,[28] then two years later in Venice, in Cesare Vecellio's costume book.[29] Giving any proper indication of the origin of the garments seems to have been an increasingly minor affair for the authors, who adapt earlier models and travel literature to suit their purposes on an ad hoc basis, and with scant regard for geographical attribution.[30]

One of the best-known manuscripts on costume was assembled between 1530 and 1540 by Christoph Weiditz (1500–1559), who in 154 coloured illustrations sought to capture distinctive properties in clothing from an international perspective.[31] In what was at the time a new literary genre, the work devoted itself to styles of clothing from a number of lands, with particular emphasis on regional dress codes. The images show men and women at different stages of life, for example attending weddings, in mourning, or on their way to market or church. By the end of the century the costume book had become a successful medium; an assortment of them still exists today.[32] Weiditz himself visited Spain and the court of Charles V in 1529. Even if its creator remains unknown, stylistically the costume book points unmistakably to Augsburg;[33] as Holy Roman Emperor, Maximilian I had previously commissioned depictions of popular costume from a range of countries for inclusion in a series of printed works created in his memory. Known as *Gedechtnus*, the originals would doubtless have been on hand in the Imperial City.[34] Weiditz's collection in particular found repeated use in other books in the genre: popular figures included the bride and the female servant, as well as women of the middle classes and from the countryside.

One of Weiditz's figures (fig. 103) is in fact reproduced in a pair of drawings that Dürer made during his journey to the Netherlands, showing two women from Burgenland (fig. 104), now in the Biblioteca Ambrosiana in Milan. The inscription on the drawings is also revealing. Weiditz annotated his drawing 'thus do the women of Vienna in Austria go about in their clothing' ('Allso gend die Frawen Zu wien in Ostreich in Irer Beklaidung'), while Dürer's inscription similarly references the origin of the woman – although the latter was wrongly attributed for many years. Writing in 1876, Thausing dated Dürer's drawing to the time of his second trip to Venice, transcribing his inscription as *Türkin* – the German term for a Turkish woman. This was amended by Ephrussi, who placed the drawing in 1521, in connection with Dürer's Livonian women. Ephrussi's own interpretation of the subject as a resident of Iceland held until Ursula Mende was able to show the clothing's origin in Bohemia, Silesia and Lower Austria, changing Thausing's original reading from *Türkin* to Bürgin, in reference to women from the region discussed by Mende.[35] Shown in simple attire, in a dress, apron and coat with fur trimming closed by a round clasp, the woman wears a headdress with a knob-like crest particular to the region. Beneath this a broad white band tightly encircles her head, ears and chin, as was prescribed for married women and when going to church.[36] To the left Dürer drew a cylindrical version of the headdress, which he demonstrably used again as a model. In the *Crucifixion in Outline*, for example, a copperplate engraving that was created after Dürer motifs, the woman to the left of the crucified Christ, behind Mary, wears the same head covering (cat. 115).[37] The figure depicted on the verso of the silverpoint drawing now in the British Museum shows an almost identical headdress (figs 154, 155),[38] as does Albrecht Altdorfer's rendition of a woman in the margin of Emperor Maximilian's prayer book.[39]

Dürer's extensive repertoire of clothing style and character heads gave him remarkable artistic freedom when it came to dressing his subjects, deploying them to new purposes or varying them. Yet his pen-and-ink drawings also represented a practical way of capturing spontaneous moments of inspiration and fleeting impressions for later use in detailed studies and larger works.[40]

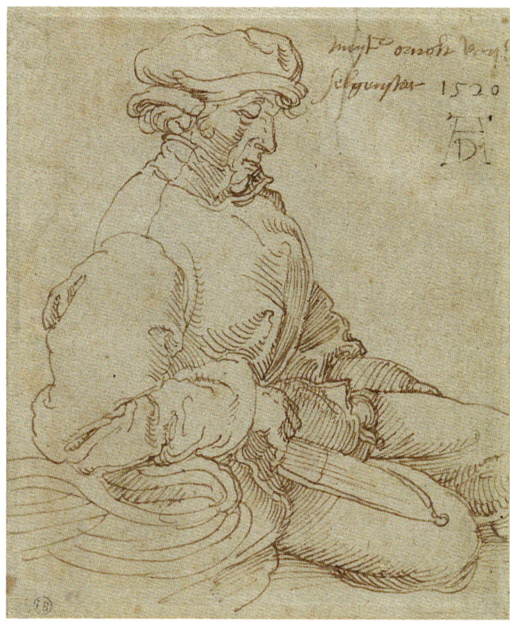

Fig. 105
ALBRECHT DÜRER
Portrait of Arnold Rucker of Seligenstadt, sleeping, 1520
Pen and brown ink on paper, 12.3 × 9.9 cm
Musée Bonnat-Helleu, Bayonne (1514)

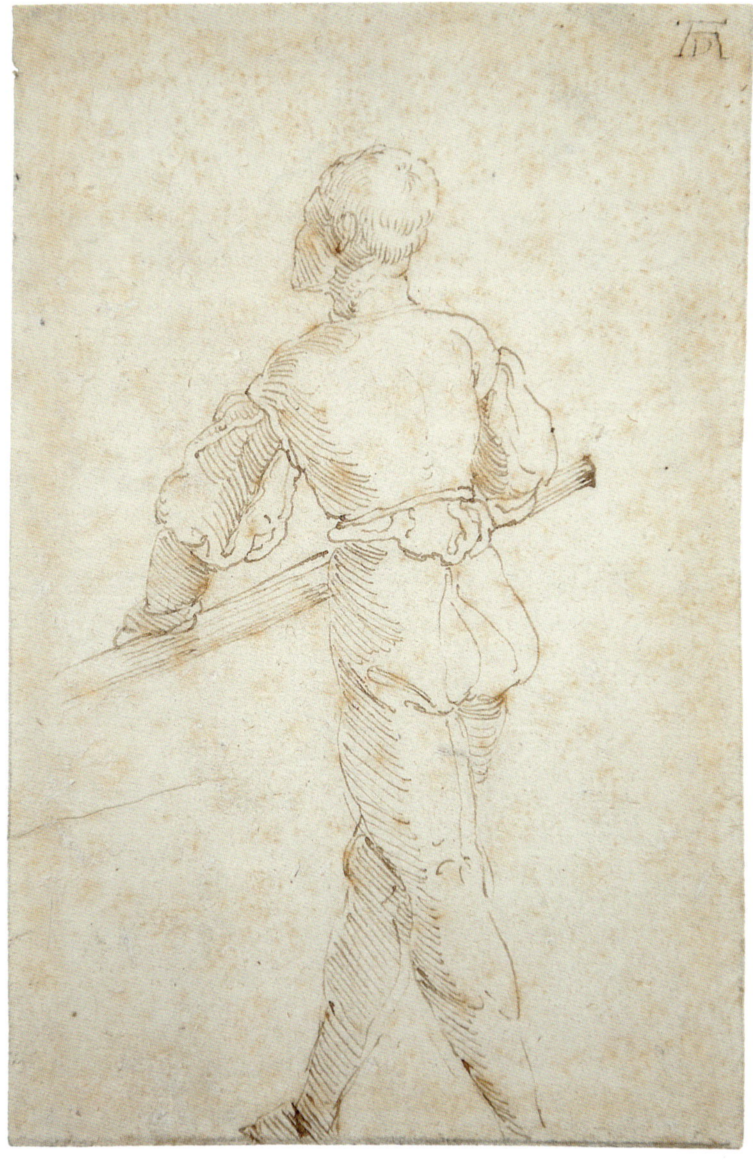

75
ALBRECHT DÜRER
A Man with an Oar, about 1520–1
Pen and brown ink on paper, 16 × 10.4 cm
The Henry Barber Trust, the Barber Institute of Fine Arts, University of Birmingham

GREAT TALENT ON A SMALL SCALE

Over the course of time, Dürer's work in pen and ink, the better part of which comprises studies of people, has either gone missing or been donated. The few drawings that remain reveal a broad palette of motifs ranging from portraits, such as those of *Captain Felix Hungersperg* (cat. 87) or the *Lady from Brussels* (cat. 89), and multiple studies of heads of bearded men both young and old, to a depiction of the *Descent from the Cross* recently attributed to this group (cats 79, 80, 81; cat. 11).[41]

Two of the earliest works from Dürer's journey are found on sheets currently housed in Bayonne and Birmingham; both mark the beginning of the trip and bear the same watermark (fig. 105; cat. 75). On 19 July 1520 he passed by Seligenstadt aboard a boat, which is presumably where he met the organ builder and innkeeper Arnold Rucker (about 1480–1538/9).[42] The rapid, loose strokes with which Dürer composes Rucker's portrait lend it the feeling of being captured on the spur of the moment, a snapshot where the shutter release has been pressed at the decisive instant. One can easily imagine how the sight of Rucker, who lies asleep peacefully and at ease, must have caught Dürer's eye, prompting him to take out his sketchbook and record the fleeting moment. A similar dynamic is at play in Dürer's depiction of *A Man with an Oar*, now in Birmingham (cat. 75).[43] Here the artist's anatomical interest takes precedence: oar in hand, the figure strikes a pose reminiscent of a nude, revealing an athletic figure with powerful calf and thigh muscles. By contrast, the oarsman's clothing distracts from this view: his upper body is covered with a garment akin to a doublet, ending in classical fashion at the waist, beneath which he wears a type of waist belt. One can further make

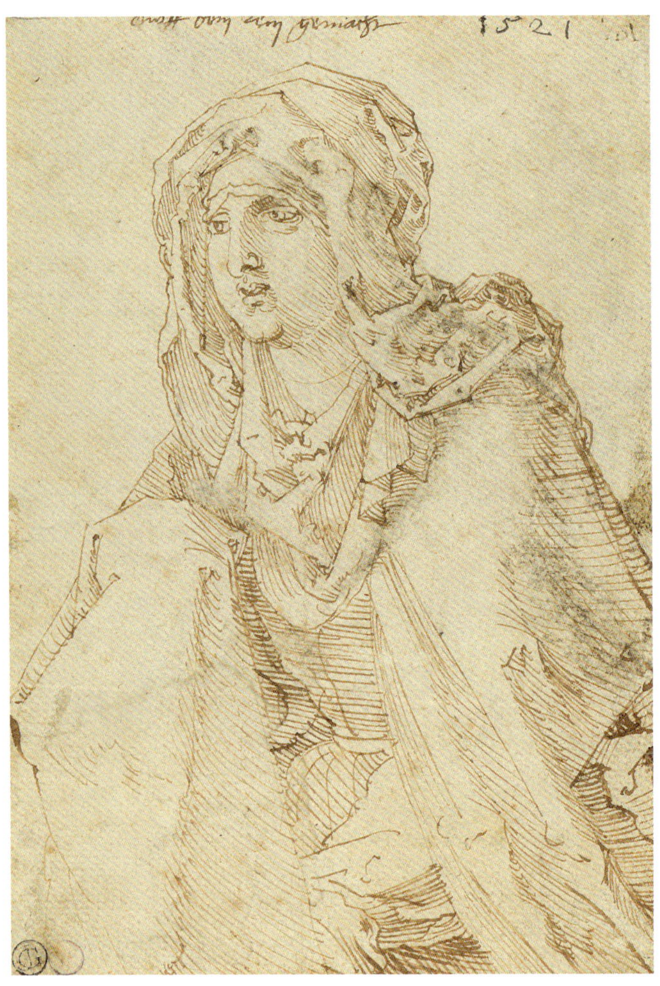

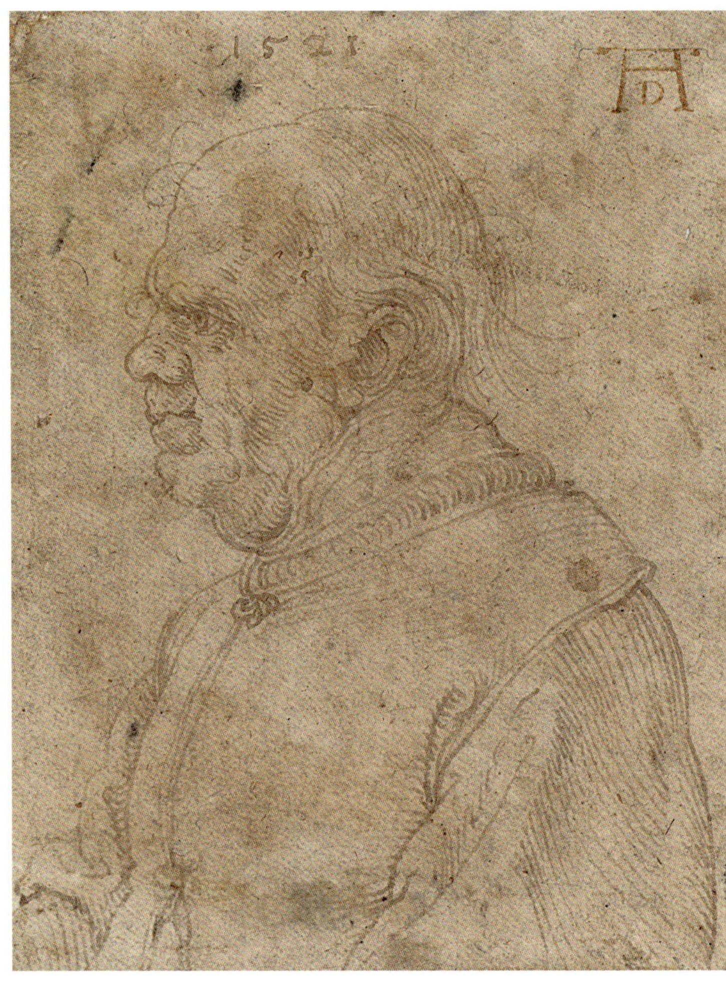

76
ALBRECHT DÜRER
Female Half-length Figure in the Type of a Mourning Virgin, 1521
Pen and brown ink on paper, 15.2 × 10.3 cm
Germanisches Nationalmuseum, Nuremberg

77
ALBRECHT DÜRER
Portrait of a Man in Profile, 1521
Pen and brown ink, 11 × 8.2 cm
The Albertina Museum, Vienna

out tight-fitting men's trousers with back leg seams, outlining the buttocks.[44]

If Dürer's Seligenstadt portraits of Rucker and the oarsman form a sort of prelude to his year-long trip, he documented its end with a *Female Half-length Figure* (cat. 76) and the noteworthy inscription 'awff dem rein gemacht',[45] which was probably drawn between Cologne and Nuremberg. In both robe and physiognomy, the woman fits the classical Marian image in his drawing *Virgin Mary with Halo*.[46] The image has also given rise to speculation, however: did the sitter actually exist, or did Dürer imagine her? Here opinion is split: for Eduard Flechsig, the heavily pleated cloth is too elaborate for the image to have been drawn from a living model.[47] Winkler maintains the opposite, seeing in the figure another passenger on ship.[48] The drawing has even been regarded as a costume study for a member of the Christian lay order known as the Beguines,[49] although this association has proved unfounded, based on a copy of Dürer's journal that has since been revised. The single original sheet from Dürer's travel journal that remains today shows the cutting pattern for a cloak described by Dürer as 'Netherlandish lady's mantle' ('nyder lendischer frawen mantel'; fig. 99), a phrase replaced in a later copy with 'the beguines' mantle' ('Peginen Mantel').[50] Still, given that veils and wimples (known as *Höcke* in German, or *huik* in Dutch) were also used among women of the middle classes at the time, it is entirely conceivable that Dürer would in fact have met his subject on board, and recorded her likeness for use as a motif in future work.[51]

Through such highly accomplished pen-and-ink drawings Dürer assembled a diverse roster of templates, including female figures like the fellow passenger mentioned above, as well as head studies that would find later use, particularly in narrative images, as with his depictions of the Passion.

The *Entombment* now in Nuremberg presents several figures familiar to us from the pen-and-ink drawings (fig. 133): the striking head of an older man shown at left in profile (cat. 77), who is recognisable as the pall bearer, for example, or the garment study in back view (fig. 99). Behind the latter we find the same youth (fig. 106) who appears in the *Lamentation in Bremen* (fig. 134), the *Road to Calvary* in Florence (fig. 131) and the *Crucifixion* in the Albertina, Vienna (cat. 104). Here Dürer uses the young man to represent John, while the variant with more

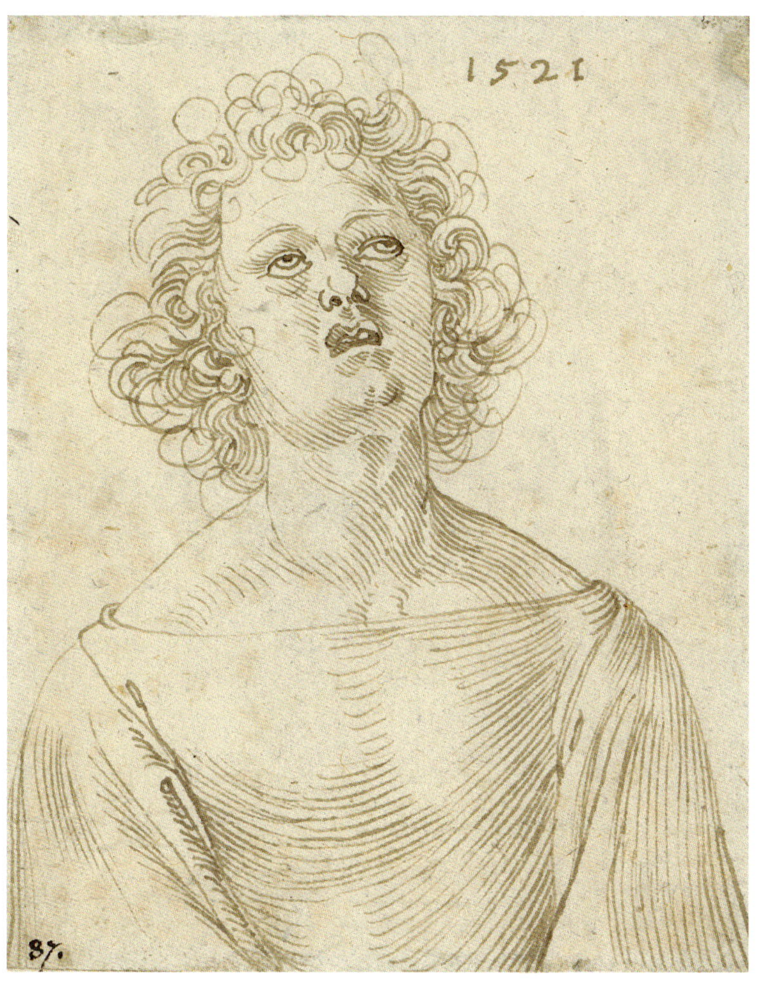

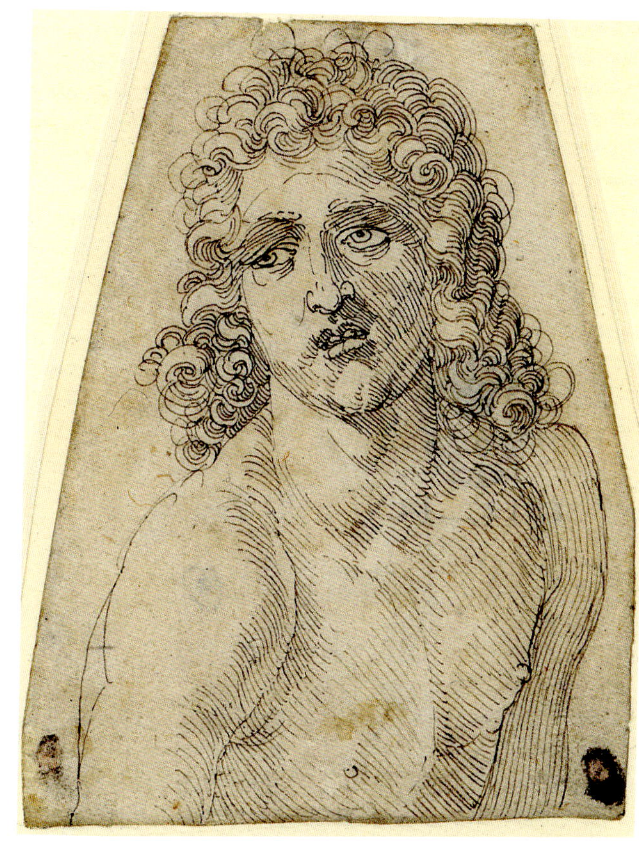

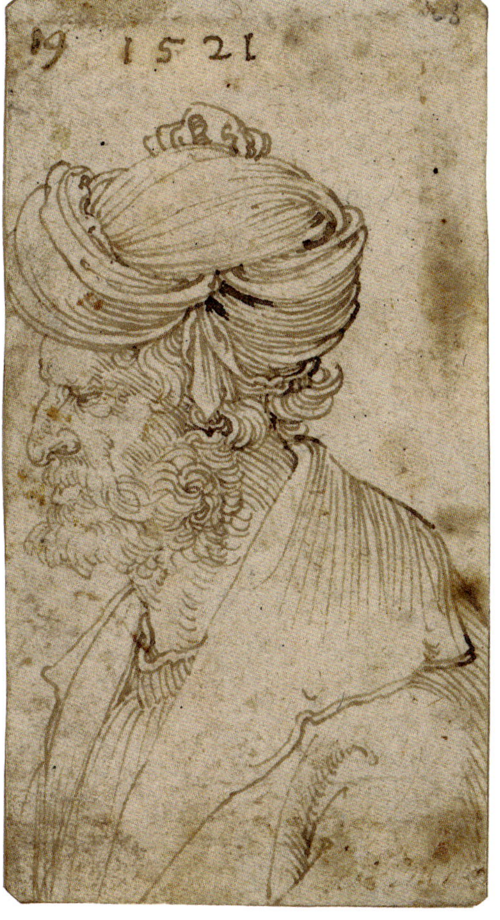

elaborate curls (cat. 78) is unquestionably an adoption and elaboration of Martin Schongauer's engraving of Saint Sebastian. Another pen-and-ink study appears in the *Lamentation* in the Liberna Collection in Mettingen (cat. 108), his *Oriental Figure* (fig. 107) – albeit with slightly altered turban.

While many of the pen-and-ink sketches Dürer completed on his trip through the Low Countries are still missing today there are bright spots, such as the rediscovery of the *Bust of an Old Man* (cat. 79).[52] At one point forming the pendant to an image of the *Virgin Mary with Halo* or *Mary as the Mother of Sorrows*, the figure may be interpreted as Joseph. Both drawings were known only through a copperplate engraving dating from 1781,[53] until the portrait of the man resurfaced in a private collection.[54] The style of the depiction especially makes it stand out: with furrowed eyebrows and a bushy beard, the old man casts a gloomier impression than is normal for Dürer's face types, such as the studies now in London (cat. 80) and Frankfurt (cat. 81). One sheet attributed to Dürer's school that makes use of the old man's distinctive physiognomy is in the Royal Collection at Windsor Castle.[55]

Fig. 106
ALBRECHT DÜRER
Young Man looking up, 1521
Pen and brown ink,
11.4 × 9.1 cm
Staatliche Museen zu Berlin, Kupferstichkabinett
(KdZ 4183)

78
ALBRECHT DÜRER
Nude Young Man, 1520–1
Pen and brown ink,
10.4 × 7.9 cm
British Museum

Fig. 107
ALBRECHT DÜRER
Oriental Figure in Profile, 1521
Pen and brown ink,
10.8 × 5.8 cm
Staatliche Museen zu Berlin, Kupferstichkabinett
(KdZ 1285)

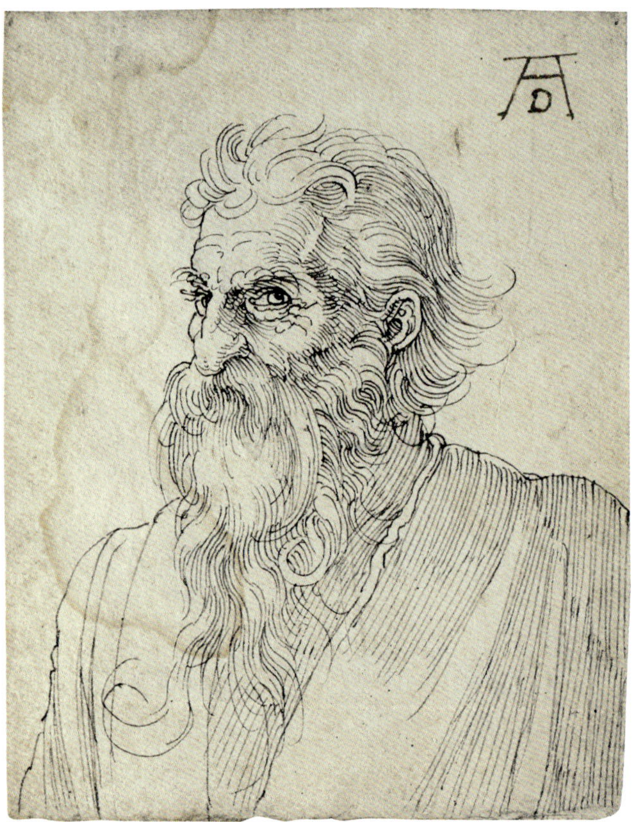

79
ALBRECHT DÜRER
Bust of an Old Man,
1520–1
Pen and black ink,
11.5 × 8.9 cm
Collection Jean Bonna,
Geneva

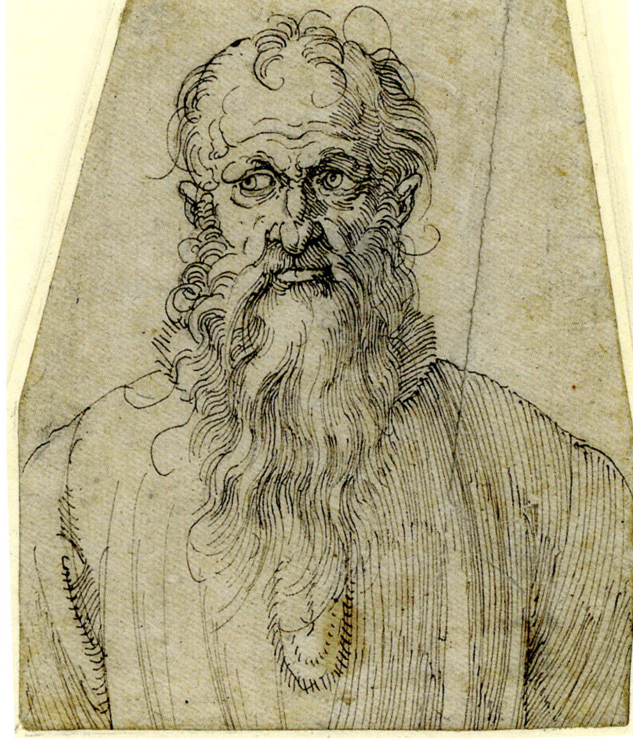

80
ALBRECHT DÜRER
Head and Shoulders of a Bearded Man,
1520–1
Pen and brown ink,
9.4 × 8 cm
British Museum

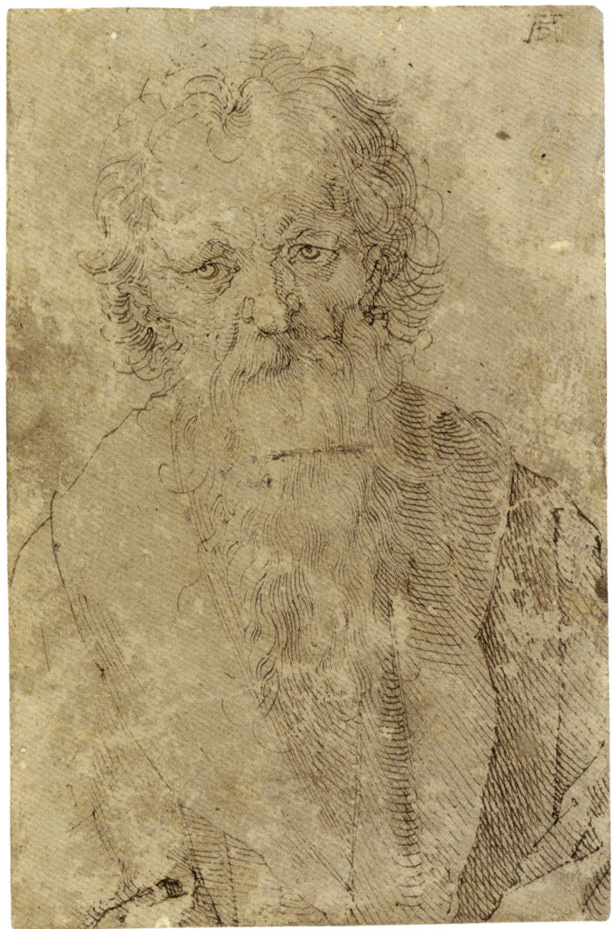

81
ALBRECHT DÜRER
Bearded Old Man,
1520–1
Pen and brown ink on paper, 16 × 10.4 cm
Städel Museum,
Frankfurt am Main

Throughout his trip Dürer's drawings in pen served primarily as a rapid way to capture what inspired or made an impression on him, as well as what he wanted to remember for use in later works. In this connection, Dagmar Hirschfelder has quite rightly noted that Dürer's pen drawings 'held a secondary purpose of being for personal use, as Dürer himself considered them'.[56]

LANDSCAPE, ANIMALS AND DISTANT TREASURES

Dürer's gift for observation and his broad mind towards people, foreign cultures and new artistic techniques are clear from the journal he kept during his trip. He attends to the landscapes in which he finds himself with a steady fascination and an evident desire for knowledge, either embedding them within his drawings or reserving for them an entire sheet as subjects in their own right. One depiction of Antwerp's harbour, which features a striking diagonal composition, reveals an almost unpopulated quay, except for a handful of tentatively sketched figures that suggest the loading of freight (fig. 108). While Dürer first mentions having left Antwerp by ship during his fourth stay in the city, and does not actually mention the harbour,[57] it was a central urban landmark that he could easily have visited beforehand. The Cathedral of Our Lady, on the other hand, is described in detail by him: Dürer's journal gives a lasting impression of the building's construction and magnificent altars, as well as the 'fine stonework' ('köstlich steinwerg').[58] His greatest enthusiasm, however, was reserved for the quality and the soundscape of the church services. While one drawing of the church has been preserved among his property bearing the inscription '1514. The large church in Antwerp' ('1514. Die groß kirch zu Anttorff') in Dürer's own hand, the work is not his (fig. 109).[59]

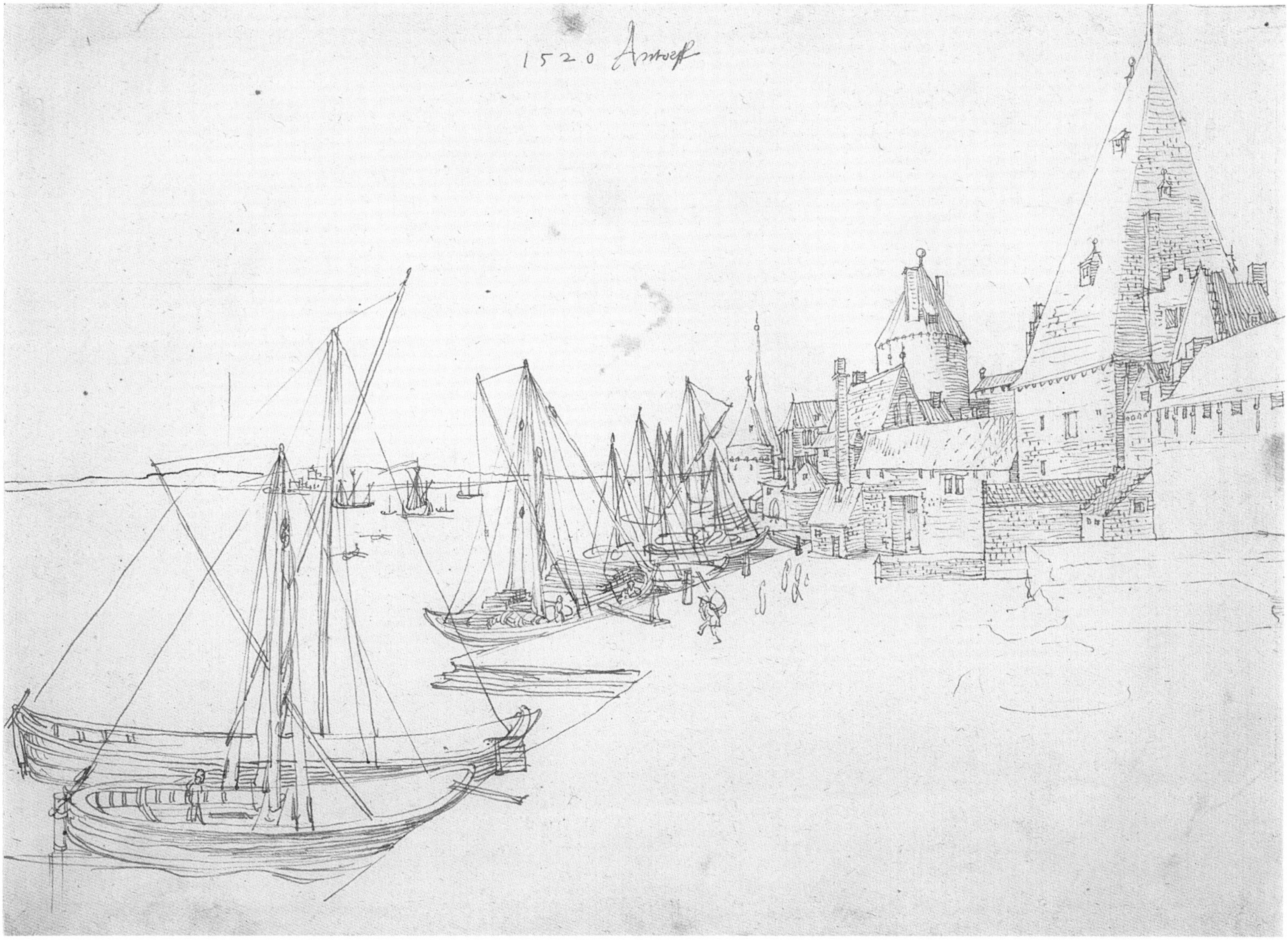

The journal also contains a written account of Dürer's visit to the zoological gardens in Brussels. This description fits perfectly with a drawing by Dürer, which shows this garden, with its labyrinth, fountain and tournament grounds (cat. 83).[60] Such parks were still a rarity in Europe

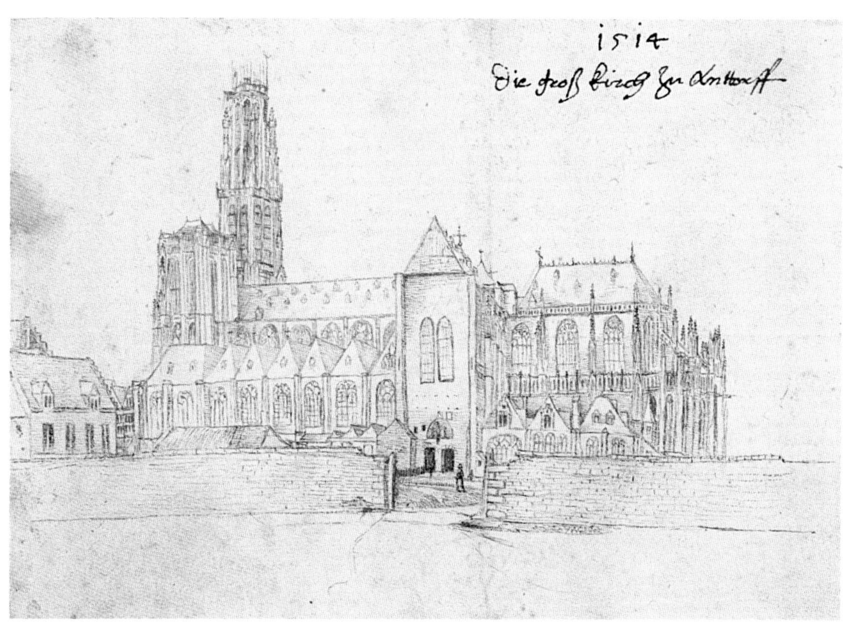

Fig. 108
ALBRECHT DÜRER
The Port in Antwerp near the Scheldepoort, 1520
Pen in brown ink, 21.3 × 28.7 cm
The Albertina Museum, Vienna (3165)

Fig. 109
ANONYMOUS ARTIST
Our Lady's Church in Antwerp, 1514
Pen and brown ink, 13 × 19.8 cm
The Albertina Museum, Vienna (3164)

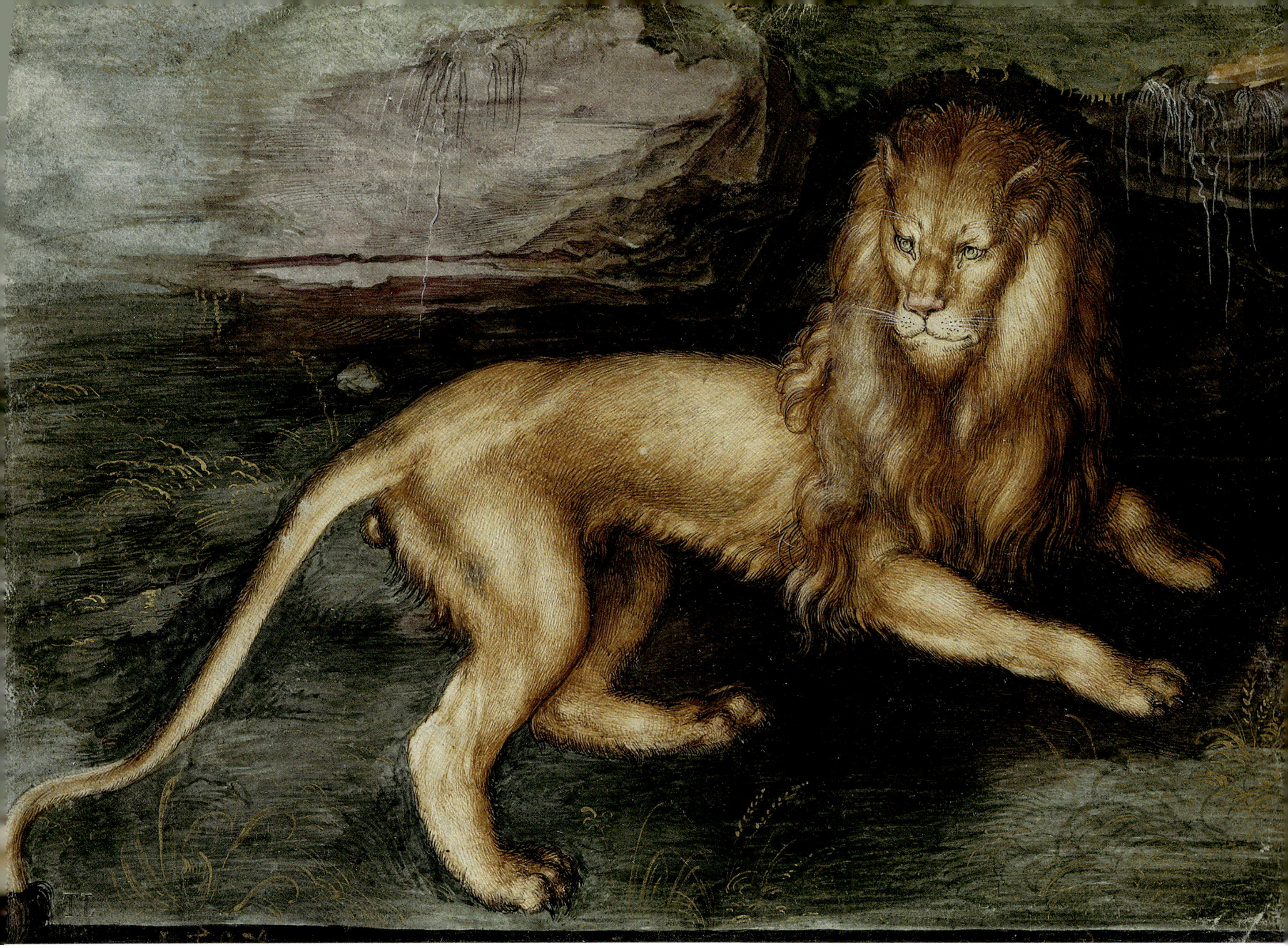

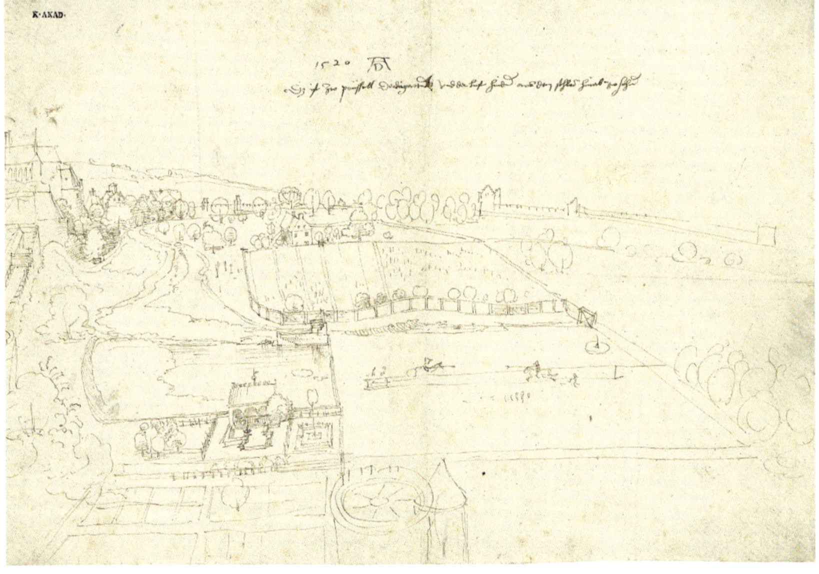

82
ALBRECHT DÜRER
A Lion, 1494
Gouache on parchment, heightened with gold, 12.6 × 17.2 cm
Hamburger Kunsthalle, Kupferstichkabinett

83
ALBRECHT DÜRER
The Brussels Zoo seen from the Royal Castle (Coudenberg Palace), 1520–1
Pen and ink on paper, 28.3 × 40 cm
Kupferstichkabinett der Akademie der bildenden Künste, Vienna

at the time: the Visconti and Gonzaga dynasties had held unusual animals since the fourteenth century, and Philip the Good founded the first of its kind north of the Alps in 1420. Around 1520 the most impressive menagerie was kept in Lisbon at the court of Manuel I, who enjoyed a virtual monopoly on overseas trade thanks to Portuguese conquests in Central and South America and East India.[61] The Holy Roman Empire also saw the establishment of animal parks.[62] While references to breeding lions in Europe do exist,[63] it seems that Dürer had not seen a living specimen before travelling to the Netherlands.[64] The animal nonetheless figures recurrently in the artist's work, and prominently as the sole motif in a landscape painted prior to Dürer's trip (cat. 82). It is the obvious model for the lion at the National Gallery's *Saint Jerome* (cat. 84), one of the few paintings from Dürer's early work to have survived. The lion appears in the painting as the attribute to the saint, in an image type that Christof Metzger has in turn set within the context of the art of the Upper Rhine valley.[65] Two other images of lions attributed to Dürer, now in Detroit and Warsaw respectively, are today viewed correctly as the work of his successors.[66] Another sheet dating from 1494/5 contains three studies of a lion's head with a marked Italian influence, much like the other drawings on the sheet (the Rape of Europa, Apollo and an Oriental figure).[67] It remains unclear whether Dürer modelled these earlier studies of lions after sculptures, paintings or prints; no direct lineage has been shown to date.[68]

Dürer's depictions of lions changed with his trip to the Netherlands as he was now able to draw studies from living animals, a fact to which his journal attests. On 10 April 1521 he notes with astonishment that he saw, and drew ('conterfeÿt'), one of the lions ('löben') in Ghent.[69] Multiple drawings have been connected with this entry, among them a depiction dating from 1521 of a standing lion,[70] a lioness[71] and silverpoint drawings now in Vienna and Berlin.[72] Another sheet with an obvious connection to Dürer's visit to the gardens has survived, showing one lion in rear view and two others, without manes and ears cropped, lying asleep (cat. 85). Whether these latter two are different lions or one and the same in different positions is unclear, as is their sex: is it a young male lion still without mane, as with the lion in *Saint Jerome in his Study* (fig. 140), or a lioness? They are accompanied by sketches of other animals, including a hamadryas baboon in colour, a chamois (a goat-antelope native to the Alpine region) and a lynx. Two landscape drawings were later additions to the sheet, of which at least parts of one were copied in reverse by Augustin Hirschvogel (1503–1553) as an independent

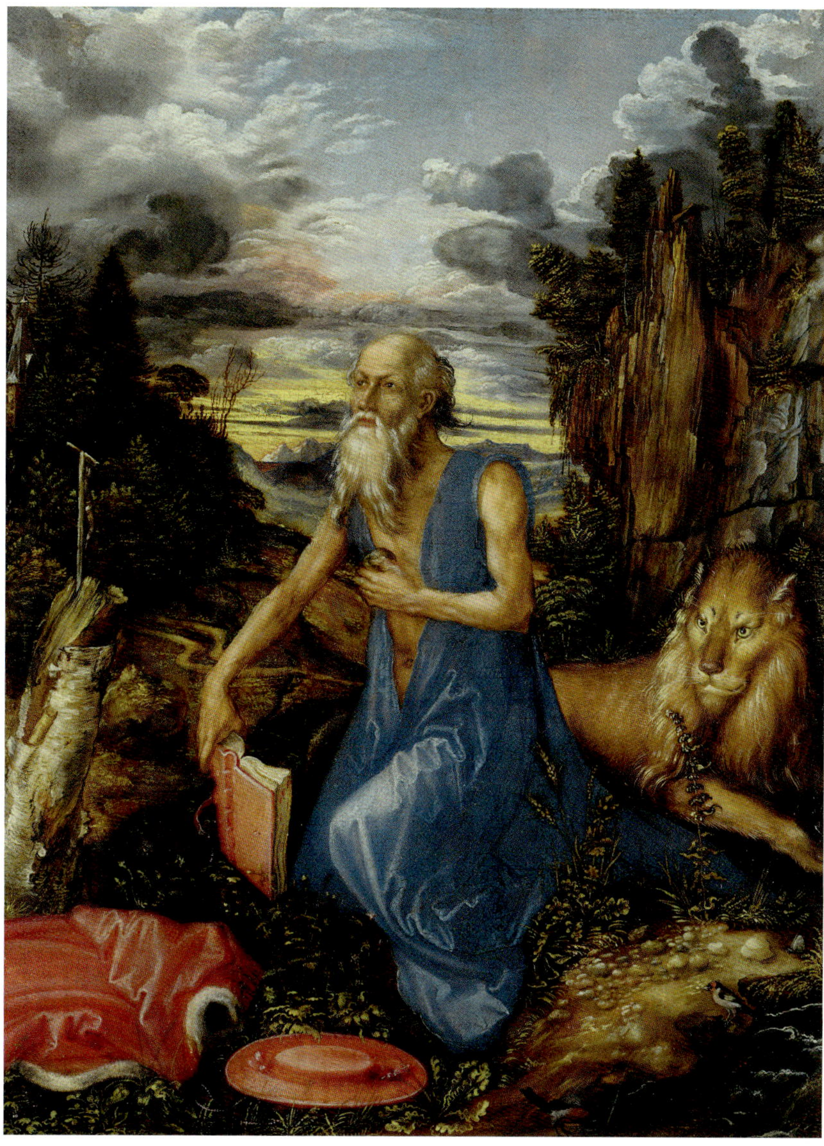

84
ALBRECHT DÜRER
Saint Jerome, about 1496
Oil on pearwood, 23.1 × 17.4 cm
The National Gallery, London

motif.[73] The topography surrounding the castle complex has not been identified: the mountains outlined in the background lead Marschall justifiably to suspect the Alpine region,[74] a landscape moreover in which the lynx and chamois would both fit in well. Nor may it have been in the Netherlands that Dürer saw his first living specimens. It remains unresolved whether or not these, too, are later additions, as Marschall supposes for the castle.

Hirschvogel's copy is not the only instance of the later use of this drawing. The animal studies and one of the castles also appear in a collected volume that Giovanna Garzoni bequeathed to the Accademia di San Luca (see fig. 83), in this case as separate images, each bearing Dürer's monogram.[75] Garzoni even replicated Dürer's original inscription above the hamadryas baboon, although it is not cut off in this case.[76] Confronted with Dürer's notoriously difficult, partially smudged

OVERLEAF
85
ALBRECHT DÜRER
Sketches of Animals and Landscapes, 1521
Pen and black ink, and blue, grey and rose wash on paper, 26.5 × 39.7 cm
Sterling and Francine Clark Art Institute, Williamstown, Massachusetts, USA

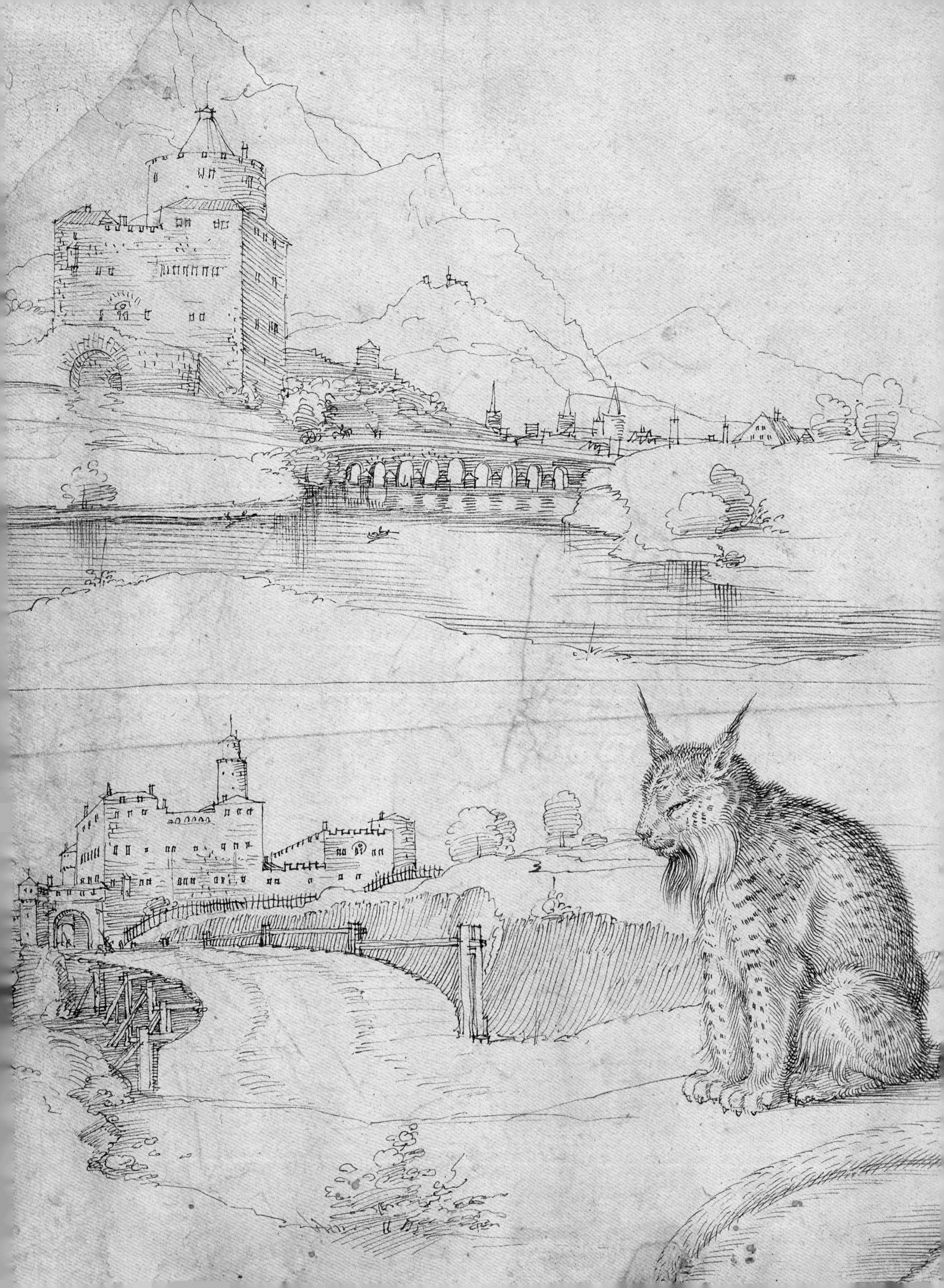

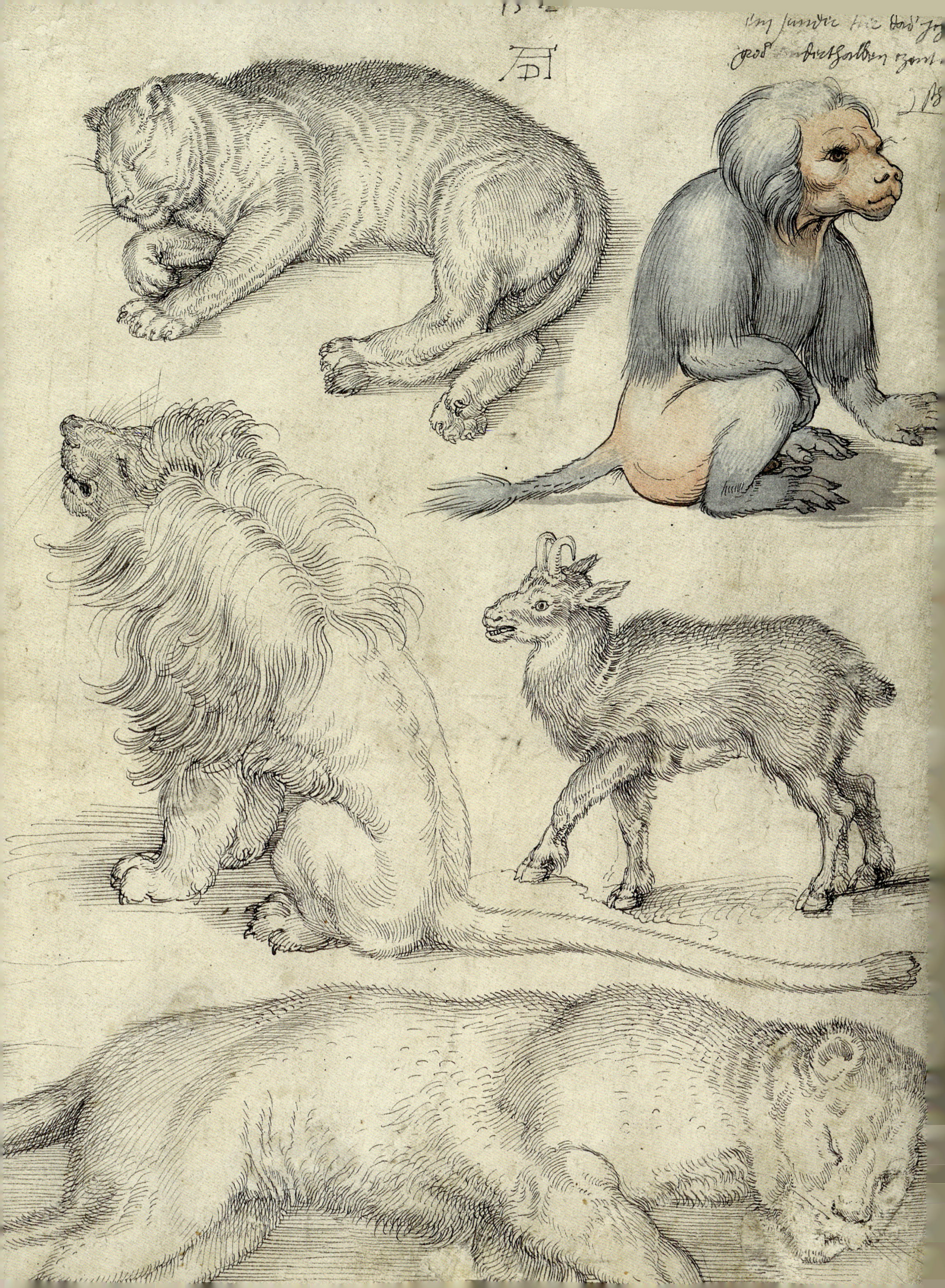

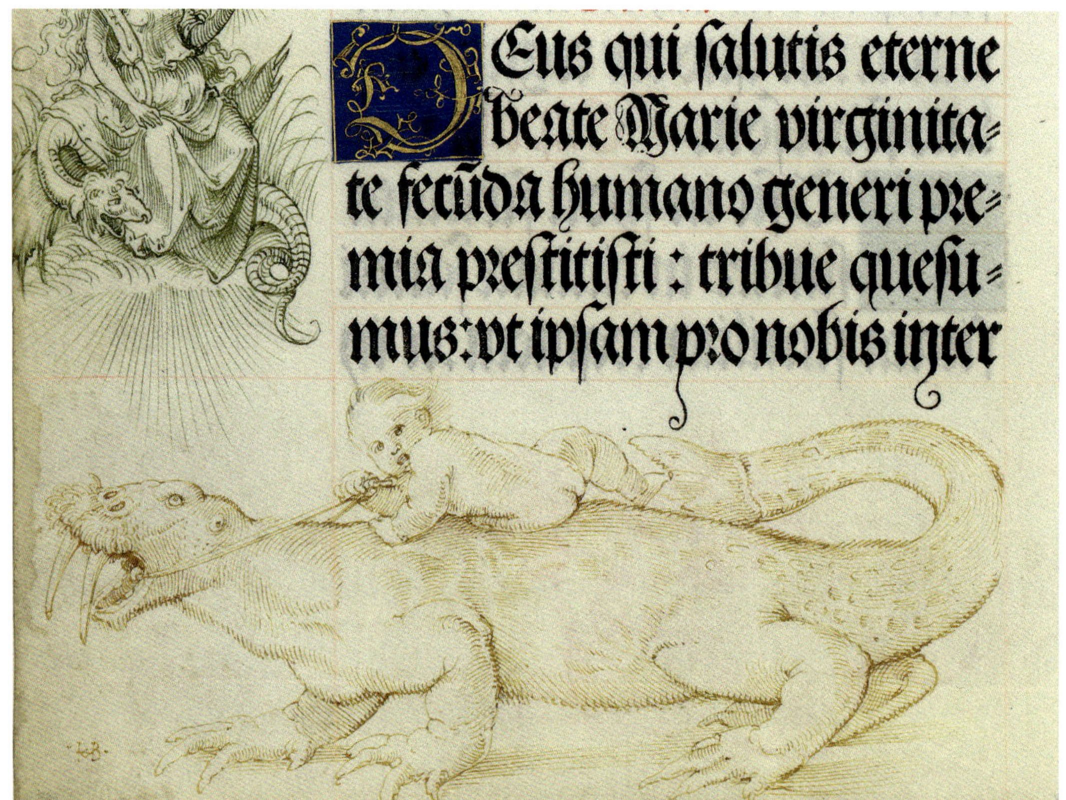
Deus qui salutis eterne
beate Marie virginita-
te fecũda humano generi pre-
mia prestitisti : tribue quesu-
mus: vt ipsam pro nobis inter

Fig. 110
HANS BALDUNG GRIEN (1484/5–1545)
Page from the *Prayer Book of Emperor Maximilian I*, about 1519
Bibliothèque municipale de Besançon

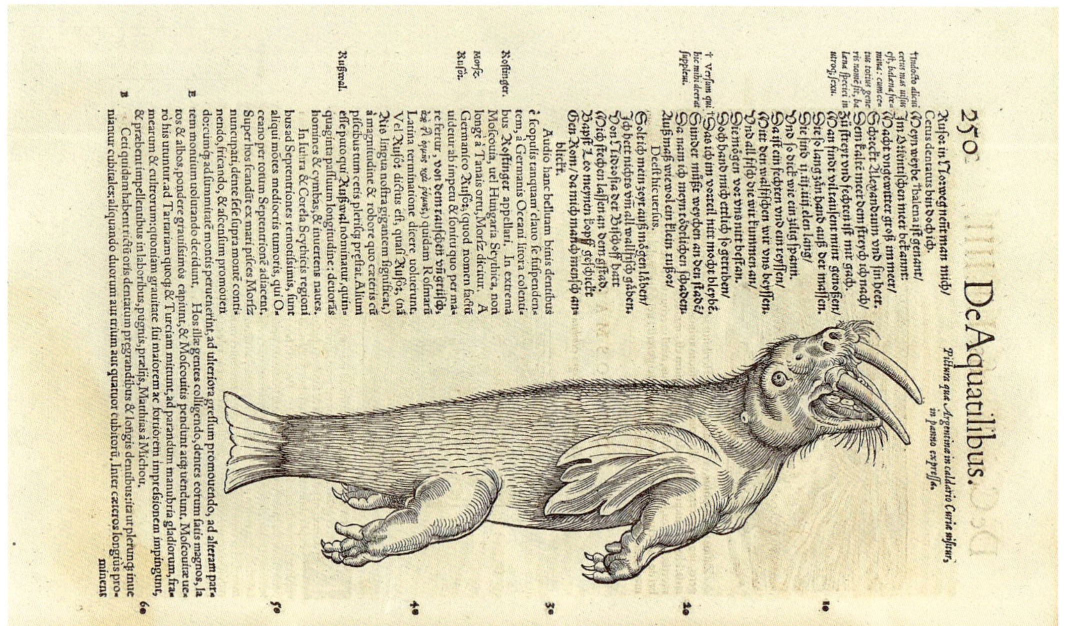
250 De Aquatilibus.

Fig. 111
CONRAD GESSNER (1516–1565)
Historiae animalium liber IV, 1551
The J. Paul Getty Museum, Los Angeles, California

handwriting, for many of the words Garzoni seems to have copied the shape of the letters but not their meaning. The wording can nonetheless now be reconstructed, and reads: 'ein sunder tür [tier] das ich sach,/ grod anderthalben zentner/schwer'.[77] A grown hamadryas baboon weighs some 30 kg, somewhat more than half a Nuremberg *zentner*, or hundredweight. Aside from his giving the weight, Dürer's interest in the baboon is signalled by his using colour for its depiction. While he mentions monkeys repeatedly in his journal, no entries can be linked to this particular drawing.

It is a striking feature of Dürer's journal that he records many more rare objects in words than in images, all the more so as he had completed his rhinoceros woodcut years earlier, in 1515, and drew images of indigenous weapons and clothing for the prayer book of Maximilian I around the same time (fig. 11).[78] The lack of non-European art by no means implies a disdain for it, as his journal entries can confirm. After seeing works of art from Central America in Brussels, for example, Dürer notes: 'I have never in my life seen anything that gave my heart such delight as these things, for I saw amongst them marvellously skilful objects and was amazed at the subtle ingeniousness of people in foreign lands.'[79] This comes as strikingly enthusiastic praise when compared to the rather reserved tone he finds for his European colleagues – if they are mentioned at all. Nonetheless, Dürer's enthusiasm was not reflected in his artistic oeuvre – at any rate, no images of these treasures, or any other kind of reference, appear in his work.

It is all the more surprising, then, that while in Strasbourg on his journey home Dürer should copy down a rare sight – a walrus – in a drawing that he would later reuse as a workshop model. The artist's annotation for the image reads: '1521/Das dosig thÿr van dem jch do das hawbt/contrefett hab ist gefangen worden/jn die niderlendischen see vnd/was XII ellen lang/brawendisch mit für fussen' (fig. 112).[80] Unlike with the hamadryas baboon, Dürer does not mention seeing the walrus for himself. This may be explained by a strikingly similar walrus found in the fourth volume of Conrad Gessner's *Historiae animalium* (fig. 111): in both drawings the animal's head is turned to the side, revealing both nostrils. Only the head could be drawn from nature;

Fig. 112
ALBRECHT DÜRER
A 'Walrus from Zeeland', 1521
Pen and brown ink, watercolour, 21.1 × 31.2 cm
British Museum (SL,5261.167)

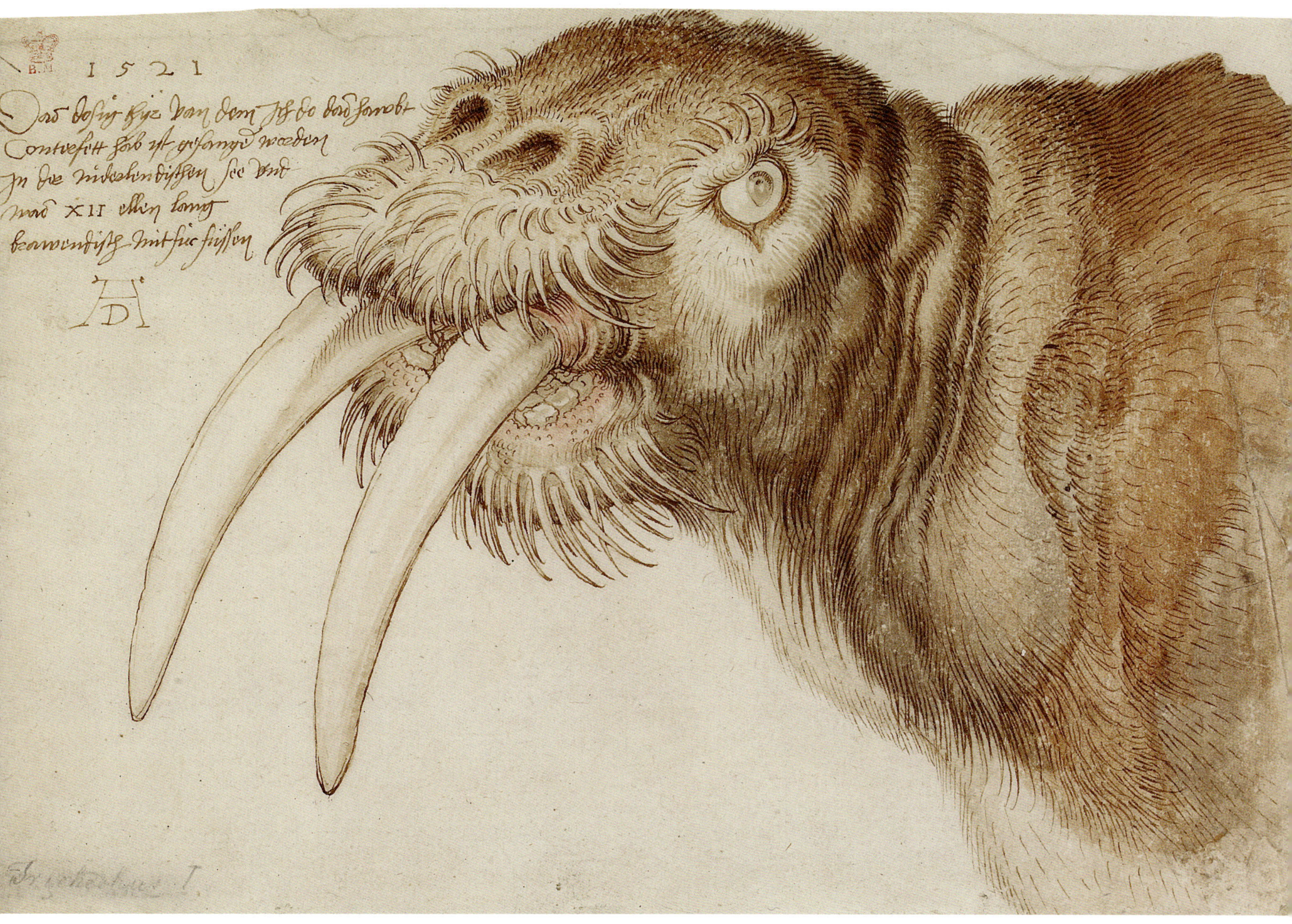

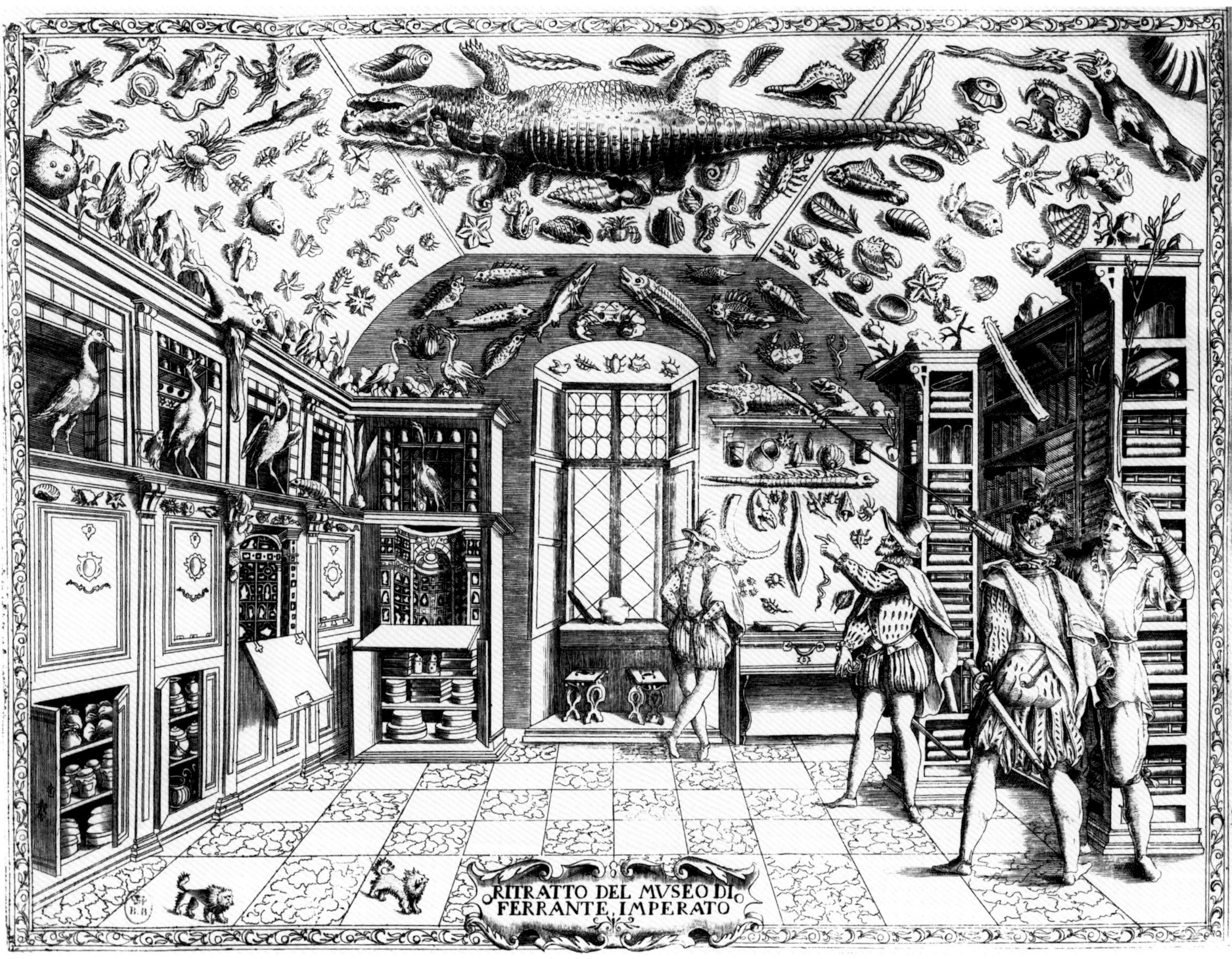

Fig. 113
FERRANTE IMPERATO
(1525–1615)
Plate from *Dell'Historia Naturale*, second edition, Venice, 1672
Engraving,
30.6 × 39.4 cm
Private collection

as Gessner reports, around 'Christmas 1519' the head of a walrus submerged in brine – a gift from the Archbishop of Trondheim, Erik von Valkendorf, to Pope Leo X – stopped over in Strasbourg on its way to Rome. The date would have been given in the 'nativity style' common at the time, which took Christmas Day to mark the new year, making it Christmas 1518 by today's reckoning. Gessner based his own work on a painting in Strasbourg town hall, which has since been lost; the animal is said to have measured 28 ft (over 8 m) in length, according to a poem on the painting that Gessner reproduced along with his image.[81] Dürer apparently converted this into the measurement standard for Nuremberg at the time, calculating 12 ells to arrive at approximately the same length. His interest clearly lay exclusively with a naturalistic representation of the head, as he would otherwise have added an imagined body. The painting in Strasbourg may have come from Hans Baldung Grien, who drew a walrus in the prayer book of Maximilian I directly after the animals passed Strasbourg in 1518–19 (fig. 110).[82]

Dürer dated his walrus with the year 1521, making it conceivable that he stopped off in Strasbourg on his way back to Nuremberg from Cologne, the final place mentioned in his journal. Whether Dürer based his version of the extraordinary creature on Baldung's or that of another artist remains obscure. In 1522 he incorporated the walrus into his *sacra conversazione*, setting at the Virgin's feet (fig. 66). The Strasbourg image of the walrus may already have achieved some notoriety; by the time of Gessner's account, however, it had acquired international repute, even if it has largely been forgotten today. In 1599 it appears with a body on the ceiling of Ferrante Imperatos's cabinet of curiosities (fig. 113),[83] hardly as a real animal in this case but in reminiscence of the famous walrus of Strasbourg.

1 The subsequent watercolour series *Design for Court Dress* (1515–17), today in the Albertina, Vienna (invs 3146–8), forms the male 'pendant' to the costume studies. Strauss 1974, vol. 3, no. 1517/10–13.
2 Städel Museum, Frankfurt, inv. 696. Strauss 1974, vol. 1, nos 1495–6; Frankfurt 2003, pp. 74–6, no. 20; Vienna 2019, no. 66.
3 See also *Saint Catherine* (cat. 25) illustrated on p. 66 in the present publication, as well as Dürer's pen-and-ink drawing from 1495, *Venetian Woman* (Albertina, Vienna, inv. 3064r), Strauss 1974, vol. 1, no. 1495/4; Vienna 2019, no. 65.
4 See Joseph Koerner's article in the present publication, pp. 43–57.
5 T. Eser, 'Gewandstudien und Sittenbilder: Dürers frühe Kostümdarstellungen', in Nuremberg 2012, p. 367.
6 Vienna 2019, p. 180.
7 Ibid., p. 180.
8 Ashcroft 2017, vol. 1, no. 162, p. 583.
9 Samuel Muller and Jan Veth see a direct connection between the two drawings: see Veth and Muller 1918, vol. 1, p. 44.
10 T. Eser in Nuremberg 2012, p. 367.
11 See also in this connection a drawing formerly in the Kunsthalle, Bremen (inv. Kl 59, *Kriegsverlust* [*Wartime Loss*]), now missing: Albrecht Dürer, *Woman kneeling on a Prayer Stool*, 1508–10 (pen and ink, 16 × 10.4 cm). The sheet likely dated from the time of Dürer's trip to the Netherlands.
12 Flechsig maintains that Dürer completed the drawing at a later point, continuing to work on it in the context of his women's costumes from Nuremberg and adding current material from Flanders and Brabant. See Flechsig 1928–31, vol. 2, p. 226. For his part, Christof Metzger finds it more likely that Dürer would have kept a stock of workshop templates, which in turn would have curtailed his free use of imagination. See Vienna 2019, p. 180.
13 Ashcroft 2017, vol. 1, no. 162, p. 569. On 3 December 1520, Dürer writes: 'Note: At Bergen bought my wife thin Dutch cloth for a headdress, cost 1 gulden 7 stuivers.'
14 See Flechsig 1928–31, vol. 2, p. 232; Strauss 1974, vol. 4, no. 1521/23; M. Mende in Vienna 2003, p. 498, no. 175.
15 Ashcroft 2017, vol. 1, no. 162, p. 612 n. 248. See also Peter van den Brink's article in the present publication, pp. 205–25.
16 Ashcroft 2017, vol. 1, no. 162, p. 558.
17 Ibid., no. 162, p. 558.
18 Ibid., no. 163.22, p. 634.
19 Loschek 1988, p. 454.
20 Ibid., p. 299.
21 Mentges 2015, p. 144.
22 A. Moraht-Fromm, 'Knopf und Kragen. Zu Kostüm und Accessoire im deutschen Porträt um 1500', in Vienna and Munich 2011, pp. 273–308, at p. 273.
23 Albrecht Dürer, *Irish Warriors and Peasants*, 1521. Kupferstichkabinett, Staatliche Museen zu Berlin, inv. KdZ 37.
24 Busch 1931, p. 7. Livonia is a historical geographical designation for present-day Estonia and Latvia.
25 J.M. Massing in Washington 1991, p. 301, no. 208; on Jobst Plankfelt see Unverfehrt 2007, p. 33.
26 Hans Weigel, *Habitus praecipuorum populorum* …, Nuremberg 1577, fol. 37/L, fol. 38/L I, fol. 39/L II.
27 Mende 1969, p. 28.
28 Jost Amman, *Im Frauwenzimmer Wirt vermeldt von allerley schönen Kleidungen und Trachten der Weiber* …, Frankfurt 1586, Bl.r S, S ij and S iij.
29 Cesare Vecellio, *De gli Habiti antichi et moderni di diverse parti del mondo*, Venice 1590.
30 Mentges 2015, p. 149.
31 See Hampe 1927. For more on Dürer's costume studies see Susanne Gattineau, "Die Trachtenstudien von Albrecht Dürer," Master's Thesis, University of Munich 1988; on the history of costume also see Rublack, Hayward and Tiramani 2015.
32 Mentges 2015, p. 145.
33 Erichsen 2019, p. 1.
34 See Augsburg 2019, cats 103, 104.
35 Mende 1969, p. 36.
36 Loschek 1988, p. 210.
37 See Giulia Bartrum's article in the present publication, pp. 267–76.
38 See Arnold Nesselrath's article in the present publication, pp. 165–83.
39 Albrecht Altdorfer, page from the *Prayer Book of Emperor Maximilian I*, fol. dd3v, 1515. Bibliothèque municipale de Besançon, inv. Res. 67633. See Lange-Krach 2017, vol. 1, pp. 83–4; vol. 2, p. 242.
40 On the history of pen-and-ink sketches, see Christof Metzger's article in the present publication, pp. 149–63. The sheets resemble each other in style, technique and format, and for the most part measure approximately 16 × 11 cm.
41 Albrecht Dürer, *Descent from the Cross*, about 1520; pen and brown ink, 14.6 × 10.3 cm (Musée des Beaux-Arts et d'Archéologie, Besançon, inv. D 256). In this context see van den Brink 2020.
42 *Portrait of Arnold Rucker of Seligenstadt, sleeping*, 1520 ('meistr ornolt von d … /Selgenstat 1520/AD' (top right); pen and brown ink, 12.3 × 9.9 cm (Musée Bonnat, Bayonne, inv. 1514). Strauss 1974, vol. 4, no. 1520/7; Ashcroft 2017, vol. 1, no. 162, p. 552; Unverfehrt 2007, p. 26. On Arnold Rucker, see Gottron 1962.
43 Strauss 1974, vol. 4, no. 1520/6.
44 Zander-Seidel 1990, p. 183.
45 'Done on the Rhine, 1521', Ashcroft 2017, vol. 1, no. 163.33, p. 638.
46 Strauss 1974, vol. 4, no. 1521/56.
47 Flechsig 1928–31, vol. 2, p. 211.
48 Winkler 1936–9, vol. 4, pp. 7, 744.
49 Strauss 1974, vol. 4, no. 1521/58, p. 2098. Hans and Erica Tietze believe the cloak to belong to the order; Panofsky, however, supposes that Dürer's travel companion served as the model for an Our Lady of Sorrows.
50 Ashcroft 2017, vol. 1, no. 162, p. 590; Rupprich 1956–69, vol. 1, p. 178.
51 Rupprich 1956–69, vol. 1, p. 202 n. 765.
52 Strauss 1974, vol. 4, nos 1521/55 and 1521/56.
53 Flechsig 1928–31, vol. 2, p. 473, nos L. VII, 879 and 880. The drawings were previously housed in the Kunstakademie, Düsseldorf.
54 Sold Christie's, New York, 24 January 2006 (lot 55).
55 School of Dürer, *The Head of a Bearded Man, facing Left*, about 1510–30; pen and brown ink, 11 × 78 cm (Royal Collection, Windsor Castle, inv. RCIN 912174).
56 Hirschfelder 2013, p. 112. Hirschfelder does not start from the premise that the drawings were assembled together in a sketchbook, as most of the sheets were used only on one side and nearly all bear the artist's monogram.
57 Ashcroft 2017, vol. 1, no. 162, pp. 554–9, 561–4, 567–9, 571–7.
58 Ibid., p. 557.
59 Evers 1974, pp. 243–4.
60 Frankfurt 2013, cat. 14.8.
61 See Berlin 2007, pp. 502–3; Gschwend 2015, pp. 11–24.
62 Werner 2013, pp. 17–18.
63 Feichtner 2011, p. 241.
64 David 1909, p. 79.
65 Vienna 2019, p. 100.
66 *Recumbent Lion*, n.d.; brush and brown ink with touches of watercolour on paper, 12.4 × 17.8 cm (Detroit Institute of Arts, inv. 1934.158). Strauss 1974, vol. 1, p. 234, no. 1494/18. The Warsaw copy is held in the library of the University of Warsaw; see Strauss 1974, vol. 4, p. 42; Winkler 1936–9, vol. 1, p. 246. My thanks to Christof Metzger for this reference.
67 Albertina, Vienna, inv. 3062. H. Widauer in Vienna 2003, pp. 168–9, cat. 25, and p. 199, cat. 73. For more lions in Dürer's work, see David 1909, p. 107. David does not mention the lioness from Paris discussed by C. Metzger in Vienna 2019, cat. 47: Musée du Louvre, Paris, Collection Rothschild, inv. 16 D.R.
68 See Stubbe 1967, p. 30; Eisler 1991, pp. 140–2; Hamburg 2001, pp. 136–7, cat. 63; H. Widauer in Vienna 2003, p. 168, cat. 25; Vienna 2019, pp. 197–8.
69 Ashcroft 2017, vol. 1, no. 162, p. 578; Rupprich 1956–69, vol. 1, p. 168, l. 73.
70 Albertina, Vienna, inv. 3173; Vienna 2019, cat. 47.
71 See note 68.
72 See Arnold Nesselrath's article in the present publication, figs 94, 95.
73 Augustin Hirschvogel, *River Landscape with Two Buildings Connected by a Bridge*, 1545. British Museum, London, inv. E,4.426. Frankfurt 2013, p. 350, cat. 14.8.
74 Ibid.
75 Cipriani 1976, pp. 241–4. Cipriani suspects Garzoni herself to have owned Dürer's drawing. She is followed in this by Roccasecca 2011. In this context, see Christof Metzger's article in the present publication, pp. 149–63.
76 Policicchio 2018, p. 226, cats 48.23–48.29.
77 'An extraordinary [animal] … Large, one-and-a-half hundredweight … heavy …', Ashcroft 2017, vol. 1, no. 163.31, p. 637.
78 Lange-Krach 2017, vol. 1, p. 46; vol. 2, p. 89.
79 Ashcroft 2017, vol. 1, no. 162, p. 560.
80 'This animal of those parts, whose head I have drawn here, was caught in the Netherlandish sea and was twelve Brabant ells long with four feet', Ashcroft 2017, vol. 1, no. 163.26, p. 636.
81 Conrad Gessner, *Historiae animalium Liber IIII. qui est de Piscium & Aquatilium animantium natura. Christof Froschauer*, Zurich 1558, p. 248.
82 Karlsruhe 2019, p. 180, cat. 109.
83 Ferrante Imperato, *Dell'Historia Naturale*, Naples 1599.

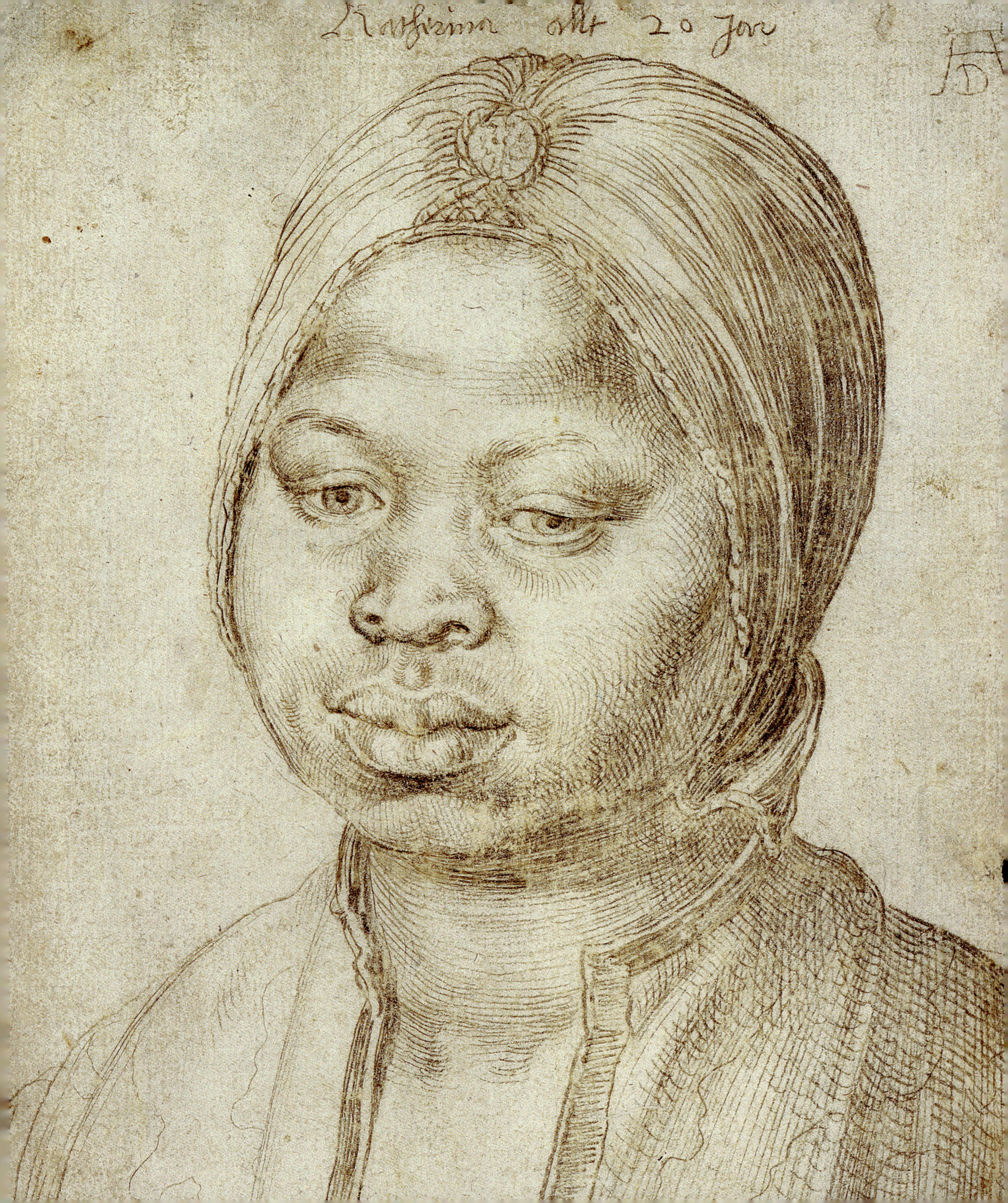
Katherina allt 20 Jor
AD

PETER VAN DEN BRINK

PORTRAIT DRAWINGS OF A TRAVELLING ARTIST
ALBRECHT DÜRER'S CREATIVE ENTERPRISE IN THE LOW COUNTRIES

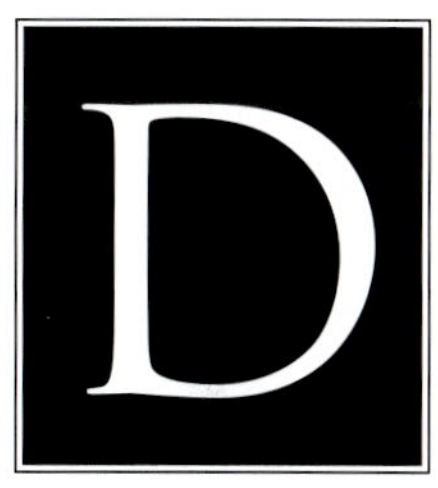

During his sojourn in the Low Countries Albrecht Dürer created a new market by producing large portrait drawings, sometimes mounted on panels, according to a specific format that made these drawings look like replacements for painted portraits. It was a very effective marketing strategy and he produced more than eighty of these finished works of art for clients and friends, but he used them especially as gifts within the so-called honour system.[1] Apart from Lucas van Leyden, no other painter adopted this marketing strategy. Dürer kept track of these portraits in a check-and-balance system recorded in his journal, unlike his smaller pen portraits. These were either replicas after large finished drawings or swift, informal portraits he kept for his own records, which would end up as part of his *Nachlass* (legacy). Dürer also made silverpoint portrait drawings, either as gifts for friends or colleagues, such as Jan Provoost, Joachim Patinir and Lucas van Leyden (fig. 118), or for study purposes, such as the drawing of the young black servant, Katharina (fig. 119). His small silverpoint book with many portraits was a treasure trove and he mentioned it time and again, out of pride rather than economic necessity. When looking at both the written journal and the surviving portraits, new angles with regard to identification and date emerge, leading to some new hypotheses.

In her excellent article of 2013 Dagmar Hirschfelder focused on the potential Dürer's portrait drawings had within his network and how these works of art helped him to achieve his goals. She presents the various social groups portrayed by Dürer, whether countrymen from Augsburg or Nuremberg, merchants from Portugal or Italy, innkeepers, fellow artists or influential people from the households of Margaret of Austria and Charles V, whom he sought to persuade to reinstate his annual imperial income of 100 guilders.[2] The portrait drawings functioned within his check-and-balance system not simply as works of art that he was able to sell for money – although that most certainly happened – but also as tools to obtain services from those portrayed or in return for gifts or invitations. The monetary value of Dürer's portrait

Detail from *Katharina, the 20-Year-Old Servant of João Brandão* (fig. 119)

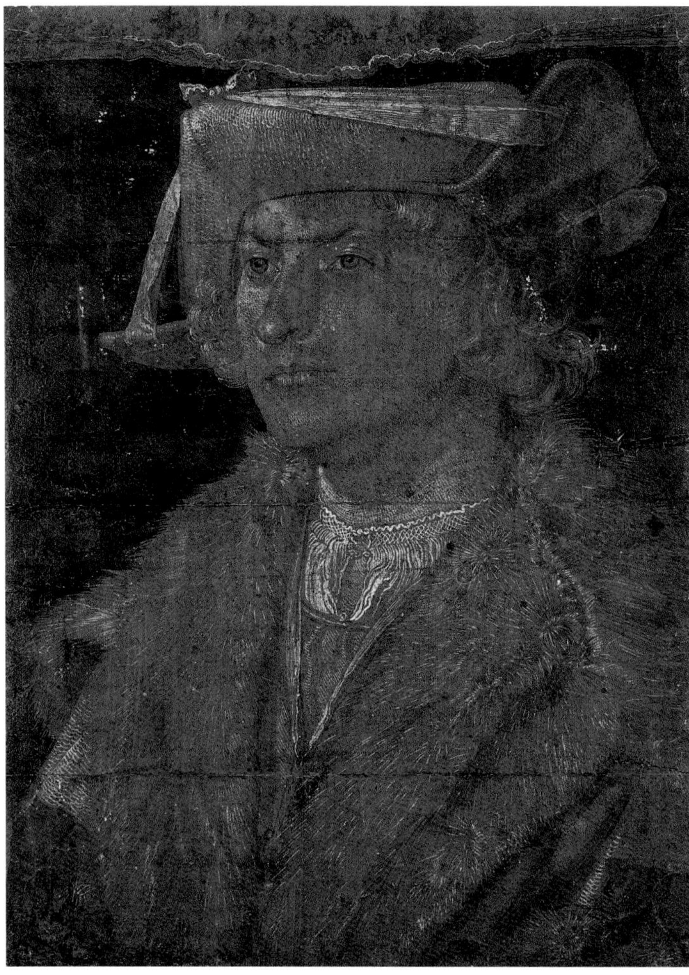

Fig. 114
ALBRECHT DÜRER
Portrait of Rodrigo Fernandes de Almada, 1521
Brush on grey-violet grounded paper, heightened with white, 37.3 × 27.1 cm
Staatliche Museen zu Berlin, Kupferstichkabinett (KdZ 40)

drawings could be estimated at between one and two guilders apiece, although in his view the real value of these precious gifts could not be expressed in terms of money.[3] This essay will try to reflect on the sheer magnitude of Albrecht Dürer's undertaking, as well as the connection between his journal and the drawings themselves.

Dürer's Netherlandish journal mentions 116 portraits produced during his journey to the Low Countries: 109 drawings and seven paintings.[4] By far the most explicit references are to portraits he presented as gifts to the sitters. Most of the drawings were executed in charcoal, some in black chalk and a few in metalpoint (*stefft*). One portrait drawing was made with the brush in black ink and white bodycolour. This is the impressive and exquisite *Portrait of Rodrigo Fernandes de Almada* made in late March 1521 (fig. 114).[5]

Dürer's journal functioned not as a diary but as a notebook in which he kept track of his profits and expenses and the balance between the two. He noted all transactions, including those in kind. Thus every work of art that had commercial value and was used by the artist in the aforementioned gift culture is *de facto* mentioned, as follows from a passage in the journal. On his first visit to Brussels a spark of frustration appears: 'Item: Six people have given me nothing for doing their portraits in Brussels'.[6] According to his journal, Dürer produced seven portrait drawings that week, three during an evening session with Conrad Meit and three at a lavish banquet organised by Bernaert van Orley a few days later, at which Dürer depicted his host and Erasmus of Rotterdam. Jean de Marnix, advisor and treasurer to Margaret of Austria, who was also present at this dinner, had been portrayed a day or two earlier. None of these sitters paid Dürer for their portrait – except van Orley of course, whose banquet the artist valued at 10 guilders, an exceptionally high sum. Dürer regarded the fact that the others gave him nothing as both an economic failure and a personal insult, since none seemed to realise or value the honour he bestowed upon them by drawing their portraits.

THE PEN DRAWINGS

Works of art that Dürer kept for himself held no relevance for the journal. Therefore, portrait drawings in pen and ink are not mentioned, with the notable exception of the portrait he made for Felix Hungersperg's *Album Amicorum*.[7] This is probably not the pen drawing now in the Albertina (cat. 86), which may have been part of Dürer's legacy and therefore likely a replica he produced for himself.[8] All other portrait drawings in pen and ink, six of which are still known today, were probably part of his journal.[9] Of these all but one are of almost identical size, and all were drawn on one side only, possibly in case the ink leaked through.[10] These pen drawings contain additional information about the sitters, unlike Dürer's large portraits in charcoal and black chalk. From the nature of these original inscriptions it is clear that the drawings were intended to remain with the artist and are not therefore mentioned in his journal.

All Dürer's pen portraits are dated 1520 and three of the sitters are identified by the artist. The first was his host in Antwerp, innkeeper Jobst Plankfelt (cat. 88). This drawing, unfortunately water-damaged, carries an inscription identifying the sitter: 'This is my landlord in Antwerp/Jobst Plankfelt 1520'.[11] The drawing is not the same as the large charcoal drawing mentioned in the journal on 6 or 7 August 1520:[12] it may be a replica but there is no way to be certain. Since the sitters he portrayed in pen and ink are mentioned in the journal, each with a large portrait, it is possible that some of the pen drawings were indeed replicas.

Although the portrait of Hans Pfaffrot (fig. 115) is somewhat marred by brown staining, it is characterised by a subtle refinement. This is Dürer's finest portrait in pen and brown ink, a combination of superlative linework

– as in the parallel strokes of the sitter's hair and the various areas of hatching – with a true sense of tranquillity in the reflective eyes and the subtly drawn nose, expertly rendered by mere suggestion. The drawing is inscribed: 'Hans Pfaffrot of Danzig 1520 a strong man'.[13] A native of the Rhineland area and apparently some sort of troubleshooter, Pfaffrot worked for the Portuguese factor Francisco Pesão, who had instructed him to retrieve consignments of goods confiscated from Portuguese merchants by their Danzig counterparts in Reval (Tallinn).[14] By August 1520 Pfaffrot had returned to Antwerp, where Dürer portrayed him in charcoal.[15]

The liveliest of all seven pen portraits is that of the one-eyed lutenist and captain of the imperial guard, Felix Hungersperg (cat. 87). The powerful pen strokes point to a swiftness of execution that is absent in the refined portrait of Hans Pfaffrot. Dürer noted in his journal: 'Item: I made a second portrait of Felix the lutenist'.[16] It is unlikely that this small pen portrait was a copy after the drawing he made between 7 and 19 August 1520, since it was apparently made on an earlier occasion. The inscription seems to fit a first encounter rather well: 'This is Captain Felix, the exquisite lutenist, done at Antwerp 1520'.[17]

The identification of the sitters in two other pen portraits, now in Berlin (fig. 116) and Vienna (cat. 89), is not as clear-cut. The former is inscribed 'a goldsmith from Mechelen, done in Antwerp 1520'.[18] During his journey Dürer portrayed four different goldsmiths. He connected very easily to this profession; his own father, his brother Endres and his cousin Niclas were goldsmiths, while his own talent for engraving had emerged during his early training in his father's Nuremberg workshop. Of the four goldsmiths he drew, three are actually linked by Dürer himself to the towns of Brussels, Bruges and Antwerp.[19] The fourth was Stefano Capello, whom he had portrayed in Antwerp during the last week of November 1520 in return for a cedarwood rosary; this was no doubt a large portrait drawing in charcoal or black chalk.[20] The inscription on the small pen drawing seems to point in the direction of this Capello, a jeweller and goldsmith in the service of Margaret of Austria.[21] It is known that in 1529 Capello actually lived in Antwerp and not in Mechelen, but the reference in the inscription might refer to Margaret's court.[22] It may seem odd that Dürer refers to Capello with his full name in the journal but only as a goldsmith from Mechelen on the pen drawing,[23] but it should not be forgotten that he may have added inscriptions to his pen drawings immediately, whereas the notes in his journal may date from a few days after he made the portraits. Moreover, it is possible that this drawing, like that of Felix Hungersperg (cat. 87), which displays the same swift and dynamic characteristics, was actually drawn earlier than the large portrait he made at the end of November, and was likewise intended as a private souvenir of a first encounter.

The portrait of a young lady from Brussels (cat. 89) carries the inscription '1520/done in Brussels',[24] a reference to Dürer's first excursion to Brussels, between 27 August and 2 September 1520. The young woman can possibly be identified as Berthelmine le Paige, Conrad Meit's wife, whom he portrayed in a drawing session at night: 'I did a night-time portrait by candlelight of Master Konrad who gave hospitality to my lords in Brussels. And at the same time I did a charcoal drawing of Dr Lamparter's son, also the host's wife'.[25] If the Albertina pen drawing was actually a replica made on the spot, Dürer must have reached the limits of his physical capacity: of all his pen-and-ink portraits this is the least inspired.

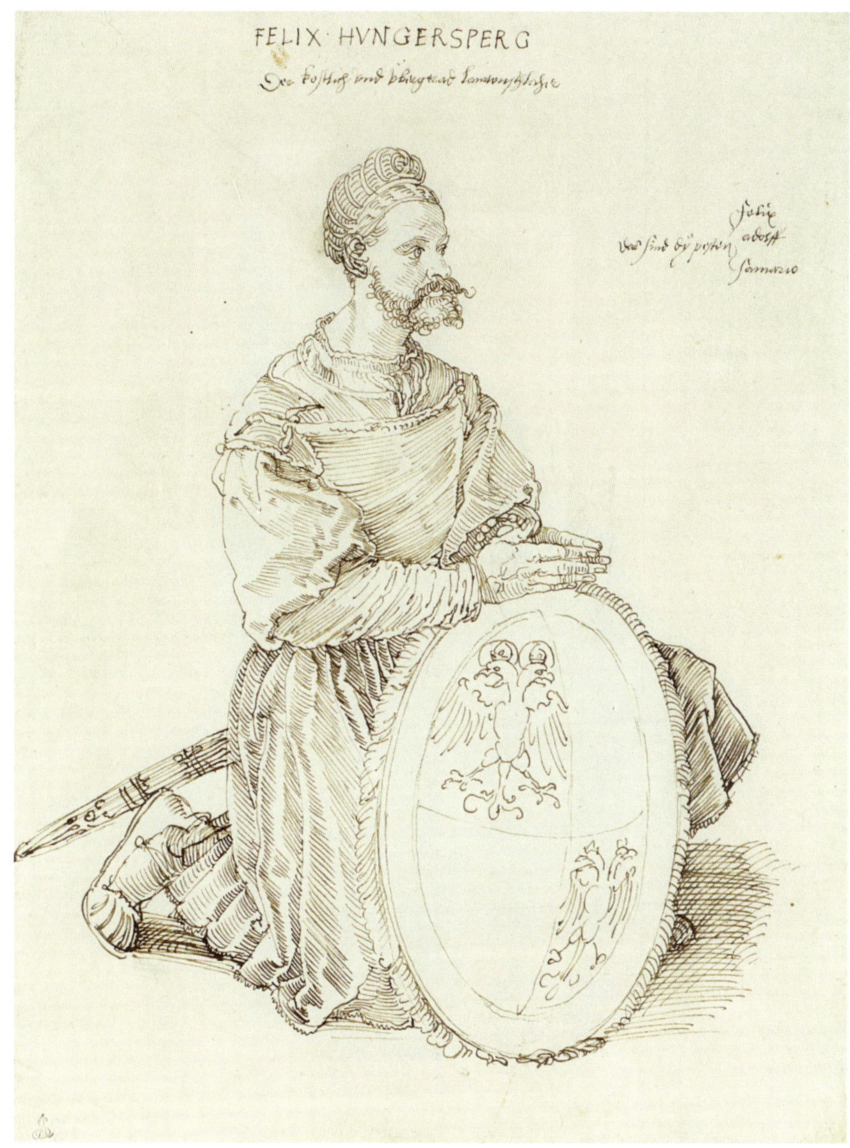

86
ALBRECHT DÜRER
The Imperial Captain Felix Hungersperg in Full Figure, 1520
Pen and brown ink on paper, 27.8 × 20.8 cm
The Albertina Museum, Vienna

87
ALBRECHT DÜRER
The Imperial Captain Felix Hungersperg, 1520
Pen and brown ink,
16 × 10.5 cm
The Albertina Museum,
Vienna

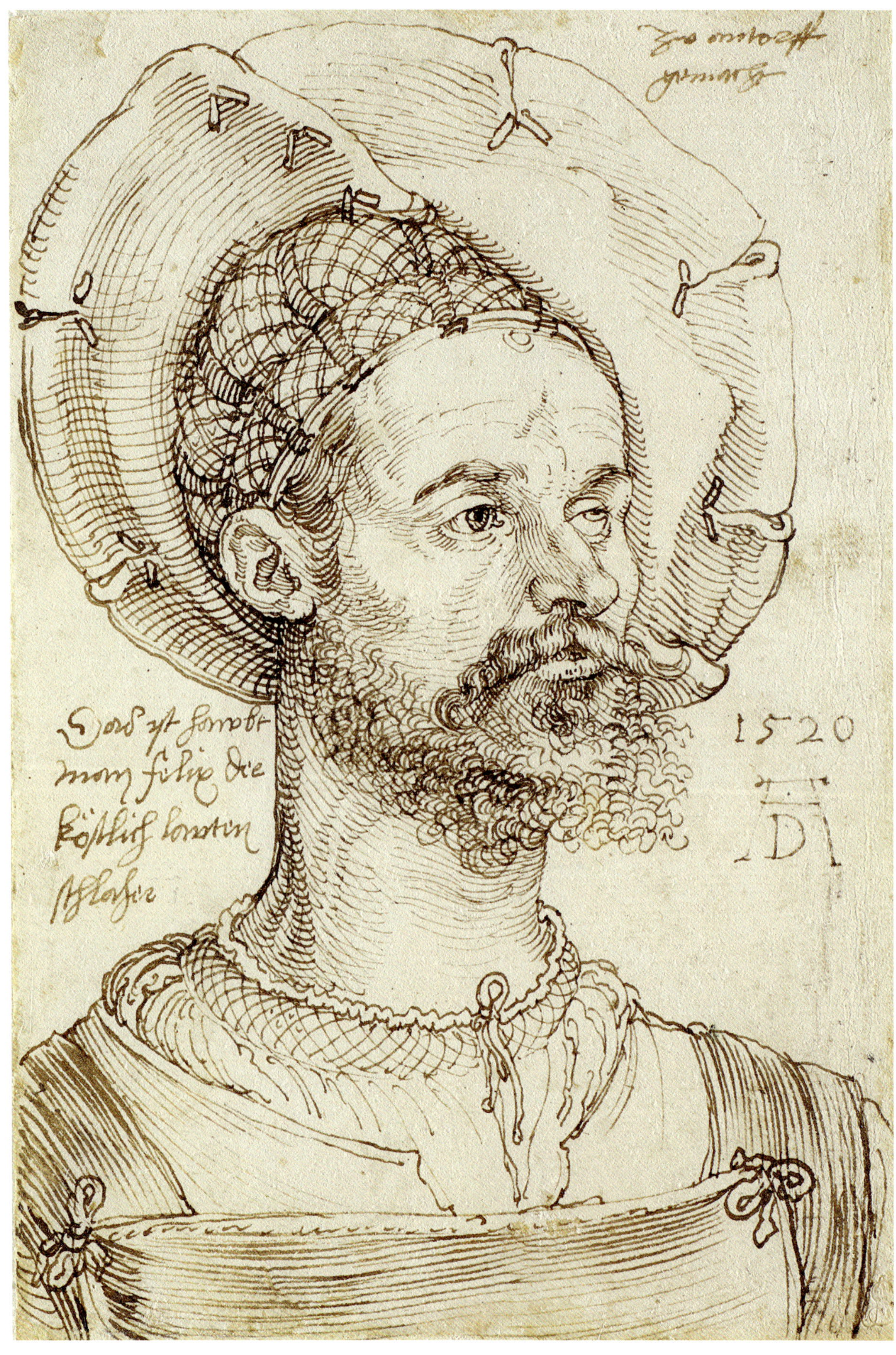

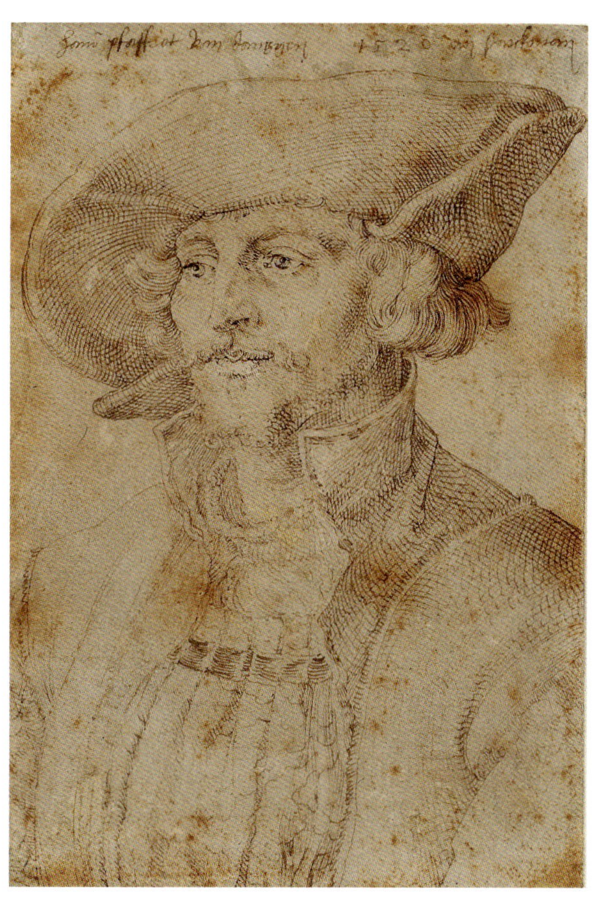

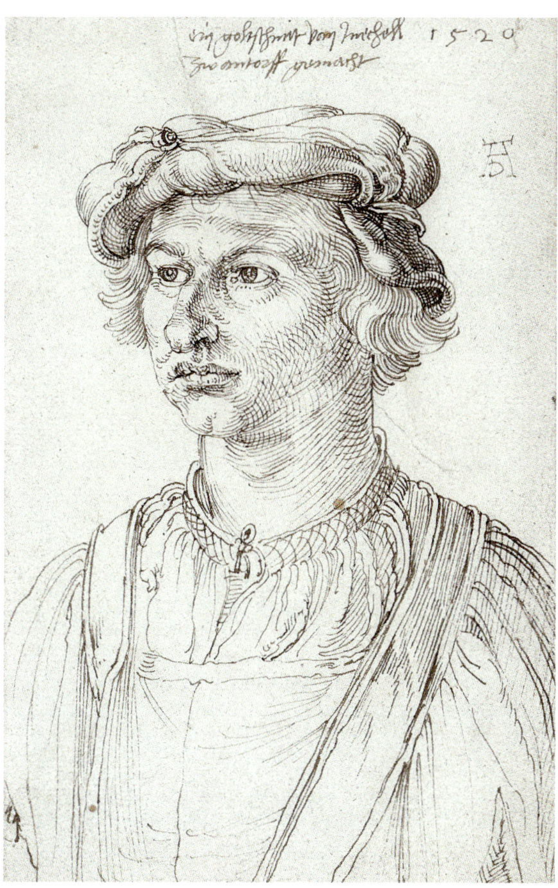

Fig. 115
ALBRECHT DÜRER
Portrait of Hans Pfaffrot from Danzig, 1520
Pen and brown ink,
16.1 × 10.6 cm
Musée du Louvre, Paris, département des Arts graphiques, collection Edmond de Rothschild (13DR)

Fig. 116
ALBRECHT DÜRER
A Goldsmith from Mechelen, possibly Stefano Capello, 1520
Pen and brown ink,
15.9 × 10.1 cm
Staatliche Museen zu Berlin, Kupferstichkabinett (KdZ 4009)

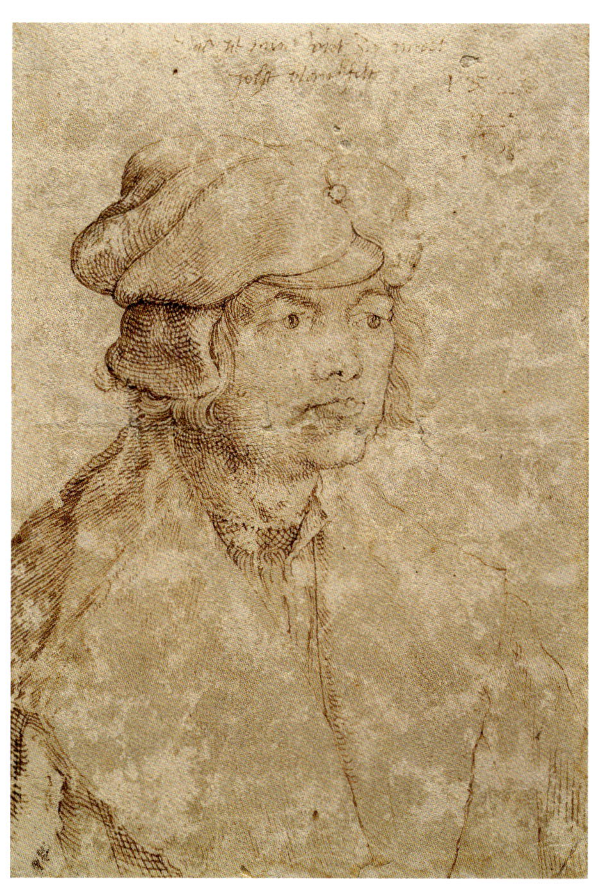

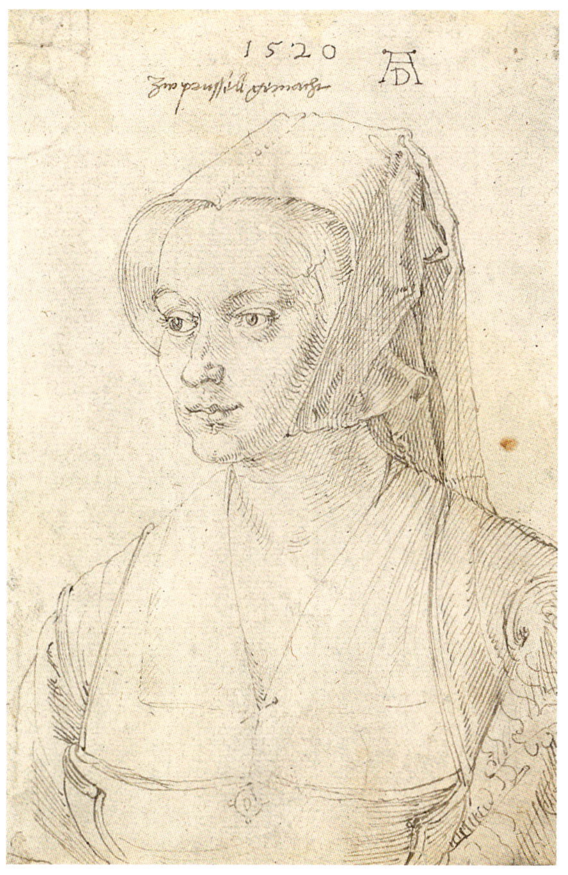

88
ALBRECHT DÜRER
Portrait of Jobst Plankfelt, 1520
Pen and brown ink on paper, 15.8 × 10.5 cm
Städel Museum, Frankfurt am Main

89
ALBRECHT DÜRER
Lady from Brussels, 1520
Pen and brown ink,
16 × 10.5 cm
The Albertina Museum, Vienna

PORTRAIT DRAWINGS WITH THE STYLUS

Dürer mentions some twenty metalpoint portrait drawings in his journal. Nineteen individual portraits drawn with a stylus have survived[26] – although this does not mean that all his silverpoint portrait drawings are extant. Many of these he drew in a small book. It was a work of art in its own right, combining silverpoint portraits drawn from life with landscapes or townscapes, to create new compositions, and Dürer refers to it with unconcealed pride.[27] The silverpoint book was intended to remain in the artist's own hands: it contained no added value to his transactions, he had no need to record them in his journal. Nevertheless, he does explicitly mention several portraits as well as other drawings from this small drawing book, such as the portraits of two eminent Nuremberg citizens, Paulus Topler and Martin Pfinzing (fig. 84) on one of the first pages.[28]

Two other portraits he made during his journey to Zeeland are also recorded. Between 3 and 7 December 1520 in Bergen op Zoom, where Dürer stayed before he set sail for Goes, he portrayed the innkeeper Jan de Haas and his family: '… and drew the maid and old woman in my sketchbook with the silverpoint'.[29] These are no doubt the two portraits on the recto of one of the three silverpoint drawings now in Chantilly.[30] Near the young woman, her eyes modestly cast downward, the inscription 'At Bergen op Zoom, feast day'[31] can be made out, a reference to Saint Nicholas Day, 6 December. These two women worked in the household of Jan de Haas; the same may be true of the portrait of a third woman from Bergen op Zoom, to the left on the verso of the same drawing. The younger woman in local costume to the right was drawn a few days later, on 8 December, when Dürer had arrived in Goes.[32]

Dürer made at least one other portrait drawing in his silverpoint book during his adventure in Zeeland, that of a young Augsburg merchant in his entourage, Markus Ulstett. He is depicted on the verso of the silverpoint drawing in Frankfurt (cat. 69). Dürer did not record Ulstett's portrait in his journal, unlike the one he drew next to it, of the 18-year-old-daughter of an Antwerp solicitor named Sebastian. There is little doubt that she was Dürer's favourite model: he drew her at least four times, three times in silverpoint and once with charcoal. On the last occasion she was portrayed with her fiancé, Gerhard Bombelli.[33]

A sixth portrait in the silverpoint drawing book that can probably be directly connected to Dürer's journal is that of Caspar Sturm, the imperial herald, who would summon and accompany Martin Luther from Wittenberg to the Diet

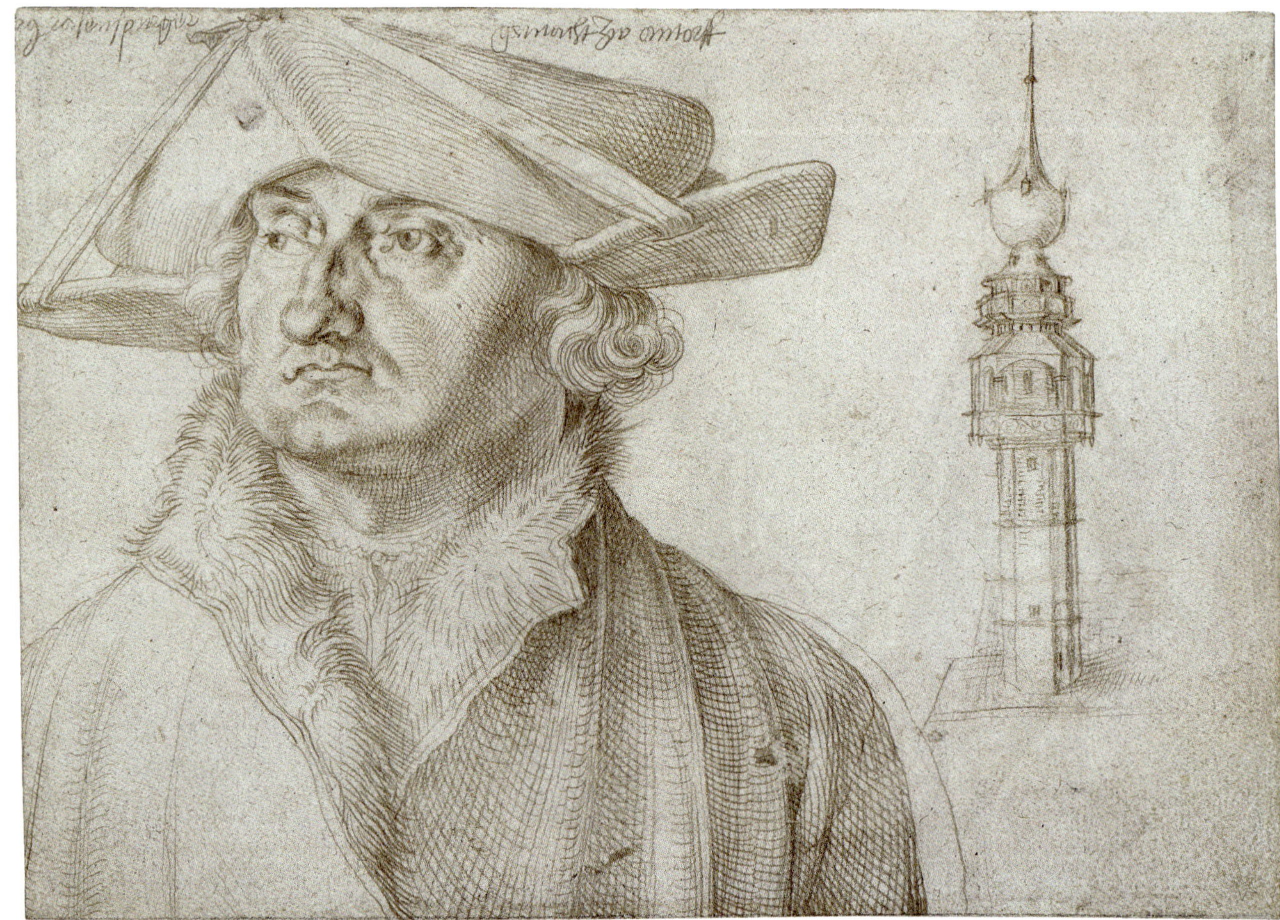

90
ALBRECHT DÜRER
Lazarus Ravensburger and the Tower of the House of Mayor Arnold van Liere in Antwerp, 1520–1
Silverpoint on ivory-coloured prepared paper, 12.4 × 17.1 cm
Staatliche Museen zu Berlin, Kupferstichkabinett

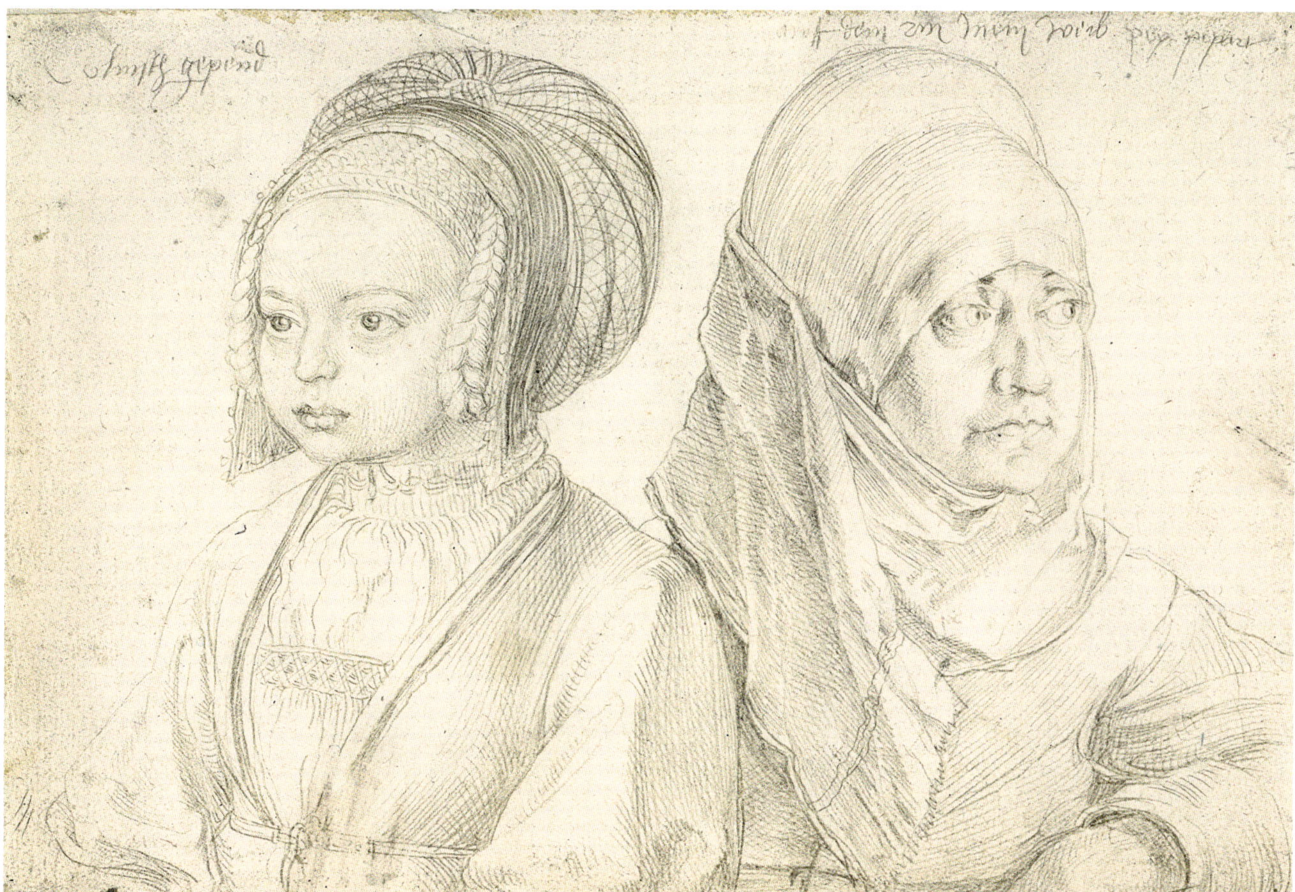

Fig. 117
ALBRECHT DÜRER
Girl in Cologne; *Agnes Dürer in Boppard*, 1521
Silverpoint on white prepared paper, 13.5 × 19.6 cm
The Albertina Museum, Vienna (22385 recto)

of Worms some five months later.[34] This is one of those compositions in which a portrait was drawn first, followed later by a landscape as a backdrop. Whereas Sturm's portrait was drawn in Aachen, the river landscape carries the inscription 'toll', a possible reference to a toll-house on the Rhine, such as Lobith. On his way back to Antwerp, in Emmerich near Lobith Dürer had to lie low for a few days because of a storm, and had time to make several drawings. However, it is possible that the two castles in the drawing actually refer to Haus Angerort and Haus Ruhrort near Duisburg, both mentioned in his journal.[35] Ruhrort was in fact a toll-house on the Rhine.

Some portrait drawings in the silverpoint book were not recorded in the journal, such as the portrait of Lazarus Ravensburger now in Berlin (cat. 90) and the beautiful heads of the young girl from Cologne and Dürer's wife, Agnes (fig. 117).[36] The drawing of the girl, in local costume and headdress ('Cölnisch gepend'), was most likely made in mid-July 1521, when the Dürers made a stop-over on their way home and where the journal comes to a halt. Agnes's portrait was done later on the way home to Nuremberg, near Boppard. It is fascinating to see how Dürer was able to suggest the sunlight on his wife's face on a warm summer's day. The double portrait is the verso rather than the recto of the sheet.[37]

The three remaining, anonymous portraits that were part of the silverpoint book, cannot be connected to Dürer's journal with any certainty either. The most interesting is the *Portrait of a 24-Year-Old Man with a View of St Michael's Abbey in Antwerp* (fig. 89).[38] Apart from his age, no reference to the sitter is noted on the drawing, but it is dated 1520. The young dandy certainly has some feminine characteristics, especially his facial type and the decorative ornament on his breast, but the headdress and the use of a hairnet mark him as a male.[39] Even the somewhat extravagant dress was not unfit for a man, as can be judged from the portraits of Hans Pfaffrot or Markus Ulstett. He may actually be the Portuguese man called Nicolao Sopalis, whom Dürer portrayed in late November 1520.[40] As Hans Mielke has demonstrated, the portrait followed directly after that of the two women in Netherlandish dress (cat. 68),[41] on the verso of the Ravensburger portrait, which was certainly drawn in Antwerp (cat. 90).[42] This places the portrait of the 24-year-old with certainty between 22 November and 3 December, when Dürer drew the beautiful view of the city of Bergen op Zoom on the verso (fig. 162). During this short interlude only three portraits are mentioned in the journal: the pen drawing of Felix Hungersperg (cat. 86) and the portraits of

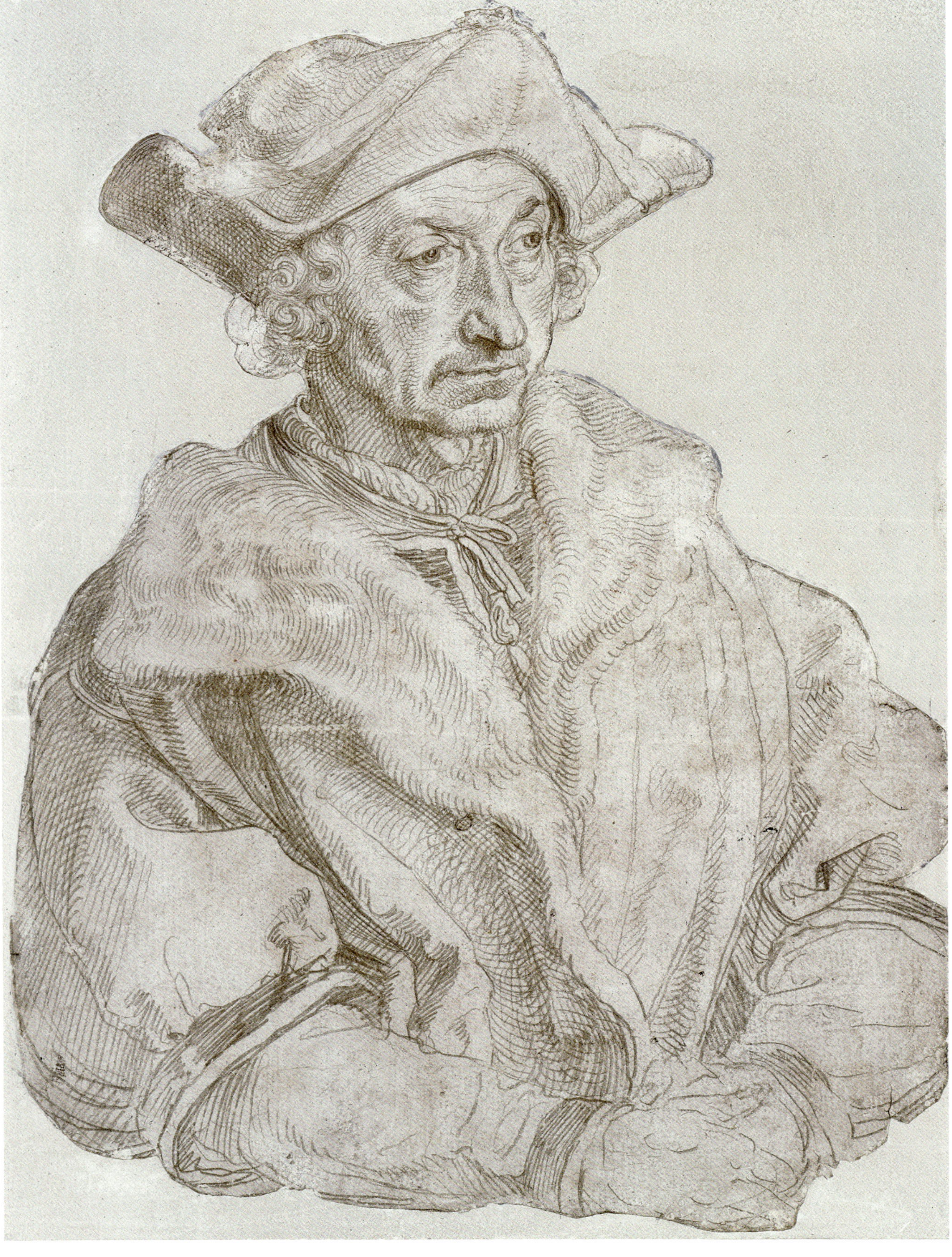

91
ALBRECHT DÜRER
Portrait of a Man, possibly Jan Provoost, about 1520–1
Silverpoint on white prepared paper, cut out around the outlines, 19.5 × 14.7 cm
Staatliche Museen zu Berlin, Kupferstichkabinett

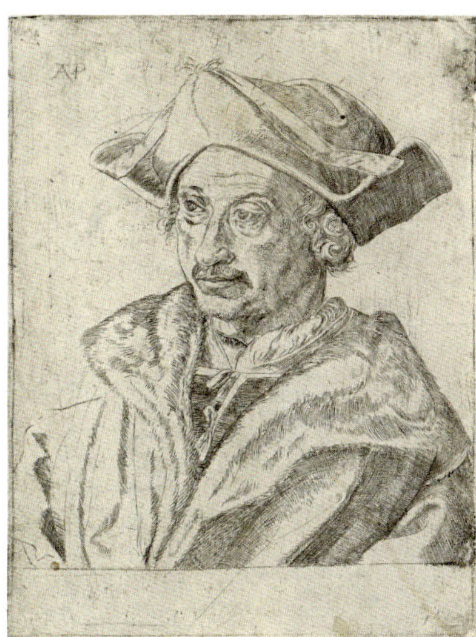

92
MONOGRAMMIST AP
Portrait of a Man, possibly Jan Provoost,
date unknown
Engraving, 16.3 × 12.2 cm
Staatliche Museen zu Berlin, Kupferstichkabinett

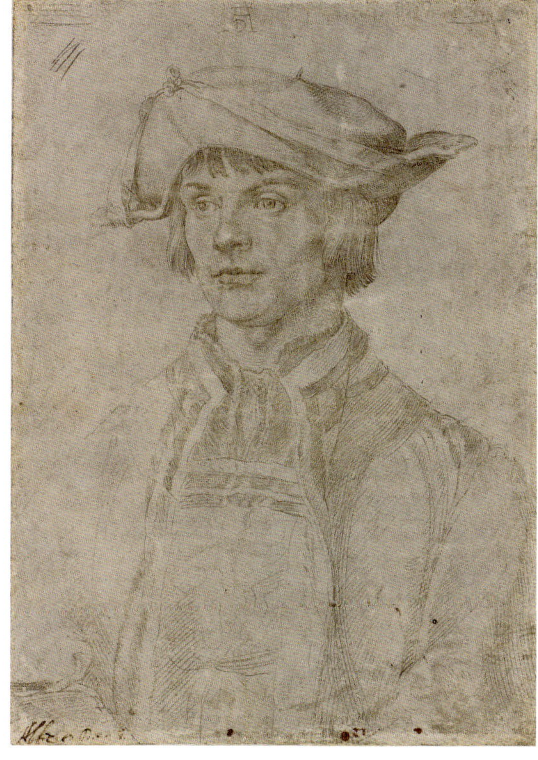

Fig. 118
ALBRECHT DÜRER
Portrait of Lucas van Leyden, 1521
Silverpoint, 24.4 × 17.1 cm
Palais des Beaux-Arts, Lille (Pl. 918)

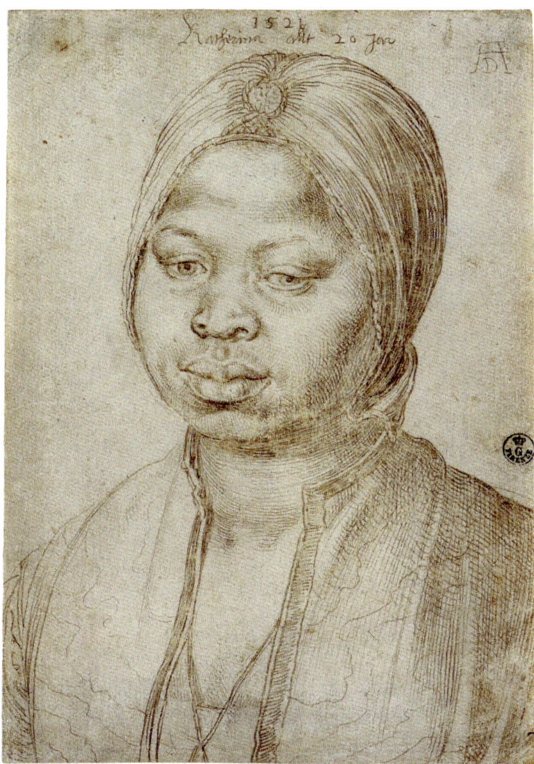

Fig. 119
ALBRECHT DÜRER
Katharina, the 20-Year-Old Servant of João Brandão, 1521
Silverpoint, 20.1 × 14.1 cm
Gabinetto dei Disegni e delle Stampe, Gallerie degli Uffizi, Florence (1060E)

Stefano Capello (the drawing given in exchange for a cedarwood rosary) (fig. 116) and Nicolao Sopalis.[43]

Dürer's larger metalpoint portrait drawings, of which four from the period have survived, had a different function and were not necessarily meant to stay in his own collection. Three of these can be traced in his journal. The portrait he made on 22 June 1521 of his colleague Lucas van Leyden (fig. 118) was no doubt intended as a gift, possibly in exchange for a portrait Lucas made of him, although Dürer left no record of this.[44] The drawing does not carry a contemporary inscription, unlike those in his silverpoint book or the pen drawings he kept for his own use. Another drawing we come across in writing is of the 20-year-old servant of João Brandão (fig. 119), whom he drew between 16 March and 5 April 1521. Black servants were probably rare in Nuremberg, although less so in Antwerp or Venice.[45] In one of the unused drafts for his 1528 posthumous published books on the theory of human proportion, he wrote the following observation, at the time an acceptable viewpoint: 'A large difference can be observed between white and Moorish people. They are still human beings and many of the proportions of these black people are usable for their beauty, although black people's faces are rarely beautiful to look at …'.[46] Dürer did not present the drawing to the young servant but kept it for potential later use.

For a long time the remarkable *Portrait of a Man* in Berlin (cat. 91) was believed to depict Sebastian Brant. The contours of this drawing have been traced, no doubt by the unknown Monogrammist AP, for the production of a mirrored engraving. There are only two known impressions of this print, of which one is in the Berlin print room (cat. 92). Following the contours of the portrayed, the drawing was cut out and mounted on another piece of paper. The sitter is warmly dressed and wears a Netherlandish hat. This is an informal portrait, suggesting that the artist and his model were well acquainted. Dürer recorded all the portrait drawings he presented as gifts in his journal, this one identifiable with a note written on 9 April 1521: 'Then early on Tuesday we departed. But first I did a metalpoint portrait of Jan

Provo[o]st and gave his wife 10 stuivers as a parting gift.'[47] Apart from the fact that the sitter is dressed up and ready to go, his age perfectly fits that of Jan Provoost, who would have been 58 or 59. The two painters knew each other well, having met in Antwerp in September the previous year, when Dürer portrayed Provoost in charcoal.[48]

The fourth large metalpoint drawing is not mentioned in the journal. It is the largest of the four, and drawn not in silverpoint but with a much softer point of lead or tin. This could be used on any paper, in this case a darkened grey violet (fig. 100).[49] The drawing depicts Agnes Dürer and has a long inscription, written in the artist's hand: 'This likeness of his wife in Netherlandish costume was drawn by Albrecht Dürer at Antwerp in the year 1521, when they had been married to each other for twenty-seven years'.[50] Her traditional headdress was a gift from her husband, acquired in Bergen op Zoom on 4 December 1520.[51] The portrait would have been made in Antwerp before their twenty-seventh wedding anniversary on 7 July 1521. On that particular day, however, they were not in Antwerp but in Brussels, a few days before returning to Nuremberg. The drawing was no doubt meant to honour the bond between Agnes and Albrecht Dürer, a loving souvenir to remember their joint enterprise. The drawing remained part of the artist's legacy and is mentioned as such in the 1588 inventory of the Imhoff collection, before it was acquired by Rudolf II.[52]

Some silverpoint drawings that are explicitly mentioned in Dürer's journal have disappeared, such as that of Wolfgang von Rogendorf, Viscount of Steyr and a marshall in imperial Habsburg service.[53] This was certainly an independent drawing presented to the sitter as a gift. Dürer made two portraits of Jakob Köpfinger's sister-in-law from Ulm during her stay in Aachen: the first was a large drawing in charcoal, the second possibly a silverpoint drawing in his drawing book.[54] The two silverpoint portraits Dürer made of Joachim Patinir, in April or early May 1521, have gone too, just as two silverpoint drawings of Gerhard Bombelli's fiancée.[55]

LARGE PORTRAIT DRAWINGS IN CHARCOAL AND BLACK CHALK

No fewer than 47 portraits Dürer made in charcoal are recorded in the journal, as well as five in black chalk. Quite a number of drawings, however, are recorded without any reference to the technique used. Many of these were probably drawn in charcoal or chalk, so it is possible that Dürer produced a total of ninety of these large portraits.[56] Already by 1503 Dürer had started to make large portrait drawings in charcoal, but only of family or friends, such as the famous profile portrait of Willibald Pirckheimer now in Berlin.[57] As far as we know Dürer made no portrait drawings during his journey to Venice in 1505–7, and hardly any in the years directly thereafter. Only in the second decade of the sixteenth century did he resume where he had left off. *The Portrait of an Unknown Man* now in Berlin, dated 1515, is the first large charcoal drawing in which Dürer places the sitter against a dark background, with a small strip at the top for his monogram and date.[58] He would later use this format for portrait drawings made during the Netherlandish journey. As Anzelewsky stated correctly, this would give the drawing a closed outlook, much closer to paintings they replaced.[59]

Although Dürer turned his hand to these large portraits on paper in 1516, 1517 and especially in the summer of 1518, which he spent at the Diet of Augsburg, nothing prepares us for the enormous outburst of productivity in his year of travelling in 1520–1. His signed portrait drawings, which he would sometimes mount on small panels, were a remarkably original and extremely effective way of cornering the market.[60] Admittedly he could earn much more money with painted portraits – somewhere between 8 and 30 guilders, to judge from his journal[61] – but these incurred considerable costs: oak panel as support, pigments, binding media and, not unimportant, a studio and an assistant for grinding the pigments and preparing the panel.[62] Furthermore, he needed much more time – at least four or five days – to paint a portrait.[63] By contrast, three large portrait drawings could be completed in a single night, enabling him to portray many more of his customers, with obvious advantages.

All 15 large portrait drawings from the Netherlandish journey that have survived were recorded in Dürer's journal, even those that can be regarded as *tronies* (facial studies) for various projects. These sitters were in fact paid models, whether a 93-year old man or a nun. The latter was recorded at the end of his stay in Cologne, between 3 and 12 November: 'I did the likeness of the nun and gave her 7 silver pence and 3 half-sheet copper engravings'.[64] This is probably the drawing referred to in the 1588 Imhoff inventory as 'A woman's head with a veil'.[65] The subject of this large charcoal drawing (cat. 93), now in the collection of the Fondation Custodia in Paris, is most certainly not the wife of Dürer's host in Bergen op Zoom, Jan de Haas, as has recently been suggested.[66] As van Gelder has proposed, the woman seems to be a 39-year-old Carmelite nun.[67] Katrin Dyballa remarks that the use of the sitter's first name, Metzgen – inscribed at the top of the drawing – 'suggests a degree of intimacy that seems unlikely if the sitter was a Beguine or even a nun';[68] this, however, is irrelevant, since the drawing was to remain in Dürer's own collection, providing another argument in favour of van Gelder's identification. Dürer added the name Metzgen – which is certainly not Dutch and possibly a diminutive of

93
ALBRECHT DÜRER
Portrait of a 39-Year-Old Woman, 1520
Charcoal, background with stump on slightly discoloured paper, 40.4 × 27.3 cm
Fondation Custodia, Collection Frits Lugt, Paris

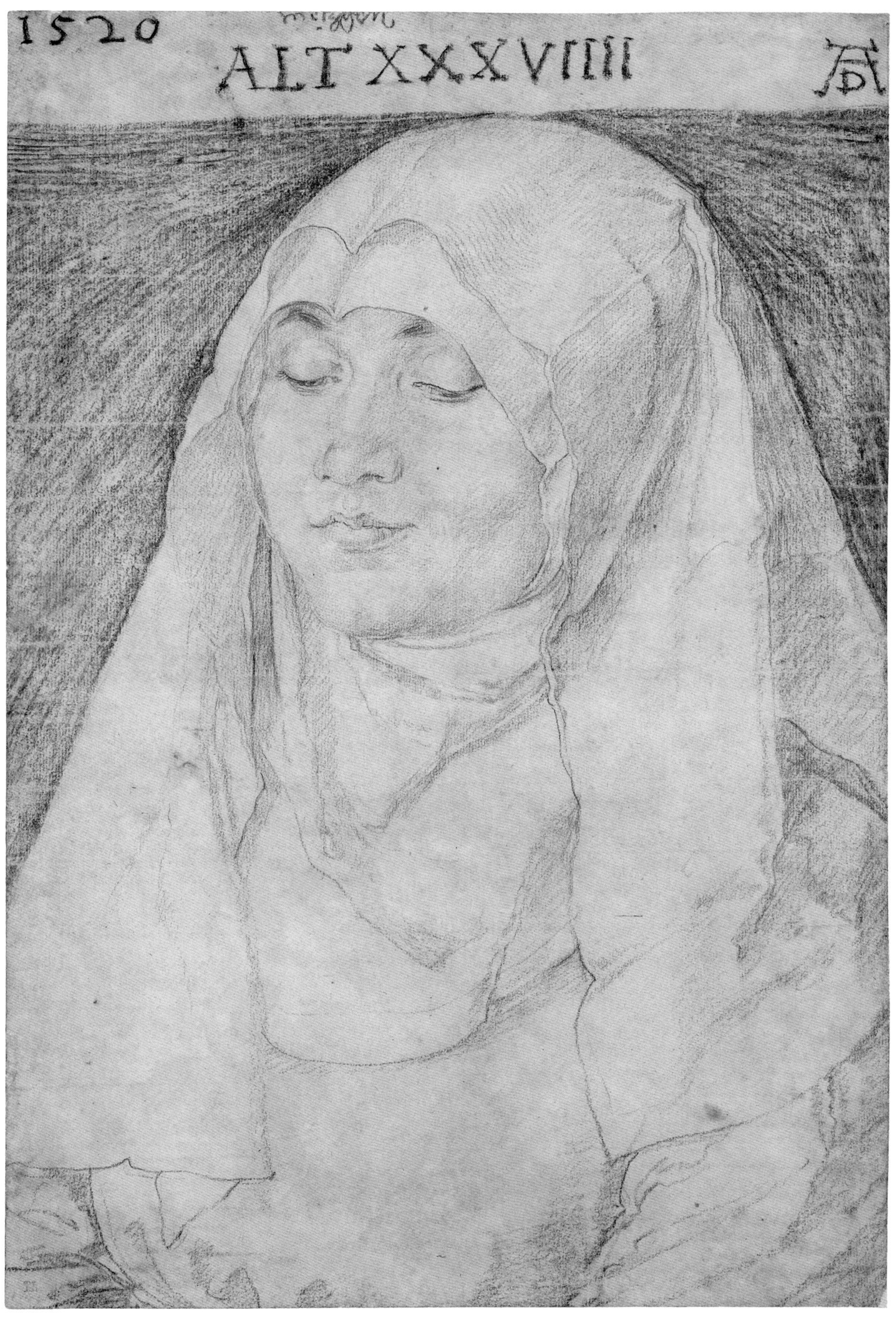

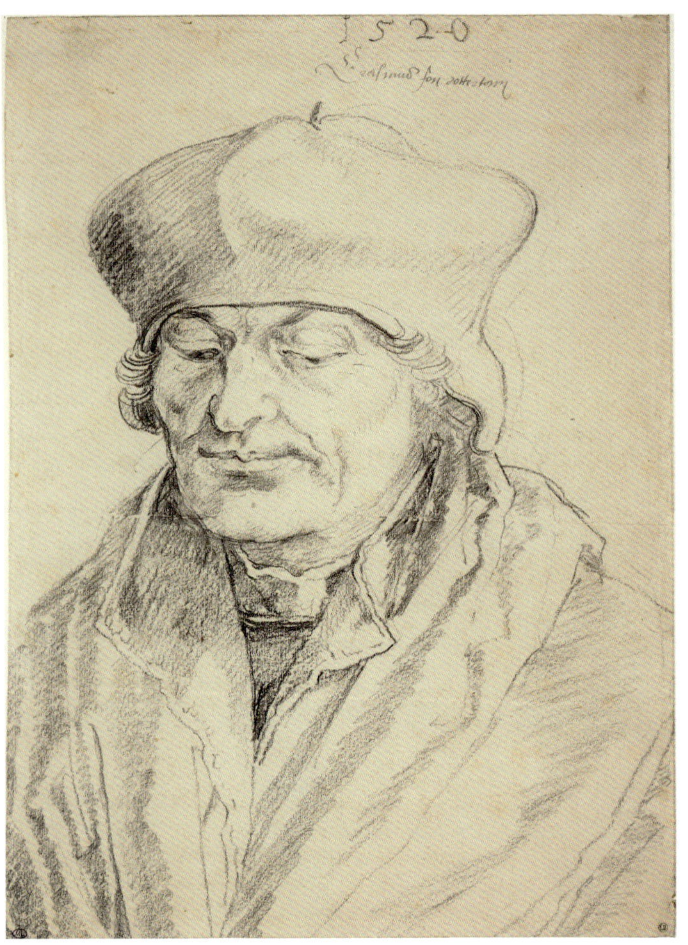

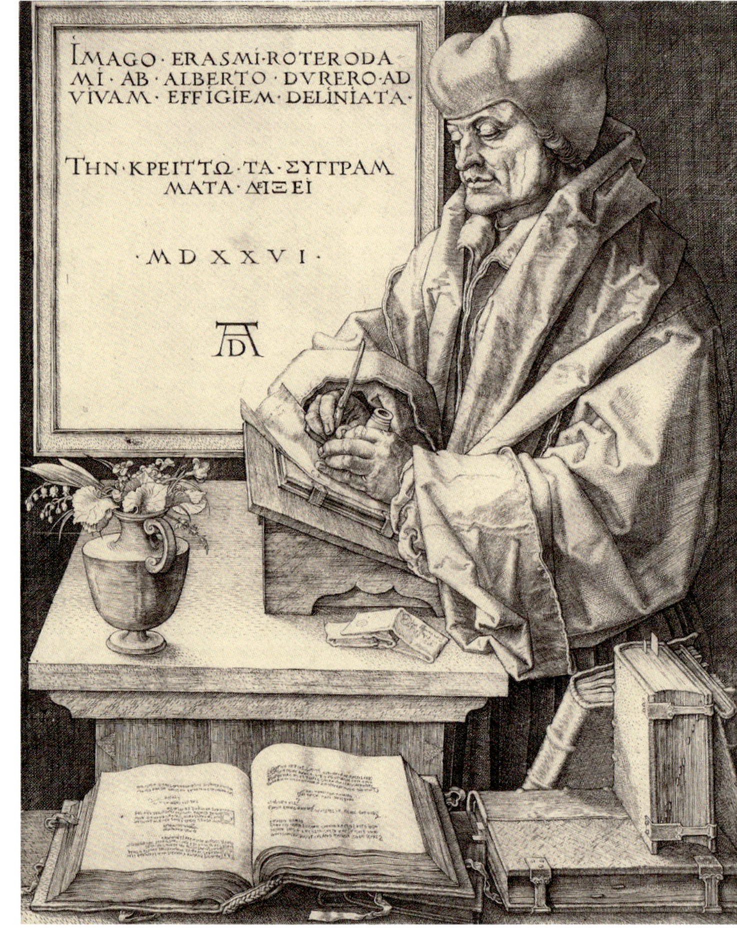

Fig. 120
ALBRECHT DÜRER
Portrait of Desiderius Erasmus, 1520
Black chalk,
37.3 × 27.1 cm
Musée du Louvre, Paris (RF4113 recto)

94
ALBRECHT DÜRER
Portrait of Erasmus, 1526
Engraving, 24.9 × 19.3 cm
Rijksmuseum, Amsterdam

95
QUINTEN MASSYS
Medal with bust of Desiderius Erasmus, 1519
Cast bronze,
diameter 10.7 cm
The Syndics of the Fitzwilliam Museum, University of Cambridge

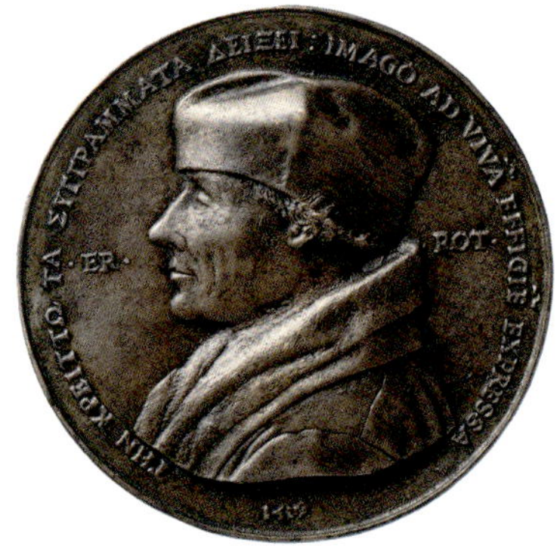

the German name Mechthild – to the drawing later. The fact that this woman, unusually, has downcast eyes may indicate that he made the drawing with a specific saint in a painting in mind.[69]

Of the remaining 13 large drawings, three are dated 1520, five 1521, and five have no date due to the removal of the upper margin. Two of these have been firmly associated with references in Dürer's journal. The first is the *Portrait of King Christian II of Denmark* (fig. 54) made on 2 July 1521, just before Dürer's return to Nuremberg.[70] This was drawn with charcoal, although now faded, making the technique hard to recognise.[71] With the exception of Fedja Anzelewsky, scholars have universally identified the sitter as the Danish king.[72] A close comparison with the many painted portraits of Christian II (cat. 53) reveals that each artist seems to have portrayed a different person. However, as Winkler rightfully asserted, Dürer's drawing is the noblest rendering of the king's features and displays a sharp contrast with the cold eyes and cruel mouth in Michael Sittow's portrait now in Copenhagen that give the king's true nature away.[73] His dignified presentation on paper may explain why Christian II was so pleased with the portrait that he commissioned a painted version; this, unfortunately, has not survived.[74] As can be judged from remarks made in his journal, Dürer was proud of the king's respect for his talents, the more so because both Charles V and Margaret of Austria failed him in that regard. It must have been a moment of triumph when he presented the king with the finished portrait at a royal banquet in Brussels on 7 July, in the presence of Margaret and her cousin; for this he received a bonus of 30 guilders.

The other securely identified drawing is the *Portrait of Desiderius Erasmus* now in the Louvre, dated 1520 (fig. 120).[75] According to his journal, Dürer met Erasmus at least three or four times during his journey in 1520–1

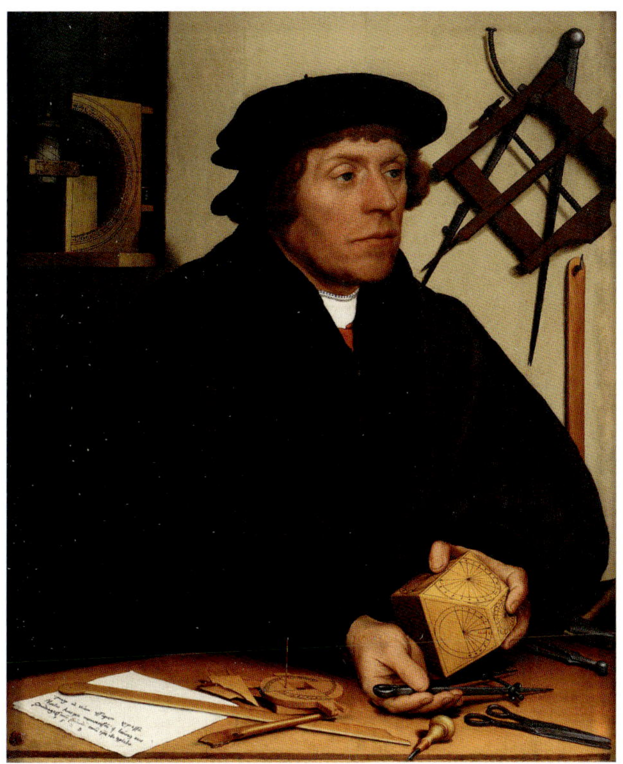

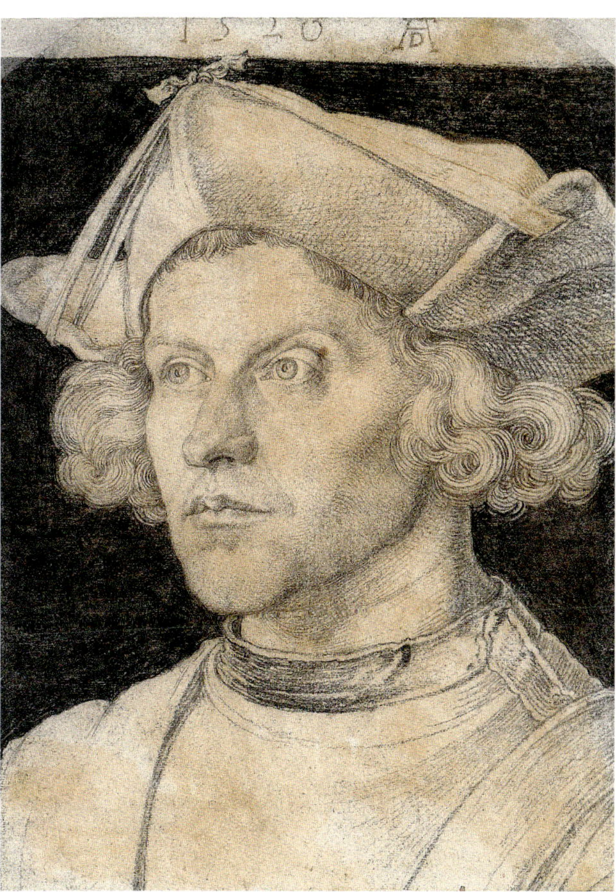

Fig. 121
HANS HOLBEIN THE YOUNGER (1497/8–1543)
Portrait of Nikolaus Kratzer, 1528
Oil on panel, 83 × 67 cm
Musée du Louvre, Paris

96
ALBRECHT DÜRER
Portrait of a Young Man, possibly Nikolaus Kratzer, 1520
Black and brownish chalk, partly worked over with the brush in grey by a later hand,
36.7 × 25.9 cm
Staatliche Museen zu Berlin, Kupferstichkabinett

but only mentions a portrait drawing once, during his first visit to Brussels: 'I did another sketch of Erasmus of Rotterdam'.[76] This suggests that he had made another portrait of Erasmus on an earlier occasion, but during their first meeting, shortly after the artist's arrival in Antwerp, no portrait drawing is mentioned.[77] It is therefore likely that this first portrait was a pen drawing, now lost, for Dürer's own documentation. Neither of the drawings passed to Erasmus, as follows from his correspondence with Willibald Pirckheimer between 1523 and 1525.[78] To Erasmus's regret, Dürer did not finish his portrait in Brussels, possibly because the session – at Bernaert van Orley's banquet (mentioned above) – was interrupted.[79] The Louvre drawing is indeed unfinished: while it is arguably the most spontaneous and informal portrait of the great humanist, compared to Dürer's other large portrait drawings it has not been fully worked out, no dark background has been added and the signature is lacking.[80] Dürer clearly kept the drawing to himself, possibly for later use. For his engraving produced in 1526 (cat. 94) he may have used Quinten Massys's medal of 1519 (cat. 95) as an additional model, at Erasmus's own suggestion, as well as his earlier pen portrait – now lost.[81]

The medium used for his portrait of Erasmus has been much debated. The meagre consensus of recent scholarship is that the drawing was made in black chalk, although in one of his letters to Pirckheimer the great philosopher clearly refers to a drawing in *carbone* (charcoal).[82] Furthermore, Dürer mentions that he portrayed the host

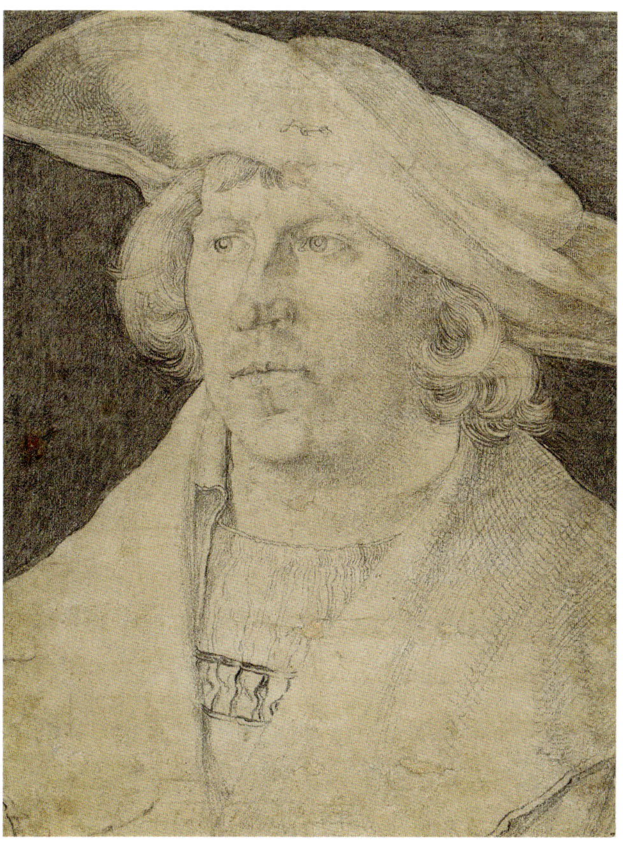

Fig. 122
ALBRECHT DÜRER
Portrait of a Man, 1520
Black chalk,
37.4 × 27.9 cm
Musée du Louvre, Paris, département des Arts graphiques, collection Edmond de Rothschild (24 DR)

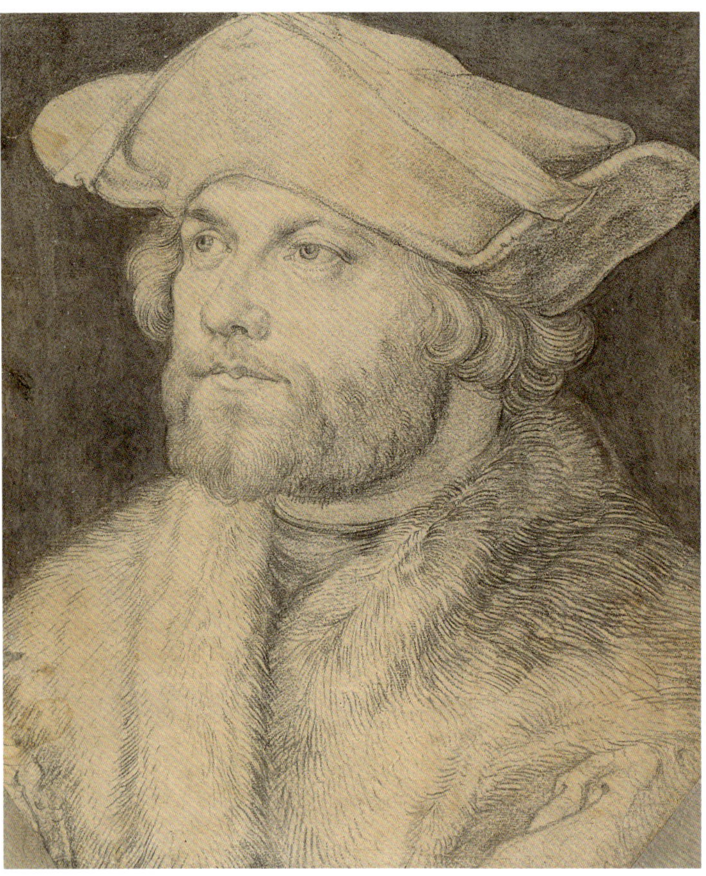

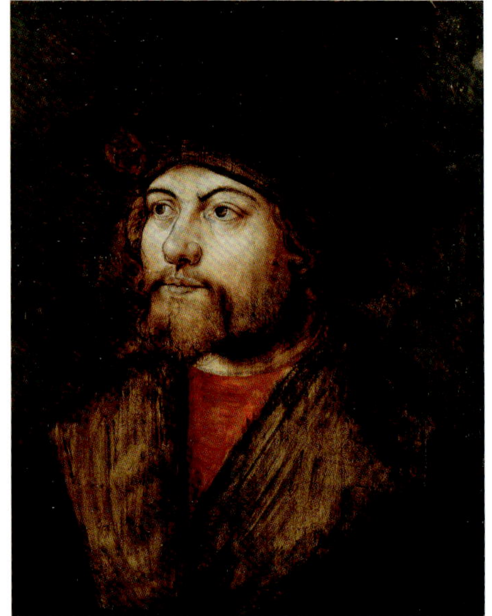

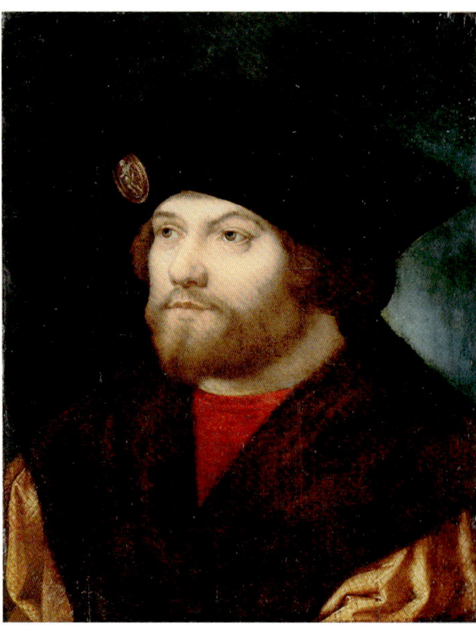

insufficient evidence to firmly identify the sitter as Nikolaus Kratzer.

A much more likely candidate for that identification is the young man in Dürer's most elaborate large portrait drawing, dated 1520, now in Berlin (cat. 96). The systematic, detailed system of parallel lines and cross-hatching, elegantly drawn curls in the young man's hair that are reminiscent of silverpoint drawings, and the use of three different types of charcoal and chalk, have led Winkler to suggest that this might be one of Dürer's earliest drawings after his arrival in Antwerp, implying that the artist would spend less time on later portrait drawings. This drawing fits the identification of the young Kratzer perfectly, his nose, mouth and chin, as well as the cropped hair on the forehead, bearing close comparison with the Holbein portrait. The level of precision and detail so praised in the Berlin drawing are missing from some of Dürer's other drawings, but it does not make the Berlin drawing 'stiff', as Winkler opined.[87] As Mielke asserted many years later, this apparent stiffness is due to the almost invisible use of a brush to add light and dark grey accents to the existing framework of lines, especially in the waves of hair, around the eyes and in the lighter hatchings in the hat. This may have been an experiment;[88] if so, Dürer was apparently satisfied with the result, since he made further use of this technique several times.

A good example is the portrait of a bearded man (cat. 97) traditionally identified as the Portuguese historian and humanist Damião de Góis (1502–1574). Stylistically the drawing fits perfectly into Dürer's Netherlandish period, although it is not his most sparkling work, due to the discoloured paper and the somewhat faded drawing.[89] The use of light grey watercolour is identical to that of the Berlin portrait (cat. 96). The drawing has been cut at the top and

97
ALBRECHT DÜRER
Portrait of a Man,
about 1520–1
Black chalk and brush on brownish paper,
35.5 × 28.5 cm
The Albertina Museum, Vienna

Fig. 123
NETHERLANDISH PAINTER AFTER ALBRECHT DÜRER
Portrait of a Man,
after 1521
Oil on oak,
43.4 × 33.5 cm
Private collection, Edinburgh

Fig. 124
NETHERLANDISH PAINTER AFTER ALBRECHT DÜRER
Portrait of a Man,
about 1550
Oil on oak,
43.6 × 33.9 cm
Phoebus Foundation, Antwerp

of the banquet, Bernaert van Orley, in charcoal and it is unlikely that he would have switched to black chalk between drawings on the same occasion.[83] Given the great difficulty of distinguishing between black chalk and charcoal, it is hardly surprising there has been some confusion in art historical literature.

A portrait drawing of a man in the Rothschild collection in the Louvre (fig. 122) is subject to similar confusion. Both Winkler and Strauss are uncertain of the material used, whereas Jean-Richard refers to *pierre noir*, a soft black chalk, for this and each of the other large portrait drawings by Dürer in the Louvre.[84] The sitter here is usually identified as Nikolaus Kratzer (1486–1550), Professor of Mathematics at the University of Oxford and from 1519 court astronomer to Henry VIII. Kratzer travelled to the Low Countries to meet Erasmus, where he witnessed the drawing session at which Dürer portrayed Erasmus in Brussels. According to Dürer's journal he portrayed Kratzer in early August 1520.[85] His identification here is based inconclusively on comparison with a painted portrait of 1528 by Hans Holbein the Younger (fig. 121).[86] However, the drawing offers no clues to date the drawing with certainty within the year of Dürer's stay in the Low Countries. The sitter's hat is likely to be of German origin, comparable to those of Hans Pfaffrot (fig. 115) and Markus Ulstett (cat. 69), but this is the background fully overpainted with the brush. The sitter cannot be Damião de Góis, since Dürer had passed away by the time de Góis had reached the age of the man portrayed here.[90] This persistent identification goes back to an engraving by Philips Galle of 1587, to which both Dürer's monogram, a Latinised version of de Góis's name and a laudatory phrase have been added.[91] Although there is little doubt that the man in the print is the same as the one in the drawing, this only proves that 60 years after Dürer's death and 13 after de Góis's, Philips Galle was under the impression that the drawing portrayed the Portuguese humanist.

The sitter must certainly have been a man of reputation, since we know of at least four painted copies, of which the two finest, both in private collections, are painted on oak panel. One of these is unfinished (fig. 124), although the face has been carefully worked out, especially the eyes, eyebrows, nose and the flesh colours.[92] The other is highly finished (fig. 123) and is a much more faithful copy of Dürer's drawing but by a less talented hand. Both paintings appear to be Netherlandish, apparently executed not long after Dürer had finished his portrait drawing.[93] This would certainly indicate that the drawing remained in the Netherlands for some time after its completion, but it does not decisively identify the sitter or his nationality. However, in the second of the painted copies the sitter wears a badge or a medal bearing the figure of Aequitas, a reference to Good Government, which might be a key to the sitter's identity: perhaps Adrian Herbouts or Cornelis Grapheus (1482–1558), both civil servants and good acquaintances of Albrecht Dürer, are portrayed here.

For his *Portrait of a Young Man with a Hat* now in the Rijksmuseum (cat. 98) Dürer made use of the Italian paper he used during his sojourn in Venice in 1505–7, although the *Portrait of Otto zu Solms Laubach* in the British Museum, dated 1516, bears the same watermark too.[94] As Kurt Löcher has argued, the unusual cap worn by the Amsterdam sitter was customary in Augsburg between 1502 and 1513 (cat. 98), whereas his clothes would point to an artisan rather than a merchant.[95] However, a date between 1502 and 1513 is stylistically inconclusive. The drawing fits with others Dürer made in Augsburg in 1518, when he visited the Imperial Diet between the end of June and early September. Several of these are closely comparable to the Amsterdam portrait, such as those of Konrad Peutinger now in Munich or Count Philipp zu Solms now in Bayonne.[96] Although the Amsterdam sitter is linked through style and fashion to Dürer's Augsburg trip, the same arguments might also suggest a date during his stay in the Low Countries, when he portrayed several Augsburg citizens.[97]

A portrait drawing in charcoal and brown chalk that offers a closer comparison to the Amsterdam portrait than any other is now in the British Museum (fig. 72). In terms of technique the drawings are closely related, although the condition of the London drawing is much better. A part of the upper strip still remains, although no remnants of a date can be made out. The striking and energetic face in this imposing drawing has been given several names in the past, having been linked to both the 1518 Augsburg Diet and the Netherlandish journey. The sitter seems to be in his forties, which would rule out previous identifications as Hans Tucher (1456–1536), Jan Provoost, Paul Hofhaimer (1459–1537) or Oswald Krell.[98] Dürer's good friend Lazarus Spengler (1479–1534) was with him on the Augsburg Diet of 1518, and Dürer no doubt painted him that year. That picture is unfortunately lost and no conclusions can be drawn from the inferior engraving of about 1750.[99]

Whereas the previously discussed portraits in Amsterdam and London may have been produced in Augsburg, and perhaps not during the 1520–1 sojourn in the Low Countries, others no doubt were. It is hardly surprising that commentators have sought to identify Dürer's sitters with well-known individuals, preferably artists he had met. However, this has led to some preposterous identifications, such as the subject of the now-lost drawing from Weimar, once identified as Joachim

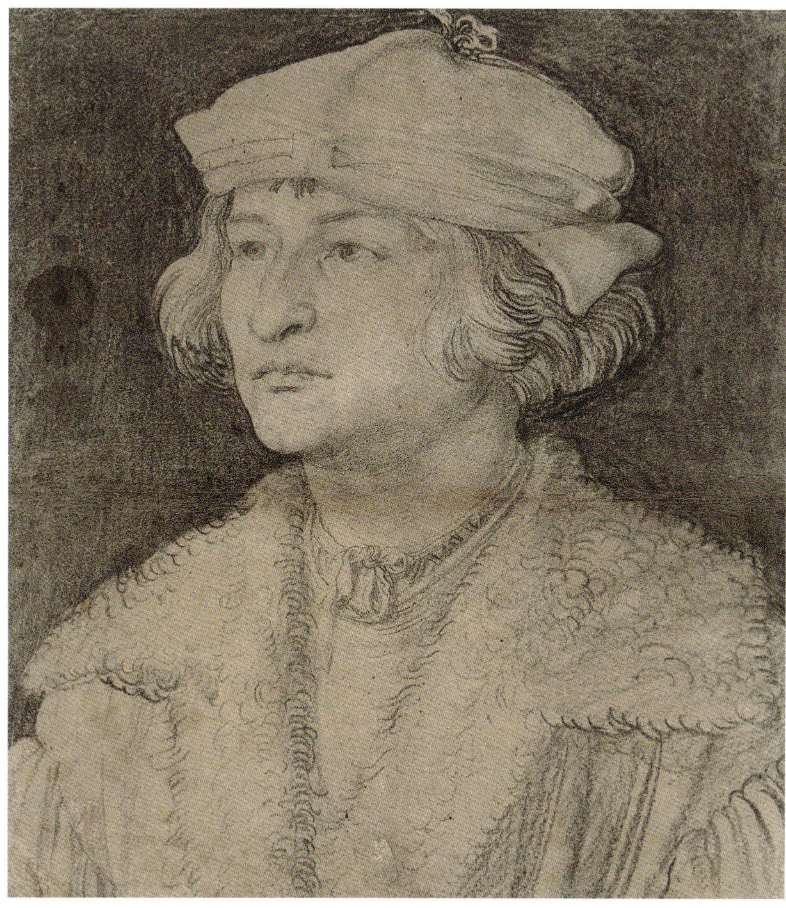

98
ALBRECHT DÜRER
Portrait of a Young Man with a Hat, probably 1518
Charcoal on paper, 33.7 × 29.7 cm
Rijksmuseum, Amsterdam

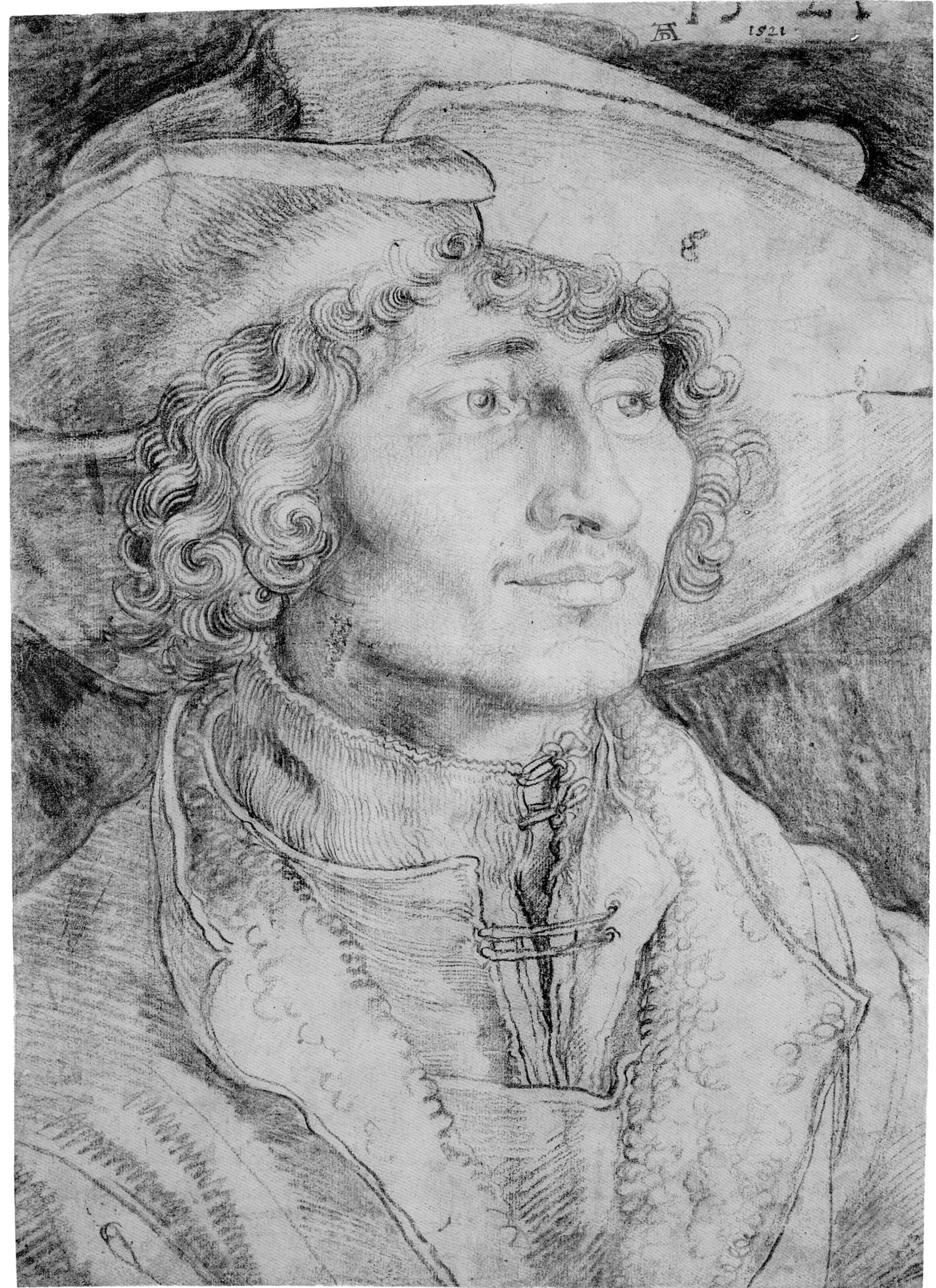

Patinir.[100] While this incorrect identification was superseded in 1913, others still linger on. For example, Dürer's largest-known portrait drawing, the very impressive *Portrait of a Young Man* (fig. 125) in the Louvre, is still regarded by several scholars as a portrait of Bernaert van Orley.[101] Dürer records in his journal that he portrayed Bernaert van Orley only once, at the festive banquet in Brussels between 27 August and 2 September 1520,[102] yet the drawing is clearly dated 1521. Moreover, the superbly characterised baby face of this dandy, with just a touch of youthful arrogance, bears no resemblance to the 1572 portrait engraving by Cornelis Cort said to represent van Orley.[103] It would be tempting to identify the young man in the Louvre with Jacob Rehlinger, the rich young heir of the famous Augsburg merchant house, who paid Dürer handsomely for his charcoal portrait on 29 or 30 June 1521, three weeks after the drawing had been produced.[104]

Lippmann mentioned the same Bernaert van Orley as the sitter in a drawing dated 1521 in the British Museum (cat. 99).[105] However, his opinion, based on a comparison with the Dresden picture at the time thought to portray van Orley (cat. 43), was not shared by anyone. Although Veth and Muller argued that the subject could not be the same man as the sitter in the Dresden painting,[106] who is now securely identified as the Danzig merchant Bernhard von Reesen, Giulia Bartrum, almost a century later, asserted that both portraits might actually represent the same individual.[107] But a comparison of the portraits precludes this. Apart from the obvious differences in facial features – nose, moustache, eyes, hair – their character is altogether different. A striking feature is the glowing light in which Dürer miraculously captures the face of the young man. The light source is to the right, positioned lower than the sitter's face but close by, as suggested by the deep shadows created by the artist. This is no doubt a portrait by candlelight, similar to those of Conrad Meit and Hans Lamparter that he drew the previous year. Such a session in 1521 is not explicitly mentioned in his journal, but Dürer did make at least one portrait in charcoal by candlelight, that of Florent Nepotis (or Fleurequin Neefs), Margaret of Austria's organist, whom he depicted at a night banquet at Shrovetide.[108]

EMPTY FOOTPRINTS

It is surprising that the commercial success of Dürer's portrait enterprise was not followed by his fellow artists in the Netherlands, indicating that few were capable of creating high-quality portrait drawings that could replace paintings. Not even skilled portrait painters such as Bernaert van Orley, Joos van Cleve and Quinten Massys would try their hands at finished portrait drawings. The one surviving example by Jan Gossaert, a portrait of Christian II, was a preparatory drawing for a print;[109] there is little doubt, however, that he made at least a few more.[110]

There may have been another reason why Dürer's lucrative business was not followed. Being a travelling painter, he would have been dependent upon his local colleagues for permission to make use of their studios and assistants. As a draughtsman he was fully independent. In addition, drawing was a much more important tool for Dürer than it was for his peers in Antwerp, who were under production duress in a city where demand always outstripped supply. Whereas Dürer's body of extant drawings is huge – more than

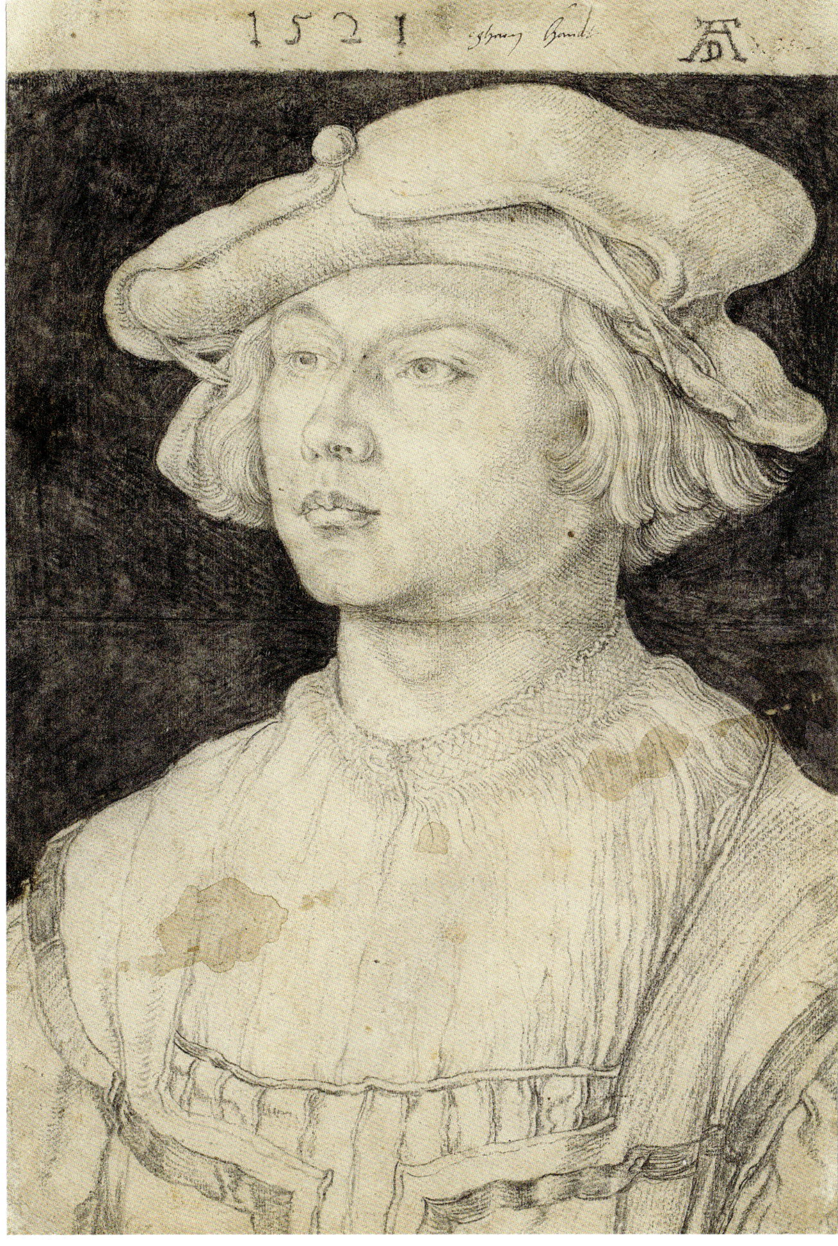

Fig. 125
ALBRECHT DÜRER
Portrait of a Young Man, possibly Jacob Rehlinger, 1521
Black chalk, 40.3 × 27.5 cm
Musée du Louvre, Paris. Collection Rothschild (23DR)

OPPOSITE
99
ALBRECHT DÜRER
Portrait of a Young Man, 1521
Charcoal, 37.8 × 27.1 cm
British Museum

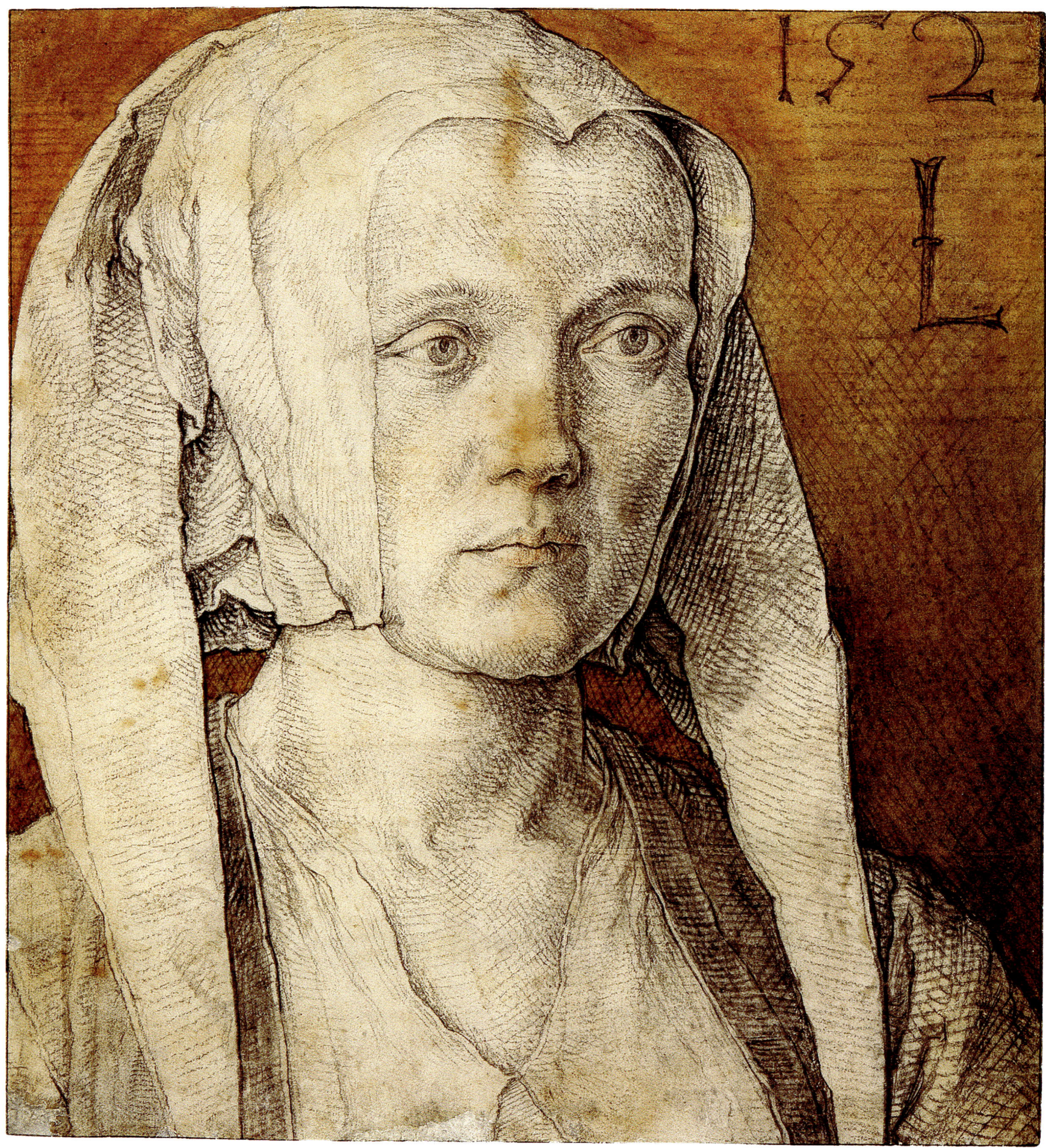
152
L

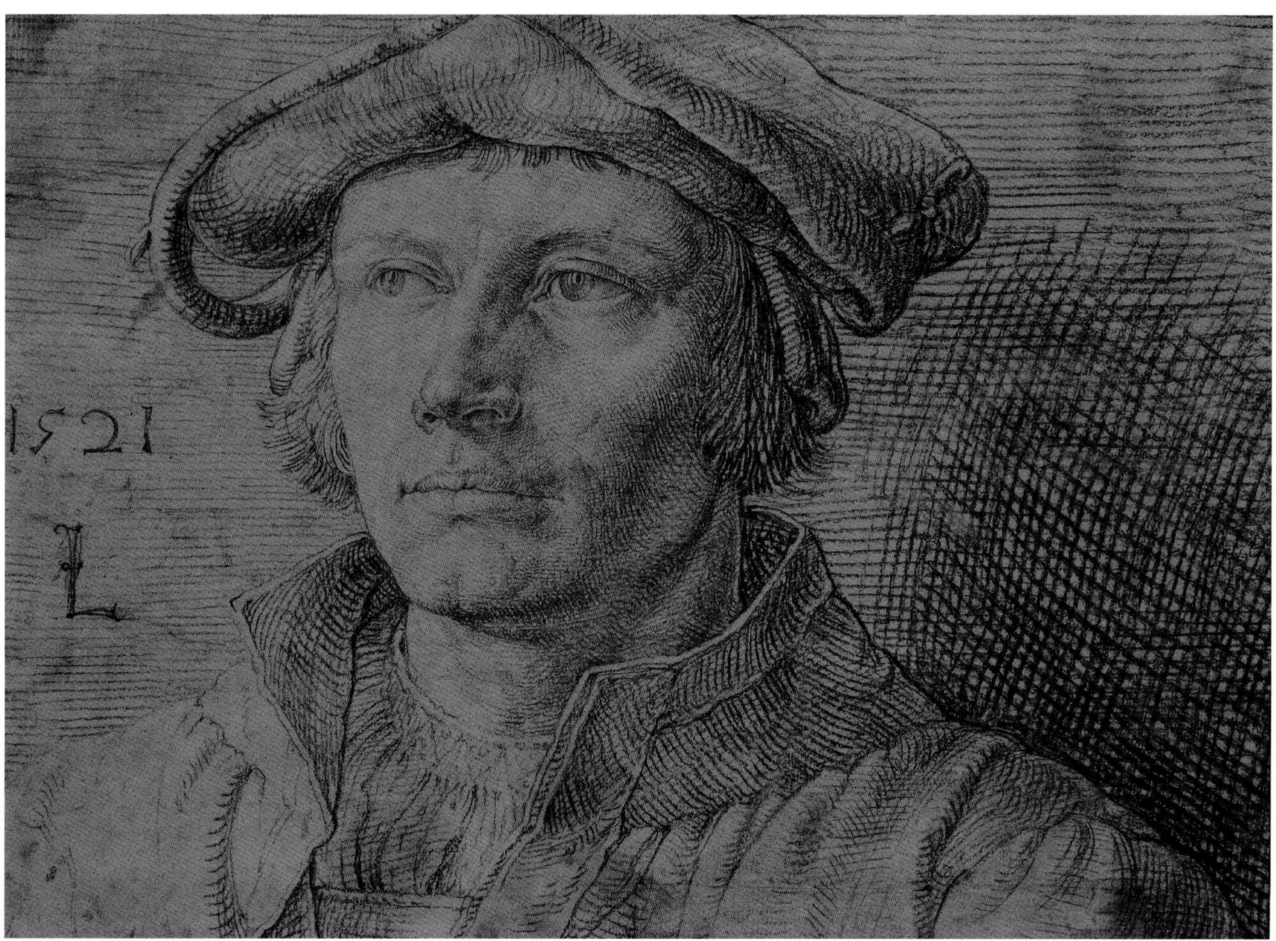

101
LUCAS VAN LEYDEN
(active 1508; died 1533)
Portrait of a Man, 1521
Black chalk on paper,
26.2 × 35.3 cm
Museum De Lakenhal, Leiden

OPPOSITE
100
LUCAS VAN LEYDEN
(active 1508; died 1533)
Portrait of a Woman with Bonnet, 1521
Charcoal and red chalk, brush in brown watercolour,
36.3 × 32.8 cm
Klassik Stiftung Weimar, Museum

nine hundred are in existence – no more than sixty are known to be by his most productive Antwerp counterpart, Dirk Vellert, and none survives by the two most notable Antwerp master painters, Quinten Massys and Joos van Cleve. It is true that many drawings may not have escaped destruction, but it is hardly conceivable that all large portrait drawings by Massys and van Cleve, or for that matter Bernaert van Orley and Jan Provoost, disappeared. In all probability such drawings were never produced.

Only Lucas van Leyden would start to make large portrait drawings on paper in a similar fashion around the time when he and Dürer met, in Antwerp in the early summer of 1521. Six finished portrait drawings by Lucas clearly pay tribute to Dürer's portraits from the Low Countries; three of these are dated 1521 and the others no doubt date from the same period.[111] The only portrait drawing Lucas had made beforehand was the virtuoso piece in pen and brush for a printed portrait of Emperor Maximilian I .[112] He was well acquainted with Dürer's prints from an early age, but he must have been extremely impressed with Dürer's portrait drawings and their enormous variety in terms of size, technique, style and function. Lucas's six large portrait drawings are approximately the same size as Dürer's, yet fundamentally different. The first and most obvious difference is their horizontal format. Furthermore, all of them are executed in black chalk, although in the most majestic and monumental drawing, the almost square *Portrait of a Woman with Bonnet* now in Weimar (cat. 100),[113] he added touches of red chalk and brown wash in imitation of Dürer's black backgrounds. Nevertheless, Lucas's portraits are more rigid than Dürer's, stripped of emotion, and their compositions are less varied. Their lighting is even, the shadows rendered meticulously with almost infinite hatching, sometimes soft, at other times bold, both parallel and in crossed variations, both straight and curved, depending on function.

At first glance the horizontal composition and the use of hatching as the prime modelling tool in Lucas van Leyden's drawings seem more closely connected to Dürer's silverpoint drawings than to his larger portraits in charcoal or black chalk. However, when we compare Dürer's highly finished *Portrait of a Young Man* now in Berlin (cat. 96) with Lucas van Leyden's male portraits now in Stockholm[114] and Leiden (cat. 101), made a year later, there are obvious similarities in the way both artists painted nose, mouth and eyes, and in their handling

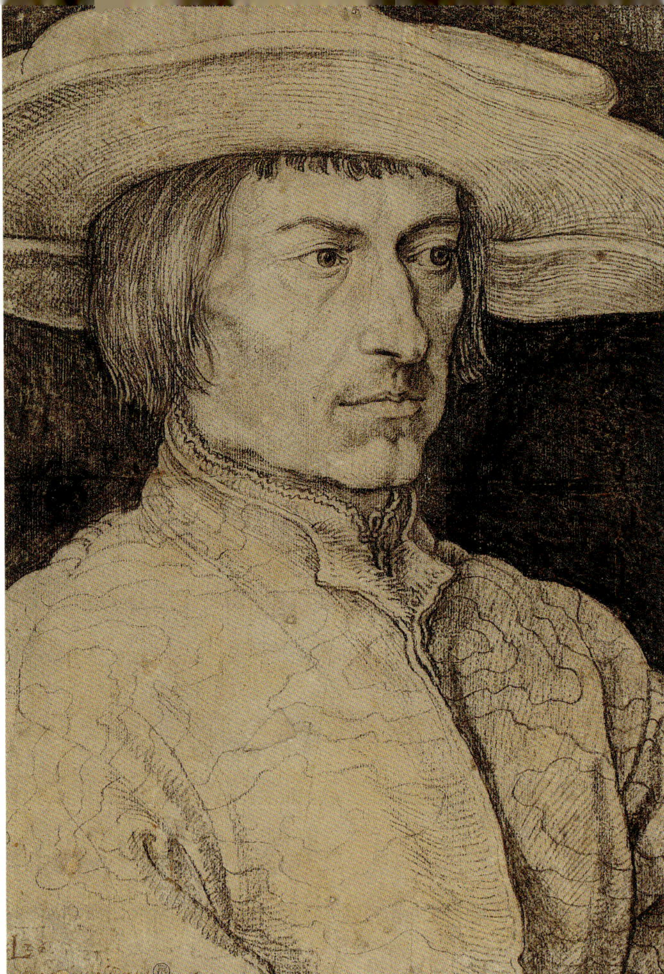

Fig. 126
ALBRECHT DÜRER
Portrait of a Man, possibly Anton von Metz, 1521
Black chalk, 36.9 × 25.4 cm
British Museum (1910,0212.103)

of light. Only Dürer's decorative elegance in rendering his model's hair and his more restrained use of hatching sets him apart from Lucas in terms of technique. Their essential difference can be seen in Dürer's much greater variety of pose, lighting and emotional response, and in his ability to give his sitters a more human outlook, whether characterised by modesty (cat. 93), arrogance (fig. 125) or cheerfulness (cat. 99). It is therefore hardly surprising that the rather stiff and sturdy-looking gentleman in another portrait now in the British Museum was long considered to be a self portrait by Lucas van Leyden (fig. 126): both Mende and Kloek point to Lucas van Leyden as the source for Dürer's more rigid and visually objective perception.[115] This would mean, however, that the drawing was made after the two artists met in June 1521. In that case the distinguished-looking gentleman may actually be Anton von Metz, Christian II's chamberlain, whom Dürer portrayed in Antwerp on 2 July 1521.[116] This would be the last large portrait drawing of Dürer's year-long sojourn in the Low Countries.

1 On Dürer, the honour system and the 'gift economy', see Sahm 2002, pp. 146–55; Honig 2008; Hirschfelder 2013.
2 Hirschfelder 2013, pp. 113–14. On Dürer's lost imperial privilege and its reinstatement, see Sahm 2002, p. 133; Unverfehrt 2007, pp. 13–16; and several other essays in the present publication.
3 Hirschfelder 2013, pp. 122–3, 128–9.
4 Dürer's original journal has not survived. See Christof Metzger's essay in the present publication, pp. 149–63. Two later copies are in the Nuremberg State Archive (about 1550) and the State Library in Bamberg (cat. 14, seventeenth century). The most precise German transcription of both texts is still Rupprich 1956–69, vol. 1, pp. 146–202. Publications that have added new insights to our knowledge of Dürer's Netherlandish journey are: Veth and Muller 1918; Goris and Marlier 1970; Brussels 1977; Sahm 2002, pp. 133–84; Unverfehrt 2007. The most recent translation in English is Ashcroft 2017, vol. 1, pp. 545–628.
5 Kupferstichkabinett, Staatliche Museen zu Berlin, inv. KdZ 40. See Ashcroft 2017, vol. 1, p. 577. On the drawing, see Strauss 1974, vol. 4, p. 2014, no. 1521/9; Hans Mielke in Anzelewsky and Mielke 1984, pp. 108–9, no. 105; and Michael Roth in Berlin 2006, pp. 150–1, 152, 156, no. 94.
6 Ashcroft 2017, vol. 1, p. 561.
7 Ibid., p. 569.
8 It is still uncertain whether the drawing was part of Dürer's *Nachlass*, but this is likely.
9 See Christof Metzger's essay in the present volume, pp. 149–63.
10 Frankfurt 2003, p. 103 n. 2. However, according to Arnold Nesselrath (verbal communication) this must have occurred much later.
11 Ashcroft 2017, vol. 1, p. 629, no. 163.2.
12 Ibid., p. 556.
13 Ibid., p. 630, no. 163.5.
14 Veth and Muller 1918, vol. 2, pp. 259–60.
15 Ashcroft 2017, vol. 1, p. 557.
16 Ibid., p. 556.
17 Ibid., p. 629, no. 163.4.
18 Ibid., p. 629, no. 163.3.
19 Ibid., pp. 566, 580 and 583.
20 Ibid., p. 569.
21 On the goldsmiths of Margaret of Austria, see Duverger 1929 and Duverger 1934.
22 Not much is known about Stefano Capello. Today just one work of art is attributed to his hand, a silver beaker in the Treasury of the Munich Residenz (Duverger 1980, p. 130; Ginzburg 2005; D. Eichberger, 'Dürer and the Netherlands: Patterns of Exchange and Mutual Admiration', in Silver and Chipps Smith 2010, pp. 149–65, at p. 159 n. 18).
23 This was remarked upon by both Panofsky and Strauss: Panofsky 1943, vol. 2, no. 1072; Strauss 1974, vol. 4, p. 1920, no. 1520/9.
24 '1520 / zw prwssell gemacht'.
25 Ashcroft 2017, vol. 1, p. 560.
26 All drawings from the small silverpoint book are actually made with a silverpoint stylus, as well as the *Portrait of a Man* in Berlin (cat. 91). See H. Guicharnaud and A. Duval, 'Analyse des dessins de Dürer à la pointe métallique au Laboratoire de Recherche des Musées de France', in Chantilly 1999, pp. 144–6; Reiche, Merchel and Radtke 2005, *passim*. On silverpoint drawings in general, see Washington and London 2015.
27 See the contribution of Arnold Nesselrath in the present publication, pp. 165–83.
28 Ashcroft 2017, vol. 1, p. 564. The drawing is in the Kupferstichkabinett, Staatliche Museen zu Berlin, inv. KdZ 4179. Strauss 1974, vol. 4, p. 1940, no. 1520/19; Hans Mielke in Anzelewsky and Mielke 1984, pp. 97–8, no. 94; Michael Roth in Berlin 2006, p. 148, no. 92.
29 Ashcroft 2017, vol. 1, p. 569. Ashcroft translates 'Büchlein' as 'sketchbook'. In fact, none of Dürer's silverpoints can be characterised as sketches.
30 Musée Condé, Chantilly, inv. 891. Strauss 1974, vol. 4, p. 1964, no. 1520/31; Chantilly 1999, pp. 58–9, no. 10r.
31 Ashcroft 2017, vol. 1, p. 633, no. 163.17.
32 Ibid., p. 569.
33 Ibid., pp. 572, 575. It is not unlikely that the pair were portrayed by Joos van Cleve, in the painted pendants in the Uffizi, Florence (*Portrait of a Man*, inv. 1643, and *Portrait of a Woman*, inv. 1644, both oil on oak panel).
34 Musée Condé, Chantilly, inv. 893. Strauss 1974, vol. 4, no. 1520/21; Chantilly 1999, pp. 52–4, no. 8v.
35 Ashcroft 2017, vol. 1, p. 566.
36 Albertina, Vienna, inv. 22385. Strauss 1974, vol. 4, no. 1521/57; Vienna 2003, pp. 496–8, no. 174r; Vienna 2019, pp. 402, 410, 412–13, 463, no. 188.
37 The wonderful lion on the recto was drawn three months earlier, in Ghent (fig. 95).
38 Musée Condé, Chantilly, inv. 892r. Strauss 1974, vol. 4, p. 1960, no. 1520/29; Chantilly 1999, pp. 55–7, no. 9r.
39 Hairnets were used by men at the time, as indicated by the portraits of Felix Hungersperg and Paulus Topler.
40 Ashcroft 2017, vol. 1, p. 567.
41 Hans Mielke in Anzelewsky and Mielke 1984, p. 100.
42 The Ravensburger portrait carries the inscription 'gemacht zw antorff' ('Done in Antwerp').
43 This may actually be the same Nicolao to whom Dürer granted three engravings two months earlier (Ashcroft 2017, vol. 1, p. 563).
44 Ibid., p. 585. Karel van Mander – who was otherwise remarkably well informed about Dürer's life – argues that both artists portrayed each other, not in Antwerp but in Leiden (K. van Mander, *Het schilder-boeck waer in voor eerst de leerlustighe ieught den grondt der edel vrij schilderconst in verscheyden deelen wort voorghedraghen*, Haarlem 1604, fol. 212v). The silverpoint portrait is kept in the Palais des Beaux-Arts in Lille, inv. Pl. 918. Strauss 1974, vol. 4, no. 1521/26; Leiden 2011, p. 279, no. 77.

45 Maria Luise Sternath in Vienna 2003, p. 386.
46 Ashcroft 2017, vol. 1, p. 635. The actual document is in the British Library, inv. Add MS 5231, fol. 79v.
47 Ibid., p. 578.
48 Ibid., p. 562.
49 Kupferstichkabinett, Staatliche Museen zu Berlin, inv. KdZ 36. Metalpoint on grey-violet prepared paper, 40.1 × 27.1 cm. Strauss 1974, vol. 4, p. 1998, no. 1521/1; Fedja Anzelewsky in Anzelewsky and Mielke 1984, pp. 109–10, no. 106; Michael Roth in Berlin 2006, pp. 148–50, no. 93.
50 Ashcroft 2017, vol. 1, p. 634, no. 163.22.
51 Ibid., p. 569: 'Note: At Bergen bought my wife thin Dutch cloth for a headdress, cost 1 gulden 7 stuivers'.
52 Budde 1996, p. 217, no. Z5; Christof Metzger in Vienna 2019, p. 466, no. 5.
53 Ashcroft 2017, vol. 1, p. 563.
54 Ibid., p. 565. Jakob Köpfinger was a solicitor from Nuremberg and an acquaintance of Dürer.
55 Dürer made two portraits of Joachim Patinir, both silverpoints. One was no doubt a gift to Patinir, the second Dürer probably kept for himself. Therefore, the translation by Ashcroft (2017, vol. 1, p. 579) is not quite correct: 'I drew Master Joachim with the silverpoint and then did a second portrait for him too'. A drawing in the Herzog Anton Ulrich-Museum in Braunschweig, inv. Z1289, is probably a direct copy after Patinir's portrait from Dürer's estate by Aegidius Sadeler, who was in the service of Rudolf II in Prague.
56 Dürer recorded only five portrait drawings in black chalk, the first being that of sculptor Jean Mone in the early spring of 1521, but that does not necessarily mean this was Dürer's first drawing in chalk. Several of the 36 unspecified portrait drawings may have been executed in black chalk. Dürer mentions it for the first time shortly after his return from Brussels in early September 1520 (ibid., p. 562: 'I paid 4 stuivers for anthracite and black chalk').
57 Kupferstichkabinett, Staatliche Museen zu Berlin, inv. KdZ 4230. Strauss 1974, vol. 2, no. 1503/4; F. Anzelewsky in Anzelewsky and Mielke 1984, p. 37, no. 34.
58 Kupferstichkabinett, Staatliche Museen zu Berlin, inv. KdZ 1528. Strauss 1974, vol. 3, no. 1515/51; F. Anzelewsky in Anzelewsky and Mielke 1984, p. 81, no. 77.
59 'Auf diese Weise erhalten die gezeichneten Bildnisse etwas Geschlossenes, was sie den Gemälden annähert, für die sie ein Ersatz sein sollten'. Anzelewsky in Anzelewsky and Mielke 1984, p. 81, no. 77.
60 On the use of panels as support for these autonomous portrait drawings, see Krischel and Schaefer 2009, p. 91; Hirschfelder 2013, p. 125. No doubt these large drawings in charcoal or chalk needed to be fixed before they were handed over to the sitter: on this complicated technique, see Koschatzky 1993, pp. 102–3; Dietz 2008, pp. 35–6, 43–6, 66–74; Hirschfelder 2013, p. 125.
61 Ashcroft 2017, vol. 1, pp. 576, 580, 589. On Dürer as a portrait painter, see Till-Holger Borchert's essay in the present publication, pp. 77–101.
62 The journal confirms that by August 1520 Joachim Patinir was letting Dürer use his pigments and allowing him to use one of his assistants (Ashcroft 2017, vol. 1, p. 557) and Dirk Vellert would provide Dürer with red pigment (ibid., p. 562). For the preparation of the portrait of Christian II he was helped by a Brussels painter and his assistants. To cover Dürer's expenses, Christian's chamberlain Anton von Metz paid him no fewer than 12 'hornisch gulden' (ibid., p. 589), more than the artist actually needed.
63 Dürer's journal reveals that he needed four days to finish the portrait of King Christian II of Denmark (ibid.). This was most certainly fast, but he had done this previously, as can be judged from the painted note on the 1506 *Christ among the Doctors* (cat. 31). See Dana Cowen's essay in the present volume, pp. 241–51.
64 Ashcroft 2017, vol. 1, p. 566.
65 'Ein Frauen-Bild mit einem Schleyer'. Heller 1827, vol. 2, part 1, p. 82, no. 43.
66 Katrin Dyballa in Frankfurt 2013, pp. 356–7, no. 14.11. The same applies for Strauss's suggestion that the 39-year-old might present Dürer's niece, although she may have been the same age (Strauss 1974, vol. 4, p. 1956, no. 1520/27).
67 Van Gelder 1971, p. 158.
68 Katrin Dyballa in Frankfurt 2013, p. 356.
69 Van Gelder 1971, p. 158. See Stijn Alsteens's essay in the present volume, pp. 129–45.
70 Ashcroft 2017, vol. 1, p. 587.
71 Based on the assumption that the drawing was done in black chalk, Veth and Muller (1918, vol. 1, p. 46) suggested that the sitter was possibly Jean Mone or Anton Honold (1466–1533), both of whom Dürer portrayed in black chalk (Ashcroft 2017, vol. 1, pp. 575, 585).
72 Anzelewsky 1971, pp. 264, 267; F. Anzelewsky in Brussels 1977, p. 78, no. 88.
73 Winkler 1936–9, vol. 4, p. 38. Only a year earlier, Christian II played a decisive role in the Stockholm Bloodbath. Shortly after his coronation as the new king of Sweden, he had nearly a hundred Swedish noblemen executed who were part of the anti-unionist party led by Sten Sture (1440–1503). Regarded in occupied Sweden as a tyrant, Christian II became known as the 'Nero of the North'. With regard to Michel Sittow's portrait in the Statens Museum for Kunst in Copenhagen (inv. Sp. 789), Weniger 2011, pp. 79–82, no. 7.
74 Christian II does not wear his Order of the Golden Fleece, which he had received in 1519, as it may have been deemed unnecessary for this rather informal portrait. No doubt he would have worn it for the more formal painted portrait. For the king's 'travel attire', see Kai Sass 1976, pp. 164–6, and Rowlands 1993, vol. 1, p. 102. It cannot be stated with any certainty whether or not the drawing was used as a preparatory study for the painting, as Hirschfelder (2013, p. 126) suggests as a reason why its condition is less satisfactory than that of most other large portrait drawings.
75 Strauss 1974, vol. 4, p. 1934, no. 1520/16; Emmanuel Starcky in Paris 1991, pp. 72–3, 75, 165, no. 66; Matthias Mende in Vienna 2003, pp. 494–5, no. 173.
76 Ashcroft 2017, vol. 1, p. 561.
77 Ibid., p. 557.
78 Peter van der Coelen in Rotterdam 2008, pp. 61–3.
79 Erasmus himself wrote in 1525 that the sitting was interrupted by the arrival of several courtiers (see John Rowlands in Bietenholz 2003, vol. 1, p. 414). One of the guests at this dinner must have been Nikolaus Kratzer, who noted on his personal copy of the very different portrait engraving Dürer made in 1526 that he was a witness to the portrait session in Brussels (Veth and Muller 1918, vol. 1, p. 17; Rowlands in Bietenholz 2003, vol. 1, p. 414; Unverfehrt 2007, p. 44; Ashcroft 2017, vol. 1, p. 595, no. 57). The present location of this particular engraving is unknown; it was auctioned as lot 579 at the sale of the collection of Henri Wolff, with Prestel in Frankfurt, 26 November 1877.
80 Dürer added the date 1520, whereas the inscription is by a later hand.
81 Peter van der Coelen in Rotterdam 2008, pp. 62, 71 n. 29.
82 Allen and Garrod 1906–58, vol. 6, p. 1536; Rupprich 1956–69, vol. 1, p. 271, no. 79; Ashcroft 2017, vol. 2, p. 748, no. 203.1.
83 Ashcroft 2017, vol. 1, p. 561.
84 Winkler 1936–9, vol. 4, no. 808; Strauss 1974, vol. 4, p. 2060, no. 1521/34; Pierrette Jean-Richard in Paris 1991, p. 75, no. 67.
85 Ashcroft 2017, vol. 1, p. 557.
86 Musée du Louvre, Paris, inv. 1343.
87 Winkler 1936–9, vol. 4, p. 33: 'Die Schönheit des Linienwerkes vermag eine gewiße Starrheit nicht zu überwinden'.
88 Hans Mielke in Anzelewsky and Mielke 1984, p. 107.
89 Winkler 1936–9, vol. 4, no. 917; Mende 1985, *passim*. I do not think that the drawing should be dated to about 1526, as Winkler did, nor do I share Mende's opinion that it is a mere copy after a lost original by a Netherlandish draughtsman from the second half of the sixteenth century. Mende's main argument against Dürer's authorship, the incorrect presentation of the typical Antwerp headdress, is unconvincing.
90 Mende 1985, pp. 109–11; Campbell 2014, vol. 1, pp. 322–3.
91 M. Leesberg and M. Sellink, 'Philips Galle', in New Hollstein Dutch, 2001, p. 103, no. 628.
92 It is still unclear why this version was abandoned before it was finished.
93 The single oak board of the unfinished painting has been subject to dendrochronological examination by Ian Tyers. According to his report, dated March 2009, the panel cannot have been used for painting before 1520.
94 Briquet 1907 (1968), no. 6281. For the Venetian drawings, see Strauss 1974, vol. 2, nos 1506/30, 39–42, 44–5. For the 1516 drawing in London, ibid., vol. 3, no. 1516/10; Rowlands 1993, vol. 1, p. 96, no. 210; and London 2002, pp. 197–8, no. 141.
95 Löcher 2004, pp. 319–22.
96 Strauss 1974, vol. 3, nos 1517/1 and 1518/22. Strauss incorrectly dated the Peutinger drawing to 1517 because he was convinced that a drawing dated 1517 from the Rothschild collection portrayed the same sitter. That sitter, however, is the Nuremberg patrician and counsellor Kaspar Nützel (1471–1529; Pierrette Jean-Richard in Paris 1991, p. 67, no. 60).
97 Lazarus Ravensburger, Markus Ulstett, Hans Lüber (before 1477–1554), Ambrosius Höchstetter (1463–1534), Jacob Rehlinger (died 1571) and Bernhard Stecher are all known to have been portrayed by Dürer at the time.
98 For an overview, see Rowlands 1993, vol. 1, pp. 97–8, no. 213, and London 2002, p. 200, no. 145.
99 Anzelewsky 1971, p. 248, fig. 103.
100 Strauss 1974, vol. 4, p. 2056, no. 1521/32.
101 Pierrette Jean-Richard in Paris 1991, p. 77, no. 70; Hirschfelder 2013, pp. 110–11, 132 n. 22, fig. 1.
102 Ashcroft 2017, vol. 1, p. 561.
103 It is not impossible that Cort's portrait is actually based on Dürer's now-lost charcoal portrait of Bernaert van Orley of 1520.
104 Ashcroft 2017, vol. 1, pp. 584, 586–7. In 1523 Dürer would portray his younger sister Anna Rehlinger in a drawing now in the Veste Coburg (Strauss 1974, vol. 4, p. 2244, no. 1523/20).
105 Lippmann 1883–1929, vol. 4, no. 287.
106 Veth and Muller 1918, vol. 1, p. 40, no. L.
107 London 2002, p. 210, no. 155. See also Rowlands 1993, vol. 1, p. 103, no. 229.
108 Ashcroft 2017, vol. 1, p. 573.
109 On the drawing and the print by Jacob Binck, see S. Alsteens, 'Gossart as a Draftsman', in New York and London 2010, pp. 89–104, at pp. 401–4, no. 111.
110 See Alsteens in New York and London 2010, pp. 97, 102 n. 63, for another example. A drawing in the Hermitage, published by Alexey Larionov as *Portrait of Christian II* by Jan Gossaert (St Petersburg 2010, pp. 147–55, 357, no. 21) is possibly by Gossaert; although there is some resemblance with other portraits of the Danish monarch, it is most certainly not an autonomous portrait, but a free facial study.
111 Kloek 1978, pp. 432, 434–5, 446–9, nos 13–18; W. Kloek in Leiden 2011, pp. 160, 162–3, 297–9, nos 91–3.
112 Kloek 1978, pp. 452–3, no. 23; Jan Piet Filedt Kok in Leiden 2011, pp. 286–7, nos 79a–b.
113 The drawing is probably cut on the left and right.
114 Nationalmuseum, Stockholm, inv. 1858/1863.
115 Matthias Mende in Vienna 2003, p. 492; Wouter Kloek in Leiden 2011, p. 298.
116 Ashcroft 2017, vol. 1, p. 587.

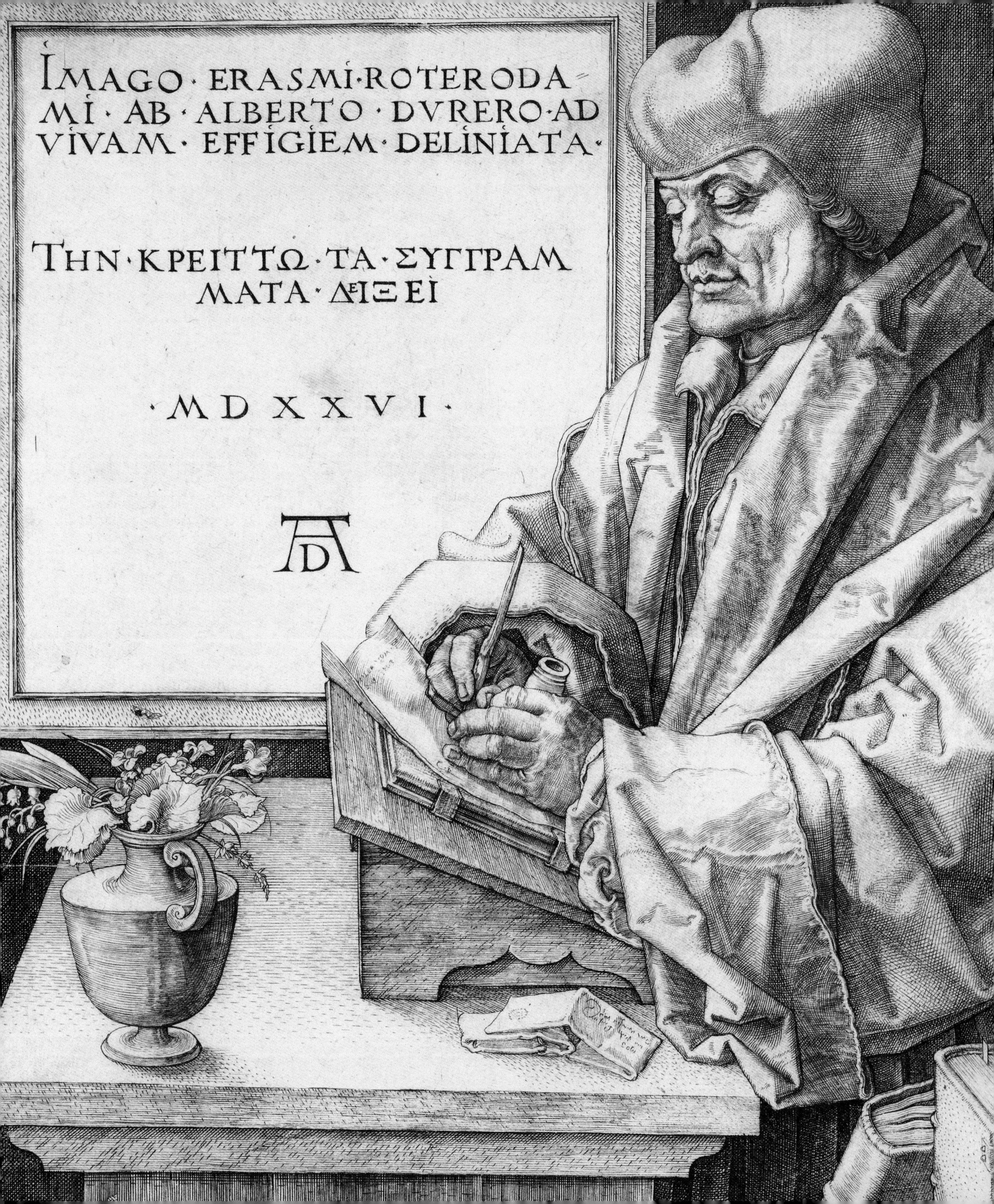
IMAGO · ERASMI · ROTERODA
MI · AB · ALBERTO · DURERO · AD
VIVAM · EFFIGIEM · DELINIATA ·
ΤΗΝ · ΚΡΕΙΤΤΩ · ΤΑ · ΣΥΓΓΡΑΜ
ΜΑΤΑ · ΔΕΙΞΕΙ
· M D X X V I ·
AD

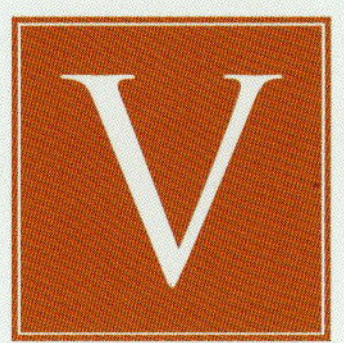

ALBRECHT DÜRER AND MARTIN LUTHER

WITHIN DÜRER'S LIFETIME, THE CHRISTIAN CHURCH underwent enormous upheaval and division. In 1517 the Augustinian friar Martin Luther published his 95 theses calling attention to abuses in the Church, such as the practice of selling indulgences, through which people effectively paid to have their time in purgatory reduced. Luther and his supporters advocated ordinary people reading the Bible in German and participating fully in the ceremony of the Mass. They emphasised Christ's teachings and questioned the role that saints and their images had come to play in Christian belief. The events that followed led to a permanent division in Christianity.

Like many others, Dürer was deeply interested in what Luther had to say: the list he made of 16 of Luther's pamphlets exemplifies the latter's challenges to the old beliefs on topics such as indulgences, sin and the real head of the Church (Christ, not the Pope). Dürer planned to make Luther's engraved portrait, although he did not proceed with this project, and acquired Lutheran broadsheets during his visit to the Low Countries. The Emperor Charles V, whose coronation in Aachen in 1520 Dürer set out to attend, was determined to challenge Lutheranism and prevent it from taking hold. Shortly after Dürer left the Low Countries the authorities clamped down on the reformers and their publications.

The adoption of new beliefs had a profound impact on the production of paintings, prints and sculpture, particularly in Germany. Although Luther himself was conservative in this respect, in Strasbourg and Basel religious images were destroyed wholesale, and in many places demand for traditional subjects representing saints and the Virgin Mary was greatly reduced. New subjects developed under Lutheran guidance, with a renewed focus on the life and teachings of Christ, and on the apostles rather than the saints. Among Dürer's last paintings were two over life-size panels with representations of four holy men: Saints John the Evangelist, Peter, Mark and Paul. Made in 1526 and inscribed with texts in German from Luther's translation of the New Testament, Dürer gave the panels to the city of Nuremberg, which espoused moderate reform. As a designer of prints, Dürer was able to choose subjects for his markets; but in his later years his drawings and prints focused on scenes from the life of Christ, the apostles or else portraits such as the long-delayed portrait of the humanist Erasmus of 1526, his last engraving, for which he had made sketches in the Low Countries. SF

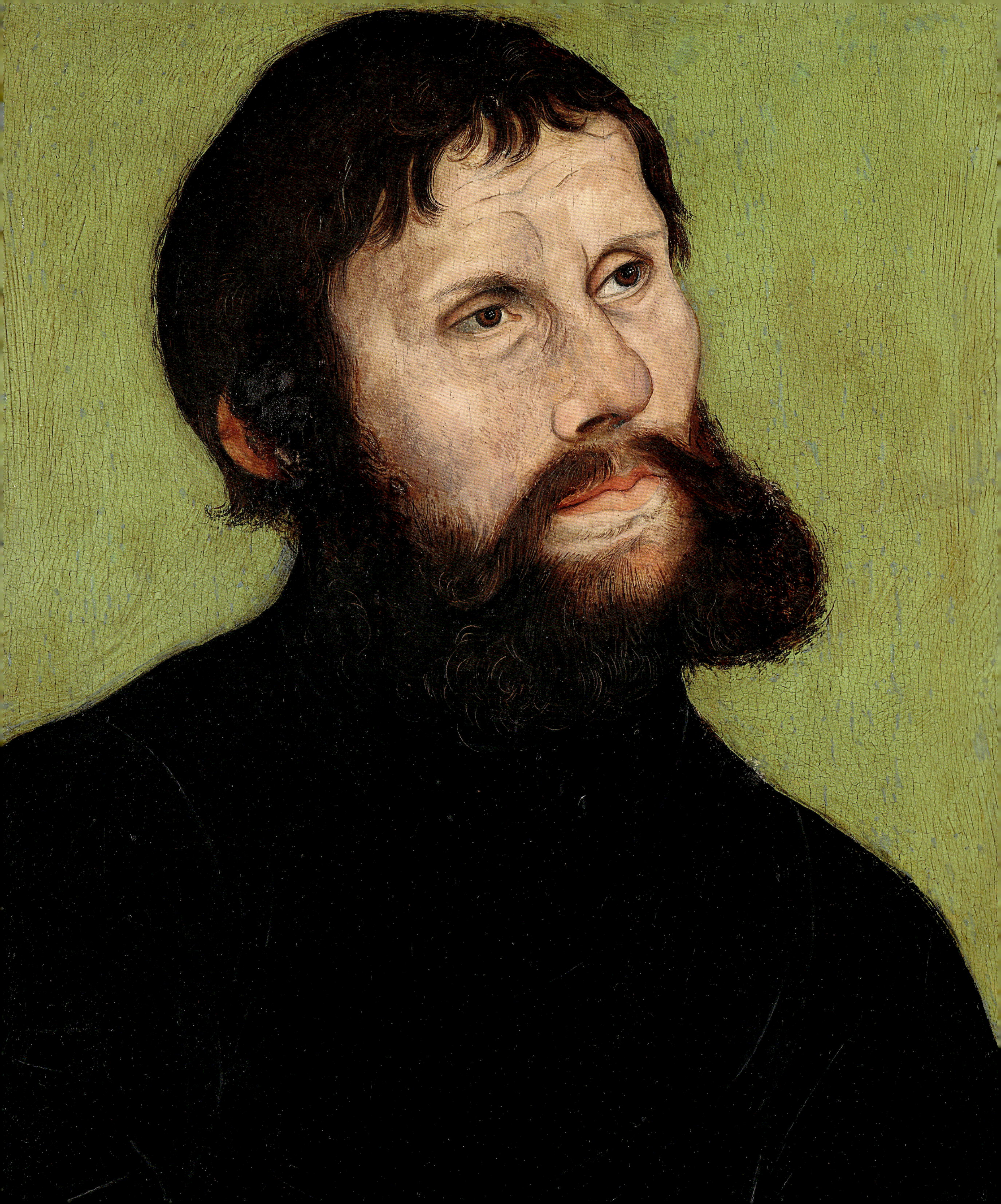

JEROEN STUMPEL

LUTHER IN DÜRER'S JOURNAL

ON THE *LUTHERKLAGE*, ITS AUTHORSHIP AND PERSECUTION IN ANTWERP

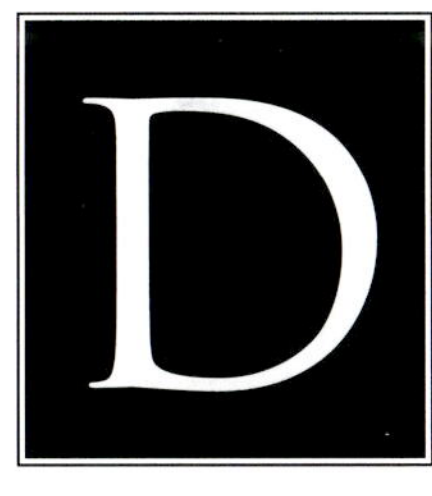

ÜRER'S TRAVEL JOURNAL CONTAINS AN astonishingly personal outburst, known as the *Lutherklage*. This 'Lament on Luther' has always been considered an important and moving document, but at times its authenticity has been questioned.[1] That doubts could arise at all is partly due to the fact that we do not have an autograph version of the journal, but just two handwritten copies made many decades after Dürer's death: one in Nuremberg and the other in Bamberg.[2] Only one folio of the original manuscript has apparently survived, now in London, showing a schematic drawing of a mantle (cat. 6).

By the beginning of the twentieth century, the text of the Lament had become generally acknowledged as a genuine elegy from Dürer himself. About fifty years ago, however, Heinrich Lutz, in an article on Protestantism in the age of Dürer, believed it to be a forgery of some sort.[3] Remarkably, his argument was largely ignored: according to the latest established opinion it could not possibly be a later fraudulent insertion and therefore must be an authentic part of the original journal.[4]

Interestingly, the Lament on Luther is probably neither a forgery nor a personal statement by Dürer. It is even possible to trace the name of the author who must really have been responsible for 'one of the greatest spontaneous prayers in World literature', as it has been called.[5] He appears to be a man who belonged to the Antwerp world that Dürer visited. Looking into this question also leads to a better understanding of some of the reasons for Dürer's long stay in Antwerp, and how events related to the Lament may have induced him to leave the town in the summer of 1521.

PREVIOUS PAGE
Detail from *Portrait of Erasmus* (cat. 94)

OPPOSITE
Detail from *Portrait of Martin Luther as 'Junker Jörg'* (cat. 102)

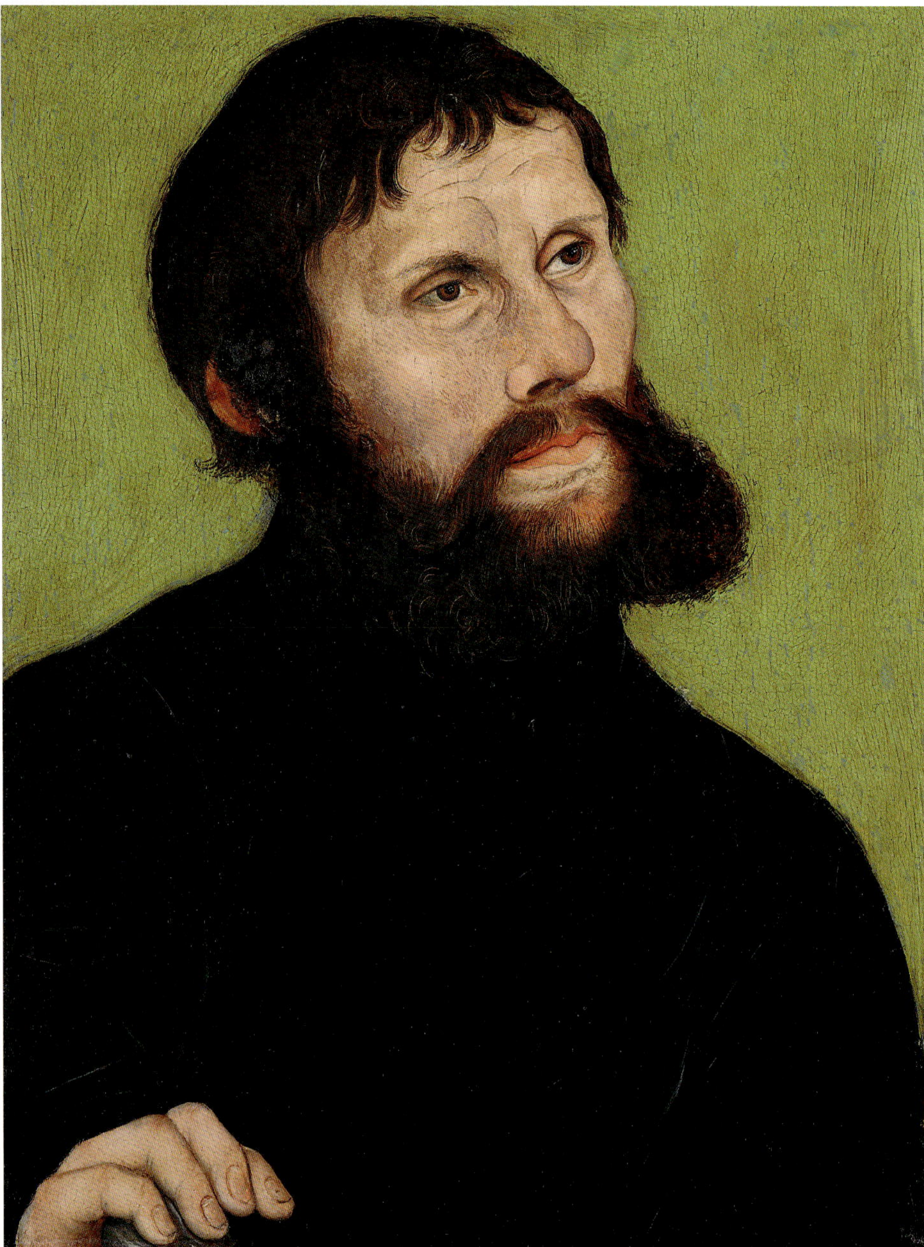

102
LUCAS CRANACH THE ELDER
(1472–1553)
Portrait of Martin Luther as 'Junker Jörg', 1521
Oil on wood, 33.5 × 25.3 cm
Museum of Fine Art, Leipzig

THE LAMENT AND ITS CIRCUMSTANCES

The passage begins with the date of 17 May 1521. Luther had been summoned to appear at the Diet of Worms in order to recant before the young Charles V. The Elector Frederick the Wise of Saxony had managed to arrange that Luther would not be arrested without a proper hearing and would be protected by a letter of safe conduct during the period of the imperial assembly.

The Diet of Worms hearing is famously considered to have been the point of no return. When Luther set out to travel back to Wittenberg on 25 April he was not arrested: he was to enjoy safe conduct for several more days. At this point Frederick the Wise initiated a ruse, with the intention of eventually bringing Luther safely back to Wittenberg without obvious damage to his own political situation. At Eisenach, where Luther arrived on 2 May 1521, he was told that he would be taken to the nearby stronghold of Wartburg. Luther had to change his priest's habit for a knight's costume and the rumour would be spread that he had been taken prisoner by supporters of the Emperor. In his safe haven at the Wartburg castle Luther assumed the false identity of 'Junker Jörg' and let his hair and beard grow. It was to be another 300 days before he would be back in Wittenberg. To commemorate this episode Lucas Cranach painted a portrait of Luther in his disguise as 'Junker Jörg' (cat. 102). Long before his return to

Fig. 127
HANS HOLBEIN THE YOUNGER
(1497/8–1543)
Portrait of Desiderius Erasmus of Rotterdam in the Round, about 1532
Oil on lime, 14.2 cm diameter
Kunstmuseum Basel

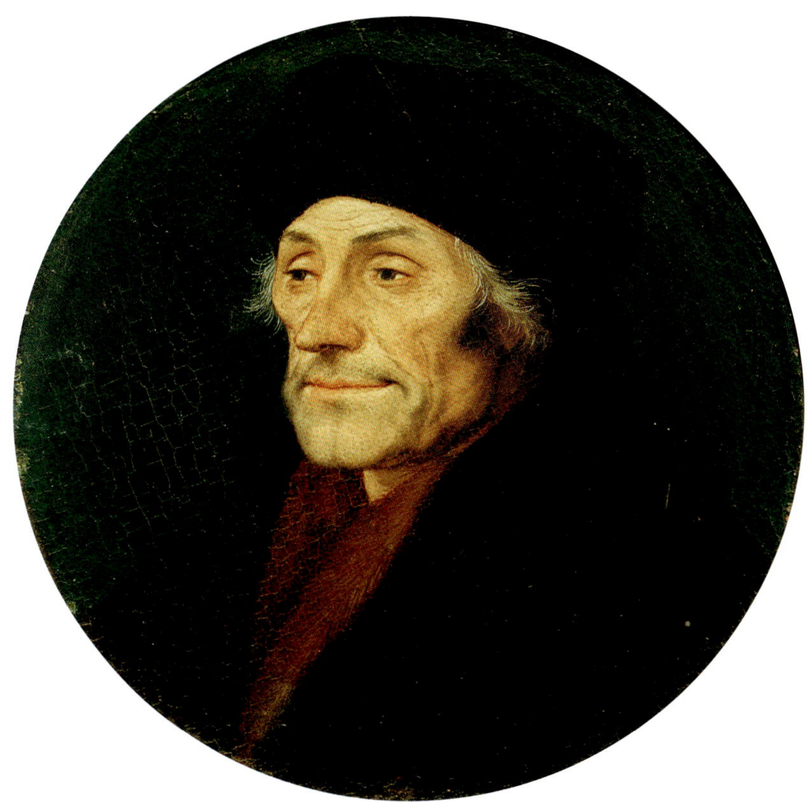

Wittenberg, however, the pretence had been abandoned. Within weeks of Luther's move to the Wartburg it had become known all over Europe that he was in fact safe.[6]

The Lament in Dürer's journal was a first response to the sensational false news of Luther's captivity. The story had reached Antwerp by 17 May, the text says, and was apparently taken very seriously indeed. In Dürer's notebook we may read, for instance, about 'this godly man, illuminated by the Holy Spirit, who was thus betrayed, but who was following in the footsteps of Christ and in the true Christian faith. And whether he is alive, or whether they have put him to death … I cannot know …'. The author was clearly on Luther's side, and had little respect for Rome: 'he has suffered that for the sake of Christian truth, and because he has denounced the unchristian Papacy'.[7]

It seems that the abduction fable was swallowed whole. The text reveals how an admirer of Luther could be deeply worried about his fate, and consider the situation tense enough even for murder. God and the Holy Spirit are in fact evoked to send or inspire a follower. Throughout the Lament we find a combination of despair at the potential loss of Luther and hopeful calls for a worthy replacement: 'If we lose this man … we pray Thee, Heavenly Father, that Thou givest thy Holy Spirit instead to another …'.[8] Elsewhere we read:

> O God, if Luther be dead, who will henceforth proclaim the Holy Gospel to us with like clarity? Ah God, what might he have written for us in ten or twenty more years! O all pious Christian folk, help me to weep for this man imbued with God's spirit, and to beseech God to send us another man who bears his light.[9]

It was this eager wish to see reparation for the assumed loss of Luther that would lead to the famous call to Erasmus (fig. 127): 'Oh, Erasmus Roterodamus, why do you hold back? See, what the unjust tyranny of worldly might and the powers of darkness are capable of? Hear us, soldier of Christ! Ride forth with the Lord Christ, defend the truth, win the martyr's crown!'[10] This is the voice of a devastated man, devoted to both Luther and his cause. His admiration – and indeed love – for Luther can also be gauged from the various passages in which he explains the clarity with which Luther could preach and write about the gospels: 'Therefore let each man see, who reads Dr Martin Luther's books, how transparently clear his teaching is when he sets forth Holy Scripture';[11] 'And if we lose this man, who has written more clearly than anyone who has lived in the last 140 years …'.[12]

This last reference to '140 years' poses the question of to whom the journal refers. We know that while the bad news was still fresh, the Lament desperately turned to Erasmus as a possible successor. But who was Luther's precursor in this perspective of Church reform? Interestingly, the reference was already explained in the first printed edition in Dutch, which followed the first German printed version of the journal of 1780. According to the commentary in the Dutch edition, it could refer to none other than John Wycliffe (about 1330–1384), the English precursor of the Reformation. This identification must certainly be correct and has also been unanimously accepted in modern scholarship.[13]

It is tempting to quote more of these earliest outpourings of a Lutheran. The whole passage in the journal expresses genuine despair, and seems to show the extent to which laymen like Dürer could feel involved in the cause of the Reformation. But is it Dürer who speaks to us here, or indeed a layman? Most probably it is neither.

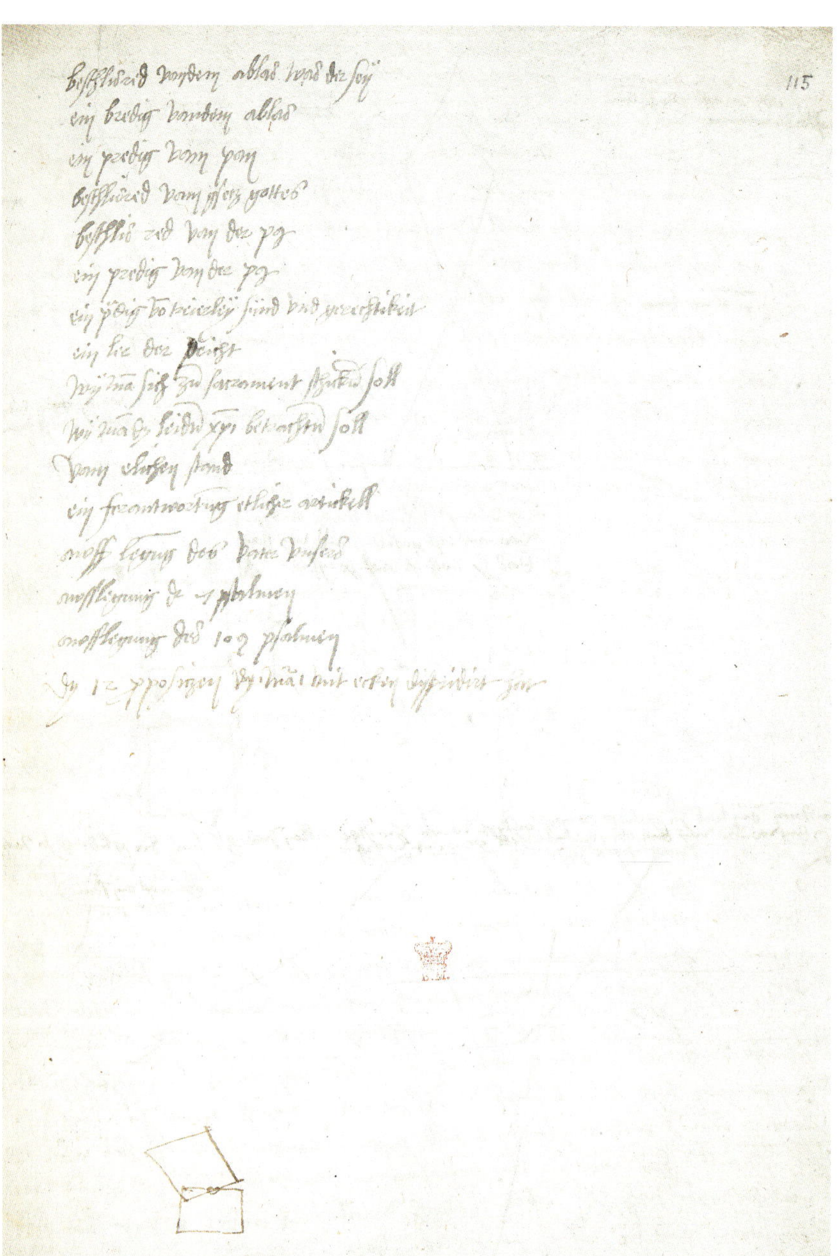

103
ALBRECHT DÜRER
List of works by Martin Luther, about 1520
Ink on paper, 32 × 22 cm
The British Library

AUTHORSHIP

There is no doubt that Dürer was interested in Luther and sympathised with his cause. In fact, just before he set off for the Low Countries in early 1520 he wrote a letter to Georg Spalatin, in which he famously expressed his wish to meet Luther in person in order to portray him and 'engrave it in copperplate as a lasting memorial of this Christian man, who has rescued me out of deep anguish'.[14] Tantalisingly, we are not informed as to what anguish he refers or how Luther helped to relieve these fears. Luther, in his turn, knew about and appreciated Dürer, as we know from a letter he wrote to Christoph Scheurl.[15] In the same year, having arrived in the Low Countries, Dürer purchased a number of Lutheran tracts. He had been acquiring such texts already before his departure to the Low Countries, and a personal list of them has survived (cat. 103).[16] But none of these is in Latin – in fact, in the aforementioned letter to Spalatin he requests to be sent texts '… whenever Doctor Martinus makes something new', adding: 'when it is German'.[17]

Dürer was not a theologian and his Latin was meagre. These facts might make one pause at the reference to Wycliffe. Apart from the problem that his writings had not yet been put into print, it is important to realise that they were in Latin, and thus all but inaccessible to Dürer.[18] So how could he have come to know about the clarity of Wycliffe's expositions of the gospels? And how could he know so precisely that Wycliffe had indeed been active 140 years earlier? Given Dürer's lack of Latin, it is perhaps also odd that he would so classically make use of the vocative case when emotionally addressing Erasmus, as well as using the Latinised form of Rotterdam correctly: '*O Erasme Roderadame*'.[19]

It has been obvious all along that the Lament stood apart from the remainder of the journal.[20] In fact, its sheer length and expressiveness is so different from the rest of it that the transition from the Lament to the usual format makes for a comical effect, especially when read aloud:

> O Christian men, pray God for help, for his judgement draws nigh and his justice shall be revealed … These are the slain who lie at the foot of God's altar and cry out for vengeance, to whom the voice of God answers: Await the full number of the innocent slain, then I will judge. Changed another 1 gulden for cash. I paid the doctor a further 8 stuivers. Note: Ate two more meals with Rodrigo. Ate with the rich canon. Cashed 1 gulden.[21]

From the manuscript in Bamberg we learn that even in 1779 the first editor, Gottlieb von Murr, had considered it wise to instruct the printer to insert a couple of white lines before and after the passage, a typographical measure followed by almost all modern editors (cat. 14 detail, below). As Max Friedländer wrote in 1921, the Lament is composed 'with an unexpectedly intense eloquence'.[22] For this reason he assumed that Dürer had written the entire text as a letter to Erasmus. This proposal still implied that the text came from Dürer himself, while acknowledging the difficulty of treating it as a proper and natural part of the journal. It would therefore have been seen as an interpolation. Friedländer's idea never met with acceptance by other scholarly commentators and his proposal would in any case not solve difficulties such as the effortless display of theological knowledge about Wycliffe.

Certainly the strangest aspect of the passage is the fact that Dürer, after such a long and intense outcry, does not return to the matter in the entire journal at all. Yet about seven days later, on 25 May, it had become known to the Venetian ambassador in Germany, to the council of Strasbourg and elsewhere in Europe, that Luther had not been captured by enemies, let alone killed, and that he was in safe hands and continued his work, even though his whereabouts had not been disclosed.[23] So it is more than likely that the news would have reached Antwerp around the same date. Given the outburst of emotion in the Lament at the news of Luther's perils, it is simply incongruent that the ensuing relief when it proved to be false news did not find expression in the journal – indeed, that it was not deemed worthy of mention at all.

Considering all this together, it seems impossible that the text should have issued from Dürer himself. Yet there

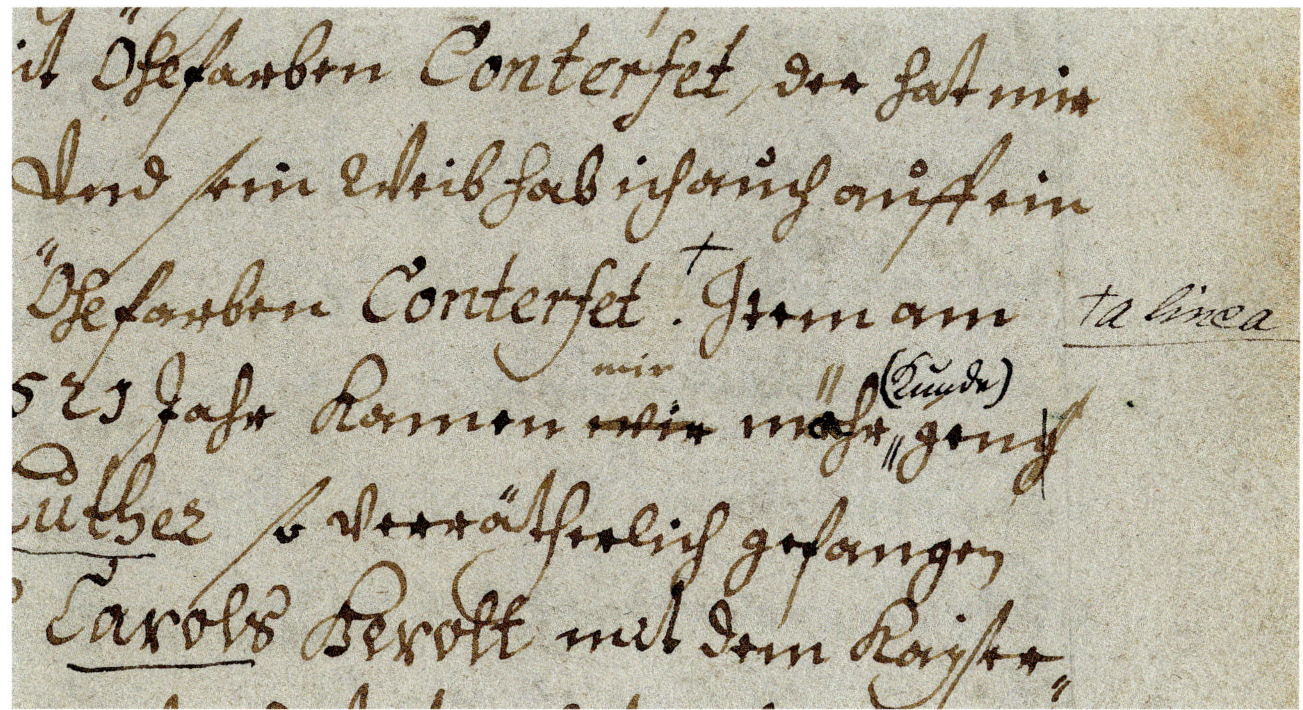

Detail from copy of Albrecht Dürer's diary of the journey to the Netherlands, about 1620 (cat. 14), fol. 47 recto

is no need to consider it a later forgery either. The dates of this very short incident of Luther's abduction fit the known data much too well. It would demand an excessive amount of philological precision on the part of a forger. This argument – that the passage is, in fact, too good to be false – is the reason why it has continued to be ascribed to Dürer.

One must conclude that the passage certainly was contemporary, and yet not composed by Dürer. It must somehow have become attached to the journal, and later absorbed by it, whether accidentally or more or less intentionally, as an easy and welcome occasion to frame Dürer as a staunch Lutheran.

AN ALTERNATIVE AUTHOR

If this theory is correct, we will have to find an author who is contemporaneous, related to Antwerp and strongly connected to the Lutheran cause. At the same time this author must not have been aware of the Wartburg ruse and therefore have accepted the false rumour as truth. As it happens, there is a strong candidate for such a position: the prior of the small convent of the Antwerp Augustinians, no more than about a thousand footsteps from the inn of Jobst Plankfelt, Dürer's Antwerp home. The name of this prior was Jacob Probst (died 1562). 'I have eaten twice with the Augustinians. Note: ate with Alexander Imhof; paid 8 stuivers at the apothecary's; ate once more with the Augustinians', Dürer wrote about the week after Corpus Christi 1521. And not much later: 'I ate again with the Augustinians'.[24] A couple of days later, just after he had 'sketched Master Lukas of Leiden with the silverpoint', he presented 'the steward of the Augustinian Priory here with a *Life of our Lady*, and his servant 4 stuivers'.[25] Before this period Dürer would have visited the convent on a number of occasions. Once in a while he mentions an Antwerp father confessor, and it has been assumed by several commentators that this could well have been the same Jacob Probst.

Small as it was, this community of Augustinians in Antwerp played a distinctive role in the early Reformation in the Low Countries, and it is worth closer scrutiny.[26] The Antwerp settlement was a special branch of the Augustinians, the so-called Augustine Observants. It had near the end of the fifteenth century split away from the regular Augustinian order, which itself dated from the thirteenth century. The new movement originated from the Germanic regions and the order was also known as the Saxon congregation. The young organisation had been granted its own vicar-general in 1503, the famous Johann von Staupitz (1460–1524), not only a friend of Luther (who was an Augustinian of the same branch) but also well known to Dürer, who actually belonged to the so-called 'Staupitz group' (Sodalitas Staupitziana) in Nuremberg, in the years just before he travelled to Antwerp.

From Germany the order of the Augustine Observants reached the Low Countries surprisingly fast, and it took hold in Holland first of all: initially Haarlem, then Enkhuizen. It must have been around 1513 that a group from Enkhuizen started a new filial in Antwerp, soon supported by the donation of money and a house through the generosity of two Antwerp burghers. The new settlement was opposed by the canons of the mighty Cathedral Church of Our Lady in Antwerp, but in 1514 official permission was granted. By this time the community consisted of a mere eight monks, the majority of whom came from the German lands and Guelders, almost all of them from Hanseatic regions. We hear names such as John of Essen, Gerard of Cologne and John of Osbach, as well references to two monks from Doetinchem, one from Deventer and one from Zutphen. The latter, named Hendrik, would later become famous as a martyr for the Lutheran cause. There was, strictly speaking, no Flemish member – except for the prior, Jacob Probst (also known as Propst, Praepositus or Jacob of Ypres, after his probable town of birth).[27] Probst's theological orientation or education was, however, German in some respects. He had been cloistered at Erfurt where the young Luther stayed – perhaps even sharing a cell with him during the period after Luther had his famous religious crisis – and he was mentored by Staupitz himself. Probst had also been studying theology in Wittenberg. It was this German-oriented Flemish monk who had been appointed prior of the new community in Antwerp at an unspecified date in the first half of 1519.

The close ties of Jacob Probst to Luther and Wittenberg are confirmed by his correspondence with Luther in 1519 (just after Probst moved to Antwerp from Wittenberg, where Luther was staying) and very clearly in a letter of Erasmus to Martin Luther of 30 May the same year (about a year before Dürer's arrival in Antwerp and about two years before the composition of the Lament). Erasmus wrote the following about Jacob Probst to Martin Luther: 'In the Augustine monastery in Antwerp is a prior, a true Christian, without falsehood, who has a glowing love for you [Luther], he was your pupil one time, of which he is proud. He is almost the only one who preaches Christianity.'[28] It is this man (with his 'glowing love' for Luther, as Erasmus wrote) who may be held responsible for the Lament on Luther in 1521. As it happens, we know that in these critical days Jacob Probst was not in Antwerp but had left his congregation to take examinations in Wittenberg. He would have

'news reached me at Antwerp that Martin Luther had been treacherously taken captive'.

departed round the end of April and sat his theological paper ('baccolaureatus') on 13 May.

It was initially disappointing to discover during this research that Probst had been far from Antwerp precisely during the time the Lament was composed, since this potentially undermined any attempt to connect him to the passage. After all, some of the dinners at the Augustinian priory mentioned above certainly took place while the prior was studying theology in Wittenberg, 700 miles from Antwerp. How could his alarmed voice concerning Luther's supposed arrest ever have reached the journal? But this very absence is the key to the entire history. Precisely because Probst was not in Antwerp, he had to communicate with his flock from a distance – via a written message.

We have seen that the Venetian ambassador in Worms heard of Luther's alleged kidnapping around 11 May, seven days after the event. This interval is related to the speed with which postal messages travelled in Renaissance Europe. It determines the rhythm of the correspondence, for instance, between Luther and Erasmus. One might assume that the false news would have reached Probst in Wittenberg at the same time. If the prior then reacted to inform his flock left in Antwerp, such a message would have reached Antwerp again six or seven days later, around 17 May: in other words, the very day it entered Dürer's journal as 'news reached me at Antwerp that Martin Luther had been treacherously taken captive'.[29]

Jacob Probst had not been told that the story about Luther was fabricated, as we learn from the correspondence of Luther himself. Luther's contact and confidant during this episode was Philip Melanchthon (1497–1560), at that time also staying in Wittenberg. Melanchthon was part of the very close inner circle informed about the plot during the first days of Luther's supposed disappearance. By 18 May the very same Venetian ambassador – seven days after he had first heard of the story – received the news of Luther's safety. By that time the news had reached the town of Wittenberg as well. That Jacob Probst, still in Wittenberg, was informed by this time is proven by the fact that he is mentioned in a letter from Melanchthon to Luther. This letter has not survived, but Luther's long reply of 26 May has.[30] In one passage he mentions Jacob Probst's eagerness to be in contact with Luther; the passage as well as the context make it clear that Probst had not been informed about the ruse. Luther's letter is in Latin but he uses a German word when Probst is first mentioned: he calls him 'Flemmichen', little Fleming. Jacob Probst had, so it seems, expressed overwhelming relief and enthusiasm upon hearing about Luther's safety; Luther's reaction to his elation is somewhat condescending.[31] At the end of the letter Probst is mentioned again. In this passage Luther tells Melanchthon that he may send greetings to various persons, among whom we encounter two members of the Antwerp Augustinians.[32] When it comes to Jacob Probst, Luther says that Melanchthon does not have to include greetings to him, as he will write to him separately. Here again he uses German rather than Latin, referring cordially to Probst (if again a little condescendingly) as 'das fette Flemmichen' ('fat little Fleming').[33]

THE INTERPOLATION

Returning to Dürer's journal, we can now venture the following hypothesis about the Lament on Luther. The phrase 'On the Friday before Whitsun, 1521, news reached me at Antwerp that Martin Luther had been treacherously taken captive', is by Dürer, as a reaction to a message of Jacob Probst, sent from Wittenberg to his congregation. The journal entry continued with: 'Changed another 1 gulden for cash. I paid the doctor a further 8 stuivers. Note: Ate two more meals with Rodrigo.'[34] There is no breach of style or change of mode here. The text of the Lament in between is probably the very message that had reached Antwerp: the letter that Jacob Probst wrote upon hearing the news that affected him so much, and that would be of great interest to the Antwerp Augustinians. The first sentence is by Albrecht Dürer while the sequel is from Jacob Probst. In fact, in the manuscript in Bamberg it can be seen that the editor, von Murr, had problems with the phrase and inserted words such as 'mir' (to me) to suggest a smooth transition between Dürer's factual text and Probst's exalted writings from Wittenberg (cat. 14 detail, p. 233).

The rhetoric, the indignation, the despair, the theological references, the use of the Latin vocative – all the features discussed above that make the document awkward when read as originating from the hand of Dürer – are completely in line with Jacob Probst's position, training and whereabouts at the given date.[35] Dürer, with his interest in matters concerning Luther, would have been struck by what at that time was a text of great historical interest. If a version had been preserved in Dürer's journal, one can well imagine how in the process of copying the entire journal, this preserved message might have become an interpolation – by accident or perhaps by intent.

If the Lament is accepted as an interpolation based on a message by the prior of the Augustinians while he was in Wittenberg, a great number of problems would be solved. The document would be authentic and of the period, providing a particularly lively insight into the reaction of a devoted friend and follower of Luther at the moment when Luther was thought to be in mortal danger. And if it was written with the possibility of publishing in mind, the rhetorical tone and public call for a successor could be explained as well. Most importantly, it would relieve Dürer scholarship of the impossible task of trying to reconcile this theological, rhetorical and zealous voice with the Dürer we know from so many other written documents.

The tone and style of the Lament comply in every respect with the letter known to have been written by Probst that was published the following year.[36] The Lament was probably also translated for publication purposes – but of course the whole text became obsolete within a week when it transpired that Luther was safe. Again, the theology, the exalted voice and the love for Luther comply perfectly well with Probst's publications at the time, and are completely at odds with anything we know to have been written by Dürer.

VIOLENCE AND THE EARLY REFORMATION IN ANTWERP

It was suggested above that the early Reformation and Luther's fate might be related to Dürer's decision to break his long stay in Antwerp and return to Nuremberg. It is helpful here to consider more closely the history of the Augustine congregation of which Jacob Probst was prior.

As it happens, the Antwerp community was not only small but also short-lived, due to its loyalty to Luther. Whether because of its German orientation or as a result of the resentment with which it had been looked upon by competing monastic communities in Antwerp from the start, the monks swiftly faced prosecution. Already in October or November 1521 (Dürer had left Antwerp two or three months earlier), a first attempt was undertaken to capture and question Jacob Probst, but this faltered. Later, on 5 December – Saint Nicholas Eve – he was lured to Brussels and imprisoned. For what happened subsequently we have a long account by Probst himself, first published in Latin (1522) and later translated into German by someone else. Here we read how Probst was rather rudely questioned, how he was pressed again and again to recant the views he had earlier expressed, that he was threatened with the stake and that on several occasions he was told that not only he but the whole city of Antwerp would suffer, in fact be set on fire, if he refused to give in. Under these threats Probst understandably yielded. He was taken to Brussels where, in front of the church of St Gudula, he publicly revoked his earlier views in a humiliating ceremony. Probst narrates how before his recantation he started to preach to the people but because of the warm reception of his words was silenced and given the list of theses he had to denounce.

This list is interesting as it gives a rather neat and compact summary of Lutheran views concerning the power of the Pope, the Sacraments and of course of Indulgences. Probst had to read from papers forced upon him ('like a child', he writes) and was pressed to go through the list both in the vernacular and in Latin. Then he was told he could not return to Antwerp but instead to Ypres, the town of his birth. The fact of his revocation was triumphantly publicised by the opponents of reformative views.[37] On hearing about all this Luther expressed his sadness in a letter. But the brave Flemish prior started preaching again very soon, making it clear that the revocation had been forced upon him and was far from genuine. Probst was again imprisoned, and this time execution at the stake seemed inevitable. But the story continues with his night-time escape, aided by a monk. He managed to reach Wittenberg and went from there to Bremen, where he spent the rest of his life as pastor of a successful Lutheran community – in fact the first pastor in this capacity. He would stay faithful to his Lutheran ideas for the rest of his life.

Probst was not the only person in Antwerp who fell victim to these very early prosecutions. In Dürer's journal mention is made more than once of Cornelis Grapheus, the learned secretary of Antwerp. This man had helped Dürer in formulating a proper plea for the renewal of his pension and had given him a booklet by Luther, as well as a printed version of a not too controversial text dating from the middle of the fifteenth century. Grapheus himself had written a preface to this edition.[38] This short but ardent introduction about the decline of true Christianity was the reason why Grapheus was subjected to the same treatment as Jacob Probst: he too was imprisoned and threatened, and he too chose to recant. He survived by doing so, but was publicly humiliated and hounded out of his profession. Later, in February 1524, he wrote a warm letter to Dürer and Willibald Pirckheimer in Nuremberg, seeking to re-establish contact. Grapheus mentions Tommaso Bombelli (whom we also know from the journal) as a mutual friend, and refers to the intense and continuous persecution in Antwerp 'about which

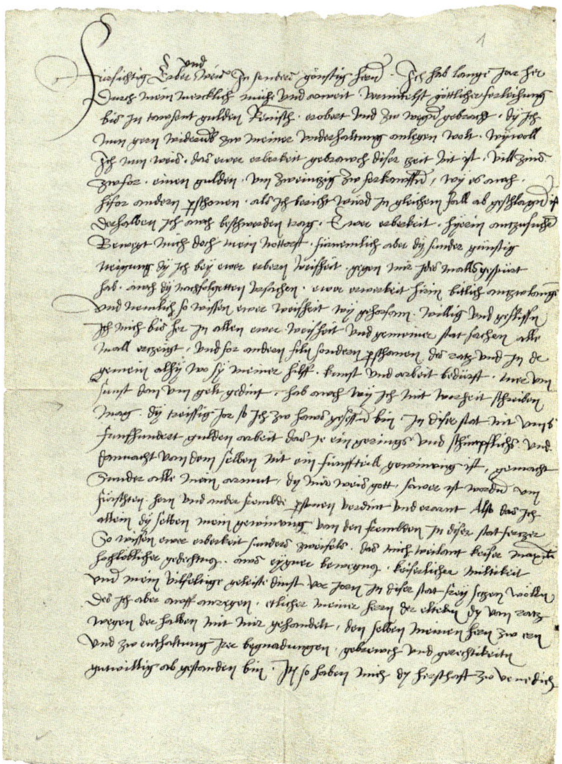

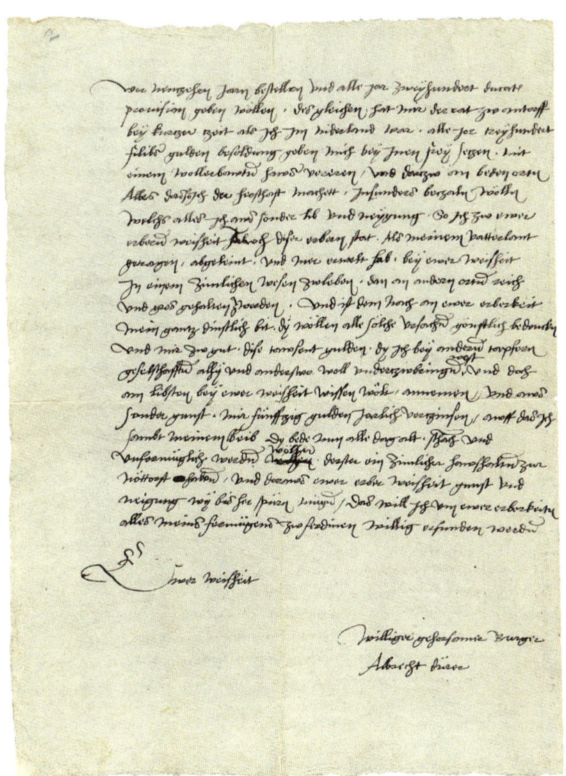

Figs 128, 129
Albrecht Dürer requests an annuity from the City Council of Nuremberg, October 1524
Pen on paper, 29.9 x 21.8 cm
Staatsarchiv Nürnberg, Reichsstadt Nürnberg, Ratskanzlei (A-Laden Akten 145/15)

these brothers will tell you more openly'. Here he must be referring to the Augustinians.[39]

The fate that befell some of these brethren was even worse than that of Grapheus. John of Essen and Henrich of Voes were executed at the stake in 1523. The same would have happened earlier to Hendrik van Zutphen had he not, like Probst before him, managed to escape, in his case with the help of large group of women who had turned up in protest against his capture. He met a gruesome martyr's death a few years later. Two other monks were also arrested; they recanted and nothing further is known of their fate.

Of the entire monastic community (which by 1521 had doubled from 8 to 16), the remaining group of about ten was defrocked. The monastery was closed and the sacred objects and holy hosts moved elsewhere. Their church was virtually demolished. Thus ended the Augustine settlement in Antwerp under the priorate of a devoted early Lutheran, a true forerunner of the Wittenberg Reformation in the Low Countries. The community's existence had spanned a mere nine years. But these years were decisive for the early Reformation in the southern Netherlands, and Dürer witnessed its heyday from very close by.

DURER'S CHOICE OF ANTWERP, AND HIS DEPARTURE

One might ask here why Dürer travelled to Antwerp in the first place. The known and accepted reason for his journey to the Low Countries was his need to have the pension, granted to him by Maximilian, reinstalled by the new young king and designated emperor. In this Dürer succeeded. But this undertaking does not suffice to explain the length of his stay – he remained many months after obtaining his pension. Nor does it explain his choice of Antwerp as a temporary domicile. Aachen, and certainly Brussels, would have been just as good – in fact much better for such an administrative, courtly matter.

Besides his pension, Dürer had another solid reason to go to Antwerp, even apart from the attraction of the town as a capital of the arts. In 1524, about three years after he went on his Netherlandish journey, in a letter to the Nuremberg council he stated that he had received a very tempting offer from the council in Antwerp to come and settle in the town. For this he would receive a yearly retainer of 300 guilders, and a house, while still being allowed to make personal profit (figs 128, 129).[40] If this offer had been made shortly before his journey, it provides an explanation for the remarkable fact that less than two days after his arrival an elaborate reception with representatives of the council and the guilds had been organised for the guest from Nuremberg. It may also account for his frequent contacts with someone like the town secretary Cornelis Grapheus; perhaps it also explains why Dürer travelled with his wife on this trip, unlike his other known journeys. And even if the offer had been made after his arrival, it helps to explain why he lingered in Antwerp. We will never know for sure, but it appears that Dürer may have considered settling in Antwerp for a longer period of time.

Among the various reasons he may have had not to do so eventually, the unrest of the burgeoning Reformation will have played a decisive role. It is, after all, strange to consider the large number of people Dürer had met in Antwerp who would fall victim to prosecution within a year, with threats even of retribution for Antwerp itself.

By 22 March 1521 the first imperial *plakkaat* or edict for the Low Countries had already been issued, ordering every magistrate to retrieve all books by Luther and his followers and have them burned in public, to the sound of trumpets, while the printing, buying, selling and possessing of such books was prohibited.[41] About seven weeks later, when the drama at Worms was evolving, we notice for the first time that Dürer starts to make preparations for a possible return. This first mention of an item that will be sent to Nuremberg dates from a few days before the story of Luther's capture and the Lament would reach Antwerp – and after the news of the events at the Diet at Worms. It is also the date of an order issued from Ghent, for all magistrates, to actually make sure that the commands of the imperial decree are carried out.

On 13 July, just one day after Dürer and his wife left Brussels for Cologne, Lutheran books and pamphlets were publicly burned in Antwerp as well, probably not for the first time. Four days later in Ghent a baker was displayed near a scaffold, next to a pile of Lutheran and other heretical texts, during the solemn procession of Saint James, attended by many high lords, among them Christian II, King of Denmark (cat. 53). The Emperor pardoned the recanting baker (ignoring the pleas of his entourage, including the King of Denmark) but the books were burned in a public ceremony.[42]

It appears that Dürer left the Low Countries just in time, not only because the first books and other materials were already being publicly destroyed, but also because the first Lutheran sympathisers were actually arrested shortly afterwards. A couple of months later Probst barely managed to escape the stake, and not much later the first victims fell – all members of the former Antwerp community. The case of Grapheus has already been mentioned, but when we read the documents around Hieronymus Aleander (1480–1542), papal nuncio and the persecutor of heretics for the young Charles V, we also encounter 'the German merchants' as direct targets – precisely Dürer's circle. The same applied to the Portuguese merchants of Jewish extraction, the so-called Maranos mentioned by Aleander and others explicitly and repeatedly as a group who held heretic ideas.[43] These were the people with whom Dürer dined and socialised, as his journal informs us. More people mentioned in the journal as associates were in clear danger of persecution – including Erasmus. Paul Kalkoff, in his 1903 study of the period, devoted an entire chapter to the way Aleander's anti-heretic activities finally drove Erasmus from the Low Countries to Basel, and he believed that Dürer's fate could have been comparable.[44] In any case, something of the atmosphere in Antwerp during the year after his departure can be felt from a letter to Erasmus in 1522 by a correspondent from the Low Countries: 'such terror has seized everyone there who had ever spared Luther a thought, that scarcely anyone thought himself safe.'[45]

In Nuremberg (and elsewhere in Germany), for all kinds of political and organisational reasons, Charles's power was much less stringent than it was in his own backyard, the personal hereditary region of the Low Countries. While Dürer could witness after his return how Nuremberg became Lutheran in 1525, the Low Countries had to wait for their Reformation following the revolt of 1566. This only succeeded for part of the provinces, and ultimately left Antwerp on the Catholic side – in spite of the wide appeal of reformative sentiments in the town when Dürer was there and in the following decades.

1 The argument as presented in this article was developed over a rather long period of time, and tentatively presented in various public lectures, in Rotterdam (2009), Dresden (2012) and Utrecht (2016).

2 Staatsarchiv, Nuremberg (inv. S.I., L. 78, no. 15, Fasz, 18); Staatsbibliothek, Bamberg (inv. 246. J.M. Msc.art I); The Digital Library of the Heidelberg Universität Bibliothek offers a digitised version, at: https://digi.ub.uni-heidelberg.de/diglit/sbbam_jhmscart1 (accessed 1 October 2019). The journal has been published in many different editions. The authoritative edition of the text is still Rupprich 1956–69, vol. 1, pp. 146–202, which also gives data on the history of the manuscript. For a recent comment on the text, see Unverfehrt 2007. For the most recent English translation, with comment, see Ashcroft 2017, vol. 1, pp. 545–628.

3 Lutz 1968, p. 32.

4 See, for instance, the important contribution by Seebass: 'Dürers Stellung in der Reformatorische Bewegung', in Hirschmann and Schnelbögl 1971, pp. 101–31. For a more recent treatment, see the careful contribution by Sahm 2002, pp. 170–82, and Unverfehrt 2007, pp. 176–80.

5 Quoted by Lutz 1968, p. 32.

6 A number of scholars devoted to Reformation history in the nineteenth and early twentieth centuries have researched this episode thoroughly, and their meticulous work has been of great value in the preparation of this article. See, for instance, Janssen 1862, de Hoop-Scheffer 1886 and Kalkoff 1903.

7 Ashcroft 2017, vol. 1, p. 580.

8 Ibid., p. 581.

9 Ibid., pp. 581–2.

10 Ibid., p. 582. This solemn appeal was immediately changed into a more colloquial one: 'Else you are nothing but a feeble old *manneken*.' He also says how he has heard that Erasmus gave himself just another two years or so to do something useful, and soon would be too old. From the phrasing it might seem that the author had heard such things not first hand from Erasmus himself but from others. This depends on the translation of 'von dir' as 'from you' or 'about you'. Somehow the latter seems truer to the text, and one would have expected more emphasis if the author had this information directly from Erasmus himself: 'I heard it from your own mouth', or something similar. But all this is subjective, and either possibility stands.

11 Ibid., p. 582.

12 See note 8.

13 Christoph Gottlieb von Murr had published the journal in 1779: 'Reisejournal Albrecht Dürers: von seiner niederländischen Reise', *Journal zur Kunstgeschichte und zur allgemeinen Litteratur*, 7 (1779), pp. 53–98. The Dutch translation with commentary appeared the following year: *Dagverhaal van Albert Durer's Nederlandsche reize, in de jaaren 1520 en 1521 gedaan/ door hemzelven beschreeven; onlangs uit zijn hs. door den heer C. G. van Murr uitgegeven: en thans op verzoek van, en ten dienste der liefhebberen van deezen beroemden kunstenaar in 't Nederduitsch overgebragt*, Amsterdam 1780. The translator is merely indicated by initials, 'A.L.'. For further data on Wycliffe and Dürer and the various discussions of this relation in the history of Dürer research, see note 19 below.

14 Ashcroft 2017, vol. 1, p. 535, no. 154; the text is dated January or February 1520. Letter from Albrecht Dürer to Georg Spalatin, from Nuremberg, beginning of 1520: 'And if with God's help I should come to Dr Martinus Luther, I will use my skill to sketch his portrait and engrave it in copperplate as a lasting memorial of this Christian man, who has rescued me out of deep anguish.'

15 Letter to Scheurl, 5 March 1518 (Ashcroft 2017, vol. 1, p. 483, no. 122).

16 For a thorough discussion of these Lutheran pamphlets, see Krodel and Brecht 2012, esp. pp. 11–33.

17 Ashcroft 2017, vol. 1, p. 535.

18 Gottfried Krodel (Krodel and Brecht 2012, pp. 47–72) has presented a thorough discussion of Dürer's possible sources of knowledge about Wycliffe, fully facing the problem of the apparent unavailability of Wycliffe's writings for Dürer and attempting a number of speculative solutions. Especially informative is the overview on pp. 118–19 (n. 370), showing the various undecided discussions of this point in Dürer scholarship, from Thausing in the nineteenth century to recent times. If, however, the Lament was not written by Dürer but by a Lutheran theologian, the entire matter would simply be resolved.

19 The entire call to Erasmus has clearly bothered scholars. Dürer after all had spoken to Erasmus several times both during at least two dinners, and at least one portrait session (see Peter van den Brink in the present volume, p. 216). But the Lament betrays no such direct knowledge. Erwin Panofsky, for instance, in his great book on the life and art of Albrecht Dürer, wrote: 'the very fact that he [Dürer] could imagine him [Erasmus] as a martyr of Luther's cause shows *a pathetic misunderstanding of the man* who was to defend the freedom of the human will against the tyranny of Luther's God' (Panofsky 1943, p. 239; my italics). For Panofsky as for others, the invocation of Erasmus is made to bear even on the supposed lack of success of Dürer's engraved portrait of Erasmus. 'Dürer had lost access to the world of Erasmus', he wrote (loc. cit.) on the basis of the passage, and this fact explained the lukewarm attempts at portrayal (as Panofsky saw it) by the Nuremberg artist. Johan Huizinga, in his biography of Erasmus, preferred a solution for the call in precisely the opposite direction: 'It expresses confidence in Erasmus's power, but at bottom is the expectation that he will not do all this. *Dürer had rightly understood Erasmus*' (Huizinga 1954, p. 149; my italics). Obviously Huizinga felt that the only way he could make sense of Dürer's view of Erasmus was by suggesting that the author of the Lament did not *actually* believe that Erasmus would ever heed such a call to martyrdom.

20 Sometimes the use of particular terms seems peculiar: for instance, the author's use of the word *meniken* in the call to Erasmus, which does not sound like Dürer's Nuremberg dialect at all, but rather typically Flemish. Phonetically this word shows an interesting divergence from his famous description of Lucas van Leyden as a *männlein* a number of pages later (Rupprich 1956–69, vol. 1 [1956], p. 174). In fact, there is another person in the journal described as small, namely Erasmus the secretary of Jakob Banisius – not Erasmus of Rotterdam – and he, too, is called *männlein* (ibid., p. 155). Of course, the author might have chosen this Flemish form to suggest a word choice of Erasmus himself.

21 Ashcroft 2017, vol. 1, p. 582.

22 Quoted by Unverfehrt 2007, p. 178, from Friedländer 1921, p. 178.

23 See Janssen 1862, pp. 67–74. For the letters of the Venetian ambassador, see Kalkoff 1898, esp. pp. 59–61.

24 Ashcroft 2017, vol. 1, p. 584.

25 Ibid., p. 585.

26 For the Augustinians, see, for example, Clemen 1901 and Janssen 1862.

27 For Probst, see Janssen 1862 and Rudloff 1985, esp. pp. 42–65 and pp. 154–7.

28 Luther 1883–2009, *Briefwechsel*, vol. 6, pp. 413–14.

29 Ashcroft 2017, vol. 1, p. 580.

30 Letter from Luther to Melanchthon, 26 May 1521, in Luther 1883–2009 *Briefwechsel*, vol. 2, pp. 346–52.

31 Ibid., p. 348: 'Iacobo Flemmichen satis est te videre, et uti ne nimio felix sit, omnia quae vellet videns'.

32 Ibid., p. 349: 'Omnes ex nomine meo salutabis, estis enim multi (M. Eisleben non salutabis, nec *das fette Flemmichen*, iis enim scribo…').

33 Apparently when Jacob Probst heard about Luther's safety (still not knowing exactly where he was) he asked Melanchthon to bring greetings and establish contact with Luther. Seven days later this request had reached Luther in the Wartburg through Melanchthon, and after another six or seven days Jacob, still in Wittenberg, would have received the letter promised by Luther in the correspondence with Melanchthon. This was around 3 June: the Antwerp community would have received their messages from Wittenberg (from Melanchthon and probably also from their own prior, Jacob Probst) again six or seven days later, around 10 June. It seems that only Luther's letter has survived, but it is the pivot of this reconstruction, referring to all these events.

34 Ashcroft 2017, vol. 1, pp. 580, 582.

35 Probst would, however, have written the message in Latin, just as he did on other occasions: for example, his message to his brethren, originally composed in Latin, to be translated into German only later, which was subsequently published in print (Probst 1522: see note 36). Given the importance of the message (at that seemingly crucial moment), the Lament was immediately translated into German as well.

36 J. Probst, *Ein schone und clegliche history Bruder Jacob Probst Augustiner Ordens vor Zeiten Prior zu Antorff, an gemeine fromme Christen wegen des Worts Gottes, und umb des heyligen Evangeliumss willen erlitten hatt*, n.p. 1522 (with a number of later editions, including Strasbourg 1524). This was the immediate translation by an unknown translator of the story as told in a Latin text by Jacob Probst: *Fratris Iacobi Praepositi Augustiniani quonda[m] Prioris Antuuerpie[n]sis historia vtriusq[ue] captiuitatis propter verbum Dei. Eiusdem etiam Epistola ad Auditores suos Anuuerpienses* [Wittenberg?] 1522.

37 Quite clearly and rather triumphantly in the booklet *Revocationes duorum Lutheraniorum: anathematizatio et revocatio fratris Jacobi Prepositi…: errores revocati per dominum Hermannum Gerardi in civitate Trajectensi*, Cologne 1522.

38 For the text of the introduction of this rare book, see for example Ullmann 1842, vol. 1, pp. 151–7 (a digitised version is provided by Google Books, https://play.google.com/books/reader?id=nTyPG59F03MC&hl=en_US&pg=GBS.PA151[accessed 10 November 2019]).

39 Ashcroft 2017, vol. 2, pp. 721–2, no. 188: 'And so farewell my dearest Albrecht! Here in Antwerp a great persecution, each day newly fomented, arises because of the Gospels, about which these brothers will tell you more openly. Once more farewell!' (The letter – in Latin – is for both Willibald Pirckheimer and Albrecht Dürer, to be translated for Dürer by the former: 'Vale mi charissime Alberte! Apud nos magna et subinde nova quotidie propter evangelium oritur persequutio, de qua re fratre isti apertius omnia narrabunt. Iterum vale!').

40 Letter from Dürer to the burgomasters and council of the town of Nuremberg, October 1524, preserved in the Staatsarchiv Nürnberg (inv. S.I, L. 79, no. 15, fasc. 9) and published in Ashcroft 2017, vol. 2, p. 734: 'Note that nineteen years ago the authorities in Venice offered me an appointment and two hundred ducats annual stipend, similarly a few years ago, when I was in the Netherlands, the Antwerp Council wanted to pay me a salary of three hundred Philip gulden a year, exempt me from tax, and provide with a fine house for nothing, and in both places pay me extra for everything I painted for the City government.'

41 Fredericq 1889–1906, vol. 1, p. 29. For a recent treatment, see, for instance, Duke 2009, esp. chaps 3 and 4 (pp. 77–119).

42 See Kalkoff 1903, esp. chaps 3 and 4.

43 Ibid.

44 Kalkoff 1897.

45 See Duke 2009, p. 80. The entire letter of November 1522 is in Mynors 1974–2003, vol. 9, no. 1318, pp. 191–2.

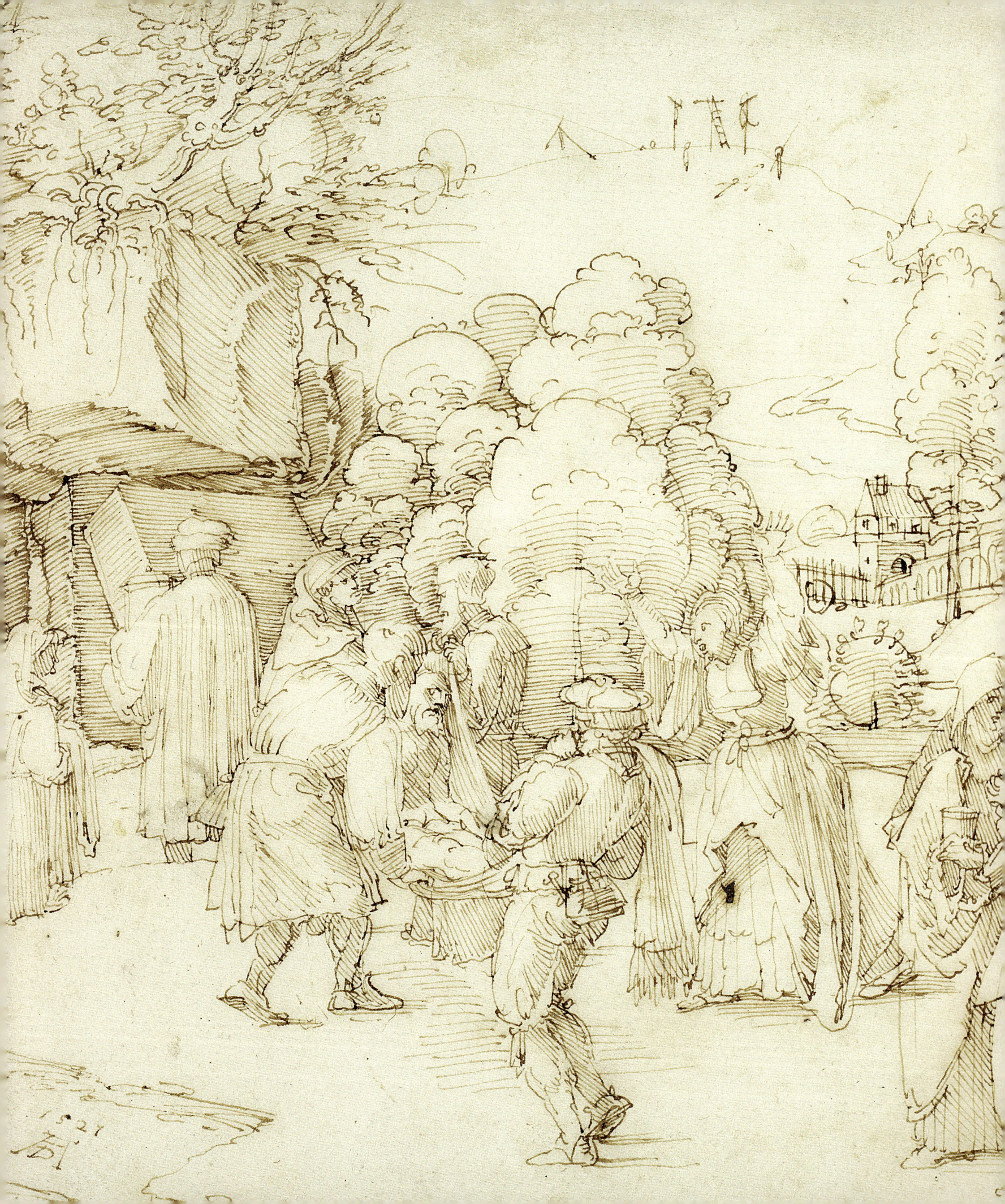
1527

DANA E. COWEN

ALBRECHT DÜRER'S LATE PASSION DRAWINGS
THE *OBLONG PASSION* IN CONTEXT

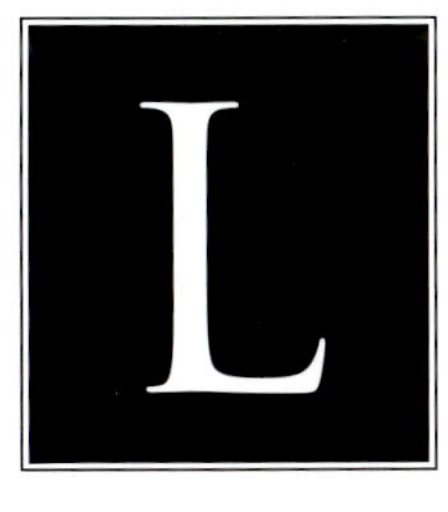

IKE COUNTLESS NORTHERN EUROPEAN artists of the late fifteenth and early sixteenth centuries, Albrecht Dürer devoted much of his career to depicting Christ's Passion. Described in all four Gospels, the Passion narrative spans the last few days of Christ's life and encompasses the events from his betrayal to his entombment. In addition to paintings, singular prints and independent drawings, Dürer produced four finished series on the subject, three of which were published. Together the *Large Passion* (1497–1511), *Green Passion* (1504), *Small Passion* (about 1509–11) and *Engraved Passion* (1507–13) reveal his differing stylistic approach and his varied interpretations of the narrative, both conceptually and visually, over a prolonged period of time and across a broad range of media.

After producing only a handful of compositions related to the subject following the completion of his *Engraved Passion* series in 1513, Dürer returned to the theme of the Passion with renewed intensity during his sojourn in the Netherlands. Several of his drawings of isolated episodes, such as the 1521 *Crucifixion* (cat. 104) and *Lamentation* (cat. 105), share the vertical format and devotional characteristics of his earlier representations. He also began a series of drawings with a landscape format, known today as the *Oblong Passion*. Quite unique among his Passion imagery, the drawings mark a significant transformation in his depiction of this narrative.

Dated between 1520 and 1524, eleven of Dürer's drawings associated with this series survive and represent four events from the Passion story. Listed in narrative order, they include one *Last Supper*, four drawings of the Christ on the Mount of Olives (cat. 106; fig. 130), two drawings of the Road to Calvary (fig. 131, 132) and three of Christ carried to the Tomb (cat. 107; figs 133, 135). A 1524 drawing of the *Adoration of the Magi*, a theme not usually included in Passion cycles, is designated by some as the preface to the entire series, while one drawing of Christ carried to the Tomb is considered a copy after a lost original or a workshop study (fig. 135).[1] Three

OPPOSITE
Detail from
Deposition of Christ
(cat. 107)

104
ALBRECHT DÜRER
The Crucifixion, 1521
Pen with brown ink,
32.3 × 22.2 cm
The Albertina Museum,
Vienna

additional Passion drawings from the period relate closely to the series: a partial *Road to Calvary* (fig. 137), which extends the composition of the Uffizi *Road to Calvary* drawing (fig. 131), and two Lamentation scenes (cat. 108; fig. 134), one which represents the only Passion drawing of this group completed in chalk (fig. 134).

Several of the *Oblong Passion* drawings were recorded in Dürer's Netherlandish journal. In a May 1521 entry the artist wrote: 'I drew 3 Christ Led Away to Calvary and 2 Mounts of Olives on 5 half- sheets'.[2] This probably refers to the two 1520 *Road to Calvary* drawings in Florence (figs 131, 132) and one evidently lost, and the two drawings of the Christ on the Mount of Olives dated 1520 and 1521 respectively (cat. 106; fig. 130). Dürer may have intended the drawings as preparatory designs for a new woodcut Passion series, although only a revised version of his *Last Supper* drawing of 1523 was published.

There are several reasons why Dürer may have abandoned the series. The artist was simultaneously preoccupied with finishing his theoretical writings and other large artistic projects.[3] Additionally, his age or declining health could have prevented him, or he may have been reluctant to publish devotional material at a time of religious upheaval.[4] From a creative point of view the presence of multiple versions of the same scene may indicate that Dürer encountered unexpected design challenges when conceiving the narrative in a landscape format, while the lack of a finished series might suggest that he was dissatisfied with the results.[5]

In each subject group the drawings vary in style and execution as well as in figure scale and viewpoint. The more finished version of the two Uffizi *Road to Calvary* drawings (fig. 132) shows a highly structured design and is assiduously executed with tight, controlled and uniform hatching and cross-hatching. The other drawing (fig. 131) appears quickly rendered, with loosely defined elements and less finish. Likewise, the Christ on the Mount of Olives drawings from 1520 and 1521 (cat. 106; fig. 130) show a similar difference in approach. Dürer's use of cross-hatching to indicate deep shadows in the 1520 rendition (cat. 106), particularly in the clothing of the disciples, recalls the *Road to Calvary* drawings created the same year (figs 131, 132). He employed a greater uniformity of line in the later *Agony in the Garden* (fig. 130), relying on parallel pen strokes and consistent hatching to model forms, a technique that extends to other drawings of 1521. Dürer also altered the scale and viewpoint between analogous compositions, including the drawings of Christ carried to the Tomb of 1521 (fig. 133; cat. 107). Here he changed the view from a direct, frontal perspective to a higher vantage point, thus

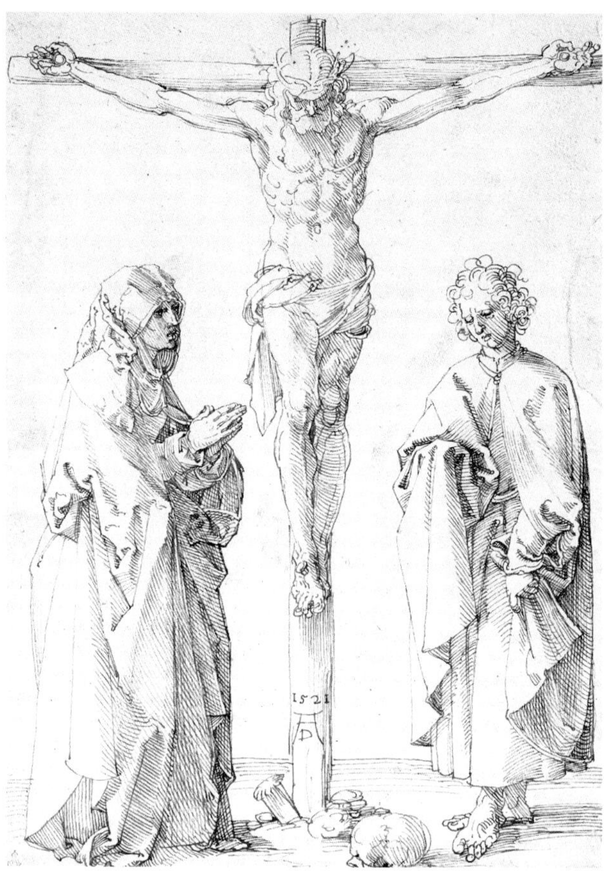

altering the viewer's position from participant to observer.

Dürer's return to the subject of Christ's Passion during this period and his experimentation with the design and execution of the drawings illustrates his desire to intellectually and artistically re-engage with the topic, perhaps as a result either of his experiences in the Netherlands or of his interest in the changing religious climate in Europe during the 1520s. His knowledge of the evangelical teachings of Martin Luther at the time of his Netherlandish journey is well documented, and he surely would have been aware of Luther's discussions of the Passion.[6] In 1519 Luther published *Ain Sermon von der Betrachtung des heiligen Leidens Christi (A Sermon on Meditating on the Holy Passion of Christ)*, which provided instructions on the appropriate and inappropriate motivations behind meditating on the Passion.[7] Reprinted in at least 25 editions over two years, the tract was extremely popular for its rejection of older forms of devotional Passion meditation that stressed a vicarious participation in Christ's suffering. This sermon was most certainly known to Dürer, being listed among the reformer's writings that the artist either owned or looked to acquire (cat. 103).[8] In 15 expository directives Luther guides the reader on how to contemplate Christ's suffering so as to model one's own life and death following

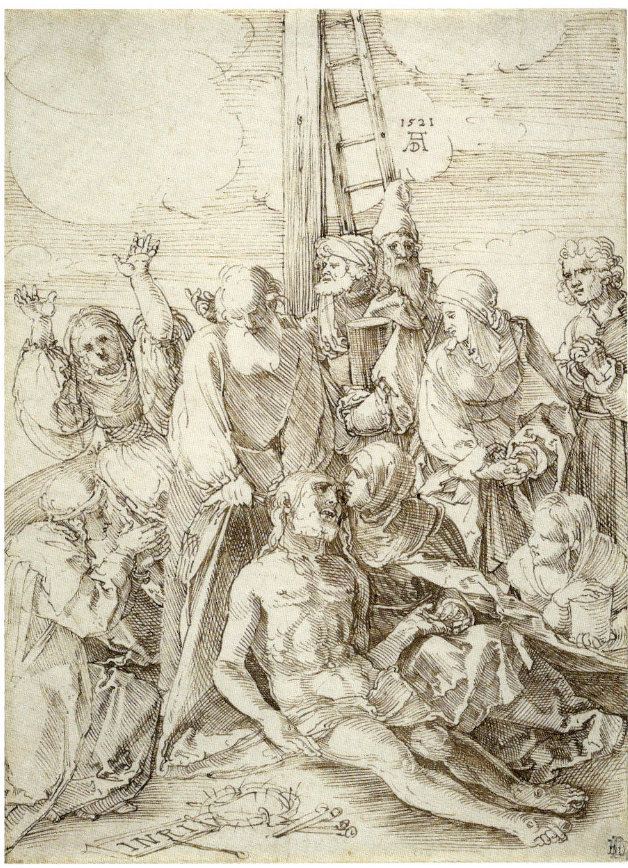

105
ALBRECHT DÜRER
The Lamentation of Christ, 1521
Brown ink on white antique laid paper, 29 × 21 cm
Harvard Art Museums / Fogg Museum

his example, to draw strength from his actions in overcoming sin in daily life, and to rectify a misguided belief in the redemptive power of one's own actions. Luther asserted that 'After your heart has thus become firm in Christ, and love, not fear of pain, has made you a foe of sin, then Christ's passion must from that day on become a pattern for your entire life. Henceforth you will have to see his passion differently.'[9] It was perhaps this declaration that partly motivated Dürer's intensive engagement with the theme of the Passion during this late stage in his career.

As the Reformation was still in its infancy during the early 1520s, interpretation of conventionally devotional subject matter through the lens of Luther's teachings is challenging. Because Dürer's Passion imagery can be traced over the entirety of his career, his late experimental drawings provide useful examples of how his approach to the subject changed. For example, his earlier treatments of the episodes and his use of space is generally consistent. His restrictive vertical compositions typically confine movement to the foreground, promoting an instant recognition of the narrative and an increased sense of immediacy. The emphasis rests heavily on Christ's suffering and the viewer's direct access to it. The shift from a vertical to a horizontal compositional arrangement in his *Oblong Passion* altered not only the space and movement of the narrative, but also the expressive intensity of the scene and the viewer's distance from it. Unlike the immediately familiar, compact and energetic renditions of his earlier versions, the landscape format of the later Passion drawings allowed the narrative of Christ's suffering and death to unfold gradually across a wide surface. The slow movement inherent in the broad composition encourages unhurried contemplation of the event. Traditionally obvious displays of grief, particularly those of the Virgin, are mitigated in the late drawings, where the pain and suffering experienced by everyone becomes more introspective and personalised.

Dürer's 1520 and 1521 *Christ on the Mount of Olives* drawings demonstrate how a reworking of the image transforms a highly emotional depiction of Christ's suffering into one that focuses on the essence of Protestant piety as laid out by Luther – the quiet submission to God's authority and faith in his word. The 1520 drawing now in Karlsruhe (cat. 106) depicts Christ with arms raised, kneeling before a jagged hillock, in torment at the prospect of his impending suffering and death. Matthew relates in his Gospel that at this point Christ pleads to God: 'My Father, if it be possible, let this chalice pass from me' (Matthew 26: 39). This wrestling with his faith and request to God for mercy is when Christ appears at his most human. In contrast, Dürer's 1521 drawing now in Frankfurt (fig. 130) shows him prostrated, face down and arms outstretched. As noted by Larry Silver, Christ's prone position in the form of a cross echoes Luther's doctrine that 'salvation lies in complete submission to faith'.[10] Christ has accepted God's plan for him, with the words 'My Father, if this chalice may not pass away, but I must drink it, thy will be done' (Matthew 26: 42). This shift in emphasis, from suffering to acceptance, from uncertainty to faith, is also reflected in the crucifix and chalice held aloft by the angel in each respective drawing.

While one of Dürer's renditions of the *Road to Calvary* (fig. 131) preserves an earlier motif of Christ's suffering under the weight of the cross and is more devotional in nature, his other version, also in the Uffizi (fig. 132), shows a less tormented scene in which Christ's apparent suffering is diminished. Rather than portray a frantic crowd jumbled with witnesses and soldiers who push and whip Christ, Dürer transforms the spectacle into an orderly and slow-moving procession. Christ's act of looking back to engage with Veronica as she presents him her veil effectively pauses time, allowing the viewer to contemplate Christ's steady approach to fulfilling God's plan.

Dürer experimented with the passage of time and distance in a scene less commonly found in the Passion

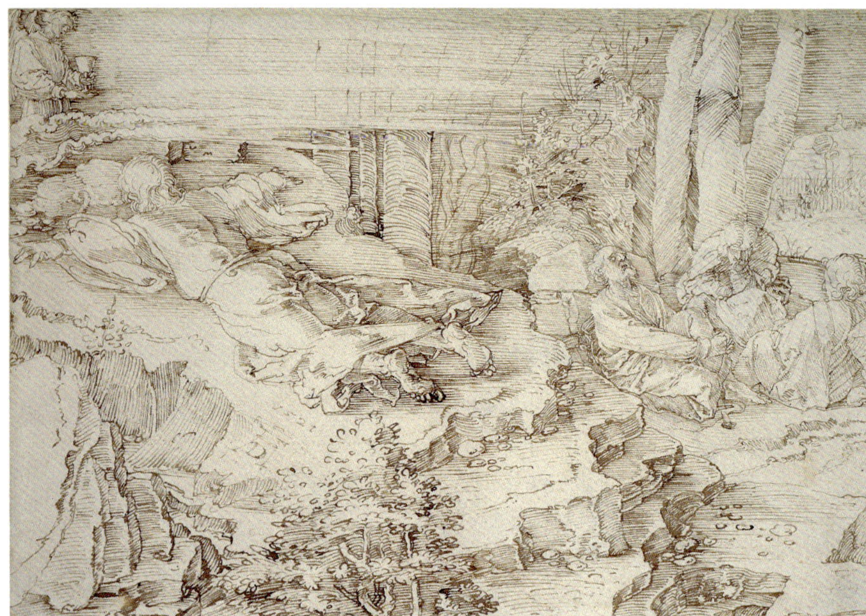

Fig. 130
ALBRECHT DÜRER
The Agony in the Garden, 1521
Pen and grey brown ink, 20.6 x 29.3 cm
Städel Museum, Frankfurt am Main (695)

106
ALBRECHT DÜRER
Christ on the Mount of Olives, 1520
Pen and brown ink, 20.9 x 27.9 cm
Staatliche Kunsthalle Karlsruhe,
Kupferstichkabinett

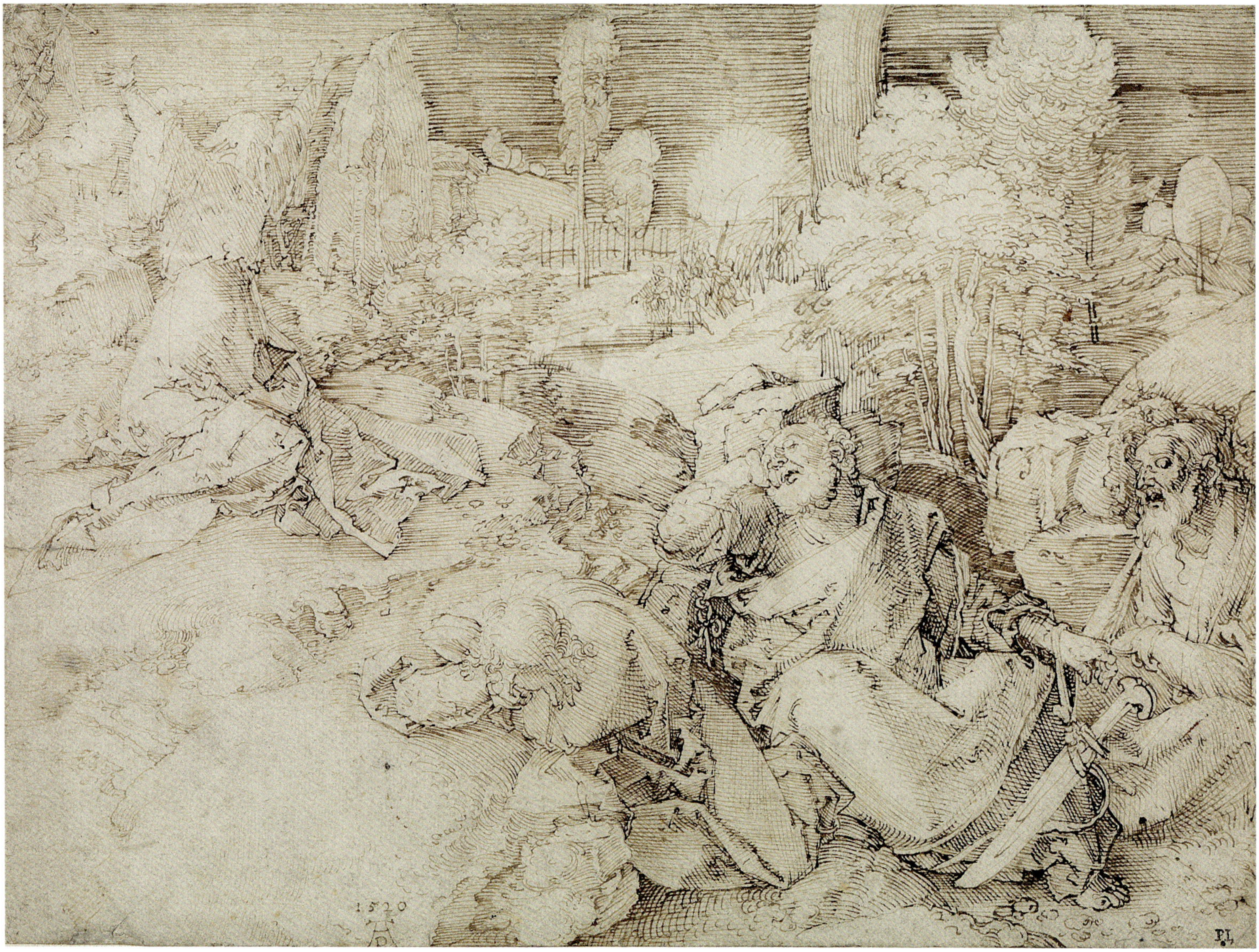

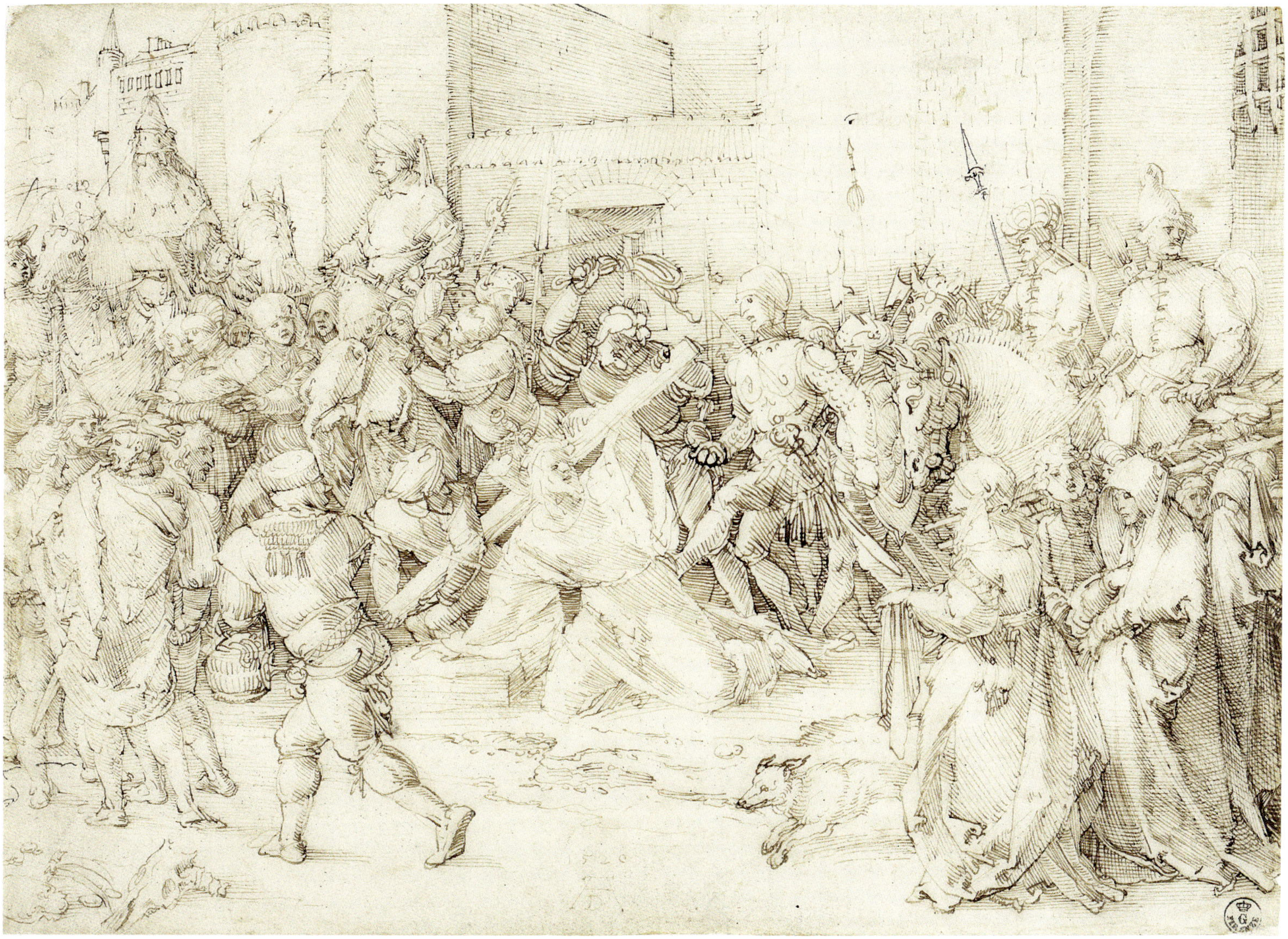

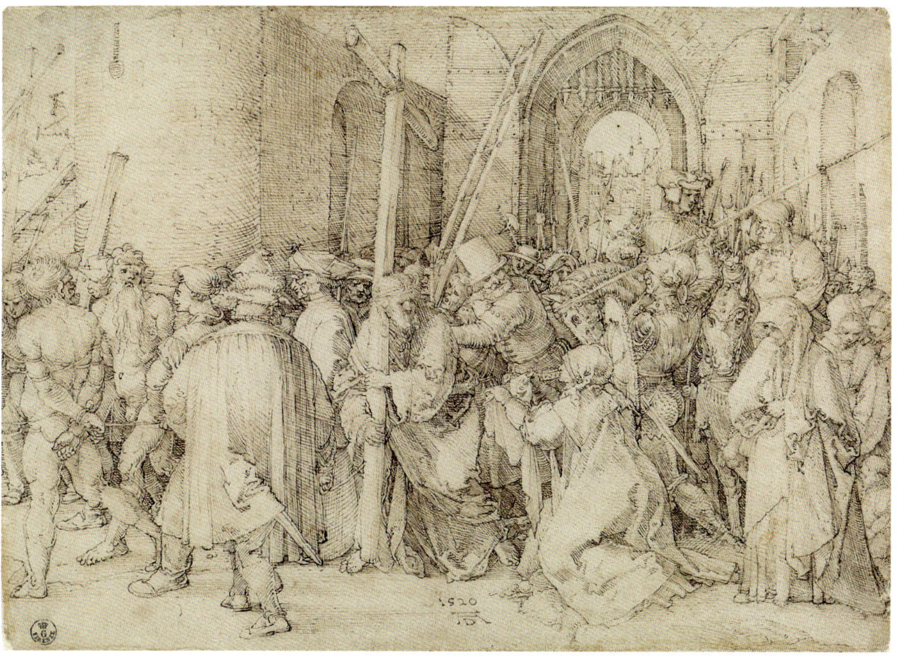

Fig. 131
ALBRECHT DÜRER
The Road to Calvary, 1520
Pen and brown ink,
20.9 x 28.6 cm
Gabinetto dei Disegni e delle Stampe, Gallerie degli Uffizi, Florence (1077)

Fig. 132
ALBRECHT DÜRER
The Road to Calvary, 1520
Pen and ink, 21 x 28.5 cm
Gabinetto dei Disegni e delle Stampe, Gallerie degli Uffizi, Florence (1078)

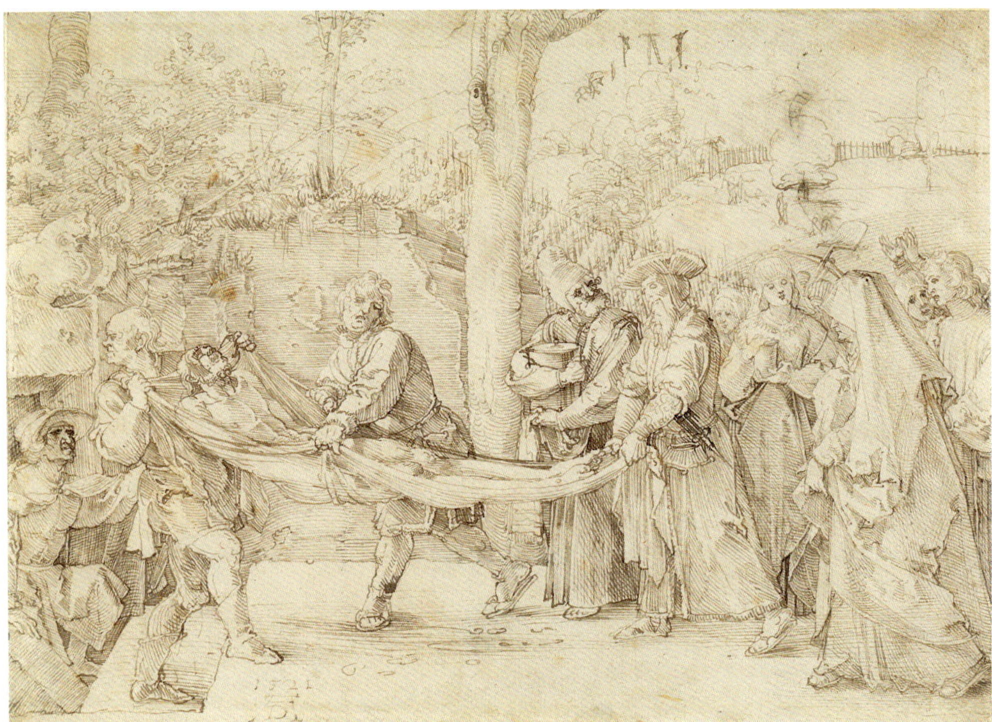

Fig. 133
ALBRECHT DÜRER
The Entombment, 1521
Pen and brown ink, 21.1 × 29.8 cm
Germanisches Nationalmuseum, Nuremberg (StN12589)

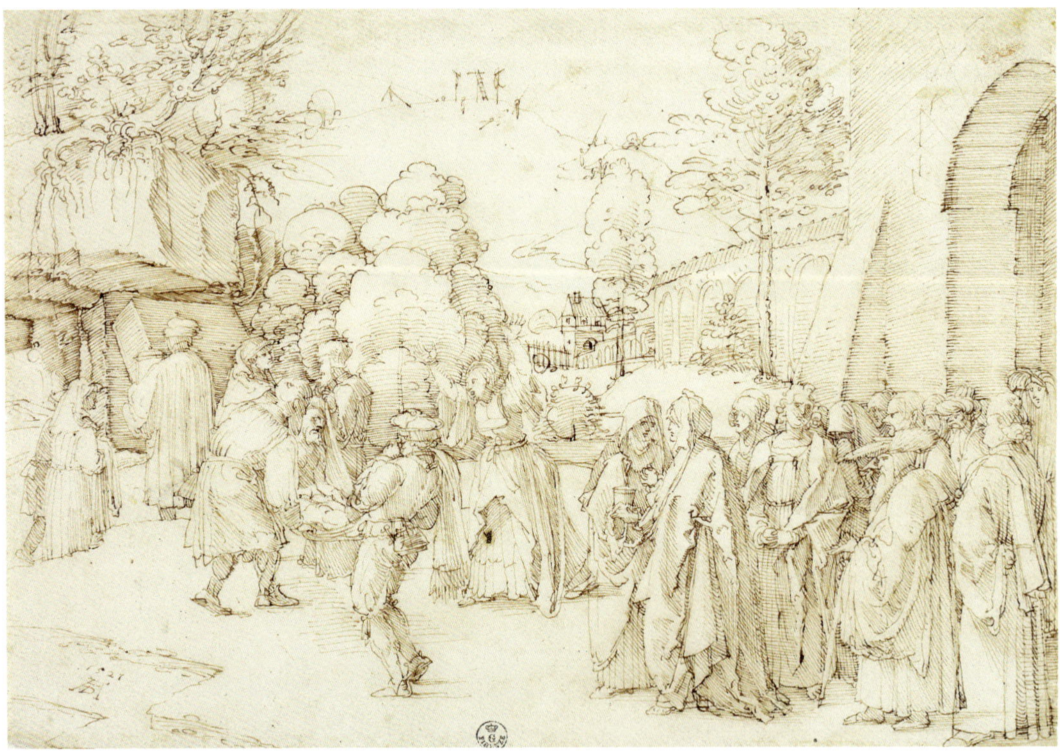

107
ALBRECHT DÜRER
Deposition of Christ, 1521
Pen and brown ink, 20.7 × 29 cm
Gabinetto dei Disegni e delle Stampe, Gallerie degli Uffizi, Florence

narrative – the liminal moment when Christ's body is carried to the tomb. In another slow-moving procession, the first of these two drawings (fig. 133) confronts the viewer with Jesus's elongated and languid corpse, emphasising the human character of his remains. The participants, including the Virgin, who trails behind the body, are subdued and convey a sense of pensive mourning rather than impassioned grief.[11] In the subsequent drawing (cat. 107) Dürer places less emphasis on Christ's body and more on the group of mourners following in its wake. The viewpoint is higher, while the scale of the figures has been minimised and their number increased. Again, there is little display of emotion, save for the central figure, who raises her arms

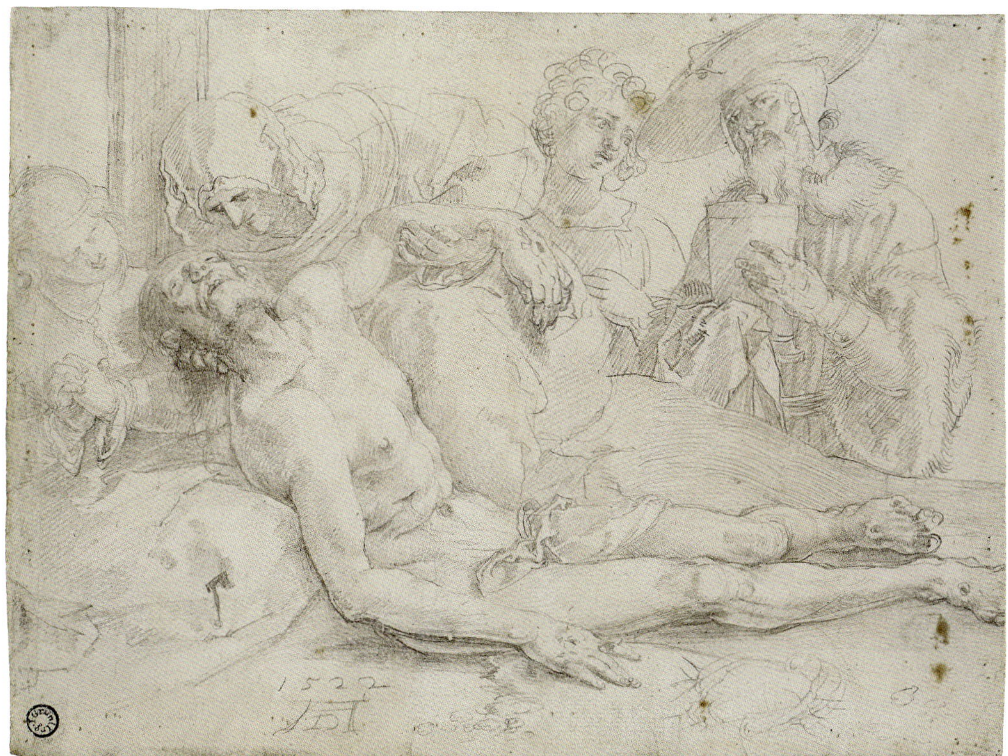

Fig. 134
ALBRECHT DÜRER
The Lamentation, 1522
Brown chalk on white grounded paper, 24.5 × 32.5 cm
Kunsthalle Bremen (TL 37117)

in consternation. The slow movement of the procession effectively relates the gravitas of the situation without overt displays of affective grief.

Dürer plays with viewpoint again in two separate Lamentation scenes (fig. 134; cat. 108), this time drawing the viewer's gaze into a scene of great intimacy. The figures are now monumental and placed close to the picture's edge, while the narrative elements have been stripped to the most essential. Once part of the Lubomirski holdings and now in the Liberna Collection housed at the Draiflessen Collection in Mettingen, the latter drawing shows a rarely depicted moment from the Passion narrative. Christ's corpse appears on a stone slab as he is prepared for burial according to Jewish custom. Emphasising direct access to Christ's corporeal presence, Dürer creates form and shadow through parallel lines with little crosshatching, similar to his 1521 Christ on the Mount of Olives (fig. 130) but with the apparent speed of execution of the partial *Road to Calvary* drawing (fig. 137). As in the other Passion drawings, there are no overt exhibits of grief in either work, but rather a quiet acceptance of God's will. By moving away from the highly charged traditional imagery of his previous Passion series, Dürer here presents a visually new way to meditate on Christ's Passion. The artist's reassessment of Christ's suffering and that of his followers directs the focus on the central narrative of evangelical Christian spirituality – faith.

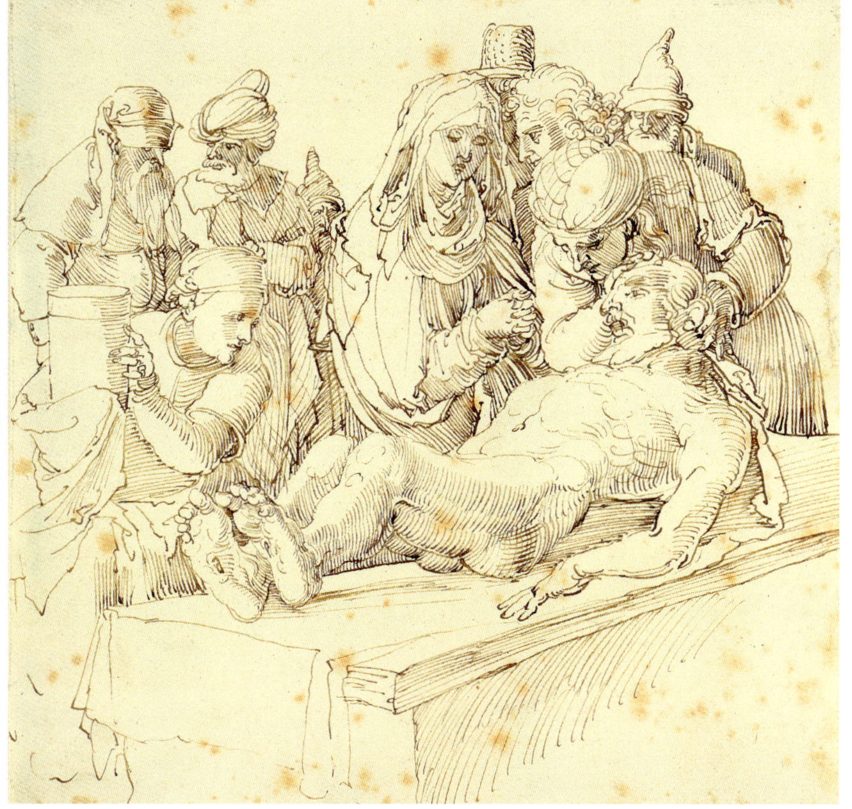

108
ALBRECHT DÜRER
The Lamentation of Christ, about 1521–8
Pen and brown ink on paper, 20.4 × 20.7 cm
Draiflessen Collection (Liberna), Mettingen

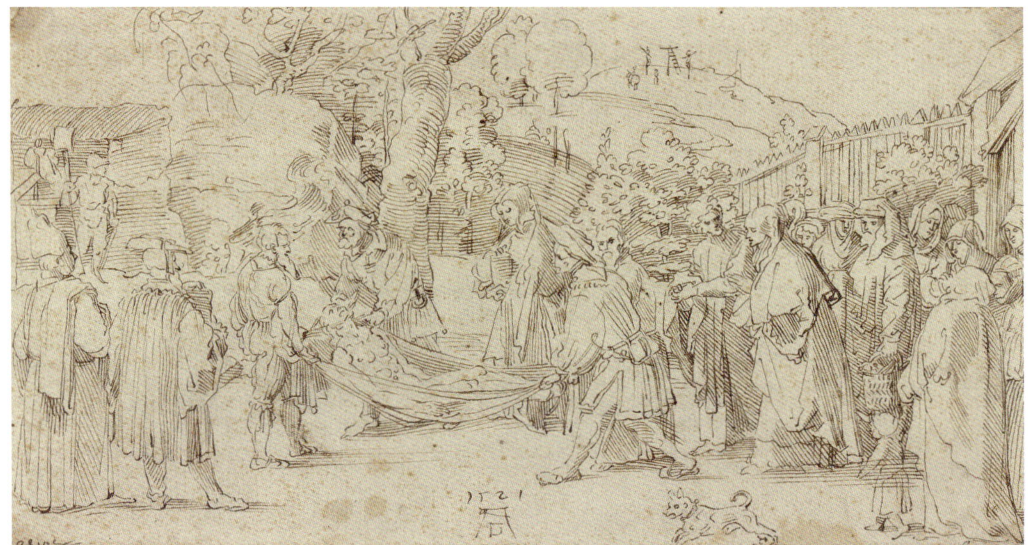

Fig. 135
AFTER ALBRECHT DÜRER
The Entombment, about 1521
Pen and brown ink, 14.5 × 27.1 cm
Städel Museum, Frankfurt am Main (716)

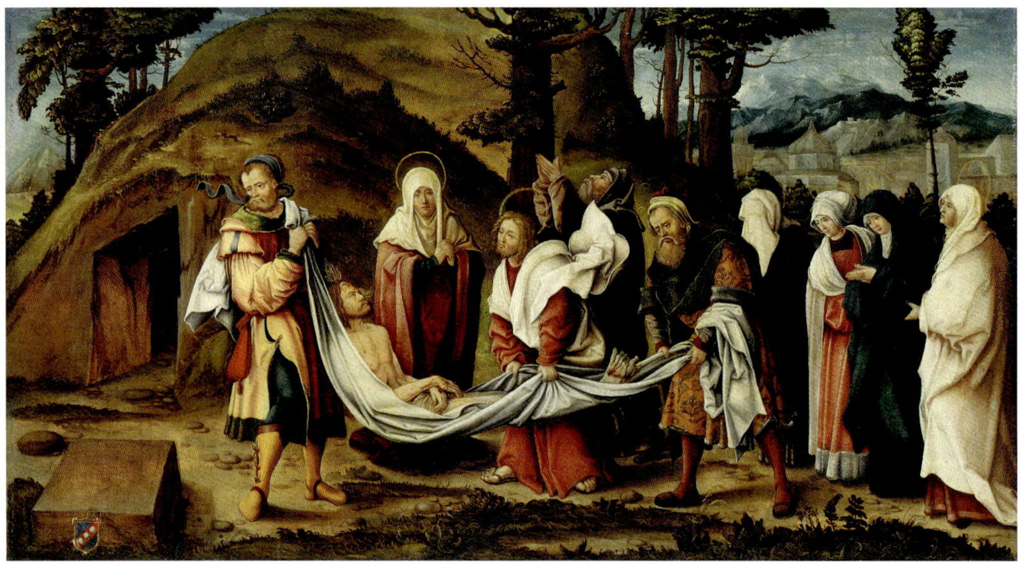

Fig. 136
HANS BURGKMAIR (1473–1531)
Christ's Body carried to the Tomb, about 1518–20
Oil on panel. 66.3 × 118.3 cm
Museo Nacional Thyssen-Bornemisza, Madrid

PAINTINGS AFTER DRAWINGS

Although Dürer's late Passion drawings were never made into a finished woodcut series, two of his *Oblong Passion* compositions (figs 133, 137) are related to two paintings, one by Dürer's contemporary from Augsburg, Hans Burgkmair, and the other by Dürer himself.

Dürer's decision to depict Christ's body carried to the tomb in his *Oblong Passion* drawings (fig. 133; cat. 107) is curious, since the theme was less common during the sixteenth century than the Deposition, Lamentation and Entombment, particularly among painters and printers who preceded him in Germany. Hans Burgkmair also painted this liminal moment in a predella panel for a lost altarpiece dated around 1520 (fig. 136), in a composition that is strikingly similar to Dürer's. The fact that Dürer's drawings and Burgkmair's painting share common elements with Italian prototypes, such as Andrea Mantegna's *Entombment* engraving of around 1465–70 and Raphael's central panel of the Baglioni Altarpiece of 1507, does not adequately account for their remarkable similarity, particularly in the positioning of the figures in a frieze, the elongation of Christ's body, the central tree that bisects the compositions, and the postures of the three bearers.[12] While Friedrich Winkler believed this to be coincidental, Isolde Lübbeke has suggested that Dürer and Burgkmair had access to similar Italian drawings available in both the Netherlands and in Augsburg.[13] It is more likely, however, that Dürer directly observed Burgkmair's early experiments with the theme while visiting Augsburg for two months during the Imperial Diet of 1518. While there he made several drawings of prominent citizens, including one of his fellow artist.[14] Burgkmair also made a portrait of Dürer, which no longer survives, suggesting that Dürer visited his workshop. If Burgkmair was working on the predella panel at that time, this may be a clearer example of artistic reciprocity than previously considered.

Sometime between 1520 and 1527, Dürer produced a rapidly executed drawing (fig. 137) in which he expanded the procession of his 1520 *Road to Calvary* (fig. 131) to include more figures. It shows three riders, the foremost of which holds a large standard bearing a single-headed eagle. In the foreground a foot soldier presses a cluster of women forward while a bound prisoner, stripped of his clothing, trails behind. Guardsmen carry large wooden crosses for the two thieves to be crucified alongside Christ. A different hand inscribed Dürer's monogram and added hatching in reddish-brown ink to several of the figures. Together, this sketch and the *Oblong Passion* drawing (fig. 131) formed the basis of what is considered to be Dürer's final painting, the *Road to Calvary* of 1527. Although the original is assumed lost, three versions of the painting survive, each executed in partial grisaille. The finest of these is generally deemed the version formerly in the Cook collection in Richmond and still in private hands (cat. 109), while the other two are located in the Accademia Carrara, Bergamo (fig. 138) and the Gemäldegalerie, Dresden (fig. 139). Although the overall figural group of each work corresponds to the drawings, the architectural elements have been elaborated to accommodate the larger scale of the painted composition. Other buildings denoting Jerusalem have been included in the distance, as well as a landscape dotted with trees and a winding road that leads to a jagged rock formation, presumably Golgotha. Additionally, a small tree now grows from the central stone buttress of the exterior wall.

Stylistic comparison between the three paintings indicates that a different artist completed each version. While the privately owned painting aligns most closely with the spirit of Dürer's style in terms of naturalism and the skilful application of light and shadow, the panel now in Dresden reproduces the original drawing with greatest accuracy and exhibits the highest level of detail. This version also lacks the added weapons and small open-mouthed figure featured in the rounded archway on the right in both the privately owned and Bergamo versions. Therefore the Dresden painting's mechanical depiction of details and its closeness to the *Oblong Passion* drawing suggest that it might be the earliest of the three versions. The Bergamo panel, which appears the most derivative, is likely the latest of the three.[15] Each of the panels bears a Latin inscription in the central foreground, written on lengths of cloth secured by wooden stakes. The privately owned and Bergamo paintings feature the same passage, which may be translated 'As for this panel in ash-grey colours, Albrecht Dürer was painting it spontaneously

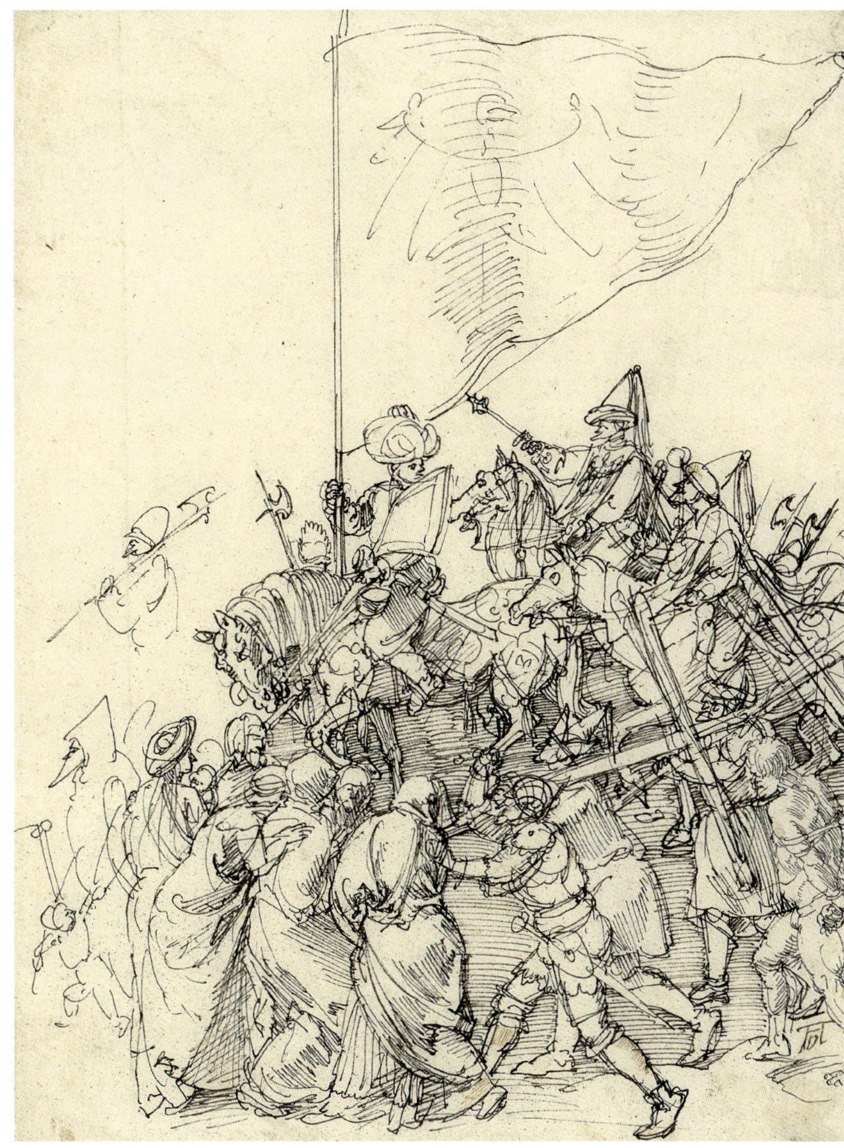

Fig. 137
ALBRECHT DÜRER
The Road to Calvary, 1520–7
Pen and brown ink, 29.4 × 21.5 cm
Staatliche Museen zu Berlin, Kupferstichkabinett (KdZ 3868)

and without any drawing based on real figures, in the year of salvation 1527 at the age of 56'.[16] In contrast, the Dresden version bears a paraphrased excerpt from the Old Testament book of Isaiah (53: 7–8): 'He is brought as a lamb to the slaughter, and as a sheep before her shearers is dumb, so he openeth not his mouth. He was taken from judgement, and who shall declare his generation?'[17]

Details surrounding this artistic project are sparse. A reference to such a composition is found in Karel van Mander's *Schilder-Boeck* of 1604, which relates that an 'excellent' painting by Dürer depicting 'the story of Christ carrying his cross … full of details and figures' was donated to Emperor Rudolf II by 'the council and the authorities of the city of Nuremberg for one reason or another', and that it could be viewed in the Emperor's palace in Prague in a gallery specifically devoted to German and Netherlandish artists.[18] Van Mander also noted that the painting was 'certainly one of the most important pieces ever made by

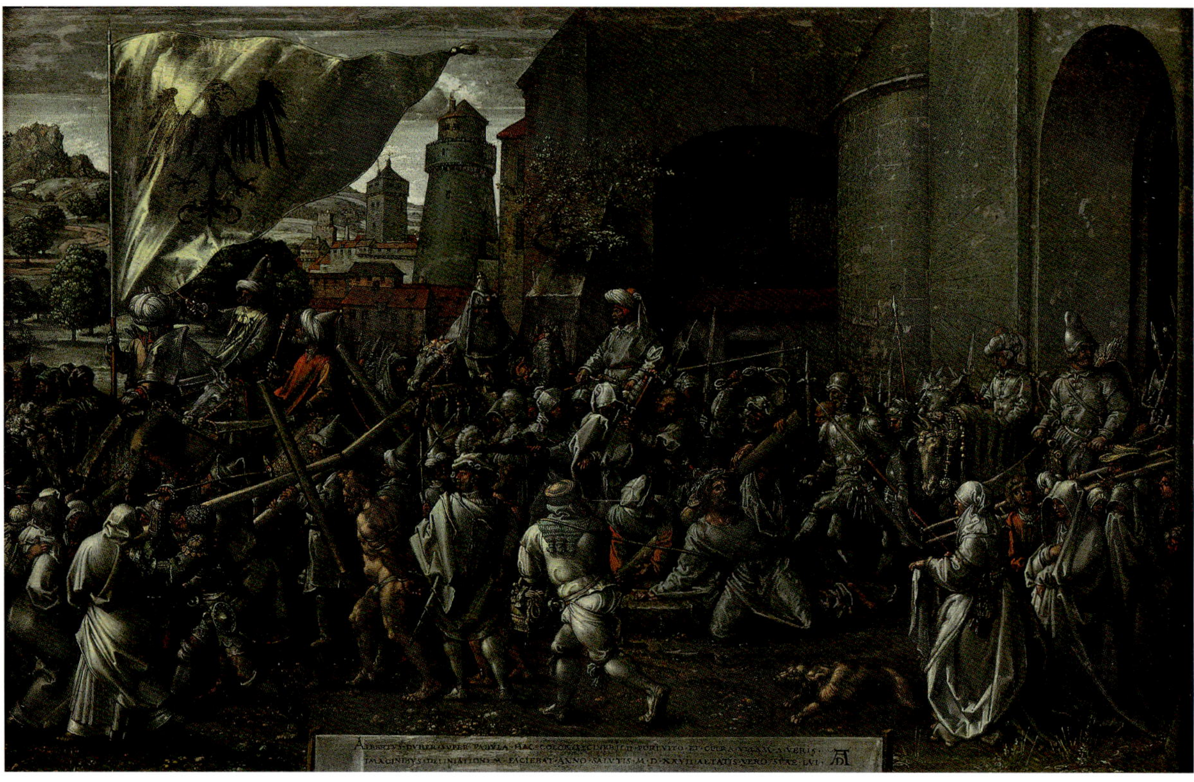

109
ATTRIBUTED TO ALBRECHT DÜRER
The Procession to Calvary, 1527
Panel, 29 × 45 cm
Private collection

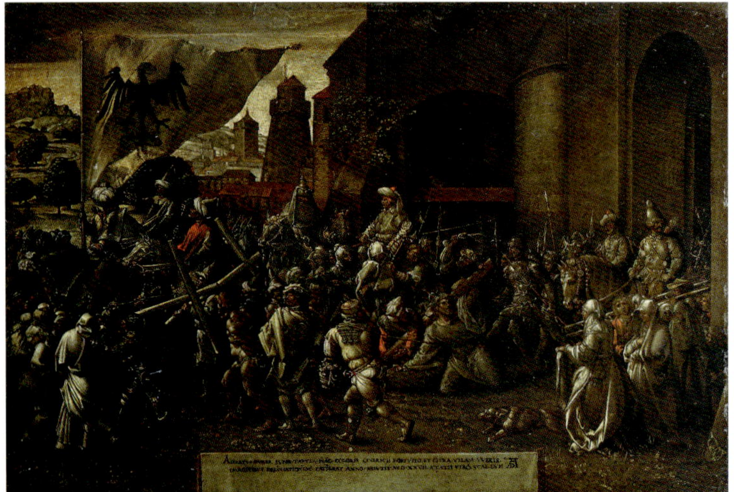

Fig. 138
AFTER ALBRECHT DÜRER
The Road to Calvary, 1527
Oil on oak, 22.7 × 47.9 cm
Accademia Carrara, Bergamo

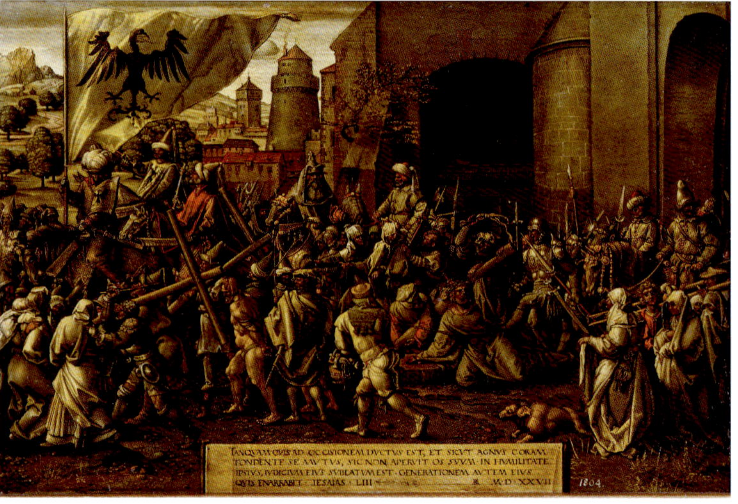

Fig. 139
AFTER ALBRECHT DÜRER
The Road to Calvary, 1527
Oil on canvas on linden wood, 30 × 45.5 cm
Gemäldegalerie Alte Meister, Staatliche Kunstsammlungen Dresden

Albert' and that 'all Nuremberg's councillors alive at that time [were] also in it, portrayed from life'. [19] Since the figures in the extant works do not appear to be portraits, either van Mander was mistaken or he was referring to a different painting. Erwin Panofsky has suggested that the Dutch writer misunderstood the large eagle in the painting to represent Nuremberg and accordingly interpreted the Roman soldiers as members of that city's civic body.[20] If Dürer's original was in the imperial collection by 1604 and the subsequent versions are based on that painting, it still remains uncertain whether the original had an inscription, and if so, whether it was one of the two possibilities found on the extant works or a different inscription entirely.

Dürer's inclusion of explanatory texts on authorship and date of execution, like those found on the private and Bergamo versions, occurs elsewhere in his oeuvre. A self portrait in his *Feast of the Rose Garlands* panel of 1506 (fig. 19) includes a sheet of paper stating 'Albrecht Dürer, a German, produced it within the span of five months. 1506.'[21] Similarly, an inscription on a bookmark in his *Christ among the Doctors* of 1506 (cat. 31) boasts that the painting was 'a work of five days'.[22] Rather than focus on time of completion, the elaborate text of the 1527 *Road to Calvary* paintings (cat. 109; fig. 138) instead emphasise the accomplishment of completing a complex multi-figured composition without extensive preparatory effort. For

Panofsky, this assertion appeared less like a signature by the artist and more like a memorial to his mastery, subsequently added in place of the original inscription to legitimise the authenticity of the later versions.[23]

The only previous example of Dürer's inclusion of an extensive religious text within a painting is found at the base of his 1526 *Four Apostles* panels (Alte Pinakothek, Munich).[24] Here the artist featured excerpts from the writings of apostles John, Peter and Paul, and the evangelist Mark, all taken from Martin Luther's *September Testament*, the first edition of his translation of the New Testament published in 1522. Dürer included his own introductory message taken from the book of Revelation warning against false prophets and the distortion of God's word.[25] The artist gifted the panels to Nuremberg's municipal leaders a year after the city's official acceptance of Lutheranism, as a reminder to consult and uphold the word of God in decisions of government and justice. If the original inscription on the 1527 *Road to Calvary* painting was indeed the passage from Isaiah found on the Dresden painting (fig. 139), it may have had a similar purpose.[26] By 1527 varying reformist positions deviated from Luther's teachings and jeopardised the religious and political unity of Nuremberg.[27] Promoters of spiritualism, for instance, challenged Luther's doctrine of justification through faith by asserting that salvation was derived from the changes the Holy Spirit makes within us rather than faith in God's promise that Christ redeems us through his sacrifice.

For the authors of the Gospels, the validity of Christ's sacrifice as told through the scriptures is clearly laid out in Isaiah 53, one of the most provocative passages of the Old Testament. In 12 verses, the author prophetically describes the suffering and death of Christ for the redemption of the sins of humankind. Dürer's possible inclusion of a passage from this chapter in his painting, an example of God's divine inspiration, serves to reiterate the supreme authority of God over the thoughts and deeds of man.

The presence of the small tree growing from the central stone buttress of the exterior wall also suggests that the passage from Isaiah was part of Dürer's original painting. The second verse of chapter 53 states: 'For he shall grow up before him as a tender plant, and as a root out of a dry ground: he hath no form nor comeliness; and when we shall see him, there is no beauty that we should desire him.'[28] Seemingly weak and insignificant, the tender plant grows and is sustained in God's presence, despite its harsh environment. As the tree is not present in the original drawing and is placed prominently in the painting, it must have been added for its symbolic significance.

The intended audience for Dürer's original painting and the subsequent versions remains uncertain. Van Mander's account that the city of Nuremberg gave the original to the emperor suggests that the city had the right to gift it. The fact that the inscriptions were altered in later versions implies that these paintings were made for patrons seeking works closely related to the painter after his death. One such panel was listed as from Dürer's workshop in the Imhoff collection inventories for 1573 to 1648.[29] Initially offered for sale to Emperor Rudolf II, this may be the version sold in Antwerp in 1633, which entered the collection of the Almada family, the descendants of Rodrigo Fernandes de Almada, envoy of the King of Portugal, who also had in his possession Dürer's *Saint Jerome* of 1521 (cat. 110).[30]

1 The *Oblong Passion* drawings are held in the following museum collections, in alphabetical order by city: Kupferstichkabinett, Staatliche Museum, Berlin: *The Agony in the Garden* (inv. KdZ 17 [W. 803]); Uffizi, Florence: *Road to Calvary* (inv. 1077 E [1520, W. 794]), *Road to Calvary* (inv. 1078 E. [1520, W. 793]), *The Entombment* (inv. 1069 E [1521, W. 795]); Städel Museum, Frankfurt: *The Agony in the Garden* (inv. 695 [1521, W. 798]), *The Agony in the Garden* (inv. 694 [1524, W. 891]), copy after Dürer, *The Entombment* (inv. 716 [W. 799]); Staatliche Kunsthalle, Karlsruhe: *The Agony in the Garden* (inv. 1978-11 [1520, W. 797]); Germanisches Nationalmuseum, Nuremberg: *The Entombment* (inv. St. Nbg. 12589 [1521, W. 796]); The Albertina Museum, Vienna: *The Last Supper* (inv. 3178 [1523, W. 889]), *The Adoration of the Magi* (inv. 4837 [1524; W. 894]). Heinrich Wölfflin and Erwin Panofsky considered Dürer's late *Adoration* drawing the prelude to the entire series. See Wölfflin 1971, p. 257; Panofsky 1955, p. 218.

2 Ashcroft 2017, vol. 1, p. 583.

3 See the essays by Stijn Alsteens (pp. 129–45) and Giulia Bartrum (pp. 267–76) in the present volume.

4 Panofsky 1955, p. 222; Strieder 1982, p. 129; Cambridge 2000, pp. 34–41; See D. McColl, 'Agony in the Garden: Dürer's "Crisis of the Image"', in Silver and Chipps Smith, 2010, pp. 166–84.

5 White 1971, p. 193.

6 See Jeroen Stumpel in the present volume, pp. 229–39.

7 Erwin 1999, pp. 258–9, 282–3.

8 Ashcroft 2017, vol. 1, p. 533, no. 152.10.

9 Pelikan and Lehman 1955–86, vol. 42, pp. 13–14.

10 Silver 1997, p. 424.

11 The Virgin's costume is modelled after a figure study by Dürer in the Albertina (fig. 99).

12 Andrea Mantegna, *The Entombment*, about 1470/1475, engraving in brown ink on laid paper, 29.9 × 44.2 cm, National Gallery of Art, Washington (inv. 1986.98.1); Raphael, *The Deposition*, 1507, oil on panel, 179 × 174 cm, Galleria Borghese, Rome (inv. 369).

13 Winkler 1936–9, vol. 2, p. 796; Lübbeke 1991, p. 177.

14 Anzelewsky 1980, pp. 194–198. *Portrait of Hans Burgkmair*, 1518, charcoal on discoloured laid paper, touched with brush and bodycolour, against a background of brown ink, 37.4 × 26.5 cm, Ashmolean Museum, Oxford (WA1863.416); Strauss 1974, vol. 3, no. 1518/21.

15 Technical investigation of the three versions, which has been undertaken in anticipation of this exhibition, will greatly enhance our understanding of the paintings and their relationship to one another. Unfortunately, the results of these scientific studies will not be available by the time this essay goes to publication.

16 Anzelewsky 1991, vol. 1, p. 289.

17 Ashcroft 2017, vol. 2, p. 832.

18 Mander 1604 (1994), fol. 209r.

19 Ibid.

20 Panofsky 1945, vol 2, p. 7.

21 Chipps Smith 2012, p. 174.

22 Ashcroft 2017, vol. 1, p. 176; '1506/AD/opus qui[n] que dierum' ('a work of five days').

23 Panofsky 1945, vol. 2, p. 8. Panofsky believed that Joachim Camerarius drafted the text.

24 *The Four Apostles*, 1526, oil on panel, 212.8 × 76.2 cm (left panel), 212.4 × 76.3 cm (right panel), Bayerische Staatsgemäldesammlungen – Alte Pinakothek, Munich (inv. 545).

25 Ashcroft 2017, vol. 2, p. 819. Revelation 22: 18–19.

26 Anzelewsky 1991, vol. 1, 289. Fedja Anzelewsky argued the verses on the Dresden painting were written by Dürer himself, thus making it the earliest of three versions.

27 Ibid., p. 289. Anzelewsky made specific reference to Andreas Osiander (1498–1552).

28 Isaiah 53: 2.

29 Ashcroft 2017, vol. 2, p. 833. See the 1630 Imhoff inventory in Ernstberger 1954, pp. 175–7, no. 26: 'Die Ausführung des H. Christi, von sehr viel Personen, kommt aus Alb. Dürers Werkstatt, und ist unserm Vater sel. oftmalen viel Geld dafür geboten worden.'

30 Anzelewsky 1991, vol. 1, p. 288.

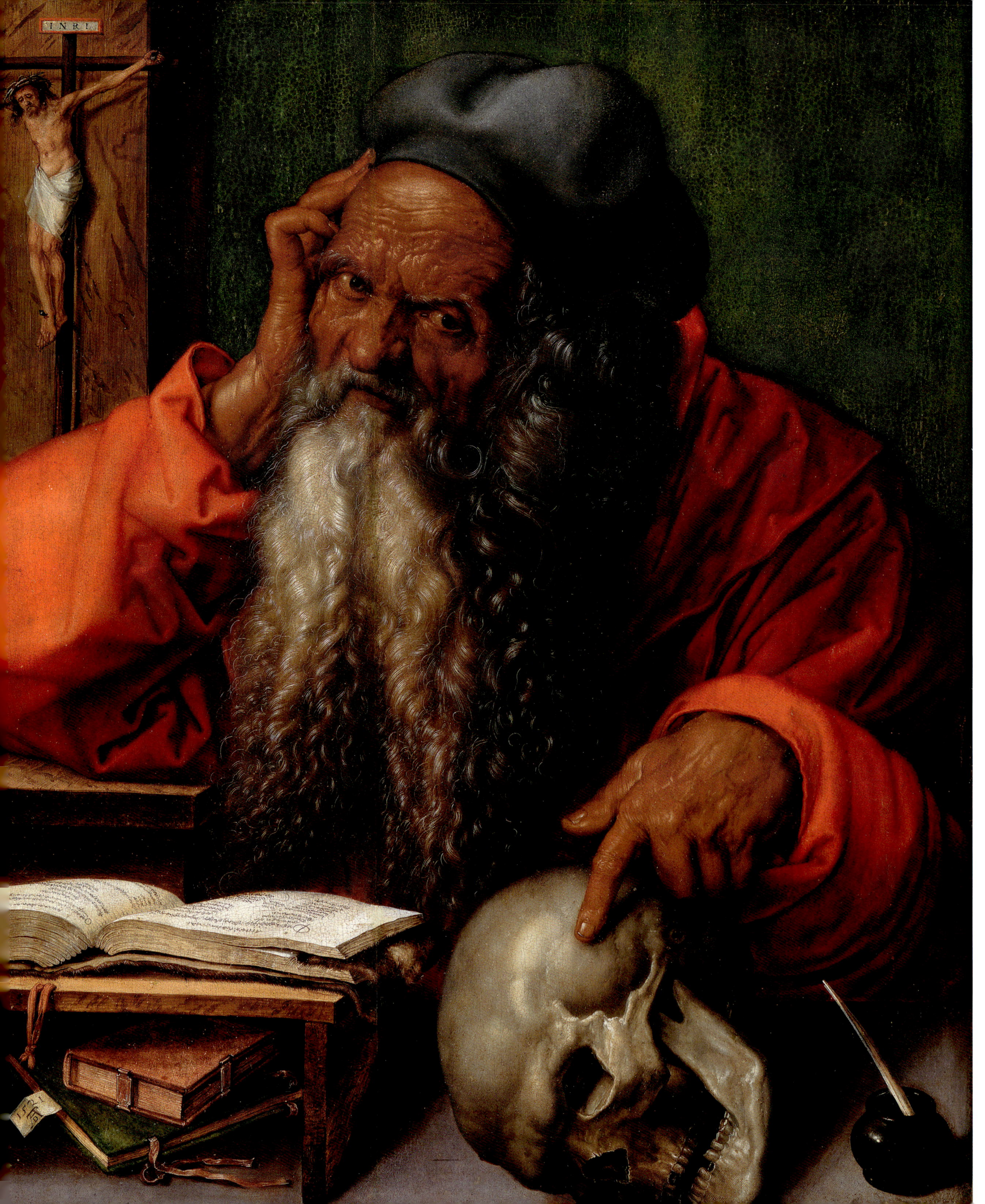
INRI

ASTRID HARTH AND MAXIMILIAAN P.J. MARTENS

ALBRECHT DÜRER'S ICONIC IMAGE OF SAINT JEROME
MAKING, MEANING AND RECEPTION

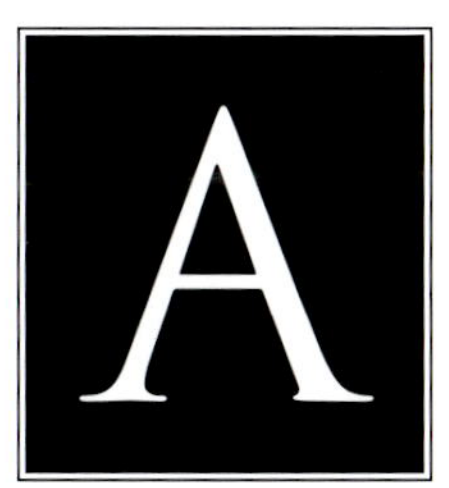

LBRECHT DÜRER'S ACTIVITY IN ANTWERP between August 1520 and July 1521 included the production of one of his most influential paintings, which fascinated two generations of Netherlandish artists.[1] It is a half-length depiction of Saint Jerome shown close-up as an aged savant pointing at a human skull (cat. 110), painted on locally available Baltic oak. The picture was made for Rodrigo Fernandes de Almada of the Antwerp Portuguese trading establishment and presented to him as a gift around mid-March 1521.[2] De Almada was one of Dürer's closest friends in Antwerp: the artist portrayed him at least twice, once in a drawing (fig. 114) and once in a painting (fig. 28).

The *Saint Jerome* painting remained in Antwerp until 1548.[3] A few years after Dürer left Antwerp in the summer of 1521, copies and variants after the Nuremberg master's image were produced in large quantities in the Netherlands. The workshops of Joos van Cleve (cat. 112; fig. 141), Pieter Coecke van Aalst (1502–1550), Jan Sanders van Hemessen (died about 1556–7; fig. 143), Marinus van Reymerswale (active 1533–45; cat. 111) and anonymous painters (fig. 142) specialised in the serial reproduction of Dürer's painting.[4] The majority of this serial output was probably disseminated on the open market in Antwerp, the mercantile and financial capital of Europe in the sixteenth century.

Dürer's image for de Almada marks a radical departure from the visual tradition of Saint Jerome. Unlike the fifteenth-century iconographical invention of Jerome in his Study, Dürer's painting bears little connection with the late medieval iconography of the saint, which emphasised his scholarly achievements as the creator of the Vulgate version of the Bible and his authority as a cardinal and Church Father.[5] Dürer jettisoned the traditional full-length format and iconographic motifs, notably the distinctive cardinal's attire, which had defined the saint's late medieval image. His famous 1514 copper engraving (fig. 140) is a fine example of this traditional iconography, in which the saint is writing at his desk with intense concentration.[6]

110
ALBRECHT DÜRER
Saint Jerome, 1521
Oil on oak,
60 × 48 cm
Museu Nacional de Arte Antiga, Lisbon

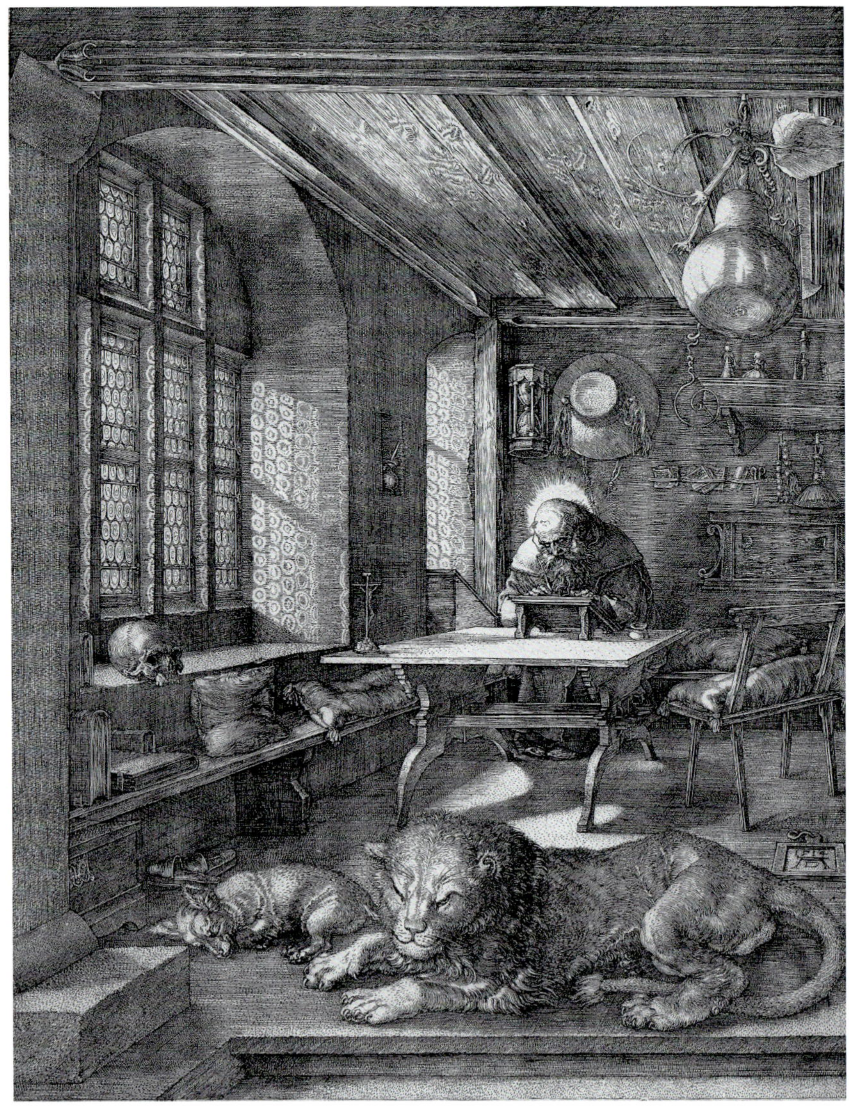

Fig. 140
ALBRECHT DÜRER
Saint Jerome in his Study, 1514
Engraving, 24.4 × 18.7 cm
Rijksmuseum, Amsterdam
(RP-P-OB-1224)

Throughout the room we see his attributes: a crucifix on his working table, a sleeping lion in the foreground, books on a bench, a skull on the windowsill and his cardinal's hat hanging behind him on the wall beside an hourglass.

In the 1521 painting only the crucifix, the lectern and books and the human skull are retained. The skull is a central motif now, moved to the top of the saint's desk between the lectern and writing utensils. In an attitude of melancholy, the elderly Church Father leans his head against his right hand and appears to be interrupted as he contemplates an open manuscript in Greek script, conspicuously pointing at the skull. This visual motif was characteristic of the other widely spread traditional representation, Saint Jerome in the Wilderness.[7]

MAKING

The design process for the *Saint Jerome* painting, now in Lisbon, is partly documented in Dürer's journal and five extant study drawings in black ink, heightened with white on grey-dyed paper (see figs 144–7).[8] Dürer started using such preliminary drawings on coloured paper after his Venetian journey (1505–7) to examine single motifs that constitute the composition. It appears that he employed this working process for large-scale commissioned altarpieces, notably the *Feast of the Rose Garlands* (1506) and the *Heller Triptych* (1507–9).[9] For the small-scale Saint Jerome he made separate study drawings of almost every individual element – the saint's head, his outstretched left arm, the pointing gesture of his left index finger, the lectern with books, and the human skull. In these study sheets he suggested volume with great precision through a meticulous modulation of light and shadow; all indicate a light source at the top left of the composition.

The preparatory drawings of the aged saint's physiognomy were made after a living model, a man 'ninety-three years old and still sane and healthy', according to Dürer's inscription on the sheet with the study of the head (fig. 147).[10] He mentions in his Netherlandish journal that the portrait session took place in Antwerp sometime in January 1521.[11] A drawing of the same man, now in Berlin, is more focused on the aged, wrinkled face and especially

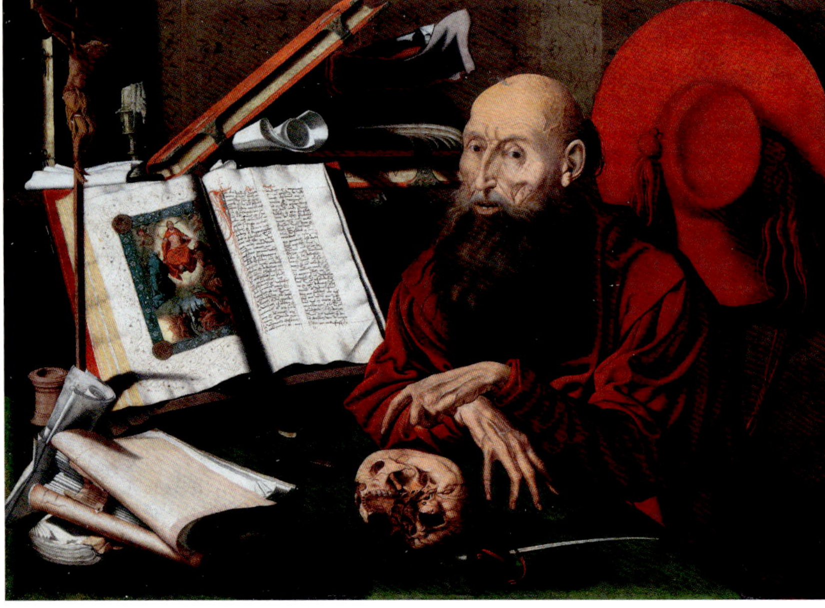

111
MARINUS VAN REYMERSWALE
(active 1533–45)
Saint Jerome in his Study, about 1535–45
Oil on panel, 80.5 × 109 cm
Rijksmuseum, Amsterdam

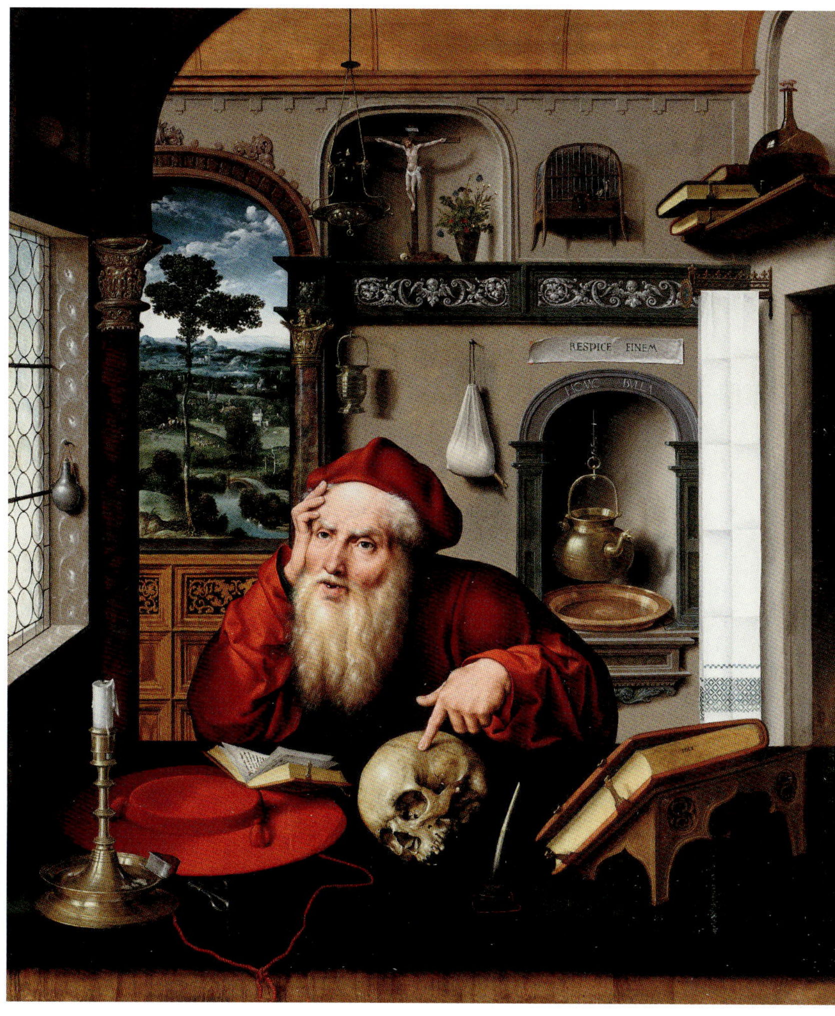

112
JOOS VAN CLEVE
(1485–1541)
Saint Jerome in his Study, 1521
Oil on panel, 99.7 × 83.8 cm
Harvard Art Museums / Fogg Museum

the concentrated gaze of the sitter (fig. 148).[12] Whether this latter version pre-dates the Viennese one or whether they were made during the same sitting is difficult to tell.[13] In any case, the Viennese drawing is a more accomplished study and is more closely related to the *Saint Jerome* painting itself. Parenthetically, this drawing later became an important work of art in its own right and was copied by Hans Hoffman (about 1530–about 1591; cat. 113).[14]

Dürer took a keen interest in the physiological signs of ageing and facial expression, such as deep wrinkles and furrows, which he modelled along the facial muscles and which, in the Berlin version, lend the subject an expression of weariness and misery. This contrasts with the old man's active, penetrating gaze of concentration, reflecting his mental vigour, as mentioned in the inscription on the Viennese study sheet. In the Berlin drawing, however, Dürer abandons the intense psychological effect of the sitter's direct stare in favour of a more modest downward gaze to suggest the saint's inward mental state of contemplation. Moreover, he opens up the tightly framed compositional scheme to present the saint as a half-length figure, characteristic of the portrait formula that he had adopted since the 1500s.[15]

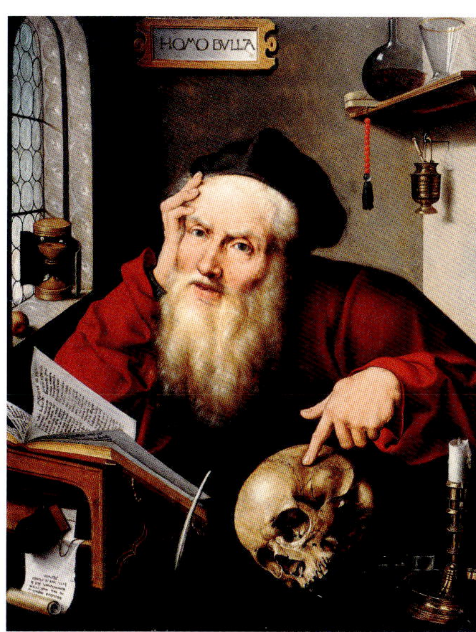

Fig. 141
JOOS VAN CLEVE
(1485–1541)
Saint Jerome in his Study, after 1528
Oil on canvas, 60.7 × 46.7 cm
Private collection

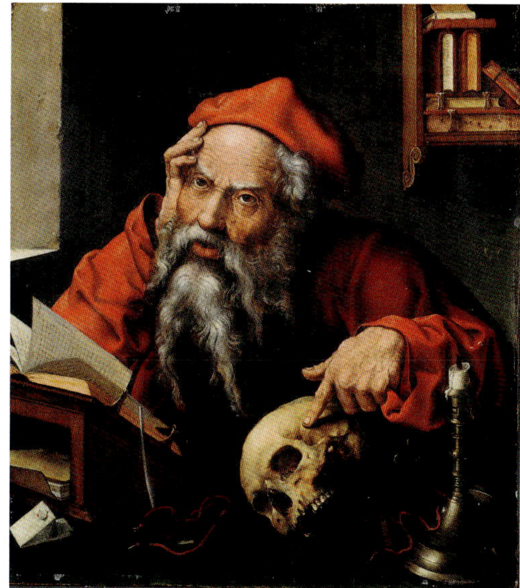

Fig. 142
AFTER JOOS VAN CLEVE
Saint Jerome in his Study, after 1521
Oil on oak, 52 × 46 cm
Private collection, Luxembourg

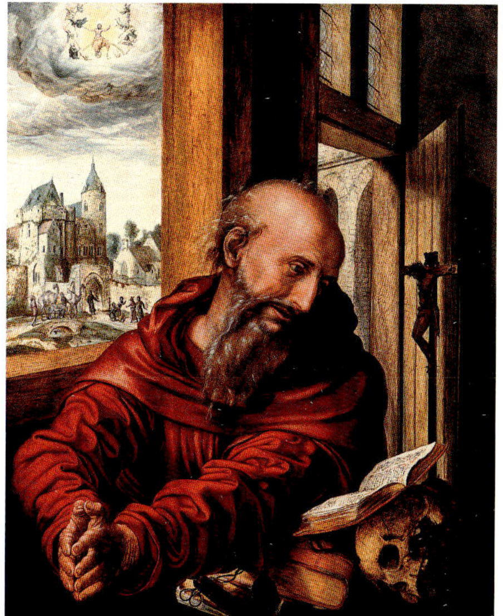

Fig. 143
JAN SANDERS VAN HEMESSEN
(about 1519/20; about 1556/7)
Saint Jerome, between 1534 and 1556
Oil on oak, 103 × 81 cm
Snijders & Rockox House Museum, Antwerp

For his *Saint Jerome* painting (cat. 110) the artist ultimately adopts the conceit of the direct outward gaze. This increases the interaction between the saint and the viewer, while the saint's hand-against-head gesture maintains the central theme of the painting: the mental activity of contemplating death.

Similarly, Dürer depicts the human skull, the central object of Jerome's meditative practice, as a highly realistic and even animated object. In the drawing (fig. 144) he positions the skull on its right lateral flank, resting on the zygomatic bone with the anterior side arranged perpendicular to the picture plane. The proportions and structure of the human skull are represented with scientific accuracy.[16] The forehead correctly merges with the rear parietal bone and the lower jaw is accurately placed behind the zygomatic bone, indicating that this particular drawing was made from a real human cranium.[17] In the painting Dürer enhances the expressive effect by turning the skull slightly towards the left to reveal more of the inner anatomical structure of the right eye orbit. Repositioning the motif also broadens its spatial potential as it now leans forward toward the viewer as much as back into the pictorial space toward the saint. Dürer thus establishes a direct physical and psychological relationship between the painting and the viewer by challenging the two-dimensionality of the pictorial plane through individual elements in the composition.

Another difference between the preparatory drawings and the Lisbon painting can be observed in the study sheet of the lectern, books and oval box (fig. 145). The original concept of this still-life feature was modified by placing it at the left edge of the composition, reducing the original arrangement of items by omitting the oval box, a container for writing utensils.[18] Thus the artist has opted to reduce the representation of Saint Jerome in his Study to its bare essentials to provide a dramatic close-up.[19]

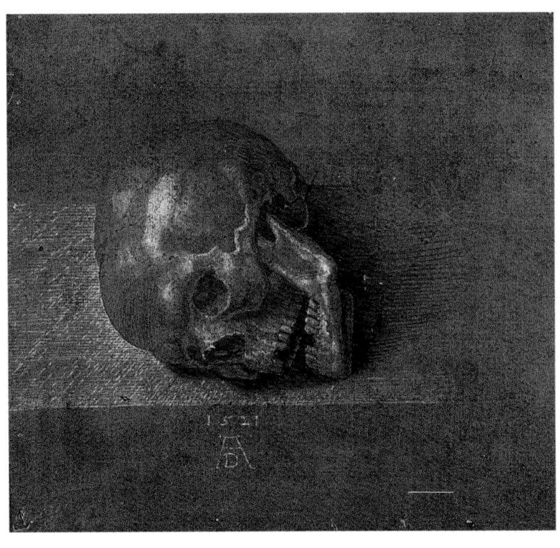

Fig. 144
ALBRECHT DÜRER
Study of a Skull, 1521
Brush in black ink, heightened with white, on grey-violet grounded paper, 18.2 × 19.4 cm
The Albertina Museum, Vienna (3175)

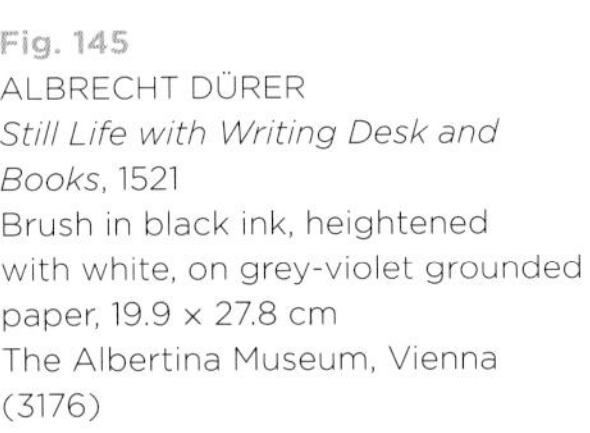

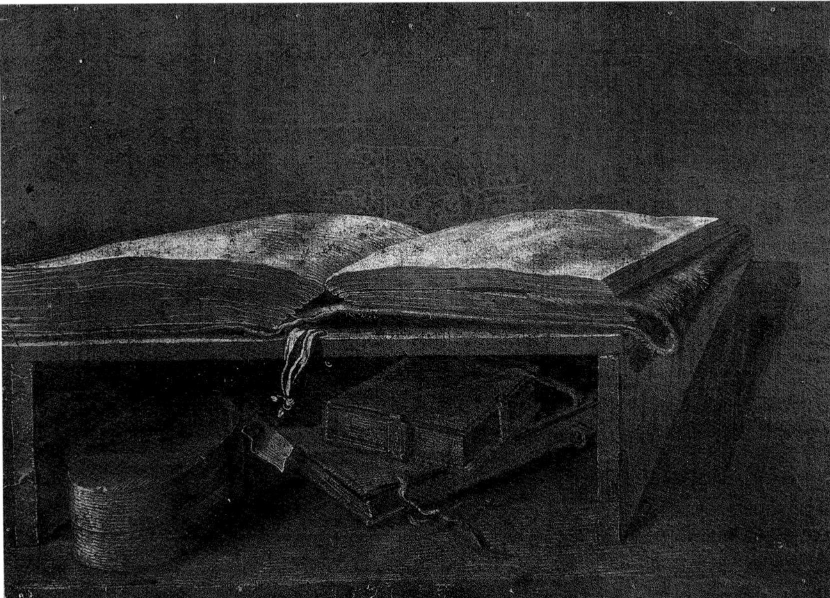

Fig. 145
ALBRECHT DÜRER
Still Life with Writing Desk and Books, 1521
Brush in black ink, heightened with white, on grey-violet grounded paper, 19.9 × 27.8 cm
The Albertina Museum, Vienna (3176)

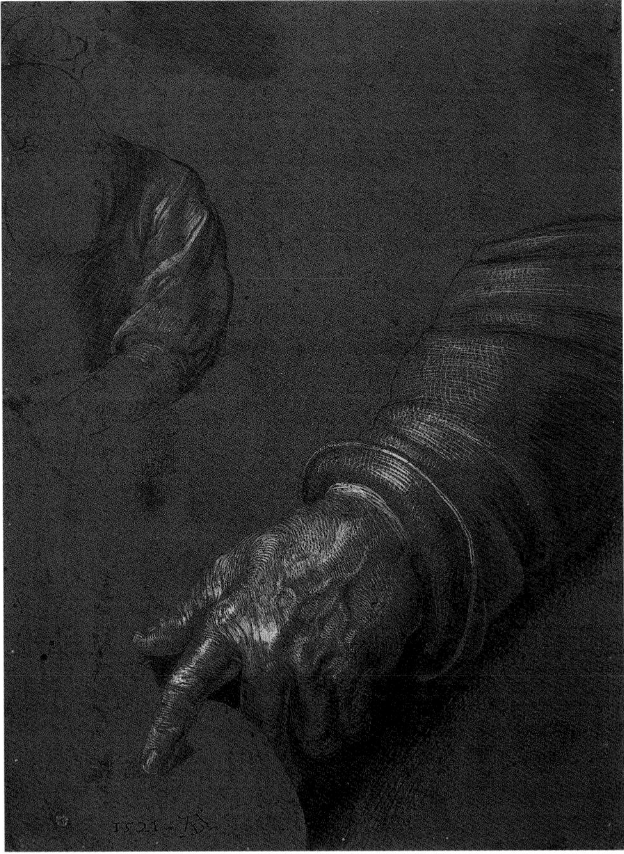

Fig. 146
ALBRECHT DÜRER
Study of an Arm, 1521
Brush in black and grey ink, heightened with white, on grey-violet grounded paper, 39.3 × 28.3 cm
The Albertina Museum, Vienna (3168)

'ninety-three years old and still sane and healthy'

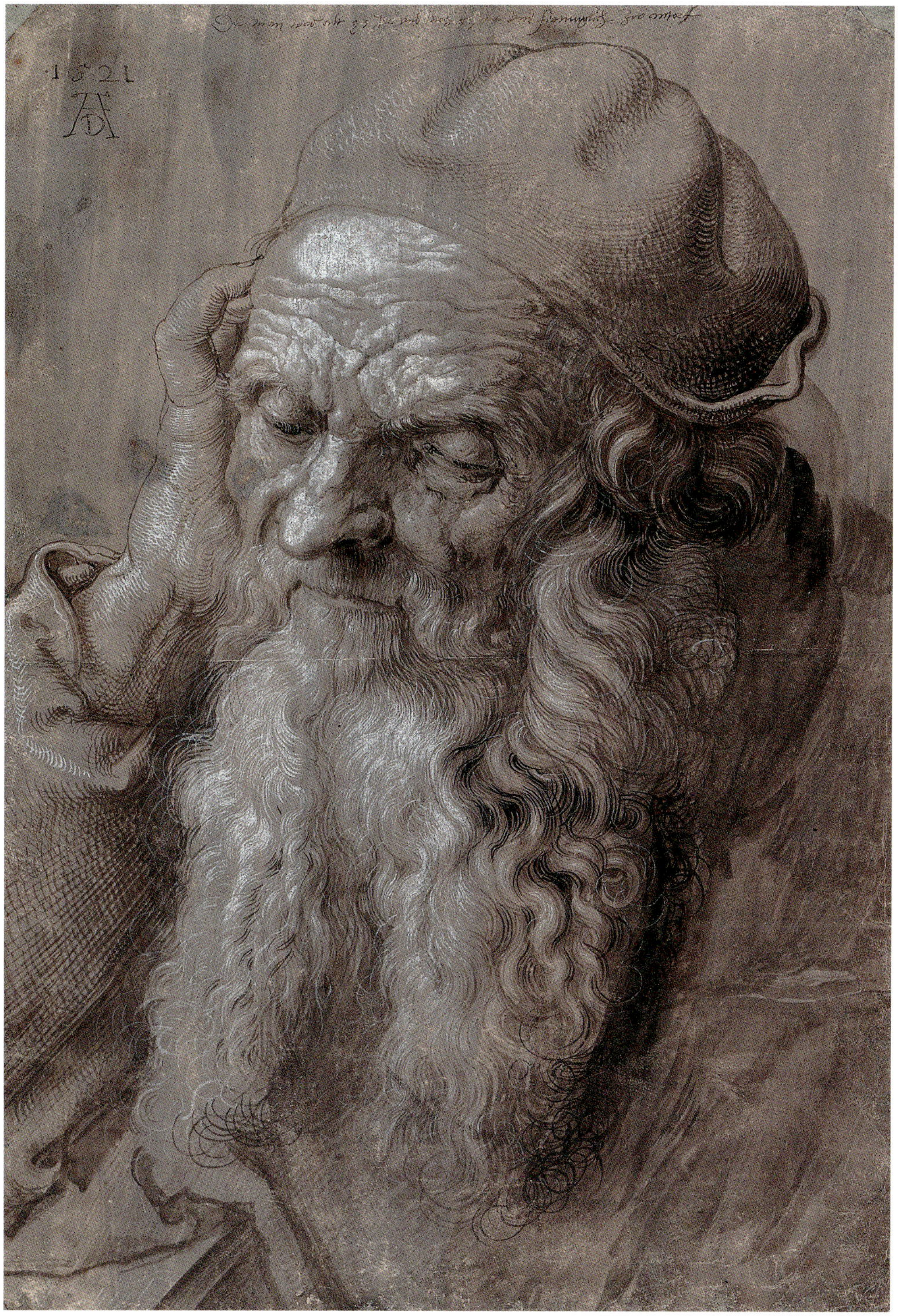

Fig. 147
ALBRECHT DÜRER
Head of a 93-Year-Old Man, 1521
Brush in black and grey ink, heightened with white, on grey-violet grounded paper, 41.5 × 28.2 cm
The Albertina Museum, Vienna (3167)

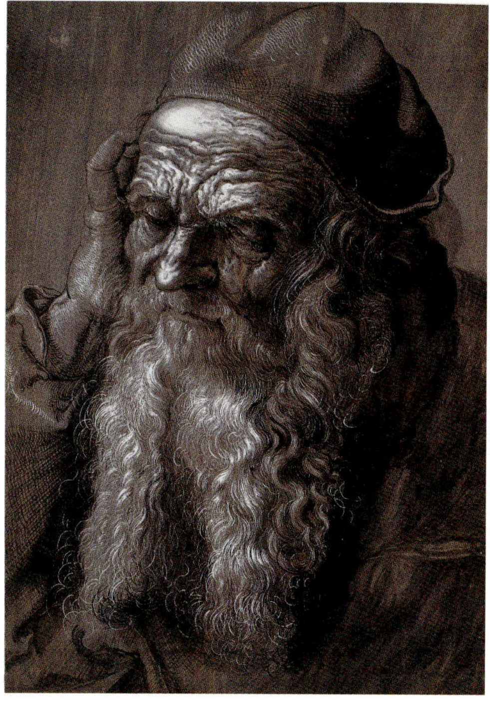

113
HANS HOFFMAN (about 1530–about 1591)
AFTER ALBRECHT DÜRER
An Old Man aged 93 (Saint Jerome), 1545–91
Brush with brown and black ink, heightened with white on a dark brown preparation, 39.5 × 27.3 cm
The Ashmolean Museum, University of Oxford

OVERLEAF
Detail of *Saint Jerome*
(cat. 110)

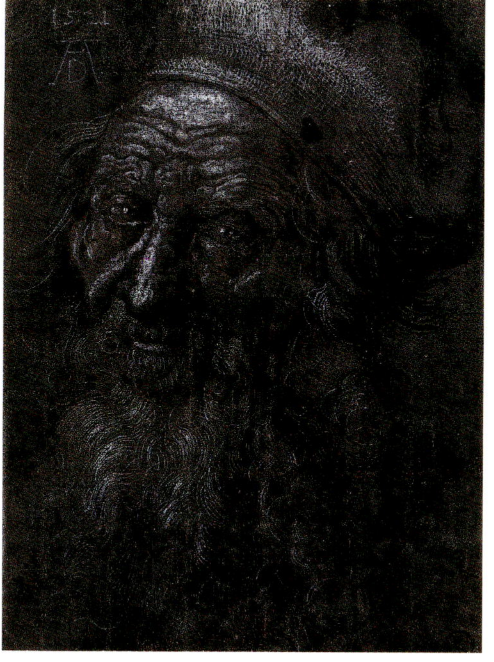

Fig. 148
ALBRECHT DÜRER
Head of an Old Man, 1521
Brush and black ink on grey-violet grounded paper, 26.9 × 19.9 cm
Staatliche Museen zu Berlin, Kupferstichkabinett (KdZ 38)

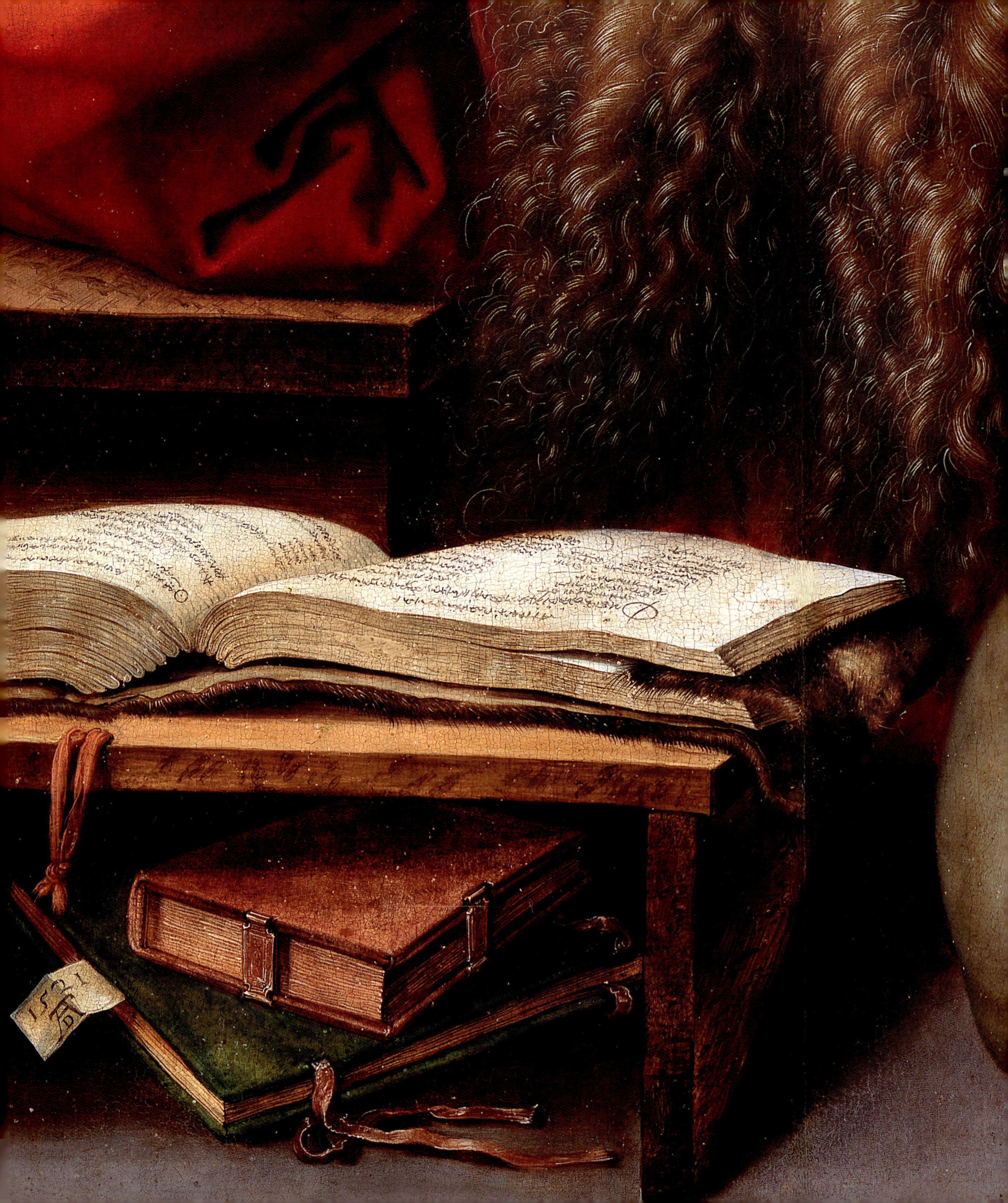
1521

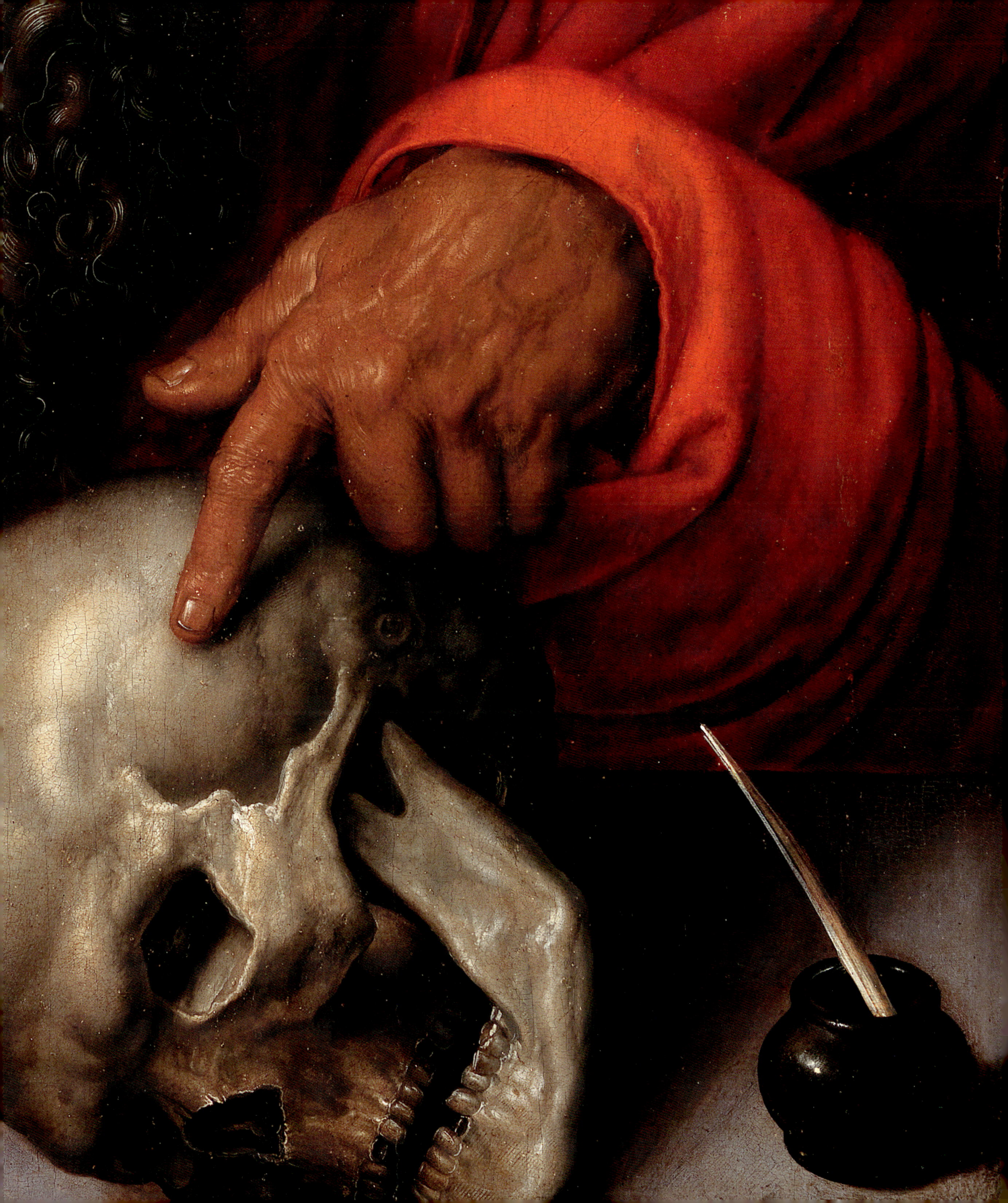

Even before Dürer created his Saint Jerome painting the skull motif featured as an attribute of the penitential saint, reflecting his awareness of his own sinful, mortal state, for which he as a follower of Christ must repent in preparation for death.[20] In the context of Jerome's own penance, the skull motif as a symbol of the transience of earthly life also refers to his 'ascetic' letters, filled with advice on moral conduct and addressed to his contemporaries, fellow clergy, friends and Roman patricians in the late fourth and early fifth centuries.[21]

The absence from the painting of any traditional symbol of penance raises questions about which actions the saint requires the spectator to undertake in preparation for death, especially in light of salvation. Is the spectator encouraged to embrace the historical Jerome's ascetic life of solitude, silence, austerity and contemplation in the wilderness or in the monastery, far from the secular world, or to conduct penitential exercises of prayer, confession, fasting and self-mortification, practices that the historical Jerome exercised himself and prescribed to his contemporaries? Or does it now suffice to singly internalise the symbolic message about the transience of earthly life?

Another significant omission from Dürer's 1521 composition is that of the saint's red cardinal's hat, the *galerus ruber*, Jerome's most familiar attribute in the visual arts since the mid-fourteenth century.[22] It has been suggested that Dürer's dismissal of the iconic motif reflects the scornful rejection of the anachronistic account of Jerome's cardinalship by Desiderius Erasmus in his critical biography, *Hieronymi Stridonensis vita* (1516).[23]

All previous attempts to understand the iconography, function and popularity of Dürer's innovative image of Saint Jerome have revolved around the same question: was Dürer influenced by the humanistic views of Desiderius Erasmus or the reformed ideas of Martin Luther?[24] Another important factor in the equation is that Rodrigo Fernandes de Almada, the recipient of the Saint Jerome painting, was a Roman Catholic.[25]

Although Dürer had travelled as a mature artist to Italy, it seems that his humanistic ideas were mainly developed and consolidated in his own town of Nuremberg. In the first decades of the sixteenth century Nuremberg was a thriving centre of humanism, home to prominent intellectuals such as Hartmann Schedel, Sixtus Tucher (1459–1507), Willibald Pirckheimer and Lazarus Spengler.[26] Dürer himself was an active participant in this humanistic milieu, with his various contributions to ambitious book projects of Nikolaus Kesler, Conrad Celtis and Lazarus Spengler.[27]

Although Dürer was passionately devoted to antiquity and to liberal arts subjects, the humanistic practice of the artist and his Nuremberg network was provoked by a perception that the popular teachings of the Latin Church had become detrimental to the spiritual health of Christian laity. Akin to the theological and philosophical endeavours of Desiderius Erasmus, Nuremberg humanists strongly advocated a return to the true teachings of Christ.[28] Within this climate of reform in Nuremberg, the figure of Saint Jerome thus not only functioned as a trope for defining humanistic scholarship but also for humanistic piety, in contrast to the immorality emanating from the popular teachings of the Latin Church.[29]

These humanistic concerns with popular piety are exemplified in the German translation of *De morte Hieronymi* (1514) by Dürer's friend Lazarus Spengler, a Nuremberg town clerk.[30] This translation was based on a pseudograph attributed to Eusebius of Cremona.[31] Spengler called this text Jerome's last 'haylsame und götliche leer' (salvific and divine teachings), which he equated in his dedicatory preface with the true teachings of Christ.[32] The title page of Spengler's translation featured a woodcut designed by Dürer. The print was made in 1512, two years before the publication of Spengler's translation, and portrayed Jerome as an elderly but still vigorous scholar, writing while contemplating a crucifix in the wilderness (fig. 149).[33] In the context of Spengler's publication, Dürer's print seemingly captures the aged saint fervently writing down his final 'salvific and divine teachings' on the ascetic life, feeling that death is near. In this respect Dürer's print can be considered a visual manifestation of the fascination with the saint's scholarship and ascetic piety that animated his humanist milieu in Nuremberg.

Besides producing imagery for humanistic publications, Dürer contributed to the dissemination of humanism among the laity by presenting large parts of his printed oeuvre, such as the three Passion books and his Saint Jerome prints, as gifts to friends, lodgers, fellow artists and patrons in the Netherlands.[34] Of course, such gift-giving was an essential part of a set of personal obligations that informed Dürer's network of support abroad.[35] Although he used his prints both as gifts and as payment, and they were considered collectibles and used by artists as models, they also retained their original religious function as objects intended for private devotion.

Here, again, a distinction must be made between the artist's earlier prints of Jerome and his painting of the saint for de Almada. The prints were created before Martin Luther initiated the Reformation in Wittenberg, Saxony, in 1517. Thus although it has been established that Dürer was an early admirer of Luther, certainly before he took up residence in Antwerp,[36] these prints are too early to be expressions of the reformer's theological thought. By the time of Luther's arrival in Antwerp, however, his writings had reached the city through printed books and leaflets,[37] and Dürer showed his enduring fascination for the reformer by buying copies of his writings.[38] Furthermore, during his stay in Antwerp the artist maintained close contact with the reformed Augustinian friars there.[39]

It should be kept in mind, however, that during this early stage of the Reformation, religious factions had not been firmly established and innovative theological ideas circulated back and forth.[40] After all, Dürer also socialised in the Netherlands with other major humanistic thinkers of his time, notably Desiderius Erasmus, as well as with traditional Catholics, such as Margaret of Austria and Rodrigo Fernandes de Almada. Nor should we assume that the new iconography of the Saint Jerome painting for de Almada is specifically linked to Luther's reformatory ideas, because he and his followers thought little of Jerome. Protestants criticised the Marian cult founded by Jerome and disapproved of his monastic lifestyle and ascetic practices of celibacy as a means to God's grace and salvation.[41] Interestingly, it has been argued that Jerome's pointing gesture towards the human skull is a reference to the faculty of reason.[42] This suggests that Dürer's new iconography of the saint was ultimately inspired by Erasmus's concept of self-knowledge.

Crucial in the question of Lutheran or Erasmian influence in this particular painting is their respective stance towards the concept of penance, which was strongly associated with Saint Jerome's traditional iconography. For both thinkers penance was contaminated by the financial corruption of the Catholic practice of selling indulgences to atone for sin, and the resulting torment and misery among ordinary Christians.[43] This latter concern also prompted Erasmus to participate in the indulgence controversy by criticising the sacrament of penance itself.[44]

The idea of Christian life as one continuous repentance prevailed throughout Luther's and Erasmus's critiques on the sacrament of penance.[45] This was based on the early Christian understanding of the concept of penance as a series of successive stages of spiritual growth, from believing in Christ's message of salvation to faithful imitation of his evangelical life.[46] For both Erasmus and Luther, 'the mark of the true Christian is not annual penance but continual penitence',[47] thus reducing the efficacy of the Catholic sacrament of penance by subordinating it to the early Christian idea of repentance as a way of life.

A distinction must be made, however, between Luther's incorporation of the concept of repentance into his theology and Erasmus's understanding of it. For Luther, the sacrament of baptism was a key element in the first step towards repentance, or spiritual conversion, while the development of faith characterised the second stage of spiritual growth. In this Luther differed from Erasmus,

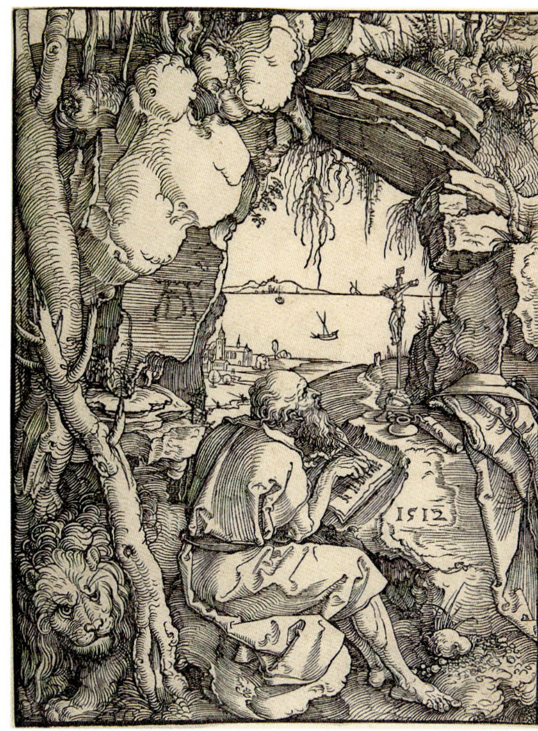

Fig. 149
ALBRECHT DÜRER
Saint Jerome in the Desert, 1512
Woodcut, 17 × 12.5 cm
The Metropolitan Museum of Art, New York. Rogers Fund, 1931 (31.57.1)

who advocated that next to faith, the development of virtues through self-knowledge is the principal teaching of the New Testament and thus the essence of penance and forgiveness.[48] For Erasmus, self-knowledge helped to shield the penitent from further temptation and brought consolation to the troubled conscience. In his *Enchiridion* (1503) he wrote: 'the only road to happiness is first to know yourself and then not to act in anything according to the passions but in all things according to the judgment of reason.'[49] For Erasmus, reason is the God-given armour by which we know ourselves and wage war against the flesh in order to attain virtue. For Luther, on the other hand, reason is not the source of self-knowledge, since human beings can only acquire it with the help of God, through divine illumination.[50]

Jerome's demonstrative request in Dürer's painting for de Almada is an appeal to the Christian viewer to pursue a moral life, in accordance with the Christian faith, by means of developing self-knowledge rather than merely performing rites of penance. Thus Dürer reflects Erasmus's humanistic ideas about Christian faith as outlined in the *Enchiridion*, rather than those of Luther. However, this is not to suggest that Luther's criticism of Saint Jerome could not have affected Dürer, since it would explain the complete omission of both symbols of penance and Marian motifs (such as a rosary).

Therefore, it does not seem far-fetched to conclude that Dürer presented *Saint Jerome* to de Almada as a devotional painting freed from the corrupted teachings of the Roman Catholic Church (cat. 110). In the context of their personal relationship, the gift may perhaps be considered as a painted argument in their intellectual exchange of ideas.

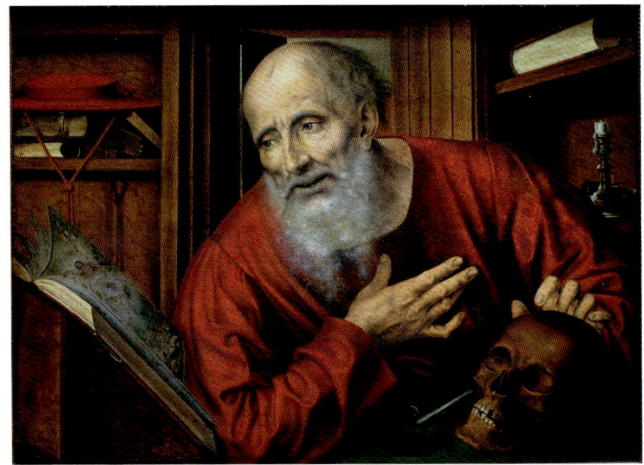

Fig. 150
QUINTEN MASSYS (1465/6–1530)
Saint Jerome, after 1521
Oil on oak, 57 × 77 cm
Kunsthistorisches Museum, Vienna

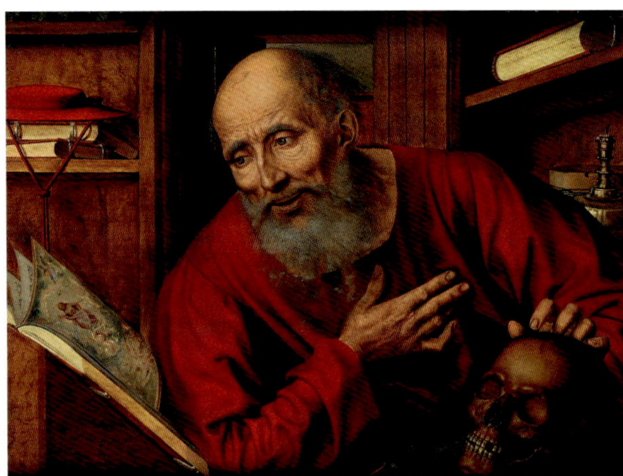

Fig. 151
JAN MASSYS (1509–1575) or QUINTEN MASSYS WORKSHOP
Saint Jerome, between 1530 and 1540
Oil on panel, 57.5 × 76.5 cm
Musée des Beaux-Arts de Rouen

RECEPTION

In the quest to understand the specific meaning of Dürer's *Saint Jerome*, the composition's reception by fellow artists in Antwerp is revealing. Although a large number of paintings produced in the city at this time have been considered as variants and copies of Dürer's painting, their relationship to it tends to be more complex.

A painting often compared with Dürer's *Saint Jerome* by art historians is *Saint Jerome in his Study*, attributed to Quinten Massys and now in Vienna (fig. 150).[51] This is probably a workshop copy after a lost original by Massys, produced after his death.[52] Silver has dated Massys's lost original before 1521, when Dürer made his painting for de Almada, based on common elements that appear in the Vienna copy and Massys's portrait of Erasmus of 1517.[53] This would suggest that the position of the skull within reach of the saint's hand may well have been an invention of Massys adapted by Dürer.

Certainly the Vienna copy is not an exact duplicate of Dürer's painting: the *memento mori* symbolism of the skull is emphasised by the extinguished candle on the right and the open manuscript on the lectern on the left, which shows the Last Judgement; no crucifix is present. Massys's Jerome makes a gesture of remorse with his right hand raised to his chest, and he seems to drum his left fingers on the skull instead of pointing it out to the viewer.[54] The presence of the cardinal's hat on the shelf is perhaps a last remaining traditional attribute, contradicting Erasmus but helping the viewer to identify the Church Father. Massys has invented a new iconography here, focusing on Saint Jerome in his study, pondering on his mortality and emphasising penance, yet still rooted in late medieval tradition.

Several other copies after Quinten Massys's lost composition are known, some of them by his son, Jan, or his workshop (fig. 151).[55] One of the finest is a version in the Prado, Madrid, in which the saint is set in a deeply receding space and points to the skull with his left index finger (following Dürer's example) and to the Last Judgement in the book with his right hand.[56] This page is visually related to that depicted in the Vienna copy: both feature Saint Michael in the centre, herding the damned into hell.[57]

A completely different approach to the subject is seen in a dramatic drawing of 1521 by Lucas van Leyden (cat. 114), whom Dürer met during his stay in the Netherlands.[58] Here Lucas focuses even more closely on the saint than does Dürer. He retains the vertical format, the pointing gesture on the skull, the crucifix (here held in the crook of his arm) and the scholar's cap. It has been assumed that Lucas knew not only Dürer's painting but also his preparatory drawing.[59] Unlike Dürer's 93-year-old man (fig. 147), Lucas's figure has his eyes open, staring resolutely sideways. Moreover, the finished drawing technique of ink heightened with white bodycolour is similar to Dürer's example. In an engraving, also dated 1521, Lucas van Leyden draws back and shows the saint in a rather awkward outstretched position leaning against his desk (fig. 152). The composition conflates Dürer's pointing gesture at the skull and Lucas's own motif of the crucifix in the crook of the arm, and reintroduces the cardinal's hat and the lion, both declared apocryphal in Erasmus's biography of Saint Jerome.

Of all Netherlandish artists, Joos van Cleve imitated Dürer's prototype most faithfully by copying the figure literally. In one version now in private hands, Jerome sits in a confined space reminiscent of a monk's cell (fig. 141).[60] The leaded window at the left is taken from Dürer's 1514 engraving, including the circular reflections on the side wall. The composition is completed with *memento mori* symbols: an extinguished candle, an hourglass and an apple on the windowsill, and the inscription 'HOMO BVLLA' (man is a bubble) on the wall. The stoppered wine carafe and the rosary beads on the wall shelf are clearly Marian references, shifting Dürer's model back into the traditional Catholic realm.[61]

The market success of this composition can be estimated from the numerous copies that have been preserved, produced for the open market by van Cleve and his workshop, and later his followers (fig. 142). However, van Cleve also painted more luxurious versions, like the

114
LUCAS VAN LEYDEN
(active 1508; died 1533)
Saint Jerome, 1521
Pen and brown ink with brown and grey wash, over black chalk, heightened with white bodycolour, on a background of blue bodycolour, laid down on paper, 37.6 × 28.1 cm
The Ashmolean Museum, University of Oxford

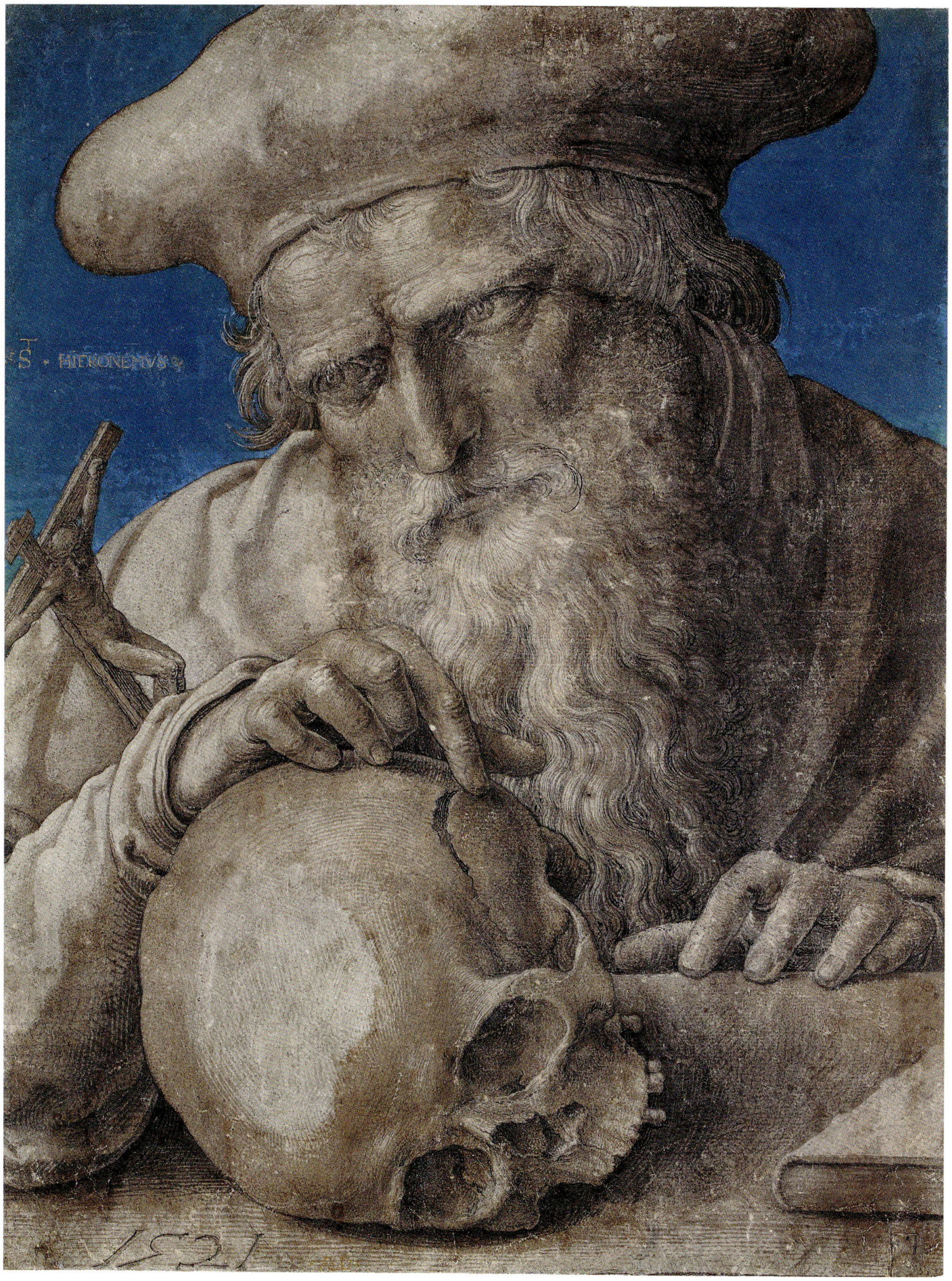

Fig. 152
LUCAS VAN LEYDEN
(active 1508; died 1533)
Saint Jerome, 1521
Engraving, 10.1 × 14.7 cm
Rijksmuseum, Amsterdam
(RP-P-OB-1696)

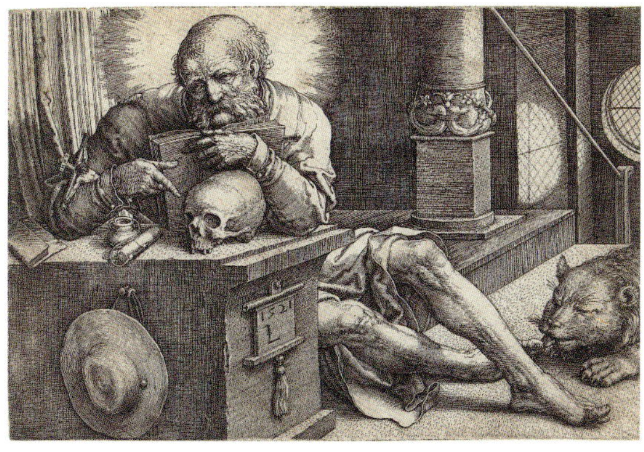

one now in the Fogg Museum (cat. 112).[62] Again, Dürer's model is followed, but the setting is now a palatial Flemish renaissance interior with a lush hilly landscape visible through the rear window. Where the cardinal's hat had been put aside by the saint, symbolising his contempt for earthly power and luxuries, here the anachronistic motif regains a prominent position in front of the saint, propping up the open book. A niche with ewer and basin and a white towel, referring to the purity of the Virgin, is a motif derived from the Annunciation scene on van Eyck's Ghent Altarpiece, thus anchoring the painting in the Flemish artistic tradition.

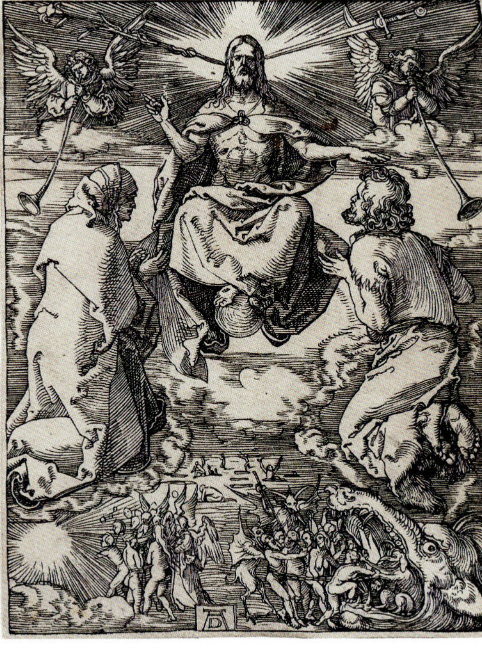

Fig. 153
ALBRECHT DÜRER
The Last Judgement
(from the *Small Passion*),
about 1496–8
Woodcut, 12.6 × 9.6 cm
Städtische Sammlung
Aachen, Suermondt-Ludwig-Museum (DK 659)

Van Cleve's niche arch is again inscribed 'HOMO BVLLA'. A scroll tacked on the wall above it with the words 'RESPICE FINEM' (consider the end), as well as a book on the shelf inscribed 'APOCALIPSIS', emphasise the theme of *memento mori*. A polychrome crucifix, enlivened with a vase of flowers next to it, stands in a niche higher up, alongside a caged bird. Also on the bookshelf is the stoppered carafe, containing the eucharistic wine, symbol of the blood of Christ and of the Virgin, the vessel who contained him. The luxury of the scene is as far removed from the late medieval penitent Saint Jerome alone in the wilderness as it is from the Erasmian humanism that permeated from Dürer's model.

However, one should not assume that the wholesale reintroduction of traditional symbolism reflects outright Catholic doctrine.[63] More precisely, Joos van Cleve inserted in several of his copies traditional Marian symbols, while simultaneously including a critical note on the financial and moral abuses of popular piety by the Latin Church (fig. 141).[64] This is contained in a text from Saint Matthew's Gospel, chapter 23, which van Cleve displays in the open book on Jerome's lectern. Here Christ condemns the scribes and Pharisees as hypocrites who in denying others entrance into heaven also deny themselves.[65] In the sixteenth-century plays of the Chambers of Rhetoric (the early Netherlandish theatre companies) the figure of the Pharisee was frequently used as a symbol of the Catholic clergy's immoral abuse of popular piety for financial gain.[66] The origin of this immoral abuse was the Latin Church's exploitation of the sacrament of penance through the practice of indulgences.

This example illustrates very well how in a period of religious transition, but before polarisation had reached the point of overt conflict, details in different versions of a composition may have been adapted to the specific ideology of the individual client. Marinus van Reymerswale conceived at least three different compositions of the representation of Saint Jerome in his Study. To judge from the number of surviving copies, the version with half-length saint gazing directly at the observer, now in the Rijksmuseum, Amsterdam, seems to have been the most successful (cat. 111).[67] Both in its horizontal format and its spatial setting, the composition is closest to Quinten Massys's prototype. From Dürer Marinus takes the direct gaze and the gesture of the hand pointing to the skull. The Last Judgement miniature in the open book, now turned more towards the viewer, is taken directly from Dürer's *Last Judgement* woodcut from the *Small Passion* of about 1496–8 (fig. 153). The crucifix is placed directly on the saint's desk, while the extinguished candle has been moved to the bookshelf. The cardinal's hat hangs prominently behind the saint on the wall to the right.

In another composition by van Reymerswale, now in a private collection, Jerome turns his full attention to the manuscript on the lectern in front of him.[68] The text he reads, hidden from view, seems to sadden him intensely. The skull lies besides him as a last remaining attribute but is no longer the centre of attention. More than in the artist's other versions, it seems to be most accurate in its anatomical detail.

Jan Sanders van Hemessen also treated the iconography of Saint Jerome in different compositional formulas. The version now in the Antwerp Rockoxhuis (fig. 143) shows the saint praying with folded hands and his book resting on a skull.[69] Through the window is a city gate, with the saint's mental image of the Last Judgement in the sky above it. The only elements of Dürer's painting of Saint Jerome for Rodrigo Fernandes de Almada retained here are the vertical format and the composition restricted to bare essentials of books, a crucifix and a skull. Van Hemessen thus foregrounds the Church Father's faith in salvation as a key aspect of penance instead of self-knowledge as presented in Dürer's iconographical concept.

These copies and variants of Netherlandish masters all illustrate how, in a period of religious transition, details in different versions of a similar composition may have been adapted to the specific ideology of the individual client. None of the extant copies and variants, however, followed Dürer's new iconographic concept of self-knowledge as a gateway to salvation. On the contrary – and perhaps inspired by Quinten Massys's approach – Netherlandish masters adhered more to the late-medieval theological understanding of penance as a series of spiritual and physical exercises of repentance to develop proper Christian virtues in preparation for death.

This essay is derived from research conducted by Astrid Harth at Ghent University for her PhD dissertation on sixteenth-century Netherlandish copying practices, under the supervision of Koenraad Jonckheere and Maximiliaan Martens. Her research was supported by the Research Foundation Flanders (FWO) and the Metropolitan Museum of Art, New York (NYC).

1 See Held 1931, pp. 139–40; Marlier 1954, pp. 179–211; Jungblut 1967, p. 93; Rice 1985, pp. 163–7; Anzelewsky 1991, vol. 1, pp. 263–5; M. Mende, 'Albrecht Dürers Lissaboner Hieronymus', in Bonn 1999, pp. 164–5; D. Eichberger, 'Dürer and the Netherlands: Patterns of Exchange and Mutual Admiration', in Silver and Chipps Smith 2010, pp. 162–5.

2 'I painted a *Jerome* in oils, taking care over it, and gave it as a gift to Rodrigo the Portuguese …', Ashcroft 2017, vol. 1, no.162, p. 576. The painting was first published in Justi 1888, p. 149.

3 For a hypothesis about the accessibility of Dürer's painting in Antwerp between 1521 and 1548, see Mende in Bonn 1999, p. 165.

4 On the copies and variants by Joos van Cleve see Hand 1990; Hand 2004, pp. 92–5, 160–4; Leeflang 2015, pp. 171–3. On Pieter Coecke van Aalst, see Marlier 1966, pp. 254–7 (esp. the Turin version, pp. 254, 255 fig. 199). On Jan van Hemessen, see Wallen 1983, pp. 37–45, 322–3, no. 57, fig. 40. On Marinus van Reymerswale, see Friedländer 1967–76, vol. 12: *Jan van Scorel and Pieter Coecke van Aelst*, pp. 40–1, 106–7, nos 162–6, pls 92–3; Mackor 1995, pp. 195–6.

5 On the iconographical theme of Jerome in his Study, see Venturi 1924; Strümpell, 1925–6, pp. 173–252; Meiss 1963; Pächt 1963; Meiss 1974; Ridderbos 1984, pp. 15–40, 63–88; Howell Jolly 1983; Rice 1985, pp. 87–9, 104–8. On the medieval cult image of Saint Jerome, see Jungblut 1967; Rice 1985, pp. 23–48.

6 Schoch, Mende, and Scherbaum 2001–4, vol. 1, no. 70.

7 On the iconographic theme of Saint Jerome in the Wilderness, see Meiss 1974; Wiebel 1988. The skull motif occurred in the iconography of the penitent Jerome during the first half of the fifteenth century, when Hieronymite orders acquired a firm institutional base in Tuscany. An early example is by Fra Filippo Lippi, *Saint Jerome in Penance*, about 1435 (Lindenau-Museum, Altenburg). See Wiebel 1988, pp. 110–12; Jeon 2005, pp. 31–46. However, the skull is not always present: see, for example, Dürer's *Saint Jerome* of about 1496 (National Gallery, London; cat. 84).

8 On the study drawings, see Matthias Mende, 'Der Heilige Hieronymus', in Vienna 2003, pp. 503-511; Jeon 2005, pp. 127–132; Julia Zaunbauer, 'Der heilige Hieronymus', in Vienna 2019, pp. 414–17.

9 On Dürer's use of preparatory studies on coloured paper, see Crawford Luber 2005, pp. 77–109. Metzger considers such drawings less as preparatory studies, for which he argues they are unsuited, than as workshop reference works: see Metzger in Vienna 2019, pp. 414–17.

10 'Der man was alt 93 jor vnd noch gesunt vnd fermuglich zw antorff'.

11 'Note: Gave 3 stuivers to the man who sat as model for a portrait', Ashcroft 2017, vol. 1, no. 162, p. 572.

12 Albrecht Dürer, *Head of an Old Man*, 1521, Kupferstichkabinett Berlin(inv. KdZ 38).

13 See Koschatzky and Strobl 1971, p. 384; Matthias Mende, 'Der Heilige Hieronymus', in Vienna 2003, p. 506; Jeon 2005, pp. 128–31.

14 On the so-called 'Dürer Renaissance' of the late 1500s, of which Hoffman was a leading representative, see Białostocki 1986; Bubenik 2013.

15 Panofsky 1955, p. 211. See Till-Holger Borchert in the present publication, pp. 77–101.

16 Jeon 2005, pp. 133–4. Dürer also recorded the ear canal located under the temporal bone. In the painting, however, scientific accuracy was partially discarded as the seam connections between the parietal and temporal bones and the parietal and frontal bones are eliminated.

17 Perhaps, as Hans Rupprich has previously argued, Dürer depended on one of the two 'todtenköpfflein' ('small skulls') that he had bought in Cologne; see Rupprich 1956–69, vol. 1, p. 188 n. 312 (Ashcroft 2017, vol. 1, no. 162, pp. 565, 606 n. 167). According to Hanho Jeon, however, these 'todtenköpfflein' were probably amulets: see Jeon 2005, p. 134.

18 According to Mende, the oval box is a *scrinium deitatis*, that is, a container for the eucharistic host: see Mende, 'Der Heilige Hieronymus', in Vienna 2003, p. 510. Rice (1985, p. 112) identified an oval box as a container for the host in Dürer's Saint Jerome engraving of 1514. Here the motif is grouped with other Marian symbols, such as the stoppered carafe and rosary beads.

19 Ringbom 1984.

20 Wiebel 1988, pp. 110–12; Jeon 2005, pp. 31–46.

21 On Jerome's morality and the letters, see Rice 1985, pp. 12–14; 23–83, Wiebel 1988, p. 20. For transcription and English translation of the letters, see Wright 1933.

22 Rice 1985, p. 37.

23 Price 2003, p. 220. The *galerus ruber* was prescribed for cardinals by Pope Innocent IV in 1245. On the anachronistic motif and its function in the visual arts, see Rice 1985, p. 37. For Erasmus's biography and his critical approach, see ibid., pp. 130–6.

24 Friedländer 1924–37, vol. 12, p. 72; Marlier 1954, p. 187; Panofsky 1955, p. 212; Bietenholz, 'Erasmus und der Kult des Heiligen Hieronymus', in Füssel and Wuttke 1989, p. 212.

25 Silver 1984, p. 63.

26 See Hamm 1990.

27 For an in-depth study of Dürer's humanistic interests and the impact on his artistic production, see Price 2003.

28 See Hamm 1990, pp. 230–3; Price 2003, pp. 97–157, 196–9; Hamm and Litz 2004, pp. 73–117.

29 Price 2003, p. 197.

30 The translation was printed in Nuremberg in 1514 by Hieronymus Höltzel and dedicated to Hieronymus Ebner, a patrician and humanist of Nuremberg. For the transcription of Spengler's publication, see Bauer 1997. On Lazarus Spengler's humanistic piety and reform-oriented enthusiasm, see Schubert and Holborn 1971; Grimm 1978; Hamm and Litz 2004, pp. 171–203.

31 See Hamm 1990, pp. 232–3; Pabel 2008, pp. 195–6; Price 2003, pp. 198–9; Jeon 2005, pp. 110–12.

32 Hamm and Huber 1995, p. 65.

33 Schoch, Mende and Scherbaum 2001–4, vol. 1, no. 232.

34 On the three Passion books and humanistic piety, see Price 2003, pp. 97–132. For the dissemination of printed work by Dürer during his Netherlandish travels, see Ashcroft 2017, vol. 1, no.162, pp. 551–90; Grigg 1986.

35 On the informal exchange of gifts by Dürer, see Grebe 2017. On informal exchange in the early modern period see Krausman Ben-Amos 2000. On the 'honour system' gift culture, see Honig 2008 and Hirschfelder 2013. See also Peter van den Brink's essay in the present publication, pp. 205–25.

36 See Dürer's handwritten list of Luther's writings in his possession (cat. 103). See also the essays by Dana Cowen (pp. 241–51) and Jeroen Stumpel (pp. 229–39) in the present publication.

37 In November 1520 a middle Dutch translation of Luther's writings on indulgences was disseminated in Antwerp: see Suykerbuyk 2017, p. 157.

38 'I have bought a pamphlet of Luther's …', Ashcroft 2017, vol. 1, no.162, p. 565; and 'Cornelius the Secretary has given me Luther's Babylonian Captivity …', ibid., p. 586. For an overview of 16 Luther pamphlets in Dürer's possession, see British Library, London, MS 5231, fol. 115r. For a complete list, see Ashcroft 2017, vol. 1, no. 152, pp. 533–4.

39 'I have eaten twice with the Augustinians … Ate once more with the Augustinian', Ashcroft 2017, vol. 1, no.162, p. 584; and 'Presented the Steward of the Augustinian Priory here with a *Life of Our Lady*…', ibid., p. 585. See also Jeroen Stumpel's essay in the present publication, pp. 229–39.

40 For the reformation in Antwerp, see the excellent study by Marnef 1996; more recently, see Christman 2015.

41 Rice 1985, pp. 138–43.

42 See Dixon, 'An Occupational Hazard: Saint Jerome, Melancholia, and the Scholarly Life', in Turnhout 1998, pp. 74–6.

43 See Bagchi, 'Luther and the sacramentality of Penance', in Cooper and Gregory 2004, pp. 119–27.

44 Tentler 1965.

45 Ibid., p. 120.

46 For examples of Luther's and Erasmus's understanding of penance, see Bagchi 'Luther and the sacramentality of Penance', in Cooper and Gregory 2004, pp. 120 and 124.

47 See ibid., p. 124.

48 Tentler 1965, p. 123.

49 *Enchiridion* 46: 22–4. For the translation, see O'Malley 1988, p. 46.

50 Zimmermann 2012, p. 253.

51 Marlier 1954, pp. 179–95; Silver 1984, pp. 218–19, cat. 28 (after Quinten Massys); Buijnsters-Smets 1995, pp. 34–5, 228, no. C-20 (attributed to Quinten Massys).

52 A dendrochronological report by Peter Klein (dated 26 May 2004, on file in the Kunsthistorisches Museum, Vienna) considers its earliest possible production date to be after 1527, and more probably from 1533, which is three years after Massys's death.

53 Silver 1984, p. 219, cat. 28. For the portrait of Erasmus, see ibid., pp. 235–6, cat. 58.

54 The Last Judgement image echoes late medieval Italian iconography of Saint Jerome as a harbinger of this final event for Christians, which became widespread in the seventeenth century under the influence of the Counter Reformation. See Rice 1985, pp. 160–72.

55 Buijnsters-Smets 1995, pp. 168–70, no. 14.

56 Museo Nacional del Prado, Madrid (inv. 2099); see ibid., p. 168, no. 13.

57 Miniatures with a similar iconography are depicted in Jerome's folio Bible by Jan Massys in two other copies, now preserved in Museé des Beaux-Arts de Rouen (inv. 975.4.14) and the Kunsthistorisches Museum in Vienna (inv. 966).

58 On the relationship between Dürer and Lucas van Leyden, see Christiaan Vogelaar's essay in the German edition of this catalogue, and published in English in the National Gallery website.

59 Wouter Kloek, 'Lucas van Leyden als tekenaar', in Leiden 2011, pp. 152–4 and 287–8, no. 80a.

60 The best-preserved version of this type is dated 1528 (Princeton University Art Museum, inv. 82-76). On these two paintings, see Hand 2004, pp. 92–5, 160–1, nos 75–6.

61 Ibid., pp. 92–3.

62 Ibid., pp. 92–5, 161–2, cat. 78.

63 On Catholics and the sixteenth-century cult of Saint Jerome around the time of reform, see Rice 1985, pp. 143–72.

64 Hand 2004, p. 161, cat. 76.

65 Ibid., pp. 6, 92.

66 Vlam 1977, p. 563.

67 Another fine version is in the Koninklijk Museum voor Schone Kunsten, Antwerp (inv. 990).

68 Marinus van Reymerswale, *Saint Jerome in his Study*, after 1521, oil on oak, 62 x 80 cm. Private collection, USA. Sold Fernando Durán, Madrid, 8 December 2015 (lot 358).

69 Although this painting is signed, Wallen (1983, p. 322, cat. 57) considered it as a copy.

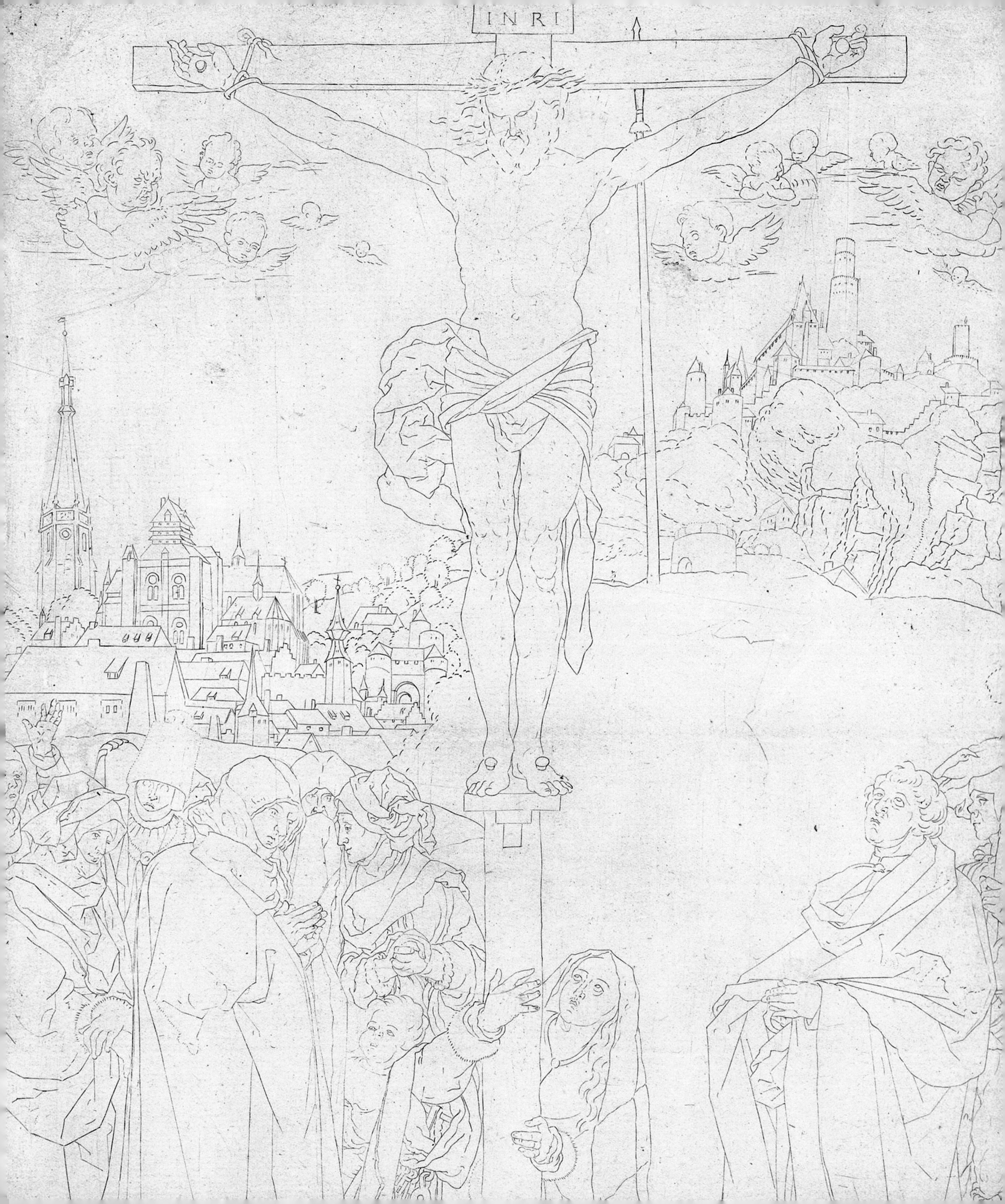
INRI

GIULIA BARTRUM

FROM DRAWING INTO PRINT
THE *CRUCIFIXION IN OUTLINE* AND DÜRER'S LEGACY

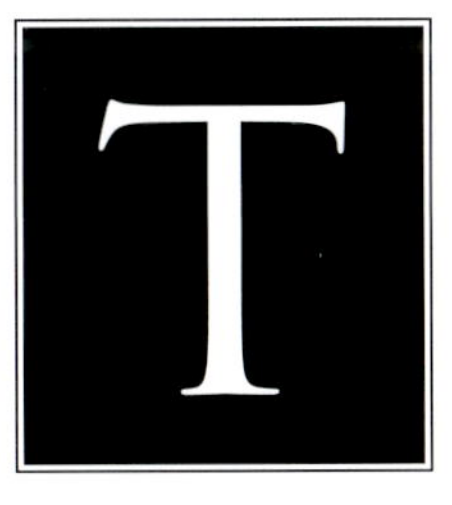

The abundance of Dürer's religious prints and his skill at creating innovative narrative and devotional scenes to appeal to a contemporary market are among the most remarkable achievements of his artistic output.

The demand for images of the Virgin and of the life of Christ in pre-Reformation Europe was paramount, and Dürer was the first artist to achieve international recognition through the circulation of his prints in this field. Between 1507 and 1513 he produced several series: 12 woodcuts for the *Large Passion*, 37 woodcuts for the *Small Passion* and 19 woodcuts for the *Life of the Virgin*; and also 16 plates in a small, elegant format for the *Engraved Passion*. A measure of Dürer's successful marketing and the wide appeal of this latter series in particular, was remarked on as early as 1512, the year in which many of them appeared, by the historian Johann Cochlaeus (1479–1552) in his *Description of Germany*: 'There are pictures of the Passion of our Lord recently painted by Albrecht Dürer which he engraved in copper and printed himself, which are so finely represented with the correct perspective that merchants across the whole of Europe are buying impressions for their artists'.[1] In particular, Dürer's representations of crucifixion scenes are striking for their different size, function and purpose.[2] Within his corpus of over a thousand drawings he treated subjects from Christ's Passion on several occasions,[3] including a highly finished set of 11 drawings in pen and ink with wash and white bodycolour on green paper, which was very likely made on commission.[4]

In terms of quantity and variety, his prints of the Passion outstrip those of his famous Dutch contemporary Lucas van Leyden, who was some twenty years younger than Dürer and whom he met in the Netherlands in 1521. It seemed that there was mutual admiration, for they both drew the same model for images of Saint Jerome;[5] and Lucas made a set of 14 engravings of the Passion in 1521, which in style, format and composition was clearly inspired by Dürer's *Engraved Passion*.[6] Lucas's remarkable prints stimulated the burgeoning collectors' market that

OPPOSITE
Detail of *Crucifixion in Outline* (cat. 115)

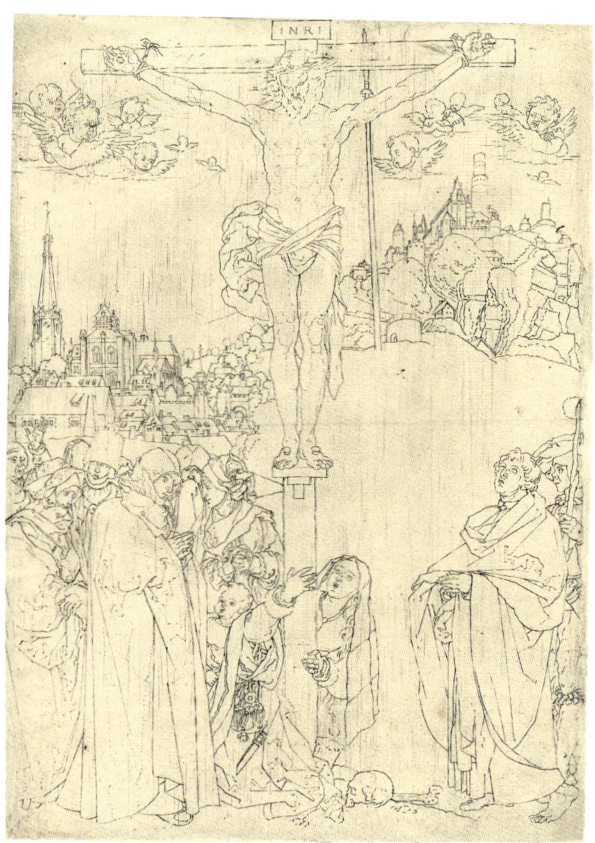

115
ANTWERP FOLLOWER OF ALBRECHT DÜRER
Crucifixion in Outline
Plate 1, about 1558–64
Engraving, 31.7 × 23.6 cm
British Museum

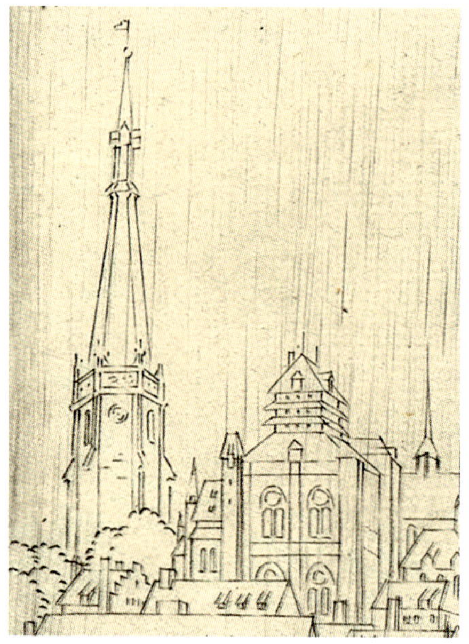

Detail from *Crucifixion in Outline* (cat. 115)

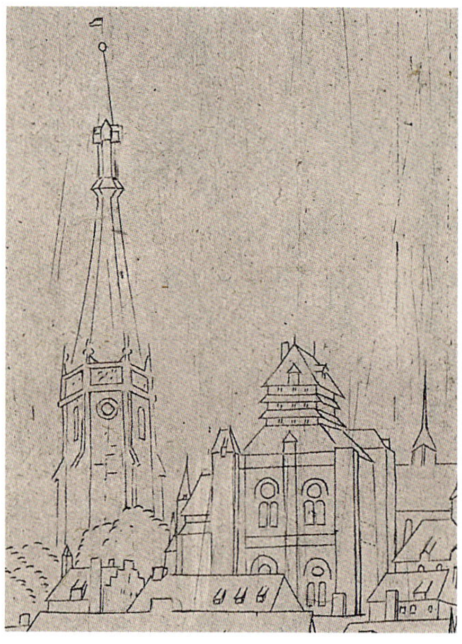

Detail from *Crucifixion in Outline* (fig. 154)

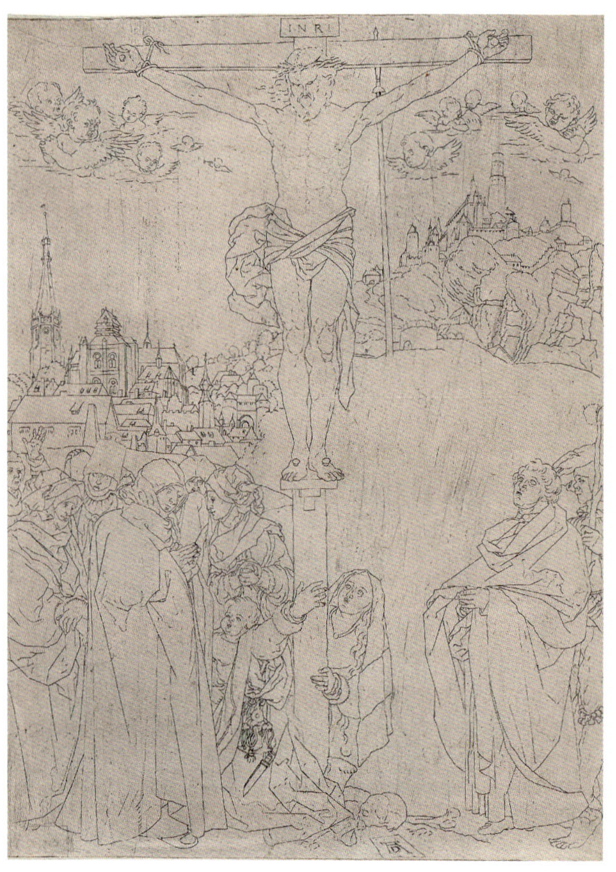

LEFT
Fig. 154
ANTWERP FOLLOWER OF ALBRECHT DÜRER
Crucifixion in Outline
Plate 2, about 1558–64
Engraving, first state with monogram, 31.6 × 22.5 cm
British Museum (E,4.47)

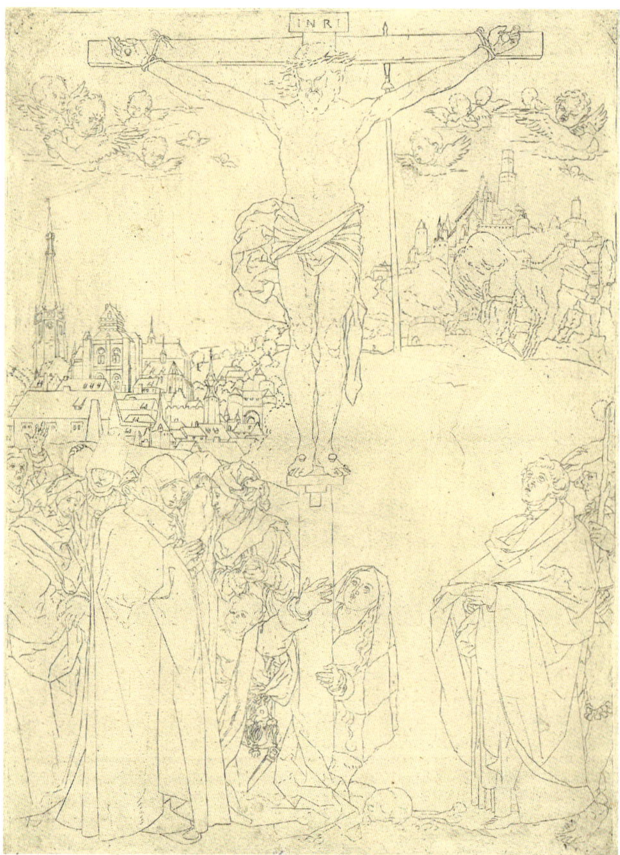

RIGHT
Fig. 155
ALBRECHT DÜRER
Crucifixion in Outline,
about 1570–1600
Engraving, second state without monogram,
31.6 × 22.5 cm
British Museum (E,4.48)

had been initiated by Dürer himself in the years around the turn of the century,[7] and like Dürer's own prints, became highly sought after in the years after his death.

Among Dürer's varied representations of Christ on the Cross there is one that has always provoked curiosity. The *Crucifixion in Outline*, also known as 'The Large Crucifixion', is an engraving executed entirely in outline, with an unfinished area on the right and a dense figural composition that shows a specific knowledge of drawings made by Dürer between 1520 and 1523. It is known in two plates: the higher-quality first version was identified by Campbell Dodgson in 1923 among the collection of duplicates at the British Museum (cat. 115).[8] Impressions of the first plate can be distinguished by a dot in the clockface of the tower on the left, and windows outlined in the building next to it (cat. 115), neither of which are present in the second plate, which is otherwise a very close copy (figs 154, 155). Few impressions of the first plate have survived[9] and it has been suggested with some plausibility that the plate cracked, which resulted in the production of the second plate soon after the first.[10] Impressions of this second version are more numerous: it is known in two states, the first with the 'AD' monogram added at the foot of the cross, and the second without it (figs 154, 155).

The print was first described by Joachim von Sandrart (1606–1688) in his *Teutsche Akademie* of 1679: 'In copper but by his [Dürer's] hand engraved and in tin designed and etched/the large Crucifixion is seen together with a procession of people'.[11] The reference to the plate being designed and etched in tin rather than copper or iron is unusual, but has not been remarked upon by subsequent scholars. As an artist and printmaker himself, Sandrart was familiar with printmaking techniques, and the outline style probably reminded him of designs etched or engraved in decorative objects made from tin by his contemporaries. Dürer never mixed the techniques of engraving and etching in one plate, and Sandrart's description 'in copper' most likely referred to an intaglio print as opposed to one cut in relief, that is, a woodcut.

Although the print was not recorded by Bartsch, it was described in 1862 by Passavant as an authentic work by Dürer.[12] Many have considered that the evident familiarity with Dürer's drawings confirmed its authenticity; these include Josef Meder, who wrote the first comprehensive catalogue of Dürer's prints in 1932 and dated it to about 1523. Erwin Panofsky, whose famous biography became a touchstone for all subsequent work on the artist, greatly admired the print and considered it 'the most complex of all Dürer's compositions', largely on the basis of the magnificent drawings, undoubtedly in the master's hand, with which it is connected.[13] Others have suggested that despite the similarity with passages in outline seen in trial proofs by Dürer, it is unusual that the engraving was never finished. The artist's few surviving trial proofs date from earlier in his career and present a different appearance. He preferred to engrave complete sections of the plate uniformly, while leaving parts in outline, as if to examine the effect of the final image (see figs 156, 157).[14]

Matthias Mende's long summary of opinions on the *Crucifixion in Outline* shows that the majority of

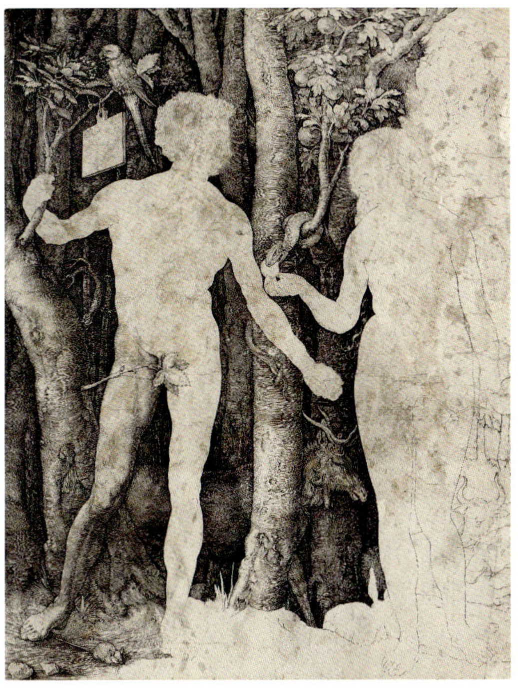

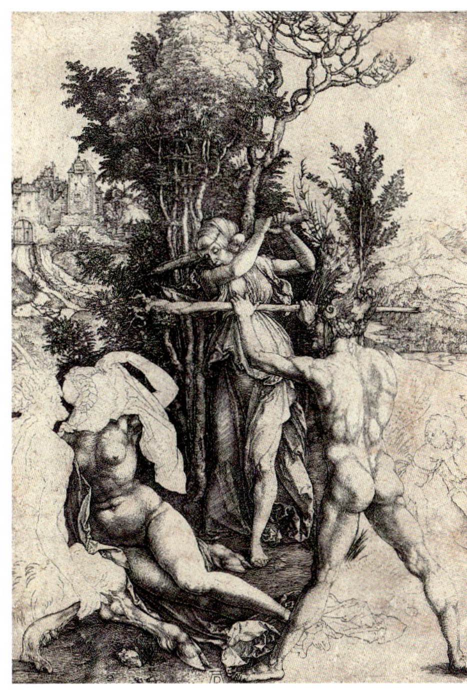

Fig. 156
ALBRECHT DÜRER
Trial Proof of *Adam and Eve*, 1504
Engraving, first state, 24.9 × 18.6 cm
British Museum (1837,0616.72)

Fig. 157
ALBRECHT DÜRER
Trial Proof of *Hercules at the Crossroads*, about 1498
Engraving, 31.7 × 22.2 cm
The Albertina Museum, Vienna (DG 1930/1523)

commentators have come down on the side of Dürer's authorship.[15] His account illustrates an obsession with attribution, when perhaps the important question to ask about the origins of this work is not who made it, but why. Mende himself considered that the engraving was made in Nuremberg during the second half of the sixteenth century, by which time many of Dürer's original plates had worn out. The extent of Dürer's popularity spread so quickly during his lifetime that anything produced in his style could be absorbed in a burgeoning market for single-sheet prints. This opinion goes back to 1887, in a long article written by Jaro Springer,[16] who was the earliest commentator to articulate the significance of the work as an amalgam of Dürer motifs, and the intense interest – especially after the artist's death in 1528 – in collecting anything remotely associated with him. The inventory of one of the earliest serious print collectors, Ferdinand Columbus (1488–1539), the son of Christopher Columbus, who worked for the Spanish court and who may have met Dürer in 1520, signals the critical significance of the artist on the development of Columbus's personal collection.[17]

A close examination of the *Crucifixion in Outline* reveals the signs of a pastiche more clearly. It is based on no fewer than 15 very different types of drawing that Dürer made between 1520 and 1523.[18] The most striking are large, carefully worked-up studies made in 1521 and 1523 in black chalk or leadpoint with white heightening on green or blue/grey prepared paper. These drawings were copied for the figures of Christ, the Virgin and other women on the left, Saint John the Evangelist on the right and the Magdalen wrapped around the foot of the cross (cat. 117; figs 158, 159 and 160).[19] The engraving shows that the Magdalen has a large tasselled purse and knife dangling from her right sleeve, which are not seen in the related drawing and which strike a discordant note in a crucifixion scene (cat. 115; fig.161). Lovers of Dürer's work, however, will instantly spot a reference to the elaborate purse with similar tassels hanging from the woman's belt in his famous engraving of 1514,

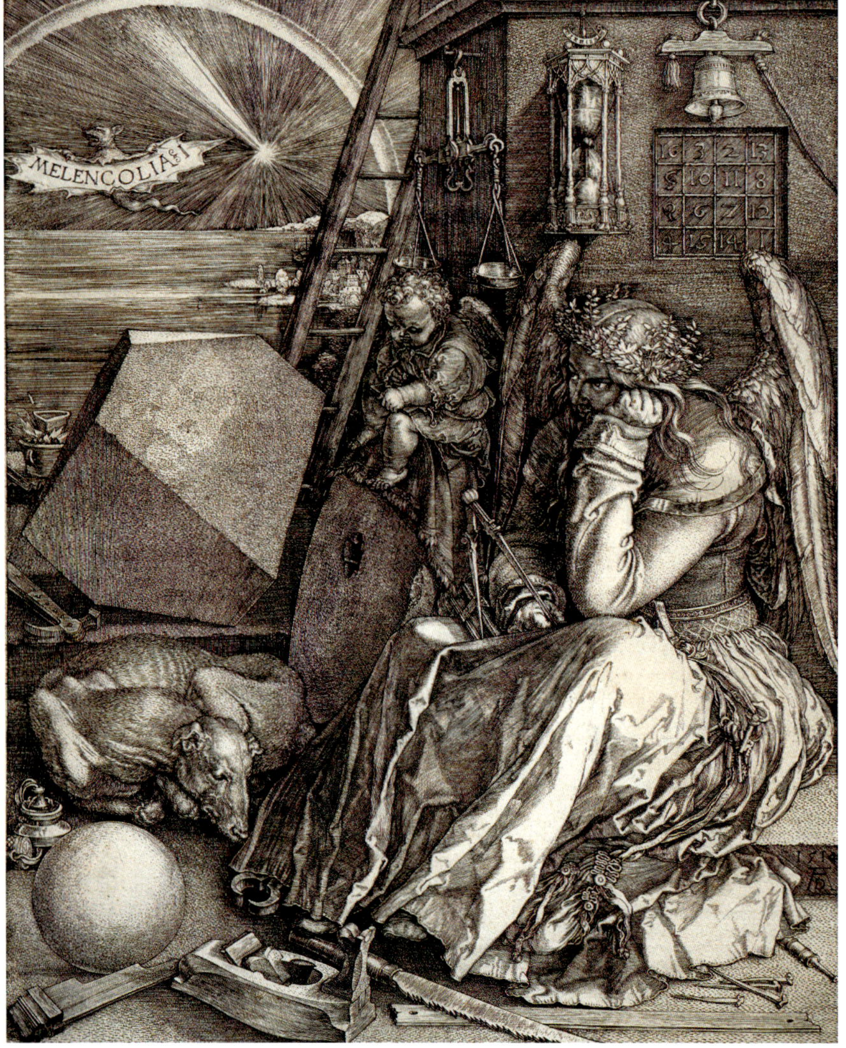

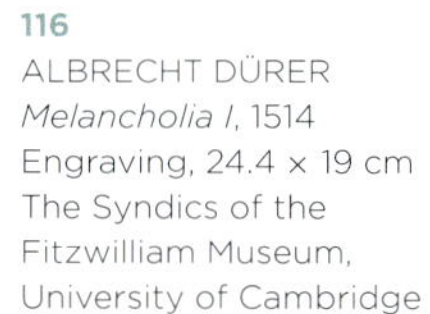

116
ALBRECHT DÜRER
Melancholia I, 1514
Engraving, 24.4 × 19 cm
The Syndics of the Fitzwilliam Museum, University of Cambridge

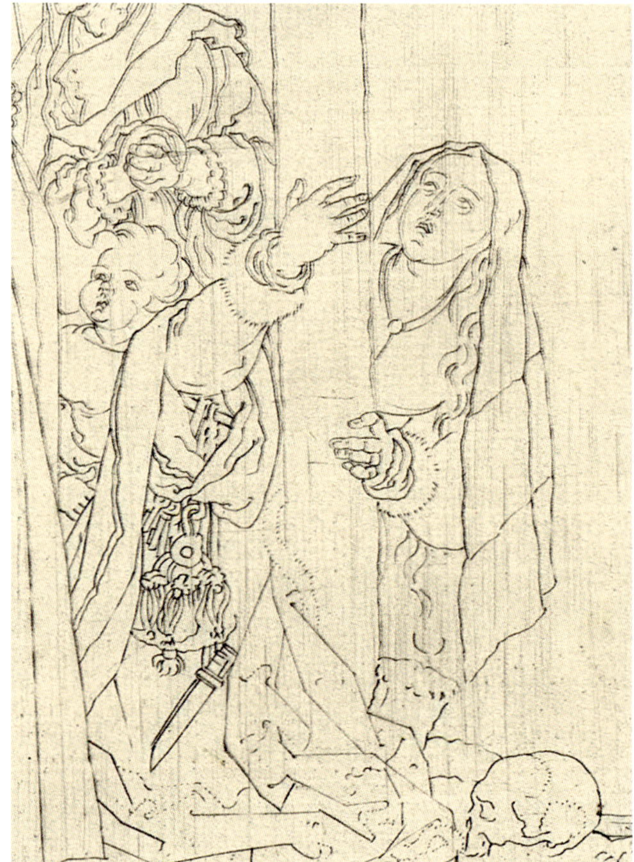

Detail from *Crucifixion in Outline* (cat. 115)

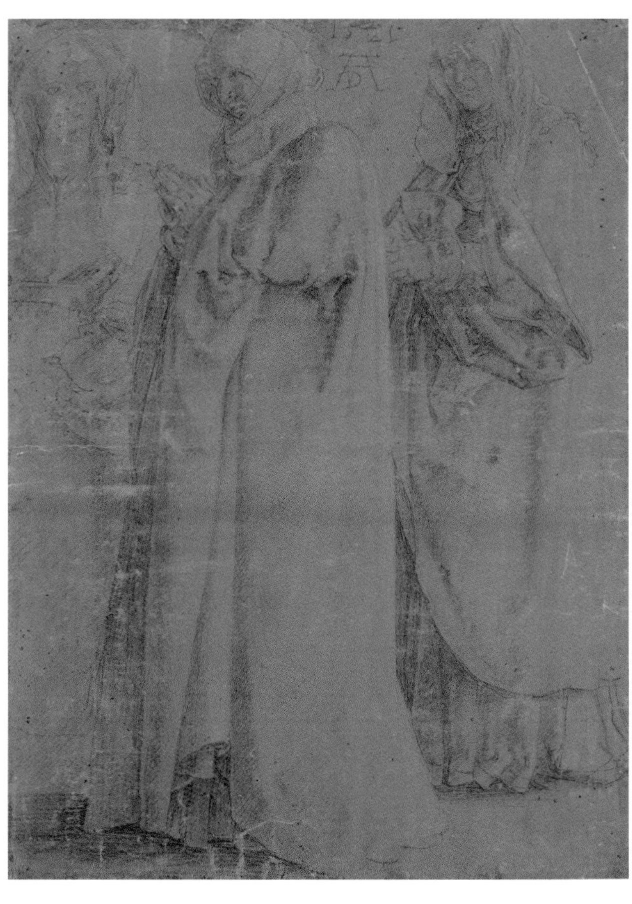

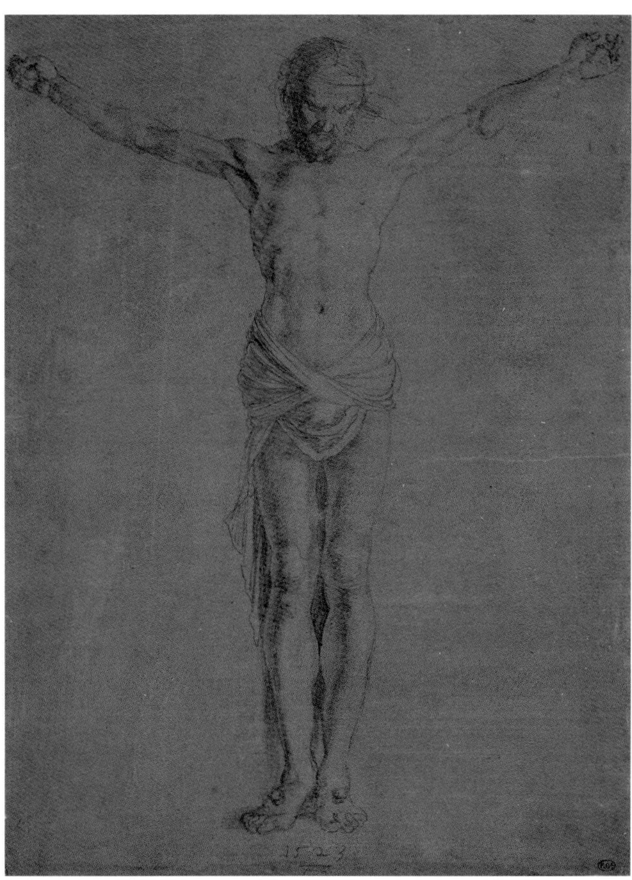

Fig. 158
ALBRECHT DÜRER
The Virgin Mary with Two Holy Women, 1521
Leadpoint with white heightening on green prepared paper,
42.4 × 31 cm
Musée du Louvre, Paris
(REC79 recto)

Fig. 159
ALBRECHT DÜRER
Christ on the Cross, 1523
Leadpoint with white heightening on green prepared paper,
41.3 × 30 cm
Musée du Louvre, Paris
(RF60 recto)

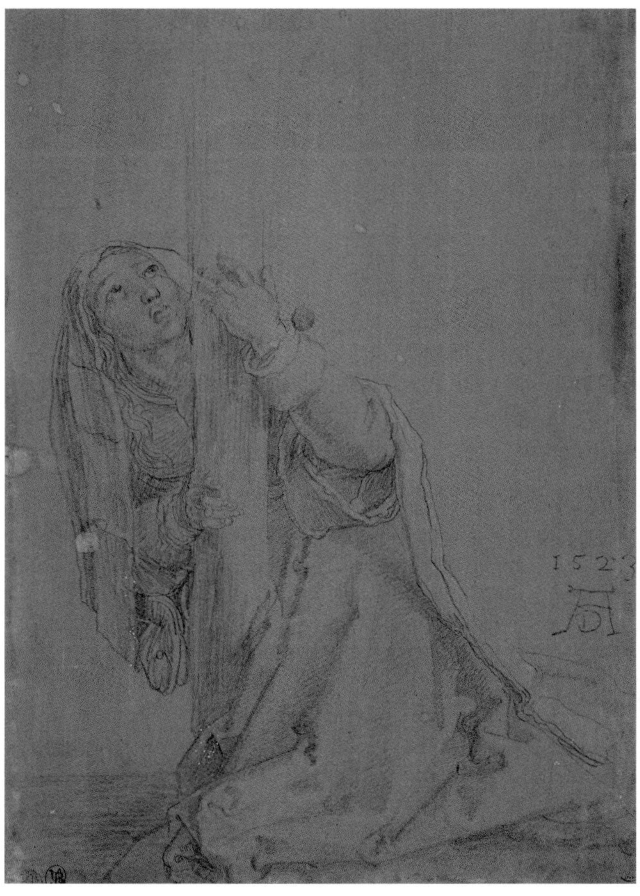

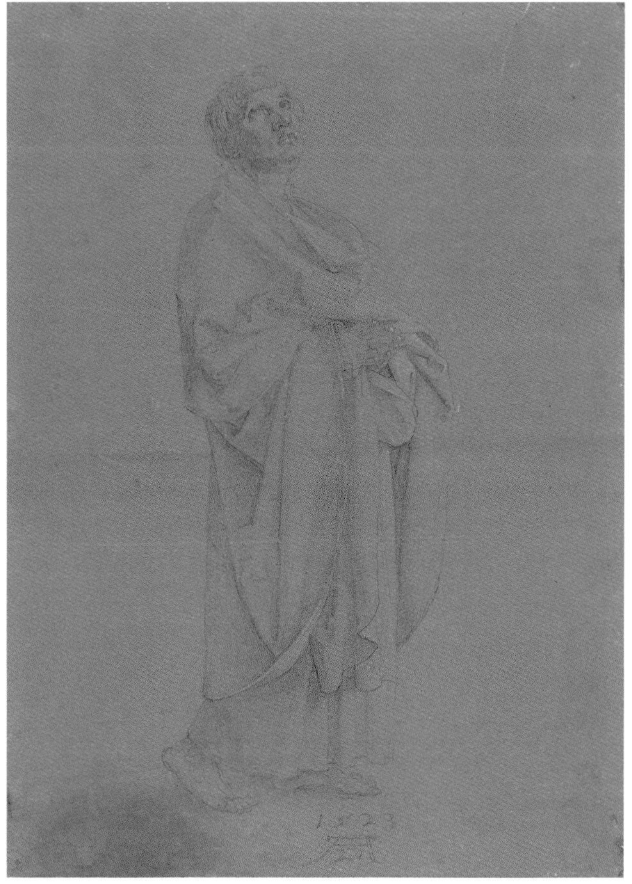

Fig. 160
ALBRECHT DÜRER
Mary Magdalene kneeling and embracing the Cross, 1523
Leadpoint with white heightening on green prepared paper,
29.2 × 20.2 cm
Musée du Louvre, Paris
(RF5168 recto)

117
ALBRECHT DÜRER
Saint John beneath the Cross, 1523
Leadpoint with white heightening on green prepared paper,
41.5 × 29.7 cm
The Albertina Museum, Vienna

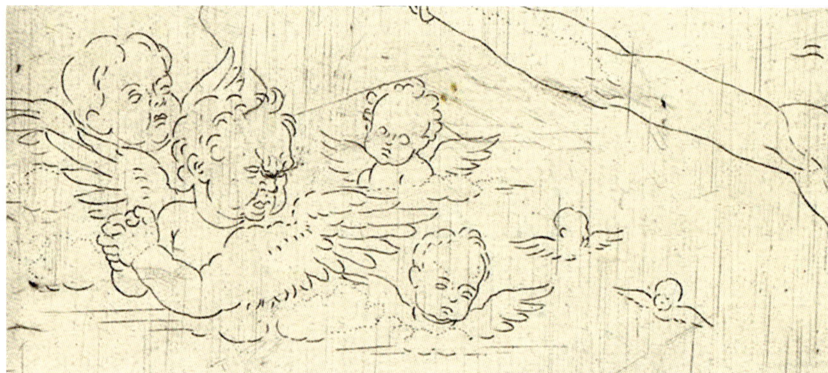

Detail from *Crucifixion in Outline* (cat. 115)

118
ALBRECHT DÜRER
Head and Shoulders of a Young Child looking upwards, 1521
Black chalk heightened with white, on greenish-blue prepared paper, 20.7 × 18.3 cm
British Museum

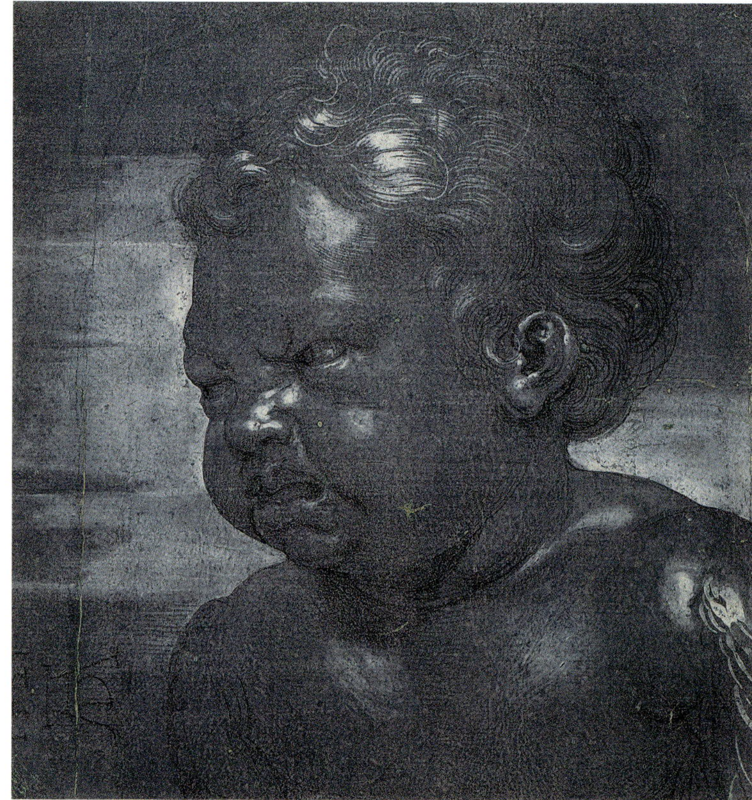

Fig. 161
ALBRECHT DÜRER
Head of a Weeping Cherub facing Left, 1521
Leadpoint with white heightening on grey-blue prepared paper, 21.4 × 19.9 cm
Staatliche Museen zu Berlin, Kupferstichkabinett (KdZ 2879)

Melancholia I (cat. 116).[20] The heads of cherubs in the sky and the face of a small child at the foot of the cross, which is an odd addition to a crucifixion scene, have been taken from a large group of heads of small children drawn by Dürer in 1521 (cat. 118; fig. 161).[21] One of Dürer's most admired idiosyncrasies in all the Passion series was his use of a variety of regional costumes and eye-catching headwear for figures throughout. *Crucifixion in Outline* shows a figure in the crowd on the left wearing a distinctive tall hat with a knob on it, which is taken directly from Dürer's pen-and-ink sketch of a woman from Burgenland,[22] repeated in silverpoint (fig. 93). The curiously anomalous town views in the background of *Crucifixion in Outline* are copied after drawings of two quite different locations: on the left, buildings at Bergen op Zoom north of Antwerp (fig. 162)[23] and on the right, the castle at Rheinfels, near Sankt Goar on the river Rhine, both drawn by Dürer in silverpoint during his journey to the Netherlands in 1520–1 (fig. 96).

Dürer was a prolific draughtsman and habitually referred to his stock of studies from nature for incidental detail, as well as making preparatory studies, often in pen and ink, for his prints. This was done in order to articulate difficult figural sections[24] and is well exemplified in his studies for the engraving *Adam and Eve*, 1504 (cat. 52).[25] It was uncharacteristic of his working method to use such a large number of different types of drawing, or to reduce them so much in scale, for the composition of a single engraving. The purpose of the highly finished drawings of 1521 and 1523, which form part of a group

Fig. 162
ALBRECHT DÜRER
Bergen op Zoom, 1520
Silverpoint on pink prepared paper, 13.3 × 19.4 cm
Musée Condé, Chantilly
(892 [315]v)

of similar figure and drapery studies, is not known. The careful preparation of the coloured paper and the use of dark leadpoint combined with white heightening to give a weighty, sculptured effect to the figures makes it likely that they were made in connection with a large altarpiece, not for a print. Perhaps, like his oblong studies for a religious composition, Dürer was thinking of an elaborate commission for Margaret of Austria that he hoped to undertake but which did not materialise.[26] His numerous studies of heads of children show similar experimentation with a chiaroscuro technique and are also more likely connected with a large figural composition. None of Dürer's authentic prints relates to his silverpoint drawings of 1520–1, which were made in a small sketchbook as records of his travels.

In terms of size and virtuoso skill, Dürer's highpoint in the engraving technique are his so-called 'Master prints' of 1513–14, *Knight Death and the Devil*[27], *Saint Jerome in his Study* (fig. 140) and *Melancholia I* (cat. 116). Along with many prints of his earlier career, he took impressions of these to the Netherlands in 1520–1 to use as gifts and in payment for bills. With dimensions of around 24 × 19 cm, they are infinitely more elaborate than any engraving made during the last few years of his life. During this period Dürer suffered from recurring bouts of a malarial type of illness first contracted in the Netherlands; while his drawing production diminished little, he made fewer prints and also worked towards publication of his writings on artistic theory. In 1521 he made a group of pen-and-ink drawings of Saint Christopher (cat. 17) and a further drawing in pen with white heightening on a dark ground (cat. 16), in addition to two small engravings of Saint Christopher[28]. His other engravings of 1521–6 show standing saints and portraits, not figural compositions; the most elaborate of these is the *Portrait of Erasmus*, with its much-admired detailed interior (cat. 94).[29] With Meder's suggested date of about 1523, the large scale and compositional diversity of *Crucifixion in Outline* looks unconvincing alongside this group.

The idea of a posthumous pastiche is supported by the fact that no surviving impression of the *Crucifixion in Outline* was taken during Dürer's life. The impression of the first plate in the British Museum shows delicate burr and plate tone (see cat. 115), indicating that it was taken at an early stage of the print run. This sheet possesses a watermark of about 1558–88,[30] suggesting the unlikely scenario that if engraved by Dürer, the plate would have remained unprinted in his studio for several decades. The first state of version 2, with the monogram, has only survived in impressions with watermarks of

Fig. 163
ATTRIBUTED TO SEBALD BEHAM (1500–1550)
Ecce Homo, 1521
Woodcut,
32.8 × 25 cm
British Museum
(E,2.211)

Fig. 164
ANONYMOUS NUREMBERG SCHOOL, PRINTED BY HANS GULDENMUND (active 1526–60)
Christ on the Cross with the Virgin and Saint John,
about 1530–40
Woodcut with tone block in green,
29.8 × 21 cm
The Metropolitan Museum of Art, New York. Purchase, Joseph Pulitzer Bequest
(1917 17.50.36)

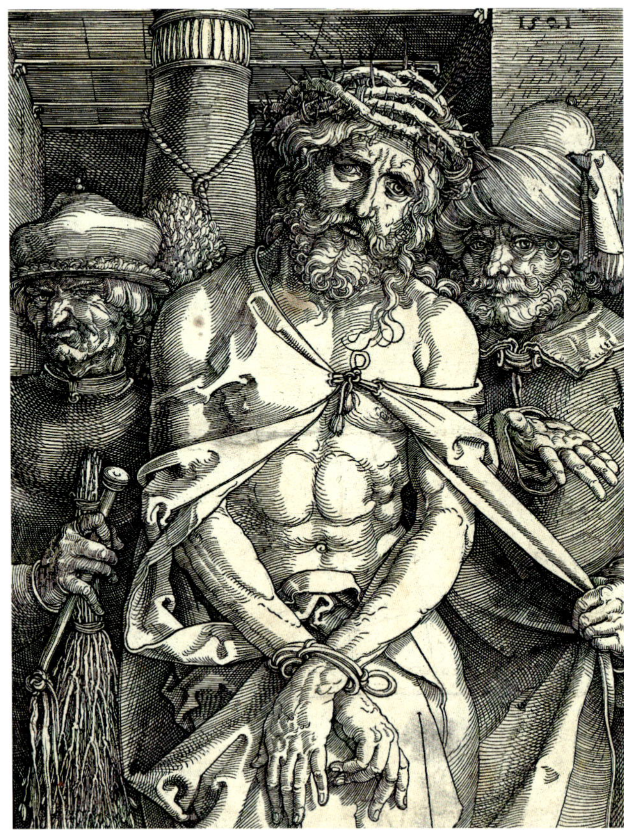

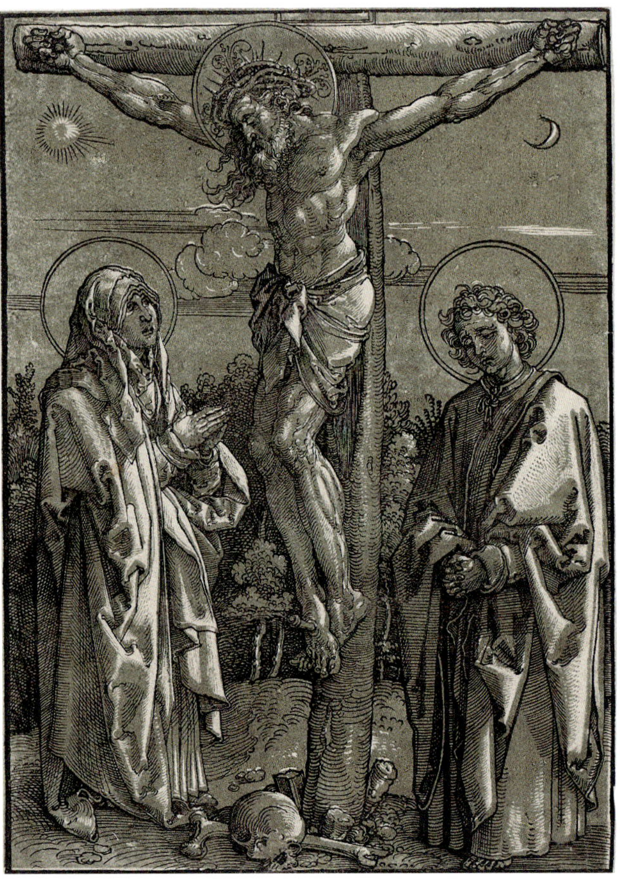

around 1570; and impressions of the second state, where the monogram has been erased, are only recorded on sheets watermarked circa 1600.

On close examination of Dürer's reputation, the abundant production of copies and pastiches of his work is put into perspective. By 1604 his engravings and woodcuts were so well known that the great biographer of early German and Netherlandish artists, Karel van Mander, did not even feel it necessary to list them: 'I do not of course, need to deal with all of his pieces in detail ... for these are known well enough by the practitioners and lovers of art'.[31] Dürer's impact in his home city of Nuremberg must have been incalculable. The heirs of his estate, particularly his sister-in-law Ursula Dürer (who died in 1560) and the grandson of Dürer's close friend Willibald Pirckheimer, Willibald Imhoff, to whom she sold all that she owned by the artist in 1557, were well aware of the marketable commodity in their possession.[32] Copies and pastiches started appearing during Dürer's life: his reputation in Italy was massively enhanced by the engraved copies of 74 of his prints circulated by Marcantonio Raimondi.[33]

In 1528, the year of Dürer's death, his former pupil Sebald Beham (1500–1550) published a treatise on the horse that plagiarised Dürer's work on the theory of proportions. This resulted in civic action against Beham, who was expelled from Nuremberg for a few months.[34] He also made a large woodcut *Head of Christ* that was considered during the nineteenth century to be one of Dürer's finest prints.[35] A striking unsigned woodcut *Ecce Homo*, dated 1521, also bears the hallmarks of Beham's imitative style (fig. 163).[36] The pose of the figure of Christ and the elaborate headwear is so redolent of Dürer that, like *Crucifixion in Outline*, it was doubtless intended to be taken as the master's work. The absence of an 'AD' monogram supports a date of production during Dürer's life, when use of his monogram was banned.[37] A poor seventeenth-century copy of it has the 'AD' monogram added in the tone block, as if, like the second plate of *Crucifixion in Outline*, there was a motive to add a reminder of the Dürer brand.[38]

Dürer's fluent pen-and-ink *Crucifixion* dated 1521 (cat. 104) also resulted in a pastiche made for the Dürer market in Nuremberg. In style and technique it is connected with rapidly executed figure compositions for scenes of the Lamentation that Dürer made at this period.[39] The pose of the figure of Christ, with one nail through his feet and not two, makes it clear that it was not used for *Crucifixion in Outline*; but the figures of the Virgin and Saint John in the Albertina drawing were used for a colour woodcut, *Christ on the Cross with the Virgin and Saint John* published around 1530–40 by the

Nuremberg printer Hans Guldenmund (active 1526–60; fig. 164). This is one of the earliest woodcuts printed in colour in Nuremberg to be associated with any work by Dürer. Like *Crucifixion in Outline*, it has survived in very few impressions and has also been attributed to the master himself.[40] Either Guldenmund or his draughtsman who designed the woodcut would have gained access to the drawing *Christ on the Cross* when it was in Nuremberg.[41] The Imhoffs were known to have encouraged copyists: Hans Hoffman established his reputation by producing superlative copies of Dürer's drawings before the collection was sold in 1589 to the Holy Roman Emperor Rudolf II in Prague.[42]

Intriguingly, it seems that the drawings on which *Crucifixion in Outline* is based were probably not in Nuremberg during the years 1558–80 – arguably the period when the print is most likely to have been made. Neither the large chiaroscuro figure drawings on prepared paper or the silverpoint landscapes are listed in the inventory drawn up in 1588 of the entire Dürer collection before it was sold to Rudolf II.[43] It is clear that the Dürer family had disposed of items before Ursula sold the bulk of the estate to Willibald Imhoff in 1557. The most notable sale amounted to around two hundred drawings, which were acquired during the 1540s or early 1550s by Cardinal Antoine Perrenot de Granvelle, bibliophile secretary to the Holy Roman Emperor, Charles V, and his son Philip II, and the de facto ruler of the Netherlands.[44] Granvelle was an ambitious collector and patron of the arts, which he displayed in an ever-expanding palace in Brussels, where he lived from 1543 to 1564. Unusually for a diplomat of his status, he took a keen interest in printmaking and commissioned a large portrait engraving in 1556 from Lambert Suavius (about 1510–1567), which is one of the most spectacular of its era (fig. 165). His knowledge of the subject, style and quality of engravings – which he markedly preferred over the woodcut technique – is made evident in correspondence of 1547 with the Italian printmaker Giovanni Battista Scultori (1503–1575), in which he discusses a commission of prints to be made after Michelangelo's frescoes in the Sistine Chapel.[45] He was also closely associated with the earliest leading print publisher, Hieronymus Cock, who between 1551 and 1562 dedicated eight magnificent engravings to him.[46] This suggests that Granvelle made a significant financial input into Cock's publishing house, 'Aux Quatre Vents', in Antwerp, perhaps from its outset in 1548.

Christof Metzger's analysis of the early inventories of Dürer drawings has shown that the large chiaroscuro figure drawings related to *Crucifixion in Outline* very likely formed part of Granvelle's collection.[47] Although

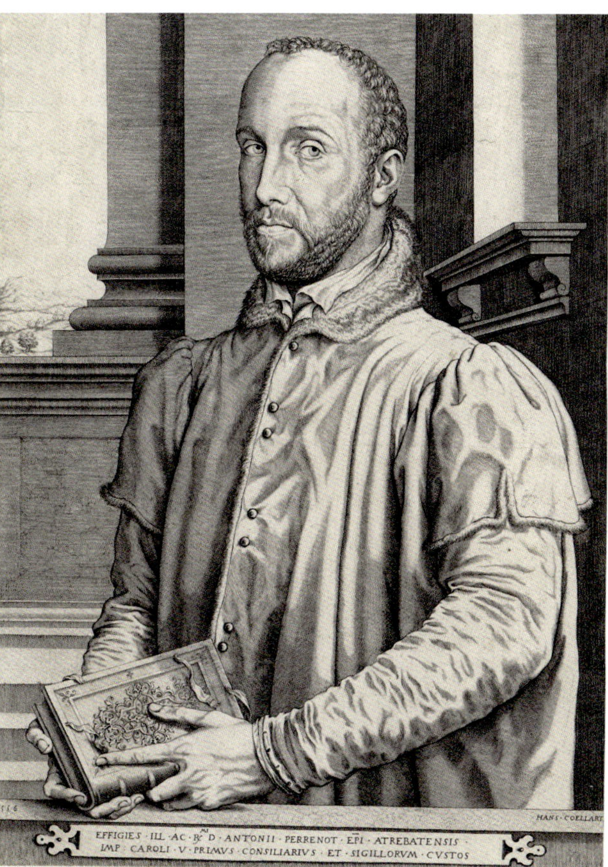

Fig. 165
LAMBERT SUAVIUS (about 1510–1567)
Portrait of Cardinal Antoine Perrenot de Granvelle, 1556
Engraving, 40 × 28.2 cm
Rijksmuseum, Amsterdam (RP-P-OB-60.635)

the engraver of *Crucifixion in Outline* is unknown, a possible scenario presents itself given the position that both Granvelle and Cock held within the intellectual and cultural society of their day. The wide repertoire of subjects that Cock published included prints in the style of earlier artists such as Hieronymus Bosch, who were much admired at the time.[48] Granvelle had the means – through Cock, who employed numerous engravers – to commission an entertaining pastiche based on drawings known personally to him, with the intention of creating an 'unfinished' print by Dürer, the most widely respected Northern artist of all, for circulation among his friends and associates. The subject of Christ on the Cross was also significant for Granvelle, who as bishop, cardinal and secretary to two sovereigns, was in the position of actively promoting Catholic orthodoxy in the face of emerging Protestantism.[49] The most likely date for its production would be around 1558–64, when Granvelle lived in the Netherlands.[50] The origin of the print within the milieu of Cock and Granvelle is supported by the survival of a drawn copy of it, made by the Liègois artist Lambert Lombard (about 1505/6–1566), who worked for Granvelle early in his career and whose designs were also published by Cock.[51] The plate for *Crucifixion in Outline* was then most likely left with Hieronymus Cock when Granvelle had no further use for it; or Cock acquired it when Granvelle departed for Rome in 1564. Either way, an item matching its description is listed among the assets of Volcxken Diericx (1525–1600), Hieronymus Cock's widow. The inventory of 1601 lists 1,607 printing plates from the publishing house, including 'A copper plate of a Crucifix and certain persons drawn (printed) by "Aelbert Dure" with a stylus'.[52] The inventory also contains five plates engraved by Jan Wierix after Dürer: 'Five plates of five Apostles after "Alber Dure"'.[53] These are examples of some fifty plates that the child prodigy Jan Wierix had made as a teenager after Dürer – roughly the same period of time that *Crucifixion in Outline* was produced – to display his bravura skill at the engraving technique. Volcxken Diericx played a key role in the establishment and running of her husband's publishing house, 'Aux Quatre Vents', and following Cock's death in 1570 managed the business successfully for thirty years during a most turbulent phase of Antwerp's history; she could easily have been responsible for the later impressions of *Crucifixion in Outline*.

Dürer's work continued to resonate in the city at the end of the sixteenth century. It was here that two volumes of his prints were assembled by another famous Antwerp publisher, Abraham Ortelius (1527–1598); these to this day constitute the earliest collection of Durer's work to have survived as a group.[54]

OPPOSITE
Detail of *Melancholia I* (cat. 116)

The author would like to thank Antony Griffiths for consultation and advice during the compilation of this article.

1 'Da gibt es Bilder von der Passion des Herrn, die kürzlich Albrecht Dürer malte, in Kupfer stach und selber abzog, so überaus fein and mit richtiger Perspective dargestellt, dass di Kaufleute sogar aus ganz Europa die Exemplare für ihre Maler kauften'. Cochlaeus 1512 (1969), pp. 88–9, cited by A. Scherbaum, 'Die Kupferstich-Passion', in Schoch, Scherbaum and Mende 2001–4, vol. 1, pp. 128–9 n. 32.
2 Five woodcuts: from the *Large Passion*, about 1498; *Small Passion*, about 1509; a *Calvary with the Three Crosses*, about 1503–4; a large devotional *Christ on the Cross with Three Angels*, about 1513; a *Crucifixion with a Border of Angels*, 1516, designed as a book illustration; and one engraving of 1508 for the *Engraved Passion*. See Schoch, Scherbaum and Mende 2001–4, vol. 2, nos 161, 210, 131, 236; vol. 3, no. 271.1; vol. 1, no. 55.
3 See articles in the present volume by Dana Cowen (pp. 241–51) and Stijn Alsteens (pp. 129–45).
4 For the *Green Passion* drawings of 1504 in The Albertina Museum, Vienna, see Strauss 1974, vol. 2, nos 1504/24, 1504/26, 1504/28, 1504/31, 1504/33, 1504/36, 1504/38, 1504/40, 1504/41, 1504/44 and 1504/46; Vienna 2019, pp. 332–51, 460–1, cats 148–61.
5 For Lucas van Leyden and Dürer's drawings of the head of a bearded old man and paintings of Saint Jerome, see the article by Maximiliaan Martens and Astrid Harth in the present volume, pp. 253–65.
6 For Passion engravings by Lucas van Leyden, see New Hollstein Dutch 1993–, nos 43–56.
7 A letter from Johann Cochlaeus of April 1520 to Willibald Pirckheimer refers to an abundance of Lucas van Leyden's prints at the Frankfurt trade-fair that year, while Dürer's were in short supply; see Ashcroft 2017, vol. 1, p. 540, no. 156.
8 *Crucifixion in Outline*, Meder 1932, no. 25; M. Mende in Schoch, Scherbaum and Mende 2001–4, vol. 1, pp. 250–2, no. A3.
9 Recorded in the British Museum, Berlin, Chatsworth, Amsterdam and St Louis.
10 Ehrenfest 1950, pp. 48–51.
11 'Im Kupfer aber von seinem Hand gestochen/geätzt und in Zinn gerissen/nebst andern die grosse Creutzigung (wovon blos der Umzug zu sehen)'. Sandrart 1679 (1994), vol. 2, p. 79.
12 Passavant 1860–4, vol. 3, p. 156, no. 109.
13 Panofsky 1955, vol. 1, p. 224; vol. 2, p. 30, no. 218.
14 There are trial impressions of *Adam and Eve* (Meder 1932, no. 1) in the British Museum and the Albertina; of *Hercules at the Crossroads* (Meder 1932, no. 63) in the Albertina and in the Kupferstichkabinett, Berlin; and a unique unfinished impression of *Enthroned Oriental Ruler* in the Rijksprentenkabinet, Amsterdam.
15 M. Mende in Schoch, Scherbaum and Mende 2001–4, vol. 1, p. 252 n. 2.
16 Springer 1887.
17 For the significance of Dürer to Ferdinand Columbus, see McDonald 2004, p. 1.
18 See Winkler 1936–9, vol. 4, nos 751, 762, 768, 858–69; Strauss 1974, vol. 4, nos 1520/25, 1520/30, 1521/59, 1521/72–1521/80, 1523/2, 1523/3, 1523/5.
19 Strauss 1974, vol. 4, nos 1521/72, 1523/2, 1523/3 and 1523/5.
20 Meder 1932, no. 75.
21 Strauss 1974, vol. 4, 1521/73–1521/80.
22 Biblioteca Ambrosiana, Milan; see Winkler 1936–9, vol. 4, no. 751.
23 *View of Bergen op Zoom*, 1520, Musée Condé, Chantilly; Strauss 1974, vol. 4, no. 1520/30.
24 See, for example, the *Fisherman's House* used in *Virgin and Child with a Monkey*, London 2002, pp. 242–3, nos 193–4; design for the figure of Fortune in the *Large Fortune*, ibid, p. 140, nos 73–4; and various studies for *Melancholia I*, ibid., pp. 188–9, nos 128–9.
25 Studies for *Adam and Eve*, 1504; see London 2002, pp. 150–3, nos 87–91.
26 See Stijn Alsteens' article in the present volume, pp. 129–45.
27 Meder 1932, no. 74.
28 Ibid., nos. 52 and 53
29 *Portrait of Erasmus*, 1526, engraving 25 × 19 cm; Meder 1932, no. 105. See Peter van den Brink in the present volume, pp. 205–25.
30 Crescent moon with four-lobed leaf and the letters 'EDMONDENISE'; see Briquet 1907 (1968), no. 5304, about 1558–88.
31 Miedema 1994–2002, vol. 1, p. 90.
32 Bubenik 2013, p. 47.
33 London 2002, pp. 247–8.
34 For Beham's plagiarism of Dürer, see London 1995, pp. 104–5, no. 94.
35 British Museum, inv. E,2.260 without the monogram, and inv. 1895,0122.757 with a new border and an oversized 'AD' monogram; see London 2002, p. 82, no. 5; M. Mende in Schoch, Scherbaum and Mende 2001–4, vol. 2, no. A18.
36 M. Mende in Schoch, Scherbaum and Mende 2001–4, vol. 2, no. A24.
37 British Museum inv. E,2.211 has a bull's head watermark that supports a date of the second or third decade of the sixteenth century; see Meder 1932, no. 69; similar to Briquet 1907 (1968), nos 15,419–15,423 (with dates 1521–34).
38 British Museum, inv. 1877,0609.70, dated by Mende around 1600–50.
39 Strauss 1974, vol. 4, nos 1521/69 and 1521/70.
40 Dodgson 1937.
41 This drawing was still in Nuremberg in 1588, when it was listed in the Imhoff inventory; see Vienna 2019, p. 470, no. 78.
42 London 2002, pp. 266–74.
43 Vienna 2019, pp. 466–71.
44 Ibid., pp. 54, 59–60.
45 Wouk 2015, p. 38.
46 Ibid., p. 31.
47 Vienna 2019, p. 60.
48 See M. Ilsink in Leuven and Paris 2013, pp. 243–60.
49 For a discussion of Granvelle's patronage of Frans Floris (1517–1570) in this respect, see Wouk 2018, p. 291.
50 Granvelle was forced to flee in 1564 on account of the deepening political and religious crisis which led to the Dutch Revolt; see Wouk 2015, p. 45.
51 Cabinet des Estampes et Dessins de Liège, Album d'Arenberg, no. 257; see Denhaene 1990, p. 304, no. 341, ill. 193. I would like to thank Ed Wouk for alerting me to this information.
52 'Een coperen plaete van een Crucifix ende seker personagien van Aelbert Dure ghetrocken metten pinsoene'. J. van Grieken in Leuven and Paris 2013, p. 25.
53 'Vyff coperen plaetkens van vyff Apostelkens nae Alber Dure'. Ibid., pp. 25, 29 n. 35.
54 The albums are in the Rijksprentenkabinet, Amsterdam, and the Rothschild collection at the Louvre, Paris; see Buchanan 1982.

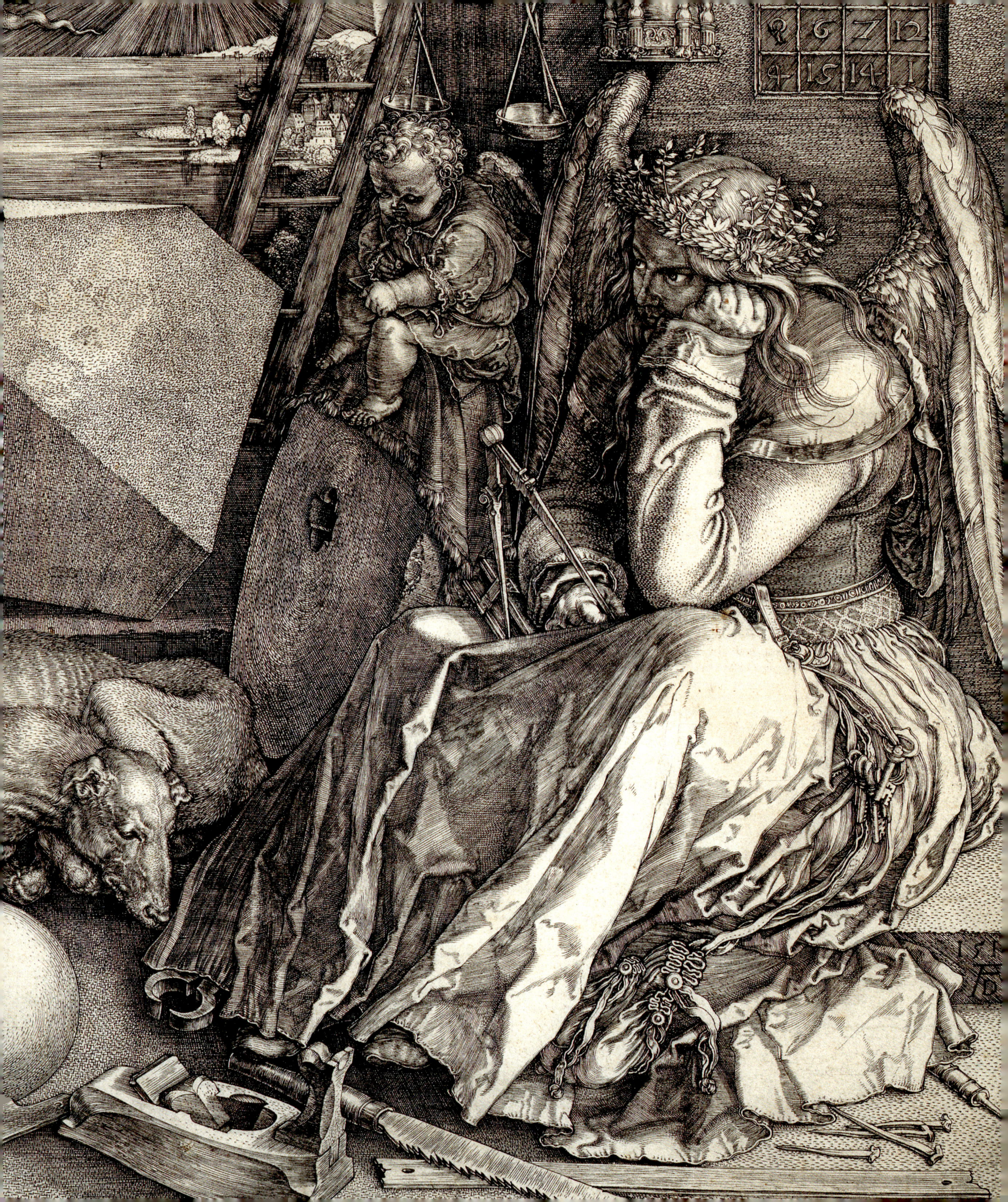
6 7 12
4 15 14 1

DÜRER'S JOURNEYS

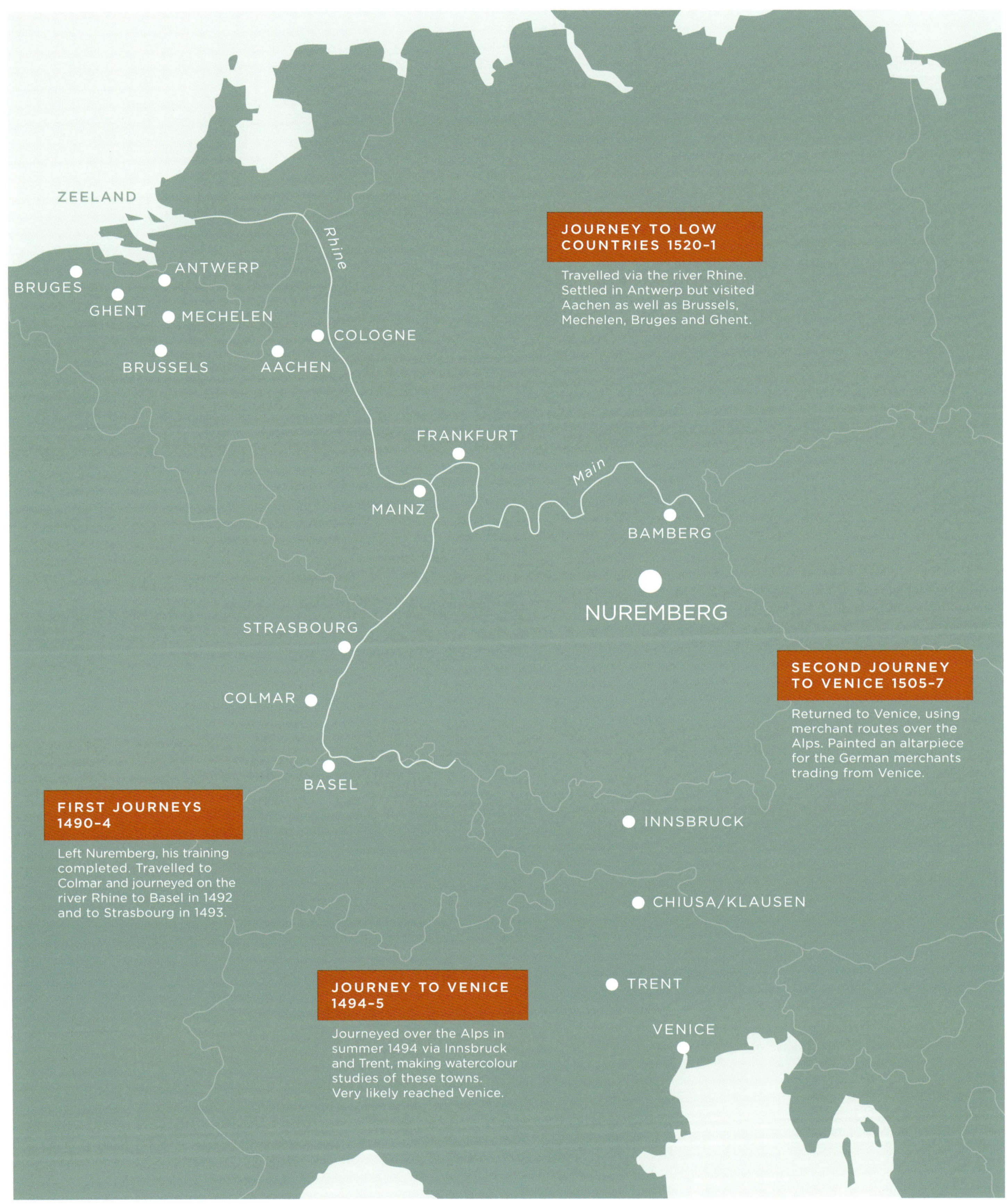

DÜRER'S LIFE AND TIMES

COMPILED BY IMOGEN TEDBURY

		ALBRECHT DÜRER		ART AND CURRENT EVENTS
1470s	**1471**	21 May. Albrecht Dürer is born in Nuremberg.	**1472**	Lucas Cranach the Elder is born in Kronach.
			1473	Michael Wolgemut, Dürer's future teacher, takes over Hans Pleydenwurff's workshop.
			1474–7	The Burgundian Wars between the Old Swiss Confederacy and the Burgundian State.
			1475	Michelangelo is born in Caprese, near Arezzo.
			1475–6	Antonello da Messina visits Venice.
			1477	Charles the Bold, Duke of Burgundy, dies. The Burgundian territories are divided between France and the Holy Roman Empire.
			1479	Venice declares peace with Sultan Mehmed II of the Ottoman Empire.
1480s	**1480s**	Apprenticed with his father Albrecht Dürer the Elder, a goldsmith, probably aged 10 or 12.	**1480s**	Sandro Botticelli paints his mythological paintings the *Birth of Venus* and *Primavera* (Gallerie degli Uffizi, Florence) around this time.
			1481	Beginning of the Spanish Inquisition against Jews, Muslims and heretics.
			1482	Mary of Burgundy, heir to deceased Duke of Burgundy Charles the Bold, is killed in a riding accident.
			1483	Raphael is born in Urbino. Martin Luther is born in Eisleben.
	1484	First *Self Portrait*, in silverpoint (fig. 16).	**1484**	Pope Innocent VIII condemns witchcraft and inquisitions are renewed in Germany.
			1485	Henry VII defeats Richard III, King of England, in the Battle of Bosworth.
	1486	30 November. Apprenticed with Nuremberg painter and woodcut designer Michael Wolgemut.	**1487**	Kaiser Friedrich III visits Nuremberg.
1490s	**1490**	April. Leaves Nuremberg to travel as a journeyman. Perhaps visits engravers near Nuremberg, the publishing warehouse of his godfather Anton Koberger in Frankfurt, publishers and printmakers in Mainz and Cologne.	**1491**	Martin Schongauer dies in Colmar.
	1492	Visits Colmar, home to recently deceased Martin Schongauer. Probably travels to Basel, home to Schongauer's brother Georg Schongauer, a goldsmith. That year a title-page woodcut of *Saint Jerome* is published in Basel, from a woodblock inscribed with Dürer's name on the reverse (cat. 22).	**1492**	Michael Sittow becomes court painter to Isabella of Castile in Toledo. Pope Alexander VI succeeds Innocent VIII. Christopher Columbus reaches the Americas.
	1493	Visits Strasbourg. Paints a pair of portraits representing Dürer's Strasbourg master and his wife, listed in the 1573 Pirckheimer family inventory. Paints *Self Portrait Holding a Thistle*, dated and inscribed (Musée du Louvre, Paris), possibly in Strasbourg.	**1493**	Anton Koberger, Dürer's godfather, prints and publishes the *Nuremberg Chronicle*, an illustrated encyclopaedia and history of the world.
	1494	Returns to Nuremberg. 7 July. Marries Agnes Frey, daughter of brassworker Hans Frey. Travels through the Alps to northern Italy, visiting Innsbruck, Trent and most likely Venice.	**1494**	September. Outbreak of plague in Nuremberg. King Charles VIII of France invades Italy.
	1495	Opens his own workshop in Nuremberg and begins to publish prints.	**1495**	Formation of the first Holy League to oppose France in Italy.
	1496	14–18 April. Frederick the Wise, Elector of Saxony, visits Nuremberg. Dürer paints his *Portrait* (Gemäldegalerie, Berlin).	**1496**	Veit Stoss returns from Crakow to Nuremberg. French troops are forced out of Italy.
	1497	Hires Konrad Schweitzer and Georg Coler as travelling agents to sell his prints.	**1497/8**	Hans Holbein the Younger is born in Augsburg.
	1498	Publishes the *Apocalypse with Pictures*, a series of 15 woodcuts illustrating scenes from the Book of Revelation. Paints his *Self Portrait* (fig. 24), signed and dated.	**1498**	Leonardo da Vinci completes the *Last Supper* (Convent of Santa Maria delle Grazie, Milan).
			1499	Expulsion of Nuremberg's Jewish community. End of the Swiss War between the Swiss Confederacy and the Holy Roman Empire.

ALBRECHT DÜRER

1500s

1500 Paints the Munich *Self Portrait* (fig. 18).
1 August. Signs a contract with a second travelling sales agent, Jakob Arnold.

1502 20 September. Dürer's father dies.

1503 Hans Baldung Grien joins Dürer's workshop, where other assistants include Hans Schäufelin, Hans Süss and Dürer's youngest brother, Hans III.

1504 Publishes engravings of *Adam and Eve* (cat. 52) and the *Nativity* (fig. 38).
Paints the *Adoration of the Magi* (fig. 10), probably for Frederick the Wise.

1505 Late summer. Travels to Venice.
His wife, Agnes, and his mother, Barbara, manage the business in Nuremberg. Agnes sells prints at the Frankfurt fair. Barbara sells prints at the Nuremberg fair.
Madonna with the Iris (cat. 34) is possibly produced by Dürer's workshop in his absence.

1506 Paints the altarpiece of the *Feast of the Rose Garlands* (fig. 19) for the German church in Venice.
Paints *Christ among the Doctors* (cat. 31), signed, dated and inscribed 'the work of five days'.

1507 Returns to Nuremberg by early February.
1507–9 Paints the Heller Altarpiece (destroyed), commissioned by merchant Jakob Heller for the Dominican church in Frankfurt.

1508 Paints the *Martyrdom of the Ten Thousand* (Kunsthistorisches Museum, Vienna), for Frederick the Wise.

1509 Buys his house in the Zisselgasse.
Becomes a member of the Great Council of Nuremberg.
Produces several woodcuts for the *Large Passion*, the *Life of the Virgin* and the *Small Passion*.

ART AND CURRENT EVENTS

1500 Portuguese explorer Pedro Álvares Cabral reaches Brazil.
1500–1 Jacopo de' Barbari spends at least a year in Nuremberg as court painter to Maximilian I.

1502 Frederick the Wise founds the University of Wittenberg.

1503 Jan Gossaert joins the Antwerp Guild.
Pope Julius II succeeds Pius III.

1504 Lucas Cranach the Elder becomes court painter to Frederick the Wise.

1505 Giovanni Bellini paints the San Zaccaria Altarpiece (San Zaccaria, Venice).

1506 *The Laocoön* is found in Rome.
Work begins on Donato Bramante's designs for St Peter's Basilica.

1508 Maximilian I succeeds his father, Frederick III, as Holy Roman Emperor.
Pope Julius II brings together the League of Cambrai, an alliance between the papal states, France, Aragon and the Holy Roman Empire, to challenge the power of the Republic of Venice.
1508–12 Michelangelo paints the Sistine Chapel.
1509 Luca Pacioli publishes *Divina Proportione*, a book on artistic and mathematical proportion.
Henry VIII becomes King of England and marries Catherine of Aragon.
Pope Julius II excommunicates the Republic of Venice.

ALBRECHT DÜRER

1510s

1511 Paints the *Adoration of the Trinity* (Kunsthistorisches Museum, Vienna) for merchant Matthaeus Landauer.
Publishes the 'Three Great Books': the *Large Passion* (12 woodcuts), the *Life of the Virgin* (19 woodcuts) and the *Apocalypse* (15 woodcuts).
Publishes the *Small Passion* (37 woodcuts).
Emperor Maximilian I grants Dürer a copyright.

1512 Drafts the introduction to his treatise *Food for Young Painters*, a lifelong project.
Publishes the *Engraved Passion* (16 engravings).
Nuremberg's City Council rules against a 'stranger' selling prints with forgeries of Dürer's monogram.
Begins to undertake commissions for Maximilian I, including several portraits, an illustrated Book of Hours, the monumental *Triumphal Arch* (fig. 51) and the *Triumphal Procession* woodcuts.

1513–14 Publishes his Master Prints, the three engravings *Knight, Death and the Devil*, *Melancholia I* (cat. 116) and *Saint Jerome in his Study* (fig. 140).

1514 Dürer's mother, Barbara, dies.

1515 Maximilian I directs the City Council of Nuremberg to pay Dürer an annual pension.

1518 Attends the Diet of Augsburg to make portraits of Maximilian I and others.

1519 January. Dürer's pension is stopped on the death of Maximilian I.

ART AND CURRENT EVENTS

1510 Giorgione dies in Venice.
League of Cambrai collapses. Pope Julius II allies himself with Venice against France, joined by the Holy Roman Empire, Spain and England in a second Holy League.

1512 Holy League expels the French from Italy.
1512–17 Fifth Lateran Council.

1513 Pope Leo X succeeds Pope Julius II.
1515 Francis I succeeds Louis XII as King of France, and recaptures Milan.
1516 Giovanni Bellini dies in Venice.
Hieronymus Bosch dies in 's-Hertogenbosch.
Leonardo da Vinci enters the service of Francis I.
Erasmus publishes his Greek New Testament and his biography of Saint Jerome.
1517 Quinten Massys paints his portrait diptych of *Desiderius Erasmus* (cat. 37) and *Peter Gillis* (cat. 38).
Luther publishes his Ninety-five Theses.
1518 Bernaert van Orley is appointed as the official court painter to Margaret of Austria, replacing Jacopo de' Barbari.
Diet of Augsburg.
1519 Leonardo da Vinci dies in Clos Lucé.
Charles V succeeds his grandfather Maximilian I as Holy Roman Emperor.
Margaret of Austria is reappointed Governor of the Netherlands.

ALBRECHT DÜRER

1520s

1520 12 July. Dürer, his wife Agnes and her maid Susanna travel to Bamberg to obtain a travel pass for their journey to the Netherlands.
14–20 July. Travel from Bamberg to Frankfurt by boat along the Main.
22 July. Travel from Frankfurt to Mainz.
23–28 July. Travel along the Rhine to Cologne, where they stay with Dürer's cousin Niclas 'the Hungarian'.
28 July–2 August. Travel from Cologne to Antwerp.
2 August. Dürer's party arrives in Antwerp.
5 August. Invited to dine at the Antwerp painters' guild.
26 August–3 September. Dürer leaves Agnes and Susanna in Antwerp to visit Mechelen (Malines) and Brussels.
Meets Margaret of Austria, Regent of the Netherlands, who promises she will intercede with Charles V on Dürer's behalf.
Visits the Royal Palace with its zoo.
Visits the exhibition of pre-Columbian art from Mexico, sent to Charles V by Captain Hernán Cortés.
Attends a banquet held by Bernaert van Orley.
3 September–4 October. Pays Raphael's pupil Tommaso Vincidor to acquire items from Raphael's estate.
Witnesses Charles V's triumphal entry into Antwerp.
3 October. Leaves Antwerp for Aachen.
23 October. Attends the Coronation of Charles V in Aachen.
28 October. Leaves Aachen for Cologne via Düren.
12 November. Receives word that his annual pension from Charles V has been granted.
14–22 November. Travels back to Antwerp via 's-Hertogenbosch and the northern Netherlands.
3–14 December. Travels to Bergen op Zoom and Zeeland to see a whale that has washed up. Nearly shipwrecked on a tour of the islands. Falls ill, probably with malaria.
14 December. Returns to Antwerp.

1521 Paints *Saint Jerome* (cat. 110) for his friend Rodrigo Fernandes de Almada.
March. Begins to tie up his affairs and send baggage home to Nuremberg.
6–11 April. Travels by boat to Bruges and Ghent with Jan Provoost. Sees Michelangelo's *Bruges Madonna* and the Ghent Altarpiece. Visits the zoo at Ghent.
11 April–17 May. Back in Antwerp. Dürer's earlier illness returns. Attends Joachim Patinir's wedding.
6–8 June. Travels to Mechelen to meet Margaret of Austria, who rejects Dürer's gift of a portrait of her father. Margaret gives Dürer a personal tour of her art collection, including Jan van Eyck's *Arnolfini Portrait* (fig. 53), works by Jacopo de' Barbari, and panels painted by Juan de Flandes and Michael Sittow for Queen Isabella of Castile (cat. 55).
8 June–2 July. Back in Antwerp. Meets Lucas van Leyden.
2 July. Christian II of Denmark arrives in Antwerp and sends for Dürer to draw his portrait. Dürer postpones his party's journey home.
3–12 July. Dürer, Agnes and Susanna travel to Brussels, where Dürer has been summoned to paint Christian II's portrait (fig. 54). Dürer attends a banquet held by Christian II for Charles V and Margaret of Austria.
12–15 July. Dürer's party set out for Nuremberg via Aachen and Cologne.
Late July. The travellers arrive home.
August–December. Dürer's designs are used in the refurbishment of Nuremberg City Hall.

1522 Works on his *Four Books on Human Proportion.*

1524 Writes the Dürer family chronicle.

1525 Publication of his introduction to geometric theory, *Underweysung der Messung* (Treatise on Measurement).

1526 Completes his engraved *Portrait of Erasmus* (cat. 94) and an engraved *Portrait of Philip Melanchthon.*

1528 6 April. Albrecht Dürer dies.
Posthumous publication of the first of his *Four Books on Human Proportion.*

ART AND CURRENT EVENTS

1520 Lucas Cranach the Elder engraves the first *Portrait of Martin Luther.*
Raphael dies in Rome.
Moctezuma II, the last Aztec ruler, dies.
Martin Luther publishes pamphlets against the Pope and the Catholic Church.

1520–3 Titian paints *Bacchus and Ariadne* (National Gallery, London).

1521 Diet of Worms. Martin Luther is summoned before Charles V and excommunicated by the Pope.
Henry VIII refutes Luther's views in his Defence of the Seven Sacraments. The Pope makes him Defender of the Faith.
Hernán Cortés conquers Mexico.

1522 Luther publishes his German translation of the New Testament.
Inquisition in the Spanish Netherlands begins.

1524 City Council in Nuremberg allows Mass to be celebrated in German.
German Peasants' War begins.

1525 William Tyndale's English translation of the New Testament is printed in Worms and smuggled into England.

1527 Mutinous troops of Charles V carry out the Sack of Rome.

1529 Suleiman the Magnificent, Sultan of the Ottoman Empire, lays siege to Vienna.

1530 Augsburg Confession.

BIBLIOGRAPHY

AACHEN 1997
C. Meifert and D. Preising, *Dürer und die Renaissance: Aspekte in der Druckgraphik*, exh. cat., Suermondt-Ludwig-Museum, Aachen 1997

AACHEN 2004
D. Preising, U. Willwock and C. Vogt (eds), *Albrecht Dürer, Apelles der Schwarz-Weiss*, exh. cat., Suermondt-Ludwig-Museum, Aachen 2004

ACHILLES 1986
K. Achilles, 'Naturstudien von Hans Hofmann in der Kunstsammlung des Nürnberger Kaufmann Paulus II. Praun', *Jahrbuch der Kunsthistorischen Sammlungen in Wien*, 82/83 (1986), pp. 243–59

ACKROYD 2000
P. Ackroyd et al., 'A Virgin and Child from the Workshop of Albrecht Dürer?', *National Gallery Technical Bulletin*, vol. 21 (2000), pp. 28–42

AINSWORTH 1998
M.W. Ainsworth, *Gerard David. Purity of Vision in an Age of Transition*, New York 1998

AINSWORTH 2020
M.W. Ainsworth, 'Portrait of a Woman', *The Met Collection Online* (www.metmuseum.org/art/collection/search/436986, accessed 21 September 2020)

AINSWORTH AND WATERMAN 2013
M.W. Ainsworth and J.P. Waterman, *German Paintings in The Metropolitan Museum of Art, 1350–1600*, New Haven 2013

ALLEN AND GARROD 1906–58
P.S. Allen, H.M. Allen and H.W. Garrod (eds), *Opus Epistolarum Des Erasmi Roterodami*, 12 vols, Oxford 1906–58

ANGEHRN 2017
E. Angehrn, *Sein Leben schreiben. Wege der Erinnerung*, Frankfurt 2017

ANTWERP 1993
J. van der Stock (ed.), *Antwerpen, verhaal van een metropool 16de–17de eeuw*, exh. cat., Hessenhuis, Antwerp 1993

ANTWERP AND MAASTRICHT 2005
P. van den Brink and M. Martens (eds), *ExtravagAnt! A Forgotten Chapter of Antwerp Painting 1500–1530*, exh. cat., Koninklijk Museum voor Schone Kunsten, Antwerp, and Bonnefantenmuseum, Maastricht, Schoten 2005

ANZELEWSKY 1980
F. Anzelewsky, *Dürer: His Art and Life*, trans. H. Grieve, New York 1980

ANZELEWSKY (1971) 1991
F. Anzelewsky, *Albrecht Dürer. Das malerische Werk*, 2 vols (1971), 2nd edn, Berlin 1991

ANZELEWSKY AND MIELKE 1984
F. Anzelewsky and H. Mielke (eds), *Albrecht Dürer. Kritischer Katalog der Zeichnungen im Kupferstichkabinett Berlin*, Berlin 1984

ASHCROFT 2017
J. Ashcroft (ed. and trans.), *Albrecht Dürer: Documentary Biography*, 2 vols, New Haven and London 2017

AUGSBURG 2019
H. Lange-Krach (ed.), *Maximilian I: 1459–1519. Kaiser. Ritter. Bürger zu Augsburg*, exh. cat., Maximilianmuseum, Augsburg, Regensburg 2019

BAKHUŸS AND COUDERT 2010
D. Bakhuÿs and M.-C. Coudert (eds), *Gérard David. La Vierge entre les vierges. Un joyau restauré*, Rouen 2010

BARTSCH
A. Bartsch, *Le Peintre Graveur*, 12 vols, Vienna 1803–21

BARTSCH 2019
T. Bartsch, *Maarten van Heemskerck. Römische Studien zwischen Sachlichkeit und Imagination*, Munich 2019

BASEL 2006
S. Kemperdick, *Das frühe Porträt: Aus den Sammlungen des Fürsten von und zu Liechtenstein und dem Kunstmuseum Basel/The Early Portrait: From the Collections of the Prince of Liechtenstein and the Kunstmuseum Basel*, exh. cat., Kunstmuseum Basel, Munich 2006

BASEL AND BERLIN 1997
G. Brunner (ed.), *Dürer, Holbein, Grünewald. Meisterzeichnungen der deutschen Renaissance aus Berlin und Basel*, exh. cat., Kunstmuseum Basel and Kupferstichkabinett, Berlin, Ostfildern 1997

BASS 2016
M.A. Bass, *Jan Gossart and the Invention of Netherlandish Antiquity*, Princeton 2016

BAUER 1997
E. Bauer, *Lazarus Spengler als Übersetzer. (Ps.-)Eusebius De morte Hieronymi Nürnberg 1514*, Heidelberg 1997

BELTING 2013
H. Belting, *Faces. Eine Geschichte des Gesichts*, Munich 2013

BERLIN 2006
M. Roth and U.B. Ullrich (eds), *Dürers Mutter. Schönheit, Alter und Tod im Bild der Renaissance*, exh. cat., Kupferstichkabinett, Staatliche Museen zu Berlin, Berlin 2006

BERLIN 2007
M. Kraus and B. Vogel, *Novos mundos – Neue Welten. Portugal und das Zeitalter der Entdeckungen*, exh. cat., Deutsches Historisches Museum, Berlin, Berlin 2007

BERTHOLD HINZ 1998
A. Berthold Hinz, *Aphrodite: Geschichte einer abendländischen Passion,* Munich and Vienna 1998

BIAŁOSTOCKI 1986
J. Białostocki, *Dürer and His Critics 1500–1971: Chapters in the History of Ideas Including a Collection of Texts*, Baden-Baden 1986

BIETENHOLZ 2003
P.G. Bietenholz (ed.), *Contemporaries of Erasmus: A Biographical Register of the Renaissance and Reformation*, 3 vols, Toronto, Buffalo and London 2003

BIRMINGHAM 2019
D. Ewing, P. van den Brink and R. Wenley (eds), *Truly Bright and Memorable: Jan de Beer's Renaissance Altarpieces*, Barber Institute of Fine Arts, Birmingham, London 2019

BLEYERVELD 2000
Y. Bleyerveld, *Hoe bedriechlijck dat die vrouwen zijn. Vrouwenlisten in de beeldende kunst in de Nederlanden circa 1350–1650*, Leiden 2000

BOBER AND RUBINSTEIN 2010
P.P. Bober and R. Rubinstein, *Renaissance Artists and Antique Sculpture: A Handbook of Sources*, 2nd edn, London and Turnhout 2010

BÖHME 1995
H. Böhme, 'Albrecht Dürers Traumgesicht von 1525', in *Grenzüberschreitungen. Friedenspädagogik, Geschlechter-Diskurs, Literatur – Sprache – Didaktik. Festschrift für Wolfgang Popp*, ed. G. Härle, Essen 1995, pp. 17–33

BONN 1999
A. Curvelo (ed.), *Museu Nacional de Arte Antiga Lissabon*, exh. cat., Kunst- und Austellungshalle der Bundesrepublik Deutschland, Bonn 1999

BONNET 2001
A.M. Bonnet, *'Akt' bei Dürer*, Cologne 2001

BOON 1992
K.G. Boon, *The Netherlandish and German Drawings of the XVth and XVIth Centuries of the Frits Lugt Collection*, 3 vols, Paris 1992

BORCHERT 2012
T.-H. Borchert, 'Form and Functions of van Eyck's Portraiture', in *Vision and Material: Interaction between Art and Science in Jan van Eyck's Time*, eds M. de Mey, M. Martens and C. Stroo, Brussels 2012, pp. 213–33

BOURG-EN-BRESSE 2018
P.G. Girault and M. Briat-Philippe (eds), *Primitifs flamands. Trésors de Marguerite d'Autriche de Jan Van Eyck à Jérôme Bosch*, exh. cat., Musée de Brou, Bourge-en-Bresse 2018

BREMEN 2012
A. Röver-Kann and M. von Miller, *Dürer-Zeit. Die Geschichte der Dürer-Sammlung in der Kunsthalle Bremen*, exh. cat., Kunsthalle Bremen, Munich 2012

VAN DEN BRINK 2006
P. van den Brink, 'The Artist at Work: The Crucial Role of Drawings in Early Sixteenth-Century Antwerp Workshops', *Jaarboek Koninklijk Museum voor Schone Kunsten Antwerpen* (2006), pp. 158–231

VAN DEN BRINK 2020
P. van den Brink, 'A Tale of Two Drawings: Albrecht Dürer and Gossart's lost Middelburg Altarpiece', *Ingenium et labor. Studia ofiarowane Profesorowi Antoniemu Ziembie z okazji 60. urodzin/Studies offered to Professor Antoni Ziemba on his 60th birthday*, ed. P. Borusowski, Warsaw 2020, pp. 109–17

BRIQUET 1907 (1968)
C.M. Briquet, *Les filigranes. Dictionnaire historique des marques du papier dès leur apparition vers 1282 jusqu'en 1600*, 4 vols, Geneva 1907 (facsimile edn, Amsterdam 1968)

BRISMAN 2016
S. Brisman, *Albrecht Dürer and the Epistolary Mode of Address*, Chicago 2016

BROWN 2018
C.J. Brown, 'Family Female Networking in Early Sixteenth-Century France. The Power of Text and Image', in *Women and Power at the French Court, 1483–1563*, ed. S. Broomhall, Amsterdam 2018 (*Gendering the Late Medieval and Early Modern World*), pp. 209–39

BRUGES 1998
M.P.J. Martens, *Memling und seine Zeit. Brügge und die Renaissance*, exh. cat., Memlingmuseum, Bruges, Stuttgart and Zürich 1998

BRUGES 2010
T.-H. Borchert (ed.), *Van Eyck bis Dürer. Altniederländische Meister und die Malerei in Mitteleuropa 1430–1530*, exh. cat., Groeningemuseum, Bruges, Tielt 2010

BRUNO 1928
L. Bruno, 'Le vite di Dante e di Petrarcha', in *Leonardo Bruni Aretino: Humanistisch-Philosophische Schriften mit einer Chronologie seiner Werke und Briefe*, ed. H. Baron, Berlin 1928

BRUSSELS 1977
F. Anzelewsky, M. Mende and P. Eeckhout, *Albrecht Dürer in de Nederlanden. Zijn reis (1520–1521) en invloed/Albert Dürer aux Pays-Bas: son voyage (1520–1521), son influence*, exh. cat., Palais des Beaux-Arts, Brussels 1977

BRUSSELS 2019
V. Bücken and I. de Meûter (eds), *Bernard van Orley*, exh. cat., Palais des Beaux-Arts, Brussels 2019

BUBENIK 2013
A. Bubenik, *Reframing Albrecht Dürer: The Appropriation of Art, 1528–1700*, Farnham 2013

BUCHANAN 1982
I. Buchanan, 'Dürer and Abraham Ortelius', *The Burlington Magazine*, 124, no. 957 (December 1982), pp. 734–41

BUCHNER 1953
E. Buchner, *Das deutsche Porträt der Spätgotik und der frühen Dürerzeit*, Berlin 1953

BÜCKEN 2019
V. Bücken, 'Bernard van Orley et la peinture à Bruxelles au temps de Pieter Coecke', *Studia Bruxellae*, 13 (2019), pp. 47–63

BUDDE 1996
H. Budde, *Die Kunstsammlung des Nürnberger Patriziers Willibald Imhoff unter besonderer Berücksichtigung der Werke Albrecht Dürers*, Münster 1996

BUIJNSTERS-SMETS 1995
L. Buijnsters-Smets, *Jan Massys: Een Antwerps schilder uit de zestiende eeuw*, Zwolle 1995

BURCKHARDT 1860
J. Burckhardt, *Die Kultur der Renaissance in Italien. Ein Versuch*, Basel 1860

BURGER 2019
D. Burger, 'Zeichnete Albrecht Dürer 1521 die fränkische Burg Virnsberg?', in *Burgen, Schlösser, Häuser. Festschrift für G. Ulrich Großmann zum 65. Geburtstag*, eds G. von Büren and M. Goer, Petersberg 2019, pp. 30–7

BUSCH 1931
N. Busch, 'Untersuchungen zur Lebensgeschichte Dürers', *Abhandlungen der Herder-Gesellschaft und des Herder-Instituts zu Riga*, 4, no. 1 (1931), pp. 1–74

CAMBRIDGE 2000
J. Kantor, *Dürer's Passions*, exh. cat., Harvard University Art Museums, Cambridge, MA 2000

CAMPBELL 1990
L. Campbell, *Renaissance Portraits*, New Haven and London 1990

CAMPBELL 1998
L. Campbell, *The Fifteenth Century Netherlandish Schools*, National Gallery Catalogues, London 1998

CAMPBELL 2010
L. Campbell, 'The Patron of Jan Gossaert's "Adoration of the Kings" in the National Gallery, London', *The Burlington Magazine*, 152, no. 1283 (February 2010), pp. 86–93

CAMPBELL 2014
L. Campbell, *The Sixteenth Century Netherlandish Paintings: With French Paintings before 1600*, 2 vols, National Gallery Catalogues, London 2014

CAMPBELL AND FOISTER 1986
L. Campbell, and S. Foister, 'Gerard, Lucas and Susanna Horenbout', *The Burlington Magazine*, 128 (1986), pp. 719–27

CARROLL 1989
M. Carroll, 'The Erotics of Absolutism: Rubens and the Mystification of Sexual Violence', *Representations*, 25 (winter 1989), pp. 3–30

CHANTILLY 1999
D. Mandrella, *Dessins allemands et flamands du Musée Condé à Chantilly. De Dürer à Rubens*, exh. cat., Musée Condé, Château de Chantilly, Paris 1999

CHIPPS SMITH 2011
J. Chipps Smith, 'Albert Dürer as Collector', *Renaissance Quarterly*, 64 (2011), pp. 7–9

CHIPPS SMITH 2012
J. Chipps Smith, *Dürer*, London 2012

CHRISTMAN 2015
V. Christman, *Pragmatic Toleration: The Politics of Religious Heterodoxy in Early Reformation Antwerp, 1515–1555*, Rochester 2015

CIPRIANI 1976
A. Cipriani, 'Giovanna Garzoni, miniatrice', *Ricerche di storia dell'arte* (1976), pp. 241–54

CLEMEN 1901
O. Clemen, 'Das Antwerpener Augustinerkloster bei Beginn der Reformation (1513–1523)', *Monatsschrift der Comenius-Gesellschaft*, 10 (1901), pp. 306–13

COBURG 2010
M. Müller et al., *Apelles am Fürstenhof: Facetten der Hofkunst um 1500 im alten Reich*, exh. cat., Kunstsammlung der Veste Coburg, Coburg 2010

COCHLAEUS 1512 (1969)
J. Cochlaeus, *Brevis germanie descriptio* (1512), ed. K. Lagosch, Darmstadt 1969

COLBORN 2005
F.D. Colborn, 'From Pre-Columbian Artifact to Pre-Columbian Art', *Record of the Art Museum, Princeton University*, 64 (2005), pp. 36–41

COOK 1913–15
F. and H. Cook (eds), *A Catalogue of the paintings at Doughty House, Richmond, and elsewhere in the collection of Sir Frederick Cook*, 3 vols, London 1913–15

COOPER AND GREGORY 2004
K. Cooper and J. Gregory (eds), *Retribution, Repentance, and Reconciliation*, Woodbridge and Rochester 2004

CRAWFORD LUBER 2005
K. Crawford Luber, *Albrecht Dürer and the Venetian Renaissance*, Cambridge 2005

CUMMINS 2010
T. Cummins, 'Through the "Devil's Looking Glass" Darkly: Brazilians, Peruvians, Aztecs, and Zemis in Europe; Serlio and Hercules in the Americas', *The Arts of South America, 1492–1850: Papers from the 2008 Mayer Center Symposium at the Denver Art Museum*, ed. D. Pierce, Denver 2010, pp. 16–46

DAVID 1909
H. David, 'Die Darstellung des Löwen bei Albrecht Dürer', dissertation, University of Halle, 1909

DAVIES 1961
M. Davies, *The Earlier Italian Schools*, National Gallery Catalogues, London 1961

DENHAENE 1990
G. Denhaene, *Lambert Lombard: Renaissance et Humanisme à Liège*, Antwerp 1990

DENKER 2015
C.W. Denker, *Vom Geist des Bauches. Für eine Philosophie der Verdauung*, Bielefeld 2015

DICKEL 2014
H. Dickel (ed.), *Zeichnen seit Dürer. Die süddeutschen und schweizerischen Zeichnungen der Renaissance in der Universitätsbibliothek Erlangen*, Petersberg and Erlangen 2014

DICKHAUT 2016
K. Dickhaut, 'Techniken des Autoporträts in Cellinis "Vita"', in *Selbst-Bild und Selbst-Bilder. Autoporträt und Zeit in Literatur, Kunst und Philosophie*, ed. B. Kuhn, Paderborn 2016, pp. 57–72

DIETZ 2008
G.J. Dietz, *Die Zeichentechnik Matthias Grünewalds. Untersuchung am Bestand des Kupferstichkabinetts Berlin*, Munich 2008

DODGSON 1937
C. Dodgson, 'A Chiaroscuro Woodcut by Dürer?', *Print Collector's Quarterly*, 24 (1937), pp. 173–83

DUKE 2009
A. Duke, *Dissident Identities in the Early Modern Low Countries*, eds J. Pollmann and A. Spicer, Farnham 2009

DÜLBERG 1990
A. Dülberg, *Privatporträts. Geschichte und Ikonologie einer Gattung im 15. und 16. Jahrhundert*, Berlin 1990

DÜRER 1977
A. Dürer, *The Painter's Manual*, ed. and trans. W.L. Strauss, New York 1977

DÜSSELDORF 1991
H. Mielke, *Albrecht Dürer. 50 Meisterzeichnungen aus dem Berliner Kupferstichkabinett*, Kunstmuseum Düsseldorf, Berlin 1991

DUVERGER 1929
J. Duverger, 'Margareta en de Noord-Nederlandsche kunstenaars, de goudsmid Michiel Mercator', *Oud Holland*, 46 (1929), pp. 188–92

DUVERGER 1934
J. Duverger, 'Fransche kunstenaars aan het Habsburgsche vorstenhof in de Nederlanden (1477–1559)', *Kunst (Handelingen van het 2de Congres voor Algemeene Kunstgeschiedenis)*, Ghent 1934, pp. 19–28

DUVERGER 1980
J. Duverger, 'Margareta van Oostenrijk (1480–1530) en de Italiaanse Renaissance', *Relations artistiques entre les Pays-Bas et l'Italie à la Renaissance. Études dédiées à Suzanne Sulzberger*, ed. N. Dacos, Brussels and Rome 1980, pp. 127–42

VAN ECK 1999
P.C.R. van Eck, *Gebrandschilderde ruitjes uit de Nederlanden 1480–1560/Painted Glass Roundels from the Netherlands 1480–1560*, Amsterdam 1999

EDINBURGH AND LONDON 2012
K. Heard and L. Whittaker, *The Northern Renaissance: Dürer to Holbein*, exh. cat., Queen's Gallery, Edinburgh and Queen's Gallery, London 2012

EHRENFEST 1950
F. Ehrenfest, 'Albrecht Dürer's "Crucifixion in Outline"', *Print Collector's Quarterly*, 30, no. 2 (1949/51), pp. 48–51

EICHBERGER 2002
D. Eichberger, *Leben mit Kunst – Wirken durch Kunst. Sammelwesen und Hofkunst unter Margarete von Österreich, Regentin der Niederlande*, Turnhout 2002

EICHBERGER 2014
D. Eichberger, 'Official Portraits and Regional Identities. The Case of Emperor Maximilian I (1459–1519)', in *The Habsburgs and their Courts in Europe, 1400–1700. Between Cosmopolitism and Regionalism*, eds H. Karner, I. Ciulisová and B.J. García, [Leuven] 2014, pp. 100–14 (www.courtresidences.eu/uploads/general/Habsburgs%202014.pdf, accessed June 2020)

EICHBERGER, LORENTZ AND TACKE 2017
D. Eichberger, P. Lorentz and A. Tacke (eds), *The Artist Between Court and City (1300–1600)/Der Künstler zwischen Hof und Stadt*, Petersberg 2017

EISLER 1991
C. Eisler, *Dürer's Animals*, Washington and London 1991

EITEL-PORTER 2006
R. Eitel-Porter (ed.), *From Leonardo to Pollock: Master Drawings from the Morgan Library*, New York 2006

ERICHSEN 2019
J. Erichsen, 'Beobachtungen zum sog. "Trachtenbuch des Christoph Weiditz"', *Anzeiger des Germanischen Nationalmuseums*, Nuremberg 2019

ERNSTBERGER 1954
A. Ernstberger, 'Kurfürst Maximilian I. und Albrecht Dürer. Zur Geschichte einer grossen Sammlerleidenschaft', in *Anzeiger des Germanisches National-Museums 1940–1953*, Nuremberg 1954

ERWIN 1999
R. Erwin, 'The Passion and Death of Christ in the Piety and Theology of the Later Middle Ages and Martin Luther', PhD dissertation, Yale University, 1999

ESER 2011
T. Eser, 'Dürers Selbstbildnisse als "Probestücke"', in *Menschenbilder: Beiträge zur Altdeutschen Kunst*, ed. A. Tacke and S. Heinz, Petersberg 2011, pp. 159–76

EVANS 1992
M.L. Evans, *The Sforza Hours*, London 1992

EVANS 2004
M. Evans, 'Dürer and Italy Revisited: The German Connection', in G. Bartrum (ed.), *Albrecht Dürer and his Legacy,* British Museum Occasional Paper no. 130, London 2004 (www.nationalarchives.gov.uk)

EVERS 1974
H.-G. Evers, 'Zur Zeichnung "1514 die grosz kirch zu Anttorff" in der Albertina', *Pantheon*, 32 (1974), pp. 243–8

EWING 2004–5
D. Ewing, 'Magi and Merchants: The Force Behind the Antwerp Mannerists' Adoration Pictures', *Jaarboek Koninklijk Museum voor Schone Kunsten Antwerpen* (2004–5), pp. 274–99

EWING 2016
D. Ewing, *Jan de Beer: Gothic Renewal in Renaissance Antwerp*, Turnhout 2016

FEHRENBACH 2019
F. Fehrenbach, *Leonardo da Vinci: Der Impetus der Bilder*, Berlin 2019

FEICHTNER 2011
D. Feichtner, 'Eine kurfürstliche Löwin: Bezugsquellen, Haltungsweisen und Haltungszweck exotischer Tiere im europäischen Mittelalter und der frühen Renaissance', *historia.scribere*, 3 (2011), pp. 235–50 (www.historia.scribere.at, accessed 17 June 2019)

FERRARI 2006
S. Ferrari, *Jacopo de' Barbari: Un protagonista del Rinascimento tra Venezia e Dürer*, Milan 2006

FILEDT KOK, GIBSON AND BRUIJNEN 2014
J.P. Filedt Kok, W. Gibson and Y. Bruijnen, *Cornelis Engebrechtsz: A Sixteenth-Century Leiden Artist and his Workshop*, Turnhout 2014

FLECHSIG 1928–31
E. Flechsig, *Albrecht Dürer. Sein Leben und seine künstlerische Entwicklung*, 2 vols, Berlin 1928–31

FOISTER 2004A
S. Foister, *Holbein and England*, New Haven and London 2004

FOISTER 2004B
S. Foister, *Dürer and the Virgin in the Garden*, London 2004

FOISTER 2004C
S. Foister, 'Dürer's Nuremberg Legacy: The Case of the National Gallery Portrait of Dürer's Father', in G. Bartrum (ed.), *Albrecht Dürer and his Legacy*, British Museum Occasional Paper no. 130, London 2004 (www.nationalarchives.gov.uk)

FOISTER 2015
S. Foister, 'Distinctive or Different? English Artistic Practices in a European Context', in T. Cooper, A. Burnstock, M. Howard and E. Town (eds), *Painting in Britain 1500–1630: Production, Influences and Patronage*, Oxford 2015, pp. 204–15

FOUCAULT 1997
M. Foucault, 'Self Writing', trans. R. Hurley, in *Ethics: Subjectivity and Truth*, ed. P. Rabinow, New York 1997, pp. 207–22

FOWLER 2016
C.O. Fowler, *Drawing and the Senses: An Early Modern History*, Turnhout 2016

FOWLER 2019
C.O. Fowler, *The Art of Paper: From the Holy Land to the Americas*, New Haven and London 2019

FRANKFURT 1981
H. Beck and B. Decker (eds.), *Dürers Verwandlung in der Skulptur zwischen Renaissance und Barock,* exh. cat., Liebieghaus Museum alter Plastik, Frankfurt 1981

FRANKFURT 2003
S. Buck, *Wendepunkte deutscher Zeichenkunst. Spätgotik und Renaissance im Städel*, exh. cat., Graphische Sammlung, Städelsches Kunstinstitut und Städtische Galerie, Frankfurt 2003

FRANKFURT 2007
B. Brinkmann, *Hexenlust und Sündenfall. Die seltsamen Phantasien des Hans Baldung Grien*, exh. cat., Städel Museum, Frankfurt 2007

FRANKFURT 2013
J. Sander (ed.), *Albrecht Dürer. His Art in Context /Dürer. Kunst – Künstler – Kontext*, exh. cat., Städel Museum, Frankfurt, Munich 2013

FRANKFURT, LEIPZIG AND BERLIN 2006
B. Brinkmann (ed.), *Albrecht Dürer. Zwei Schwestern*, exh. cat., Städel Museum, Frankfurt, Museum der bildenden Künste, Leipzig and Gemäldegalerie, Berlin, Frankfurt 2006

FREDERICQ 1889–1906
P. Fredericq, *Corpus documentorum Inquisitionis haereticae pravitatis Neerlandicae. Verzameling van stukken betreffende de pauselijke en bisschoppelijke Inquisitie in de Nederlanden*, 10 vols, Ghent 1889–1906

FRIEDLÄNDER 1921
M.J. Friedländer, *Albrecht Dürer*, Leipzig 1921

FRIEDLÄNDER 1924–37
M.J. Friedländer, *Die Altniederländische Malerei*, 14 vols, Berlin and Leiden 1924–37

FRIEDLÄNDER 1967–76
M.J. Friedländer, *Early Netherlandish Painting*, 12 vols, Leiden and Brussels 1967–76

FÜSSEL AND WUTTKE 1989
S. Füssel and D. Wuttke (eds), *Poesis et Pictura. Festschrift für Dieter Wuttke zum 60. Geburtstag*, Baden-Baden 1989, pp. 191–221

GALAND 2013
A. Galand, *The Flemish Primitives*, vol. 6: *The Bernard van Orley Group*, Brussels and Turnhout 2013

VAN GELDER 1971
J.G. van Gelder, '"Sister Metzgen", a portrait by Dürer', *Master Drawings*, 9, no. 2 (1971), pp. 154–9, 208

GINZBURG 2005
C. Ginzburg, 'Hybrids: Learning from a Gilded Silver Beaker (Antwerp, *c.*1530)', in *Renaissance Go-Betweens: Cultural Exchange in Early Modern Europe,* eds A. Höfele and W. von Koppenfels, Berlin 2005, pp. 121–38

GOLDBERG, HEIMBERG AND SCHAWE 1998
G. Goldberg, B. Heimberg and M. Schawe (eds), *Albrecht Dürer: Die Gemälde der Alten Pinakothek*, Munich 1998

GORIS AND MARLIER 1970
J.A. Goris and G. Marlier (eds), *Albrecht Dürer 1520–1521. Das Tagebuch der niederländischen Reise. Mit dem Silberstift-Skizzenbuch und den während der Reise ausgeführten Bildern und Zeichnungen*, Brussels 1970

GORIS AND MARLIER 1971
J.A. Goris and G. Marlier (eds), *Albrecht Dürer: Diary of his Journey to the Netherlands 1520–21,* Greenwich, CT, 1971

GÖRRES 2017
D. Görres, 'Der Mönch und der Maler – Luther und Cranach als Vermittler eines neuen Glaubens', in *Lucas Cranach der Ältere. Meister – Marke – Moderne,* eds G. Heydenreich, D. Görres and B. Wismer, exh. cat., Stiftung Museum Kunstpalast, Düsseldorf 2017, pp. 44–51

GOTTRON 1962
A. Gottron, *Arnold Rucker. Orgelmacher von Seligenstadt*, Mainz 1962

GREBE 2017
A. Grebe, 'Marketing favours: Formal and informal criteria for pricing Albrecht Dürer's works between 1500 and 1650', *Journal for Art Market Studies*, 1 (2017), pp. 6–20

GRIGG 1986
R. Grigg, 'Studies on Dürer's Diary of his Journey to the Netherlands: The Distribution of the Melencolia I', *Zeitschrift für Kunstgeschichte*, 49 (1986), pp. 398–409

GRIMM 1978
H.J. Grimm, *Lazarus Spengler: A lay leader of the Reformation*, Columbus, OH, 1978

GRIMM 1854–1960
J. and W. Grimm (eds), *Deutsches Wörterbuch*, 16 vols, Leipzig 1854–1960

GROSSMANN 2009
G.U. Grossmann (ed.), *Buchmalerei der Dürerzeit – Dürer und die Mathematik. Neues aus der Dürerforschung, Dürer-Forschungen*, vol. 2, Nuremberg 2009

GRÜNDLER 2015
H. Gründler, 'The Necessity of Disorder: Scribbles and Sketches between Episteme and the Writing of the Self', in *Theologisches Wissen und die Kunst. Festschrift für Martin Büchsel*, eds R. Müller, A. Rau and J. Scheel, Berlin 2015, pp. 177–90

GSCHWEND 2015
A.J. Gschwend, 'Geliebte Gefährten, Maskottchen und Haustiere. Die Haltung wilder Tiere im Portugal der Renaissance', in *Echt tierisch! Die Menagerie des Fürsten*, ed. S. Haag, exh. cat., Kunsthistorisches Museum, Vienna and Schloss Ambras, Innsbruck, Vienna 2015, pp. 11–24

GUASTI 1887
C. Guasti, *Santa Maria del Fiore. La costruzione della chiesa e del Campanile secondo i documenti*, Florence 1887

HAMBURG 2001
P. Roettig, A. Stefes and A. Stolzenburg (eds), *Von Dürer bis Goya. 100 Meisterzeichnungen aus dem Kupferstichkabinett der Hamburger Kunsthalle*, exh. cat., Hamburger Kunsthalle, Hamburg 2001

HAMM 1990
B. Hamm, 'Hieronymus-Begeisterung und Augustinismus vor der Reformation: Beobachtungen zur Beziehung zwischen Humanismus und Frömigkeitstheologie', in *Augustine, the Harvest, and Theology (1300–1600): Essays dedicated to Heiko Augustinus Oberman*, ed. K. Hagen, Leiden 1990, pp. 154–243

HAMM AND HUBER 1995
B. Hamm and W. Huber, *Lazarus Spengler Schriften. Band 1 Schriften der Jahre 1509 bis Juni 1525*, Gütersloher 1995

HAMM AND LITZ 2004
B. Hamm and G. Litz, *Lazarus Spengler (1479–1534): der Nürnberger Ratsschreiber im Spannungsfeld von Humanismus und Reformation, Politik und Glaube*, Tübingen 2004

HAMPE 1927
T. Hampe, *Das Trachtenbuch des Christoph Weiditz von seinen Reisen nach Spanien (1529) und den Niederlanden (1531/32)*, Berlin 1927

HAND 1990
J.O. Hand, '"Saint Jerome in His Study" by Joos van Cleve', *Record of the Art Museum, Princeton University*, 49 (1990), pp. 2–10

HAND 1993
J.O. Hand with S.E. Mansfield, *German Paintings of the Fifteenth through Seventeenth Centuries*, The Collections of the National Gallery of Art, Washington, Cambridge 1993

HAND 2004
J.O. Hand, *Joos van Cleve: The Complete Paintings*, New Haven and London 2004

HAND 2013
J.M. Hand, *Women, Manuscripts and Identity in Northern Europe, 1350–1550*, Farnham and Burlington, VT, 2013

HEIDRICH 1906
E. Heidrich, *Kunstgeschichtliche Monographien*, vol. 3: *Geschichte des Dürerschen Marienbildes*, Leipzig 1906

HELD 1931
J. Held, *Dürers Wirkung auf die niederländische Kunst seiner Zeit*, The Hague 1931

HELLER 1827
J. Heller, *Das Leben und die Werke Albrecht Dürers*, vol. 2, Bamberg 1827

HESS, HIRSCHFELDER AND VON BAUM 2019
D. Hess, D. Hirschfelder and K. von Baum (eds), *Die Gemälde des Spätmittelalters im Germanischen Nationalmuseum. Franken*, 2 vols, Regensburg 2019

HEYDENREICH 2007
G. Heydenreich, *Lucas Cranach the Elder*, Amsterdam 2007

HINDRIKS 2019
S. Hindriks, *Der 'vlaemsche Apelles': Jan van Eycks früher Ruhm und die niederländische 'Renaissance'*, Petersberg 2019

HIRSCHFELDER 2013
D. Hirschfelder, 'Bildniszeichnungen als Tauschobjekte und Freundschaftsgaben. Dürers Strategien der Beziehungspflege in den Niederlanden', *Wallraf-Richartz Jahrbuch*, 74 (2013), pp. 107–36

HIRSCHMANN AND SCHNELBÖGL 1971
G. Hirschmann and F. Schnelbögl (eds), *Albrecht Dürers Umwelt: Festschrift zum 500. Geburtstag Albrecht Dürers am 21. Mai 1971*, Nuremberg 1971

HOLLSTEIN GERMAN 1954–
Hollstein's German Engravings, Etchings and Woodcuts c.1400–1700, 89 vols to date, Ouderkerk aan den Ijssel 1954 [continuing]

HONIG 2008
E. Honig, 'Art, Honor, and Excellence in Early Modern Europe', in *Beyond Price: Value in Culture, Economics, and the Arts*, eds M. Hutter and D. Throsby, Cambridge 2008, pp. 89–105

DE HOOP-SCHEFFER 1886
J.G. de Hoop-Scheffer, *Geschichte der Reformation in den Niederlanden von ihrem Beginn bis zum Jahre 1531*, Leipzig 1886

HOWELL JOLLY 1983
P. Howell Jolly, 'Antonello da Messina's *Saint Jerome in His Study*: An Iconographic Analysis', *The Art Bulletin*, 65 (June 1983), pp. 238–53

HUIZINGA 1954
J. Huizinga, *Erasmus and the Age of Reformation*, New York and London 1954 [1st published as *Erasmus of Rotterdam*, New York and London 1924]

HUTCHISON 1990
J. Campbell Hutchison, *Albrecht Dürer: A Biography*, Princeton 1990

ISHIKAWA 2004
C. Ishikawa, *The Retablo de Isabel la Católica by Juan de Flandes and Michel Sittow*, Turnhout 2004

JANSSEN 1862
H.Q.Q. Janssen, *Jacobus Praepositus. Luthers leerling en vriend*, Amsterdam 1862

JEON 2005
H. Jeon, *Meditatio mortis. Zur Ikonographie des heiligen Hieronymus mit dem Totenschädel unter besonderer Berücksichtigung des Lissaboner Gemäldes von Albrecht Dürer*, PhD dissertation, Westfälischen Wilhelms-Universität, Münster, 2005

JUNGBLUT 1967
R. Jungblut, *Hieronymus: Darstellung und Verrehrung eines Kirchenvaters*, Tübingen 1967

JUSTI 1888
C. Justi, 'Die portugiesische Malerei des 16. Jahrhunderts', *Jahrbuch der Königlich Preussischen Kunstsammlungen*, §9 (1888), pp. 137–59

KAI SASS 1976
E. Kai Sass, 'A la recherche d'un portrait disparu de Christian II, roi de Danemark, peint par Albrecht Dürer en 1521', *Hafnia: Copenhagen Papers in the History of Art* (1976), pp. 163–84

KALKOFF 1897
P. Kalkoff, 'Zur Lebensgeschichte Albrecht Dürer's', *Repertorium für Kunstwissenschaft*, 20 (1897), pp. 443–63

KALKOFF 1898
P. Kalkoff, *Briefe, Depeschen und Berichten über Luther von Wormser Reichstage 1521*, Halle 1898

KALKOFF 1903
P. Kalkoff, 'Die Anfänge der Gegenreformation in den Niederlanden', *Schriften des Vereins für Reformationsgeschichte*, 21 (1903), 2 vols, nos 79, 81

KARLSRUHE 2007
J. Mack-Andrick (ed.), *Grünewald und seine Zeit*, exh. cat., Staatliche Kunsthalle Karlsruhe, Munich and Berlin 2007

KARLSRUHE 2019
H. Jacob-Friesen (ed.), *Hans Baldung Grien – heilig, unheilig*, Staatliche Kunsthalle Karlsruhe, Berlin 2019

KATHKE 1997
P. Kathke, *Porträt und Accessoire. Eine Bildnisform im 16. Jahrhundert*, Berlin 1997

KEMPERDICK 2004
S. Kemperdick, *Martin Schongauer: Eine Monographie*, Petersberg 2004

KIM 2014
D. Kim, *The Traveling Artist in the Italian Renaissance: Geography, Mobility, and Style*, New Haven and London 2014

KLOEK 1978
W. Kloek, 'The drawings of Lucas van Leyden', *Lucas van Leyden Studies. Nederlands Kunsthistorisch Jaarboek*, eds J.P. Filedt Kok, W.T. Kloek and I.M. Veldman (eds), 29 (1978), pp. 425–58

KOERNER 1993
J.L. Koerner, *The Moment of Self-Portraiture in German Renaissance Art*, Chicago 1993

KOERNER 2010
J.L. Koerner, 'Epiphanies of the Black Magus at 1500', in *The Image of the Black in Western Art*, 3, no. 1: *The Sixteenth through Eighteenth Centuries*, ed. D. Bindman, Cambridge, MA, 2010, pp. 7–92

KONOWITZ 1990–1
E. Konowitz, 'Drawings as Intermediary Stages: Some Working Methods of Dirk Vellert and Albrecht Dürer re-examined', *Simiolus*, 20 (1990–1), pp. 142–52

KOPP-SCHMIDT 2004
G. Kopp-Schmidt, 'Mit den Farben des Apelles. Antikes Künstlerlob in Dürers Selbstbildnis von 1500', *Wolfenbütteler Renaissance-Mitteilungen*, 28 (2004), pp. 1–24

KORENY 1985
F. Koreny, *Albrecht Dürer und die Tier- und Pflanzenstudien der Renaissance*, Munich 1985

KORENY 2008
F. Koreny, 'Alberto Durero y los Países Bajos [Albrecht Dürer und die Niederlande]', in *El Siglo de Durero. Problemas historiográficos*, ed. M. del Mar Borobia Guerrero, Madrid 2008, pp. 160–79

KOSCHATZKY 1993
W. Koschatzky, *Die Kunst der Zeichnung: Technik, Geschichte, Meisterwerke*, Salzburg and Vienna 1993

KOSCHATZKY AND STROBL 1971
W. Koschatzky and A. Strobl, *Die Dürer Zeichnungen der Albertina*, Salzburg 1971

KRAUSMAN BEN-AMOS 2000
I. Krausman Ben-Amos, 'Gifts and Favors: Informal Support in Early Modern England', *The Journal of Modern History*, 72 (June 2000), pp. 295–338

KRISCHEL AND SCHAEFER 2009
R. Krischel and I. Schaefer, 'Ein unbekanntes Gemälde des Jacob Cornelisz. van Oostsanen', *Wallraf-Richartz-Jahrbuch*, 70 (2009), pp. 81–118

KRODEL AND BRECHT 2012
G.G. Krodel and M. Brecht (eds), 'Dürers Luther-Bücher: Ein Beitrag zur Dürer-Biographie', *Schriften des Vereins für Reformationsgeschichte*, vol. 123, Heidelberg 2012

LANDAU AND PARSHALL 1994
D. Landau and P. Parshall, *The Renaissance Print 1470–1550*, New Haven and London 1994

LANGE-KRACH 2017
H. Lange-Krach, *Das Gebetbuch Kaiser Maximilians I: meisterhafte Zeichnungen der deutschen Renaissance*, 2 vols, Lucerne 2017

LEEFLANG 2015
M. Leeflang, *Joos van Cleve: A Sixteenth-Century Antwerp Artist and his Workshop*, Turnhout 2015

LE GLAY 1839
A.J.G. Le Glay (ed.), *Correspondance de l'Empereur Maximilien Ier et de Marguerite d'Autriche, sa fille, gouvernante des Pays-Bas*, vol. 2, Paris 1839

LEHMANN 2002
A.-S. Lehmann, 'Adam en Eva. De paradenaakten van het noorden', in *Kunstschrift*, 46 (2002), pp. 18–27

LEIDEN 2011
C. Vogelaar, J.P. Filedt Kok, H. Leeflang and I.M. Veldman (eds), *Lucas van Leyden en de Renaissance*, exh. cat., Museum De Lakenhal, Leiden 2011

LEUVEN 2016
J. van der Stock (ed.), *In Search of Utopia: Art and Science in the Era of Thomas More*, exh. cat., M-Museum Leuven, Leuven 2016

LEUVEN AND PARIS 2013
J. van Grieken, G. Luijten and J. van der Stock (eds), *Hieronymus Cock: The Renaissance in Print*, exh. cat., Illuminare – Centre for the Study of Medieval Art, Leuven, and the Institut Néerlandais, Paris, English edn, Brussels 2013

LEVEY 1959
M. Levey, *The German School*, National Gallery Catalogues, London 1959

LIPPMANN 1883–1929
F. Lippmann (ed.), *Zeichnungen von Albrecht Dürer in Nachbildungen*, 7 vols, Berlin 1883–1929

LÖCHER 1997
K. Löcher (ed.), *Die Gemälde des 16. Jahrhunderts* (Germanisches Nationalmuseum, Nuremberg), Ostfildern-Ruit 1997

LÖCHER 2004
K. Löcher, 'Zu Dürers Skizzenbuch der Reise in die Niederlande 1520/1521. Der Augsburger Kaufmann Markus Ulstett', *Wallraf-Richartz-Jahrbuch*, 65 (2004), pp. 315–24

LONDON 1995
G. Bartrum, *German Renaissance Prints 1490–1550*, exh. cat., British Museum, London 1995

LONDON 2002
G. Bartrum, *Albrecht Dürer and his Legacy: The Graphic Work of a Renaissance Artist*, exh. cat., British Museum, London 2002

LONDON 2008
L. Campbell et al., *Renaissance Faces: Van Eyck to Titian*, exh. cat., National Gallery, London 2008

LONDON 2010
M. Evans, C. Browne and A. Nesselrath, *Raphael: Cartoons and Tapestries for the Sistine Chapel*, exh. cat., Victoria and Albert Museum, London 2010

LONDON 2013
S. Buck and S. Porras (eds), *The Young Dürer: Drawing the Figure*, exh. cat., Courtauld Institute Galleries, London 2013

LONDON AND BERLIN 2018
C. Campbell et al., *Mantegna and Bellini: A Renaissance Family*, exh. cat., National Gallery, London, and Gemäldegalerie, Berlin, London 2018

LONDON AND LOS ANGELES 2003
T. Kren and S. McKendrick, *Illuminating the Renaissance: The Triumph of Flemish Manuscript Painting in Europe*, exh. cat., Getty Museum, Los Angeles and Royal Academy of Arts, London 2003

LORENZ 1904
L. Lorenz, *Die Mariendarstellungen Albrecht Dürers* (*Studien zur deutschen Kunstgeschichte*, vol. 55), Strasbourg 1904

LOSCHEK 1988
I. Loschek, *Reclams Mode- und Kostümlexikon*, 2 vols, Stuttgart 1988

LÜBBEKE 1991
I. Lübbeke, *The Thyssen-Bornemisza Collection: Early German Painting, 1350–1550*, London 1991

LUGT 1968
F. Lugt, *Inventaire general des dessin des écoles du nord. Maîtres des anciens Pays-bas né savant 1550*, Paris 1968

LUTHER 1883–2009
M. Luther, *D. Martin Luthers Werke: kritische Gesamtausgabe*, 127 vols, Weimar 1883–2009

LUTZ 1968
H. Lutz, 'Albrecht Dürer in der Geschichte der Reformation', *Historische Zeitschrift*, 206 (February 1968), pp. 22–44

MCDONALD 2004
M. McDonald, *The Print Collection of Ferdinand Columbus (1488–1539): A Renaissance Collector in Seville*, London 2004

MACKOR 1995
A. Mackor, 'Marinus van Reymerswale: Painter, Lawyer and Iconoclast?', *Oud Holland*, 109 (1995), pp. 191–200

MADRID 2007
A. Vergara (ed.), *Patinir: Essays and Critical Catalogue*, exh. cat., Museo Nacional del Prado, Madrid 2007

MADRID, BRUGES AND NEW YORK 2005
T.-H. Borchert (ed.), *Memling and the Art of Portraiture*, exh. cat., Museo Thyssen-Bornemisza, Madrid, Groeningemuseum, Brügge and The Frick Collection, New York, Stuttgart 2005

MANDRELLA 1999
D. Mandrella, *Dessins allemands et flamands du musée Condé à Chantilly. De Dürer à Rubens*, Paris 1999

MARLIER 1954
G. Marlier, *Erasme et la peinture flamande de son temps*, Domme 1954

MARLIER 1966
G. Marlier, *La Renaissance flamande: Pierre Coecke d'Alost*, Brussels 1966

MARNEF 1996
G. Marnef, *Antwerp in the Age of Reformation: Underground Protestantism in a Commercial Metropolis, 1550–1577*, Baltimore 1996

MATTEI 2019
F. Mattei, 'I disegni dell'Anonimo A nel "Taccuino Mantovano" di Berlino. Antichità e architettura moderna al nord delle Alpi', in *Disegnare l'antico, riproporre l'antico nel Cinquecento*, eds S. Ferrari and A. Pattanaro, Padua 2019, pp. 41–60

MECHELEN 2005
D. Eichberger (ed.), *Women of Distinction: Margaret of York and Margaret of Austria*, exh. cat., Lamot, Mechelen, 2005

MEDER 1932
J. Meder, *Dürer-Katalog. Ein Handbuch über Albrecht Dürers Stiche, Radierungen, Holzschnitte, deren Züstande, Ausgabe und Wasserzeichen*, Vienna 1932

MEISS 1963
M. Meiss, 'French and Italian Variations on an Early Fifteenth Century Theme: Saint Jerome in His Study', *Gazette des Beaux-Arts*, 62 (1963), pp. 147–70

MEISS 1974
M. Meiss, 'Scholarship and Penitence in the Early Renaissance: The Image of St. Jerome', *Pantheon* 32 (1974), pp. 134–40

MENDE 1969
U. Mende, 'Dürers Zeichnungen livländischer Frauentrachten und seine sogenannte Türgin', in *Kunstgeschichtliche Aufsätze*, ed. J. Gaus, Cologne 1969, pp. 24–41

MENDE 1983
M. Mende, 'Albrecht Dürer d. Ä', *Allgemeines Künstlerlexikon*, vol. 30, Munich, Leipzig and Berlin 1983

MENDE 1985
M. Mende, 'Dürer's so-called Portrait of Damião de Góis: Toward a Reconstruction of a Lost Painting of 1521', in *Tribute to Lotte Brand Philip, Art Historian and Detective*, ed. W.W. Clarke, New York 1985, pp. 103–11

MENSGER 2002
A. Mensger, *Jan Gossaert*, Berlin 2002

MENTGES 2015
G. Mentges, 'Mode, Städte und Nationen: Die Trachtenbücher der Renaissance', in *In Mode. Kleider und Bilder aus Renaissance und Frühbarock*, ed. J. Zander-Seidel, exh. cat., Germanisches Nationalmuseum, Nuremberg, Nuremberg 2015, pp. 144–51

METTINGEN 2012
G.T. Clark and M. Kordhanke (eds), *Von der Schönheit der Präzision: Faszination Buchkunst und Grafik mit der Liberna Collection*, exh. cat., Draiflessen Collection, Mettingen 2012

MICHAELIS 1995
R. Michaelis, *Staatliche Museen zu Berlin – Preußischer Kulturbesitz. Dokumentation der Verluste*, vol. 1: *Gemäldegalerie*, Berlin 1995

MIEDEMA 1994–2002
H. Miedema (ed.), *Karel van Mander: The Lives of the Illustrious Netherlandish and German Painters, from the first edition of the Schilder-boeck (1603–), preceded by the lineage, circumstances and place of birth, life and works of Karel van Mander, painter and poet and likewise his death and burial, from the second edition of the Schilder-boeck (1616–1618)*, 6 vols, Doornspijk 1994–2002

MILAN 2018
B. Aikema (ed.), *Dürer e il Rinascimento tra Germania e Italia*, exh. cat., Palazzo Reale, Milan 2018

MINNEAPOLIS, NEW YORK AND ATLANTA 2016
K. Herbst, *Martin Luther: Treasures of the Reformation*, exh. cat., Minneapolis Institute of Art, Morgan Library and Museum, New York, and Pitts Theology Library, Emory University, Atlanta, Dresden 2016

MUNICH 2006
R. Eikelmann (ed.), *Conrat Meit. Bildhauer der Renaissance*, exh. cat., Bayerische Nationalmuseum, Munich 2006

MUYLAERT 2011–12
S. Muylaert, 'De Brugse goud- en zilversmeden in de late middeleeuwen: een prosopografische Studie', MA thesis, University of Ghent 2011–12

MYNORS 1974–2003
R.A.B. Mynors et al., *The Correspondence of Erasmus*, 12 vols, Toronto 1974–2003

NASH 2008
S. Nash, *Northern Renaissance Art*, Oxford 2008

NESSELRATH 1986
A. Nesselrath, 'I libri di disegni di antichità. Tentativo di una tipologia', in *Memoria dell'antico nell'arte italiana*, ed. Salvatore Settis, Turin 1986, vol. 3, pp. 87–147

NESSELRATH 1993A
A. Nesselrath, *Das Fossombroner Skizzenbuch*, London 1993

NESSELRATH 1993B
A. Nesselrath, 'Raphael's Gift for Dürer', in *Master Drawings*, 31, no. 4: *Essays in Memory of Jacob Bean (1923–1992)*, New York 1993, pp. 376–89

NESSELRATH 2011A
A. Nesselrath, 'A Little Gift from an Old Friend: Dürer's Drawings by Fra Giocondo', *Print Quarterly*, 28: *Festschrift für Antony Griffiths* (September 2011), pp. 244–8

NESSELRATH 2011B
A. Nesselrath, 'Raffael und die Meister des Nordens', in *Himmlischer Glanz. Raffael, Dürer und Grünewald malen die Madonna*, eds A. Henning and A. Nesselrath, exh. cat., Gemäldegalerie Alte Meister, Dresden, Munich 2011, pp. 78–85

NESSELRATH 2014
A. Nesselrath, *Der Zeichner und sein Buch – Die Darstellung der antiken Architektur im 15. und 16. Jahrhundert*, Mainz 2014

NESSELRATH 2019
A. Nesselrath, 'The Acts of the Apostles: Raphael's Design Process for Tapestries in the Sistine Chapel', *Studia Bruxellae*, 13 (2019), pp. 311–23

NESSELRATH 2020A
A. Nesselrath, 'Raffael und Dürer. Dialog und Wertschätzung über weite Fernen', in *Raffael. Macht der Bilder – Die Tapisserien und ihre Wirkung*, ed. S. Koja, Dresden 2020, pp. 176–85

NESSELRATH 2020B
A. Nesselrath, 'Disegni e cartoni – i materiali preparatori per gli arazzi di Raffaello', in *Leone X e Raffaello in Sistina. Gli Arazzi degli Apostoli Arazzi*, ed. A.M. De Strobel, vol. 1, Vatican City 2020, pp. 87–116

NEW HOLLSTEIN DUTCH 1993–
The New Hollstein: Dutch and Flemish etchings, engravings and woodcuts 1450–1700, Amsterdam 1993 [continuing]

NEW YORK 2004
H. Evans (ed.), *Byzantium: Faith and Power*, exh. cat., Metropolitan Museum of Art, New York 2004

NEW YORK 2012
S. Alsteens and F. Spira (eds), *Dürer and Beyond: Central European Drawings in The Metropolitan Museum of Art, 1400–1700*, exh. cat., Metropolitan Museum of Art, New York 2012

NEW YORK 2019
C. Jenkins, N. Orenstein and F. Spira, *The Renaissance of Etching*, exh. cat., Metropolitan Museum of Art, New York 2019

NEW YORK AND LONDON 2010
M.W. Ainsworth, *Man, Myth, and Sensual Pleasures: Jan Gossart's Renaissance: The Complete Works*, exh. cat., Metropolitan Museum of Art, New York, and National Gallery, London, New Haven and London 2010

NEW YORK AND WASHINGTON 1994
S.K. Scher, *The Currency of Fame: Portrait Medals of the Renaissance*, exh. cat., Frick Collection, New York, and National Gallery of Art, Washington, New York 1994

NUREMBERG 1971
Albrecht Dürer 1471–1971, exh. cat., Germanisches Nationalmuseum, Nuremberg, Munich 1971

NUREMBERG 2012
D. Hess and T. Eser (eds), *The Early Dürer/Der frühe Dürer*, exh. cat., Germanisches Nationalmuseum, Nuremberg 2012

NUREMBERG 2019
B. Baumbauer, D. Hirschfelder and M. Teget-Welz (eds), *Michael Wolgemut: Mehr als Dürers Lehrer*, exh. cat., Albrecht-Dürer Haus, Nuremberg, Regensburg 2019

O'MALLEY 1988
J.W. O'Malley (ed.), *Collected Works of Erasmus: Spiritualia, Enchiridion, De contemptu mundi, De vidua christiana*, vol. 66, Toronto 1988

ORENSTEIN 1996
N.M. Orenstein, *Hendrick Hondius and the Business of Prints in Seventeenth-Century Holland*, Rotterdam 1996

OSNABRÜCK 2003
T. Schauerte, *Albrecht Dürer. Das grosse Glück*, exh. cat., Kulturgeschichtliches Museum, Osnabrück 2003

OSTEN 1935
G. von der Osten, *Der Schmerzensmann*, Berlin 1935

OXFORD 2017
C. Whistler and B. Thomas (eds), *Raphael: The Drawings*, exh. cat., Ashmolean Museum, Oxford 2017

PABEL 2008
H. Pabel, *Herculean Labours: Erasmus and the Editing of Saint Jerome's Letters*, Leiden and Boston 2008

PÄCHT 1963
O. Pächt, 'Zur Entsteing des Hieronymus im Gehäuse', *Pantheon*, 22 (1963), pp. 131–42

PANOFSKY 1915
E. Panofsky, *Dürers Kunsttheorie vornehmlich in ihrem Verhältnis zur Kunsttheorie der Italiener*, Berlin 1915

PANOFSKY 1943
E. Panofsky, *Albrecht Dürer*, 2 vols, Princeton 1943 (rev. edn 1945)

PANOFSKY 1945
E. Panofsky, *Das Leben und die Kunst Albrecht Dürers*, Princeton 1945 (rev. edn 1995)

PANOFSKY 1955 (2005)
E. Panofsky, *The Life and Art of Albrecht Dürer*, 2 vols (1943; 2nd edn 1945), 4th edn, Princeton 1955 (rev. edn ed. J. Chipps Smith, Princeton 2005)

PANOFSKY 1971
E. Panofsky, *Early Netherlandish Painting: Its Origin and Character*, 2 vols, New York 1971

PARIS 1991
E. Starcky et al. (eds), *Dessins de Dürer et de la Renaissance germanique dans les collections publiques parisiennes*, exh. cat., Cabinet des Dessins, Musée du Louvre, Paris 1991

PARIS 2017
C. Scailliérez (ed.), *François Ier et l'art des Pays-Bas*, exh. cat., Musée du Louvre, Paris 2017

PASSAVANT 1860–4
J.D. Passavant, *Le Peintre Graveur: contenant l'histoire de la gravure sur bois, sur métal et au burin jusque vers la fin du XVI siècle*, 6 vols, Leipzig 1860–4

PASZTORY 1989
E. Pasztory, 'Identity and Difference: The Uses and Meanings of Pictorial Styles', *Studies in the History of Art*, 27 (1989), pp. 14–40

PEARSON 2005
A. Pearson, *Envisioning Gender in Burgundian Devotional Art, 1350–1530: Experience, Authority, Resistance* (*Women and Gender in the Early Modern World*), Farnham and Burlington, VT, 2005

PELIKAN AND LEHMAN 1955–86
J. Pelikan and H.T. Lehman (eds), *Luther's Works, American Edition*, 55 vols, Philadelphia 1955–86

PETRIOLI TOFANI 1987
A. Petrioli Tofani, *Gabinetto disegni e stampe degli Uffizi, Inventario*, vol. 2: *Disegni esposti*, Florence 1987

PHILADELPHIA 2006
M. Cole (ed.), *The Early Modern Painter-Etcher*, exh. cat., Ross Gallery, Philadelphia 2006

PLAGEMANN 2002
V. Plagemann, 'Tod in Bologna. Hans Cranachs Reise 1537. Zur Frühgeschichte der Künstlerreisen nach Italien', *Niederdeutsche Beiträge zur Kunstgeschichte*, 41 (2002), pp. 37–155

POLICICCHIO 2018
G. Policicchio, 'Het album met miniaturen en tekeningen van Giovanna Garzoni uit de Accademia di San Luca', in *De dames van de barok. Vrouwelijke schilders in het Italië van de 16de en 17de eeuw, les dames du baroque. Femmes peintres dans l'Italie du XVIe et XVIIe siècle*, eds V. de Beir, F. Solinas and A. Tapié, exh. cat., Museum voor Schone Kunsten, Ghent, Ghent 2018, pp. 188–226

PONTORMO 1984
J. Pontormo, *Il libro mio*, ed. S.S. Nigro, Genoa 1984

PRAGUE 2006
O. Kotková (ed.), *Albrecht Dürer: The Feast of the Rose Garlands*, exh. cat., Národní Galerie v Praze, Prague 2006

PRANGE 2007
P. Prange, *Die Sammlunger der Hamburger Kunsthalle, Kupferstichkbainett* (2 vols), vol. 1: *Deutsche Zeichnungen, 1450–1800*, Cologne, Weimar and Vienna 2007

PRICE 2003
D. Price, *Albrecht Dürer's Renaissance: Humanism, Reformation and the Art of Faith*, Ann Arbor 2003

PUGLISI AND BARCHAM 2013
C. Puglisi and W. Barcham (eds), *New Perspectives on the Man of Sorrows*, Kalamazoo 2013

VAN REGTEREN ALTENA AND FRERICHS 1965
J.Q. van Regteren Altena and L. C. J. Frerichs, *Selected Drawings from the Printroom*, Amsterdam 1965

REICHE ET AL. 2002
I. Reiche et al., 'Non-Destructive Investigations of Dürer's Silverpoint Drawings by PIXE and SR-XRF', in *Art* 2002, pp. 1–8

REICHE ET AL. 2004
I. Reiche et al., 'Spatially Resolved Synchrotron-Induced X-Ray Fluorescence Analyses of Metal Point Drawings and Their Mysterious Inscriptions', *Spectrochimica Acta Part B: Atomic Spectroscopy*, 59 (2004), pp. 1657–62

REICHE, MERCHEL AND RADTKE 2005
I. Reiche, S. Merchel and M. Radtke, 'Auf den Spuren Albrecht Dürers – Zerstörungsfreie Spurenanalyse mit ortsaufgelöster Synchrotronstrahlungs-*induzierter* Röntgenfluoreszenzanalyse', *ZfP-Zeitung*, 96 (2005), pp. 40–5

RICE 1985
E.F. Rice, *Saint Jerome in the Renaissance*, London 1985

RIDDERBOS 1984
B. Ridderbos, *Saint and Symbol: Images of Saint Jerome in Early Italian Art*, Groningen 1984

RINGBOM 1984
S. Ringbom, *Icon to Narrative: The Rise of the Dramatic Close-Up in Fifteenth-Century Devotional Painting*, Doornspijk 1984

ROBERT 2003
J. Robert, *Konrad Celtis und das Projekt der deutschen Dichtung. Studien zur humanistischen Konstitution von Poetik, Philosophie, Nation und Ich*, Tübingen 2003

ROCCASECCA 2011
P. Roccasecca, 'Il ruolo della teoria düreriana nella formazione degli artisti nell'Accademia del Disegno di Roma', in *Dürer, l'Italia e l'Europa*, eds S. Ebert-Schifferer and K. Herrmann Fiore, Milan 2011, pp. 88–97

ROMDAHL 1928
A.L. Romdahl, 'Dürer und die Apokalypse', in *Albrecht Dürer. Festschrift der internationalen Dürer-Forschung*, Leipzig and Berlin 1928, pp. 15–28

ROME 2007
K. Hermann Fiore, *Dürer e l'Italia*, exh. cat., Scuderie del Quirinale, Rome 2007

ROME AND FLORENCE 2020
M. Faietti and M. Lafranconi (eds), *Raffaello 1520–1483*, exh. cat., Scuderie del Quirinale, Rome and Galleria degli Uffizi, Florence, Milan 2020

ROTTERDAM 2008
P. van der Coelen and M. Bol, *Images of Erasmus*, exh. cat., Museum Boijmans Van Beuningen, Rotterdam 2008

ROWLANDS 1993
J. Rowlands, *Drawings by German Artists and Artists from German-Speaking Regions of Europe in the Department of Prints and Drawings in the British Museum: The Fifteenth Century, and the Sixteenth Century by Artists born before 1530*, 2 vols, London 1993

RUBLACK, HAYWARD AND TIRAMANI 2015
U. Rublack, M. Hayward and J. Tiramani, *The First Book of Fashion: The Book of Clothes of Matthaeus and Veit Konrad Schwarz of Augsburg*, London 2015

RUDLOFF 1985
O. Rudloff, 'Bonae Litterae et Lutherus. Texte und Untersuchungen zu den Anfängen der Theologie des Bremer Reformators Jakob Propst', published as vol. 14 of the *Hospitium Ecclesiae: Forschungen zur bremischen Kirchengeschichte*, Bremen 1985

RUPPRICH 1956–69
H. Rupprich (ed.), *Dürer. Schriftlicher Nachlass*, 3 vols, Berlin 1956–69

SAHM 2002
H. Sahm, *Dürers kleinere Texte. Konventionen als Spielraum für Individualität*, Tübingen 2002

SALZMANN 1991
S. Salzmann (ed.), *Dokumentation der durch Auslagerung im 2. Weltkrieg vermißten Kunstwerke der Kunsthalle Bremen*, Bremen 1991

SANDRART 1679 (1994)
J. von Sandrart, *Teutsche Academie der Edlen Bau- Bild- und Mahlerey-Künste. Nürnberg 1675–1680*, reproduction of original with an introduction by C. Klemm, 3 vols, Nördlingen 1994

SAVILLE 1920
M.H. Saville, 'The Earliest Notices Concerning the Conquest of Mexico by Cortés in 1519', *Indian Notes and Monographs*, 9, no. 1 (1920)

SCHAUERTE 2001
T. Schauerte, *Die Ehrenpforte für Kaiser Maximilian I. Dürer und Altdorfer im Dienst des Herrschers*, Berlin 2001

SCHAUERTE 2006
T. Schauerte, 'Dürer und Spranger: Ein Autographenfund', in *Mitteilungen des Vereins für Geschichte der Stadt Nürnberg*, 93 (2006), pp. 25–69

SCHAUERTE 2012
T. Schauerte, *Dürer. Das ferne Genie. Eine Biographie*, Stuttgart 2012

SCHAUERTE 2015
T. Schauerte, *Dürer und Celtis. Die Nürnberger Poetenschule im Aufbruch*, Munich 2015

SCHMID 2003
W. Schmid, *Dürer als Unternehmer. Kunst, Humanismus und Ökonomie in Nürnberg um 1500*, Trier 2003

SCHMIDT 2018
S. Schmidt, *Abbild Selbstbild. Das Porträt in Nürnberg um 1500*, Wiesbaden 2018

SCHOCH, MENDE AND SCHERBAUM 2001–4
Albrecht Dürer. Das Druckgraphische Werk, vol. 1: *Kupferstiche, Eisenradierungen und Kaltnadelblätter* (2001); vol. 2: *Holzschnitte und Holzschnittfolgen* (2002); vol. 3: *Buchillustrationen* (2004), Munich 2001–4

SCHÖNHERR 1884
D. Schönherr, 'urkunden und regesten aus dem k. k. Statthalterei-Archiv in Innsbruck', *Jahrbuch der kunsthistorischen Sammlungen des Allerhöchsten Kaiserhauses*, 2 (1884), pp. i–clxxii

SCHUBERT AND HOLBORN 1971
H. von Schubert and H. Holborn, *Lazarus Spengler und die Reformation in Nürnberg*, vol. 17: *Quellen und Forschungen zur Reformationsgeschichte*, Leipzig 1971

SEEBASS 1971
Gottfried Seebass, 'Dürers Stellung in der Reformatorischen Bewegung', in *Albrecht Dürers Umwelt. Festschrift zum 500. Geburtstag Albrecht Dürers am 21. Mai 1971*, Nuremberg 1971, pp. 101–31

SHEARMAN 1972
J. Shearman, *Raphael's Cartoons in the Collection of Her Majesty the Queen and the Tapestries for the Sistine Chapel*, London 1972

SILVER 1984
L. Silver, *The Paintings of Quinten Massys*, Oxford 1984

SILVER 1986
L. Silver, '*Figure nude, historie, e poesie: Jan Gossaert and the Renaissance Nude in the Netherlands*', *Nederlands Kunsthistorisch Jaarboek*, 37 (1986), pp. 1–40

SILVER 1987
L. Silver, 'The "Gothic" Gossaert: Native and Traditional Elements in a Mabuse Madonna', *Pantheon*, 45 (1987), pp. 58–69

SILVER 1997
L. Silver, 'The Influence of Anxiety: The Agony in the Garden as Artistic Theme in the Era of Dürer', *Umení*, 45 (1997), pp. 420–9

SILVER 2008
L. Silver, *Marketing Maximilian: The Visual Ideology of a Holy Roman Emperor*, Princeton 2008

SILVER 2009
L. Silver, 'Full of Grace: "Mariolatry" in Post-Reformation Germany', in *The Idol in the Age of Art*, eds M. Cole and R. Zorach, Farnham 2009, pp. 289–315

SILVER AND CHIPPS SMITH 2010
L. Silver and J. Chipps Smith (eds), *The Essential Dürer*, Philadelphia 2010

SPRING 2018
M. Spring (ed.), *National Gallery Technical Bulletin*, vol. 39, London 2018

SPRINGER 1887
J. Springer, 'Dürer und die Umrissstiche "Die Kreuzigung"', *Jahrbuch der Königlich Preussischen Kunstsammlungen*, 8 (1887), pp. 56–66

SPUFFORD 2002
P. Spufford, *Power and Profit: The Merchant in Medieval Europe*, London 2002

ST PETERSBURG 2010
A. Larionov, *From Gothic to Mannerism: Early Netherlandish Drawing in the State Hermitage Collection*, exh. cat., State Hermitage Museum, St Petersburg 2010

STEER 1982
J. Steer, *Alvise Vivarini, his art and influence*, Cambridge and New York 1982

STEINBERG 1983
L. Steinberg, *The Sexuality of Christ in Renaissance Art and in Modern Oblivion*, New York 1983

STRAUSS 1974
W.L. Strauss, *The Complete Drawings of Albrecht Dürer*, 6 vols, New York 1974

STRIEDER 1982
P. Strieder, *Albrecht Dürer: Paintings, Prints, Drawings*, trans. N.M. Gordon and W.L. Strauss, New York 1982

STRIEDER 2012
P. Strieder, *Dürer*, 3rd rev. edn, Königstein im Taunus 2012

STROBEL AND KOSCHATZKY 1971
A. Strobel and W. Koschatzky, *Die Dürer Zeichungen der Albertina*, Vienna 1971

STRÜMPELL 1925–6
A. Strümpell, 'Hieronymus im Gehäuse', *Marburger Jahrbuch für Kunstwissenschaft*, 2 (1925–6), pp. 173–252

STUBBE 1967
W. Stubbe, *Hundert Meisterzeichnungen aus der Hamburger Kunsthalle 1500 bis 1800*, vol. 5, Hamburg 1967

SUCKALE 2009
Robert Suckale, *Die Erneuerung der Malkunst vor Dürer*, 2 vols, Petersberg 2009

SULZBERGER 1959
S. Sulzberger, 'Dürer a-t-il vu à Bruxelles les cartons de Raphaël?', *Gazette des Beaux-Arts*, 54 (1959), pp. 177–84

SUYKERBUYK 2017
R. Suykerbuyk, *The Matter of Piety: Material Culture in Zoutleeuw's Church of St Leonard (c.1450–1620)*, PhD dissertation, University of Ghent, 2017

SWOBODA 2009
G. Swoboda, 'Tausch bei Hofe: Über die Gemäldesammlung Erzherzog Ferdinand Karls und den Kulturtransfer zwischen Florenz und Innsbruck im 17. Jahrhundert', in *Ferdinand Karl: Ein Sonnenkönig in Tirol*, ed. S. Haag, exh. cat., Schloss Ambras, Vienna, Innsbruck and Vienna 2009, pp. 103–15

TENTLER 1965
T.N. Tentler, 'Forgiveness and Consolation in the Religious Thought of Erasmus', *Studies in the Renaissance*, 12 (1965), pp. 110–33

TIETZE AND TIETZE-CONRAT 1938
H. Tietze and E. Tietze-Conrat, *Kritisches Verzeichnis der Werke Albrecht Dürers* (2 vols), vol. 2: *Der reife Dürer*, Basel and Leipzig 1938

TRUSTED 1990
M. Trusted, *German Renaissance Medals: A Catalogue of the Collection in the Victoria and Albert Museum*, London 1990

TURNHOUT 1998
L.S. Dixon (ed.), *In Detail: New Studies in Northern Renaissance Art in Honor of Walter S. Gibson*, Turnhout 1998

ULLMANN 1842
C. Ullmann, *Reformatoren vor der Reformation, vornehmlich in Deutschland und den Niederlanden*, 2 vols, Hamburg 1842

ULLMANN 1994
E. Ullmann, 'Albrecht Dürer – Selbstbildnisse und autobiographische Schriften als Zeugnisse der Entwicklung seiner Persönlichkeit', in *Sitzungsberichte der Sächsischen Akademie der Wissenschaften zu Leipzig, Phil.-hist. Klasse*, 133, no. 3 (1994), pp. 3–20

UNVERFEHRT 2003
G. Unverfehrt, *Wein statt Wasser. Essen und Trinken bei Jheronimus Bosch*, Göttingen 2003

UNVERFEHRT 2007
G. Unverfehrt, *Das sah ich viel köstliche Dinge. Albrecht Dürers Reise in die Niederlande*, Göttingen 2007

VELDMAN 2015–16
I.M. Veldman, 'Portrait of an art collector: Pieter S piering van Silvercroon', *Simiolus*, 38, no. 4 (2015–16), pp. 228–49

VENICE 1999
B. Aikema and B. Brown (eds), *Renaissance Venice and the North: Crosscurrent in the Time of Dürer, Bellini and Titian*, exh. cat., Palazzo Grassi, Venice 1999

VENTURI 1924
A. Venturi, *L'arte a S. Gerolamo*, Milan 1924

VERMEYLEN 2003
F. Vermeylen, *Painting for the Market: Commercialization of Art in Antwerp's Golden Age,* Turnhout 2003

VETH AND MULLER 1918
J. Veth and S. Muller, *Albrecht Dürers Niederländische Reise*, 2 vols, Berlin and Utrecht 1918

VIENNA 1959
Präkolumbische Kunst aus Mexiko und Mittelamerika, exh. cat., Künstlerhaus Wien, Vienna 1959

VIENNA 1994
K. Schütz, *Albrecht Dürer im Kunsthistorischen Museum*, exh. cat., Kunsthistorisches Museum, Vienna 1994

VIENNA 2003
K.A. Schröder and M.L. Sternath (eds), *Albrecht Dürer*, exh. cat., Albertina, Vienna 2003

VIENNA 2012
E. Michel and M.L. Sternath (eds), *Kaiser Maximilian I und die Kunst der Dürerzeit* (*Emperor Maximilian I and the Age of Dürer*), exh. cat., Albertina, Vienna, Munich 2012

VIENNA 2019
C. Metzger (ed.), *Albrecht Dürer*, exh. cat., Albertina, Vienna, Munich 2019

VIENNA AND MUNICH 2011
S. Haag (ed.), *Dürer – Cranach – Holbein. Die Entdeckung des Menschen: das deutsche Porträt um 1500*, exh. cat., Kunsthistorisches Museum, Vienna, and Kunsthalle der Hypo-Kulturstiftung München, Munich 2011

VLAM 1977
G.A.H. Vlam, 'The Calling of Saint Matthew in Sixteenth-Century Flemish Painting', *The Art Bulletin*, 59 (December 1977), pp. 561–70

WALDECK 2016
A. Waldeck, 'Vincenzo Catena and Giorgione, Reconsidered', *Artibus et Historiae*, 37, no. 74 (2016), pp. 59–71

WALDMANN 1920
E. Waldmann, *Albrecht Dürers Handzeichnungen*, Leipzig 1920

WALDMANN 1933
E. Waldmann, *Albrecht Dürer. Sein Leben und seine Kunst*, Leipzig 1933

WALLEN 1983
B. Wallen, *Jan Van Hemessen: An Antwerp Painter Between Reform and Counter-reform*, Ann Arbor 1983

WASHINGTON 1991
J.A. Levinson (ed.), *Circa 1492: Art in the Age of Exploration*, exh. cat., National Gallery of Art, Washington, New Haven and London 1991

WASHINGTON 1999
From Schongauer to Holbein: Master Drawings from Basel and Berlin, exh. cat., National Gallery of Art, Washington, 1999

WASHINGTON 2013
A. Robison and K.A. Schröder, *Albrecht Dürer: Master Drawings, Watercolors, and Prints from the Albertina*, exh. cat., National Gallery of Art, Washington, 2013

WASHINGTON AND ANTWERP 2006
J. Hand, C. Metzger and R. Spronk, *Prayers and Portraits: Unfolding the Netherlandish Diptych*, exh. cat., National Gallery of Art, Washington, and Koninklijk Museum voor Schone Kunsten, Antwerp, New Haven and London 2006

WASHINGTON AND LONDON 2015
S. Sell and H. Chapman, *Drawing in Silver and Gold: Leonardo to Jasper Johns,* exh. cat., National Gallery of Art, Washington, and The British Museum, London, Princeton and Oxford 2015

WASHINGTON AND NEW YORK 1986
J.O. Hand, J.R. Judson, W.W. Robinson and M. Wolff, *The Age of Brueghel: Netherlandish Drawings in the Sixteenth Century*, exh. cat., National Gallery of Art, Washington, and Morgan Library & Museum, New York, Cambridge 1986

WEIAND 1993
C. Weiand, *Libri di famiglia« und Autobiographie in Italien zwischen Tre- und Cinquecento. Studien zur Entwicklung des Schreibens über sich selbst*, Tübingen 1993

WEIDEMA AND KOOPSTRA 2012
S. Weidema and A. Koopstra, *Jan Gossart: The Documentary Evidence*, Turnhout 2012

WEIXLGÄRTNER 1903
A. Weixlgärtner, 'Dürer und die Gliederpuppe', *Beiträge zur Kunstgeschichte. Franz Wickhoff gewidmet*, Vienna 1903, pp. 80–90

WELCH 2005
E. Welch, *Shopping in the Renaissance: Consumer Cultures in Italy 1400–1600*, London and New Haven 2005

WENIGER 2011
M. Weniger, *Sittow, Morros, Juan de Flandes. Drei Maler aus dem Norden am Hof Isabellas der Katholischen*, Kiel 2011

WERNER 2013
P. Werner, 'Die Menagerie des Landgrafen Karl. Ein Beitrag zur Einheit von Natur und Kunst im Barockzeitalter', dissertation, University of Kassel, 2013

WHITE 1971
C. White, *Dürer: The Artist and His Drawings*, New York 1971

WIEBEL 1988
C. Wiebel, *Askese und Endlichkeitsdemut in der italienischen Renaissance. Ikonologische Studien zum Bild des heiligen Hieronymus*, Weinheim 1988

WIESENER WOOD 1981
M. Wiesener Wood, 'Women in the Distributive Trades in Early Modern Nuremberg', *Sixteenth Century Journal*, 12,no. 2 (1981), pp. 3–13

WINKLER 1936–9
F. Winkler, *Die Zeichnungen Albrecht Dürers*, 4 vols, Berlin 1936–9

WINKLER 1957
F. Winkler, *Albrecht Dürer, Leben und Werk*, Berlin 1957

WÖLFFLIN 1971
H. Wölfflin, *The Art of Albrecht Dürer,* trans. Alastair and Heide Grieve, 3rd edn, New York 1971

WÖLFFLIN 1984
H. Wölfflin, *Die Kunst Albrecht Dürers* (1905, 2nd edn 1908), Munich 1984

WOUK 2015
E.H. Wouk, 'Antoine Perrenot de Granvelle, the Quatre Vents press, and the patronage of prints in early Modern Europe', *Simiolus*, 38, no. 1/2 (2015–16) pp. 31–61

WOUK 2018
E.H. Wouk, 'Frans Floris (1519/20–1570): Imagining a Northern Renaissance', *Brill's Studies in Intellectual History*, vol. 19, Leiden and Boston 2018

WRIGHT 1933
F.A. Wright, *Select Letters of Saint Jerome with an English Translation*, London and New York 1933

ZANDER-SEIDEL 1990
J. Zander-Seidel, *Textiler Hausrat. Kleidung und Haustextilien in Nürnberg von 1500–1650*, Munich 1990

ZIMMERMANN 2012
J. Zimmermann, *Recovering Theological Hermeneutics: An Incarnational-Trinitarian Theory of Interpretation*, Oregon 2012

ZINK 1968
F. Zink, *Die deutschen Handzeichnungen*, vol. 1: *Die Handzeichnungen bis zur Mitte des 16. Jahrhunderts*, Nuremberg 1968

LIST OF EXHIBITED WORKS

PROVENANCE AND REFERENCES COMPILED BY IMOGEN TEDBURY

A complete record of works included in the exhibition at the National Gallery, London. Works are listed alphabetically by artist, then by title, and then chronologically. Dimensions are given height followed by width.

Jacopo de' Barbari
A Sparrowhawk, 1510s
Oil on oak, 17.8 × 10.8 cm
The National Gallery, London. Layard Bequest, 1916 (NG3088)
[cat. 35]
PROVENANCE
Count Bertolazone d'Arache, Turin; Count Castellani, Turin, by whom sold around 1859; by 1869 presented by Sir James Hudson to Sir Austen Henry Layard, by whom bequeathed in 1916.
SELECTED LITERATURE
Davies 1961, pp. 43–4; Ferrari 2006, pp. 108–10, no. 17; Coburg 2010, pp. 220–2, no. 1.4.08.

Giovanni Bellini
The Assassination of Saint Peter Martyr, about 1505–7
Oil on wood, 99.7 × 165.1 cm
The National Gallery, London. Presented by Lady Eastlake, 1870 (NG812)
[cat. 33]
PROVENANCE
Seen by Sir Charles Lock Eastlake in the studio of Natale Schiavone, Venice, in 1854 and purchased from him that year; presented by Lady Eastlake in 1870.
SELECTED LITERATURE
Davies 1961, pp. 65–7; London and Berlin 2018, pp. 226–7, 238, 291–2; Spring 2018.

Hans Burgkmair
Standing Black Youth Dressed in a Feather Skirt, Cape and Headdress, 1520–30
Pen and black ink, with grey, brown and green wash, 15 × 16.1 cm
British Museum. Bequeathed by Sir Hans Sloane, 1753 (SL,5218.129)
[cat. 9]
PROVENANCE
Bequeathed by Sir Hans Sloane in 1753.
SELECTED LITERATURE
London 1988, p. 187, no. 158(b); Rowlands 1993, p. 47, no. 100; Frankfurt 2013, pp. 367–72.

Vincenzo Catena
Portrait of a Young Man, probably about 1510
Oil on wood, 30.5 × 23.5 cm
The National Gallery, London. Bought 1882 (NG1121)
[cat. 41]
PROVENANCE
Dukes of Hamilton, Hamilton Palace, perhaps as early as 1643; purchased in the Hamilton Palace sale, 24 June 1882, lot 344.
SELECTED LITERATURE
Gould 1975, pp. 52–3; Waldeck 2016, p. 68.

Joos van Cleve
Saint Jerome in his Study, 1521
Oil on panel, 99.7 × 83.8 cm
Harvard Art Museums / Fogg Museum, Gift of Howland Warren, Dr Richard P. Warren and Mrs Grayson M.P. Murphy (1961.26)
[cat. 112]
PROVENANCE
Possibly sold through Galerie Stern, Düsseldorf, June 11, 1932, lot 136; Joseph Warren by 1942; by descent to Joseph Warren, Jr, 1946; by descent to Howland Warren, Nahant, Massachusetts, Dr Richard Warren, Dedham, Massachusetts, and Mrs Grayson M.P. Murphy, New York, in 1957.
SELECTED LITERATURE
Hand 2004, pp. 92–5, 161–2, no. 78; Leeflang 2015, pp. 171–3.

Lucas Cranach the Elder
Portrait of Martin Luther as 'Junker Jörg', 1521
Oil on wood, 33.5 × 25.3 cm
Museum of Fine Art, Leipzig
[cat. 102]
PROVENANCE
Recorded in the Leipzig municipal library in 1761; lost in 1852 and rediscovered in 1883; transferred to the museum in 1921.
SELECTED LITERATURE
Heydenreich 2007, p. 75 n. 7, 335–6; Görres 2017, p. 46, no. 96.

Gerard David
The Virgin and Child with Saints and Donor, probably 1510
Oil on oak, 105.8 × 144.4 cm
The National Gallery, London. Bequeathed by Mrs Lyne Stephens, 1895 (NG1432)
PROVENANCE
Painted for the Church of St Donatian, Bruges, where it may have remained until 1793; perhaps with the Giustiniani family, Rome and Genoa; sold at Hôtel Drouot, Paris, 18 January, 1877, lot 7, to a dealer who sold it to Lebrun; by 1878, Etienne Martin, Baron de Beurnonville, Paris; sold at Beurnonville sale, Paris, 14–16 May 1881, lot 287; by 1888, Yolande Marie Louisa Lyne-Stephens (née Duvernay), Paris, by whom bequeathed in 1895.
SELECTED LITERATURE
Campbell 1998, pp. 146–57; Ainsworth 1998, pp. 3, 18, 20, 83, 184, 320, 198, 286, 201.

After Albrecht Dürer
The Painter's Father, 1497
Oil on lime, 51 × 40.3 cm
The National Gallery, London. Bought 1904 (NG1938)
[cat. 19]
PROVENANCE
Presented to Charles I by the City of Nuremberg in November 1636 and sold in the Charles I sale, July 1650; by 1903, Louisa, Lady Ashburton; by descent to the Marquess of Northampton, from whom purchased in 1904.
SELECTED LITERATURE
Levey 1959, pp. 26–32; Anzelewsky 1991, p. 29, no. 48; Foister 2004c; Vienna and Munich 2011, pp. 86–91, no. 39.

After Albrecht Dürer
Virgin and Child Enthroned, Six Saints and Music-making Angels, 1521
Pen and brown ink, 31.6 × 43.8 cm
Musée du Louvre, Paris, département des Arts graphiques (inv. 18604)
[cat. 64]
PROVENANCE
Everhard Jabach, Cologne and Paris; acquired for the royal collection in 1671.
SELECTED LITERATURE
Winkler, IV/6; Strauss 1521/82; Paris 1991, p. 91, no. 88.

Antwerp Follower of Albrecht Dürer
Crucifixion in Outline
Plate 1, about 1558–64
Engraving, 31.7 × 23.6 cm
British Museum. Bequeathed by Joseph Nollekens, 1834 (E,2.160)
[cat. 115]
PROVENANCE
Bequeathed by Joseph Nollekens through Francis Douce in 1834.
SELECTED LITERATURE
Hollstein German 25; Schoch, Mende and Scherbaum 2001–4, vol. 1, no. A3; Nuremberg 1971, pp. 126–8, no. 223; Cambridge 2000, p. 45.

Attributed to Albrecht Dürer
The Procession to Calvary, 1527
Panel, 29 × 45 cm
Private collection
[cat. 109]
PROVENANCE
Perhaps Imhoff family, Nuremberg, until sold in Antwerp in 1633; by 1871, Saldanha Collection, Lisbon, when it became part of the Cook Collection; by descent, private collection.
SELECTED LITERATURE
Cook 1913–15, pp. 111–4, no. 482; Anzelewsky 1991, vol. 1, pp. 288–92, no. 187.

Albrecht Dürer
A Lion, 1494
Gouache on parchment, heightened with gold, 12.6 × 17.2 cm
Hamburger Kunsthalle, Kupferstichkabinett (23005)
[cat. 82]
PROVENANCE
Willibald Imhoff, Nuremberg; to Emperor Rudolf II in 1588; imperial collection, Prague and Vienna; lost after transfer to Duke Albert of Saxe-Teschen in 1796, perhaps sold or stolen in 1809; perhaps sold by François Lefebvre, Vienna; Sir Thomas Lawrence, London, until at least 1834; George Ernst Harzen, Hamburg, by whom bequeathed in 1863.
SELECTED LITERATURE
Winkler 65; Strauss 1494/17; Prange 2007, pp. 144–6, no. 289; Vienna 2003, pp. 212–17, no. 44; Nuremberg 2012, pp. 516–17, 520, no. 182; Vienna 2019, pp. 98–103, 447, no. 20.

Albrecht Dürer
A Man with an Oar, about 1520–1
Pen and brown ink on paper, 16 × 10.4 cm
The Henry Barber Trust, the Barber Institute of Fine Arts, University of Birmingham
[cat. 75]
PROVENANCE
Endres and Ursula Dürer, Nuremberg; probably Antoine Perrenot de Granvelle, Antwerp and Madrid; from 1589, imperial collection, Prague and Vienna; from 1809, Prince Henryk Lubomirski, Lemberg and Vienna; Lubomirski Princes Museum, Lviv; taken from the Lubomirski Princes Museum by the Nazis in 1941; recovered by the Allies in 1945 and restored in May 1950 to Jerzy Rafał Lubomirski, by whom sold; purchased in 1954.
SELECTED LITERATURE
Winkler 760; Strauss 1520/6; Ashcroft 2017, vol. 1, pp. 551–4.

Albrecht Dürer
Recto: *A Table and Jugs, and a Slight Sketch of a Horse in Trappings*; verso: *A Chest and a Firedog*, 1520
Recto: silverpoint on pale pink prepared paper; verso: silverpoint on pink prepared paper, 11.5 × 16.7 cm
British Museum (1921,0714.2)
[cats 66, 67]
PROVENANCE
Endres and Ursula Dürer, Nuremberg; Willibald Imhoff, Nuremberg; Antoine Perrenot de Granvelle, Antwerp and Madrid; from 1588 until 1809, imperial collection, Prague and Vienna; purchased from Dr J. Law Adam in 1921.
SELECTED LITERATURE
Winkler 784, Strauss 1521/43; Rowlands 1993, pp. 99–100, no. 218; London and Washington and London 2015, pp. 71, 93, 94, no. 31; Ashcroft 2017, vol. 1, p. 564.

Albrecht Dürer
Adam and Eve, 1504
Engraving, 25.1 × 19.2 cm
Rijksmuseum, Amsterdam (RP-P-OB-1155)
[cat. 52]
PROVENANCE
Probably Jonkheer J. de Witte van Citters, The Hague, by whom bequeathed in 1877.
SELECTED LITERATURE
Bartsch 1; Hollstein German 1; Schoch, Mende and Scherbaum 2001–4, vol. 1, no. 39; Bruges 2010, p. 425, no. 236; London 2002, p. 150, no. 87; Schauerte 2012, pp. 128–34, 244–5; Vienna 2019, p. 454, no. 93.

Albrecht Dürer
Apocalypse Woodcut – Babylonian Whore, 1511 (originally published 1498)
Woodcut, 39.2 × 28.1 cm
The Syndics of the Fitzwilliam Museum, University of Cambridge. Bequeathed by the Rev. R. E. Kerrich 1872
PROVENANCE
Collection of Revd Thomas Kerrich; by descent to Revd Richard Edward Kerrich, by whom bequeathed in 1872. Received in 1873.
SELECTED LITERATURE
Bartsch 73; Hollstein German 177; Schoch, Mende and Scherbaum 2001–4, vol. 2, no. 125; London 2002, pp. 126–7, no. 59; Vienna 2003, pp. 219–24, no. 49.

Albrecht Dürer
Bearded Old Man, 1520–1
Pen and brown ink on paper, 16 × 10.4 cm
Städel Museum, Frankfurt am Main (700)
[cat. 81]
PROVENANCE
Endres and Ursula Dürer, Nuremberg; probably Antoine Perrenot de Granvelle, Antwerp and Madrid; from 1588 until 1809, imperial collection, Prague and Vienna; Etienne-Barthélemy Garnier, Rome; acquired in 1845.
SELECTED LITERATURE
Winkler 750; Strauss 1521/47; Frankfurt 2003, pp. 102–3, no. 30.

Albrecht Dürer
Bernhard von Reesen, 1521
Oil on oak, 45.5 × 31.5 cm
Gemäldegalerie Alte Meister, Staatliche Kunstsammlungen Dresden
[cat. 43]
PROVENANCE
Acquired from Le Leu, Paris, in 1734; first recorded in the Royal Art Gallery, Dresden, in 1754.
SELECTED LITERATURE
Anzelewsky 1991, vol. 1, p. 265, no. 163; Rome 2007, p. 127, no. I.15; Bruges 2010, pp. 428–9, no. 239.

Albrecht Dürer
Burkhard of Speyer, 1506
Oil on panel, 31.7 × 26 cm
The Royal Collection / HM Queen Elizabeth II
[cat. 42]
PROVENANCE
Charles I; Ralph Grynder and Dividend, Commonwealth sale, 23 October 1651; recovered at the Restoration.
SELECTED LITERATURE
Anzelewsky 1991, vol. 1, pp. 205–6, no. 97; Crawford Luber 2005, pp. 40–3; Rome 2007, p. 122, no. 1.11; Edinburgh and London 2012, pp. 74–7, no. 23; Frankfurt 2013, pp. 186, 189, no. 6.10.

Albrecht Dürer
Bust of an Old Man, 1520–1
Pen and black ink, 11.5 × 8.9 cm
Collection Jean Bonna, Geneva
[cat. 79]
PROVENANCE
Carl Philipp Theodor von Sulzbach, Elector of Bayern, Count Palatine and Elector of the Pfalz and Duke of Jülich-Berg; private collection, Nancy; sold at Christie's, New York, 24 January 2006, no. 55.
SELECTED LITERATURE
Winkler 758; Strauss 1521/55; Nuremberg 1971, p. 86, no. 120; Rowlands 1993, vol. 1, p. 105; Madrid 2007, p. 352, no. 156.

Albrecht Dürer
Christ among the Doctors, 1506
Oil on panel, 64.3 × 80.3 cm
Museo Nacional Thyssen-Bornemisza, Madrid
[cat. 31]
PROVENANCE
Barberini collection, Rome, by 1634; acquired in 1934 by Heinrich Baron Thyssen-Bornemisza, Reichnitz and Lugano; by descent to Baron Hans Heinrich Thyssen-Bornemisza, Lugano; collection acquired by the Spanish state 1993.
SELECTED LITERATURE
Anzelewsky 1991, pp. 206–10, no. 98; Lübbeke 1991, pp. 218–41, no. 50; Crawford Luber 2005, pp. 11–12; Rome 2007, pp. 270–1, no. VI.1; Vienna 2019, pp. 252–62, 456–7, no. 104.

Albrecht Dürer
Christ on the Mount of Olives, 1520
Pen and brown ink, 20.9 × 27.9 cm
Staatliche Kunsthalle Karlsruhe, Kupferstichkabinett
[cat. 106]
PROVENANCE
Peter Lely, London; Lord Hampton, Waresley Court; P. & C. Colnaghi & Co., London; by April 1928, Robert von Hirsch, Frankfurt and Basel; his sale, Sotheby's, London, 20 June 1978, lot 20, where purchased for Karlsruhe by Walter Feilchenfeld, Zurich.
SELECTED LITERATURE
Winkler 797; Strauss 1520/39.

Albrecht Dürer
Deposition of Christ, 1521
Pen and brown ink, 20.7 × 29 cm
Gabinetto dei Disegni e delle Stampe, Gallerie degli Uffizi, Florence (1069 E)
[cat. 107]
PROVENANCE
Listed in the inventory of 1687.
SELECTED LITERATURE
Winkler 795; Strauss 1521/17; Petrioli Tofani 1987, p. 448, no. 1069E; Cambridge 2000, pp. 34–40, 54, no. 89; Frankfurt 2013, pp. 362–3, no. 14.16; Ashcroft 2017, vol. 1, p. 583.

Albrecht Dürer
Descent from the Cross, about 1520
Pen and iron gall ink on paper, 14.6 × 10.2 cm
Musée des Beaux-Arts et d'Archéologie, Besançon
[cat. 11]
PROVENANCE
Possibly Endres and Ursula Dürer, Nuremberg; possibly Antoine Perrenot de Granvelle, Antwerp and Madrid; from 1589 until 1809, imperial collection, Prague and Vienna; Jean-François Gigoux, Paris and Besançon, by whom bequeathed in 1894.
SELECTED LITERATURE
Winkler II/5; Strauss 1504/43.

Albrecht Dürer
Ecce Homo, about 1509
Woodcut, 12.7 × 9.8 cm
Städtische Sammlung Aachen, Suermondt-Ludwig-Museum (DK 645)
PROVENANCE
Acquired from the Schiffers-Krauthausen collection, Aachen, in 1878.
SELECTED LITERATURE
Bartsch 35; Hollstein German 144; Schoch, Mende and Scherbaum 2001–4, vol. 2, no. 205; Aachen 2004, pp. 131–2, no. 49.

Albrecht Dürer
Female Half-length Figure in the Type of a Mourning Virgin, 1521
Pen and brown ink on paper, 15.2 × 10.3 cm
Germanisches Nationalmuseum, Nuremberg
[cat. 76]
PROVENANCE
Endres and Ursula Dürer, Nuremberg; probably Antoine Perrenot de Granvelle, Antwerp and Madrid; from 1588 until 1809, imperial collection, Prague and Vienna; Count Antoine-François Andréossy, Montauban; Sir Thomas Lawrence, London; Jean François Gigoux, Paris; Baron Etienne Edmond Martin de Beurnonville, Paris; Henry Oppenheimer, London; purchased by Frits Lugt at his sale, Christie's, London, 10 July 1936, no. 367, for Franz Koenigs, Haarlem; by descent to Koenigs' heirs; purchased at Sotheby's, London, 26 June 1969, lot 71.
SELECTED LITERATURE
Winkler 744; Strauss 1521/58; Brussels 1977, p. 78, no. 89.

Albrecht Dürer
Flight into Egypt, about 1504
Woodcut, 29.9 × 20.9 cm
Städtische Sammlung Aachen, Suermondt-Ludwig-Museum (DK 672)
PROVENANCE
Acquired from the Schiffers-Krauthausen collection, Aachen, in 1878.
SELECTED LITERATURE
Bartsch 89; Hollstein German 201; Schoch, Mende and Scherbaum 2001–4, vol. 2, no. 179; Aachen 2004, pp. 85–7, no. 24.

Albrecht Dürer
Four Naked Women (The Four Witches), 1497
Engraving, 19.2 × 13.4 cm
Städtische Sammlung Aachen, Suermondt-Ludwig-Museum (DK 618)
PROVENANCE
Acquired from the Schiffers-Krauthausen collection, Aachen, in 1878.
SELECTED LITERATURE
Bartsch 75; Hollstein German 69; Aachen 1997, p. 10, no. 3; London 2002, p. 227, no. 176; Aachen 2004, pp. 166–9, no. 69; Nuremberg 2012, pp. 474, no. 152.

Albrecht Dürer
Hand with Book (study for *Christ among the Doctors*), 1506
Brush, heightened with white on light-blue paper, 19 × 25.1 cm
The Albertina Museum, Vienna
[cat. 30]
PROVENANCE
From 1589, imperial collection, Prague and Vienna; from 1796, Duke Albert of Saxe-Teschen, whose collections became the Albertina Museum.
SELECTED LITERATURE
Winkler 406; Koschatzky and Strobl 1971, pp. 162–3, no. 59; Crawford Luber 2005, pp. 18, 77–125; Silver and Chipps Smith 2010, pp. 22–3, 110–11; Washington 2013, pp. 161–5, no. 51; Vienna 2019, pp. 252–62, 456, no. 107.

Albrecht Dürer
Head and Shoulders of a Bearded Man, 1520–1
Pen and brown ink, 9.4 × 8 cm
British Museum. Bequeathed by Sir Hans Sloane, 1753 (SL,5218.16)
[cat. 80]
PROVENANCE
Bequeathed by Sir Hans Sloane in 1753.
SELECTED LITERATURE
Winkler 756; Strauss 1521/48; Nuremberg 1971, p. 120, no. 215; Rowlands 1993, p. 106, no. 235.

Albrecht Dürer
Head and Shoulders of a Young Child looking upwards, 1521
Black chalk heightened with white, on greenish-blue prepared paper, 20.7 × 18.3 cm
British Museum. Bequeathed by Sir Hans Sloane, 1753 (SL,5218.40)
[cat. 118]
PROVENANCE
Bequeathed by Sir Hans Sloane, 1753.
SELECTED LITERATURE
Winkler 866; Strauss 1521/74; London 1971, p. 43, no. 277; Rowlands 1993, p. 104, no. 230.

Albrecht Dürer
Head of a Woman, 1520
Brush drawing in black and grey bodycolour, heightened with white, 32.4 × 22.8 cm
British Museum. Bequeathed by Sir Hans Sloane, 1753 (SL,5218.43)
[cat. 13]
PROVENANCE
Bequeathed by Sir Hans Sloane in 1753.
SELECTED LITERATURE
Winkler 576; Strauss 1520/5; Rowlands 1993, pp. 98, no. 215; London 2002, pp. 206–7, no. 150.

Albrecht Dürer
Head of a Woman and Study of Two Hands, 1522
Black chalk heightened with white on green prepared paper, 17.5 × 29 cm
Musée du Louvre, Paris, département des Arts graphiques (RF 1080)
[cat. 62]
PROVENANCE
Endres and Ursula Dürer, Nuremberg; probably Antoine Perrenot de Granvelle, Antwerp and Madrid; from 1588 until 1809, imperial collection, Prague and Vienna; Count Antoine-François Andréossy, Montauban; Sir Thomas Lawrence, London; William Coningham, London, by whom sold to P. & D. Colnaghi, 8 July 1846; Jacques Édouard Gatteaux, Paris, by whom bequeathed in April 1881.
SELECTED LITERATURE
Winkler 857; Strauss 1522/3; Paris 1991, pp. 80–1, no. 75.

Albrecht Dürer
Head of a Sleeping Child, 1520
Black chalk, black bodycolour heightened with white, 25.9 × 18.2 cm
Hamburger Kunsthalle, Kupferstichkabinett (23911)
[cat. 12]
PROVENANCE
Thomas Dimsdale, London; George Ernst Harzen, Hamburg, by whom bequeathed in 1863.
SELECTED LITERATURE
Winkler 832; Strauss 1519/6; Paris 1991, p. 59, no. 47; Vienna 2003, p. 480, no. 168; Prange 2007, pp. 152–3, no. 296.

Albrecht Dürer
Head of the 12-Year-Old Christ (study for *Christ among the Doctors*), 1506
Brush and grey ink, heightened with white, on blue paper, 27.5 × 21.1 cm
The Albertina Museum, Vienna
[cat. 29]
PROVENANCE
From 1589, imperial collection, Prague and Vienna; from 1796, Duke Albert of Saxe-Teschen, whose collections became the Albertina Museum.
SELECTED LITERATURE
Winkler 404; Strauss 1506/34; Koschatzky and Strobl 1971, no. 58; Crawford Luber 2005, pp. 11–12, 123–4; Vienna 2019, pp. 252–62, 456, no. 110.

Albrecht Dürer
Head of the Lute-playing Angel (study for the *Feast of the Rose Garlands*), 1506
Brush and black and grey ink, grey wash, heightened with white, on blue paper, 27 × 20.8 cm
The Albertina Museum, Vienna
[cat. 27]
PROVENANCE
Willibald Imhoff, Nuremberg; to Emperor Rudolf II in 1588; imperial collection, Prague and Vienna; from 1796, Duke Albert of Saxe-Teschen, whose collections became the Albertina Museum.
SELECTED LITERATURE
Winkler 385; Strauss 1506/19; Koschatzky and Strobl 1971, pp. 158–9, no. 57; Crawford Luber 2005, pp. 18, 77–125; Schauerte 2012, pp. 135–41; Washington 2013, pp. 157–8, no. 48; Vienna 2019, pp. 252–62, 456, no. 109.

Albrecht Dürer
Kneeling Donor, 1506
Brush and black ink and wash, with white opaque watercolour, with pen and dark ink, on blue paper, 32.4 × 19.8 cm
The Morgan Library & Museum, New York. Purchased by Pierpont Morgan (1837–1913) in 1909
[cat. 28]
PROVENANCE
Count Antoine-François Andréossy, Montauban; Sir Thomas Lawrence, London; Robert Staynor Holford, sold at his sale, Christie's, London, 11–14 July 1893, lot 630, to Charles Fairfax Murray; Baron Adalbert von Lanna, Prague; sold at his sale in Stuttgart, 6–11 May 1910, part II, lot 220, to Gutekunst, who possibly sold it to Colnaghi; purchased in 1909.
SELECTED LITERATURE
Winkler 384; Strauss 1506/18; Eitel-Porter 2006, pp. 112–13, no. 52.

Albrecht Dürer
Lady from Brussels, 1520
Pen and brown ink, 16 × 10.5 cm
The Albertina Museum, Vienna
[cat. 89]
PROVENANCE
Endres and Ursula Dürer, Nuremberg; probably Antoine Perrenot de Granvelle, Antwerp and Madrid; from 1589, imperial collection, Prague and Vienna; from 1796, Duke Albert of Saxe-Teschen, whose collections became the Albertina Museum.
SELECTED LITERATURE
Winkler 746; Strauss 1520/13; Koschatzky and Strobl 1971, p. 292, no. 120; Brussels 1977, p. 71, no. 68; Ashcroft 2017, vol. 1, pp. 559–61.

Albrecht Dürer
Large Fortune, about 1501–2
Engraving, 32.5 × 22.9 cm
The Syndics of the Fitzwilliam Museum, University of Cambridge
PROVENANCE
Dr August Sträter, Aachen; probably sold by H.G. Gutekunst in Stuttgart, 10–14 May 1898; given by Arthur W. Young in 1934.
SELECTED LITERATURE
Bartsch 77; Hollstein German 72; Schoch, Mende and Scherbaum 2001–4, vol. 1, no. 33; London 2002, pp. 138–40, no. 72; Crawford Luber 2005, p. 60; Nuremberg 2012, pp. 464–7, 475, no. 153.

Albrecht Dürer
Recto: *Lazarus Ravensburger and the Tower of the House of Mayor Arnold van Liere in Antwerp*; verso: *Two Young Women in Netherlandish Costume*, 1520–1
Silverpoint on ivory-coloured prepared paper, 12.4 × 17.1 cm
Staatliche Museen zu Berlin, Kupferstichkabinett
[cats 90, 68]
PROVENANCE
Endres and Ursula Dürer, Nuremberg; probably Antoine Perrenot de Granvelle, Antwerp and Madrid; from 1588 until 1809, imperial collection, Prague and Vienna; unknown collection, possibly Italian; Ambrois Firmin Didot, Paris; acquired in 1877.
SELECTED LITERATURE
Winkler 774; Straus 1520/35; Anzelewsky and Mielke 1984, pp. 99–100, no. 95; Washington 1999, pp. 169–72, no. 72; Ashcroft 2017, vol. 1, p. 592.

Albrecht Dürer
Letter to Willibald Pirckheimer from Venice, 23 September 1506
Ink on paper, 30 × 21 cm
The British Library (Harley MS 4935, f. 41)
PROVENANCE
Edward Harley, 2nd Earl of Oxford and Mortimer; by bequest to his wife, Henrietta Cavendish Harley (née Holles), Countess of Oxford and Mortimer and their daughter Margaret Cavendish Bentinck, Duchess of Portland; by whom sold to the nation for £10,000 under the Act of Parliament that established the British Museum in 1753.
SELECTED LITERATURE
Hutchison 1990, p. 94; Crawford Luber 2005, pp. 112, 121–3; Ashcroft 2017, vol. 1, pp. 163–6, no. 29.9.

Albrecht Dürer
List of works by Martin Luther, about 1520
Ink on paper, 32 × 22 cm
The British Library (Add MS 5231, f. 115)
[cat. 103]
PROVENANCE
Possibly Willibald Pirckheimer; possibly the Imhoff family, Nuremberg; possibly Earl of Arundel; Sir Hans Sloan, whose collections were purchased and incorporated into the British Museum in 1753.
SELECTED LITERATURE
Krodel and Brecht 2012, esp. pp. 11–33; Ashcroft 2017, vol. 1, pp. 533–4, no. 152.

Albrecht Dürer
Recto: *Madonna and Child*; verso: *Lot and his Daughters*, about 1496–9
Oil on panel, 52.4 × 42.2 cm
National Gallery of Art, Washington, Samuel H. Kress Collection (1952.2.16.a and 1952.2.16.b)
[cats 7, 8]

PROVENANCE
Probably a member of the Haller family, Nuremberg; possibly Paul von Praun and descendants, Nuremberg, until at least 1778; Charles à Court Repington, Amington Hall, Warwickshire; Mrs Phyllis Loder, London; sold at Christie, Manson & Woods, London, 29 April 1932, lot 51, as by Bellini, possibly to Vaz Dias; by 1934 acquired by Baron Heinrich Thyssen-Bornemisza, Villa Favorita, Lugano; purchased by the Samuel H. Kress Foundation in 1950 through Rudolf Heinemann, Pinakos, Inc., and M. Knoedler & Co., New York.
SELECTED LITERATURE
Anzelewsky 1991, pp. 142–4, no. 43; Hand 1993, pp. 52–60; Crawford Luber 2005, pp. 52–3; Rome 2007, p. 244, no. IV.20.

Albrecht Dürer
Melancholia I, 1514
Engraving, 24.4 × 19 cm
The Syndics of the Fitzwilliam Museum, University of Cambridge
[cat. 116]
PROVENANCE
Dr August Sträter, Aachen; probably sold by H.G. Gutekunst in Stuttgart, 10–14 May 1898; given by Arthur W. Young in 1934.
SELECTED LITERATURE
Bartsch 74; Hollstein German 75; Schoch, Mende and Scherbaum 2001–4, vol. 1, no. 71; Grigg 1986; London 2002, p. 128, no. 128; Vienna 2019, pp. 360–2, 461, no. 168.

Albrecht Dürer
Music-making Angels, 1521
Pen and brown ink, 16.9 × 22.3 cm
The Metropolitan Museum of Art, New York. Gift of Mrs William H. Osborn, 1961 (61.257)
[cat. 59]
PROVENANCE
Sir Peter Lely, London; Sir Hans Sloane, London; J.B.J. Achtienhoven, Amsterdam, sold 6 September 1802, lot B18; Sir Thomas Lawrence, London; Francis Turner Palgrave, London; John Postle Heseltine, London; sold in his sale at Knoedler and Co., Paris, 7 July 1916, lot 2; Johnston L. Redmond, New York; by descent to his wife, Katherine Redmond, known as Mrs William H. Osborn after her second marriage, by whom given in 1961.
SELECTED LITERATURE
Winkler 836; Strauss 1521/84; New York 2012, pp. ix, x, 24–7, no. 10.

Albrecht Dürer
Nine Studies of Saint Christopher, 1521
Pen and black ink, 22.9 × 40.7 cm
Staatliche Museen zu Berlin, Kupferstichkabinett
[cat. 17]
PROVENANCE
Count Antoine-François Andréossy, Montauban; Duval collection; acquired in 1910.
SELECTED LITERATURE
Winkler 800; Strauss 1521/14; Anzelewsky and Mielke 1984, p. 104, no. 100; Washington 1999, p. 177, no. 76; Bruges 2010, p. 432, no. 241.

Albrecht Dürer
Nude Young Man, 1520–1
Pen and brown ink, 10.4 × 7.9 cm
British Museum. Bequeathed by Sir Hans Sloane, 1753 (SL,5218.14)
[cat. 78]
PROVENANCE
Bequeathed by Sir Hans Sloane in 1753.
SELECTED LITERATURE
Winkler 755; Strauss 1521/52; Rowlands 1993, p. 106, no. 235.

Albrecht Dürer
Page from Dürer's original diary of the Netherlandish journey, 1520
Ink on paper, 22.5 × 16 cm
The British Library (Add MS 5229, f. 50)
[cat. 6]
PROVENANCE
Possibly Willibald Pirckheimer, Nuremberg; possibly the Imhoff family, Nuremberg; possibly Earl of Arundel; Sir Hans Sloan, whose collections were purchased and incorporated into the British Museum in 1753.
SELECTED LITERATURE
Ashcroft 2017, vol. 1, pp. 558–9, 561, no. 162.

Albrecht Dürer
Portrait of a 39-Year-Old Woman, 1520
Charcoal, background with stump on slightly discoloured paper, 40.4 × 27.3 cm
Fondation Custodia, Collection Frits Lugt, Paris
[cat. 93]
PROVENANCE
Endres and Ursula Dürer, Nuremberg; probably Antoine Perrenot de Granvelle, Antwerp and Madrid; from 1588 until 1809, imperial collection, Prague and Vienna; Count Antoine-François Andréossy, Montauban; Sir Thomas Lawrence, London; Samuel Woodburn, London; Lord Henry Seymour, Paris, as a gift from Pauline Viardot, Paris; Pierre Deschamps, Paris; by inheritance to his pupil, Marie Fauque de Jonquières, Toulon; acquired on 22 October 1929 by Frits Lugt, Maartensdijk and Paris.
SELECTED LITERATURE
Winkler IV/32; Strauss 1520/27; Boon 1992, vol. 1, pp. 482–4, no. 280; Ashcroft 2017, vol. 1, p. 566; Frankfurt 2013, pp. 356–7, no. 14.11.

Albrecht Dürer
Portrait of a Man, about 1520–1
Black chalk and brush on brownish paper, 35.5 × 28.5 cm
The Albertina Museum, Vienna
[cat. 97]
PROVENANCE
From 1589, imperial collection, Prague and Vienna; from 1796, Duke Albert of Saxe-Teschen, whose collections became the Albertina Museum.
SELECTED LITERATURE
Winkler 917; Strauss XW.917; Koschatzky and Strobl 1971, no. 143; Mende 1985; Berlin 2007, pp. 526–7, no. IX.31.

Albrecht Dürer
Portrait of a Man, 1521
Oil on oak, 50 × 36 cm
Museo Nacional del Prado, Madrid
[cat. 46]
PROVENANCE
Possibly Charles I before being acquired by Philip IV of Spain on Charles's death; in the Spanish royal collection by 1686.
SELECTED LITERATURE
Panofsky 1943, vol. 1, p. 240; vol. 2, no. 85; Nuremberg 1971, p. 296, no. 550; Anzelewsky 1991, p. 267, no. 165; Madrid 2005, pp. 287–9, no. 79; Bruges 2010, pp. 427–8, no. 238; Frankfurt 2013, pp. 354–5, no. 14.10.

Albrecht Dürer
Portrait of a Man in Profile, 1521
Pen and brown ink, 11 × 8.2 cm
The Albertina Museum, Vienna
[cat. 77]
PROVENANCE
Endres and Ursula Dürer, Nuremberg; probably Antoine Perrenot de Granvelle, Antwerp and Madrid; from 1589, imperial collection, Prague and Vienna; from 1796, Duke Albert of Saxe-Teschen, whose collections became the Albertina Museum.
SELECTED LITERATURE
Winkler 757; Strauss 1521/50; Zink 1968, pp. 88.

Albrecht Dürer
Portrait of a Man, possibly Jan Provoost, about 1520–1
Silverpoint on white prepared paper, cut out around the outlines, 19.5 × 14.7 cm
Staatliche Museen zu Berlin, Kupferstichkabinett
[cat. 91]
PROVENANCE
Acquired in 1881.
SELECTED LITERATURE
Winkler 817; Strauss 1920/42; Anzelewsky and Mielke 1984, p. 110, no. 107; Ashcroft 2017, vol. 1, p. 578; Leuven 2016, pp. 148–51, no. 17.

Albrecht Dürer
Portrait of a Young Man, 1506
Oil on panel, 46 × 35 cm
Musei di Strada Nuova-Palazzo Rosso, Genoa (PR 47)
[cat. 44]
PROVENANCE
Giuseppe Maria Durazzo, Genoa; by descent to his daughter Maria; by descent to her nephew Giovanni Francesco 'giuniore' Brignole-Sale; given by his descendants with the Palazzo Rosso to the Comune of Genoa in 1874.
SELECTED LITERATURE
Anzelewsky 1991, vol. 1, pp. 204–5, no. 96; Rome 2007, pp. 124–5, no. I.13; Milan 2018, pp. 248–9, 361–2, no. 4/2.

Albrecht Dürer
Portrait of a Young Man, 1521
Charcoal, 37.8 × 27.1 cm
British Museum. Bequeathed by Sir Hans Sloane in 1753 (SL,5218.54)
[cat. 99]
PROVENANCE
Bequeathed by Sir Hans Sloane in 1753.
SELECTED LITERATURE
Winkler 807; Strauss 1521/28; Rowlands 1993, pp. 103, no. 229; London 2002, p. 210, no. 155.

Albrecht Dürer
Portrait of a Young Man with a Hat, probably 1518
Charcoal on paper, 33.7 × 29.7 cm
Rijksmuseum, Amsterdam (RP-T-00-712)
[cat. 98]
PROVENANCE
In the national collection from an early date, certainly by 1906.
SELECTED LITERATURE
Winkler 812; Strauss 1507/2; Van Regteren Altena and Frerichs 1965, p. 22, no. 17.

Albrecht Dürer
Portrait of a Young Man, possibly Nikolaus Kratzer, 1520
Black and brownish chalk, partly worked over with the brush in grey by a later hand, 36.7 × 25.9 cm
Staatliche Museen zu Berlin, Kupferstichkabinett
[cat. 96]
PROVENANCE
By 1853, Swedish ambassador Freiherr von Hochschild, Berlin; John Charles Robinson, London; acquired in 1880.
SELECTED LITERATURE
Winkler 804; Strauss 1520/17; Anzelewsky and Mielke 1984, p. 107, no. 103; Washington 1999, pp. 167–9, no. 71; Ashcroft 2017, vol. 1, p. 557.

Albrecht Dürer
Portrait of a Young Woman in a Red Beret, 1507
Parchment on panel, 32.5 × 22.3 cm
Staatliche Museen zu Berlin, Gemäldegalerie, Property of the Kaiser Friedrich Museumsverein (557 I)
[cat. 26]
PROVENANCE
Possibly the Imhoff family, Nuremberg, until 1622, when sold to dealer Abraham Bloemart, Amsterdam; gift from dealers P. and D. Colnaghi in 1899.
SELECTED LITERATURE
Anzelewsky 1991, vol. 1, pp. 211–12, no. 102; Budde 1996, pp. 172–4; Rome 2007, p. 131, no. I.18.

Albrecht Dürer
Portrait of Erasmus, 1526
Engraving, 24.9 × 19.3 cm
Rijksmuseum, Amsterdam
(RP-P-OB-1281)
[cat. 94]
PROVENANCE
Probably Jonkheer J. de Witte van Citters, The Hague, by whom bequeathed in 1877.
SELECTED LITERATURE
Bartsch 107; Hollstein German 105; Schoch, Mende and Scherbaum 2001–4, vol. 1, no. 102; Vienna 2003, pp. 528–9, no. 188; Rotterdam 2008, pp. 61–3, 77, no. 4.

Albrecht Dürer
Portrait of Jobst Plankfelt, 1520
Pen and brown ink on paper, 15.8 × 10.5 cm
Städel Museum, Frankfurt am Main, (699)
[cat. 88]
PROVENANCE
Endres and Ursula Dürer, Nuremberg; probably Antoine Perrenot de Granvelle, Antwerp and Madrid; from 1588 until 1809, imperial collection, Prague and Vienna; Etienne-Barthélemy Garnier, Rome; acquired in 1845.
SELECTED LITERATURE
Winkler 747; Strauss 1520/8; Ashcroft 2017, vol. 1, p. 554; Frankfurt 2003, pp. 102–3, no. 29.

Albrecht Dürer
Proportion Drawings of Infants, before 1513
Ink on paper, 28 × 20 cm
The British Library (Add MS 5228, 186v-187r)
[cat. 1]
PROVENANCE
Possibly Willibald Pirckheimer, Nuremberg; possibly the Imhoff family, Nuremberg; possibly Earl of Arundel; Sir Hans Sloan, whose collections were purchased and incorporated into the British Museum in 1753.
SELECTED LITERATURE
Strauss HP 1513/38 and HP 1513/39.

Albrecht Dürer
Reading Virgin, 1521
Leadpoint on green prepared paper, white heightening, 29.5 × 21.1 cm
The Albertina Museum, Vienna
PROVENANCE
Endres and Ursula Dürer, Nuremberg; probably Antoine Perrenot de Granvelle, Antwerp and Madrid; from 1589, imperial collection, Prague and Vienna; from 1796, Duke Albert of Saxe-Teschen, whose collections became the Albertina Museum.
SELECTED LITERATURE
Winkler 885; Strauss 1521/65; Koschatzky and Strobl 1971, no. 131, p. 316; Vienna 2019, pp. 434–6, 464, no. 200.

Albrecht Dürer
Ruin of an Alpine Shelter, 1514
Metalpoint and watercolour, heightened with white, 37.2 × 26.6 cm
Veneranda Biblioteca Ambrosiana, Pinacoteca, Milan
[cat. 24]
PROVENANCE
Endres and Ursula Dürer, Nuremberg; probably Antoine Perrenot de Granvelle, Antwerp and Madrid; from 1589 until 1809, imperial collection, Prague and Vienna; Federico III Fagnani, Marchese di Gerenzano, Milan, by whom bequeathed in 1841.
SELECTED LITERATURE
Winkler 635; Strauss 1495/38; Coleman 1984, p. 184, no. 80; Venice 1999, pp. 274–5, no. 42; Rome 2007, p. 19, no. III.4; Milan 2018, p. 357, no. 3/11.

Albrecht Dürer
Saint Catherine, about 1494
Pen and light grey ink, 23.4 × 20.1 cm
Wallraf-Richartz-Museum and Fondation Corboud, Cologne
[cat. 25]
PROVENANCE
Acquired by 1900.
SELECTED LITERATURE
Winkler 73; Strauss 1495/8; Nuremberg 1971, p. 108, no. 184; London 2013, pp. 207–14, no. 26.

Albrecht Dürer
Saint Catherine, 1521
Black chalk on green grounded paper, 26.6 × 19.7 cm
Veneranda Biblioteca Ambrosiana, Pinacoteca, Milan
[cat. 60]
PROVENANCE
Endres and Ursula Dürer, Nuremberg; probably Antoine Perrenot de Granvelle, Antwerp and Madrid; from 1589 until 1809, imperial collection, Prague and Vienna; Federico III Fagnani, Marchese di Gerenzano, Milan, by whom bequeathed in 1841.
SELECTED LITERATURE
Winkler 847; Strauss 1521/96; Coleman 1984, pp. 194–5, no. 85.

Albrecht Dürer
Saint Christopher, about 1521
Pen and black ink, heightened with white, on dark grey prepared paper, 18.6 × 14 cm
British Museum. Bequeathed by Sir Hans Sloane, 1753 (SL,5218.178)
[cat. 16]
PROVENANCE
Bequeathed by Sir Hans Sloane in 1753.
SELECTED LITERATURE
Winkler 891; Strauss 1521/15; London 1988, pp. 106–7, no. 77; Rowlands 1993, p. 106, no. 236.

Albrecht Dürer
Saint Christopher, 1521
Engraving, 11.8 × 7.5 cm
Städtische Sammlung Aachen, Suermondt-Ludwig-Museum (DK 621)
PROVENANCE
Acquired from the Schiffers-Krauthausen collection, Aachen, in 1878.
SELECTED LITERATURE
Bartsch 52; Hollstein German 52; Aachen 1997, p. 15, no. 13; London 2002, p. 213, no. 160; Aachen 2004, pp. 205–6, no. 86.

Albrecht Dürer
Saint Eustace, about 1499–1503
Engraving, 35.9 × 26.1 cm
Rijksmuseum, Amsterdam
(RP-P-OB-1219)
[cat. 50]
PROVENANCE
Probably Jonkheer J. de Witte van Citters, The Hague, by whom bequeathed in 1877.
SELECTED LITERATURE
Bartsch 57; Hollstein German 60; Schoch, Mende and Scherbaum 2001–4, vol. 1, no. 32; London 2002, pp. 140–2, no. 74; Rome 2007, pp. 342–3, no. VII.16; Nuremberg 2012, p. 523, no. 183.

Albrecht Dürer
Saint Jerome, 1492
From *Epistolare beati Hieronymi*, published by Nikolaus Kesler
Woodcut, 13.5 × 19.1 cm
Syndics of Cambridge University Library (Peterborough D.11.1)
[cat. 22]
PROVENANCE
By the 1720s, White Kennett, Bishop of Peterborough; Library of Peterborough Cathedral, by whom deposited in 1970.
SELECTED LITERATURE
Schoch, Mende and Scherbaum 2001–4, vol. 3, no. 261.1; London 2002, p. 99, no. 29; Nuremberg 2012, pp. 426–7, no. 112.

Albrecht Dürer
Saint Jerome, about 1496
Oil on pearwood, 23.1 × 17.4 cm
The National Gallery, London. Bought with the assistance of the Heritage Lottery Fund, the Art Fund and Mr J. Paul Getty Jr through the American Friends of the National Gallery, London, 1996 (NG6563)
[cat. 84]
PROVENANCE
Sir Edmund Bacon, Raveningham Hall, Norfolk; purchased in 1996.
SELECTED LITERATURE
Anzelewsky 1991, pp. 127–8, no. 14; London 2002, pp. 114–16, no. 47; Frankfurt 2013, pp. 72–3, no. 2.26; Vienna 2019, pp. 98–103, 447, no. 19.

Albrecht Dürer
Saint Jerome, 1521
Oil on oak, 60 × 48 cm
Museu Nacional de Arte Antiga, Lisbon
[cat. 110]
PROVENANCE
Commissioned by Rodrigo Fernandez d'Almada, Antwerp, by whom taken to Portugal; by descent to Alberto Henriques Gomes de Oliveira, from whom purchased in 1880.
SELECTED LITERATURE
Marlier 1954, pp. 187–93, 199–206; Rice 1985, pp. 163–7; Anzelewsky 1991, vol. 1, pp. 263–5, no. 162; Strieder 2012, pp. 129–30, 140–4, no. 147; Frankfurt 2013, pp. 338–9, no. 14.1; Vienna 2019, pp. 414–17, 425, 464, no. 196.

Albrecht Dürer
Saint Jerome in his Study, 1514
Engraving on laid paper, 24.8 × 18.7 cm
The Ashmolean Museum, University of Oxford. Bequeathed by G.O. Farrer through the Art Fund, 1946
PROVENANCE
Bequeathed by Gaspard Oliver Farrer through the Art Fund, 1946.
SELECTED LITERATURE
Bartsch 60; Hollstein German 59; Schoch, Mende and Scherbaum 2001–4, vol. 1, no. 70; London 2002, p. 189, no. 130; Price 2003, pp. 209–14; Grossmann 2009; Vienna 2019, pp. 360–3, 461, no. 167.

Albrecht Dürer
Saint Jerome in Penitence in the Wilderness, 1496
Engraving, 32.3 × 22.6 cm
The Syndics of the Fitzwilliam Museum, University of Cambridge
PROVENANCE
Bequeathed by Charles Brinsley Marlay in 1912.
SELECTED LITERATURE
Bartsch 61; Hollstein German 57; Schoch, Mende and Scherbaum 2001–4, vol. 1, no. 6; London 2002, p. 114, no. 46; Nuremberg 2012, pp. 385, 393, no. 91; Vienna 2019, pp. 100, 447, no. 18.

Albrecht Dürer
Saint John beneath the Cross, 1523
Leadpoint with white heightening on green prepared paper, 41.5 × 29.7 cm
The Albertina Museum, Vienna
[cat. 117]
PROVENANCE
Endres and Ursula Dürer, Nuremberg; probably Antoine Perrenot de Granvelle, Antwerp and Madrid; from 1589, imperial collection, Prague and Vienna; from 1796, Duke Albert of Saxe-Teschen, whose collections became the Albertina Museum.
SELECTED LITERATURE
Winkler 859; Strauss 1523/5; Koschatzky and Strobl 1971, p. 324, no. 135; Karlsruhe 2007, pp. 286–8, no. 89.

Albrecht Dürer
Saint Joseph, 1521
Leadpoint, heightened with white on dark-grey prepared paper, 20.7 × 18.3 cm
British Museum. Bequeathed by Sir Hans Sloane, 1753 (SL,5218.42)
[cat. 61]

PROVENANCE
Bequeathed by Sir Hans Sloane in 1753.
SELECTED LITERATURE
Winkler 848; Strauss 1521/95; Rowlands 1993, pp. 104–5, no. 232; London 2002, pp. 210–11, no. 156.

Albrecht Dürer
Sea Monster, 1498
Engraving, 25.3 × 19.1 cm
The Syndics of the Fitzwilliam Museum, University of Cambridge
PROVENANCE
Given by Arthur W. Young in 1934.
SELECTED LITERATURE
Bartsch 71; Hollstein German 66; Schoch, Mende and Scherbaum 2001–4, vol. 1, no. 21; London 2002, p. 121, no. 53; Nuremberg 2012, pp. 465–6, 472, no. 150.

Albrecht Dürer
Sketches of Animals and Landscapes, 1521
Pen and black ink, and blue, grey and rose wash on paper, 26.5 × 39.7 cm
Sterling and Francine Clark Art Institute, Williamstown, Massachusetts, USA
[cat. 85]
PROVENANCE
Earl of Pembroke and Montgomery, Wilton House, Salisbury; sold at his sale, Sotheby's, London, 5–6 and 9–10 July 1917, lot 298; Colnaghi, London, from whom purchased by Robert Sterling Clark in 1919.
SELECTED LITERATURE
Winkler I/23; Strauss 1521/40; Eisler 1991, p. 331; Ashcroft 2017, vol. 1, p. 560.

Albrecht Dürer
Recto: *Study of a Female Nude seen from the Front with Construction Lines and Alteration to her Left Leg*;
verso: *Study of a Female Nude seen from the Front with a Foreshortened Circle*, 1500
Recto: pen and brown ink; verso: pen and brown ink with green wash, 33 × 43.6 cm
British Museum. Bequeathed by Sir Hans Sloane, 1753 (SL,5218.184)
[cats 3, 4]
PROVENANCE
Bequeathed by Sir Hans Sloane in 1753.
SELECTED LITERATURE
Winkler 411; Strauss 1500/29; Rowlands 1993, pp. 70–1, no. 149; London 2002, pp. 137–8, no. 70; Nuremberg 2012, pp. 499–503, no. 170.

Albrecht Dürer
The Brussels Zoo seen from the Royal Castle (Coudenberg Palace), 1520–1
Pen and ink on paper, 28.3 × 40 cm
Kupferstichkabinett der Akademie der bildenden Künste Wien/Graphic Collection of the Academy of Fine Arts Vienna
[cat. 83]
PROVENANCE
Antoine Perrenot de Granvelle, Antwerp and Madrid; from 1588 until 1809, imperial collection, Prague and Vienna; Franz de Paula Neumann, Vienna; acquired in 1816.
SELECTED LITERATURE
Winkler 822; Strauss 1520/15; Brussels 1977, p. 71, no. 67; Frankfurt 2013, pp. 350–1, no. 14.8; Ashcroft 2017, vol. 1, p. 560.

Albrecht Dürer
The Crucifixion, 1521
Pen with brown ink, 32.3 × 22.2 cm
The Albertina Museum, Vienna
[cat. 104]
PROVENANCE
Endres and Ursula Dürer, Nuremberg; possibly Willibald Imhoff, Nuremberg; probably to Emperor Rudolf II in 1588; from 1589, imperial collection, Prague and Vienna; from 1796, Duke Albert of Saxe-Teschen, whose collections became the Albertina Museum.
SELECTED LITERATURE
Winkler 880; Strauss 1521/71; Koschatzky and Strobl 1971, p. 302, no. 124; Budde 1996, no. Z/78; Washington 2013, pp. 272–3, no. 110.

Albrecht Dürer
The Imperial Captain Felix Hungersperg, 1520
Pen and brown ink, 16 × 10.5 cm
The Albertina Museum, Vienna
[cat. 87]
PROVENANCE
Endres and Ursula Dürer, Nuremberg; probably Antoine Perrenot de Granvelle, Antwerp and Madrid; from 1589, imperial collection, Prague and Vienna; from 1796, Duke Albert of Saxe-Teschen, whose collections became the Albertina Museum.
SELECTED LITERATURE
Winkler 749; Strauss 1520/10; Koschatzky and Strobl 1971, pp. 294–5, no. 121; Brussels 1977, p. 71, no. 66; Vienna 2003, pp. 490–1, no. 171; Washington 2013, pp. 252–3, no. 102.

Albrecht Dürer
The Imperial Captain Felix Hungersperg in Full Figure, 1520
Pen and brown ink on paper, 27.8 × 20.8 cm
The Albertina Museum, Vienna
[cat. 86]
PROVENANCE
Endres and Ursula Dürer, Nuremberg; probably Antoine Perrenot de Granvelle, Antwerp and Madrid; from 1589, imperial collection, Prague and Vienna; from 1796, Duke Albert of Saxe-Teschen, whose collections became the Albertina Museum.
SELECTED LITERATURE
Winkler 819; Strauss 1520/28; Koschatzky and Strobl 1971, pp. 296, no. 122; Ashcroft 2017, vol. 1, p. 569; Vienna 2019, pp. 402, 405, 463, no. 183.

Albrecht Dürer
The Knight, Death and the Devil, 1513
Engraving, 24.3 × 18.8 cm
The Syndics of the Fitzwilliam Museum, University of Cambridge
PROVENANCE
Given by Arthur W. Young in 1934.
SELECTED LITERATURE
Bartsch 98; Hollstein German 74; Schoch, Mende and Scherbaum 2001–4, vol. 1, no. 69; London 2002, pp. 186–7, no. 126; Vienna 2019, pp. 360–2, 461, no. 166.

Albrecht Dürer
The Lamentation of Christ, 1521
Brown ink on white antique laid paper, 29 × 21 cm
Harvard Art Museums / Fogg Museum, Bequest of Meta and Paul J. Sachs (1965.339)
[cat. 105]
PROVENANCE
Baron Dominique Vivant Denon, Paris; possibly Thomas Lawrence; Pierre Defer and Henri Dumesnil, Paris; sold Paris, 10–12 May 1900, lot 38; Leboeuf de Montgermont, Paris; sold at the Galerie Georges Petit, Paris, 16–19 June 1919, lot 232; purchased from Féral by Paul J. Sachs.
SELECTED LITERATURE
Winkler 881; Strauss 1521/69; Cambridge 2000, pp. 54, no. 92.

Albrecht Dürer
The Lamentation of Christ, about 1521–8
Pen and brown ink on paper, 20.4 × 20.7 cm
Draiflessen Collection (Liberna), Mettingen
[cat. 108]
PROVENANCE
Endres and Ursula Dürer, Nuremberg; probably Antoine Perrenot de Granvelle, Antwerp and Madrid; from 1589 until 1809, imperial collection, Prague and Vienna; Prince Henryk Lubomirski, Lemberg and Vienna; Lubomirski Museum, Lviv; taken from the Lubomirski Princes Museum by the Nazis in 1941; recovered by the Allies in 1945 and restored in May 1950 to Jerzy Rafał Lubomirski, by whom sold; from about 1953/4, Liberna Collection, Hilversum, which became part of the Draiflessen Collection in 2012.
SELECTED LITERATURE
Winkler 882; Strauss 1521/70; Mettingen 2012, pp. 344–5, no. 11.

Albrecht Dürer
Recto: *The New Choir of St Gertrudis, the So-called Groote Kerk, in Bergen op Zoom*; verso: *Marx Ulstat; The Beautiful Young Woman of Antwerp*, 1520–1
Silverpoint on ivory-coloured prepared paper, 12.9 × 18.8 cm
Städel Museum, Frankfurt am Main (15269)
[cats 70, 69]
PROVENANCE
Endres and Ursula Dürer, Nuremberg; Antoine Perrenot de Granvelle, Antwerp and Madrid; from 1588 until 1809, imperial collection, Prague and Vienna; Dominique-Vivant Denon, Paris; acquired in 1930.
SELECTED LITERATURE
Winkler 772; Strauss 1520/33; Ashcroft 2017, vol. 1, pp. 569–71; Frankfurt 2013, pp. 352–3, no. 14.9.

Albrecht Dürer
The Prodigal Son, about 1496
Engraving, 24.7 × 19 cm
Victoria and Albert Museum, London (E. 584-1940)
[cat. 32]
PROVENANCE
Bequeathed by Miss Alice G.E. Cardew in 1940.
SELECTED LITERATURE
Bartsch 28; Hollstein German 28; Schoch, Mende and Scherbaum 2001–4, vol. 1, no. 9; London 2002, p. 111, no. 42; Nuremberg 2012, p. 462, no. 144; London 2013, pp. 154–9, no. 11; Spring 2018.

Albrecht Dürer
The Temptation of Saint Anthony, 1521
Leadpoint with white heightening on green prepared paper, 31.6 × 42.6 cm
The Albertina Museum, Vienna
[cat. 71]
PROVENANCE
Endres and Ursula Dürer, Nuremberg; probably Antoine Perrenot de Granvelle, Antwerp and Madrid; from 1589, imperial collection, Prague and Vienna; from 1796, Duke Albert of Saxe-Teschen, whose collections became the Albertina Museum.
SELECTED LITERATURE
Winkler 884; Strauss 1521/68; Koschatzky and Strobl 1971, p. 314, no. 130; Berthold Hinz 1998, pp. 192–4.

Albrecht Dürer
Trintperg – Dosso di Trento, 1495
Watercolour and bodycolour, 17 × 21.2 cm
Kunsthalle Bremen – Der Kunstverein in Bremen. Repurchased with additional funds from the Federal Republic of Germany (1981/306)
[cat. 23]
PROVENANCE
Josef Grünling, Vienna; H. Schulz, Hanover; Museum für Kunst und Landesgeschichte, Hanover; Fritz Nathan, Zurich, and Christoph Bernoulli, Berne; Robert von Hirsch, Frankfurt and Basel; his sale, Sotheby's, London, 20 June 1978, lot 14, where purchased for Bremen by Walter Feilchenfeld, Zurich.
SELECTED LITERATURE
Strauss 1495/34; Grossmann 2009, pp. 221–35; Bremen 2012, pp. 42–3, no. 5; Nuremberg 2012, p. 225, no. 3; Frankfurt 2013, p. 178, no. 6.3.

Albrecht Dürer
Two Drapery Studies, 1521
Metalpoint on green prepared paper, 29.6 × 41.3 cm
Hamburger Kunsthalle, Kupferstichkabinett (23004)
[cat. 58]
PROVENANCE
Perhaps Endres and Ursula Dürer, Nuremberg; perhaps Antoine Perrenot de Granvelle, Antwerp and Madrid; from 1589, perhaps imperial collection, Prague and Vienna; from 1809, perhaps Josef Grünling, Vienna; Thomas Dimsdale, London; George Ernst Harzen, Hamburg, by whom bequeathed in 1863.
SELECTED LITERATURE
Winkler 841; Strauss 1521/86; Prange 2007, p. 153, no. 297.

Albrecht Dürer
Two Livonian Women, 1521
Pen and brown ink, watercolour, 18.4 × 19.5 cm
Musée du Louvre, Paris, département des Arts graphiques, collection Edmond de Rothschild (20DR)
[cat. 74]
PROVENANCE
Endres and Ursula Dürer, Nuremberg; Willibald Imhoff, Nuremberg; Antoine Perrenot de Granvelle, Antwerp and Madrid; from 1588 until 1809, imperial collection, Prague and Vienna; Count Antoine-François Andréossy, Montauban; sold in Paris, 13–16 April 1864, lot 72, to Baron Édouard de Rothschild, by whom given in 1935.
SELECTED LITERATURE
Winkler 828; Strauss 1521/38; Busch 1931, p. 7; Paris 1991, p. 78, no. 72.

Albrecht Dürer
Virgin and Child, 1519
Engraving, 11.6 × 7.4 cm
Städtische Sammlung Aachen, Suermondt-Ludwig-Museum (DK 695)
PROVENANCE
Acquired from the Schiffers-Krauthausen collection, Aachen, in 1878.
SELECTED LITERATURE
Bartsch 36; Hollstein German 39; Aachen 1997, p. 15, no. 12; Aachen 2004, pp. 198–200, no. 82.

Albrecht Dürer
Virgin and Child Enthroned, Fourteen Saints, a Female Donor and Music-making Angels, 1521–2
Pen and brown ink, 31.2 × 44.5 cm
Musée du Louvre, Paris, département des Arts graphiques (RF 1079)
[cat. 63]
PROVENANCE
Endres and Ursula Dürer, Nuremberg; Antoine Perrenot de Granvelle, Antwerp and Madrid; from 1588 until 1809, imperial collection, Prague and Vienna; Baron Dominique Vivant Denon; sold in Paris, 1 May 1826, no. 603; Jacques Édouard Gatteaux, by whom bequeathed in April 1881.
SELECTED LITERATURE
Winkler 838; Strauss 1521/83; Anzelewsky 1991, vol. 1, p. 53; Paris 1991, pp. 79–80, no. 74; Rome 2007, p. 241, no. IV.17.

Albrecht Dürer
Virgin and Child Seated in a Landscape with an Angel playing the Violin, 1519
Pen and black ink, with revisions in brown ink, 30.3 × 21.2 cm
The Royal Collection / HM Queen Elizabeth II
[cat. 65]
PROVENANCE
In the Royal Library at Windsor Castle by around 1810.
SELECTED LITERATURE
Winkler 536; Strauss 1519/13; London 2002, p. 203, no. 149; Edinburgh and London 2012, p. 106, no. 45.

Albrecht Dürer
Young Woman in Netherlandish Dress, 1521
Brush and brown and white ink on grey-violet prepared paper, 28.3 × 19.8 cm
National Gallery of Art, Washington, Widener Collection, 1942
[cat. 73]
PROVENANCE
Count Antoine-François Andréossy, Montauban; Baron Arthur de Schickler, Martinvast, Normandy; by inheritance to his son-in-law, Count Hubert de Pourtalès, Hôtel de l'Imperatrice, Faubourg Saint-Honoré, Paris; Duveen Brothers, New York; Joseph E. Widener, Elkins Park Hall, PA, by whom given in 1942.
SELECTED LITERATURE
Winkler 820; Strauss 1521/23; Vienna 2003, pp. 498–9, no. 175; Silver and Chipps Smith 2010, p. 115; Strieder 2012, pp. 166–7, no. 194.

Juan de Flandes
Christ appearing to the Virgin with the Redeemed of the Old Testament, about 1499–1500
Oil on oak, 21.2 × 15.4 cm
The National Gallery, London. Bought 1889 (NG1280)
[cat. 55]
PROVENANCE
Queen Isabella of Castile until her death in 1504; presumably owned by Margaret of Austria; Professor Henry Attwell, Leiden and Surrey, from whom purchased in 1889.
SELECTED LITERATURE
Campbell 1998, pp. 260–6; Ishikawa 2004, pp. 37–9; Weniger 2011, pp. 224–5.

Matthes Gebel
Medal with bust of Albrecht Dürer, about 1528
Brass and copper, diameter 3.9 cm
Victoria and Albert Museum, London (201-1866)
PROVENANCE
Purchased at the posthumous sale of Revd Dr Henry Wellesley, at Sotheby's, London, 1 June 1866.
SELECTED LITERATURE
Trusted 1990, p. 42; Vienna 1994, p. 113, no. 30.

Jan Gossaert (Jean Gossart)
Adam and Eve, about 1507–8
Oil on board, 56.5 × 37 cm
Museo Nacional Thyssen-Bornemisza, Madrid
[cat. 51]
PROVENANCE
Possibly Hans Wagner of Kulmbach; Neumann collection, Nuremberg; Professor Hartmann; Heinrich Wilhelm Campe, Leipzig; purchased by Prince Leopold Friedrich Franz von Anhalt-Dessau through H. Beck at Börner, Leipzig, 24 September 1827, lot 301; Gotisches Haus, Wörlitz; Jacques Goudstikker, Amsterdam; by 1930, Baron Heinrich Thyssen-Bonremisza, Reichnitz and Lugano, and by descent to Baron Hans Heinrich Thyssen-Bornemisza, Lugano, who founded the Museo Nacional Thyssen-Bornemisza, Madrid, in 1992.
SELECTED LITERATURE
Brussels 1977, pp. 164–5, no. 350; Silver 1986, pp. 1–3; Mensger 2002, pp. 136–9; New York and London 2010, pp. 114–17; Bass 2016, pp. 10–11.

Jan Gossaert (Jean Gossart)
An Elderly Couple, about 1520
Oil on parchment laid down on canvas, 48.1 × 69.2 cm
The National Gallery, London. Bought 1900 (NG1689)
[cat. 47]
PROVENANCE
Possibly sold at Christie's, 21 May 1808, lot 120, by Sir Charles Merrik Burrell, MP; purchased by dealer Philip Hill, Soho; in the collection of William Wells, Kent, by 1824; sold in his sale at Christie's, 13 May 1847, lot 76; purchased by Seguier for Maria Louisa Whyte (née Simpson), Barrow Hill; bequeathed to her niece Louisa Jane Finch Dawson (née Simpson); inherited by her son Captain Arthur Finch Dawson; purchased in 1900 through Ayerst Hooker Buttery, London.
SELECTED LITERATURE
Campbell 2014, pp. 326–35; New York and London 2010, pp. 276–9, no. 53.

Jan Gossaert (Jean Gossart)
The Adoration of the Kings, 1510–15
Oil on oak, 179.8 × 163.2 cm
The National Gallery, London. Bought with a special grant and contributions from the Art Fund, Lord Glenconner, Lord Iveagh and Alfred de Rothschild, 1911 (NG2790)
[cat. 49]
PROVENANCE
Probably commissioned by Daniel van Boechout, Lord of Boelare; Albert and Isabella, rulers of the Spanish Netherlands, Brussels until 1731; from 1744, Charles of Lorraine; sold in his posthumous sale in 1781 to Emanuel-Marie de Cock, Brussels; M. van Fulnes, The Hague; sold by auctioneer John Greenwood, London, on 26 April 1788; in the possession of Michael Bryan by 1795; from 1796 Frederick Howard, 5th Earl of Carlisle, Castle Howard, Yorkshire, and thence by descent to George Howard, the 9th Earl; sold to the National Gallery by his widow, Rosalind Frances (née Stanley), in 1911–12.
SELECTED LITERATURE
New York and London 2010, pp. 145–50, no. 8; Campbell 2010; Campbell 2014, pp. 352–83.

Johann Christoph Hauer (?)
Copy after Albrecht Dürer's diary of the journey to the Netherlands, about 1620
Pen on paper, 30 × 20.5 cm
Staatsbibliothek, Bamberg (JH.Msc.Art.1)
[cat. 14]
PROVENANCE
By 1822 Hans Albrecht von Derschau, Nuremberg; in 1825 purchased by Joseph Heller, Bamberg, by whom bequeathed on his death in 1849.
SELECTED LITERATURE
Heller 1827; Goris and Marlier 1971, pp. 50–110; Grigg 1986; Ashcroft 2017, vol. 1, pp. 545–628.

Hans Hoffman after Albrecht Dürer
An Old Man aged 93 (Saint Jerome), 1545–91
Brush with brown and black ink, heightened with white on a dark brown preparation, 39.5 × 27.3 cm
The Ashmolean Museum, University of Oxford. Purchased, 1953
[cat. 113]
PROVENANCE
Purchased from William Hartnup in 1953.
SELECTED LITERATURE
Brussels 1977, p. 186, no. 404; Leiden 2011, p. 288, no. 80b.

Gerard Horenbout
The Virgin and Child Enthroned with Angels, from the *Sforza Hours*, about 1519–21
Tempera on parchment, 13 × 10 cm
The British Library (Add MS 34294, vol. 3, fol. 177v)
PROVENANCE
Bona of Savoy, Duchess of Milan; by whom given or bequeathed to her nephew Philibert II, Duke of Savoy; from whom passed to his wife, Margaret of Austria; by whom possibly bequeathed to her nephew Charles V, Holy Roman Emperor; in Spain around 1600; purchased from an unknown Spanish noble in October 1871 by Sir John Charles Robinson, London; John Malcolm of Poltalloch, by whom presented to the British Museum in 1893.
SELECTED LITERATURE
Evans 1992; London and Los Angeles 2003, pp. 428–31, no. 129.

Gerard Horenbout
The Virgin Mary as Queen of Heaven holding the Christ Child, from the *Sforza Hours*, about 1519–21
Tempera on parchment, 13 × 10 cm
The British Library (Add MS 34294, vol. 2, fol. 133v)
[cat. 56]
PROVENANCE
Bona of Savoy, Duchess of Milan; by whom given or bequeathed to her nephew Philibert II, Duke of Savoy; from whom passed to his wife, Margaret of Austria; by whom possibly bequeathed to her nephew Charles V, Holy Roman Emperor; in Spain around 1600; purchased from an unknown Spanish noble in October 1871 by Sir John Charles Robinson, London; John Malcolm of Poltalloch, by whom presented to the British Museum in 1893.
SELECTED LITERATURE
Evans 1992; London and Los Angeles 2003, pp. 428–31, no. 129.

Andries Jacobsz Stock after Tommaso Vincidor
Portrait of Albrecht Dürer, 1629
Etching and engraving, 24.2 × 16.4 cm
Rijksmuseum, Amsterdam. Purchased with the support of the F.G. Waller-Fonds (RP-P-1967-1010)
[cat. 10]
PROVENANCE
Purchased at auction, at Veiling Vendu Notarishuis, Rotterdam, in 1967.
SELECTED LITERATURE
New Hollstein Dutch, vol. 28, p. 94, no. 18; Orenstein 1996, p. 187, no. 272.

Lucas van Leyden
A Man aged 38, about 1521
Oil on oak, 46.7 × 40.8 cm
The National Gallery, London. Presented by the children of Lewis Fry in his memory, through the Art Fund, 1921 (NG3604)
PROVENANCE
Probably owned by Claes Adriaensz van Leeuwen; probably by descent to Cornelis van Doeswerff until 1686; Alexander Le Breton van Doeswerff; his sale, Leiden, 31 July 1775 and the following days, lot 1; purchased by Abraham Delfos, Leiden; sold at Leiden, 26 August 1788, lot 79; acquired in the mid-nineteenth century by the family of Lewis Fry, Clifton, Bristol; presented by his children in his memory, through the National Art-Collections Fund, in 1921.
SELECTED LITERATURE
Leiden 2011, pp. 302–3, no. 96; Campbell 2014, vol. 1, pp. 420–3.

Lucas van Leyden
Portrait of a Man, 1521
Black chalk on paper, 26.2 × 35.3 cm
Museum De Lakenhal, Leiden
[cat. 101]
PROVENANCE
Bequest of Charles Marius Dozy in 1901.
SELECTED LITERATURE
Brussels 1977, pp. 177–8, no. 380; Kloek 1978, p. 446, no. 13; Leiden 2011, pp. 297–8, no. 91a.

Lucas van Leyden
Portrait of a Woman with Bonnet, 1521
Charcoal and red chalk, brush in brown watercolour, 36.3 × 32.8 cm
Klassik Stiftung Weimar, Museum (KK 1558)
[cat. 100]
PROVENANCE
Acquired from Johann Friedrich Rochlitz in 1839.
SELECTED LITERATURE
Brussels 1977, pp. 178–9, no. 382; Kloek 1978, p. 447, no. 15; Leiden 2011, p. 299.

Lucas van Leyden
Saint Jerome, 1521
Pen and brown ink with brown and grey wash, over black chalk, heightened with white bodycolour, on a background of blue bodycolour, laid down on paper, 37.6 × 28.1 cm
The Ashmolean Museum, University of Oxford. Purchased, 1953
[cat. 114]
PROVENANCE
Purchased from William Hartnup in 1953.
SELECTED LITERATURE
Kloek 1978, pp. 449–50, no. 19; London 2002, p. 237, no. 191; Rotterdam 2008, pp. 94–5; Leiden 2011, p. 287, no. 80a; Frankfurt 2013, pp. 340–1, no. 14.2.

Master of the Bruges Passion Scenes
Christ presented to the People, about 1510
Oil on oak, 93.4 × 41.5 cm
The National Gallery, London. Bequeathed by Mrs Joseph H. Green, 1880 (NG1087)
PROVENANCE
By 1831, Karl Aders, London; sold at Foster's, 1 August 1835, lot 104; sold at the Aders Trust sale, Christie's, London, 26 April 1839, lot 58; Joseph Henry Green and his widow, Anne Eliza (née Hammond), from whom received as a bequest in 1880.
SELECTED LITERATURE
Campbell 1998, pp. 316–21.

Quinten Massys
Desiderius Erasmus, 1517
Oil on oak panel, 50.5 × 45.2 cm
The Royal Collection / HM Queen Elizabeth II
[cat. 37]
PROVENANCE
Thomas More, London; Vincenzo II Gonzaga, Duke of Mantua; purchased by Charles I of England in 1628 and sold after his death in 1649; recovered at the Restoration.
SELECTED LITERATURE
Silver 1984, pp. 235–7, no. 58; London 2008, p. 168, no. 42; Leuven 2016, pp. 130–7, no. 13a.

Quinten Massys
Medal with bust of Desiderius Erasmus, 1519
Cast bronze, diameter 10.7 cm
The Syndics of the Fitzwilliam Museum, University of Cambridge
[cat. 95]
PROVENANCE
Purchased at Spink, Zürich, 28 November 1979, auction no. 2, lot 280.
SELECTED LITERATURE
London 2008, pp. 170–1, no. 43; New York and Washington 1994, pp. 349–50, no. 157; Rotterdam 2008, pp. 60–1, no. 3.

Quinten Massys
Portrait of Aegidius (Peter Gillis), 1517
Oil on panel, 74.5 × 53.4 cm
Longford Castle Collection
[cat. 38]
PROVENANCE
Thomas More, London; Vincenzo II Gonzaga, Duke of Mantua; purchased by Charles I of England in 1628 and sold after his death in 1649; Thomas Rawlinson, London; Dr Richard Mead, London, at whose posthumous sale 22 March 1755, lot 2, purchased by Jacob Bouverie, 1st Viscount Folkestone; thence by descent.
SELECTED LITERATURE
Silver 1984, pp. 235–7, no. 58; London 2008, pp. 168–9, no. 42; Leuven 2016, pp. 130–7, no. 13b

Quinten Massys
Portrait of a Man with a Rosary, about 1520
Oil on panel, 48.2 × 41.9 cm
Private collection, Antwerp
[cat. 39]
PROVENANCE
By 1901, Franz Seraph von Lenbach, Munich; Consul H.C. Bodmer, Zurich; by descent to Mrs H. von Schulthess-Bodmer, Schloss Au, from thence by descent; sold at Christie's, London, 6 December 2007, lot 29.
SELECTED LITERATURE
Silver 1984, p. 237, no. 60; Campbell 1990, pp. 34, 36–7, 65, 109, 248; Ainsworth 2020.

Quinten Massys
Portrait of a Woman, about 1520
Oil on wood, 48.3 × 43.2 cm
The Metropolitan Museum of Art, New York. The Friedsam Collection. Bequest of Michael Friedsam, 1931 (32.100.47)
[cat. 40]
PROVENANCE
By 1807, Philip Hill; sold Christie's, London, 20 June 1807, no. 11; Goudstikker, Amsterdam, and Kleinberger, Paris and New York, until 1928; Michael Friedsam, New York, by whom bequeathed in 1931.
SELECTED LITERATURE
Silver 1984, p. 237, no. 60; Campbell 1990, pp. 34, 36–7, 65, 109, 248; Ainsworth 2020.

Quinten Massys
Portrait of King Christian II of Denmark, 1522
Oil on paper glued to a thin oak board, 38.5 × 32 cm
Archbishopric Olomouc
[cat. 53]
PROVENANCE
In the Kroměříž collection by 1680.
SELECTED LITERATURE
Friedländer 1967–76, vol. 7, p. 81, suppl. 172; Silver 1984, pp. 238–9, no. 62.

Conrad Meit
Adam and Eve, 1515
Glazed boxwood, Adam: 36 × 15.8 × 9 cm; Eve: 33.7 × 14.5 × 5.3 cm
Stiftung Schloss Friedenstein Gotha (P21 and P22)
[cat. 48]
PROVENANCE
Acquired in Nuremberg in 1817 for the Kunstkammer of Herzog August von Sachsen-Gotha-Altenburg, Schloss Friedenstein, Gotha; by descent until 1856, when Herzog Ernst II von Sachsen-Coburg und Gotha relinquished ownership of the family art collections.
SELECTED LITERATURE
Gotha 1994, pp. 64–5, 91, no. 1.34; Munich 2006, pp. 68–71, no. 1; Minneapolis, New York and Atlanta 2016, pp. 90–91, nos. 75 and 76.

Monogrammist AP
Portrait of a Man, possibly Jan Provoost, date unknown
Engraving, 16.3 × 12.2 cm
Staatliche Museen zu Berlin, Kupferstichkabinett
[cat. 92]
PROVENANCE
Baron Hans Albrecht von Derschau, Nuremberg; possibly Frederick William III, King of Prussia; certainly acquired before 1878.
SELECTED LITERATURE
Anzelewsky and Mielke 1984, p. 110, no. 107; Leuven 2016, pp. 148–51, no. 17.

Jan Mostaert
Portrait of a Man, about 1520
Oil on oak, 44.6 × 30.9 cm
Staatliche Museen zu Berlin, Gemäldegalerie (591)
[cat. 45]
PROVENANCE
In the imperial collection by 1830, when the Gemäldegalerie opened as a museum.
SELECTED LITERATURE
Friedländer 1967–76, vol. 10, p. 72, no. 34; Koreny 2008.

Bernaert van Orley
Portrait of a Secretary of Charles V, after 1519
Oil on oak panel, 54.9 × 45.6 cm
Royal Museums of Fine Arts of Belgium, Brussels (2968)
[cat. 36]
PROVENANCE
Acquired at the J. Hollender sale, Brussels, in 1884.
SELECTED LITERATURE
Friedländer 1967–76, vol. 8, p. 72, no. 149; Galand 2013, pp. 274–81; Brussels 2019, pp. 252–3, no. 72.

Bernaert van Orley
Portrait of Charles V, 1516
Oil on oak panel, 37 × 26.5 cm
The Royal Monastery of Brou, Bourg-en-Bresse, on loan from Musée du Louvre, Paris
[cat. 54]
PROVENANCE
Pierre Révoil; acquired by King Charles X in 1828; deposited by the Louvre at the Musée de Brou, Bourg-en-Bresse after 1854.
SELECTED LITERATURE
Bourg-en-Bresse 2018, pp. 146–7, no. 19; Bücken 2019; Brussels 2019, pp. 154–5, no. 28.

Bernaert van Orley
Portrait of Margaret of Austria, about 1518
Oil on wood, 37 × 27 cm
The Royal Monastery of Brou, Bourg-en-Bresse
[cat. 57]
PROVENANCE
Delporte collection, Brussels, by 1935; William Tudor Wilkinson, Paris, 1958; sold at Hotel Drouot sale, July 1969, lot 80; Norton Simon collection, New York; sold to Frederick Mont, New York, in 1973; purchased by Bourg-en-Bresse with a subsidy from the state in 1975.
SELECTED LITERATURE
Eichenberger 2002, pp. 33–6; Galand 2013, pp. 301–10; Bourg-en-Bresse 2018, pp. 136–78, no. 14; Bücken 2019.

Joachim Patinir
Landscape with the Destruction of Sodom and Gomorrah, about 1520
Oil on panel, 22.5 × 30 cm
Museum Boijmans Van Beuningen, Rotterdam (on loan from the Cultural Heritage Agency of the Netherlands)
[cat. 72]
PROVENANCE
In the possession of Pieter de Boer, Amsterdam, by 1925; Dirk Albert Hoogendijk, Amsterdam; Charles-Albert de Burlet, Berlin, by 1927; Franz Koenigs Collection, Haarlem, on loan to the Museum Boijmans van Beuningen, Rotterdam, between 1935 and 1940; purchased by dealer Jacques Goudstikker in April 1940 and soon after appropriated by Herman Göring; recuperated by the State of the Netherlands by 1948, when it was lent to the Museum Boijmans van Beuningen once more.
SELECTED LITERATURE
Friedländer 1967–76, vol. 9., no. 219; Madrid 2007, pp. 164–9, no. 2; Frankfurt 2013, pp. 346–7, no. 14.5.

Joachim Patinir
River Landscape with Saint Christopher, date unknown
Pen in brown ink with blue wash, 13.4 × 20 cm
Staatliche Museen zu Berlin, Kupferstichkabinett
[cat. 15]
PROVENANCE
Acquired in 1914.
SELECTED LITERATURE
Madrid 2007, pp. 141–2.

Marinus van Reymerswale
Saint Jerome in his Study, about 1535–45
Oil on panel, 80.5 × 109 cm
Rijksmuseum, Amsterdam. M.I.E.V., Countess von Oberndorff-de Stuers Bequest, Lausanne (SK-A-3123)
[cat. 111]
PROVENANCE
Alphonse Lambert Eugène Ridder de Stuers, Paris; by inheritance to his daughter, Marguerite I.V.E. Countess von Oberndorff-de Stuers, Lausanne; bequeathed to the Rijksmuseum in 1931; on loan since 2001 to the Bonnefantenmuseum, Maastricht.
SELECTED LITERATURE
Mackor 1995, pp. 195–6; Rotterdam 2008, pp. 91–6, 111, no. 24.

Martin Schongauer
Christ as Teacher, 1469
Pen and black ink, 20.7 × 12.4 cm
British Museum (1854,0628.23)
[cat. 21]
PROVENANCE
Probably Albrecht Dürer, Nuremberg; by 1810, Conrad Martin Metz, London; sold T. Philipe, 5 May 1801, lot 77; purchased by William Young Ottley; sold T. Philipe, 10 July 1807, part of lot 546; sold T. Philipe, 17 June 1814, lot 1254; Sir Thomas Lawrence, London; Samuel Woodburn, London; sold at Christie's, 21 June 1854, lot 1132, no. 4; purchased through Walter Benjamin Tiffin.
SELECTED LITERATURE
Rowlands 1993, p. 9, no. 13; London 2002, pp. 96–7, no. 25; Bruges 2010, p. 308, no. 142; Chipps Smith 2011; Nuremberg 2012, p. 315, no. 35.

Martin Schongauer
The Road to Calvary, about 1475
Engraving, 28.6 × 42.5 cm
The Syndics of the Fitzwilliam Museum, University of Cambridge
[cat. 20]
PROVENANCE
Given by Arthur W. Young in 1934.
SELECTED LITERATURE
Bartsch 21; Hollstein German 9; Kemperdick 2004, pp. 100–1, 259, no. 14.

Style of Martin Schongauer
The Virgin and Child in a Garden, 1469–91
Oil on lime, 30.2 × 21.9 cm
The National Gallery, London. Presented by Queen Victoria at the Prince Consort's wish, 1863 (NG723)
[cat. 18]
PROVENANCE
Prince Ludwig Kraft Ernst von Oettingen-Wallerstein; purchased by Prince Albert, 1848; presented by Queen Victoria at Albert's wish, 1863.
SELECTED LITERATURE
Levey 1959, p. 101; Foister 2004b, pp. 9–10; Kemperdick 2004, pp. 257–8.

Unknown Netherlandish artist
River Landscape with Saint Christopher, date unknown
Pen in brown, brown washes, heightened with white on blue grounded paper, 27 × 34.2 cm
Musée du Louvre, Paris, département des Arts graphiques (inv 18976)
PROVENANCE
Entered the Louvre collection in 1827.
SELECTED LITERATURE
Lugt 1968, pp. 45–6, no. 151; Madrid 2007, pp. 141–3.

Dirk Vellert
A Woman bathing holding a Brush and a Small Bucket, about 1521
Pen and brown ink, 27.9 × 12.5 cm
Musée du Louvre, Paris, département des Arts graphiques (inv 18804)
[cat. 2]
PROVENANCE
Probably Paul Bourgevin Vialart, Count of Saint Morys; entered the Louvre during the French Revolution.
SELECTED LITERATURE
Lugt 1968, p. 35, no. 107; Brussels 1977, pp. 167–8, no. 356; Washington and New York 1986, p. 289, no. 113.

Dirk Vellert
The Flight into Egypt, about 1532–40
Stained-glass panel, grisaille, silver stain and lead, diameter 28.8 cm
Rijksmuseum, Amsterdam (Bk-NM-12969)
PROVENANCE
Acquired by exchange, probably from Johan Adriaan Frederiks, The Hague, in 1922.
SELECTED LITERATURE
Van Eck 1999, no. 18, pp. 48–9; New York 1995, p. 153, no. 76; Konowitz 1990–1, p. 143.

Hans Weiditz after Albrecht Dürer
Emperor Maximilian I, 1519
Woodcut on parchment, 54.8 × 37.8cm
The Albertina Museum, Vienna
[cat. 5]
PROVENANCE
Old stock of the imperial court library, Vienna; from 1796, Duke Albert of Saxe-Teschen, whose collections became the Albertina Museum.
SELECTED LITERATURE
Bartsch 153; Schoch, Mende and Scherbaum 2001–4, vol. 2, no. 252; Rome 2007, p. 253, no. V.1; Augsburg 2019, pp. 276–7, no. 60.

Workshop of Albrecht Dürer
The Virgin and Child ('The Madonna with the Iris'), about 1500–10
Oil on lime, 149.2 × 117.2 cm
The National Gallery, London. Bought through the Art Fund, 1945 (NG5592)
[cat. 34]
PROVENANCE
By 1821, Felsenberg collection, Vienna; P.H. Desvignes, sold by his son in 1891; acquired by Sir Francis Cook in 1892; Sir Frederick Cook; purchased from the Trustees of the Cook collection in 1945.
SELECTED LITERATURE
Ackroyd 2000; Foister 2004b; Vienna 2019, pp. 154–9, 450, no. 54.

INDEX

PHOTOGRAPHIC CREDITS

AACHEN
Städtische Sammlung Aachen, Suermondt-Ludwig-Museum / photo Anne Gold, Aachen: figs 41, 42, 44, 46, 153.

AMSTERDAM
© Rijksmuseum, Amsterdam: cats 10, 50, 52, 94, 98, 111; figs 12, 13, 38, 43, 47, 50, 75, 79, 92, 140, 152, 165.

ANTWERP
© KBC, Snijders & Rockox House Museum, Antwerp: fig. 143.

© Museum aan de Stroom, Collection City of Antwerp, MAS – Photo: Bart Huysmans & Michel Wuyts: fig. 5.

© The Phoebus Foundation: fig. 124.

BAMBERG
Staatsbibliothek, Bamberg / photo Gerald Raab: cat. 14.

BASEL
© Kunstmuseum Basel: fig. 73; © akg-images: fig. 127.

BAYONNE
Musée Bonnat-Helleu, Bayonne © Bayonne, musée Bonnat-Helleu / photo A. Vaquero: figs 64, 105; © RMN-Grand Palais / René-Gabriel Ojéda: figs 65, 66.

BERGAMO
© Accademia Carrara, Bergamo: fig. 138.

BERLIN
Gemäldegalerie, Staatliche Museen zu Berlin-Preussischer Kulturbesitz © Annette T. Keller, artIMAGING, art documentation & multispectral imaging, Berlin / Firenze: fig. 85.

© Photo Scala, Florence / bpk, Bildagentur für Kunst, Kultur und Geschichte, Berlin: cat. 26; fig. 70; © Photo Scala, Florence / bpk, Bildagentur für Kunst, Kultur und Geschichte, Berlin / photo Jörg P. Anders: cats 17, 68, 90, 91, 96; figs 34, 35, 37, 59, 76, 84, 90, 91, 94, 100, 114, 116, 148, 161; © Photo Scala, Florence / bpk, Bildagentur für Kunst, Kultur und Geschichte, Berlin / photo Dietmar Katz: cats 15, 92; figs 4, 106, 107, 137; © Photo Scala, Florence / bpk, Bildagentur für Kunst, Kultur und Geschichte, Berlin / photo Christoph Schmidt: cat. 45.

BESANÇON
© Bibliothèque municipale de Besançon, 67633 RILL: fig. 110.

© Musée des Beaux-Arts et d'Archéologie, Besançon: cat. 11.

BIRMINGHAM
© The Henry Barber Trust, The Barber Institute of Fine Arts, University of Birmingham: cat. 75.

BOSTON, MASSACHUSETTS
© Isabella Stewart Gardner Museum, Boston, Massachusetts: fig. 28.

BOURG-EN-BRESSE
© Monastère royal de Brou, Bourg-en-Bresse: cats 54, 57.

BREMEN
© Kunsthalle Bremen: figs 8, 56, 58, 62, 134; © Kunsthalle Bremen – Die Kulturgutscanner – ARTOTHEK: cat. 23: fig 7.

BRUSSELS
© Royal Museums of Fine Arts of Belgium, Brussels / J. Geleyns - Art Photography: cat. 36.

BUDAPEST
© The Museum of Fine Arts Budapest / Scala, Florence: fig. 49.

CAMBRIDGE
© Fitzwilliam Museum, Cambridge: cats 20, 95, 116. University Library © akg-images: cat. 22.

CAMBRIDGE, MASSACHUSETTS
© President and Fellows of Harvard College: cats 105, 112.

CHANTILLY
© RMN-Grand Palais (domaine de Chantilly) / Gérard Blot: figs 63, 87; © RMN-Grand Palais (domaine de Chantilly) / Thierry Le Mage: figs 89, 162.

COLOGNE
Wallraf-Richartz-Museum & Fondation Corboud, Cologne © Rheinisches Bildarchiv, Cologne, rba_c004659: cat. 25.

DRESDEN
Gemäldegalerie Alte Meister, Staatliche Kunstsammlungen Dresden © Staatliche Kunstsammlungen Dresden / photo Hans-Peter Klut: fig. 139; © Photo Scala, Florence / bpk, Bildagentur für Kunst, Kultur undGeschichte, Berlin: cat. 43.

ERLANGEN
© Universitätsbibliothek Erlangen-Nürnberg: fig. 17.

FLORENCE
Gabinetto dei Disegni e delle Stampe, Gallerie degli Uffizi, Florence © Soprintendenza Speciale per il Polo Museale Fiorentino, Gabinetto Fotografico, Ministero per i Beni e le Attività Culturali: cat. 107; figs 131, 132; © Photo Scala, Florence: fig. 119.

Gallerie degli Uffizi, Florence © Photo Scala, Florence – courtesy of the Ministero Beni e Att. Culturali: figs 10, 23.

FRANKFURT AM MAIN
© Städel Museum, Frankfurt am Main: figs 1, 135; © Städel Museum, Frankfurt am Main / ARTOTHEK: cats 69, 70, 81, 88; figs 14, 130.

GENOA
© Copyright Musei di Strada Nuova / photographer: Luigino Visconti: cat. 44.

GOTHA
© Stiftung Schloss Friedenstein Gotha / Foundation Castle Friedenstein Gotha: cat. 48; fig. 52.

HAMBURG
Hamburger Kunsthalle, Hamburg © Photo Scala, Florence / bpk, Bildagentur für Kunst, Kultur und Geschichte, Berlin / photo: Christoph Irrgang: cats 12, 58, 82; figs 2, 69.

KARLSRUHE
Staatliche Kunsthalle Karlsruhe © Photo Scala, Florence / bpk, Bildagentur für Kunst, Kultur und Geschichte, Berlin / Photo: Annette Fischer / Heike Kohler: cat. 106; © Photo Scala, Florence / bpk, Bildagentur für Kunst, Kultur und Geschichte, Berlin / photo Wolfgang Pankoke: fig. 29.

KASSEL
© Gemäldegalerie Kassell: fig. 30.

LEIDEN
© Stedelijk Museum de Lakenhal Leiden: cat. 101.

LEIPZIG
© Museum der bildenden Künste Leipzig: cat. 102.

LILLE
Musée des Beaux-Arts, Lille © RMN-Grand Palais / Stéphane Maréchalle: fig. 118.

LISBON
Museu Nacional de Arte Antiga, Lisbon (National Museum of Ancient Art, Lisbon) © Instituto Portugues de Museus, Minstero da Cultura, Lisbon: cat. 110.

LONDON
© British Library Board. All Rights Reserved / Bridgeman Images: cats 1, 6, 56, 103: fig. 78.

© The Trustees of The British Museum: cats 3, 4, 9, 13, 16, 21, 61, 66, 67, 78, 80, 99, 115, 118; figs 54, 72, 86, 88, 93, 112, 126, 154, 155, 156, 163.

© The Samuel Courtauld Trust, The Courtauld Gallery, London / Bridgeman Images: fig. 15.

© The National Gallery, London: cats 18, 19, 33, 34, 35, 41, 47, 49, 55, 84; fig. 53.

Royal Collection Trust / © Her Majesty Queen Elizabeth II 2021: cats 37, 42, 65.

© V&A Images / Victoria and Albert Museum, London: cat. 32.

LONGFORD CASTLE
Longford Castle Collection © Photo courtesy of the owner: cat. 38.

LOS ANGELES
© The J. Paul Getty Museum, Los Angeles, California: figs 98, 111.

MADRID
Museo Nacional del Prado, Madrid © Photographic Archive Museo Nacional del Prado: cat. 46; fig. 24.

© Copyright Museo Thyssen-Bornemisza, Madrid: cats 31, 51; fig. 136; © Copyright Museo Thyssen-Bornemisza / Scala, Florence: fig. 20.

MILAN
© Veneranda Biblioteca Ambrosiana: cat. 24; © Veneranda Biblioteca Ambrosiana – Milano / De Agostini Picture Library: fig. 104; © Veneranda Biblioteca Ambrosiana / Gianni Cigolini / Mondadori Portfolio / Bridgeman Images: cat. 60.

MUNICH
Bayerische Staatsgemäldesammlungen, Munich © Copyright Photo Scala, Florence / BPK, Bildagentur für Kunst, Kultur und Geschichte, Berlin: figs 18, 25.

© Staatsbibliothek, Munich: fig. 11.

NEW YORK
© The Metropolitan Museum of Art, New York: cats 40, 59; figs 39, 51, 60, 68, 149, 164.

© The Morgan Library & Museum, New York: cat. 28.

NUREMBERG
© Germanisches Nationalmuseum Nüremberg: figs 96, 102, 103; © Germanisches Nationalmuseum Nüremberg/ photo Monika Runge: cat. 76; figs 55, 74, 133; Germanisches Nationalmuseum, Nüremberg © De Agostini Picture Library / Artothek / Bridgeman Images: fig. 21.

Staatsarchiv Nürnberg: figs 128, 129.

OLOMOUC
Photo © Olomouc Museum of Art, Markéta Lehečková: cat. 53.

OXFORD
© Copyright in this Photograph Reserved to the Ashmolean Museum, Oxford: cats 113, 114; © Bridgeman Images: fig. 97.

PALERMO
© Galleria interdisciplinare Regionale della Sicilia di Palazzo Abatellis, Palermo: fig. 40.

PARIS
© Fondation Custodia, Collection Frits Lugt, Paris: cat. 93.

Musée Petit Palais, Paris © Bridgeman Images: fig. 22.

Musée du Louvre, Paris © RMN-Grand Palais (musée du Louvre) / Thierry Le Mage: cat. 74; figs 101, 115, 122, 125; © RMN-Grand Palais (musée du Louvre) / Michel Urtado: cat. 64; figs 57, 120, 159, 160; © RMN-Grand Palais (musée du Louvre) / Adrien Didierjean: cat. 63; © RMN-Grand Palais (musée du Louvre) / Michèle Bellot: cat. 62; fig. 33; © Musée du Louvre, Dist. RMN-Grand Palais / Martine Beck-Coppola: cat. 2; © RMN-Grand Palais (musée du Louvre) / Tony Querrec: fig. 3; © Musée du Louvre, Dist. RMN-Grand Palais / Angèle Dequier: fig. 121; © RMN-Grand Palais: fig. 158.

PRAGUE
National Gallery, Prague © Bridgeman Images: fig. 19.

PRIVATE COLLECTIONS
Geneva, Jean Bonna Collection © courtesy of the owner / photo Patrick Goetelen, Geneva: cat. 79.

Private collection © Bridgeman Images: fig. 113

Private collection © Christie's Images / Bridgeman Images: fig. 141.

Private collection © Christie's Images, London / Scala, Florence: fig. 9.

Private collection © Photo by Andy Le Gresley Photography: cat. 109.

Private collection Edinburgh © Photo courtesy of the owner: fig. 123.

Private collection, Luxemburg © Photo courtesy of the owner: fig. 142.

Private collection © The Metropolitan Museum of Art, Paintings Conservation Department: cat. 39.

© Draiflessen Collection (Liberna), Mettingen D 60 (Photo: Stephan Kube): cat. 108

ROME
© Accademia Nazionale di San Luca: fig. 83.

ROTTERDAM
© Museum Boijmans Van Beuningen, Rotterdam: cat. 72; fig. 71.

ROUEN
Musée des Beaux-Arts de Rouen © C. Lancien, C. Loisel / Réunion des Musées Métropolitains Rouen Normandie: fig. 151.

'S-HERTOGENBOSCH
Het Noordbrabants Museum, 's-Hertogenbosch © Heritage Images / Fine Art Images / akg-images: fig. 31.

VALENCIA
Real Colegio del Corpus Christi, Valencia © Album\Scala, Florence: fig. 48.

VENICE
© Museo Correr: fig. 61.

VIENNA
© Albertina, Vienna: cats 5, 27, 29, 30, 71, 77, 86, 87, 89, 97, 104, 117; figs 16, 26, 67, 77, 80, 95, 99, 108, 109, 117, 144, 145, 146, 147, 157.

© Bibliothek der Akademie der Kunste, Vienna, Kupferstichkabinett, Sammlung Abbe Neumann: cat. 83.

Kunsthistorisches Museum, Vienna © akg-images / Erich Lessing: fig. 32; © Photo Austrian Archives / Scala Florence: fig. 27; © Bridgeman Images: fig. 36; © Photo Fine Art Images / Heritage Images / Scala, Florence: fig. 45; © KHM-Museumsverband: fig. 6; © Leonard de Selva / Bridgeman Images: fig. 150.

© LIECHTENSTEIN. The Princely Collections, Vaduz–Vienna: fig. 82.

WEIMAR
© Klassik Stiftung Weimar: cat. 100; fig. 81.

WASHINGTON, DC
Image courtesy of the Board of Trustees, National Gallery of Art, Washington, DC: cats 7, 8, 73.

WILLIAMSTOWN, MASSACHUSETTS
© Sterling and Francine Clark Art Institute, Williamstown, Massachusetts, USA: cat. 85.

LENDERS TO THE EXHIBITION

AACHEN
Städtische Sammlung Aachen, Suermondt-Ludwig-Museum

AMSTERDAM
Rijksmuseum

BAMBERG
Staatsbibliothek Bamberg

BERLIN
Staatliche Museen zu Berlin:
Gemäldegalerie
Kupferstichkabinett

BESANÇON
Musée des Beaux-Arts et d'Archéologie

BIRMINGHAM
The Henry Barber Trust, The Barber Institute of Fine Arts, University of Birmingham

BOURG-EN-BRESSE
The Royal Monastery of Brou

BREMEN
Kunsthalle Bremen – Der Kunstverein in Bremen

BRUSSELS
Royal Museums of Fine Arts of Belgium

CAMBRIDGE
Syndics of Cambridge University Library
The Syndics of the Fitzwilliam Museum, University of Cambridge

CAMBRIDGE MA
Harvard Art Museums / Fogg Museum

COLOGNE
Wallraf-Richartz-Museum & Fondation Corboud

DRESDEN
Gemäldegalerie Alte Meister, Staatliche Kunstsammlungen

FLORENCE
Gallerie degli Uffizi

FRANKFURT
Städel Museum

GENEVA
Collection Jean Bonna

GENOA
Musei di Strada Nuova – Palazzo Rosso

GOTHA
Stiftung Schloss Friedenstein

HAMBURG
Hamburger Kunsthalle, Kupferstichkabinett

KARLSRUHE
Staatliche Kunsthalle Karlsruhe, Kupferstichkabinett

LEIDEN
Museum De Lakenhal

LEIPZIG
Museum of Fine Art Leipzig

LISBON
Museu Nacional de Arte Antiga

LONDON
The British Library
British Museum
The National Gallery
Her Majesty The Queen
Victoria and Albert Museum

MADRID
Museo Nacional del Prado
Museo Nacional Thyssen-Bornemisza

METTINGEN
Draiflessen Collection (Liberna)

MILAN
Veneranda Biblioteca Ambrosiana, Pinacoteca

NEW YORK
The Metropolitan Museum of Art
The Morgan Library & Museum

NUREMBERG
Germanisches Nationalmuseum

OLOMOUC
Archbishopric Olomouc

OXFORD
The Ashmolean Museum, University of Oxford

PARIS
Fondation Custodia
Musée du Louvre

ROTTERDAM
Museum Boijmans Van Beuningen

SALISBURY
Longford Castle Collection

VIENNA
The Albertina Museum
Kupferstichkabinett der Akademie der bildenden Künste Wien/Graphic Collection of the Academy of Fine Arts Vienna

WASHINGTON DC
National Gallery of Art

WEIMAR
Klassik Stiftung Weimar, Museum

WILLIAMSTOWN
Sterling and Francine Clark Art Institute

Private collection
Private collection, Antwerp

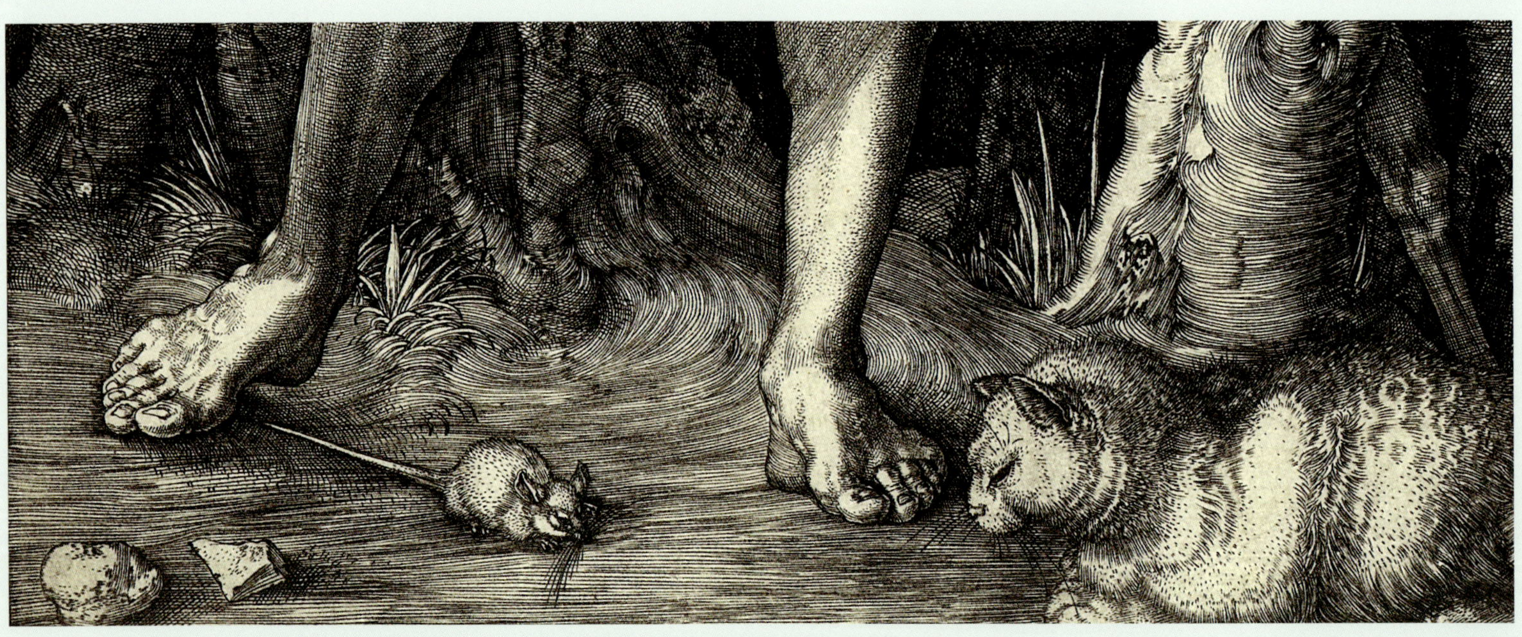